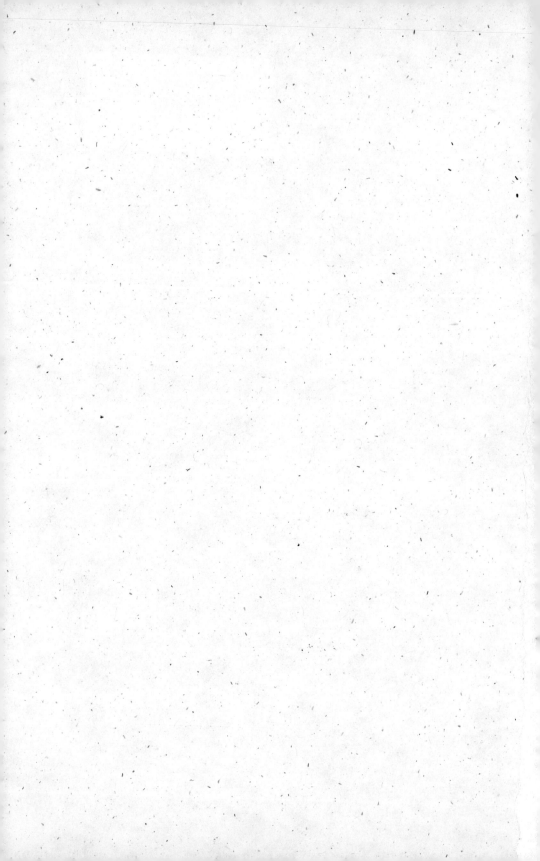

GLORIOUS IN PERSECUTION

"I glory in persecution."
Joseph Smith, May 26, 1844

GLORIOUS IN PERSECUTION

JOSEPH SMITH | AMERICAN PROPHET

1839-1844

MARTHA BRADLEY-EVANS

SMITH-PETTIT FOUNDATION
SALT LAKE CITY

To Bob

Printed on acid-free paper. Composed, printed, and bound in the United States of America. Distributed by Signature Books Publishing LLC. www.signaturebooks.com

Designed by Jason Francis.

Frontispiece: Water color portrait of Joseph Smith, ca 1844, by Sutcliffe Maudsley. All illustrations, unless otherwise noted, are courtesy of the Smith-Pettit Foundation.

2020 2019 2018 2017 2016 5 4 3 2 1

LIBRARY OF CONGRESS CATALOGING-IN-PUBLICATION DATA

Names: Bradley-Evans, Martha, author.

Title: Glorious in persecution : Joseph Smith, American prophet, 1839-1844 / Martha Bradley-Evans.

Description: Salt Lake City: Smith-Pettit Foundation, 2016. | Includes bibliographical references and index.

Identifiers: LCCN 2015041614 | ISBN 9781560852643 (alk. paper)

Subjects: LCSH: Smith, Joseph, Jr., 1805-1844. | Church of Jesus Christ of Latter-day Saints–Presidents–Biography. | Mormons–United States–Biography.

Classification: LCC BX8695.S6 B73 2016 | DDC 289.3092–dc23 LC record available at http://lccn.loc.gov/2015041614

CONTENTS

Introduction

... deep water is what I am wont to swim in; it has all become second nature to me.

–Joseph Smith, in History of the Church, *5:143*

I cannot remember a time when the world as I knew it was not shaped in some way by the Mormon prophet Joseph Smith (1805-44). For members of The Church of Jesus Christ of Latter-day Saints (LDS or Mormon) and sister churches, Joseph is where everything begins. He embodies what makes Mormonism worth living for. Joseph is an icon, larger than life, who said he knew God and wrapped his life around that knowledge. It is unrealistic to believe that a Mormon could write a biography about Joseph without this lifetime effect shadowing it. Regardless of the measures I have taken to step back from this immensely interesting subject, the truth is that I bring my own life and experiences to my interpretation of Joseph.

My father was a member of an LDS ward bishopric–a lay appointment–in Lavonia, Michigan, when I was young, but our relatives lived in Utah. Each year, we traversed the distance between Michigan and Utah in a series of cars created by American Motors, moving through the spaces of the Mormon narrative of persecution and exodus. My father's stories about the 1840s Mormon boomtown Nauvoo, Illinois, kept us awake for miles; and when we stopped and walked up wooden stairs to trace our fingers along holes in the Carthage jail (Illinois) that we imagined had been made by bullets barely missing Joseph, this narrative became our narrative. It contributed to our identity, our sense of who we were. Stories about a mob crashing through the door to shoot beloved brothers Joseph and older sibling Hyrum (1800-44) were too hideous to believe, yet my three brothers and I begged our father to tell the story over and over again.

I have written this account of Joseph's final years as if peering through a series of layers, struggling to see what is clearest on the surface, what is hidden behind lines of propriety or privacy, and what is intentionally obscured.

The Prophet-Narrative

The first layer of narrative is most evident, like the skin on one's face shaped by but covering a structure of bones, muscles, and sinews. This layer consists of the basic chronology of public events noted by Joseph's contemporaries. The next layer is Joseph's private relationships at home–the world created by Joseph and his wife, Emma Hale (1804-79), with children, parents, brothers and sisters, and close associates. The third layer is the set of experiences and associations that Joseph concealed from the public, even from insiders.

I believe that Joseph saw himself as a genuine prophet of God and spent much of his time trying to explain to himself and to others what that meant. His experience with what he understood to be transcendence changed him. In part because of this, Joseph identified closely with God–with his understanding of God–and believed that he and the rest of humanity were, literally, gods in embryo. This awareness colored everything he did, suspended him above earthly rules, and transported him into an imagined world of heaven. His was not an ordinary, commonplace identity, either in conception or achievement.

Psychologists sometimes talk about one's "narrative." The way men and women talk about themselves reveals patterns and traces of who they think they are or ought to be. When Joseph tells his story, he talks about how others must live, and often uses himself as the model of what others may become. "Be like me," he seems to say, and "you too can speak with God." The way he talked about himself helped him to grapple with and to understand his prophetic reality. In telling the Latter-day Saints about his role as prophet, he also told himself what he had learned about being a prophet.

Joseph's story became crucial to the creation and maintenance of Mormon identity. It furnished legitimacy to the Saints' efforts to build a new Zion in preparation for the second advent of Jesus Christ. Moreover, such narratives define what has the "right to be said and done."[1] In Joseph's case, the prophet-narrative not only helped to explain his behavior and choices but to justify them.

Narrative comes from the Indo-European root *gna,* meaning to "tell" and to "know." Joseph obtained his self-knowledge–what it meant to be a

1. Jean-Francois Lyotard, *The Postmodern Condition*, 23.

prophet–in part, through telling his story. His retellings changed not only him, but the ways he embraced the world, related to others, and how he operated in a world of rules, obligations, and responsibilities. Did the role of prophet provide him with a release from earthly concerns? Or did it confine him in ways he struggled to resist? Nineteenth-century expectations about leadership and authority also impacted Joseph's understanding, as did his explorations of what it meant to be a man in nineteenth-century America.[2]

Joseph's narrative is composed of both "sacred" and "mundane" tales; where the former are ineffable and cannot be "directly related at all," the latter presents the sacred in "an objective form."[3] Joseph's sacred/mundane story demonstrates the self-shaping quality of human thought, the way stories create and refashion one's identity. British philosopher R. G. Collingwood elaborates:

> As historians, social scientists, or (for that matter) prophets and bards weave narratives ... that connect individual minds to the social world[,] they create artifacts that soon take on a life of their own. These stories, told and retold, furnish the stock from which individual life narratives can be constructed. In other words, the story of an individual life usually plays off of one or more historically and socially transmitted narratives, which serve as prototypes for the elaboration of personal identity.[4]

In addition, such stories forge social bonds and create communities. Communities constituted by stories maintain a degree of coherence, identity, and meaning that help members to know what they must do with their lives.

Stories such as Joseph's place events in a sequential order with a beginning, middle, and end, a sequence that adds up to something particular and sensical. Joseph wove events together with meaningful interconnections that organized his experiences in the world and located his spiritual self in them. Those who study narratives try to find terms to describe the way this process works, terms such as "paradigms," "capsule views of reality," "interpretive

---

2. Historian Gail Bederman argues that gender definitions stem from an ideological process that results in a set of "truths"–what a man or a woman can and cannot do. "With that positioning as 'man' or 'woman' inevitably comes a host of other social meanings, expectations and identifies. Individuals have no choice but to act upon these meanings–to accept or reject them, adopt or adapt them–in order to be able to live their lives in human society." Bederman, *Manliness and Civilization*, 7.

3. Stephen Crites, qtd. in Hinchman and Hinchman, *Memory, Identity, Community*, xxi.

4. R. G. Collingwood, qtd. in Hinchman and Hinchman, *Memory, Identity, Community*, xxii-xxiii.

devices," or "world views." Although Joseph's narrative ultimately dealt with heaven, it began with everyday life and the prophet's role.

What some might term "creative genius" also impacted the development of Joseph's narrative. Studies suggest that those with heightened creativity tend to be more open and moody, have an inflated sense of self-importance, and generate a constant stream of ideas and thoughts, engaging lavishly in the world surrounding them.[5] According to historian Lawrence Foster, prophets struggle more with cognitive dissonance as they "seek with unusual intensity to try to make sense of both their personal lives and their world."[6] Such individuals exhibit emotion beyond the norm and seize on the emotions of others. They are physically and intellectually vibrant, often swinging between ranges of choices–whether emotional, perceptual, or behavioral. Life is unrestrained by imagination or convention. Creative genius banks on sharp contrasts, boundlessness, and the sense that rules do not apply.

Joseph did not see himself as an ordinary man, certainly not one ultimately confined by human law. Rather, he saw himself as exploring uncharted territory, including godhood itself. Despite moments of doubt, such explorations functioned as points of equilibrium to which he persistently returned. They drew him through the darkest nights, providing shape and meaning in his sometimes confusing anomie. I hope to show that this powerful concept/self-concept was demonstrated in, and helps to make understandable, Joseph's practice of plural marriage, what may have been the pinnacle of his theological program.

Joseph found religious and apocalyptic significance in every offense and persecution–actual or imagined–and wove these slights into his prophet-narrative. Insults became badges of honor, confirmation that his life was playing out on a mythic stage of opposition. By the time Joseph led his people to Illinois, he had lived with the adulation of followers and the vilification of enemies for more than a decade. Joseph's worst challenges often proved to be his greatest triumphs. He forged devotion through disaster, faith through depression. Joseph interpreted each new event as God's will set against manifestations of evil opposed to the restoration of all things. This

5. For discussions of creative genius, see Harold Bloom, *The American Religion;* Michael Michalko, Cracking Creativity; William James, *The Varieties of Religious Experience;* Lawrence Foster, *Women, Family, and Utopia,* 161-67; Jan Shipps, "The Prophet Puzzle"; Gary James Bergera, "Joseph Smith and the Hazards of Charismatic Leadership," 33-42; and Kay Redfield Jamison, *Touched with Fire,* 240-60.

6. Lawrence Foster, "The Psychology of Religious Genius," in Bryan Waterman, ed., *The Prophet Puzzle,* 184-85.

consciousness of a larger Mormon drama flowered especially in Nauvoo, coloring Joseph's interpretation of his life course, the people in it, and the way a hostile world battled the Mormons in their pursuit of truth.

Efforts to unravel the story of the Latter-day Saint prophet are complicated by his own record, begun in the 1830s and continuing until his death. Most of what we attribute to Joseph was dictated to, or created by, scribes or assistants. It is impossible to see this record as absolutely representational, since Joseph's scribes routinely interpreted what he said. Conscious of his story's significance, he created a narrative. Equipped with little more than a rudimentary education, his own writing, like that of others from his time, was marked by what he called "imperfections."[7] He lamented the almost "toteal darkness of paper pen and ink and a crooked broken scattered and imperfect language."[8] During the last years of his life, Joseph often had scribes with him, actively making a record of his life. He said on one occasion, "The history must continue and not be disturbed, as there are but few subjects that I have felt a greater anxiety about."[9]

Joseph perhaps more than any other Mormon of his generation anticipated the future, knowing that his was a story that would be retold. From his letters, missives, and epistles–and especially from his memory–he self-consciously composed a narrative compelling enough to be proof of revelation and scripture. Like the story of other religious traditions, it took on cosmic significance, transcending space and time and pitting evil against good in the confrontations the Mormon people survived. Joseph made no attempt to split off his own history from that of his church's. Joseph was at the center of all stories at virtually every turn.

Joseph's sense of wonder at his own life course often surfaced in sermons and in writings. On September 1, 1842, he wrote to the Latter-day Saints: "As for the perils which I am called to pass through, they seem but a small thing to me, as the envy and wrath of man have been my common lot all the days of my life; and for what cause it seems mysterious, unless I was ordained from before the foundation of the world, for some good end, or bad. ... But, nevertheless, deep water is what I am wont to swim in; it has all become second nature to me."[10]

7. Joseph Smith, Letter to Emma Smith, Mar. 21, 1839, in Dean C. Jessee, ed., *The Personal Writings of Joseph Smith,* 449.

8. Joseph Smith, Letter to William W. Phelps, Nov. 27, 1832, in Jessee, *Personal Writings of Joseph Smith,* 287.

9. *History of the Church,* 6:66 (Nov. 7, 1843).

10. Ibid., 5:143.

In the most-often cited of such moments, eleven weeks before he died, Joseph exclaimed to followers: "You don't know me; you never knew my heart. No man knows my history. I cannot tell it: I shall never undertake it. I don't blame anyone for not believing my history. If I had not experienced what I have, I would not believe it myself."[11] Joseph was aware of his differentness and searched to understand the meaning of that difference.

Accounts of Nauvoo and Joseph that appeared in national newspapers enhanced his sense of his role in American religion and his impact on people around him. His speculations about the role of prophets in society evolved into a theory of government that grounded his empire-building efforts. "The great and wise of ancient days have failed in all their attempts to promote eternal power, peace, and happiness," he proclaimed in mid-1842. But where others had failed, Joseph would succeed. As God's prophet, he would establish a government founded on righteous principles.[12] This type of government "is the only thing that can bring about the restitution of all things spoken of by all the holy Prophets."[13]

Was it confusing for Joseph's followers to listen to him grapple with the contradictions in his life? He struggled for understanding in a speech in mid-1843: "God judges men according to the use they make of the light which he gives them." He then launched into a memorable comparison: "I am like a huge, rough stone rolling down from a high mountain … [and] will become a smooth and polished shaft in the quiver of the Almighty … I could explain a hundred fold more than I ever have of the glories of the kingdoms manifested to me in the vision, were I permitted, and were the people prepared to receive them."[14] For Joseph, the story of his final years is the unfolding of a narrative, in metaphor, in perceived but undisclosed revelation, and in the actions and lives of the Mormon people themselves.

When the Mormons gathered in Zion, creating boundaries between them and "Babylon," they became a covenant people. They performed the theology they believed. They restored ancient practices and made them current. The story of the Mormons in Zion was the manifestation of ancient prophecy, anchoring their efforts in a sacred story that began before they were born and guaranteed them a future in which they would draw Jesus down from heaven for his second coming.

11. Ibid., 6:317 (Apr. 7, 1844).
12. Ibid., 5:62 (July 15, 1842).
13. Ibid., 64.
14. Ibid., 401-402.

The revelation of new scripture provided conceptual maps that legitimated contemporary efforts to build Zion. Ordinances became rituals which embodied prophecy and were enacted in a social community. They asserted the continuation of revelation beyond the New Testament. On every Sunday when they gathered in the temple grove for preaching, they were in touch with Heaven; on every Monday morning when they went to the quarries to bring out stone for the temple, they created a future of redemption and hope.

Joseph's life mirrors that of other charismatic men and women. Psychologist Len Oakes's work on prophets places Joseph in a broader context of individuals who generate trust and inspire those who hear their message. Standing out from ordinary people, the charismatic prophet seems sketched by some larger design. His role is rendered meaningful through his relationships with others,[15] with God to be sure, but also with those whose lives are changed under the impact of his story. Max Weber, the pioneering German sociologist, went so far as to say that the prophet's followers are sovereign, interpreting his power in ways that create it. Without them, the prophet is not.[16]

Joseph's *joie de vivre* is typical of the prophet. Oakes suggests that the "grandiose self-confidence of charismatic leaders is legendary." This was certainly true of Joseph who moved from moments of confidence to periods of self-doubt.[17] An accompanying fearlessness, paired with this self-confidence that "makes everything they say seem authoritative,"[18] marked Joseph as it does other prophets. Joseph acknowledged the confusing distance between the moments of inspiration when God's light bloomed in his mind and those dark moments when it did not. Those around him proposed him as always a prophet, always on stage, always subject to evaluation. But Joseph was also a man who faltered as he sought to understand his life and what he asked of his people.

Humor, "social insight," and "detached availability" are other characteristics of Joseph that are typical of prophetic leaders.[19] These traits prepared Joseph for each conversation with potential converts or with those who had already changed their lives to be near him. For believers, the most potent characteristic of all was Joseph's charisma.[20]

For those who followed him, Joseph's charisma was as seductive as any

15. Len Oakes, *Prophetic Charisma.*
16. Max Weber, *Economy and Society,* 1:242.
17. Oakes, *Prophetic Charisma,* 13.
18. Ibid.
19. Ibid., 18-19.
20. Ibid., 20.

drug. It drew them to him for advice, for doctrinal understanding, and for direction about how to live their lives. One of the followers of controversial Indian mystic Bhagwan Shree Rajneesh (1931-90) described the feeling of well-being that such devotion brings. "Once you had experienced it, you had to go back for more, to try and regain that feeling of harmony and being at one with the universe. It is similar to a drug-induced high, except that there is no artificial chemical at work."[21] Many of Joseph's followers would have agreed.

Kingdom-building

Sociologist Peter Berger's work *Sacred Canopy* is useful in understanding Joseph's kingdom-building efforts.[22] For Joseph, the Mormon community was building a sacred world. The parameters of God's kingdom–what Joseph called Zion–represented in part Joseph's conception of life's meaning–a social interaction bringing believers into a conversation with God and his prophet. This type of world, Berger says,

> encompasses the biography of the individual, which … is objectively real only insofar as it may be comprehended within the significant structures of the social world. … The individual may have any number of highly subjective self-interpretations, which will strike others as bizarre or as downright incomprehensible. Whatever these self-interpretations may be, there will remain the objective interpretation of the individual's biography that locates the latter … within a social world that itself has the character of objective reality.[23]

For Joseph, this social world emerged from the web of relationships he formed with his family, his plural wives and their families, the membership of the Church as a whole, and even his critics. The emotion, loyalty, and devotion he engendered in male friends and followers carved this world in full relief. The establishment of family networks that extended beyond the grave included systems of relationships that had even greater significance in the life hereafter. Joseph's autobiography unified them, explained them, gave them hope of eternal exaltation.

At the heart of the story of Nauvoo is the expansion of the idea of Zion.

21. Oakes, *Prophetic Charisma,* 17. Weber added two important criteria to this definition: First, charisma is a religious concept and implies a "form of spiritual energy oriented to otherworldly ideals. Second, the charismatic process is one of intense emotional arousal and great pathos; charismatic belief revolutionizes people from within. In sum, charisma is a revolutionary spiritual power." Qtd. in ibid., 28.

22. See Peter Berger, *The Sacred Canopy,* 3, 6.

23. Ibid., 13-14.

Inherent in this phase of Joseph's Zion-building efforts was the reality that he had failed earlier in Ohio and in Missouri to call forth God's kingdom. In Nauvoo, he modified Zion to fit a changed conceptual map. It emphasized ordered lives, the primacy of doctrine and ritual, and the centralization of religious power and authority. Zion became the place of this prophetic vision, rather than a literal location.

The way Joseph fashioned his story about Zion had profound implications for the Mormon people–how they behaved in the spaces they created, and what those spaces meant to them. As he told his story of Zion, Joseph filled it with interesting and potent characters–Church leaders, Saints, and enemies–each a guardian or defiler of sacred space. These characters played their roles wherever they appeared: in the temple grove, in new converts, in the upper room of Joseph's red brick store, on the unfinished walls of the Nauvoo temple, on the banks of the Mississippi River, in the comings and goings of missionaries, in the physical labor on Illinois's farms, in political maneuverings in the state capitol, in the outrage of exposés and denunciations, in the privacy of bedrooms.

Joseph built conflict into the narrative as well as crisis and resolution. His stance as prophet created a unique vantage point that privileged his information. This awareness enhanced both the story and the way it played out. Through his characterizations and descriptions of settings and meanings, his particular emphasis or imagery, his narrative shaped how people reacted. As converts became Mormons, they learned about Joseph's role, identified with him, and were shaped by him. His life expressed realities that they believed were true about God.[24] In the process of formation of identity, "the individual keeps 'talking back,'" Berger says, "to the world that formed him and thereby continues to maintain the latter as reality."[25]

The raw material for the broader narrative of Zion came from the real world. Cultural geographer Yi-Fu Tuan's study *Space and Place* describes such narrative places as "mythical space." He suggests that there are two kinds of

24. Berger explains the believer's role as that of an active participant in the creation of meanings. This pattern is visible in Joseph Smith's life. "The individual … is formed in the course of a protracted conversation (a dialectic, in the literal sense of the word) in which he is a participant. That is, the social world … is not passively absorbed by the individual, but actively appropriated by him. … Furthermore, once the individual is formed as a person, with an objectively and subjectively recognizable identity, he must continue to participate in the conversation that sustains him as a person in his ongoing biography. … No matter how small his power to change the social definitions of relation may be, he must at least continue to assent to those that form him as a person" (18).

25. Ibid., 19.

space: one is pragmatic and empirically known, the other is the "spatial component of a world view, a conception of localized values within which people carry off their practical activities."[26]

Through selection and emphasis, Joseph wove a narrative that told the Saints what to remember. It was a narrative filled with powerful memories, deep fears, passionate hopes, intense angers, visionary dreams, and a profound sense of space.[27] This is not to say that the events in Joseph's story were untrue, but their retellings reflected a series of strategic rhetorical choices. Joseph's narrative blended a past of conversion and persecution with a present of restoring the ancient order and a future of millennial hopes. A belief in Zion rendered Joseph powerful and layered his encouragement to build homes and towns with mythic gravity.

I suggest in this work that ritual carried Joseph into an anomic state[28] that gave him, on occasion, a taste of heaven's "potentialities," to borrow a term from anthropologist Victor Turner. I am not the first to propose this approach, but I make it a central paradigm for understanding why Joseph was willing to step away from fact-based "truth" in favor of "truths" composed of elaborate and subtle secrets, codes, and subterfuges. This second kind of "truth" covered the practice of plural marriage, the political Council of Fifty, Joseph's anointing as earthly "king," and other developments that existed *sub rosa.* As Joseph constructed a new world of ostensibly ancient ritual models, he ushered the Church into that same state of anomie. Previous frames of reference, identity, or meaning were discarded. The possibilities of how individuals might reconstruct their own identities and, as a result, how the Church became a timeless creation were endless.

For Turner, religious rituals are "fundamentally a response to the divisiveness, alienation, and exploitation that are associated with everyday social structure."[29] Ritual creates "social conflict by relaxing or suspending some of the requirements of everyday social structure, making possible alternative social arrangements." As a result, ritual becomes a "force for social change."[30]

---

26. Yi-Fu Tuan, *Space and Place,* 86.

27. Ibid.

28. Anomie is a theory with explanatory power for how Joseph operated outside traditional norms of behavior. As a sociological concept, anomie was developed by Emile Durkheim, who argued that human desires are held in check by societal control. Durkheim, *Suicide,* 248. During crises or transitional periods that are disruptive, society loses its ability to perform according to past expectations. Despite its risks, anomie helps society change by freeing up the rules or systems of control.

29. This is according to Bobby C. Alexander, *Victor Turner Revisited,* 2.

30. Ibid., 1.

We see in the Mormon experience how ritual transcends the limitations of social distinction by creating community and, more importantly, by saturating everyday life with communitarian values.[31]

Turner's work also focuses on the way liminality[32] explains how rituals move from the "day-to-day, ordinary frameworks by which daily experience is organized to an ambiguous context in which the everyday world is symbolically transformed and its rigid determinativeness is relaxed."[33] Liminality is ritual's ability to transcend "the everyday world while exploring alternative arrangements."[34] The liminality of rituals assures that they become transformative processes. Ritual transforms the "understandings and processes" of prophets like Joseph, where we might observe the "potential in mankind which has yet been externalized and fixed in structure."[35]

Much of Mormon Nauvoo centered on the performance of rituals that embodied religious ideas about community, gender, and heaven. All-female Relief Society meetings moved women into a select group that heard tailor-made sermons and received validation for their communal relief efforts. All-male priesthood quorum gatherings, through conducting business and listening to sermons, forged fraternal relationships, inspired secret-keeping, and raised loyalty to a prime virtue. A thin veil of the sacred fell on even the most ordinary everyday activities of building Zion. Nursing the sick, writing letters or in journals, tilling the soil, or building a family home all took on added significance, different from one's ordinary life.

For Mormons, ritual held the hope that their lives mattered greatly and lifted them up to a new relationship with God.[36] Through ritual, the flow of "action and interaction … may … generate new symbols and meanings, which may be incorporated into subsequent performances."[37]

Before Joseph was martyred in mid-1844, ritual brought him a new sense of what was possible. It transformed his relationship with the earth, its

---

31. See ibid., 2.

32. The word *limen* is Latin for "threshold." Key to the ritual process, liminality is the transition, the potentiality of what is "going to be" as well as what "may be." Victor Turner and Edith L. B. Turner, *Image and Pilgrimage in Christian Culture,* 3. See also Alexander, *Victor Turner Revisited,* 18.

33. Alexander, *Victor Turner Revisited,* 4.

34. According to ibid., 24.

35. Victor Turner, *The Ritual Process,* 128; see also Turner, *Dramas, Fields, and Metaphors,* 266, 268; and his "Variations on a Theme of Liminality," 46-47.

36. See also Turner, *The Forest of Symbols,* 97. In his *Dramas, Fields, and Metaphors,* 13-14, Turner explains: "Liminality represents the possibility of … formulating a potentially unlimited series of alternative social arrangements."

37. Turner, *From Ritual to Theater,* 79.

laws and organizations, and even some of the persons he had known along the way. Nauvoo ritual incorporated the trials of Ohio and Missouri into a new story. For Mormons, Joseph's story expressed their culture, the interwoven pattern of beliefs, values, practices that defined who they were. Ritual freed them from what they had experienced as Americans, allowing them to identify with Joseph's new world.[38]

Plurality

It is important to recognize how Joseph rhetorically positioned his doctrine of a plurality of wives and how the doctrine related to his other teachings.[39] Plurality permitted Joseph to explore familial and societal organizations in new spaces. Plurality moved beyond the private space of traditional nuclear families to connect strangers in new religio-familial networks, creating–on earth and in heaven–expanding networks and even dynasties.

Joseph's exploration of his role as prophet/model/mentor, his creativity and its ability to release him from traditional rules, and the relationship of his millennial world view and kingdom-building inevitably took a male form in his relationships with women. This sexualized context helps to explain, I believe, why Joseph manifested a sense of super-entitlement, how he justified creating an alternative ethics, how his masculine identity related to his concept of what it meant to be a prophet, and how he challenged

38. This pattern was true, in broader ways, for the larger American landscape. Historian Robert V. Remini characterizes Jacksonian America as an anomic society:

> Starting early in the nineteenth century, the country burst its narrow confines. Within a few decades the nation was converted from an insulated, agrarian society sprawled across a three-thousand-mile continent. Gone were the old ties of family, church, and community; gone, too, was the security they provided. ... There was a restless, driving desire to be better off, and this was the ambition of all classes of society, none excepted. ... There was only one way to describe them. Restless, searching, driving. By the time of [Andrew] Jackson's inauguration ... it was the prevailing mood of the country. Remini, *The Revolutionary Age of Andrew Jackson,* 4-5.

39. LDS historians Eugene Campbell and Bruce Campbell were the first to point out that "Mormon polygamy developed within a context of normlessness or anomie." Campbell and Campbell, "Divorce among Mormon Polygamists," 191. Making a more sustained argument, Lawrence Foster characterizes Nauvoo as "a brief but disruptive interregnum when neither set of standards was operative and the basis of social authority was unclear." The liminal period was characterized by "apparent discrepancies between belief and practice." Therefore, moving from the insecurity and disorientation that comes with anomie and an initial lack of social cohesion, the liminal period produced a greater sense of egalitarian community, strong identification with it, and willing, even eager, submission to the leader's authority. According to Foster, the anomic period of freedom ended by 1852–when Joseph's successor Brigham Young had plural marriage announced publicly in the Great Salt Lake Valley. "And in its place emerged a highly authority-conscious and strongly centralized Church-type structure of government." Foster, *Religion and Sexuality,* 161, 179.

institutional religion in Nauvoo to create a sovereignty that competed with mainstream American power structures.

According to LDS historian Kathryn Daynes, "The practice of plural marriage was accepted among Mormons because they believed that God had commanded it through his prophet Joseph Smith …"[40] The isolation, seclusion, and secrecy accompanying plurality created heightened demands for loyalty, obviated traditional moral or ethical stances, redefined order and government law, and was indubitably male centered. It was ritual conducted outside the "law," even above the "law" of religion. Participants felt free to make decisions based on their own sense of correctness within the boundaries of the doctrine itself. Joseph engaged in the new familial form with different norms and rules than those operationalized by his plural wives. Above all, because of Joseph's murder in 1844, plurality initiated a series of beginnings that could be completed only in the next life.

In narrating Joseph's last years, I adopt a more or less chronological approach, but I also sometimes embark upon brief detours, jumping forwards and backwards in time, that I believe make better sense of Joseph, man and prophet. I hope that in these instances, readers will agree that such narrative digressions are useful. I have tried to produce a work that both accurately recounts the important biographical details of the last five years of Joseph's life and begins to explain the appeal of his prophet-narrative.

Although the limitations of Joseph's published multi-volume autobiographical *History of the Church* are well known, I believe it achieves the purpose of presenting Joseph's prophet-narrative and captures the socially constructed performance of Mormon history as God's persecuted but faithful people. For these reasons, I cite it often, trusting that more documentary-inclined readers will understand my reasons for referencing it more frequently than the original holographs upon which it is based.[41]

Acknowledgments

To express my gratitude for the help I have received in producing this manuscript, I should be able to pinpoint some particular moment in time

40. Kathryn M. Daynes, *More Wives Than One,* 191.

41. The best scholarly edition of Joseph's holographs is that currently underway by the LDS Church History Library. See "The Joseph Smith Papers" at www.josephsmithpapers.org. For a study of the published *History of the Church* and the documentary sources upon which it is based, see Dan Vogel, ed., *History of Joseph Smith and of The Church of Jesus Christ of Latter-day Saints: A Source- and Text-Critical Edition,* 8 vols. (Salt Lake City: Smith-Pettit Foundation, 2015).

and say, "Thank you for this!" or "Thank you for that!" But I find it impossible to do so, for the experience and research that led to this interpretation of Joseph's life extends, as is true for the narrative I attempt to describe, through time and space. Some of the files I used for this project were filled with penciled notations I made in 1984 when I first traveled to the Huntington Library in San Marino, California. I remember sitting in the courtyard outside the library proper and the overpowering smell of orange trees, so exotic for a woman who had lived much of her life in the arid landscapes of Utah. I have read hundreds of diaries since that time, held tattered leather-bound notebooks the size of the palm of my hand, and squinted to decipher the handwriting containing the secrets of another's life. I have always considered this undertaking a sort of sacred heritage that brings with it an obligation to take what the diarists wrote with seriousness and respect.

The women and men who staff the quiet archives of the Huntington Library, the Bancroft and the New York Public Libraries, at Yale University, the University of Utah, Brigham Young University, and the LDS Church History Library have been immeasurably patient and kind with me–pointing me toward sources, decoding the evolving systems of organization, explaining processes and permissions. As always, individuals such as Bill Slaughter and Jeff Johnson not only helped in my search but made my life better, becoming friends through my process of trying to make sense of the past.

What amounts to a lifetime of reading has also brought me to this point, and I would be inattentive to the impact this has made on my thinking if I did not acknowledge the authors whose works I have read and studied. These include Thomas G. Alexander, James B. Allen, Lavina Fielding Anderson, Maureen Ursenbach Beecher, Gary James Bergera, Richard Lyman Bushman, Eugene E. Campbell, Todd Compton, Jill Mulvay Derr, Robert B. Flanders, Lawrence Foster, Brian D. Hales, Klaus J. Hansen, B. Carmon Hardy, Marvin S. Hill, Michael W. Homer, Dean C. Jessee, Roger D. Launius, Glen M. Leonard, Carol Cornwall Madsen, William Mulder, D. Michael Quinn, Jan Shipps, George D. Smith, Dan Vogel, and Richard S. Van Wagoner.

I wish to pay special tribute to Lavina Fielding Anderson. Her encouragement, her criticism, her careful eye, and the heart and intelligence she brings to everything she touches has not only made my work better but inspired in me an immense respect for the power and influence of religious thought. I am also grateful to Gary James Bergera–for his friendship, kindness, and continuing encouragement of my work. His careful touch strengthened this manuscript and helped me to think more carefully about the story I was trying to tell. Jani Fleet helped to prepare the index; Jason Francis designed and typeset the manuscript. The support of the Smith-Pettit Foundation helped to make it possible to devote my time to this project. In addition, the following readers provided helpful critiques: Todd Compton, Brian D. Hales, Joseph Johnstun, Nicholas Literski, and Dan Vogel. Finally, this book would not exist without the support, encouragement, and friendship of George D. and Camilla Smith, matchmakers extraordinaire, who have blessed my life with goodness. As much as all these people, and many others, have helped to improve this work, I alone am responsible for all errors of fact and interpretation.

Writing about Mormon history and my work at the University of Utah are both incredibly important to me. Even so, my real world is a circle of children and family. My amazing children–Jason, Elizabeth, Rachael, Emily, Katelyn, and Patrick–shared me with Joseph for more than a decade. My grandchildren give me hope and faith that anything is possible, my own sort of liminal place. Aspen, Krissie, Dylan, Stella, Ruby, Jaxon and Aliya Juel are lovely beyond measure. I am doubly blessed by having a second set of sons and daughters in my life: Sean, Scott and Malisa, Jake and Naiomi, and Aly Evans, and grandchildren Akolea, Toshiro, Noe, and Chloe Mags grace me with their kindness and love. Last, and best of all, is he who completed our circle and helped it all to make sense: my good, late husband, Bob Evans.

CHAPTER I

A Sustainable Prophet

> *Sustainable heroism comes ... in moments and glimpses ... in which the universe lights up.*
>
> *–Patricia Nelson Limerick,* Something in the Soil, *315*

A "sustainable" hero, writes Patricia Nelson Limerick, noted historian of the American West, possesses a particular type of staying power, weathering tremendous storms or conflicts while maintaining the devotion of followers over time and across space. "While inconsistency can disqualify a conventional hero," Limerick explains, "a degree of inconsistency is one of the essential qualifications of a sustainable hero. ... this kind of [inconsistent] heroism is resilient, credible, possible, reachable."[1]

A "prophet," continues Len Oakes, a cultural psychologist, "espouses a message of salvation" and attracts people "who look to him for guidance in their daily lives."[2] A prophet portrays in often exaggerated way the anxieties and neuroses of an age. These anxieties include the pressures society places on the individual and the way some individuals challenge mainstream norms.

Joseph Smith was both sustainable hero and prophet, an inconsistent human being whose followers adored him and whose enemies wanted to destroy him. He inspired devotion and hatred with equal ease and intensity. And in the end, both strains colored his life, conditioned his choices, and, ultimately, proved that he was indeed sustainable and prophetic.

Part of Joseph's attraction was his charisma.[3] Joseph's charisma was "pure," based on an intense, personal connection between him and his followers. "Pure" charisma requires trust, duty, and love.[4] "Devotion to the charisma of the prophet ... means that the leader is personally recognized

1. Patricia Nelson Limerick, *Something in the Soil,* 315.
2. Len Oakes, *Prophetic Charisma,* 2.
3. See Max Weber, *Economy and Society,* 241.
4. Albert Schweitzer, *The Age of Charisma,* 38, 327.

as the innerly called leader of men," according to Max Weber. "Men do not obey him by virtue of statute, but because they believe in him."[5]

The charismatic prophet claims leadership in three ways. Some capture their prophetic authority in a particular social context, rather than waiting for a human authority to bestow it. Others receive authority through an emotional, demonstrative style of preaching. Or the charismatic prophet may describe the way to salvation, a revelatory path he owns.[6] At times, Joseph seized his authority in the Latter-day Saint world by force of personality. At other times, he rose to new heights, buoyed by the faith of his followers. The sect, and eventually church, that formed around Joseph's charismatic leadership validated his role as a prophet and operationalized his message.

In many ways, Joseph's life was the performance of a prophetic identity. Like other prophets, Joseph demonstrated his strength as easily in debates or oratorical arguments with rival ministers as in wrestling matches with hardy workmen fresh from the field. Signifying his "endurance, robustness of character, and strong will," Joseph's physical strength became a metaphor for what he could produce for the Latter-day Saints more generally.[7]

Wherever Joseph went, Mormons and non-Mormons alike clamored to see him, to listen to him, to debate his truth claims, or to chat with him over a fence. Joseph was a man's man, ready to grapple with a challenger in the dust, but also a lady's man, a flirt, and a compassionate man ready to swoop up a child, tickling him into laughter. Joseph loved people.

Few who confronted Joseph did so on neutral ground. The air around him seemed charged with an energy that inspired admiration or rejection. The stories people told about such encounters mapped their effort to understand the Mormon prophet and his position in the world. At the same time and in a similar way, Joseph's own prophet-narrative depicted the highs and lows of his personal journey.[8] Joseph's claim to a divine mission and his radical doctrines launched a sort of social revolution for those who followed him. Joseph became a before-and-after line of demarcation, separating the sacred terrain of the Mormon world from the profane.

Like others who believed Joseph's story, eleven-year-old Matthias Cowley, a resident of Warsaw, Illinois, was eager to meet the Mormon prophet and convinced his father to take him to Nauvoo. There they met a man who

5. Max Weber, qtd. in ibid., 33.
6. Weber, *On Charisma and Institution Building,* 258-61; also Oakes, *Prophetic Charisma,* 38.
7. Oakes, *Prophetic Charisma,* 16.
8. See Oakes, *Prophetic Charisma,* 14.

said he knew Joseph well enough to arrange for an introduction. "We spent some time in conversation, on matters and things as they came along and we found the Prophet to be, what a man bearing that title ought to be;–a man of God in every respect, in word, and in deed, publicly, and privately, and was loved by every good man, woman, and child, we then felt very well satisfied after seeing the Prophet of the Most High God, Joseph Smith."[9]

LDS historian Juanita Brooks in her biography of Mormon convert John D. Lee notes that Lee "thought Joseph Smith carried an air of majesty that made him taller than his six feet as he faced the audience, and more handsome and commanding than an ordinary man," she wrote, trying to capture the essence of Joseph's appeal. Joseph drew "every eye and [held] every heart by the sheer magnetism of his personality, he played upon the congregation as though it were a musical instrument responsive to his slightest touch. When he spoke of the beauties and mysteries of the kingdom, he brought out the melody in deep, strong tones, into which with great skill were interspersed occasional light, sparkling tones of humor." Lee himself said Joseph was "the man who was more dear to us than all the riches and honors that could be conferred upon us by a thousand such worlds as the one we now inhabit."[10]

British convert William Clayton struggled to communicate his impressions of the prophet: "He is … a man of sound judgment, and possessed of [an] abundance of intelligence and whilst you listen to his conversation you receive intelligence which expands your mind and causes your heart to rejoice." Joseph answered Clayton's questions with wit and candor, and seemed, Clayton believed, pleased to engage in friendly badinage. He was well versed in the scriptures and conversant on many topics. Clayton found him possessed by integrity and honesty. "He has a great measure of the spirit of God, and by this means he is preserved from imposition." Joseph told Clayton and others that, even though he was a prophet, he was a "man of like passions with yourselves."[11] Clayton became Joseph's friend, confidante, and clerk, serving from 1842 until the prophet's death.

"I first saw the Prophet in 1842," wrote Elias Cox, recalling that initial encounter from the distance of fifty-eight years. Cox was only seven at the time, but had an indelible impression of Joseph's centrality to those who

9. Matthias Cowley, "Autobiography," not paginated.

10. Juanita Brooks, *John D. Lee,* 30, 31, 61.

11. William Clayton, "Historian's Corner: To the Saints in England: The Impressions of a Mormon Immigrant," 475-80; spelling and punctuation modernized.

gave up everything to join the faith. "He was a very handsome man, with blue eyes, and a countenance gleaming with beauty from his pure thoughts and enlightened work."[12] The Coxes moved to Hancock County, Illinois, in 1844, and Elias remembered Joseph's demonstration of personal power when he delivered a funeral sermon shortly before his own death: "I call to mind one prophecy which was immediately fulfilled," Elias wrote. "A severe storm arose. We grew very frightened and were preparing for home. Joseph told us to just arise to our feet, and the storm wouldn't hurt us. We obeyed. The storm soon passed away, the sun shone warm and the President resumed his speaking."[13]

Coincidence or miracle, Joseph's followers believed their own subjective experiences were objective proof of all that he spoke. For those who believed, Joseph spoke with God and delivered his message. This divine possibility loaded every moment they spent near Joseph with heightened significance, the closest thing they might hope to experience to conversing with God themselves. Many of the experiences preserved in print about Nauvoo were reminiscent accounts that had occurred when the speaker was a child or a young adult, yet they seem to have told the story over and over throughout their lives, until it acquired mythic significance.

Perhaps it was a fatal flaw, but Joseph was almost incurably optimistic about the intentions of those he cared about, even those he did not know well enough to judge. And this trait sometimes got him into trouble. When he judged incorrectly, both he and his people suffered; yet over and over, when some of Joseph's most trusted and seemingly loyal confidants betrayed him (as he and his followers interpreted their actions), he welcomed them back and made room for their repentance when they asked for it, rarely holding a grudge for long.

Though Thomas Ford was not one of Joseph's admirers, he described him in 1854 as physically prepossessing but flawed in character. He published this final evaluation of the martyred Mormon prophet:

> Thus fell Joe Smith, the most successful impostor in modern times; a man who, though ignorant and coarse, had some great natural parts, which fitted him for temporary success, but which were so obscured and counteracted by the inherent corruption and vices of his nature, that he never could succeed in establishing a system of policy which looked to

---

12. Elias Cox, "Joseph Smith, the Prophet," 544.
13. Ibid.

> permanent success in the future. . . . The strong cravings of the animal nature will never give fair play to a fine understanding, the judgment is never allowed to choose that good which is far away, in preference to enticing evil near at hand. And this may be considered a wise ordinance of Providence, by which the counsels of talented but corrupt men, are defeated in the very act which promised success.

In 1842 at age fifty-two, Ford became governor of Illinois. When he wrote his own history of Mormon Nauvoo, he had the benefit of hindsight and, furthermore, had even acted on its tumultuous stage. He was unforgiving in laying the responsibility for both the persecution of the Mormon people and the deaths of Joseph and his older brother Hyrum at the feet of Joseph himself. Believing that Joseph was crafty but clever, charismatic but dishonest, he saw genius of a sort in Joseph, but genius that was dangerous and complicated.

> It must not be supposed that the pretended Prophet practiced the tricks of a common imposter; that he was a dark and gloomy person, with a long beard, a grave and severe aspect, and a reserved and saintly carriage of his person; on the contrary, he was full of levity, even to boyish romping; dressed like a dandy, and at times drank like a sailor and swore like a pirate. He could, as occasion required, be exceedingly meek in his deportment; and then again rough and boisterous as a highway robber; being always able to satisfy his followers of the propriety of his conduct.[14]

More neutral–but more positive–was the assessment of a non-Mormon observer of Joseph's oratory who crossed his path just once. Mathew L. Davis, a visitor to Washington, D.C., was drawn by curiosity to hear Joseph preach publicly on Wednesday, February 5, 1840. He wrote the next day to his wife in New York City:

> He is a plain, sensible, strong minded man. Everything he says, is said in a manner to leave an impression that he is sincere. There is no levity, no fanaticism, no want of dignity in his deportment. He is apparently from forty to forty-five years of age, rather above the middle stature, and what you ladies would call a very good looking man. In his garb there are no peculiarities; his dress being that of a plain, unpretending citizen. He is by profession a farmer, but is evidently well read.

Davis remembered that Joseph accurately summarized the criticisms

14. Thomas Ford, *History of Illinois . . .*, 2:213-14.

against him: Some claimed that he pretended to be a "Savior, a worker of miracles." On the contrary, Joseph asserted, "[h]e made no such pretensions. He was but a man, ... a plain, untutored man; seeking what he should do to be saved." Joseph began simply with a short course on Mormon belief. "[T]here is a God," he said, "possessing all the attributes ascribed to Him by all Christians of all denominations ... all are subject to His power." Joseph continued, "We teach nothing but what the Bible teaches. We believe nothing, but what is to be found in this book." According to Davis, Joseph believed "that a man is a moral, responsible, free agent; that although it was foreordained he should fall, and be redeemed ..." In conclusion, Joseph insisted that "all who would follow the precepts of the Bible, whether Mormon or not, would assuredly be saved." *"I have changed my opinion of the Mormons"* after hearing Joseph speak, Davis reported. "They are an injured and much-abused people."[15]

Another devotee of Joseph was Parley P. Pratt, who was a member of the prophet's original Quorum of Twelve Apostles. He wrote of Joseph in near worshipful tones: "there was something connected with the serene and steady penetrating glance of his eye, as if he would penetrate the deepest abyss of the human heart, gaze into eternity, penetrate the heavens, and comprehend all worlds."[16] Pratt felt the impact on his own life of Joseph's message, so it was easy for him to believe the prophet possessed the ability to change the entire world for the good. "[H]ad [Joseph] been spared a martyr's fate till mature manhood and age, he was certainly endowed with powers and ability to have revolutionized the world in many respects, and to have transmitted to posterity a name associated with more brilliant and glorious acts than has yet fallen to the lots of mortals."[17]

A long-time Latter-day Saint and employee in the newspaper offices of both the *Nauvoo Neighbor* and the *Times and Seasons,* twenty-one-year-old Lyman O. Littlefield described the force of Joseph's message. Joseph "struck through the heart, and, like the thunder of the cataract, declared at once the dignity and matchless supremacy of the Creator." Littlefield felt he had met someone destined to change his life. "There was something in his manner, his countenance and spirit that not associated with mortal man that we had looked upon before."[18] One of Joseph's scribes, twenty-five-year-old, Howard Coray,

15. M. L. Davis, qtd. in *History of the Church,* 4:78-79 (Feb. 6, 1840).
16. Parley P. Pratt, *Autobiography,* 45.
17. Ibid., 46.
18. Lyman O. Littlefield, "Autobiography (1819-1848)," 35-36, at www.boap.org/LDS/

was "completely carried away with his indescribable eloquence, [and his] power of expression–speaking as I have never heard any other man speak."[19]

In Nauvoo, revelations came in the context of sermons as often as they were couched in the more formal, commanding language of "thus saith the Lord." Joseph expounded on new doctrine in letters or in informal conversations, in speeches delivered at the stand in the shadow of the temple or while leaning against the stone mantle of someone's fireplace. When Joseph spoke, he bore witness of heaven and transmitted sacred messages to the Saints. As a result, those who believed he was a prophet listened attentively, cherished every word, carefully interpreted it, and reshaped their lives to accommodate and obey it.

In both private and public, Joseph comported himself as if he was fulfilling a script dictated by God. His plans for the expansion of Nauvoo fell into this frame, as did his sermons about baptism for the dead or the temple endowment ritual. They weighed on him, were conceived by him as revelations, and were uttered as mandates that required prompt, specific courses of action.

Charles Root Dana solicited Joseph's help when his wife was "sick, nigh unto death." "How long has she been sick?" Joseph asked as he walked around the room of the log house that Dana and his wife shared with another family in Nauvoo. "I began to fear that he considered her past recovery," confessed Dana, "but he finally went to the fire, warmed his hands, throwed his cloak off, went to the bed, laid his hands on her, and while in the midst of his administering to her, he seemed to be baffled. The disease or evil spirit rested upon him; but he overpowered it and pronounced great blessings upon her."[20] She lived to make the journey west.

Stories of healings were legend in Joseph's wake. Phoebe Carter Woodruff, whose husband, Wilford, would become the LDS Church's fourth president, dated the beginning of her own testimony of Joseph from the summer of 1840, when the work of clearing swampland endangered Nauvoo's health. "The Prophet had the sick borne into his house and door-yard, until his place was like a hospital. At length, even he succumbed to the deadly contagion, and for several days was as helpless as the rest of our people ... But the Spirit of the Lord came upon Joseph commanding him to arise and

Early-Saints/LLittlefield.html (June 6, 2013).

19. Howard Coray, Letter to Martha Jane Lewis, Aug. 2, 1889. Coray was twenty-five in 1842.

20. Charles Root Dana, "An Abridged Account of the Life: Travels Etc., of Elder Charles R. Dana Written by Himself at Ogden City in the A.D. 1859," 28-29, LDS Church History Library.

stay the pestilence."[21] As Phoebe recalled, Joseph went to the doorway of his home and, standing there, commanded the sick in the name of Jesus to "arise and be made whole, and they were healed according to his word."[22]

It was important to believers that Joseph could see into heaven, through and beyond the veil. "As Prophet he seemed to understand, and was able to foretell the mysteries of the future with a marked degree of accuracy, and nearly as much readiness as the ordinary individual could relate the happenings of the past," convert Jane S. Richards recalled. "As Seer and Revelator he was fearless and outspoken, yet humble, never considering that he was more than the mouthpiece through whom God spoke."[23]

Joseph helped them process their questions and find their way to answers. Wandle Mace, who turned thirty-three in 1842, described the way Joseph engaged in conversation, sometimes stopping to talk with workers at the temple site. Someone would say, "Brother Joseph talk to us." And Joseph would answer, "What do you want me to talk about, start something." Inevitably, a question would surface, a sort of challenge for Joseph to take on. Mace said he loved to listen to such exchanges, when Joseph "would unravel the scriptures and explain doctrine as no other man could."[24]

Many anecdotes capture Joseph's warmth, enthusiasm for life, and optimism about people. He had the custom of going to the dock to welcome new Saints to the city. The arrival of these ships constituted quasi-social occasions for many residents of the city, so the spirit of excitement was significant. Robert Crookston remembered the rush of one of these occasions when he had felt himself a much welcomed newcomer: "As we approached the landing place to our great joy we saw the Prophet Joseph Smith there to welcome his people who had come so far. We were all so glad to see him & set our feet upon the promised land so to speak. It was the most thrilling experience of my life for I know I was with the Prophet of the Lord."[25]

Jewish immigrant and Mormon convert Alexander Neibaur, who reached Nauvoo in 1841, also wrote about the strong sense of sanctuary he felt upon arrival. "A number of the brother[s] was ready to receive us; they

21. Phoebe C. Woodruff, "Autobiographical Sketch."

22. Ibid.

23. Jane S. Richards, "Joseph Smith, the Prophet," 550. Jane Snyder, age thirty-seven in 1840, was born in Jefferson County, New York, married Apostle Franklin D. Richards, and was a member of the Relief Society in Nauvoo.

24. Wandle Mace, Journal, typescript, 101-102. Mace, a farmer from New York State, was one of Parley P. Pratt's converts. He served missions in the Catskill Mountains and in Missouri, and started an iron foundry in Nauvoo.

25. Robert Crookston, "Autobiography of Robert Crookston Senior," 65.

kindly offered their houses, many slept in a large stone building belonging to one of the brethren ... others kept up a large fire all night and stayed with our luggage. Some of the brethren that had come here before us kept us company. Early in the morning a number of the brethren came to Inquire whether all of us had obtained habitations. We got in very comfortable with a Brother."[26] Apostle Heber C. Kimball, returning from his British mission, included the welcoming scene in his report to the *Millennial Star:* "We landed in Nauvoo on the 1st of July, [1841] and when we struck the dock I think there was about three hundred Saints there to meet us, and a greater manifestation of love and gladness I never saw before. President [Joseph] Smith was the first one that caught us by the hand."[27]

Joseph himself spoke of the emotion and power that such moments evoked, the performance of community, faith, and devotion. After weeks of exhausting travel, the convert must have looked toward the wharf with enormous relief. Standing at the dock were literally hundreds of new brothers and sisters, offering love and help. The central figure was Joseph, who rushed up to the boat to greet his new followers, his enthusiasm seemingly untainted by the burden of disappointments he had endured. Each new boatload of converts was hope, proof of the power of the word of God and a prophet's voice, and reason enough to find a way to make Zion materialize.

Joseph's belief in his prophetic calling gave him the authority to demand great sacrifices of believers. When Brigham Young was preparing to leave on his first proselytizing mission in England in 1839, one of his children was sick and his wife, Mary Ann, was still in bed, having given birth only ten days earlier. Nor was their housing–abandoned barracks–even remotely adequate. Brigham had no money or supplies to leave with Mary Ann. Understandably, he was torn. Joseph said, trying to comfort his friend, "If you will go, I promise you, that your family shall live, and you shall live, and you shall know that the hand of God is in calling you to go and preach the Gospel of life and salvation to a perishing world."[28] Brigham rose to the occasion, even though he was too weak to rise from the wagon-bed that carried him away; and his commitment to his prophet sustained him until the end of his own life.

Perhaps Joseph's greatest power was his ability to craft his people's self-image, even when challenged by the judgments of outsiders. His word

26. Alexander Neibaur, Journal, 12.
27. Orson F. Whitney, *Life of Heber C. Kimball,* 323.
28. Brigham Young, July 24, 1854, JD 2:19.

empowered them in both dangerous and positive ways. Typically followers of charismatic leaders yearn "for some moral absolute."[29] Finding it in their leader, they become devoted to him as both person and symbol. Reinforcing their individual commitment is the strength of the group; those drawn by a common belief in Joseph's prophet-narrative felt their own faith buttressed by others who had similarly changed their lives in equally dramatic ways. The force and power of a group dedicated to their prophet swept them along in a current that dropped them into a future undeniably uncertain but which held heavenly potentiality. Despite the severe challenges of being a despised people, the social rewards of becoming a Saint were immense. The fraternal/sororal relationship within the community of Saints connected them to a new network. In common, they shared the belief that God had marked them for special blessings. The prophet-narrative supplied a script that was both demanding and supportive.

Their faith oriented the Saints toward Joseph and the new world he imagined. Once they made the all-or-nothing decision to hand over their lives to the greater Mormon narrative, the decisions that followed were clear.[30] For the faithful, Joseph was "proof that the divine life is attainable." As they projected their hopes onto Joseph–the "embodiment of their ultimate concerns," the "exemplar of a sacred lifestyle," the "fount of divine truth"[31]–he became a catalyst for their own belief in the meaning of their lives in the context of heaven.

---

29. Alun J. Jones and Robert M. Anservitze, "Saint-Simone and Saint-Simonism," 1104.
30. Oakes, *Prophetic Charisma,* 128.
31. Ibid., 128.

CHAPTER 2

Refuge

Central to [Joseph] Smith's religious vision was the conviction that the men of God must be men of affairs, fashioning the Kingdom of Heaven into a kingdom of this world. Nauvoo was his supreme effort to accomplish that end.

–Robert B. Flanders, Nauvoo, *vi*

Joseph wove a story in the dark, dank cavity of Liberty Jail (Missouri), where he and others were held prisoner for treason. That narrative was anchored in fact but mythic in its construction of identity. Still reeling from a round of persecution that seemed cosmic, from predictions of apocalyptic doom fulfilled in the bucolic landscapes of Missouri, and from a series of unsuccessful efforts at building Zion, Joseph began to reformulate his story. It was a story he would repeatedly lay before governors, presidents, senators, and anyone who he thought might listen. But it was also a story that would ultimately lead him to death.[1]

Although jailed from December 1838 until April 1839, Joseph struggled mightily to maintain a voice and to draw the Latter-day Saints together. Depending on his Twelve Apostles to lead the Saints in his absence and to clean up the mess left in Missouri, he wrote to Apostles Heber C. Kimball and Brigham Young, contextualizing his request for help in the larger drama of Zion building. The letter, signed by Joseph and his two counselors in the Church's governing First Presidency on January 16, 1839, conflates their sufferings with the gospel: "Let the elders preach nothing but the first principles of the gospel. and let them publish our afflictions. the injustice and

1. For a history of the Church in Missouri, see Mark A. Scherer, *The Journey of a People: The Era of Restoration, 1820 to 1844* (Independence, Missouri: Community of Christ, Seminary Press, 2013), 165-233, 279-342. See also Leland H. Gentry and Todd M. Compton, *Fire and Sword: A History of the Latter-day Saints in Northern Missouri, 1836-39* (Salt Lake City: Greg Kofford Books, 2011).

cruelty thereof upon the house tops. Let them write it and publish it in all the papers where they go." It was signed in a way that captured the tie that bound them as a group, "Brethren we remain yours in hope of Eternal life."[2]

Joseph's need of a forum for communication to preserve the story of what was happening is apparent. One theme running through the narrative of Joseph's life is his orientation toward the future. Joseph plotted what came next even as he dealt with the wet straw and winter frost of Liberty Jail. Less than certain that he indeed had a future, he nevertheless planned for the migration of the Saints to a new Zion, a place carved out of a swamp on the banks of the Mississippi that would become the sacred terrain of a religious community. Critical to Joseph's efforts were friends whom he hoped would help accomplish his goal of securing a new home for the Church.

Brigham Young was in Illinois, after leaving Far West, Missouri, on February 14, 1839, because "his life was so diligently sought for."[3] In his role as president of the Quorum of Twelve Apostles, he headed the Church committee responsible for organizing the Saints' exodus out of Missouri. Persecution had mounted to a feverish pitch, poisoning the winter of 1838-39. Beginning in February 1839, a flood of as many as 10,000 Saints surged across the Mississippi River and moved into Quincy, Illinois, and surrounding hinterland where civic-minded residents gave them shelter.[4] Illinois Governor Thomas Carlin lived in Quincy, a town of 1,600 residents when the Saints arrived.[5]

While Joseph remained in jail, he communicated his vision for the future in at least six letters. His wife, Emma, and their children had left Missouri in mid-February 1839. They arrived at the "Mississippi, opposite Quincy after a journey of almost insupportable hardships," according to Joseph's record of February 15.[6] At Quincy, non-Mormons Sarah Kingsley Cleveland and her husband, John, took the mother and children into their home located three miles from town. Some Mormon refugees found shelter in abandoned Fort Montrose on the Iowa side of the river fifty miles north of and across from Commerce. Quincy was already the area's largest municipality, and some Saints decided to stay there. By 1840, Quincy was "most

2. Joseph Smith, Letter to Heber C. Kimball and Brigham Young, Jan. 16, 1839, in Dean C. Jessee, ed., *Personal Writings of Joseph Smith,* 425.

3. *History of the Church,* 3:261 (Feb. 14, 1839).

4. James B. Allen and Glen M. Leonard, *The Story of the Latter-day Saints,* 145.

5. By 1842, the town boasted 2,319 citizens. See *The American Almanac and Repository of Useful Knowledge for Year 1842* (Boston: David H. Williams, 1842), 251.

6. *History of the Church,* 3:262 (Feb. 15, 1839).

picturesquely situated about 125 feet above the river of which commands a fine view";[7] on October 25, the Church organized the Quincy Stake.[8]

As Joseph fretted behind bars, he sent emissaries to seek a new refuge. Thirty-three-year-old Isaac Barlow traveled upriver to Commerce during the winter of 1838-39 to investigate the possibility of renting some of the town's buildings, became lost, and ended up penniless some distance from the mouth of the Des Moines River. Someone introduced him to Isaac Galland, a land promoter. Galland, born May 15, 1791, in Somerset County, Pennsylvania, had spent most of his life in a frontier community at Marietta, Ohio; had studied at William and Mary College's divinity school and medicine in Indiana; and had also made an unsuccessful bid for the Iowa State Legislature.[9] Barlow told Galland the Saints' story, and their encounter became "a providential introduction of the Church to Commerce ... and its vicinity."[10] Barlow went to Quincy and told those he met there, including David White Rogers, about his conversation with Galland.[11]

Barlow had long before proven his loyalty to Joseph, who had ordained him a seventy in 1835.[12] Rogers, age fifty-two, was an experienced frontiersman. His family had lived in Montreal, Canada, and in Chautauqua County, New York, before 1830 when they moved to New York City. Equipped with a range of skills, he embodied Frederick Jackson Turner's notion of the American frontiersman in his versatility, moving from working as a fur trapper, farmer, lumberman, and eventually cabinetmaker.[13]

When Galland met Barlow and Rogers, Commerce consisted primarily of forty dwellings. Across the Mississippi were the military barracks of Fort Des Moines, constructed to house troops during the Black Hawk War but now available for another fifty families.[14] Galland owned land in both Iowa and Illinois near Commerce. Three cousins of Mormon apostle Heber C. Kimball–Hiram, Ethan, and Phineas Kimball–had already purchased land in the Military Tract for their father, Phineas, and most likely knew

---

7. Andrew Jenson, *Historical Record,* 8:733.

8. Ibid., 739.

9. Lyndon W. Cook, "Isaac Galland–Mormon Benefactor," 261-62.

10. *History of the Church,* 3:265 (Feb. 25, 1839).

11. See Isaac Galland, Letter to D. W. Rogers, Feb. 26, 1839, in *History of the Church,* 3:265.

12. Andrew Jenson, *LDS Biographical Encyclopedia,* 4:687.

13. See Frederick Jackson Turner, "The Significance of the Frontier in American History," www.h-net.org/~hst203/documents/turner.html (Oct. 10, 2011).

14. David W. Rogers, Statement, Feb. 1, 1839; Wandle Mace, Autobiography. Barlow and Rogers most likely surveyed other sites as well. David E. Miller and Della S. Miller, *Nauvoo,* 21; *History of the Church,* 3:365-66.

Galland.[15] In 1804 and 1816, the federal government had acquired sites on both sides of the Mississippi by treaty for forts and also for settlement. The Illinois Military Bounty Tract included the region south of Rock Island between the Illinois and Mississippi Rivers where War of 1812 veterans wishing to become permanent settlers could claim 160 acres each.[16]

Barlow returned to Missouri, carrying Galland's message to Joseph. Joseph encouraged him to continue negotiations. The most immediate questions were: Should the Church establish a strong central gathering point or should the Mormons disperse across a wider landscape? If the former, where could they find land and the money to purchase it? Joseph wanted his people together. Rogers and Barlow reported Joseph's authorization to Church leaders William Marks, Elias Higbee, Sidney Rigdon, and Edward Partridge on February 11, 1839.[17] In the absence of the Twelve Apostles, these men conducted the Church's business. Rigdon presided over the meeting held in Quincy to discuss Galland's offer.

Although the Mormons must have looked like shaky prospects, Galland's offer was an attractive one: 20,000 acres at $2 per acre at no interest, payable in twenty annual installments. While it is uncertain why he made such an irresistible offer, it was the beginning of an important, though complicated, relationship.[18] Barlow and Rogers also reported on "Commerce City," a village that had never been incorporated, sold land, or been settled. Horace Hotchkiss and John Gillett, two Connecticut speculators, promoted the Hotchkiss Syndicate, which had advertised Commerce City lots for sale in 1837 even though the lots did not have clear title.

Galland kept negotiations alive in a letter to Rogers dated February 26.[19] He estimated that the area could absorb fifty families or more, pledged his friendship, and offered to help them "collectively, as a people."[20] Rogers had the assignment of selling Church holdings in Missouri. "The little knowledge which I have as yet of the doctrine, order or practice of the Church," Galland wrote, "leaves me under the necessity of acting in all this matter as a stranger, though, as I sincerely hope, as a friend, for such, ... I feel that I am assuming a very great responsibility in this undertaking, and I wish to

15. Orson F. Whitney, *Life of Heber C. Kimball,* 260; Stanley B. Kimball, *Heber C. Kimball,* 79n.
16. Robert Flanders, *Nauvoo,* 16.
17. Minutes of Church Conference, Quincy, Illinois, Feb. 1839, in *History of the Church,* 3:260.
18. Ibid., 260, 265-67.
19. Isaac Galland, Letter to D. W. Rogers, Feb. 26, 1839, in *History of the Church,* 3:265-66.
20. Ibid., 267.

be governed by the dictates of wisdom and discretion." Galland concluded with a flourish: "Accept, dear sir, for yourself and in behalf of the Church and people, assurance of my sincere sympathy in your sufferings and wrongs, and deep solicitude for your immediate relief from present distress."[21]

Marks questioned whether the Church should pledge its credit to buy land for the Saints. But simultaneously he committed support to the Church "providing that it was the will of the Lord that we should again gather together." In Joseph's absence, Marks encouraged candor, saying that if "the brethren would speak their minds, the Lord would undoubtedly manifest His will by His Spirit." Barlow expressed his belief that the Saints had brought their problems on their own heads through their disobedience in "building according to the pattern, that we had thus been scattered." Partridge also "thought it was not expedient under the present circumstances to collect together, but thought it was better to scatter into different parts and provide for the poor, which would be acceptable to God." His remarks swayed Higbee; and by the time they voted, they unanimously judged "that it would not be deemed advisable to locate on the lands for the present."[22] Partridge reported to Joseph: "It is not wisdom to effect a trade ... at present; possibly it may be wisdom hereafter." He added, "This place is full of our people, yet they are scattering off nearly all the while."[23]

A month earlier, the Quincy Democratic Association had joined LDS leaders to organize relief efforts. After February 27, 1839, J. W. Whitney headed a special committee to assess local resources and needs. Whitney, with Higbee's help, identified two dozen destitute widows and families. "We have been robbed of our corn, wheat, horses, cattle, cows, hogs, wearing apparel, houses and homes, and, indeed, of all that renders life tolerable," Higbee wrote. "We think that to give us employment, rent us farms, and allow us the protection and privileges of other citizens, would raise us from a state of dependence, liberate us from the iron grasp of poverty, put us in possession of a competency, and deliver us from the ruinous effects of persecution, despotism, and tyranny."[24] On the basis of this report, the committee promised the Mormons that Illinois would be "guided and directed by that charity which never faileth."[25] The committee raised $100 to alleviate the

21. *History of the Church,* 3:267 (Feb. 26, 1839).
22. Ibid., 260-61 (Feb. 11, 1839).
23. Edward Partridge, Letter to Joseph Smith, Mar. 5, 1839, in *History of the Church,* 3:272.
24. *History of the Church,* 3:269-70.
25. Minutes of the Democratic Association, Feb. 27-28, 1839, in *History of the Church,* 3:268.

most pressing suffering. The willingness of the Mormons to work also made them attractive refugees.

Despite Galland's aggressive salesmanship, Joseph's representatives in Commerce remained unconvinced. On March 1839, a courier brought a bundle of letters to Liberty Jail, including messages from Galland and from Partridge, who continued to urge caution.[26]

Joseph must have been dismayed that the leaders had not yet fixed on a gathering place. Fearing that the Church was splintering in his absence, he drafted an epistle on March 25 warning against "aspiring men"–those focused on their own individual well-being. "The rights of the Priesthood are inseparably connected with the powers of heaven," he explained. "The powers of heaven cannot be controlled nor handled only upon the principles of righteousness. … Everything should be discussed with a great deal of care and propriety."[27]

Joseph visualized himself cutting through the hesitation, the temporizing, and the fear–gathering up the collective will of the Saints and hurling it like an arrow into a better future. His frustration gnawed at him. At this point, his incarceration was nearing its fifth month.

Throughout his time in Liberty Jail, Joseph and those imprisoned with him received a series of visits from family and friends. For Joseph, such visits had a powerful impact on his morale and ability to endure. For his visitors, seeing their prophet in such wretched conditions was acutely painful. Presendia Huntington Buell, a woman who later would be sealed to Joseph as a plural wife, visited Joseph twice, once with her father, William, and another time with Frederick G. Williams. She later recounted her impressions of what for her became a sacred event. "We were watched very closely, lest we should have tools to help the prisoners escape. I took dinner with the brethren in prison; they were much pleased to see the faces of true friends; but I cannot describe my feelings on seeing that man of God there confined in such a trying time for the saints."[28] Joseph followed her visit with a letter on March 15: The trials suffered by his people, he affirmed, "will only give us that knowledge to understand the minds of the Ancients for my part I think I never could have felt as I now do if I had not suffered

26. Cook, "Isaac Galland–Mormon Benefactor," 269; *History of the Church,* 3:272-73 (Mar. 10, 1839).

27. *History of the Church,* 3:299-301 (Mar. 25, 1839).

28. Presendia Huntington Buell Smith Kimball, qtd. in Edward Tullidge, *The Women of Mormondom,* 209.

the wrongs that I have suffered all things shall work together for good to them that love God."[29]

Emma poured her own anguished feelings into carefully worded letters carried to the jail by friends. "I shall not attempt to write my feelings altogether," she confessed to her husband, "for the situation in which you are, the walls, bars, and bolts, rolling rivers, running streams, rising hills, sinking vallies and spreading prairies that separate us, and the cruel injustice that first cast you into prison and still holds you there, with many other considerations, places my feelings far beyond description." Marriage to a prophet brought with it extraordinary highs as well as difficulties beyond measure. "No one but God knows the reflections of my mind and the feelings of my heart," she continued, "when I left our house and home, and almost [sic] all of every thing that we possessed excepting our little children, and took my journey out of the State of Missouri, leaving you shut up in that lonesome prison. But the recollection is more than human nature ought to bear."[30]

Brigham Young, who reached Quincy in mid-February, quickly assessed the advantage in keeping the Saints together in groups rather than diffusing their solidarity both spatially and socially. He promptly set to work to reverse the uncertainty; and on March 17, he encouraged a congregation of Saints to "unite together as much as possible in extending the hand of charity for the relief of the poor, who were suffering for the Gospel's sake," and to do what "would prove for the general good of the whole Church." Acknowledging that others disagreed with this recommendation, he nevertheless strongly asserted his influence.[31] This moment was, in some ways, Young at his best.

Almost simultaneously, Joseph was taking action in Missouri. The restraints of Liberty Jail gave him time to ponder his next move and to place it in the larger narrative of persecution. On March 20, he dictated a letter to "the Church of Latter-day Saints at Quincy, Illinois and scattered abroad and to Bishop [Edward] Partridge in Particular."[32] It was apparent that he had thought deeply about the significance of the past several months. Although all the prisoners–who, besides Joseph, were Hyrum Smith, Lyman Wight, Alexander McRae, and Caleb Baldwin–signed it, the missive was

29. Joseph Smith, Letter to Presendia Huntington Buell (Mrs. Norman Buell), Mar. 15, 1839, in Jessee, *Personal Writings of Joseph Smith,* 427.

30. Emma Smith, Letter to Joseph Smith, Mar. 7, 1839.

31. "Minutes of the Conference at Quincy," *History of the Church,* 3:283 (Mar. 17, 1839).

32. Joseph Smith, Letter to the Church of Latter-day Saints, Quincy, Illinois, Mar. 20, 1839, in Jessee, *Personal Writings of Joseph Smith,* 430; D&C 121-23. See also *History of the Church,* 3:289 (Mar. 25, 1839).

clearly from Joseph himself, described in it as a "prisoner for the Lord Jesus Christ's sake." The letter situated its audience as Saints "taken and held by the power of mobocracy under the exterminating reign of his excelancy [sic] the [Missouri] Governor Lilburn W. Boggs." Joseph's letter colored meanings of "Missouri" for Latter-day Saints ever since.

The hapless men were charged falsely, held unjustly, denied common comforts, "smitten without cause," and cruelly separated "from the love of God, and fellowship with the community of Saints." Yet the persecution had only made them grow closer, becoming stronger. Almost incoherent with outrage, Joseph's accusation tumbled out, providing a glimpse into his use of language:

> [The] unrelenting hand the inhumanity and murderous disposition of this people it shocks all nature it beggers and defies all discription. it is a tail [tale] of wo a lamentable tail [tale] yea a sorrifull tail [tale] too much to tell too much for contemplation too much to think of for a moment to much for human beings it cannot be found among the hethans it cannot be found among the nations where Kings and tyrants are inthroned it cannot be found among the savages of the wilderness yea and I think it cannot be found among the wild and ferocious beasts of the forist that a man should be mangled for sport. . . . that they have their last morsel for subsistence and then be violated to gratify the hell[i]sh desires of the mob and finally left to perish with their helpless off spring clinging around their necks.[33]

"O God," Joseph lamented, "where art thou and where is the pavilion that covereth thy hiding place how long shall thy hand be stayed and thine eye yea thy pure eye behold . . . and thine ear be penetrated with their c[r]yes yea o Lord how long shall they suffer these rongs and unlawful oppressions before thine hart shall be softened towards them and thy bowels be moved with compassion to-wards them."[34]

Concluding, Joseph promised the Saints that he would be with them again soon, that all the prisoners were "determined to indure tribulation as good soldiers unto the end." Adding an additional few pages of reflection, Joseph encouraged them to place this most recent experience in context, remembering the promise "that all these things shall give thee experience." He turned their attention away from brooding by assigning them to create a

33. Jessee, *Personal Writings of Joseph Smith,* 431.

34. Ibid. Richard Lyman Bushman, *Joseph Smith,* 380, describes how this letter turns the "raw Missouri experience into a theology of suffering. The passage interwove Joseph's ongoing feelings about his own past with the struggle in Missouri."

committee that would gather statements, affidavits, and any other materials to prove the severity of their suffering.[35]

Sick much of the time, Joseph must have felt conflicted. His heart was in Quincy with Emma. His wife shared with him the burden that came with prophethood, and he in exchange shared some of his most intimate thoughts with her. On March 21, the day after finishing his epistle to the Church, he wrote privately to Emma, telling her to read the letter he had sent to the Church and to make sure that his own parents read it as well. He fretted over his inability to provide for her and their children, expressing the hope that the Clevelands would let them share their home until matters were resolved. Empathically, he wrote: "I very well know your toils and simpathise with you," and promised, "if God will spare my life once more to have the privelege of takeing care of you I will ease your care and indeavour to cumfort your heart." Anxious to assure the children that he was not voluntarily absent, he begged Emma to tell them that he was in prison so "that their lives might be saved." He concluded by positioning his plight in an eternal context: "God ruleth all things after the council of his own will my trust is in him the salvation of my soul is of the most importants to me for as much as I know for a certainty of Eternal things if the heveans linger it is nothing to [me]."[36]

It is true that stories represent variations on a repertoire of narrative themes that legitimate the tellers' personal choices, such as those that had brought Joseph to the Liberty Jail. But it is also true that narrative interprets community and guarantees its continued existence. Joseph's story of the Missouri persecutions was, at its core, self-legitimizing and unifying, making the Mormons' experience biblical theater performed on the American Midwest frontier. In it, identity, memory, and community overlap at various points, each mutually influencing and reinforcing the others.

For the Mormons, nothing short of the transformation of society was sufficient. Choosing to leave the world as they had known it and to cleave to each other as Saints in Zion, they consciously formed with their actions a social commentary that articulated what they thought worked and what did not. Restoration of an ancient religious tradition positioned this discourse in patterns long established and seized authority while forging an identity of difference, of being God's chosen people. In some ways a manifestation of the Second Great Awakening, the Mormon story was an emergence of

35. Jessee, *Personal Writings of Joseph Smith,* 438, 442.

36. Joseph Smith, Liberty, Missouri, Letter to Emma Smith, Mar. 21, 1839, in Jessee, *Personal Writings of Joseph Smith,* 448-49.

possibilities that pointed to new understandings about moral and social orders. It created a new cultural mythos of persecution, dualities which pitted them against Satan's armies and placed them in a favored position near God and his prophet.

It is easy to see why this sacred narrative created conflict wherever the Mormons went. Self-consciously designated as the "other," Mormons preached a different religious message, couched it in a different set of understandings, and challenged nearly everyone around them. The only choices were conversion or disobedience to God. The demonization involved in this dichotomy created outrage that ended in bloodshed at its worst but, even at its best, produced gaps that eventually became unbridgeable.

Mormonism was one of many groups that experimented during this period with a better way of being in the world and religious efforts at building new worlds.[37] The Mormon version questioned the culture it rejected and the social disjunction it caused. Shifts in systems of authority, economic and social power dislocations, and confused and disjointed traditions stimulated new cultural norms for converts to Joseph's message. Perceiving those outside the faith who rejected conversion as wilfully corrupt, the Mormons proposed a new moral and social order. Conflict with those who did not accept Joseph's story or vision for the good life was inevitable.[38]

In his dungeon, Joseph seized upon the opportunity that Galland held out and optimistically saw only advantages. Within a few years, his optimism would be tainted by the sharper realities of questionable land titles and Galland's own questionable honesty. The mass movement of a religious people was in some ways too good to be true, a perfect audience for Galland's performance as beneficent businessman. Moreover, Galland's dubious land titles foretold the complicated history of land deals the Church would have from that time forward. But in 1839, Galland seemed like a gift from God, designed to save the Saints.

Joseph urged the Church to seize this opportunity. While he paid lip service to caution, he counseled "friendly feelings" toward Galland and a

37. For a discussion of Jacksonian America as an age characterized by "boundlessness"–a radical sovereignty unleashing innovation and experimentation–see John Higham, *From Boundlessness to Consolidation;* see also Daniel J. Boorstin, *The Americans: The National Experience.*

38. John E. Hallwas and Roger D. Launius, eds., *Cultures in Conflict,* 8, comment: "Conflict between these groups arose because of their strikingly different cultural values. The experience of people in Hancock County [Illinois] during the 1840s demonstrates the inevitable conflict between theocratic and democratic government, the danger of demonizing other people, and the self-deceptions fostered by the myths of innocence and political righteousness."

strong relationship with Iowa's territorial governor, Robert Lucas, "he shall prove himself to be a man of honor and a friend to humanity. We really think that [Galland's] letter breathes that kind of spirit if we may judge correctly. … Governor Lucas also. We [suggest] the ideah of praying fervently for all men who manifest any degree of sympathy for the suffering children of God. … It seems to be deeply impressed on our minds that the saints ought to lay hold of every door that shall seem to be opened for <unto them> to obtain foot … hold on the Earth and to be making all the preperations that is within the power of posibles for the terible storms that are now gethering in the heavens."[39] Joseph was naive in trusting Galland; but in reality, the Mormons' friends of any type were limited.

Although an experienced land broker, Galland, called "Doctor" by some, was a quintessential frontier booster of new settlements. Thomas Ford later described him as a member of the "Marsac Gang" (implying he was an outlaw), once indicted for perjury in Hancock County (never tried), and newspaper editor (1835-46). Regardless of whether he had engaged in a life of crime, Galland was facile in his ability to strike a deal. Although never tried in court, he was "no pretender to integrity," according to Ford.[40] Capturing the spirit of the land boom of the 1830s and 1840s, Galland turned to real estate.[41]

Twenty-five years before the Saints came to the area, the Sac and Fox Indians had formed an agreement with Congress to create the so-called Half-Breed Tract. Located south of Fort Madison (Iowa), the territory after 1842 spanned the distance between the Mississippi and Des Moines Rivers and was shaped like a piece of pie. The government originally designated the space to protect the "half breed" offspring of the first wave of frontier settlers living on the reservation. Despite the government's restrictions regarding ownership of the land, many settlers applied to purchase lots.

The 119,000-acre tract opened to a flood of land speculators in 1834.[42] The Wisconsin Claims Commission tried to straighten out the land deals formed after the creation of Iowa territory,[43] but Iowa's legislature subsequently

39. Joseph Smith, Letter from the Liberty Jail, Mar. 25, 1839, in Jessee, *The Personal Writings of Joseph Smith,* 439.

40. Thomas Ford, *History of Illinois,* 2:294-95.

41. Ibid. See also Nelson C. Roberts and Samuel W. Moorehead, *History of Lee County, Iowa,* 308, 1216; Dean Depew McBrien, "The Influence of the Frontier on Joseph Smith," 249; Thomas Gregg, *History of Hancock County, Illinois,* 240, 392.

42. Roberts and Moorhead, *History of Lee County, Iowa,* 165.

43. Ibid.

prohibited the commission approach and put the tract on the market. Not long afterwards, an entrepreneurial Keokuk attorney, Hugh Reid, seized the opportunity and purchased the land for five cents per acre, or $5,773.32.[44] After twelve years of litigation, the Iowa Supreme Court ruled in Reid's favor. From that point forward, the court said, the land would be divided equally into 101 shares. The decision did not sit well in the highly speculative environment of the western prairies, and the U.S. Supreme Court overturned the decision in 1850.[45] By then, it was no longer an issue for the Mormons.

On March 22, 1839, Joseph wrote to Galland: "I know them [my people] to be an honorable, a virtuous, and an upright people. ... They have been fallen upon by a gang of ruffians and murders, three times, in the state of Missouri; and entirely broken up, without having committed the first offence ..." It was his personal misfortune, Joseph continued, "to be made a severe sufferer, by the hands of the above mentioned rascals; they are supported by some portions of the authorities of the State ... or else they themselves, are the fathers and instigators, of the whole diabolical and murderous proceeding." Joseph's denunciation rose to familiar rhetorical heights:

> Myself and those who are in prison with me, were torn from our houses, with our wives and children clinging to our garments, under the awful expectation of being exterminated. At our first examination, the mob found one or two persons, of low and worthless character, whom they compelled, at the peril of their lives, to swear some things against us: which things, if they had been ever true, were nothing at all, and could not have so much as disgraced any man under heaven.[46]

Joseph was alluding to apostates, men whom he had loved but who turned against him. As a result, he and his fellow prisoners had been jailed "on a pretended charge of treason." Believing in due process of law, Joseph "petitioned a habaeas corpus: but were thrust back again into prison, by the rage of the mob; and our families robbed, and plundered: and families, and witnesses, thrust from their homes, and hunted out of the State, and dare not return for their lives." He raged: "[W]here is liberty? Where is humanity?

---

44. Benjamin F. Gue, *History of Iowa,* 1:170.

45. Roberts and Moorehead, *History of Lee County, Iowa,* 165-66. See also Jacob Van Der Zee, "The Half-Breed Tract," *Iowa Journal of History and Politics* 13 (Apr. 1915): 151-64; and Gue, *History of Iowa,* 1:169-72. See Flanders, *Nauvoo,* 29, for these land transactions and legal actions.

46. Joseph Smith, Letter to Isaac Galland, Mar. 22, 1839, in Jessee, *Personal Writings of Joseph Smith,* 455.

Where is patriotism? Where has the genius of the pedistal of the laws and constitution of our boasted country fled?"[47]

This was almost certainly more information than Galland wanted, but Joseph continued at length. Feeling compelled to teach Galland the core doctrines of his faith, he used the rhetoric of "rights" to describe Mormonism as

> hav[ing] a right to embrace all, and every item of truth, without limitation or without being circumstanced or prohibited by the creeds or superstitious notions of men, ... when the truth is clearly demonstrated to our minds, and we have the highest degree of evidence of the same; we feel ourselves bound by the laws of God, to observe and do strictly, with all our hearts, all things whatsoever is manifest unto us by the highest degree of testimony that God has committed us, as written in the old and new Testament, or any where else, by any manifestation ... to us, being adapted to our situation and circumstances; age, and generation of life; and that we have a perfect, and indefeasible right, to embrace all such commandments ... We believe that no man can administer salvation through the gospel, to the souls of men, in the name of Jesus Christ, except he is authorized from God, by revelation ...[48]

Joseph finally got to the point that Galland must have thumbed impatiently through the letter to find: "If Bishop [Edward] Partridge, or if the church have not made a purchase of your land, and if there is not anyone who feels a particular interest in making the purchase, you will hold it in reserve for us; we will purchase it of you at the proposals you made to Mr. [Isaac] Barlow."[49]

Joseph wanted to believe that Galland was an honorable man. He considered Galland as "one of our benefactors," and later described him as one who had

> opened both his heart and his hands ... He is the honored instrument the Lord used to prepare a home for us, when we were driven from our inheritances, having given him control of vast bodies of land, and prepared his heart to make the use of it the Lord intended he should. Being a man of extensive information, great talents, and high literary fame, he devoted all his powers and influence to give us a standing.[50]

47. Ibid., 455.
48. Ibid., 458-59.
49. Ibid., 462.
50. "A Proclamation of the First Presidency of the Church to the Saints Scattered Abroad," Jan. 8, 1841, in *History of the Church,* 4:270-71.

Church membership provided certain advantages that Galland was quick to recognize, and on July 3, 1839, he would be baptized. By September 1839, he would be working as a land agent for the Church, empowered to trade for land and handle payments to Hotchkiss. From the first, this arrangement proved to be complicated, with Galland making a series of agreements that he failed to keep.[51] It is possible that he viewed his baptism more in the light of agreeably accepting an unusual form of hospitality offered by an importunate host rather than as a change of heart.

Accepting Galland's offer narrowed the potential field for Zion to two counties facing each other from opposite sides of the Mississippi River. To the east, a city would be built on the slope rising above a wide bend in the river–a city Joseph would call the New Jerusalem (from the Bible)–and to the west on the landscape of the Half-Breed Tract, a new version of Zion.

But this still lay in the future. In early April 1839, the prisoners remained in jail. On April 4, as negotiations with Galland were proceeding hopefully, Joseph again wrote to Emma. It had been five months and six days since his imprisonment, and he made little attempt to restrain either his disgust or his outrage.

> I have been under the grimace ~~of~~ a guard night and day, and within the walls grates and screeking ~~of~~ iron dors, of a lonesome dark durty prison. With immotions known only to God, do I write this letter, the contemplations, of the mind under these circumstances, defies the pen, or tounge, or Angels, to discribe, or paint, to the human ~~mid mind~~ being, who never expriance[d] what ~~I~~ we experience. This night we expect; is the last night we shall try our weary Joints and bones on our dirty straw counches in these walls, let our case herafter be as it may, as we expect to start to morrow for … our trial.[52]

He concluded with some carefully worded advice that reveals the challenges Emma was confronting and how Joseph assessed her resources: "One thing let [me adm]onish~~ed~~ by way of my duty, do not [be] self willed, neither harber a spirit of revevenge [sic]: and again remember that he who is my enemy~~s~~, is yours also, and never give up an old tried friend, who has waded through all manner of toil, for your sake, and throw him away becau[se]

51. Flanders, *Nauvoo,* 132.

52. Joseph Smith, Letter to Emma Smith, Apr. 4, 1839, in Jessee, *Personal Writings of Joseph Smith,* 463.

fools may tell you." Joseph acknowledged his faults but urged her to remain silent about them and to remember him with a "pure mind."[53]

Finally, after enduring unspeakable privations, the prisoners were taken out of jail and set out, under a guard of fifteen, on April 6, for Daviess County, Missouri, and their trial.[54] They reached Gallatin on the 8th, heckled en route by "the most ignorant of Adam's race, and more," according to Hyrum Smith. "They [are] the most savage race that dwells on the earth. May God grant that we may be delivered out of their hands."[55]

The next day, the Mormon men stood before a grand jury of their "peers" in the main room of Elisha Greekmore's house. Presiding was Austin A. King, whom they described as "drunk as the jury; for they were all drunk together."[56] Witnesses included Sampson Avard, who had headed the Danites (a kind of Mormon vigilante group), then turned state's evidence when he was captured. The defendants had been indicted for "murder, treason, burglary, arson, larceny, theft, and stealing," but were granted a change of venue to Judge Thomas C. Burch in Boone County.[57]

During the night of April 11-12, Joseph reportedly "fell into a trance. I call it a trance. I heard a voice which said, 'Joseph, fear not, you and all your friends shall be delivered without harm, and shall yet stand upon the hills of Zion.' When I awoke out of the trance, I aroused Elder [Sidney] Rigdon, who was by the side of me, and said, I have a revelation, we shall all escape. Elder Rigdon shouted, and told it to the next one."[58] It was enough to give them all new hope.

The next morning, the party started for Boone County under the supervision of Sheriff William Morgan of Daviess County and a four-man guard. Their journey was difficult and plagued by foul weather. On April 15, the Mormons bought two horses, "and paid for one of them in our clothing which we had with us, and for the other we gave our note," according to Hyrum.[59] They also bought whiskey for the guards. Morgan confided to the prisoners that Burch had told him not to reach Boone County since

53. Ibid., 465.

54. *History of the Church,* 3:321n (Apr. 15-17, 1839).

55. Hyrum Smith, Daily Record, Apr. 8, 1839 (Affidavit of Hyrum Smith given before Municipal Court of Nauvoo, July 1, 1843).

56. *History of the Church,* 3:309 (Nov. 11, 1838).

57. Ibid., 315 (Apr. 11, 1839).

58. "The Prairies, Nauvoo, Joe Smith, the Temple, the Mormons, &c.," *Pittsburgh Weekly Gazette,* 3, in Hallwas and Launius, *Cultures in Conflict,* 41.

59. *History of the Church,* 3:423 (Apr. 15, 1839).

it would be certain death for the prisoners. Morgan then announced that he was going to "take a good drink of grog and go to bed, and you may do as you have a mind to." The implication was clear. Once the guards were soundly asleep, "two of us mounted the horses, and the other three started on foot, and we took our change of venue for the state of Illinois."[60] Taking turns walking and riding, they pressed on for nine or ten days.[61]

Hyrum and Joseph reached the Mississippi River and crossed it at different times. Emma asked Joseph's trusted friend Dimick Huntington to ride three miles to the Quincy boat landing and wait on the morning of the 22nd. When the ferry docked about 8:00 a.m., Dimick scanned the debarking crowd. Eventually, he spied a disheveled traveler who leaned against the side rail with his head turned away. Ragged pants were tucked inside old boots full of holes. He wore a blue cloak with the collar turned up to hide his face, and a wide-brimmed black hat drooped over his unkempt beard. Dimick approached the ferry as the man guardedly raised his head. "My God!" Huntington exclaimed. "Brother Joseph, is that you?"[62]

Joseph insisted, "Take me to my family as quick as you can." Dimick found a horse, and Joseph slouched in the saddle as they moved through the streets. When they came to the Cleveland house, Dimick fell back to allow Joseph to precede him. Emma looked through the door, recognized Joseph, and ran through the gate.[63]

It is easy to imagine the relief the Saints felt at Joseph's presence. Having orchestrated the land purchase from jail, Joseph stood poised to build yet another Zion. Within three days of his arrival, Joseph and other members of the "Committee on Removal" examined "a location for the Saints," looking

60. Ibid., 423 (Apr. 15, 1839).

61. Ibid. Morgan's return is told in "History of Daviess County" (1882), and quoted in *History of the Church,* 3:321-22n4: "The sheriff alone returned on horseback, the guard who accompanied him returning on foot, or riding and tying by turns. The sheriff reported that the prisoners had all escaped in the night, taking the horses with them, and that a search made for them proved unavailing. The people of Gallatin were greatly exercised, and they disgraced themselves by very ruffianly conduct. They rode the sheriff on a rail, and Bowman was dragged over the square by the hair of the head. The men guilty of these dastardly acts, accused sheriff Morgan and ex-Sheriff Bowman of complicity in the escape of the Mormon leaders; that Bowman furnished the horses, and that Morgan allowed them to escape, and both got well paid for their treachery. The truth of history compels us to state that the charges were never sustained by any evidence by the persons who committed this flagrant act of mob law."

62. Dimick B. Huntington, Statement, qtd. in Miller and Miller, *Nauvoo,* 26. Huntington does not mention if Hyrum accompanied Joseph. See also Joseph Smith, "Journal Extract November 1839," in Jessee, *Personal Writings of Joseph Smith,* 470-82, for the full account of their escape.

63. Linda King Newell and Valeen Tippetts Avery, *Mormon Enigma,* 81; see also Miller and Miller, *Nauvoo,* 26.

at the land in the Half-Breed Tract that Galland had described to them, going on to ride over land in Lee County, Iowa, and Commerce's hinterland.[64] Sidney Rigdon's son-in-law, George W. Robinson, signed the deeds for Commerce, although it is unclear if he was acting for himself or for the Church as a whole. Less than a year later, thousands of acres had passed from non-Mormon to Mormon hands.

The site was an imposing one, with land stretching up from the riverbank to surmount a bluff that overlooked the river in a sweeping arch. Standing on the bluff, one could see across the river to Montrose, Iowa, a town as hopeful as others situated sporadically along the river in both directions. Traveling to the south, the closest towns were Keokuk, twelve miles south, and Warsaw, a few miles more traveling along the edge of the Mississippi. Farther by some fifty-three miles was Quincy, a long day's journey by wagon. The largest real "city" was St. Louis, a significant supply station for the journey into the American West, located 191 miles downriver.

The Saints' move was characterized by both hope and fear. "They came as exiles, lived as strangers in a hostile land," said historian Robert Flanders.[65] Of particular importance was the political situation. Beyond the immediate economic boom promised by the influx of Mormons into the region, local politicians saw the potential for tipping the balance between Jacksonian Democrats and Whigs by wooing this as-yet-uncommitted force. The ambiguity appeared in the *Quincy Whig*'s conflicted assessment: criticizing the Democratic persecution of the Mormons in Missouri, yet condemning the charity of Quincy Democrats as politically motivated.[66] Obviously a sensitive situation resulted, in which skillful political maneuvering could position the Church favorably or expose it to new vulnerabilities.

Lyman Wight, a forty-three-year-old New Yorker who had converted to Mormonism in its first year, published three letters in the *Quincy Whig* in May 1839 that criticized the Missouri Democrats. Even though these letters did not represent the Church, their Mormon authorship offended Illinois Democrats, the Church's new potential allies. Wight was, according to his biographer, "unswervingly committed to establishing an American Zion in Jackson County, Missouri," convinced that the "Kingdom of God would be created to prepare them for the Second Coming of Christ."[67] Wight's

64. *History of the Church,* 3:336, 341 (Apr. 25, 1839).
65. Flanders, *Nauvoo,* 1.
66. Marvin S. Hill, *Quest for Refuge,* 107.
67. Melvin C. Johnson, *Polygamy on the Pedernales,* 3.

action effectively preempted Joseph's attempt to position the Church as politically neutral. To manage the situation, Joseph published a letter signed by all three members of the First Presidency which acknowledged Wight's right to his personal opinion but also stated: "We disclaim any intention of making a political question of our difficulties with Missouri, believing that we are not justified in so doing."[68] Privately, Joseph wrote to Wight, advising him not to let "the Church appear as either supporting or opposing you in your politics."[69]

The new version of Zion that Joseph called into being on the banks of the Mississippi was essentially a boomtown. It would not be long before the Saints forgot what the area first looked like when they arrived; but in those initial weeks, the "peninsula," as it was locally known, was little more than a snarled mass of vines, bushes, and low-growing trees, with ground made muddy by springs cascading from the bluffs to the west.

Once again, prophet and followers began the impossible work of building the kingdom of God.

---

68. First Presidency, Letter to *Quincy Whig,* May 17, 1839, in *History of the Church,* 3:355; First Presidency, Letter to Robert B. Thompson, May 25, 1839, in *History of the Church,* 3:363-64; Joseph Smith, Letter to Lyman Wight, May 27, 1839, in *History of the Church,* 3:366.

69. Smith, Letter to Wight, May 27, 1839, in *History of the Church,* 3:366. See also Joseph's comments on tolerance and compassion in his letters to Emma, Apr. 4, 1839, and to W. W. Phelps, July 22, 1840, in Jessee, *Personal Writings of Joseph Smith,* 509-10.

CHAPTER 3

The City Beautiful

Every human society is an enterprise of world-building. Religion occupies a distinctive place in this enterprise.
–Peter Berger, The Sacred Canopy, *25*

Until Nauvoo, the Mormon Zion existed primarily in the imagination. Sketched only on plat maps in Missouri, Zion had yet to become a tangible reality. The lived space of Zion suggested by theology and discourse was seen best with the mind. But the spatial rhetoric created in Nauvoo told the story of Mormon lives on the ground. It expressed a belief that Zion was indeed possible, a complex, hierarchical, spatial vision of the world summoned into being by a charismatic prophet. Joseph proposed a new version of the good life that played out in an inclusive community that limned strong boundaries against the outside world and reshaped ideas about family, community, and self. It had always been true that Mormons seized sacred space wherever they settled and rendered it meaningful. Space helped members live together in fellowship and carry forward a particular interpretation of history. As the City of Zion, Nauvoo was the center of the Church, but the doctrines that originated there of proxy baptism for the dead, eternal marriage sealings, and the saving the millions of spirits who had already lived and died made it the center of the universe.

Nauvoo crowned a rising plain and bluff that jutted out from the east side of the Mississippi River. Created over centuries by erosion, this strong peninsula stretched toward the river, running two miles north to south, one mile from east to west, and marked the beginning of the Des Moines Rapids of the Mississippi. Then twelve miles of limestone and blue clay rock face made navigation treacherous and created a natural obstacle course. A low, flat floodplain that stepped gradually toward bluffs at the eastern edge, it was laced by streams cascading from the higher land to the east and yearning toward the river. A variety of trees–oak, walnut, maple–provided wood for homes.

A state since 1818, Illinois was an island of fertile land edged by the Mississippi River to the west, the Great Lakes to the north, and the lower Wabash and Ohio Rivers to the south. In Illinois, the great currency was land. State or national government shored up immigration by making land available for settlement with a series of treaties or other agreements. Land speculation promised quick profits.[1] For most of the decade, values held constant in Illinois, and healthy sales encouraged speculation. The seemingly limitless supply of new settlers promised prosperity and growth. Thomas Ford, Illinois's governor when Joseph Smith was killed, noted that by 1836, the

> story of the sudden fortunes made [in Chicago] excited at first wonder and amazement, next a gambling spirit of adventure, and lastly, an all-absorbing desire for sudden and splendid wealth. … But as enough did not come to satisfy the insatiable greediness of the Chicago sharpers and speculators, they frequently consigned their wares to eastern markets … at less cost than a barrel of flour. In fact, lands and town lots were the staple of the country, and were the only articles of export.[2]

The 1837 agricultural depression drove many of the original land holders in Illinois to other areas. Thus, it was a buyer's market for the Saints, ranging from good opportunities to deals of dubious legality.

Reunited with his people for less than three weeks, Joseph called a "general conference" for May 4-6, 1839, in Quincy. They began with "some preliminary observations … concerning a certain purchase of land in the Iowa Territory, made for the Church by the [First] Presidency." Members voted unanimously to "entirely sanction" the purchase. Joseph appointed William Marks to preside "over the Church at Commerce, Illinois," while Bishop Newel K. Whitney was appointed to "go to Commerce, and there act in unison with the other Bishops of the Church."[3] The conference also issued a resolution to those "living in the Eastern States … to move to Kirtland [Ohio], and again settle that place as a stake of Zion, in preference to their moving farther west."[4]

Another item of business was Orson Hyde's conflicts with Joseph, which had begun in Missouri.[5] Joseph had ordained Hyde an apostle on February

1. See Robert B. Flanders, *Nauvoo,* 14; David E. Miller and Della S. Miller, *Nauvoo,* 39.
2. Thomas Ford, *History of Illinois,* 1:279-80.
3. *History of the Church,* 3:345 (May 4, 1839).
4. Ibid.
5. By June 25, 1839, Elder Wilford Woodruff recorded Hyde's full repentance: The "horrors of hell has rolled o'er his soul, even to the wasting of his flesh, and he has now humbled himself in

15, 1835. Hyde had served a mission to Great Britain in 1837-38 and, with colleague Heber C. Kimball, had helped to bring thousands of converts into the Church. But when he returned, he questioned whether God was still working with the Church and had aligned himself with Apostle Thomas B. Marsh, then also in dissent. On October 24, 1838, Marsh drafted an affidavit in Richmond, Missouri, which both signed, summarizing their criticisms of Joseph.[6] The affidavit contributed to the persecution the Mormons experienced over the next few months; as a result, the Church expelled Marsh on March 17, 1839, and dropped Hyde from the Twelve two months later on May 4. The principal business of May's conference, however, was all-male priesthood meetings, followed by the ordinations of a half dozen men to priesthood offices.[7]

A week after the conference, on May 12, Joseph met "in council with the twelve [apostles] & the quorums of the Seventies." Another step was taken in regulating missionary work by requiring that the seventies go out with "a recommend from their presidency" and, perhaps even more important, by selecting a committee "to see to the families of the Seventies" on missions. Joseph continued meeting over the next few weeks with members of the Twelve, equipping them with new doctrine and instruction for missions to Great Britain, a move that would expand the membership of the Church. Joseph positioned the apostles' obedience in the context of the larger schema of the Kingdom of God. Joseph told them to "go over the great waters, and there promulgate my gospel" (D&C 118:4). They were to be "special witnesses of the name of Christ in all the world" (107:23).[8] The nine apostles who made it to Europe by January 1840 averaged thirty-one years old. They had limited education, but some had rhetorical styles that

the dust, desiring to return to the church ... a more humble and penitant man I never saw." Scott G. Kenney, ed., *Wilford Woodruff's Journal,* 1:340 (June 25, 1839); hereafter Woodruff, *Journal.* On June 27, "Br Orson Hyde, made his confession [to the Twelve] and was restored to the Priesthood again." Dean C. Jessee, ed., *The Papers of Joseph Smith,* 2:424. See also Woodruff, *Journal,* 1:341 (June 27, 1839); Jessee, Ashurst-McGee, and Jensen, *Joseph Smith Papers: Revelations and Translations, Manuscript Revelation Books,* 1:343; Scott H. Faulring, *An American Prophet's Record,* 236-37; also Gary James Bergera, ed., "The Personal Cost of the 1838 Mormon War in Missouri." Orson and wife Marinda made a home in Nauvoo; and by the end of the year, Marinda gave birth to their third child. Their first two children had died.

6. See Thomas Marsh, "Affidavit of Thomas Marsh," in *Document Containing the Correspondence, Orders &c. in Relation to the Disturbances with the Mormons ...* , 58.

7. *History of the Church,* 3:344-46 (May 4, 1839).

8. This was "the only time in the history of the [LDS] church that the Quorum of the Twelve as a body has been called to travel outside America for such an assignment." James B. Allen, Ronald K. Esplin, and David J. Whittaker, *Men with a Mission,* 2.

expressed "powerful and compelling personalities," particularly John Taylor and the Pratt brothers (Parley and Orson). "Before their conversion to Mormonism, most of the early apostles were 'seekers,'" explain LDS historians James B. Allen, Ronald K. Esplin, and David J. Whittaker. "That is, they were believers in God and Christ but were not satisfied that traditional Christian churches taught or practiced the ancient gospel of Christ in its simple purity, and they were seeking a restoration of that gospel," which they found in Joseph and his teachings.[9] Together they helped to establish the groundwork for the expansion of the Church and Nauvoo with a story of what would be possible for converts once they gathered in their new Midwestern home.

Even though Nauvoo would be the Church's principal settlement in Illinois, in 1839 much of the land purchased was actually in Iowa, on the other side of the river. With no obvious reason to do otherwise, Joseph trusted Isaac Galland's word on the legality of the contracts for Half-Breed Tract land and sent Oliver Granger and Vinson Knight to negotiate a purchase. Representing Joseph and the Church, the two men, starting on May 3, spent the next five weeks finalizing the deal. The resulting package included 2,638 acres for $6,600 and another 12,745 acres in the tract for $32,243.22. Rather than transfer the land itself with a deed, Galland convinced the Mormons to buy stock in what he called the "Half Breed Land Company."[10] Joseph learned quickly the ease of buying on credit. There were no banks or lending institutions in Nauvoo. Land itself was a form of capital. Joseph considered the arrangement a fair deal, one that would guarantee them indisputable title to the land and reasonable terms for credit. Joseph himself mortgaged real estate and loaned money to others who were financially strapped.

Besides the land offered by Galland, Joseph and Sidney Rigdon bought between 400 and 500 acres from Hotchkiss and Gillett–the entire site of the city.[11] According to Joseph, it comprised "all the land lying north of the White purchase to the river and thence on the river south, including the best steamboat landing, but is the most sickly part of Nauvoo."[12] Although the purchase price was high, the terms favored the specie-poor Saints–no money down and two notes: one for $25,000 maturing in ten years, and another $25,000 in twenty years.[13] The deed would not transfer until the debt

9. Ibid.,4.

10. Flanders, *Nauvoo,* 36.

11. Important to Joseph's acquiring all the land in the townsite, the Hotchkiss Purchase would prove to be an enduring challenge for the Church. Flanders, *Nauvoo,* 41n44.

12. *History of the Church,* 4:408.

13. Flanders, *Nauvoo,* 42; see also Lyndon W. Cook, "Isaac Galland," 271-72.

was paid in full. Ideally, a continuing flow of new settlers meant new money, new investments, and the production of goods for export or for trade. But in practical terms, land soaked up virtually all new money that came into Nauvoo, leaving little for investment in production or manufacturing.

On May 10, Joseph fixed his own residence in the new city, recording in his journal: "I arrived with my family at the White purchase and took up my residence in a small log house on the bank of the river, and about one mile south of Commerce City, hoping that I and my friends may here find a resting place for a little season at least."[14] Not even three weeks after his arrival in Illinois, Joseph was finally home.

Known as the Homestead, the Smiths' house had an unobscured view of the Mississippi River to the south. It was no mansion, to be sure. A simple and functional two-story house, its spaces held special meaning because they were the backdrop to the prophet's home life. It was constructed with rough-hewn logs and stones gathered from surrounding fields. The center of the home and the business of running a household occupied the first level. A narrow staircase brought visitors to another main room located upstairs. Emma and the series of girls who lived with the family–several of whom would eventually be counted among the prophet's plural wives–hauled water from a well in the yard. A summer kitchen, built against the back wall, provided a room for Joseph's aged parents. Joseph and Emma rapidly outgrew the original house and added a two-story addition to the back.[15]

Emma was thirty-five. Their children were eight-year-old adopted Julia, seven-year-old Joseph III, three-year-old Frederick, and year-old Alexander. Emma left behind, near other Smith family homes, the graves of three infants: Alvin and twins Thaddeus and Louisa. In Nauvoo, Emma would give birth to three more children: Don Carlos, who was born in 1840 and died within the year, another son born in 1842 who died too soon to receive a name, and David Hyrum, born in late 1844, four months after Joseph's death. Emma would remain in Nauvoo when Brigham Young led the majority of Saints west in 1846, remarry in 1847, raise the illegitimate son of her second husband in her home, become a member of the church that chose her son Joseph III as its president in 1860, and die in 1879 at age seventy-five in Nauvoo. Nauvoo was thus Emma's home for more than three decades,

14. *History of the Church,* 3:349 (May 10, 1839).

15. At http://josephsmith.net/josephsmith/v/index.jsp?vgnextoid=70dcf7a14ee52010VgnVCM1000001f5e340aRCRD; www.dcsites.com/home.pdf (both Feb. 2, 2009); Newell and Avery, *Mormon Enigma,* 83.

longer than any place she had lived in her life, longer than any home she had had during her marriage to Joseph.

After a month in his new home, in June 1839, Joseph described Nauvoo, in part, for rhetorical effect, as a "wilderness." The magnitude of its challenges heightened the magnitude of the Saints' determination to transform it: "The land was mostly covered with trees and bushes, and much of it so wet that it was with the utmost difficulty that a footman could get through, and totally impossible for teams. Commerce was so unhealthful very few could live there; but believing it might become a healthful place by the blessing of heaven to the Saints, and no more eligible place presenting itself, I considered it wisdom to make an attempt to build up a city."[16] Nauvoo was beautiful enough to served the Church's interests in the wake of the Missouri persecution.

Joseph first documented the platting of Nauvoo on June 11, 1839, noting the desirability of a nearby lot for a family of newcomers. The city would be organized by the cardinal points with streets running north-south/east-west, except over bluffs or swamps, in an orthogonal pattern that imposed order on the earth's geography. Unlike Missouri's 1833 plat of the City of Zion, Nauvoo's plat did not reserve a special block for public buildings. In fact, even the temple lot was then still owned privately by Daniel H. Wells. Gustavus Hills's 1842 engraving of the city plat designated Main Street and Water Street at widths of 87 and 64 feet, respectively. Again, unlike Joseph's plan for Missouri, which offered no space for a commercial center, in Nauvoo trade would enhance the formula for a city of God. Reflecting the memory of eastern towns that circulated persons and products for trade, a canal running down Main Street was part of Hill's imagined map. A momentous albeit humble symbol of local progress occurred on June 13 when "Theodore Turley raised the first house built by the Saints in this place; it was built of logs."[17]

Joseph used priesthood quorum meetings to conduct Church business and, not surprisingly, to solidify his influence and power. The business of handling land transactions, settling people so they could raise a crop before the season progressed too far, and the challenges of building homes signified the critical nature of such gatherings of Church leaders. Even informal meetings constructed connections central to the well-being of the Church.

16. *History of the Church,* 3:375 (June 11, 1839).
17. Ibid.

A description by one of Joseph's disciples illustrates how infectious the prophet's enthusiasm was and how his narrative inspired those around him with the same vision. In April 1839, the day after Joseph arrived incognito from Missouri, Wandle Mace, a thirty-year-old merchant from New York City, "spent the day ... with Joseph." Although Mace was not one of the twelve apostles, he was welcomed to their meeting in which "We received much Council from Joseph." Mace felt Joseph's pain as he gazed out at the refugees assembled in this new place. "To look upon the Saints who had been driven from their homes, and scattered as they were, among strangers, ... with so much spirit, showing their love and confidence in the gospel, and the pleasure he felt in meeting with them. He could scarcely refrain from weeping." Mace also recorded that Joseph's younger brother William, who had been suspended from the Twelve earlier in the month, "was restored to his [place in the] Quorum."[18]

On Sunday, May 25, Joseph was again surrounded by men who hung on his every word. It was heady to find themselves walking with a prophet of God and hearing from his own lips the secrets of heaven. Mace returned to Nauvoo Sunday morning. "Joseph gave his house up to the sick, and moved his family into a large tent."[19] The importance of large gatherings of Saints cannot be doubted; but these more intimate, selective events were critical in forging personal loyalty to Joseph, developing a shared sense of identity, and spreading Joseph's understanding of new doctrine.

Simultaneously, Joseph picked up the threads of his own personal narrative. On June 11, James Mulholland, a convert from Ireland recruited as Joseph's clerk, recorded that Joseph "commenced dictating my history." It continued an 1838 history begun by clerk George Robinson, and this new manuscript contained Joseph's best-known account of his First Vision.[20] Joseph had written the first account of the First Vision in 1832.[21] With each subsequent retelling, he provided additional details and emphases. In 1838,

18. Wandle Mace, Journal, 37-38, at http://www.boap.org/LDS/Early-Saints/WMace.html (June 29, 2013).

19. Ibid., 41.

20. *History of the Church,* 3:375 (June 11, 1839). The Robinson draft of Joseph's history is apparently not extant, but most likely included an account of the First Vision that James Mulholland copied in Nauvoo in Book A-1 of the multi-volume Manuscript History of the Church (upon which the *History of the Church* is based). Mulholland's draft published in Jessee, *Personal Writings of Joseph Smith,* 240-48, begins with the baptisms of Joseph and Oliver Cowdery in May 1829 and ends with a Church conference held on September 26, 1830. It is probable that Robinson's draft finished where Joseph's begins, Mulholland using both as the foundation of Book A-1.

21. "History of the Life of Joseph Smith," in Jessee, *Personal Writings of Joseph Smith,* 9-14.

he reported seeing "two personages standing in the air" before him, whom he identified as God the Father and Jesus Christ. This version, which functioned to solidify his power against dissenters who spoke against his leadership in Missouri, was the version eventually drafted into the official published history of the Church.[22]

The progress that mattered most to the Saints building new lives on the banks of the Mississippi was spiritual. Brigham Young, meeting with five other apostles on July 4, recorded the sentiment of the gathering: "now is the time of trial, soon the victory will be ours; now may be a day of lamentation, then will be a day of rejoicing; now may be a day of sorrow, but by and bye we shall see our Lord, our sorrow will be turned to joy."[23]

Joseph met with the Twelve on June 25 (in Montrose, Iowa) and on June 26 (in Nauvoo), when they welcomed back into fellowship Orson Hyde, who had made "an humble Confession & acknowledgement of his Sins."[24] Joseph then instructed the men in a "vast number of the Keys [i.e., spiritual knowledge] of the Kingdom of God," according to Wilford Woodruff:

> When an angel of God appears unto man face to face in personage & reaches out his hand unto the man & he takes hold of the angels hand & feels a substance the Same as one man would in shaking hands with another he may then know that it is an angel of God, & he should place all Confidence in him. Such personages or angels are Saints with there resurrected Bodies. But if a personage appears unto man & offers him his hand & the man takes hold of it & he feels nothing or does not sens any substance he may know it is the devel, for when a Saint whose body is not resurrected appears unto man in the flesh he will not offer him his hand for this is against the law given him & in keeping mind these things we may detect the devil that he deceived us not.[25]

Such instruction moved Joseph's followers to an imagined stage where they, armed with newly restored apostolic keys, could wrestle the powers of darkness. This knowledge, not available in the scriptures but only through their living prophet, assured them that God walked with them.

On June 23, Joseph spoke to Saints who had crowded into the front room of a Brother Wilcox. "So eager were they to hear" that they had braved

22. *History of the Church,* 1:5.

23. Elden Watson, ed., *Manuscript History of Brigham Young, 1801-1844,* 44 (July 4, 1839), 44.

24. Woodruff, *Journal,* 1:341 (June 27, 1839); see also Joseph Smith, Diary, June 27, 1839, in Jessee, *Papers of Joseph Smith,* 2:323-24; Faulring, *An American Prophet's Record,* 236-37.

25. Woodruff, *Journal,* 1:341 (June 27, 1839); see also Ehat and Cook, *Words of Joseph Smith,* 4.

a rainstorm.[26] As was often was the case, Joseph described his own experience with God. "A person may profit by noticing the first intimation of the spirit of revelation; for instance, when you feel pure intelligence flowing into you, it may give you sudden strokes of ideas, so that by noticing it you may find it fulfilled the same day or soon;" then, he continued, "those things that were presented unto your minds by the Spirit of God, will come to pass; and thus by learning the Spirit of God and understanding it, you may grow into the principle of revelation, until you become perfect in Christ Jesus."[27]

Joseph's millennialistic, restorationist theology centered on the literal establishment of the Kingdom of God, with priesthood holders holding political and ecclesiastical power. He interpreted Daniel's dream (Dan. 2:24-44; 7:13-14, 21-22) of cutting a stone out of a mountain without his body to refer to the power of the restored priesthood. It was a metaphoric image that wove through Joseph's narrative of a church rolling forth to fill the earth, fragmenting rival kingdoms in preparation of the return of Jesus. It was a glittering vision, one that created and maintained the Saints as a people. Social regulation or Church governance was related in every way to priesthood hierarchies, which Joseph said mirrored relationships the Saints would enjoy in heaven. Obviously as the narrator of this history, he wielded influence and power. Bolstered by his claim that he spoke with God, and with new scriptures as proof, he created a system of authority that could be transmitted to other Mormon leaders. Women, though excluded from the priesthood, also exercised authority though their manifestation of spiritual gifts. All of this evidence showed that the line separating earth and heaven was permeable.

Joseph's vision of theocratic government developed over time and became increasingly exclusive. Its boundaries ran sharply between Saints and outsiders. It was inevitable, in each of the places where they carved out communities, that this exclusiveness would create conflict with neighbors and eventually result in backlash and persecution.

But in June 1839, the kingdom had begun to roll forth. Apostle Parley P. Pratt had announced in 1837: "Now, when we speak of the kingdom of God, we wish it to be understood that we mean His organized government on the earth." This included a king, duly commissioned officers, a governing code of laws, and subjects.[28] Although it was possible to argue that the king was Jesus, the day-to-day reality in Nauvoo positioned Joseph as king and the

26. *History of the Church,* 3:378 (June 23, 1839).

27. Ibid., 381.

28. Parley P. Pratt, *A Voice of Warning and Instruction to All People,* 49.

code of laws–a "living constitution"–was situated in his evolving doctrines. By February 1843, Joseph was announcing to a gang of workmen who had gathered at the Nauvoo temple site: "'Tis right, politically, for a man who has influence to use it. … From henceforth I will maintain all the influence I can get."[29]

The largest town in Hancock County was Warsaw, organized in 1825 when the federal government abandoned Fort Edwards (founded in 1814). It was known as an export center that transhipped grain and livestock to St. Louis, and by 1840 counted 800 inhabitants. At the heart of the county was Carthage, the county seat, founded in 1837 and plated in 1838. Nauvoo would compete with both towns for population and importance.

Among the handful of settlers in Commerce who greeted debarking Mormons was thirty-three-year-old Hiram Kimball, who had arrived from Vermont in 1835. Kimball established a small mercantile business but, also importantly, bought discounted land to sell for a profit.[30] Thirty-nine-year-old Daniel H. Wells, a native of New York, reached Commerce in 1834 where he bought an eighty-acre parcel of land on the bluff that provided the most dramatic view of both the river and the town below.[31]

Joseph quickly changed the name of the town from Commerce to Nauvoo which, he said, meant "beautiful situation" or "place."[32] The landscape offered ready access to the river. It made the town visible to all those who traveled downriver and facilitated trade. Health risks aside, it was a beautiful site for building God's kingdom.

Nauvoo became the hub of a series of Mormon settlements. Always searching for new opportunities for the Saints moving into the area, Joseph on July 2, 1839, rode out with a group of friends to survey the Half-Breed Tract, especially Vinson Knight's purchase of acreage four miles downriver

29. *History of the Church,* 5:286 (Feb. 21, 1843).

30. Andrew Jenson, *LDS Biographical Encyclopedia,* 2:372; Thomas Gregg, *Portrait and Biographical Record of Hancock, McDonough and Henderson Counties,* 353.

31. Jenson, *LDS Biographical Encyclopedia,* 1:62-66.

32. Joseph Smith, Sidney Rigdon, and Hyrum Smith, "Proclamation to the Saints Scattered Abroad," Jan. 15, 1841, *History of the Church,* 4:268 (Jan. 8, 1841): "The name of our city (Nauvoo,) is of Hebrew origin, and signifies a beautiful situation, or place, carrying with it, also the idea of rest; and is truly descriptive of this most delightful situation." Louis C. Zucker, "Joseph Smith As a Student of Hebrew," *Dialogue: A Journal of Mormon Thought* 3 (Summer 1968): 48, explains the meaning of Nauvoo: "Many have scoffed at the assertion that the name is Hebrew, but it is. … The first word the Authorized Version [of the Bible] renders 'becometh' (Psalms 93:5), and the word *nauvoo* is rendered 'are beautiful' (Isaiah 52:7), 'are comely' (Song of Solomon 1:10). This verb may be used of person, thing, or place. The idea of rest may have stolen in from idyllic verse two of the Twenty-Third Psalm, where a homonymous root is used meaning 'pastures' (ne-ot or ne-oth)."

on the Iowa side. Joseph saw, approved, and announced the establishment of a town to be named Zarahemla, enscribing a reference from the Book of Mormon on the landscape.[33]

During late June and early July, Joseph invested enormous energy in boosting Nauvoo, promoting its interests, and writing a series of letters summoning Saints throughout the East. The rhetoric of the reward that awaited the faithful ran through one July circular:

> God has called you to an important office; He has laid you an onerous duty; He has called you to an holy calling, even to be the priests of the Most High God, messengers to the nations of the earth; and upon your diligence … hang the destinies of the human family. You are the men that God has called to spread forth His kingdom; He has committed the care of souls to your charge, and when you received this priesthood, you became the legates of heaven; and the Great God demands it of you, that you should be faithful; and inasmuch as you are not, you will not be chosen; but it will be said unto you, "Stand by and let a more honorable man than thou art take thy place, and receive thy crown."[34]

Joseph used letters like this to unify the Saints and to remind them of the narrative that dedicated their lives to God. Positioning the gathering in the context of the persecution story, he sympathized with what they had experienced: "Although you have had indignities, insults and injuries heaped upon you till further suffering would seem to be no longer a virtue; we would say, be patient … You have been tried in the furnace of affliction; the time to exercise patience is now come; and we shall reap, brethren, in due time, if we faint not."[35] Communicating that he understood the frustration and despair that colored their effort to move forward, he worked to inspire followers to try once again to construct their version of him.

In addition to city-building efforts, Joseph's repeated instructional sessions with the Twelve and seventies about missionary work was a second prong in his people-assembling program. On the same afternoon that he called Zarahemla into being, he met in Montrose with the Twelve and some of the seventies who were about to leave for Great Britain. After singing hymns and praying, the First Presidency ordained two new members of the Twelve, Wilford Woodruff and George A. Smith, and as a seventy Theodore Turley.

33. *History of the Church,* 3:382 (July 2, 1839).
34. Ibid., 395 (July 3, 1839).
35. Ibid., 393-94.

Woodruff later hosted the group at dinner where, in addition to blessing the apostles, Joseph and his counselors blessed the wives of some of the departing missionaries. Brigham Young summarized the culminating sermon, delivered by Joseph: "Joseph taught many important and glorious principles calculated to benefit and bless them on their mission, unfolding keys of knowledge whereby to detect Satan and preserve us in the favor of God."[36]

Woodruff in his diary gave an almost verbatim report: "If we were faithful we had the promise of again returning to the bosom of our families & being blessed on our mission & having many Souls as seals of our ministry." Although Joseph had shared some esoteric doctrines, he cautioned that, in their public ministry, it would be "best to say nothing but repentance to this generation or at least to preach the first principles of the gospel as that was as much as this generation could endure."[37]

Two formerly dissident apostles, Orson Hyde and William Smith, had been welcomed back into the quorum, and Joseph probably had them in mind as he instructed the Twelve to "forgive our brother on the first intimations of repentance & asking forgiveness & should we even forgive our brother or our enemy before they ask it our heavenly father would be equally as merciful unto us." Woodruff concluded that "we ought to be willing to repent of & confess all of our own sins & keep nothing back, & let the Twelve be humble & not be exalted & beware of pride & not seek to excell one above another but act for each others good & honorably make mention of each others name in our prayrs befor the Lord & before our fellow men, & not backbite & devour our brother." Joseph then painted a dazzling portrait of the cosmic consequences of the roles they were playing: They would stand "before the Congregations of the earth & they preach in the power & demonstration of the Holy Ghost & the people are astonished & confounded at the doctrin ..." Praising God for "the power of the Holy Priesthood & the Holy Ghost" would assure their continued righteousness. Joseph concluded by reminding them of the importance of maintaining their loyalty to him and to the work. "O ye Twelve and all Saints, ... see to it that you do not betray heaven, that you do not betray Jesus Christ, that you do not betray your Brethren, & that you do not betray the revelations of God ... or any of the word of God."[38]

This passage reveals the applicability of Joseph's message to everyday

36. Watson, *Manuscript History of Brigham Young,* 42-43.

37. Woodruff, *Journal,* 1:342 (July 2, 1839).

38. Ibid., 347-48 (July 2, 1839).

situations. "Remember who you are," he might have said. "Remember why you are here, and that God will reward you." Joseph had a knack for weaving an elaborate, sensuous picture of doctrine that positioned each individual in a critical station. He made heavy demands on their commitment, but most associates felt blessed to bear the burden.

Five days later on July 7, the Twelve held a farewell meeting with about a hundred Saints, thus engaging a wider range of persons in this rite of passage. "This is an important day & worthy of record," Woodruff noted.[39] Joseph had confided his instructions, his convictions, and his most fervent hopes to the Twelve. He had blessed them and would pray for them. Now he watched with pride as they stepped forward to do the same. Sidney Rigdon paid tribute to the missionaries' sacrifice, describing in a very "feeling manner" the motivation that would "induce men to leave their families and their homes to travel over all the earth amidst persecutions and trials such as always followed the preaching of this gospel."[40] Woodruff portrayed Rigdon's remarks as "appealing to our affections, in parting with our wives, and Children, & the pecularity of our mission, the perils that we might meet with, & the blessings that we should receive, &c. that tears was brought from many eyes."[41]

The meeting continued, with only a break for lunch, until 5:15 p.m., when the group adjourned to the river where three new Church members were baptized.[42] The climax was Joseph's own parting blessing, capping what was already a rich mix. Perhaps his most important contribution was comparing their experience to his own: "If you are imprisoned Brother Joseph has been imprisond before you. If you are placed whare you can ownly see your Brethren through the grates of a window while in Irons because of the gospel of Jesus Christ remember Brother Joseph has been in like circumstances also."[43] For men who loved Joseph, the identification made persecution and imprisonment marks of honor.

Such meetings cemented the bonds between the Twelve and Joseph. Although Joseph typically engaged in lengthy discourse on virtually every religious topic pertinent to the Saints' lives, the other men did as well. Joseph's model and discourse formed a rhetorical frame for their discussions and for

39. Woodruff, *Journal,* 1:344 (July 7, 1839). *History of the Church,* 4:1-3; Scott H. Faulring, ed., *An American Prophet's Record,* 238.

40. Faulring, *An American Prophet's Record,* 239.

41. Woodruff, *Journal,* 1:345 (July 7, 1839).

42. Faulring, *An American Prophet's Record,* 239.

43. Woodruff, *Journal,* 1:345 (July7, 1839).

their understanding of heaven. Important as both a type of rally and worship service, such gatherings, under the nondescript term "meetings," were settings for the performance of religious identity–critical to the effectiveness of the missionary endeavor and to the unification of the Church leadership. The language of such identity performance was typically Mormon: the bearing of testimonies, exhortations to avoid sins, and expressions of loyalty.

Furthermore, as Brigham Young's and Wilford Woodruff's records show, Joseph was not the only man conscious of the important history he was writing with his life. So were those closest to him. As Young and Woodruff described their daily lives, they narrated Joseph's as well. When they accompanied Joseph on even the most trivial errands, they wove their story with his. In this way, it is possible to flesh out how Joseph spent his time in Nauvoo. Significantly, throughout this event-crowded summer, Joseph stole moments either to write notes about his history or to dictate the journal he had commenced in September 1838.[44]

Although this dramatic meeting on July 7, 1839, climaxed with baptisms, making a picture-perfect send-off, the first departures did not take place for another month. On July 12, Woodruff paddled back across the river with John Taylor to contribute to the production of the first issue of the *Times and Seasons,* then being edited in less than favorable conditions by Don Carlos Smith, Ebenezer Robinson, and Robert B. Thompson.[45] With Joseph and Hyrum Smith, Sidney Rigdon, and Heber C. Kimball, they spent the afternoon "visit[ing] the sick & administer[ing] unto them by the laying on of hands." According to Woodruff: "We found quite a number that were sick." One of the ailing was Joseph Smith Sr., who spent his sixty-eighth birthday "nigh unto death." During the blessing, Woodruff thought "that the Lord would add unto his life fifteen years." (Joseph Sr. died a year later, on September 14, 1840). A piece of "glorious intelligence" was Parley P. Pratt's escape from Missouri after seven months in prison.[46]

---

44. Mulholland died late in 1839. After that point Willard Richards, Robert Thompson, W. W. Phelps, Thomas Bullock, and others acted as scribes for Joseph. As was sometimes true when Joseph dictated his journal or relied on scribes, the Mulholland journal describes Joseph's comings and goings but is heavily interpreted by Mulholland himself. Both Mulholland and Richards often recorded their own observations about events occurring in Joseph's life.

45. Although Woodruff records this event in his diary (1:346, July 12, 1839), the issue must have been an experimental proof-sheet to test the workings of the press only, for the first issue is actually dated November 22. *History of the Church,* 4:23 (Nov. 22, 1839). George Robinson and William Smith explain that illness was the reason for the delay ("To the Patrons of the Times and Seasons," *Times and Seasons* 1 (Nov. 1839): 16.

46. Woodruff, *Journal,* 1:346 (July 12, 1839).

Joseph framed his landscape with a utopian lens that looked past marshy soil and brutal weather. Instead, he saw a holy city crowned by a temple, and a river bringing wealth, converts, and contact with the world. Saints fought weakness and chills as they began to build houses and feed their families. They developed what Mormons called "the meanest of all diseases," the ague, actually malaria from the anopheles mosquito that flourished in the swamplands.[47] Ill and exhausted from the exodus they had just made, they were particularly vulnerable. When Zina Baker Huntington died on July 8, 1839, the third fatality in Nauvoo, her three children, Dimick, Oliver, and Zina Diantha, struggled to care for their desperately ill father and two brothers, William and John. "We were a pitiful set and none to pity us but God and his prophet," Oliver recalled. "Brother Joseph seeing that we still grew worse, told father William that we would all die if we stayed there, and that he must take the team and bring us down to his own house. So he took us all into his own family."[48] Emma and Joseph welcomed all who needed help, even including a small child named Jane, finding the energy and space to care for them.

Constructing a mythology of misfortune and despair, Joseph's followers recounted their personal drama of illness and their prophet's self-sacrifice and ability to rally despite his own physical condition. Apostle John Taylor's wife, Leonora Taylor, described the scene in Nauvoo after her husband's departure for missionary work to the east. "This has been a distressed place since you left, with Sickness. Allmost evry individual in evry Family sick."[49]

Like Leonora, Elizabeth Ann Whitney's family, including Joseph's future plural wife, Sarah Ann Whitney, was "all sick with ague, chills and fever," and were "only just barely able to crawl around and wait upon each other." "Under these trying circumstances," she remembered later when her ninth child was born, "Joseph upon visiting us and seeing our change of circumstances, urged us at once to come and share his accommodations. … [We] went to live in the Prophet Joseph's yard in a small cottage."[50]

Malaria both tested the Saints and gave Joseph the chance to see how they stood under pressure. He had seen how they fought off persecution. But this new trial was now tied to the space they inhabited. "One day coming

47. Qtd. in Linda King Newell and Valeen Tippetts Avery, *Mormon Enigma,* 83.

48. Oliver B. Huntington, Journal, 2:42 (July 28, 1839): "The prophet was our only doctor, and he visited us everyday. … He would lay on hands and apply simple prescriptions" (ibid.).

49. Ronald K. Esplin, "Sickness and Faith, Nauvoo Letters," http://byustudies.byu.edu/PDFLibrary/15.4EsplinSickness-d6770236-b4d2-454a-9606-7d57d34efe2.pdf,2 (July 10, 2013).

50. Elizabeth Ann Whitney, "A Leaf from an Autobiography," 91.

out of the house into the yard," Whitney recalled, "the remembrance of a prophecy Joseph Smith had made to me ... flashed through my mind like an electric shock; it was this: that even as we had done by him, in opening our doors to him and his family when he was without a home, even so should we be received by him into his house."[51]

According to LDS historian Fred E. Woods, the Nauvoo cemetery record kept by William D. Huntington between 1839 and 1846 demonstrates that malaria was the most common cause of death in Nauvoo.[52] Joseph's journal records for July 8-10, 1839: "This week and the following were generally spent in visiting the sick and administering to them; some had faith enough and were healed; others had not."[53] Although cooler weather in the fall brought relief, the summer of 1840 proved to be even worse, and far too many died. Survivors who benefitted from Emma and Joseph's kindness remembered it the reminder of their lives.

During this time, Joseph, whose capital base was generated largely from land he deeded to himself, then used as collateral or sold to new residents, maintained an unsteady relationship with Galland. Although Galland was the beneficiary of Joseph's call to gather, he foresaw that the Mormon prophet had set the Church on yet another collision course with society. In a letter to an associate on July 22, he warned that the Mormons would succeed in buying land and building up the area "until they again ... induce the surrounding [people] to rob them again; at which time they will no doubt have to renounce their religion; or submit to a repetition of similar acts of violince, and outrage as have already been."[54]

Sometime in July 1839, Joseph fell ill but recovered enough to get up and attend to others by July 22. It was a month when many suffered. Twenty-year-old Benjamin F. Johnson helped Emma care for Joseph, and recalled carrying a tin bucket of "composition," a mild but nourishing gruel (essentially watered-down porridge), from bed to bed, feeding the sick who still filled the house and yard.[55] Despite his illness, Joseph "arose in great power ... went to Bro. [Sidney] Ridgon, rebuked his fearful and complaining spirit,

51. Ibid.

52. Fred E. Woods, "The Cemetery Record of William D. Huntington, Nauvoo Sexton," 131.

53. By "administration," Joseph probably meant the religious rite of anointing with consecrated oil and prayer using the laying on of hands. Joseph Smith, Diary, July 8-10, 1839, in Jessee, *Papers of Joseph Smith,* 2:328.

54. Isaac Galland, Letter to Samuel B. Swasey, July 22, 1839, Community of Christ Library-Archives.

55. Benjamin F. Johnson, *My Life's Review,* 50-51.

and told him to repent, or a scourge from the Lord awaited him." Although the gruel did nothing for the malaria, it provided protein and replaced some of the body liquids lost through sweating and purging. Eighteen-year-old Charles Lowell Walker wrote a semi-comic poem about this disease in Nauvoo: "Dear sufferer, it is for your sake\ I give the description of a shake;\ You first feel cold and very queer,\ And then you shake, oh dear, oh dear;\ Next, fever burns with glowing heat\ And you are parched from head to feet.\ All those that shake say this is true,\ And so does C. L. W."[56]

Heber C. Kimball's account corroborates Johnson's: After several days of experiencing chills and fever, Joseph "arose from his bed, ... [going] from house to house and from tent to tent, upon the bank of the river, healing the sick ... until he arrived at the upper stonehouse," where he crossed the river in a boat, accompanied by several of the Twelve, and landed in Montrose. There he visited the cabin in which Brigham Young lay sick and commanded him, "in the name of Jesus Christ, to arise and be made whole." Next he went to the home of Elijah Fordham,[57] who was unable to speak and seemingly unconscious.[58] Parley P. Pratt, who was present, recalled a man summoned back from near-death: "His eyes were sunk in their sockets, his flesh was gone, and the paleness of death was upon him." Joseph asked Fordham if his faith was great enough to be healed. Fordham said he feared it was too late. Joseph took his hand and loudly said, "In the name of Jesus Christ arise and walk!" According to Pratt, Fordham "leaped from his bed, shook off the onion poultices and bandages from his feet, put on his clothes so quick that none got a chance to assist him, and ... walked with us from house to house visiting other sick beds."[59] It was, in Young's words, "a day never to be forgotten."[60]

Woodruff likewise remembered July 22, 1839, as "a day of Gods power." He recorded: "There was many Sick among the Saints on both sides of the river & Joseph went through the midst of them taking them by the hand & in a loud voice Commanding them in the name of Jesus Christ to arise from their beds & be made whole & they leaped from their beds made whole by the power of God."[61] Even more miraculously, according to Kimball, a

56. Charles Walker, "Ode to the Ague."

57. Heber C. Kimball, July 22, 1839, in Orson F. Whitney, *Life of Heber C. Kimball,* 262-63; *History of the Church,* 4:4.

58. Qtd. at http://www.boap.org/LDS/Early-Saints/WMace.html (June 29, 2013).

59. Parley Parker Pratt, *Autobiography,* 293-94.

60. Watson, *Manuscript History of Brigham Young,* 50.

61. Woodruff, *Journal,* 1:347-48 (July 22, 1839); see also *History of the Church,* 4:3-5.

stranger begged Joseph to heal her three-month-old twins. Joseph could not go but ordered Woodruff: "You go and heal those children," he told him, "and take this pocket handkerchief, and when you administer to them, wipe their faces with it, and they shall recover."[62] The touch of the red silk handkerchief and the prophet's power effected the cure. Joseph's personal record was modest for July 22-23: "The sick were administered unto with great success, but many remain sick, and new cases occurring daily."[63]

The following Sunday, July 28, Joseph linked illness to disobedience, admonishing his audience "to partake of the Sacrament in order that by our obedience to the ordinances, we might be enabled to prevail with God against the destroyer."[64] The next Sunday, without explicitly mentioning malaria, he again instructed about "the necessity of being righteous, and clean at heart before the Lord."[65]

Cast in these terms, the faith of the missionaries was clearly being tested. They responded. In September, John Taylor and Wilford Woodruff departed. Woodruff left a sick wife and children with food for only four days and was himself so "feebl[e]" that "when I landed, I laid down upon the bank of the river on a side of sole leather." Joseph came up to him and told him that he looked "more fit for a … dissecting room." But Joseph was also encouraging: "Go ahead in the name of the Lord, and you shall be healed and blessed on your mission."[66] George A. Smith, Reuben Hedlock, and Theodore Turley left on September 21. Brigham Young and Heber C. Kimball followed on October 4, both so ill that they had to lie down in the wagon that drove them away.[67] As committed as Joseph was to the expansion of the Church, these men were his closest friends and he must have grieved with them as they made superhuman efforts to do God's will.

October 1839 conference convened in Nauvoo and spanned three days. Surely Joseph felt validated about his decision to give the Church a new center place as he rose on the hastily erected stand and looked out at the crowd seated on makeshift benches or on blankets. He used his pulpit to weave the hope of Zion in the minds of believers. He spoke of "the situation of the Church; the difficulties they have had to contend with; and the manner in which they had been led to this place; and wanted to know the views of the

62. Heber C. Kimball, in Whitney, *Life of Heber C. Kimball,* 264.
63. *History of the Church,* 4:3 (July 22-23, 1839).
64. Ibid., 5 (July 28, 1839).
65. Ibid., 5 (Aug. 4, 1839).
66. Wilford Woodruff, "History of Wilford Woodruff," 326-27.
67. *History of the Church,* 4:10, 11 (Sept. 14, 1839).

brethren, whether they wished to appoint this a Stake of Zion or not; that he thought it was a good place, and suited for the Saints."[68] The unanimous vote was no surprise.

The conference continued, naming William Marks officially as Nauvoo Stake president, creating three local wards presided over by Bishops Newel K. Whitney, Edward Partridge, and Newel Knight, and designating nearby Mormon settlements. Lyman Wight had the less exalted task of appealing for funds to make the land payment that was coming due. Building organizational structure with an overlay of space and spirit, these men had proven their loyalty to Joseph.

Joseph was only one of many agents buying land for the Church and its members. And by October 1839, it became apparent that some regularization of process had to take place. The Nauvoo Stake High Council, which governed secular affairs until a city council could be installed, voted on October 20 to make Joseph the treasurer of the Church, equipped with the power to establish prices and sell lots.[69] The council's action made official what had already been true for months. Others might assist Joseph, but it became the prophet's role to regulate the process.

Land deals were greedy in terms of Joseph's time and energy.[70] Throughout his years in Nauvoo, Joseph continued to purchase, sell, and exchange land both for the Church and himself, although it is difficult to assess where the line between the two was drawn. Using the device of "trustee-in-trust" to distinguish between the two might have worked for some, but in the end it was hopelessly confused. At the same time land business was about positioning converts and supporting the poor, it was also about speculation–in fact, speculating in land and in persons was the Church's central business in Nauvoo. Joseph acknowledged this, saying, "Suppose I sell some land for ten dollars an acre, and I gave three, four, or five dollars per acre, then some persons may cry out 'you are speculating;' Yes, I will tell them: I buy other lands and give them to the widow and the fatherless. If the speculators run against me, they run against the buckler of Jehovah."[71]

The October conference also designated Joseph, Sidney Rigdon, and Elias Higbee as a committee to represent the Church's claims for redress from Missouri persecutions to the federal government in Washington,

68. Ibid., 12, 13 (Oct. 5-6, 1839).
69. Ibid., 16-17 (Oct. 20, 1839).
70. Flanders, *Nauvoo,* 120.
71. *History of the Church,* 5:356 (Apr. 13, 1843).

D.C.[72] It was an intriguing proposition: the Lord's prophet negotiating with the nation's top secular leaders. The three men almost immediately began preparations for their departure.

The Nauvoo High Council held its first meeting on October 20, and one of its first items of business, besides appointing Joseph treasurer, was determining that Joseph "and his family [would] be exempt from receiving in future such crowds of visitors as have formerly thronged his house." The Homestead was modest in size and unquestionably overcrowded out of the generosity of the Smiths who could not turn away either the sick or the curious. Emma became pregnant this month with her seventh child. She was thirty-five years old, and much of her life had been serving those who clamored for Joseph's attention. Nauvoo was no different. Before the Saints arrived, only 483 persons lived in Hancock County; this number grew to 9,912 by 1840.[73] Thomas Ford estimated that, by the mid-1840s, the population in Nauvoo alone had swelled to 12,000. Another 4,000 Mormons lived in other parts of Hancock County.[74]

Following up on Joseph's position as Church treasurer, the Nauvoo High Council named Joseph as city treasurer as well. His clerks were James Mulholland and Henry G. Sherwood. Sherwood was a land surveyor who had converted to Mormonism in New York State. In Nauvoo, he served on the high council and as city marshal. The council stipulated that the average price should be $500 per lot, none selling for less than $200 or more than $800, although it is not possible to determine how closely these guidelines were followed.[75] For devoted Saints who had been wounded or impoverished in Missouri, Joseph arranged free lots. In gratitude for John and Sarah Cleveland's hospitality, he gave them a lot across the street from his own home.

With the apostles gone and Joseph and Sidney Rigdon preparing to leave for Washington, D.C., the high council assumed both civic and ecclesiastical tasks; William Marks and his council were competently filling what would otherwise have been a power vacuum.

On October 29, Joseph and Rigdon, accompanied by Orrin Porter Rockwell and Elias Higbee, took their leave from the city. The nation's

72. Ibid., 4:13 (Oct. 5, 1839).

73. Miller and Miller, *Nauvoo,* 75.

74. Ford, *History of Illinois,* 2:144.

75. Nauvoo High Council Minutes, Oct. 20, 1839, in *History of the Church,* 4:16-17; see also Flanders, *Nauvoo,* 119.

capital was 980 miles away, and traveling by private conveyance was certainly more convenient (though perhaps less speedy) than the combination of boats and stagecoaches that most travelers resorted to. Normally such a trip took weeks, and Joseph should have been driven by anxiety to return home quickly. Instead, he was relaxed, not returning to Nauvoo until March 4, 1840, some four months and a few days later.

Rigdon was the original architect of the plan to bring the Mormon case before the U.S. Congress, buttressed by 491 personal petitions of Mormons who had lost property or suffered harm in Missouri. The goal was to "impeach" Missouri for its violations of constitutional government. Rigdon had secured letters of introduction from Governor Robert Lucas of Iowa territory addressed to Wilson Shannon, Ohio's governor, and to U.S. President Martin Van Buren. Driving for retribution but also hopeful of financial remuneration, Joseph and Rigdon planned to present, in addition to the petitions of grievances, a bill of damages amounting to $1,381,044 and "a multitude more of similar bills hereafter to be presented," "which, if not settled immediately, will ere long amount to a handsome sum, increasingly by compound interest."[76] Apparently they seem never to have considered a lawsuit.

Robert D. Foster, a physician and recent convert, traveled with them some of the way to tend to Rigdon who was ill. Within a week, Rigdon was so sick that the group paused in Springfield, Illinois, where they found shelter with Church member John Snider.[77] There they also encountered William Law, a new convert from Canada, en route to Nauvoo. Joseph preached in Springfield a few times and caught up on some correspondence.[78] For instance, on November 7, Joseph wrote to land agent Henry Sherwood, instructing him to conduct a land exchange to "bear our expences on the road."[79] Two days later, he affectionately wrote to Emma: "I shall be filled with constant anxiety about you and the children until I hear from you and in a perticular maner little Frederick it was so painful to leave him sick." He then went on to exhort his pregnant wife: "I hope you will wa[t]ch over those tender offspring in a manner that is becoming a mother and a saint and try to cu[l]tiveate their minds and learn them to read and be

76. *History of the Church,* 4:74 (Jan. 3, 1840).

77. Ibid., 19 (Nov. 1, 2, 1839).

78. Ibid., 20 (Nov. 4, 1839).

79. Joseph Smith, Letter to Henry G. Sherwood, Nov. 7, 1839, in Jessee, *Personal Writings of Joseph Smith,* 483.

sober do not let them be exposed to the wether to take cold and try to get all the rest you can it will be a long and lonesome time during my absence from you and nothing but a sense of humanity could have urged me on to so great a sacrafice."[80]

The party made slow progress toward Columbus, Ohio, perhaps because of the winter weather.[81] The roads were treacherous, pitted, and rough. They fell behind schedule, so Joseph and Higbee continued from Columbus by stagecoach, leaving Rockwell, Rigdon, and Foster to follow.

Joseph demonstrated his bravura on the ride through the hilly terrain some distance from Washington, D.C. The stagecoach had stopped at a tavern so that the driver could "take his grog," according to Joseph's account. The passengers were patiently waiting his return inside the coach when something spooked the horses and they took off without the driver. Joseph quickly told the others to be calm and to restrain a hysterical woman from throwing "her infant out of the coach." Everyone was panicked; but, moving quickly, Joseph flung the door open, seized the top rail, and hauled himself into the driver's seat. Retrieving the reins, he brought the horses under control. "My course was spoken of in the highest terms of commendation," he wrote with pride, "and no language could express the gratitude of the passengers."[82]

On November 28, Joseph and Higbee reached Washington and took lodging at the Gadsby Hotel on the corner of Missouri and Third Streets, described "as cheap boarding as can be had in this city."[83] Joseph may have been counting on his charm, as well as the pathos of his people's plight, to win favorable decision. Peter Burnett, who had been one of his attorneys the year before in Missouri, appraised Joseph: "His views were so strange and striking, and his manner was so earnest, and apparently so candid, that you could not but be interested. There was a kind, familiar look about him, that pleased you." Burnett made particular note that Joseph, unlike Rigdon, was not argumentative: "He was very courteous in discussion, readily admitting what he did not intend to controvert, and would not oppose you abruptly, but had due deference to your feelings."[84]

The Mormons found the White House to be a "very large and splendid palace, surrounded with a splendid enclosure, decorated with all the fineries

80. Joseph Smith, Letter to Emma Smith, Nov. 9, 1839, in Jessee, *Personal Writings of Joseph Smith*, 485.

81. *History of the Church*, 4:21 (Nov. 8, 1839).

82. Ibid., 23-24 (Nov. 27, 1839).

83. Ibid., 24, 40 (Nov. 28, 1839).

84. Peter H. Burnett, *Old California Pioneer*, 40-41.

and elegancies of this world." They marched to the front door, knocked, and asked to see Van Buren. On November 29, they were taken to the residence on the second floor, where the president received them and took from them their letters of introduction.

Joseph's charisma did not win over the nation's chief executive. According to Joseph's account, Van Buren read the letters, looked up, and asked, "What can I do? … If I do anything I shall come in contact with the whole state of Missouri." While the Mormons' cause was just, he said, he had no power to change their situation.[85] It was technically true. Until the Civil War and the passage of the 14th Amendment, federal intervention in sovereign states was prohibited. Van Buren also admitted that he would lose Missouri votes, which he needed, if he sided with the Mormons.[86] In fact, Joseph's visit not only failed in its purpose but had a backlash effect: Missouri continued to pursue him as an escaped prisoner. Joseph's letterbooks contain a description of Van Buren:

> He is a small man, sandy complexion, and ordinary features; with frowning brow, and considerable body, but not well proportioned as to his arms and legs; and to use his own words, is "quite fat." On the whole we think he is without body or parts, as no one part seems to be proportioned to another;–therefore instead of saying body and parts, we say body and part, or partyism if you please to call it. And in fine, to come directly to the point, he is so much a fop or a fool (for he judged our cause before he knew it) we could find no place to put truth into him.
>
> We do not say the Saints shall not vote for him, but we do say boldly … that we do not intend he shall have our votes.[87]

The Mormons spent the rest of their time in Washington meeting with members of the House of Representatives. The Illinois delegation planned a meeting for December 5 to hear the memorials and to consult with them about the best plan for bringing the case before the Congress.[88] Joseph received a note from Rigdon that same day that he and Foster would stay a day or two at Ridgon's brother's home in Pennsylvania where he could further recuperate. Joseph wrote to Hyrum and asked him to send funds. "For God's sake, … arm us with all the power possible, for now is the time or never,"

85. *History of the Church*, 4:40 (Dec. 5, 1839).

86. See *History of the Church*, 6:216, for a later attack on Van Buren.

87. Joseph Smith, Letter to Hyrum Smith, Dec. 5, 1839, http://josephsmithpapers.org/paperSummary/letter-to-hyrum-smith-5-december-1839 (June 16, 2013).

88. *History of the Church*, 4:40 (Dec. 5, 1839).

he wrote urgently. "We want you should get all the influential men you can of that section of the country, of Iowa, and of every other quarter, to write letters to the members of Congress, using their influence in our behalf, and to keep their minds constantly upon the subject."[89]

On December 7, Henry Clay and John T. Stuart, a Whig Senator from Illinois, unsuccessfully raised the issue of the Mormon petitions. Joseph had explained to the delegation the "injuries" that the Mormons had received, summarized their fruitless appeals to date, and explained why they thought it ill-advised to appeal to Missouri courts. But overall, Joseph and Higbee were unimpressed with the House of Representatives, describing it so unorganized that it delayed any progress that might have been made.[90]

The same day that Clay and Stuart spoke on the Mormon petitions in the Congress, Emma wrote Joseph another newsy letter. Orson and Marinda Hyde had moved into the Smith home the day after Joseph left, both of them ill with a "ravaging disease" (probably malaria). When James Mulholland fell ill, his wife, Sarah, also brought him to Emma. Emma had nursed him for five weeks, but he died on November 3. Little Frederick's fever had broken shortly after Joseph's departure, but Joseph III had taken the "chill fever" and was recuperating slowly. Emma also moved beyond these pressing domestic concerns to communicate an astute interest in larger affairs. She warned Joseph: "Business does not go on quite as well since you left as when you were here." Finally, she passed on Don Carlos's request to know where a letter "containing the names of a number of subscribers [to the *Times and Seasons*]" had gone, some manifestation of the present disarray in Joseph's office, and closed, "Yours affectionately, Emma Smith."[91]

Discouraged, on December 21, Joseph left Higbee to observe the Senate Judiciary Committee while he went to Philadelphia to visit Parley P. Pratt, the Saints, and to preach. Nine days later, Joseph departed with Pratt's younger brother, Orson, not to return to Washington, but to visit on December 30 the Monmouth, New Jersey, branch of the Church, some thirty-five-plus miles away.[92] Joseph continued to travel through the area until January 9, 1840, when he returned to Philadelphia to preach and visit friends. Rigdon and Foster arrived in Philadelphia on January 14.[93]

89. Ibid., 41 (Dec. 5, 1839).
90. Ibid., 43-44 (Dec. 7, 1839).
91. Emma Smith, Letter to Joseph Smith, Dec. 6, 1839.
92. *History of the Church,* 4:47, 49 (Dec. 30, 1839).
93. Ibid., 75, 76 (Jan. 14, 1840).

Joseph's wanderings appear almost random. He was obviously reluctant to return to Washington, but seems equally intent on avoiding Nauvoo. He was in a world that did not recognize him as a prophet; but by traveling with and visiting other Mormons, he clearly was not trying to conceal his prophethood either. He seems to be treading in a liminal space where, for four months, he was free to be as much the prophet as he wished to be–or not.

CHAPTER 4

Gathering In

They shall be gathered in unto one place upon the face of this land, to prepare their hearts and be prepared in all things against the day when tribulation and desolation are sent forth upon the wicked.

–Doctrine and Covenants 28:2

It is astounding how hopeful Joseph had been as he anticipated meeting with the president of the United States and members of the Congress about redressing the Saints' claims against Missouri. But by the time 1840 began, it was clear that, despite their efforts to gather hundreds of supporting affidavits, to articulate clearly the narrative of the devastating Missouri war, and to politic with the influential figures they had met, their efforts had come to nothing. Moreover, Joseph would experience great personal loss in 1840: his father would die in September. The balance set against such loss may have been some success in building Zion on the banks of the Mississippi, but he began the year in the East.

On January 1, 1840, Joseph spoke at a small conference of the Church in Philadelphia, attended by apostle-brothers Parley and Orson Pratt. For believers, Joseph spoke the word of God; for newcomers, he was a curiosity. According to Benjamin Winchester, Joseph bore his testimony of the Book of Mormon and about how it was "doing much good."[1] Two weeks later, Joseph met with the Philadelphia Branch of the Church, instructing "that the travelling Elders should be especially cautious of incroaching on the ground of stationed & presiding Elders and rather direct their efforts to breaking up and occupying new ground that the Churches generally refuse to burthened

1. Benjamin Winchester, Letter to Ebenezer Robinson and Don Carlos Smith, Feb. 10, 1840, *Times and Seasons* 1, no. 7 (May 1840): 104.

with the support of unprofitable and dilatory labourers."[2] Although addressing primarily organizational issues, Joseph was telling them how to live as Saints.

Parley Pratt, who had been proselytizing in Philadelphia since November, attended another meeting that featured the Mormon leader. His description, though recorded years after the fact and shaped by Pratt's memory of the now-martyred prophet, nonetheless captures some of the spectacle this type of event became.

> ... about three thousand people assembled to hear him. ... brother Joseph arose like a lion about to roar; and being full of the Holy Ghost, spoke in great power, bearing testimony of the visions he had seen, the ministering of angels which he had enjoyed; and how he had found the plates of the Book of Mormon, and translated them by the gift and power of God.

According to Pratt, "The entire congregation was astounded; electrified, as it were, and overwhelmed with the sense of the truth and power by which he spoke, and the wonders which he related." Reportedly, many were baptized because of this speech; and as for those who were not: "I bear witness," Pratt concluded, "that he, by his faithful and powerful testimony, cleared his garments of their blood."[3]

In Chester County, Pennsylvania, Joseph penned a lonesome letter to Emma on January 20. Between the lines is a plea for reassurance that he had not failed the Church. The story of the Missouri persecution was becoming a defining myth that captured the Church's–and Joseph's–inability to build Zion. Baffled at the lack of response to what he considered a valid argument, he was not going to wait while Congress considered "my business." Instead, he was "determined to st[art] for home in a few days," going first to Washington and "from there home as soon as pos[s]ible." His heart raced before him, filled with "constant anxiety" for his "little ones." "[M]y dear Emma," he continued, "... tell all the chi[l]dren that I love them and will come home as soon as I can." He signed the missive, "[Y]ours in the bonds of love your Husband u[n]till Death &c."[4]

Joseph had plenty of time to reflect on his failed mission. Two days later, still in Pennsylvania, he signed a forceful letter to the *Chester County*

2. "Philadelphia Branch Minutes," Jan. 13, 1840, in Andrew F. Ehat and Lyndon W. Cook, eds., *The Words of Joseph Smith,* 31.

3. Parley P. Pratt, *Autobiography* ..., 298-99.

4. Joseph Smith, Letter to Emma Smith, Jan. 20, 1840, in Dean C. Jessee, ed., *Personal Writings of Joseph Smith,* 490. I have silently omitted strike-outs in quotations from Jessee's edition. Note that Joseph says nothing about the possibility of marriage lasting beyond death.

[Pennsylvania] Register and Examiner about the proper role of government: "governments were instituted of God for the benefit of man and that he holds men accountable for their acts in relation to them ..." His expectation of Missouri's punishment was implicit. It was natural to blame the government officials with whom he had met but who had failed to see the truth of his claims: "I believe that no government can exist in peace except such laws are framed and held inviolate as will secure to each individual the free exercise of conscience the right and controll of property and the protection of life." In every way, Joseph's position was a reaction to Missouri.[5] His understanding of constitutional and statute law was simple: It existed to protect the liberties and civil rights of citizens. When it failed, when the law did not create an atmosphere of fairness, or when the agents of the law failed its citizens, individuals could act for themselves–redress was every citizen's right.

While in Philadelphia, Joseph received a visit from a Wilkinson family, non-Mormons who were curious about the thirty-four-year-old prophet and invited him to sign their family album. While nothing more is known about this visit, in the undated entry, Joseph wrote:

> Virtue is one of the most prominant principles that enables us to have confidence in approaching our Father who is in heaven in order to ask wisdom at his hand therefore if thou wilt cherish this principle in thine heart thou mayest ask with all confidence before him and it shall be poured out upon thine head and thou shalt not lack any thing that [thy] soul desires in truth and again the [Lord] shall bless this house and none of them shall fail because they turned not away the servents of the Lord from their doors even so Amen.[6]

On Saturday, January 25, Joseph presided over a conference of elders held in the Brandywine Branch, Chester County, Pennsylvania, where "Great harmony prevailed."[7] Two elders and two priests were ordained. "The Saints in that place appear determined to keep the commandments of God," the report of the conference continued, and Joseph's visit "tended much to strengthen, and confirm them in the faith of the everlasting gospel."[8] While

5. Joseph Smith, Letter to Mr. Editor, Jan. 22, 1840, in Jessee, *Personal Writings of Joseph Smith,* 493-96.

6. Joseph Smith, Inscription, in ibid., 497.

7. Lorenzo Barnes, "Letter," *Times and Seasons* 1, no. 5 (Mar. 1840): 79.

8. Ehat and Cook, *Words of Joseph Smith,* 32. The branch records are located in the Community of Christ Library-Archives (Independence, Missouri).

it was not possible to be everywhere and visit with every Saint, the effect of the prophet's personal contact was profound.

Robert Foster had accompanied Sidney Rigdon as far as Philadelphia where they joined Joseph. Foster continued with Joseph to Washington on January 27, leaving Rigdon with the Pratts to continue his recuperation. Furious over the treatment he had received from the country's top official, Joseph blistered Martin Van Buren in his history: "His whole course went to show that he was an office-seeker, that self-aggrandizement was his ruling passion, and that justice and righteousness were no part of his composition."[9] The petition and memorial caused considerable debate in the Congress on January 28.[10] Henry Clay, senator from Kentucky, announced, "I am indifferent as to the motion; but … inquiry should be made by the [Judiciary] Committee whether Congress has any power to redress."[11] Clay did, in fact, submit the question, but, predictably, it received no follow up.

Joseph departed Washington on February 9 with Foster and Orrin Porter Rockwell, leaving Elias Higbee behind to meet with the Senate Committee on February 20. The next day, the committee "refused to consult on the subject," ruling definitively on February 26 that "redress can only be had in Missouri, the courts and legislature."[12] Some four years later, Joseph would propose himself as a candidate for U.S. president, but he never again set foot in Washington nor went more than 150 miles from Nauvoo. From then on, Nauvoo was his life.

Rockwell left the party in Dayton, Ohio, but Foster and Joseph concluded their "wearisome" journey, arriving in Nauvoo on March 4, 1840.[13] Everywhere he spoke on his return to Nauvoo, Joseph expressed neither understanding of nor sympathy for the technicalities of the jurisdictional dilemma and failure of the government to resolve the Church's problems. Joseph reportedly repudiated Van Buren in public and advised against voting him into any office of trust.[14] In Nauvoo, Joseph relieved his mind by foretelling a calamitous future for the negligent nation: "I see, by the visions of the Almighty, the end of this nation, if she continues to disregard the cries and petitions of her virtuous

9. *History of the Church,* 4:80 (Feb. 6, 1840).

10. "The Mormons in Western Illinois," *Niles National Register,* Feb. 1, 1840.

11. Ibid.

12. *History of the Church,* 4:85, 88 (Feb. 20-21, 26, 1840).

13. Ibid., 9-89 (Mar. 4, 1840). These eighty pages describe Joseph and Sidney's trip to Washington. Joseph purchased three new suits, Sidney four, as well as clothing for their wives and children.

14. Ibid., 89 (Mar. 4, 1840).

citizens, as she has done, and is now doing."[15] Four months later in July, he added: "the Lord has begun to vex this nation. ... A hailstorm has visited South Carolina ... which swept crops, killing some cattle. Insects are devouring crops on the high lands, where the floods of the country have not reached, and great commercial distress prevails everywhere. ... [God] will continue to do so except they repent; for they now stand guilty of murder, robbery, and plunder, as a nation, because they have refused to protect their citizens, and execute justice according to their own constitution."[16]

For Joseph, the Nauvoo he envisioned was just the beginning of an endless chain of cities in the landscape of Zion. Seven years earlier at the 1833 dedication of the Kirtland, Ohio, House of the Lord, Joseph and Oliver Cowdery had testified to seeing heaven's veil lifted–that Moses passed to them the keys of the gathering of Israel, charging them also to build temples to redeem the dead (D&C 10:11-16). Based on an Old Testament conviction that Jesus would visit the earth when the temple had been prepared, temples from this point on became the principal "work" of the Mormons; but community building and temple building were part of the same design motif. At the figurative and actual center of the city plat, the temple became the center of worship, cosmology, and social practice.

Cultural historian William Mulder points out: "While other millenarians set a time, the Mormons appointed a place. Joseph Smith split the Hebrew metaphor of Zion and Jerusalem: he saw Judah returning to Jerusalem, Israel to Zion. And America was the land of Zion. ... all history had been prologue."[17] The Zion narrative represented the Mormon interpretation of Manifest Destiny. It wove America's future into the same design as the Mormon pattern. Certainly nothing new, it was, nevertheless, in terms of magnitude and dimension, a powerful manifestation of a belief system. In this narrative, the failure of the U.S. government to respond favorably to the Missouri petitions was only a minor setback, and did not persuade Joseph to deviate from the course he had chosen.

Mormon memory at mid-nineteenth-century was bounded by Missouri and Nauvoo. Each stood as a point in a series of events that located the Mormon experience in a biblical stream of history. This story justified, explained, and even insisted on persecution as part of a larger design. These particular images linked scenes in the imaginative world of the Mormons,

---

15. Ibid.
16. Ibid., 145 (July 3, 1840).
17. William Mulder, *Homeward to Zion*, 21.

making them real for the increased numbers who had not themselves experienced Missouri. The leitmotif that emerged represented as surely who the Mormons had been as who they hoped to be. The result was a culture based in part on the tension between memory and contemporary experience.

In some ways Nauvoo worked as a metaphoric middle ground–a liminal space–bestowing on the Saints mythic understandings before they entered the real world beyond. The metaphors contained by the narrative itself helped the Saints to understand the momentous events that transpired during Joseph's lifetime. It would be possible to describe the liminality of the Nauvoo experience as an ordeal, a transition, a painful initiation, a trauma that passed the Mormons from one world to a new one. By sometimes using the biblical metaphor of Egypt or the desert, and the exodus out of Missouri to the Promised Land–the process of making their final transition to the good life–the Saints understood that they had *had* to give something up. Their sacrifice gave them the right to claim a biblical-type exodus as their own. In the Bible, the years of Israel's wandering in the desert represented a period of heightened engagement with God despite the difficulty and danger it presented. For Joseph, the experience of the Church was more of the same.

The doctrine of the gathering functioned to build Zion in literal and figurative ways. In 1836, Joseph's scribe noted the importance the prophet assigned to "the gathering of the elect of the Lord out of every nation on earth, and bringing to the place of the Lord of Hosts, when the city of righteousness shall be built, and where the people shall be of one heart and one mind, when the Savior comes; ... we want all honest men to have a chance to gather and build up a city of righteousness, where even upon the bells of the horses shall be written *Holiness to the Lord.*"[18]

The gathering brought converts from one reality into another and turned them into Latter-day Saints. "There is no other way for the Saints to be saved in these last days," Joseph and his counselors explained, "for it is written ... –'the sons of God shall be *gathered* from far, and his daughters from the ends of the earth:' it is also the concurrent testimony of all the prophets, that this gathering together of all the Saints, must take place before the Lord comes to 'take vengeance upon the ungodly,' and 'to be glorified and admired by all those who obey his gospel.'"[19] In Zion, Latter-day Saints became citizens of a new world.

18. *History of the Church,* 2:357-58 (Jan. 6, 1836).

19. "Proclamation, to the Saints Scattered Abroad," *Times and Seasons* 2, no. 6 (Jan. 15, 1841): 276.

Joseph believed that Nauvoo had the potential to become the largest city west of the Appalachians and an important port on the Mississippi River. He had grown up, first near Vermont's major river, next close to the commercial artery of the Erie Canal, so he saw the advantages for Nauvoo as a transfer point for the large steamers that would be halted by the rapids at Warsaw. He also proposed building a wing dam in the Mississippi that would benefit the town with water power for industry and create a harbor.[20]

Meeting on March 6, 1840, with the Zarahemla High Council (Iowa), Joseph spoke on the topic of consecration.[21] This theological teaching of shared ownership was inseparably entwined with economic and social policies. The Nauvoo High Council had seized control of the Montrose ferry from the Iowa Church, but, Joseph said, "it was the will of the Lord that we should desist from trying to keep it; and if persisted in, it would produce a perfect defeat of its object, and that he [Joseph] assumed the whole responsibility of not keeping it until proposed by himself." The situation in Iowa was dire–land titles were basically invalid and Church leaders were pulling the group toward extreme policies such as living the Law of Consecration which led to infighting.[22]

Because Joseph had been back only two days before he left for Iowa, it seems fair to say that the situation there had reached a crisis point while Nauvoo seemed calmer. On March 11, Joseph penned an optimistic note to Robert Foster in Beverly, Illinois: "Our Town is improveing very fast. It is almost incredible to see what amt. [amount] of labor has been performed here during the winter past. There is now every prospect of our haveing a good society, a peaceable habitation and a desirable residence here."[23] Joseph added the news that his father had rallied. Joseph had given two speeches and had incorporated them into his master-narrative. He claimed that the Mormons "have gained friends and influence," even as he acknowledged what amounted to a total lack of results. He blamed corrupt officials: "When we can see a disposition in our chief magistrate to sacrifice the rights of the poor at the shrine of popularity, it is high time to cast off such an individual."[24] It was a political manifesto that would harden as the months passed.

---

20. Dennis Rowley, "Nauvoo: A River Town," *BYU Studies* 18, no. 2 (1978): 1-16.

21. *History of the Church,* 4:93-94 (Mar. 6, 1840).

22. "Extract from the Minutes of the Iowa High Council," Mar. 6, 1840, in *History of the Church,* 4:93.

23. Joseph Smith, Letter to Robert D. Foster, Mar. 11, 1840, in Jessee, *Personal Writings of Joseph Smith,* 500.

24. Joseph Smith, Letter to Robert Foster, Mar. 11, 1840, in ibid., 499-500.

Perhaps nothing soured Joseph on the business of real estate more than the Hotchkiss indebtedness. After the abortive attempt to establish the Kirtland Bank in the mid-1830s, the Hotchkiss Purchase was the largest entrepreneurial deal Joseph had entered into in the name of the Church. His series of letters with Horace Hotchkiss detail his reliance on a tale of justification, persecution, and hope. Hotchkiss held Joseph's note for the debts on the Iowa land; the contract allowed the Church to take possession of the land but not the deeds until after the debt–a total of $114,500–was paid completely off.[25] For Joseph, land speculation enabled the building of Zion. Yet the complexity of the deal, multiplied by dozens of similar arrangements, intruded on Joseph's ability to function as a prophet.

Because it was in his best interests to do so, Hotchkiss watched carefully the political situation of the Church and Joseph's efforts to receive restitution for the losses of Missouri. On March 17, when Joseph was back in Nauvoo, Hotchkiss inquired whether Joseph could command any influence "in the House or in the Senate," and suggested the need for "friends ... who will bring forward your case ... Milk and water friends in Congress are good for nothing."[26] Joseph had no such friends.

Hotchkiss wrote again two weeks later. He refused to take hints that the first payment might not be made: "The greatest reliance you have for regaining your wealth is in the honorable conduct of your people–their indefatigable industry–their untiring perseverance–and their well directed enterprise. These constitute a capital which can never be shaken by man." Almost recklessly, he offered an additional 12,000 acres in nearby Sangamon, Mercer, and Henry Counties, "provided from twenty to forty families, valuable for their prudence, industry, and good habits from your society, can be found to form a small colony of practical farmers."[27]

Joseph managed to pay the first two notes and then, ingeniously, conceived a plan to capitalize upon the strength provided by the influx of newcomers. Converts in the East would give Hotchkiss title to their land, then be given acreage in or near Nauvoo when they immigrated. Hotchkiss agreed.

Joseph was encouraged by newspaper editor John Wentworth's report, simultaneously sympathetic and cynical, in the *Chicago Democrat* on March 25: "We will not go so far as to call the Mormons martyr-mongers, but we

25. Deed Book 12G, 399, 400; Deed Book H, 510, qtd. in Robert B. Flanders, *Nauvoo,* 42. The First Presidency (Joseph and Hyrum Smith, and Sidney Ridgon) were agents for the deed.

26. *History of the Church,* 4:98 (Mar. 17, 1840).

27. Ibid., 101 (Apr. 1, 1840).

believe they are men of sufficient sagacity to profit by anything in the shape of persecution," commented Wentworth. "Let Illinois repeat the bloody tragedies of Missouri and one or two other States follow, and the Mormon religion will not only be known throughout our land, but will be very extensively embraced."[28] This comment was one of the first by an outsider to note both the shape of the Mormon narrative and its utility.

In April, one of two visitors from Iowa published a partly satirical report of their visit to Nauvoo in the *Quincy Whig*. The unnamed visitors crossed the Mississippi and were greeted by Joseph on horseback. Joseph alighted, not by swinging himself down by the stirrup, but by throwing one leg over the horse's head and jumping to land on both feet. Handing the bridle to a man waiting for him, Joseph's presence silently assembled a small crowd of men who awaited his words. "His bearing towards them was like one who has authority; and the deference which they paid him convinced us that his dominion was deeply seated in the empire of their consciences," the visitor wrote. "To our minds, profound knowledge of human nature had evidently taught him that, of all principles, the most omnipotent is the religious principle, and to govern men of certain classes, it is only necessary to control their religious sentiments."[29]

After speaking to the cluster of men, Joseph led his two guests on a tour of his house, drawing their attention to a room on the upper level where he pulled aside a curtain and displayed the Egyptian mummies purchased in Kirtland in 1835. "The embalmed body that stands near the centre of the case," Joseph was quoted as saying, "is one of the Pharaohs, who sat upon the throne of Egypt, and the female figure by it was probably one of the daughters." Joseph inquired whether his visitors could read Hebrew. They could not. From the top of the mummies' display case, he took down a small Hebrew grammar, which he showed to them, then took some picture frames from the opposite wall that enclosed sections of papyrus. "These ancient records," he stated, "throw great light on the subject of Christianity. ... My time has been hitherto too much taken up to translate the whole of them, but I will show you how I interpret certain parts. He then pointed to a certain design which he identified as '*the signature of the patriarch Abraham.*'"[30] The claim blended both the secular work of translation with the religious work of recovering the revelations of the ancient prophets. Joseph was nothing if not confident.

28. John Wentworth, *Chicago Democrat,* Mar. 25, 1840; rpt. in *Times and Seasons* 2, no. 7 (Feb. 1, 1841): 303.

29. "A Glance at the Mormons," *Quincy Whig* (from the *Alexandria Gazette),* Oct. 17, 1840, 1.

30. Ibid.

In both April and October, Joseph positioned such secular issues as real estate investment and politics in the larger landscape of religious ideas. The Church's semi-annual general conference began on April 6 and continued through the 8th; the agenda discloses some of the young city's problems. Although the minutes are formal and general, the "pecuniary affairs of the Church" were evidently in poor shape, since Joseph "requested the brethren to step forward, and assist in liquidating the debt on the town plot, so that the poor might have an inheritance." He described the gathering to Nauvoo as having been "set forth in the Holy Scriptures." Somewhat unexpectedly, considering the recent disarray in Iowa, he added: "It had been wisdom for the greater body of the Church to keep on this side of the river, in order that a foundation might be established in this place; but … now, it was the privilege of the Saints to occupy the lands in Iowa, or wherever the Spirit might lead them."[31]

Joseph ended the conference on a note that lifted the Saints' imagination beyond money worries: he called Orson Hyde to dedicate Jerusalem for the return of the Jews. Joseph set the apostle apart to be the "servant of the public in distant and foreign countries, for Christ's sake."[32] Wilford Woodruff recorded that Hyde was to lay "the foundation of a great work in that land. This is the first mission that any man has taken to the land of Asia belonging to the Church of Christ of Latter-day Saints. "[33] Hyde, who had been firmly returned to the bosom of the Church for less than seven months, would bring the Church into the landscape of the Bible. Joseph and Robert B. Thompson, as chair and clerk of the conference respectively, drew up credentials, identifying Hyde as an official Church representative, to present to all international dignitaries.[34]

Joseph's sermon on the final day of the conference analyzed John 3, "throwing a flood of light on the subjects which were brought up to review," according to the description in the *Times and Seasons.* He spoke briefly to the elders preparing to leave for the mission field, advising them to provide for their families before leaving and to "teach the gathering."[35]

Joseph's next two months were absorbed by personal and Church

---

31. "Commerce, Illinois, April, 1840," *Times and Seasons* 1, no. 6 (Apr. 1840): 93, 94. See also Ehat and Cook, *Words of Joseph Smith,* 35; *History of the Church,* 4:109 (Apr. 7, 1840).

32. *History of the Church,* 4:113 (Apr. 8, 1840).

33. Scott G. Kenney, ed., *Wilford Woodruff's Journal, 1833-1898,* 2:86 (Apr. 7, 1841).

34. *History of the Church,* 4:112-13 (Apr. 7, 1840); Arnold H. Green, "Jews in LDS Thought," 137-64.

35. "Commerce, Illinois, April, 1840," 94.

business. In May, forty-seven-year-old Edward Partridge died of malaria, leaving his widow, Lydia, with six children ranging in age from twenty to seven. Emma Smith, then eight months pregnant with Don Carlos, took in twenty-year-old Eliza and sixteen-year-old Emily Partridge, to help with the work of a busy household. "About this time Emma sent for me to come and live with her and nurse her baby," Emily remembered. "This pleased me very much, for tending babies was my delight. Emma was very kind to us."[36]

In Nauvoo, the Smiths never had the privacy that others had in their own homes; instead a steady stream of visitors and hired help lived periodically with the family. By the spring of 1840, they had overgrown the Homestead and Joseph organized a crew of men to build a two-story extension on the back of the house. Over time, the two rooms in the original building, which had served as the parlor, became bedrooms. An indication that Joseph saw himself as living with danger was that he had a private hideaway built under the stairs large enough for two people to either sit or lie.[37]

Joseph III, then eight, recalled another vignette of his father's kindness that summer. The Smith family was accustomed to unannounced visitors. A train of curious Saints and needy outsiders came to the Homestead. Joseph III remembered one morning when Emma stood at the stove and a black man knocked on the door. His story was tragic. After introducing himself as "Jack," he told Emma how his arm had been damaged. In the midst of a 4th of July celebration, a cannon had backfired , ripping his arm off to his elbow. Sick and penniless, he had been out of work for a long time, and had run out of options. Joseph found a buckskin suit and gave it to the man so he could clean up to apply for work. Years later, Jack remembered Joseph's kindness and returned to try to pay Joseph back, but Joseph politely refused.[38]

By June, Nauvoo had 250 houses, "a few framed, and many more are in course of construction." By August, the population reportedly stood at "nearly three thousand, and … fast increasing." Joseph conceded that it was "sickly in the summer," like other river towns, but boasted, "There is every prospect of its becoming one of the largest cities on the river."[39] The advantages of the site outweighed the problems posed by the swampland.

Letters streamed back from Brigham Young, and the other apostle-missionaries in England, sometimes directly to Joseph or to the apostles'

36. Emily Dow Partridge Young, "Incidents in the Early Life of Emily Dow Partridge," 4.

37. Linda King Newell and Valeen Tippetts Avery, *Mormon Enigma,* 89.

38. Joseph Smith III, qtd. in Newell and Avery, *Mormon Enigma,* 90.

39. *History of the Church,* 4:133 (June 1, 1840); Smith, Letter to John C. Bennett, Aug. 8, 1840, ibid., 178.

wives but also containing messages for the First Presidency.[40] Joseph kept in close contact with the missionaries and strategized with them about growth.

In England, the *Latter-day Saints Millennial Star,* the first LDS periodical outside the United States, was published for the first time on June 27, 1840. That same week, the first organized group of British converts left for Nauvoo. Eventually 4,733 immigrant converts would reach Nauvoo from the British Isles, comprising a third of Nauvoo's population.[41] According to Robert Flanders, the "number of new members recorded in 1840, 1841, and 1842 was 8,425, six times the number for the preceding three years."[42] Describing this growth in metaphoric terms, Heber C. Kimball wrote on April 17, 1840, from Preston, England:

> The Gospel is spreading, the devils are roaring. As nigh as I can learn, the priests are howling, the tares are binding up, the wheat is gathering, nations are trembling, and kingdoms are tottering; "men's hearts failing them for fear, and for looking for those things that are coming on the earth." The poor among men are rejoicing in the Lord, and the meek do increase their job. The hearts of the wicked do wax worse and worse, deceiving and being deceived.[43]

The gospel message gave hope to the poor and weak, succor to those who suffered, and comfort to the fearful.

Joseph worked vigorously throughout March, April, and May 1840 to arrange for land to accommodate the ranks of Mormons. But by June 18, he petitioned the Nauvoo High Council to "relieve him from the anxiety and trouble necessarily attendant on business transactions by appointing some one … to take charge of the City Plot." He asked for a stable income so he could turn his attention to the spiritual matters of the Church so that "the Choisest blessings of Heaven will be poured upon us and that the Glory of the Lord will overshadow the inheritances of the Saints."[44] He cast his petition in formal prose, speaking in third person, and thereby communicating the burden he labored under that might otherwise have sounded like complaining.

The high council urged him to change his mind. They suggested providing him with an assistant, Henry G. Sherwood, and agreed to compensate

40. Bryan J. Grant, "The Church in the British Isles," 1:228.

41. Flanders, *Nauvoo,* 79.

42. Ibid., 64.

43. *History of the Church,* 4:115 (Apr. 17, 1840).

44. Joseph Smith, Letter to Nauvoo High Council, June 18, 1840, in Jessee, *Personal Writings of Joseph Smith,* 502-503.

him for the money he had used to support his family since the sales had produced funds for the Church's general operations.[45] But the real reason, whether articulated privately or understood only intuitively, was that Joseph stood at the center of the Mormon kingdom. Emotionally, spiritually, and politically, those claiming their inheritance in Zion needed to receive it, at least metaphorically, from his hands.

William W. Phelps, excommunicated in Missouri for testifying against Joseph, wrote a pleading letter on June 29, seeking fellowship with the Church again and, even more importantly, Joseph's personal forgiveness: "I am as the prodigal son, though I never doubt or disbelieve the fullness of the Gospel." The fault was his own, he confessed. "I ask forgiveness in the name of Jesus Christ of all the Saints, for I will do right, God helping me."[46] Joseph responded warmly, telling Phelps that when Hyrum and he read the letter, "our hearts were melted into tenderness and compassion." Joseph reassured Phelps that his repentance would allow him to "be brought into the liberty of God's dear children, and again take your stand among the Saints of the Most High." When he read Phelps's letter to the Saints, they unanimously welcomed him back. Joseph continued: "Believing your confession to be real and your repentance genuine, I shall be happy once again to give you the right hand of fellowship, and rejoice over the returning prodigal." In a gesture of personal generosity, he concluded: "Come on dear Brother since the war is past, For friends at first are friends again at last."[47] As this letter shows, much of Joseph's experience in Nauvoo was about relationships and his abundant gift for friendship.

On the personal front, Don Carlos, Joseph and Emma's sixth child and fifth son, was born on June 14. Although he would live only one year, the child gave the couple tangible cause for celebration and hope. Husband and wife faced the future in a moment of shared happiness, believing that the riches sent to them from heaven would be grand indeed and that God would surely protect them from all enemies.

45. *History of the Church,* 4:144 (July 3, 1840).

46. W. W. Phelps, qtd. in Walter Dean Bowen, "The Versatile W. W. Phelps," 84-101; see also Jessee, *Personal Writings of Joseph Smith,* 508.

47. Joseph Smith, Letter to W. W. Phelps, July 22, 1840, in Jessee, *Personal Writings of Joseph Smith,* 509-10.

CHAPTER 5

A Hiding Place from the Tempest

> *Once the individual is formed as a person, with an objectively and subjectively recognizable identity, he must continue to participate in the conversation that sustains him as a person … [and] must at least continue to assent to those that form him as a person.*
>
> –*Peter Berger,* The Sacred Canopy, *18*

Joseph sketched a sacred universe in the minds of the Saints each time he addressed them. Everyday routines became extraordinary and sometimes to be feared. Joseph challenged the Saints to confront the sacred, to enter it, to make it their own. Sociologist Peter Berger suggests that this delineation between sacred and profane helps to keep anomie at bay: "To be in a 'right' relationship with the sacred cosmos is to be protected against the nightmare threats of chaos."[1] By rendering even the most mundane activities of Zion sacred, Joseph provided his people with an ultimate sense of rightness. Berger writes, "When roles, and the institutions to which they belong, are endowed with cosmic significance, the individual's self-identification with them attains a further dimension [and] …. becomes correspondingly deeper and more stable. He is whatever society has identified him as by virtue of a cosmic truth, as it were, and his social being becomes rooted in the sacred reality of the universe."[2]

Joseph's business maneuvers were always hampered by inadequate capital. The tremendous expense of resettling the Church, the loss of property in Missouri, and persistent debts remaining from Kirtland made it difficult to accomplish all that he needed to do; nor, it must be admitted, did Joseph show any particular financial acumen. When Horace Hotchkiss inquired

1. Peter Berger, *The Sacred Canopy*, 26.
2. Ibid., 37.

about the status of the petitions to the federal government and, even more anxiously, about the Church's ability to pay the two notes of $1,500 each due in August 1840, Joseph responded on July 28:

> Having had considerable difficulty (necessarily consequent on a new settlement) to contend with, as well as poverty and considerable sickness, our first payment will be probably somewhat delayed, until we again get a good start in the world. ... However, every exertion on our part shall be made to meet the demands against us, so that if we cannot accomplish all we wish to, it is our misfortune, and not our fault.[3]

A general letter addressed to the "Saints Scattered Abroad," on August 8, made it clear that the "work of the Lord in these last days, is one of vast magnitude, and almost beyond the comprehension of mortals." In Joseph's mind, God's goodness was demonstrated in "having secured a location upon which we have again commenced operations for the good of His people." Joseph told the Saints to

> unite our energies for the upbuilding of the Kingdom ... The work which has to be accomplished in the last days is one of vast importance, and will call into action the energy, skill, talent, and ability of the Saints, so that they may roll forth with that glory and majesty described by the prophet; and will consequently require the concentration of the Saints, to accomplish works of such magnitude and grandeur.
>
> The work of the gathering spoken of in the Scriptures will be necessary to bring about the glories of the last dispensation.[4]

It was a visionary letter intended to bring before the Saints the powerful image that actuated Joseph in his ideal city. In it, Joseph inscribed the gathering with theological significance. He asserted Nauvoo's prominence, competing with larger cities on the Mississippi for beauty and potential. In a letter to non-Mormon John C. Bennett weeks before, he had promoted Nauvoo energetically, calling it

> probably the best and most beautiful site for city on the river ... a situation in every respect adapted to commercial and agricultural pursuits. ...
>
> The number of inhabitants is nearly three thousand, and is fast increasing. If we are suffered to remain, there is every prospect of its becoming one of the largest cities on the river, if not in the western world.[5]

3. *History of the Church,* 4:171 (July 28, 1840).
4. Ibid., 185-86 (Aug. 31, 1840).
5. Ibid., 177-78.

Joseph also asked Church members to help fund "the printing and circulation of the Book of Mormon, Doctrine and Covenants, hymn-book, and the new translation of the Scriptures,"[6] as well as the building of a temple. The temple–the holiest building in the holy city–would ultimately encapsulate the prophet's narrative of Zion. Joseph urged working "as though the whole labor depended on themselves alone." He explained:

> To those who feel thus interested, and can assist in this great work, we say, let them come to this place; by so doing they will not only assist in the rolling on of the Kingdom, but be in a situation where they can have the advantage of instruction from the Presidency and other authorities of the Church, and rise higher and higher in the scale of intelligence until they can "comprehend with the Saints what is the breadth and length, and depth and height; and to know the love of Christ which passeth knowledge."[7]

The pressure to provide land, arrange funding, and sustain the Saints complicated Joseph's life with an impossibly difficult burden to carry; and since he always acted as Church president, the line between transactions formed to benefit the Church and personal arrangements was often undetectable. As he constructed Zion on the banks of the Mississippi, he bought farmland in parcels that ranged in size which he resold to land-seeking immigrants, weaving the metaphoric landscape of the Kingdom of God with the literal geography of Illinois. Joseph bought land from both speculators and friends. Robert Thompson, his secretary, sold him fifty lots in the city for $10,000.[8] Sometimes, when Joseph identified a particularly good deal, he earmarked small tracts for the members of his family. Thus, Emma and the children helped him to buy and sell land in which personal and corporate lives became inextricably entangled.[9] Probably for Joseph, the distinction between family and friends lacked any real meaning. When he saw that those around him needed land, he did what he could to insure that they would be provided for. He did the same for his family.

As July 1840 began, Joseph continued a series of meetings, visits to surrounding towns, and sermons to diverse audiences. Although Joseph was the spiritual leader of the Church, he also had considerable work as an

6. Robert J. Matthews, *A Bible! A Bible!,* 139.
7. *History of the Church,* 4:186 (Aug. 31, 1840).
8. Robert B. Flanders, *Nauvoo,* 120.
9. Linda King Newell and Valeen Tippetts Avery, *Mormon Enigma,* 91.

administrator. On July 11, he instructed the Nauvoo High Council on how to conduct meetings and hold judicial or special councils.[10] Two days later, he met with other Nauvoo citizens to discuss the "kidnapping" or arrest of Alanson Brown and Benjamin Boyce by Missouri officials and helped to draft a memorial to Illinois Governor Thomas Carlin asking for his help in returning the two men.[11] The Nauvoo High Council met again on July 2, July 17, and July 20, learning with pleasure that the first party of Mormon converts from Great Britain arrived at New York.[12] Joseph's life in Nauvoo was an exhilarating brew of business, intrigue, and challenges.

At this point, with a new baby in the house and the Nauvoo High Council reluctant to release him from the tedious duty of managing land sales, a mesmerizing new colleague appeared. On July 25, 1840, John C. Bennett, writing from Fairfield, Wayne County, 300 miles away, introduced himself to Joseph as someone who could help both the Church and the city achieve political and military power: "I hope to remove to Commerce and unite with your Church next spring. I believe I should be much happier with you."[13]

After Bennett arrived in Illinois in 1838, he had played a role in persuading the Illinois legislators to establish the "Invincible Dragoons." Exhibiting a penchant for military involvement, Bennett became brigadier general and quartermaster, which gave him access to arms and munitions. Not least, these appointments let him indulge his love of costumes, pageantry, and titles.[14] The dragoons were a militia company of Edwards, White, and Wabash Counties, all located in southeastern Illinois. In addition, Bennett claimed to be an instructor of "midwifery" in a small Ohio college,[15] was secretary of the Illinois Medical Society, and in January 1833 had been listed as one of the incorporators of the Christian College in New Albany, Indiana.[16] At age thirty-five, he was Joseph's exact contemporary. He may have first encountered Mormon missionaries a hundred miles away from Nauvoo, in 1832 in Springfield, Illinois, but if so had been unmoved by their message.[17]

10. *History of the Church,* 4:154 (July 11, 1840). For an annotated compilation of both the city council's and the high council's minutes, see John S. Dinger, ed., *The Nauvoo City and High Council Minutes,* Foreword by Morris A. Thurston (Salt Lake City: Signature Books, 2001).

11. *History of the Church,* 4:157, 159 (July 13, 1840).

12. Ibid., 162 (July 20, 1840).

13. Ibid., 168-69 (July 25, 1840).

14. Andrew F. Smith, Introduction to John C. Bennett, *The History of the Saints,* vi-xi; and Andrew F. Smith, *The Saintly Scoundrel,* 1-50.

15. Frederick C. Waite, "The First Medical Diploma Mill in the United States," 495-96.

16. Andrew Smith, *Saintly Scoundrel,* 13-16.

17. Bennett may have met Mormon missionaries, possibly even Joseph Smith, in 1832. See

Bennett's first letter, written on state Quartermaster General letterhead on July 25, 1840, was addressed to both "Reverend and Dear Friends [Joseph] Smith and [Sidney] Rigdon." He may have written an earlier letter during "your difficulties with the Missourians," he told Joseph, although this letter has not been found. He pointedly told them: "You are aware that at the time I held the office of 'Brigadier-General of the Invincible Dragoons' of this state, and profered you my entire energies for your deliverance from a ruthless and savage, but cowardly foe ... but the Lord came to your rescue, and saved you with a powerful arm." Because Bennett's letters seemingly came out of nowhere, he was careful to lay out a common history and set of understandings.

This letter, ingratiating and arrogant simultaneously, reveals Bennett as important and busy, yet also apparently receptive to the prophet's message and ostensibly humble enough to bow to his instructions. Was such impatience flattering or irritating to Joseph?

Before Joseph could have received the letter, Bennett wrote again on July 27: "I am with you in spirit, and will be in person as soon as circumstances permit, and immediately if it is your desire." Gone was the stately schedule of visiting Nauvoo in five months and moving there in a year. "Wealth is no material object with me," assured Bennett. "I desire to be happy, and am fully satisfied that I can enjoy myself better with your people ... I hope that in time your people will become my people, and your God my God."[18] To a proselytizing prophet, Bennett's offer was tempting.

Bennett cannily threw all of his weight into endorsing Joseph's already public policy of the "gathering": "It would be my deliberate advice to you to concentrate all of your Church at one point. If Hancock County, with Commerce as its commercial emporium, is to be that point, well; fix upon it. Let us cooperate with a general concerted action." Tempering this demanding tone, he added: "I have many things to communicate which I would prefer doing orally; and I propose to meet you in Springfield on the first Monday in December next, as I shall be there at the time on state and United States business."[19]

Bennett then laid out an ambitious plan of his activity in Nauvoo–if Joseph approved. He would not resign as state quartermaster-general and he would also "practice my profession; [presumably as a physician] but at

---

Jan Shipps and John W. Welch, eds., *The Journals of William E. McLellin, 1831-1836,* 69. For Bennett in Nauvoo, see Gary James Bergera, "John C. Bennett, Joseph Smith, and the Beginnings of Plural Marriage in Nauvoo."

18. *History of the Church,* 4:169 (July 27, 1840).

19. Ibid., 168-70 (July 25, 1840). The earlier letter (or letters) to which Bennett refers is not in *History of the Church* and may not be extant.

the same time your people shall have all the benefits of my speaking powers, and my untiring energies in behalf of the good and holy faith. *Un necessariis unitas, in non necessariis libertas, in omnibus charitas,* shall be my motto, with–*suaviter in modo, fortiter in re.*"[20]

Bennett followed with an exuberant third written only three days later on July 30: "My anxiety to be with you is daily increasing, and I shall wind up my professional business immediately, and proceed to your blissful abode …"[21] By then Bennett had convinced himself that Nauvoo was his future; and he was straining to go, anxious to launch his life's next act.

On Thursday, July 30, even while Bennett was posting his missive, Joseph was in Nauvoo, where, according to his uncle, John Smith, he addressed a small group of Mormons who were fasting in anticipation of their regular prayer and fast meeting. He promised to pray for them. Then, his tone became serious as he condemned the recurring problem of "Speaking evil of one another," including "the Seer." If they would "cease from these bickerings & murmurings & be of one mind," he promised, "the Lord would visit them with health & every needed good." "This is the voice of the Spirit," Joseph concluded.[22]

Peppered with three Bennett letters in less than a week, Joseph responded with cautious cordiality on August 8: "Were it possible for you to come here this season to suffer affliction with the people of God, no one will be more pleased to give you a more cordial welcome than myself." He stressed that Bennett should not expect special treatment or advantages: "My general invitation is, Let all that will, come, and partake of the poverty of Nauvoo freely."[23] Bennett wrote also on August 8, his fourth letter, assuring the man from whom he had not yet received a letter: "I shall be with you in about two weeks, and shall devote my time and energies to the advancement of the cause of truth and virtue, and the advocacy of the holy religion which you have so nobly defended, and so honorably sustained."[24] There is no record that Joseph answered, perhaps waiting to see if Bennett's hopes might be chilled by Joseph's lukewarm response of August 8.

Besides, the prophet had his hands full with other matters. He had reported to Bennett that Illinois's legislature had granted the city a railroad

20. Ibid., 170. The Latin motto translates into English as: "In essentials, unity; in non-essentials, liberty; in all things, charity. … Gentle in manner, resolute in action."

21. Ibid., 172 (July 30, 1840).

22. John Smith, Diary, July 30, 1840, LDS Church History Library.

23. *History of the Church,* 4:178 (Aug. 8, 1840).

24. Ibid., 179.

charter and predicted that the railroad would run about twenty miles between Nauvoo and Warsaw, where material coming upriver by boat had to be off-loaded "immediately below the rapids of the Mississippi."[25] If this railroad had been built (it never was), the line would have connected Nauvoo with the Des Moines Rapids Railroad and with another proposed line–the Warsaw, Peoria, and Wabash Railroad, which was planned to run from Warsaw along the Mississippi through Carthage.

On Sunday, August 9, Joseph and Hyrum both preached on the "first Principles of the gospel," including "Resurrection from the dead & eternal Judgement also the Doom of Murderers & Adulterers &c."[26] It would be six days later, on Saturday, August 15, when Joseph would make his important first discourse on the necessity of baptism for the dead. Obviously, his Sunday sermon was an introductory warm-up to his expansive new understanding of the empowering relationship between the living and the dead to which he would give concrete form in a new ordinance.

The August 15 sermon commemorated the life and death of Seymour Brunson, a member of the Nauvoo High Council who had expired at age forty on August 10.[27] Although he was in England at the time, Heber C. Kimball heard about the funeral from his wife, Vilate. According to Vilate, Brunson's funeral procession stretched a mile, and "the R[o]om was full of Angels that came after him to waft him home." Funerals gave Joseph the opportunity to frame one's earthly existence with a specific promise of heaven. Linking sacred ordinances and a righteous way of living with the kingdom of heaven, he opened the imagined landscape of the afterlife and asked his audience to consider it with him. Kimball quoted his wife on the effect of Joseph's sermon: "A more joyfull Season she never Saw be fore on the account of the glory that Joseph set forth."[28] Simon Baker, also present, said that to make his argument, Joseph pointed to a widow in the congregation whose son had died before he was baptized, and read the scripture: "Except a man be born of water and the spirit he cannot enter the kingdom of heaven" (John 3:5). Joseph then announced "that this widow should have glad tidings in that thing. He also said the Apostle was talking to a people who understood Baptism for the Dead, for it was practiced among them. He

25. Ibid., 178.

26. John Smith, Diary, Aug. 9, 1840. See also "Sermon delivered in Lee County, Iowa on August 9, 1840," http://www.boap.org/LDS/Parallel/1840/9Aug40.html; July 26, 2013.

27. Ibid., 37; *History of the Church,* 4:179 (Aug. 8, 1840).

28. Heber C. Kimball, qtd. in Ehat and Cook, *Words of Joseph Smith,* 49n1.

went on to say that people could now act for their friends who had departed this life, and that the plan of salvation was calculated to save all who were willing to obey the requirements of the law of God." It was, for Baker, "a very beautiful discourse."[29]

Although this articulation of doctrine should have opened the way for immediate baptisms for the dead, none were recorded for the next four weeks. A month after Joseph first taught the doctrine, on September 12, Harvey Olmstead officiated in the first baptism for the dead when Jane Neyman (also Neymon and Nyman) was baptized on behalf of her deceased son. Vienna Jacques, while riding her horse near the river, witnessed the scene.[30] Baptism for the dead broadened Joseph's and the Saints' understanding of the kingdom of God to include both the living and the dead in a continuum that stretched through generations, and fulfilled the scriptural exhortation to "turn the hearts of the children to their fathers" (Mal. 4:6). It also opened the door to eternal marriage sealings, including plural marriages, for both the living and the dead.

The river landing at Main Street saw numerous proxy baptisms for the dead.[31] This type of public setting made baptisms a community event. In addition to those who participated, others watched from the bank. Robert Horne remembered seeing "the Elders baptizing for the dead in the Mississippi River. This was something new to me and the beauty of this great principle dawned upon me. I had never heard of such a doctrine then. Orson Pratt was baptizing. Brother Joseph stood on the banks."[32] Many years later, Aroet Hale recalled: "Then the apostles and other elders went into the river and continued the same ordinance. Hundreds were baptized there."[33]

At the end of August, Joseph sermonized on "eternal Judgement and the eternal duration of matter."[34] He remained in Nauvoo for the next

---

29. Simon Baker, reminiscence, qtd. in Journal History, Aug. 15, 1840. Joseph may have had his own mother and oldest brother, Alvin (who had died in 1823), in mind.

30. See Nauvoo Baptisms for the Dead, Book A, attached note, microfilm no. 183,376, LDS Church History Library; see also Jane Neyman and Vienna Jacques, Statement, November 29, 1854, in Journal History, Aug. 15, 1840. Alexander Baugh, "'For This Ordinance Belongeth to My House,'" 49, notes that baptism for the dead was an "evolutionary" doctrine and changed over time. In this first case, a woman was baptized for a man; the witness was a woman and did not hold the priesthood. Later, men would be baptized for men and women for women, and witnesses would hold the priesthood.

31. M. Guy Bishop, "'What Has Become of Our Fathers?,'" 87, calculated that 6,818 baptisms for the dead were performed in Nauvoo. The majority before the end of 1841 were in the river, and thereafter in the basement of the Nauvoo temple.

32. Robert Horne, "Reminiscences of the Church in Nauvoo," 585.

33. Aroet Hale, Autobiography, 7.

34. John Smith, Diary, Aug. 30, 1840.

thirty-nine weeks, until July 1841, expounding further on Church doctrine, while also attending to his family's and the Church's business.

Meanwhile, in Great Britain, seven members of the Quorum of the Twelve struggled with many of the same issues that Joseph confronted daily in Nauvoo. Brigham Young and Willard Richards wrote to the First Presidency on September 5 that they worried about money, having used their own credit to help converts immigrate. "[W]e have done all we could to help as many off as possible to land where they may get a morsel of bread, & serve God according to his appointment; & we have done it cheerfully as unto the Lord, & we desire to ask you have we done right?" Other questions included: "Have we done right in Printing a hymn book?" "Are we doing right in Printing the book of Mormon?" "Are we doing right in staying here & leaving our families to be a burden to the Church?" "We have heard … that Brothers Joseph & Hyrum are coming to England next season. Is this good news true?"[35]

Despite the substance of their questions, the apostles were receiving important organizational training. Isolated from Joseph except for weekly letters, they began publishing the monthly *Latter-day Saints' Millennial Star*. This periodical provided news for members all over the country, instructions for missionaries, encouraging reports of progress, and, not least in significance, a permanent historical record. The apostles also organized the beginnings of an immigration system and developed a successful method for spreading the word about a living prophet, new scripture, and the Second Coming that fueled the need to gather. Forced to be relatively independent in England, they learned to make decisions framed by Joseph's understandings of the relationship of their work in the field and his work in Nauvoo.

While Joseph's apostles were abroad, John Bennett arrived in Nauvoo on September 1. Although neither man left a record of that first meeting, the consequences suggest an instant attraction. Joseph invited Bennett to share his home, and Bennett accepted. There he fascinated Joseph with a power probably not seen since Sidney Rigdon had first enchanted the prophet in New York. Joseph III, who was eight years old in September, later recalled: "While Doctor Bennett was boarding at our house every effort was made for his comfort. … Mother would set a loaf of bread down in front of the wood fire until its end would be toasted a pleasing brown. Then she would slice

35. Ronald W. Walker, ed., "The Willard Richards and Brigham Young Letter to Joseph Smith from England to Nauvoo, 5 September 1840," 473-74.

that part off, thinly, and replace the loaf before the fire. … prepared just as he [i.e., Bennett] liked it."[36]

What Emma thought of the doctor does not appear in any known contemporary document, but she was gracious and accommodating. Bennett, clever enough to know that his future hinged at this moment on Joseph's favor, worked his way into the prophet's confidence, and recorded no objection to any of Mormonism's doctrines. Joseph baptized him soon after his arrival.[37]

This new intimate was described as having a stately bearing, short in stature but thickly built. Most distinctive, a full head of black hair, peppered with gray, framed a face dominated by a large, stately nose. When he smiled, he exposed a wide gap where his two upper front teeth were missing. This seemed not to impede his persuasive oratory, however, and many acquaintances were more struck by his intense, knowing gaze.[38] "He is a big man and I hope a good one," Vilate Kimball described him in a letter to Heber. "He is a great warrior. Many of our brethren have got the same spirit." She added, somewhat dubiously, "I expect it is all right."[39]

Later, after he had been expelled from the Church, Bennett insisted that he "never believed in them [i.e., the Mormons] or their doctrines," but it seems likely that he was equally flattered by the confidence that Joseph almost immediately placed in his abilities.[40] After Bennett's baptism, Hyrum, who had been Church patriarch for only a week (see below), pronounced an expansive patriarchal blessing on Bennett's head on September 21, 1840. These blessings included

> the holy priesthood, with all its graces, and gifts, and with wisdom in all the mysteries of God. Thou shalt have knowledge given thee, and shalt understand the keys by which all mysteries shall be unlocked. Thou shalt have great power among the children of men, and shalt have influence among

36. Mary Audentia Smith Anderson and Bertha A. Anderson Hulmes, eds., *Joseph Smith III and the Restoration,* 58.

37. Bergera, "John C. Bennett, Joseph Smith, and the Beginnings of Plural Marriage in Nauvoo," 55. The date of Bennett's baptism is not known for certain. Hyrum Smith gave him a patriarchal blessing (perhaps the first he bestowed as Church patriarch) on September 21, 1840. It seems unlikely he would have done this if Bennett had not yet been baptized. Thomas Gregg, *The Prophet of Palmyra,* 173, gives October 1, 1842, as the baptismal date, but provides no documentation.

38. Anderson and Hulmes, *Joseph Smith III and the Restoration,* 57-58; Bergera, "John C. Bennett."

39. Vilate Kimball, Letter to Heber C. Kimball, Oct. 11, 1840.

40. John C. Bennett, *The History of the Saints,* 5.

> the great and the noble, even to prevail on many, and bring them to the knowledge of the truth. Thou shalt prevail over thy enemies ... The Holy Spirit shall rest upon thee, insomuch, that thy voice shall make the foundation on which thou standest to shake–so great shall be the power of God.
>
> His favor shall rest upon thee in dreams and visions, which shall manifest the glory of God. Beloved brother, if thou art faithful, thou shalt have power to heal the sick; cause the lame to leap like an hart; the deaf to hear; and the dumb to speak, and their voice shall salute thine ears; thy soul shall be made glad and thy heart shall rejoice in God. Thou shalt be like unto Paul, who, according to his own words, was like "one born out of due time," and shalt have the visions of heaven open, even as they were to him.[41]

In mid-September, Joseph's nemesis came stalking again out of Missouri. It had been only seventeen months since he had fled the state, and now a Missouri sheriff descended on Nauvoo, accompanied by a demand from Illinois Governor Thomas Carlin, that Joseph and others yield themselves to extradition as fugitives.[42] Tragically, as Joseph avoided arrest, his father, Joseph Sr., fell gravely ill. In the absence of his son, Joseph Sr., from his deathbed, appointed Hyrum as his successor on September 14 (an appointment Joseph Jr. confirmed the following January 24). According to Hyrum's biographer, Jeffrey O. Driscoll, "Hyrum's calling as patriarch to the Church would soon be formalized, but he had already accepted some responsibility and had apprenticed under the direction of his father."[43] Joseph Jr. was still in hiding from the Missouri sheriff on September 15 when Robert B. Thompson preached Father Smith's funeral sermon.[44] Hyrum's new appointment left a vacancy in the First Presidency, which William Law filled on January 30, 1841, when he joined Sidney Rigdon as Joseph's other counselor.

On October 3, 1840, during the Saturday morning meeting of October's churchwide general conference, Joseph surfaced to express his indignation that "there had been several depredations committed on the citizens of Nauvoo." He called for a committee to "search out the offenders, and bring them to justice." He also recommended building up Kirtland so that Saints moving from the East could gather there instead of Nauvoo and suggested "that some one should be appointed from this conference to preside over that

41. Hyrum Smith, Patriarchal blessing, qtd. in John C. Bennett, *The History of the Saints,* 42-44.

42. *History of the Church,* 4:198-99; "Nauvoo, Ill.: Sept., 1840," *Times and Seasons* 1, no. 11 (Sept. 1840): 170.

43. Jeffrey O. Driscoll, *Hyrum Smith: A Life of Integrity* (Salt Lake City: Deseret Book, 2003), 231.

44. *History of the Church,* 4:189-97 (Sept. 14, 1840).

stake."[45] The Church still owned property in Kirtland, and enough Saints continued to live there to maintain a viable unit.

Joseph spoke again in the Sunday morning session, October 4, taking as his topic baptism for the dead, "which was listened to with considerable interest, by the vast multitude assembled."[46]

A particular highlight of the conference was Bennett's address. He had been in the city for only a month, been a member for less than a month, and was attending his first Mormon conference, but he rose to the occasion with aplomb. He had obviously internalized Joseph's signature message. His theme was "the oppression to which the Church had been subjected," from which he argued "that it was necessary for the brethren to ... resist every unlawful attempt at persecution."[47] The next morning, October 5, he assured his audience that "many persons had been accused of crime, and been looked upon as guilty, when on investigation it has been ascertained that nothing could be proved against them."[48] Joseph publicly praised Bennett as a "superior orator, and like Paul [the New Testament apostle] is active and deligent, always employing himself in doing good to his fellow men."[49]

At that same October conference, Joseph sounded another of his perennial themes: the gathering. He pronounced a prophetic blessing to welcome "the polished European; the degraded Hottentot, and the shivering Laplanders; persons of all languages. ... and of every color; who shall with us worship ... in His holy temple and offer up their orisons in his sanctuary."[50] He obliquely responded to critics who had complained that the land purchases in Illinois and Iowa "appeared to be large and uncalled for": "[W]e shall soon have to say, 'This place is too straight ; give us room that we may dwell.' We therefore hope that the brethren ... will aid us in liquidating the debts which are now owing, so that the inheritances may be secured to the Church, and which eventually will be of great value."[51] The "inheritance" in Zion promised to new converts was pitched as a good investment.

Joseph also devoted part of one conference address to his restoration theology: "God purposed in Himself that there should not be an eternal fullness until every dispensation should be fulfilled and gathered together in

45. "Nauvoo, Illinois, October, 1840," *Times and Seasons* 1, no. 12 (Oct. 1840): 185.
46. Ibid., 186.
47. *History of the Church,* 4:205 (Oct. 3, 1840); Smith, *The Saintly Scoundrel,* 58.
48. *History of the Church,* 4:206 (Oct. 5, 1840).
49. Smith, *Saintly Scoundrel,* 61; Ehat and Cook, *Words of Joseph Smith,* 59.
50. *History of the Church,* 4:213 (Oct. 5, 1840).
51. Ibid., 214.

one[,] and that all things whatsoever that should be gathered together in one in those dispensations unto the fullness and eternal glory should be in Christ Jesus, therefore He set the ordinances to be the same for Ever and ever."[52] In addition to providing a grand schemata of dispensational history, Joseph positioned himself as *the* essential conduit of authority (see D&C 22).

From baptism, it was an easy step to assert that marriage–or, as Joseph termed, "sealing"–could endure unbroken through death and into eternity. Three years later in 1843 (if not earlier), Joseph would assert that the dead required the same set of ordinances, including marriage, as the living:

> All covenants, oaths, vows, performances, connections, association, or expectations, that are not made and entered into and sealed by the Holy Spirit of promise, of him who is anointed, … are of no efficacy, virtue, or force in and after the resurrection from the dead. …
>
> Therefore, if a man marry him a wife in the world, and he marry her not by me nor by my word, … they are not bound by any law when they are out of the world. (D&C, 132:7, 15)

This October 1840 conference proved to be an important rhetorical moment, one that validated Joseph's authority, rendering him powerful as a judge of the validity of civil marriages. In the context of this new template for salvation, priesthood power trumped civil power in marriage relations.

As the conference continued on Monday, October 5, Joseph linked an individual's ability to enter into the highest degree of heaven to this order of the priesthood via an understanding that gave family relations or even social relationships new–even eternal–significance. Parley P. Pratt later described his exhilaration when Joseph taught him about "the first idea of eternal family organization, and the eternal union of the sexes in those inexpressibly endearing relationships which none but the highly intellectual, the refined and pure in heart, know how to prize, and which are at the very foundation of everything worthy to be called happiness."[53]

This important sermon, given on the last day of conference, was evidently one of the very few that Joseph wrote out completely, with Robert Thompson acting as scribe.[54] But Joseph did not deliver it in person. Thompson read this "treatise on Priesthood" to the Saints. Howard Coray, another

52. Ibid., 208.

53. Parley P. Pratt, *Autobiography,* 297.

54. "Oct. 5, 1840, Original manuscript in the hand of Robert B. Thompson," in Ehat and Cook, *Words of Joseph Smith,* 38-44.

of Joseph's clerks, was in Joseph's office the morning they were working on the draft and later recalled the episode as part of his fervent testimony about Joseph's prophetic powers. He thought they "were examining or hunting in the manuscript of the new translation of the Bible for something on Priesthood, which Joseph wished to present, or have read to the people the next Conference." According to Coray, they did not find what they were looking for, so Joseph instead "put the manuscript" to the side, and said, "take some paper and I will tell you what to write." Thompson picked up a piece of paper and got ready to transcribe the text. Then, "the Spirit of God descended upon him [Joseph], and a measure of it upon me, insomuch that I could fully realize that God, or the Holy Ghost, was talking through him. I [n]ever before or since, have felt as I did on that occasion. I felt so small and humble I could have freely kissed his feet."[55]

In what he knew would be an important discourse, the following day after he made the announcement of his plans for the Nauvoo temple, Joseph described two priesthoods mentioned in scripture–Aaronic and Melchizedek–and explained their functions. But his most important elaboration was on priesthood "keys," the head of the priesthood who holds the highest authority "which pertains to the Priesthood" and to the "Kingdom of God in all ages of the world to the latest posterity on the earth." Important because "keys" provide the "channel through which all knowledge, doctrine, the plan of salvation and every important matter is revealed from heaven," Joseph's comments explained doctrine to which he had earlier only alluded. Significantly, he located priesthood keys in his own person and in his role as prophet. The keys had been the "channel through the Almighty commenced revealing his glory at the beginning of the creation of this earth," and to Joseph's time when he "continued to reveal himself to the children of men … and through which he will make known his purposes to the end of time."[56] Thus, Joseph's life was part of a continuum–if not the culmination–of priesthood authority and communication with God. Joseph expounded on Adam, on Abel and Cain, and more importantly on Enoch, with whom he identified and whose Old Testament story seemed to parallel aspects of his own. He used Enoch to teach about the doctrine of "translation," which he considered to grow out of the blessings accompanying priesthood.[57] Faith

55. Howard Coray, "Autobiography," 5.

56. *History of the Church,* 4:207.

57. According to Joseph, "The doctrine of translation was a doctrine whereby men were taken immediately into the presence of God, and into an eternal fullness." *History of the Church,* 4:210.

played a central role in this dynamic, for "without faith it is impossible to please God, for he that cometh to God must believe that he is, and that he is a revealer to those who diligently seek him."[58]

Secular-oriented business at the conference included a motion to establish a committee to draft "a bill for the incorporation of the town of Nauvoo, and for other purposes," with Joseph as chair and Bennett and Thompson as committee members.[59] In fact, the three had already more or less drafted a charter, so they held a pro forma meeting that afternoon to authorize Bennett to report its "outlines" to the conference, which endorsed it without debate. Bennett then spearheaded the proposal when the Illinois state legislative session began in late November.

On October 19, Joseph responded to Brigham Young's earlier letter from Great Britain, asking whether British converts should gather to Nauvoo. He clearly saw converts as key in the city's growth:

> Inasmuch as this place [Nauvoo] has been appointed for the gathering of the Saints, it is necessary that it be attended to in the order that the Lord intends. … [T]here are great numbers of the Saints in England who are extremely poor, and not accustomed to the farming business, who must have certain preparations made for them before they can support themselves in this country, therefore, to prevent confusion and disappointment when they arrive here, let those men who are accustomed to make machinery, and those who can command capital, though it be small, come here as soon as convenient, and put up machinery, and make such other preparations as may be necessary, so that when the poor come, they may have employment to come to. This place has advantages for manufacturing and commercial purposes, which but very few can boast of; and the establishing of cotton factories, foundries, potteries, etc.,

58. Ibid., 209. Three months later on January 19, 1841, Joseph said he received a revelation to tell Hyrum Smith and William Law about "keys … whereby [they] may ask and receive, and be crowned with the same blessing, and glory, and honor, and priesthood, and gifts of the priesthood, that once were put upon him that was my servant Oliver Cowdery" (D&C 124:95, 97). Orson Pratt elaborated on these keys in a footnote to his 1879 LDS edition of the Doctrine and Covenants: They were "the order of God for receiving revelations," or in other words, the keys to the oracles of God. Six days before administering what would become the LDS temple endowment for the first time, Joseph told a meeting of the Relief Society sisters on April 28, 1842, that he would soon deliver "the keys of the Priesthood to the Church, and said that the faithful members of the Relief Society should receive them with their husbands, that the Saints whose integrity has been tried and proved faithful, might know how to ask the Lord and receive an answer." *History of the Church,* 4:207. Married women received the benefits of the priesthood through their righteous husbands, but how single women might access priesthood was less certain.

59. *History of the Church,* 4:205 (Oct. 4, 1840).

> would be the means of bringing in wealth, and raising it to a very important elevation.[60]

Nauvoo never did become the industrial center the prophet anticipated, although British converts came by the thousands.

Joseph also instructed the apostles to return to Nauvoo the next spring. (Parley P. Pratt had left for England on August 29.) Not only did Joseph need them back home, but hinted at social unrest in England: "There have been whisperings of the spirit that there will be some agitations, excitements, and trouble in the land where you are now laboring."[61] By 1840, 4,743 converts had been baptized in Great Britain, but only 240 had joined the Church in Nauvoo by the end of the year.[62]

Not long after arriving in Nauvoo, British convert Francis Moon recruited his relatives in England on November 4, 1840, to come to the Latter-day Saint center. Moon saw Nauvoo as a refuge where the people of God gathered together in Zion. "[T]he Lord has helped me, and brought me safely through; and now I have the privilege of being acquainted with the mysteries of the kingdom of God." He described wages that promised economic prosperity–a dollar a day on a farm, a half dollar more for artisans. "If one is disposed to keep a cow, (and but few are without two or three) they may keep them free of expense, by sending them out to graze on the neighboring plains, and for the winter's keep they are at liberty to cut as much grass as they please." He had obviously caught Joseph's vision of the gathering as a replication of the biblical themes, as this passage is studded with scriptural allusions:

> We live in a time in which the Lord is going to gather his people, to that land [America] that was promised to Joseph and his seed, which is a choice land above all lands. … [T]here are two important things in the gathering … first it is the design of the Lord to deliver his people from the troubles that are coming upon the earth, for it is far from him to destroy the righteous with the wicked; and for the benefit of his people he has prepared an hiding place from the tempest. … Another reason … is … that they may build a sanctuary to the name of the Most High … and attend to such ordinances and receive such blessings as they could not while scattered …[63]

60. Ibid., 228 (Oct. 19, 1840).
61. Ibid., 227-28 (Oct. 19, 1840).
62. Robert B. Flanders, *Nauvoo,* 69.
63. Francis Moon, Letter, Nov. 4, 1840, *Millennial Star* 1, no. 10 (Feb. 1841): 253.

Moon believed that Joseph had "revealed a most glorious principle, which has been hid from the children of men for many generations"–this may be a reference to baptism for the dead–"but those who desire to receive these blessings must be tried even as Abraham. … You will be tried by the reports of those who … will speak evil of … the good land … and all that appertain to it." "My fellow Englishmen and brethren," Moon closed, "you may rely on what I say. … In this place there is a prospect of receiving every good thing both of this world and that which is to come: then be faithful, for the Lord has said his saints shall inherit the earth."[64]

Newly arrived British convert William Clayton wrote a no less enthusiastic but more realistic depiction of his impressions of Joseph himself on December 10, 1840:

> He is … a man of sound judgment and possessed of an abundance of intelligence, and whilst you listen to his conversation you receive intelligence which expands your mind and causes your heart to rejoice. He is very familiar and delights to instruct the poor saint. I can converse with him just as easily as I can with you … He seems exceedingly well versed in the scriptures, and whilst conversing upon any subject, such light and beauty is revealed as I never saw before.[65]

In November 1840, the Mormons voted Whig with the single exception of electing for the state legislature Democrat James H. Ralston, an individual who had already helped Joseph somewhat in Illinois. To do this, they scratched out the last name on the ballot (Abraham Lincoln's) and wrote in "Ralston."[66] Courted by all parties, Joseph vowed friendship according to expediency. Such a procedure was, and remains, American politics, but the fact that Joseph could deliver a large–and ever-growing–bloc of votes carried increasingly dangerous consequences.

But in late 1840, there was almost an innocence about Mormon ventures into politics, as shown by the successful effort to get a city charter for Nauvoo. Joseph's affinity for Bennett may seem naive in hindsight. But at the time, some of Joseph's most trusted colleagues were in England, and he needed a skilled entrepreneur to help him organize a city. Bennett seemed made-to-order. Toward the end of November, Bennett represented the Church in Springfield, proposing that the state legislature create three

64. Ibid.
65. William Clayton, Letter to "Beloved Brothers and Sisters," Dec. 10, 1840.
66. *History of the Church,* 4: 249 (Dec. 16, 1840).

charters: the first for the city of Nauvoo, a second for the Nauvoo Legion, and the third for the University of the City of Nauvoo.[67] Bennett himself addressed the legislature, stimulating sympathy for the Mormon people by recounting the tale of their sufferings in Missouri. Stephen A. Douglas, a Democrat serving as secretary of state and wielding considerable influence, supported Bennett's three charters.[68] Whig Senator Sidney H. Little of McDonough County to the east cast an affirmative vote as well.[69] At this point, there was no reason to question what Bennett seemed to offer.

Illinois's twelfth general assembly passed forty-seven acts of incorporation, including seven other city charters that year. Despite the fact that the bill traveled through the Upper House, the Judiciary Committee, the House of Representatives, the Senate and the Council of Revision, before passage on December 16, Bennett's proposal apparently never once received a close reading. Illinois was generally optimistic about the great future that lay ahead, enthusiastically welcomed new settlers, and saw organized groups as particularly desirable.

Historians Roger Launius and John Hallwas propose two explanations for why passage of Nauvoo's charter occurred so quickly: "(1) the sympathy of fellow Americans for the plight of the Mormons following their expulsion from Missouri, and (2) the awareness by politicians of the potential strength of the Mormons as a voting bloc."[70] Triumphantly, Bennett wrote to Joseph on the day of passage: "Every power we asked has been granted, every request gratified, every desire fulfilled." Bennett mentioned that even Abraham Lincoln, the candidate the Mormons had eliminated on the ballot, "had the magnanimity to vote for our act ... and cordially congratulated me on its passage."[71] The charter would take official effect on February 1, 1841.

Illinois Governor Thomas Ford recognized Bennett's role in insuring the charter's passage and also the means he used: "He flattered both sides with the hope of Mormon favor," Ford later wrote, "and both sides expected to receive their votes."[72] Bennett also claimed that none of its provisions was "anti-republican"–rather, that it simply established the respected Jeffersonian

67. Ibid., 239 (Dec. 16, 1840).

68. John E. Hallwas and Roger D. Launius, eds., *Cultures in Conflict,* 21; *History of the Church*, 4:248 (Dec. 16, 1840).

69. Flanders, *Nauvoo,* 96. See also Frank E. Stevens, "Life of Stephen A. Douglas," *Journal of the Illinois State Historical Society* 16 (1923-24): 340, 341.

70. Hallwas and Launius, *Cultures in Conflict,* 21.

71. *History of the Church,* 4:248-49 (Dec. 16, 1840).

72. Thomas Ford, *History of Illinois ...*, 2:63-64.

principle of locating significant power in the hands of local government.[73] This strength was, in fact, the charter's weakness. The Nauvoo City Council could also function as a municipal court. The militia (the Nauvoo Legion) answered only to the mayor,[74] who crossed into the judicial branch by having "exclusive jurisdiction in all cases arising under the ordinances of the corporation." This provision thus erased an important check on the executive.[75]

Joseph later stressed that the city charter was "my own plan and device. I concocted it for the salvation of the Church, and on principles so broad, that every honest man might dwell secure under its protective influence without distinction of sect or party."[76] But in a proclamation issued on January 8, 1841, the First Presidency praised Bennett as one of the principal "instruments in … in procuring the city charter. He is a man of enterprise, extensive acquirements, and of independent mind, and is calculated to be a great blessing to our community."[77]

While it would be possible to look at Nauvoo as a typical fledgling American river town, it was not. Unlike the economic base and ambition that fueled most nineteenth-century towns under the umbrella of more-or-less generally accepted political ideals, Nauvoo's residents were bound together by faith in Joseph's prophetic mission, by distinctive interpretations of the Bible, by new scripture, and by the everyday performance of religious rituals. They moved within a penumbra of self-awareness that they were God's chosen people. This identity provided a sort of armor that assured them of their specialness as it exacted sacrifice and secrecy.

Joseph's letter to the Twelve Apostles on December 15, 1840, testified of the importance of their work. "A man filled with the love of God," he wrote prescriptively, "is not content with blessing his family alone but ranges through the world, anxious to bless the whole of the human family. This has been your feelings and caused you to forego the pleasures of home, that you might be a blessing to others, who are candidates for immortality but who were strangers to the principals of truth …"[78] In addition to the mundane news of Nauvoo's progress and economic opportunities for the converts, he spelled out reminders of the vision before them:

---

73. Ibid., 66.

74. *History of the Church,* 4:240 (Dec. 16, 1840).

75. Ibid., 242.

76. Ibid., 249 (Dec. 16, 1840).

77. Ibid., 270 (Jan. 8, 1841).

78. Joseph Smith, Letter to the Twelve, Dec. 15, 1840, in Dean C. Jessee, ed., *Personal Writings of Joseph Smith,* 517.

the enemies we have to contend against are subtle and well skilled in maneuvering, it behooves us then to be on the alert, to concentrate our energies, and that the best feelings should exist in our midst, and then by the help of the Almighty we shall go on from victory to victory and from conquest unto conquest, our evil passions will be subdued, our prejudices depart, we shall find no room in our bosoms for hatred, vice will hide its deformed head, and we shall stand approved in the sight of heaven and be acknowledged "the sons of God."[79]

79. Ibid., 520-21.

CHAPTER 6

The New City Steps Out

We feel to urge its necessity, and say, let the Saints come here—THIS IS THE WORD OF THE LORD, and in accordance with the great work of the last days.

—First Presidency, "A Proclamation, to the Saints Scattered Abroad," Millennial Star *1 (March 1841): 273*

On New Year's Day 1841, Joseph formally appointed Hyrum to be a "Prophet and Revelator" and confirmed Joseph Sr.'s ordination of him as Patriarch of the Church. Throughout Hyrum's life, he stood in Joseph's shadow; but rather than resenting his secondary role, Hyrum mostly supported and sustained his younger brother as the presiding prophet.[1] Before the month's end, Joseph had also reorganized the First Presidency, with Sidney Rigdon as first counselor, William Law as second, and Hyrum as assistant president (in addition to being presiding patriarch).[2]

When Joseph and the circle of men around him invited converts to gather to Nauvoo, they explained that life in Zion was the surest defense against the world's evil and the best preparation for the millennial reign of Jesus Christ. Joseph linked Zion to citizenship, industry, prosperity, and faith, all in the same package. On January 15, the First Presidency commented that the Nauvoo Legion, the city-wide security force that formed a critical part of this new Mormonism, "will enable us to show our attachment to the state and nation, as a people, wherever the public service requires our aid, thus proving ourselves obedient to the paramount laws of the land, and [being] ready at all times to sustain and execute them."[3]

1. *History of the Church,* 4:286 (Jan. 24, 1841).

2. Ibid.

3. "Proclamation of the First Presidency of the Church to the Saints Scattered Abroad," *History of the Church,* 4:269 (Jan. 15, 1841).

In this same "Proclamation … to the Saints Scattered Abroad,"[4] the First Presidency reassured:

> This place [i.e., Nauvoo] has been objected to by some, on account of the sickness which has prevailed in the summer months, but it is the opinion of Doctor [John C.] Bennett, a physician of great experience and medical knowledge, that Hancock County, and all the eastern and southern portions of the City of Nauvoo, are as healthy as any other portions of the western country, or the world, to acclimated citizens; whilst the northwestern portion of the city has experienced much affliction from ague and fever, which, however, he thinks can be easily remedied by draining the sloughs on the adjacent islands in the Mississippi.[5]

The proclamation combined the spiritual and the temporal. An important aspect of the proclamation was economic encouragement: "Every facility is afforded, in the city and adjacent country, in Hancock County, for the successful prosecution of the mechanical arts, and the pleasing pursuits of agriculture. The waters of the Mississippi can be successfully used for manufacturing purposes, to an almost unlimited extent."[6] Despite the reality that Nauvoo never became a center of industry, the hope embedded in the missive is impressive.

Economics was only part of the predicted progress. The University of the City of Nauvoo would "enable us to teach our children wisdom, to instruct them in all the knowledge and learning, in the arts, sciences, and the learned professions" and be "one of the great lights of the world." The teaching would be "of practicable utility, and for the public good, and also for private and individual happiness." Even more important was the Nauvoo temple, then under construction: "Let us now concentrate all our powers, … and strive to emulate the action of the ancient covenant fathers and patriarchs."[7]

Despite the optimistic tone, the proclamation cautioned converts that life in Zion might challenge their faith:

> when they come here, they must not expect perfection, or that all will be harmony, peace, and love; if they indulge these ideas, they will undoubtedly be deceived, for here there are persons, not only from different states, but from different nations, who, although they feel a great attachment to

---

4. Ibid., 267-73.
5. Ibid., 274.
6. Ibid., 268.
7. Ibid., 269.

> the cause of truth, have their prejudices of education, and consequently, it requires some time before these things can be overcome.[8]

It was inevitable that the less desirable elements of society would also gather to Nauvoo.

More powerfully, the statement positioned the Saints' Zion-building efforts in a larger narrative, the course of history portrayed in part by the Book of Mormon and sketched by Joseph himself. "We have to congratulate the Saints on the progress of the great work of the 'last days'; for not only has it spread through the length and breadth of this vast continent; but on the continent of Europe, and on the islands of the sea."[9]

The proclamation also recapitulated the Saints' recent political history. Exiled from their Missouri homes, they found in Illinois "an asylum, and were kindly welcomed by persons worthy of the characters of freemen." Expressing particular gratitude to the governor and state legislature, the proclamation identified the Nauvoo City Charter as securing "all those great blessings of civil liberty, which of right appertain to all the free citizens of a great civilized republic–'tis all we ever claimed."[10]

Joseph Fielding, one of the thousands of British converts who gathered, wrote a letter of first impressions about his new home to believers in England. Toward the end, he turned to the temple and the Nauvoo House (which was intended to function as an inn or hotel): "I can truly say that the place, in general, exceeds my expectations; in short, one could hardly believe it possible that a town of such extent, could have been built in so short a time, especially by a people generally poor–there are many log, many frame, and many brick houses."[11]

Particularly significant was the temple, then composed of a basement and partially constructed walls. According to Fielding, the temple would eventually rise 150 feet toward the heavens. He wrote, "The whole is vaulted and what I call the vault, is in part occupied by the baptismal font, supported by twelve oxen." He enthused, "It would be vain to attempt to describe my feelings on beholding this interesting sight, but if you have the same faith as myself in the great work of God, and consider that the things on earth are patterns of things in heaven, at the same time look back on the form of

---

8. Ibid., 272-73.

9. Ibid., 267.

10. Ibid.

11. Joseph Fielding, Letter to Parley Pratt, Jan. [n.d.], 1842, *Millennial Star* 3 (Aug. 1842): 77-78.

the temple and font, you may judge of my feelings."[12] As he discerned, the temple was both a structure and a symbol that captured the Saints' hope for a celestial kingdom.

Fielding was reading into the physical structure the spiritual creation Joseph had enacted in his revelation of January 19, 1841, which promised temple rituals: "I will show unto my servant Joseph Smith all things pertaining to this house, and the Priesthood thereof; and the place whereon it shall be built."[13] The voice of the Lord assured the Saints: "Verily I say unto you, that your anointings, and your washings … and endowment, … are ordained by the ordinance of my holy house which my people are always commanded to build unto my holy name" (D&C 124:39).[14] The revelation continued with specific instructions to build the temple and the Nauvoo House simultaneously–one in which the Saints would engage the things of God, the other the things of the world.[15]

Despite the rapidly unfolding events of the month, Joseph found time, beginning on January 19, to have scribes start to compile sources for inclusion in "The Book of the Law of the Lord." This records-oriented effort, which continued until April 7, included copies of letters, significant revelations, minutes of meetings held in Nauvoo and elsewhere, as well as records of tithing and other donations. These documents provided one of the bases for what would, in 1902-12, be re-edited and published as the multi-volume *History of the Church* (undertaken by LDS general authority B. H. Roberts). Their collection demonstrates how Joseph and those around him viewed the history they were making.[16] They knew they were engaged in a "marvelous work and a wonder" and built a narrative centered on their prophet. The esteem given to these records is indicated by the fact that the first entry in the

12. Ibid.

13. *History of the Church,* 4:278 (Jan. 19, 1841).

14. Joseph began administering these rites in 1842. Between the time the Nauvoo temple officially opened on December 10, 1845, and when the Saints left Nauvoo for the West in early 1846, some 5,000 men and women received their endowments. See Devery S. Anderson and Gary James Bergera, eds., *The Nauvoo Endowment Companies: 1845-1846,* xi-xii. The instruction given in LDS temples, which believing Latter-day Saints consider to be too sacred to be discussed in any detail outside a temple, relates generally to the "creation and peopling of the earth" and to things that "must be done … in order to gain exaltation in the world to come." Bruce R. McConkie, *Mormon Doctrine,* 226.

15. *History of the Church,* 4:274-86 (Jan. 19, 1841).

16. Roberts used the various manuscript and published records provided by Joseph's scribes and other contemporary accounts to assemble the *History of the Church*. For a detailed analysis of the construction of Joseph's *History,* see Dan Vogel, ed., *History of Joseph Smith and of The Church of Jesus Christ of Latter-day Saints: A Source- and Text-Critical Edition,* 8 Vols. (Salt Lake City: Smith-Pettit Foundation, 2015).

Book of the Law of the Lord later became official canon as Section 124 of the Doctrine and Covenants (LDS edition).[17]

Joseph returned repeatedly to the historical drama unfolding around him. At year's end, he would muse: "Since I have been engaged in laying the foundation of the Church of Jesus Christ of Latter-day Saints, I have been prevented in various ways from continuing my journal and history in a manner satisfactory to myself or in justice to the cause." Interpreting even the simplest detail of his life as part of a larger pattern, he now hoped to leave "to posterity a connected memorandum of events desirable to all lovers of truth." This was his motivation for "keep[ing] up a journal in the best manner my circumstances would allow … so that the labors and suffering of the first Elders and Saints of this last kingdom might not wholly be lost to the world."[18]

Through gathering, the Saints had built other cities; but for the first time, they gathered to a city of Zion that had legal corporate existence. Under the Nauvoo Charter that became operational on February 1, 1841, the city sought a high ideal–to establish itself as a theocracy under the rule of civil law–although the ideal would run into bruising realities in practice.

Nauvoo's charter closely followed that of Springfield's, then two years old. The sections enumerating the privileges of the city council were, in fact, copied verbatim. However, the motives and purposes underlying the two sets of similar language were very different. Advised at virtually every step by John C. Bennett, Joseph used the charter to create an autonomous city-state with unique social and communitarian objectives.

Nauvoo's civil government included three basic tiers: a mayor, a city council with nine members, and four aldermen, each with his own set of responsibilities and distinctions. In the charter, Joseph merged the executive, judicial, and legislative branches, forming a theocratic system that stood in contrast to traditional American governmental values. The mayor was both a participating member of the city council and the chief justice of the municipal court. The city council's power was, according to Section 11, to "make, ordain, establish and execute all such ordinances not repugnant to the Constitution of the United States or of this State, as they may deem necessary for the peace, benefit, good order, regulation, convenience, and cleanliness, of said city."

17. For a brief discussion of "The Book of the Law of the Lord," see http://josephsmithpapers.org/paperSummary/the-book-of-the-law-of-the-lord (retrieved July 15, 2015). See also Alex D. Smith, "The Book of the Law of the Lord," *Journal of Mormon History* 38 (Fall 2012), no. 4:131-63.

18. *History of the Church,* 4:470 (Dec. 11, 1841).

The four aldermen and nine city councilors functioned as associate justices. Sections 16 and 17 sonorously spelled out these powers:

> The Mayor and Aldermen shall be conservators of the peace within the limits of said city, and shall have all the powers of Justices of the Peace therein …
>
> The Mayor shall have exclusive jurisdiction in all cases arising under the ordinances of the corporation, and shall issue such process as may be necessary to carry said ordinances into execution, and effect; appeals may be had from any decision of judgment of said Mayor or Aldermen, arising under the city ordinances, to the Municipal Court, under such regulations as may be presented by ordinance; which court shall be composed of the Mayor as Chief justice, and the Aldermen as Associate Justices, and from the final judgment of the Municipal Court, to the Circuit Court of Hancock county, in the same manner as appeals are taken from judgements of Justices of the Peace.[19]

Beneath the rhetoric ran the reality of power. Under the charter, the mayor as chief justice heard appeals of decisions made by the mayor and aldermen in their role at the municipal court, effectively cancelling any meaningful system of checks and balances. Beginning in mid-May 1842, Joseph would become mayor (in the messy wake of Bennett's downfall), and Church leaders filled most of the other leadership positions.

However, the most significant departure from other charters–as well as the Nauvoo City Charter's most beneficial provision–was the clause that empowered the municipal court to grant writs of habeas corpus "in all cases arising under the ordinances of the City Council."[20] Habeas corpus was a legal concept embedded in British common law. Either a court or judge orders that when a person is arrested and taken into custody, he must be brought before a legal body to judge whether the writ or his detention is legal. As Robert Flanders describes its use: "The habeas corpus provision was designed to make Nauvoo an island of legal safety in which Mormons arrested by 'outsider' civil officers could be freed by legal process. The net result was not only to help protect the Mormons from legal persecution, real or imagined, but also to make 'outside' law enforceable in Nauvoo only if the city government concurred."[21] For instance, when Missouri marshals arrested

19. Ibid., 242-43 (Dec. 16, 1840).
20. Ibid., 243.
21. Robert B. Flanders, *Nauvoo,* 99.

Joseph, he simply declared himself under the jurisdiction of the Nauvoo city court, which then freed him by issuing a writ of habeas corpus. Between 1841 and 1844, the Nauvoo city council issued five writs of habeas corpus for Joseph.[22] It was a shrewd technicality; but from the outside, it looked like an extra-legal gimmick by which Joseph evaded the legitimate claims of the law. Springfield's charter guaranteed the same power, but only Nauvoo used routinely it to secure the safety of a religious leader.

The first municipal election, held on February 1, 1841, installed Bennett as mayor with Nauvoo Stake President William Marks, Nauvoo Bishop Newel K. Whitney, Joseph's younger brother Samuel Harrison Smith, and non-Mormon merchant Daniel H. Wells as aldermen. The three members of the First Presidency formed the core of the city council, plus Charles C. Rich, John T. Barnett, Wilson Law, Don Carlos Smith, John P. Greene, and Vinson Knight.[23] No candidates opposed this slate of officers.[24] The March city council meeting added a "collector of the city," a "weigher and sealer," a "market master," a surveyor and engineer, four constables, and a "supervisor of streets."[25] The council enthusiastically passed ordinances, many of them designed to maintain the peace and create an orderly community. They guaranteed religious toleration and prohibited disrupting religious meetings.[26]

Even before the charter took formal effect, city ordinances embedded religious tolerance into the community's fabric. On January 3, the city announced that "the Catholics, Presbyterians, Methodists, Baptists, Latter-day Saints, Quakers, Episcopals, Universalists, Unitarians, Mohammedans, and all other religious sects and denominations, whatever, shall have free toleration, and equal privileges."[27] A $300 fine and six-month imprisonment punished anyone convicted of ridiculing a person's religious beliefs. This provision was unusual at a time when nativism was rampant and when prejudice against Catholics and Jews was still common. The Saints' experience had tested the constitutional guarantees of religious freedom–and found them wanting. Yet this passionate adherence to religious toleration was braided with the Latter-day Saint world view that looked at all non-Mormons as potential Mormons.

---

22. Edwin Brown Firmage and Richard Collin Mangrum, *Zion in the Courts,* 94-105.

23. *History of the Church,* 4:287 (Feb. 1, 1841).

24. Ibid.

25. Ibid., 307 (Mar. 1, 1841).

26. Ibid., 306-308 (Mar. 1, 1841); 447 (Nov. 13, 1841); 461 (Nov. 26, 1841).

27. Nauvoo City Council, Minutes, Jan. 3, 1841, in *History of the Church,* 4:306. The city passed another ordinance, with Joseph's sponsorship, on March 1, 1841, allowing "free toleration and equal privileges" to all visiting religious ministers or denominations.

One of the more disquieting elements of the charter–because it was the most public–was Section 25: "The City Council may organize the inhabitants of said city, subject to military duty, into a body of independent military men to be called the 'Nauvoo Legion,' the Court Martial of which shall be composed of the commissioned officers of said Legion." Creating an armed body of fighters had been authorized when the council met on February 3, only two days after its election. Joseph keenly felt the need to protect the Mormons and to ensure against a repetition of the Missouri experience. Bennett, as mayor, commented on February 3: "early facilities should be afforded the court martial for perfecting their plans of drill, rules, and regulations. Nothing is more necessary to the preservation of order and the supremacy of the laws." He topped his oration with a Latin tag: *Sicut patribus sit Deus nobis,* which he translated: "'As God was with our fathers, so may He be with us'–to fight the battles of our country, as victors, and as freemen; ... or the spirit of insubordination should never enter our camp–but we should, ever stand, as a united people–one and indivisible."[28] It is easy to imagine the impact of his potent image of military strength on the minds of those rendered impotent in Missouri.

As a regular unit of the Illinois militia, the legion followed state procedures in officers' commissions. The state of Illinois issued arms to the legionnaires. Terms of service followed state guidelines. Although the legion had its own officers, the city charter allowed it to provide extra muscle to the mayor "in executing the laws and ordinances of the city corporation."[29] It is easy to judge the immediate benefit such an armed force would play in Joseph's world–two thousand men ordered in twenty-six companies of soldiers, modeled on the United States military. Marveling at the sight of his legionnaires, Joseph described them as "the pride of Illinois, one of its strongest defenses, and a great bulwark of the western country."[30]

Illinois Governor Thomas Ford subsequently conceded that the charter "gave [the Saints] power to pass ... ordinances ... not repugnant to the Constitution ... of this State" but complained that they appropriated "power ... to erect a system of government for themselves."[31] It was this "stretching" that would contribute to the resistance the Saints generated among neighbors, a hatred that would turn murderous in less than four years.

---

28. *History of the Church,* 4:291 (Feb. 3, 1841).
29. Ibid., 244 (Dec. 16, 1840).
30. Ibid., 5:383-84.
31. Thomas Ford, *History of Illinois ...,* 2:64.

In hindsight, the trajectory that led to tragedy seems clear; but in the early months of 1841, Nauvoo's confidence ran high. Recognizing the need for a more diversified economy, in February 1841, the same month the city charter became operational, Joseph established the Nauvoo Agricultural and Manufacturing Association. In a switch from the previous year, he asked newcomers to put their money into mills instead of real estate. Within three years, the city had two steam sawmills and one flour mill. Reflecting Joseph's desire for manufacturing and production, a tool factory and foundry expanded what was available locally. English converts helped to plan a chinaware factory that men from the Staffordshire potteries would run. Others who had no wealth or property worked on a large cooperative farm outside the city limits, and the temple site absorbed a number of skilled and unskilled hands, paid out of donations to the temple tithing office. In addition, each adult male Mormon was expected to donate one day in ten to work on the temple or to donate goods that could be used in the construction.

As a result, the kingdom of God rapidly acquired the same literalness as the red bricks that became shops and two-story residences. Hard work and sacrifice demonstrated faith in God and Joseph, expressing personal worthiness in ways that mattered greatly. The social world of Nauvoo was not passively absorbed by individual members but actively appropriated. Each person continued to be a co-producer of the Mormon world.

As part of Nauvoo's economy, the Church elected Joseph as trustee-in-trust on January 30, 1841.[32] In some ways, this identification was simply an accommodation to state law regulating the way religious corporations conducted business. This designation gave Joseph power to "receive, acquire, manage or convey property, real, personal, or mixed, for the sole use and benefit of said church …"[33] The legal person of trustee-in-trust would handle the financial obligations of the Church, not Joseph as an individual. Ideally, transferring the property and accompanying obligations to the trustee would untangle the complicated ownerships. However, only some properties were transferred, and Joseph continued to straddle the line between individual and corporate ownership.

Attempting to order the new city that his land deals helped to create, Joseph literally redrew the geometries of Nauvoo to conform to his vision. On March 1, 1841, the Nauvoo City Council voted to vacate both

32. *History of the Church,* 4:286 (Jan. 30, 1841).
33. Ibid., 287 (Feb. 1, 1841).

the Commerce and Commerce City plats, which were recorded as "Joseph Smith's Addition to Nauvoo." It simultaneously vacated the addition of speculators "Herringshaw and Thompson" because it would "make the streets regular and uniform and materially to beautify this city." The new plat imposed a unified logic on the landscape. Ignoring legal complications, city officials laid off the town in four-acre blocks with streets and alleys dividing the blocks into four lots. Streets intersected at right angles.[34]

Nauvoo, as a cornerstone of Zion, became its lodestone as well. On March 20, the First Presidency, "anxious to promote the prosperity of [the] Church," issued another epistle, summoning members outside Hancock County "to come in without delay. ... all the Stakes, excepting those in this county, in Lee County, Iowa, are discontinued, and the Saints [are] instructed to settle in this county as soon as circumstances will permit." Zarahemla Stake in Iowa Territory was specifically excepted and reconfirmed as a gathering place.[35] Unfortunately for the Saints, title to as many as 250 parcels of land sold to Mormons in this area would eventually be invalidated.

About March 20, Joseph received a revelation (D&C 125) about Iowa. Couched in the rhetoric of revelation, it was directed to those "who call themselves by my name, and are essaying to be my Saints." To please the Lord, they should "gather themselves together, unto the place which I shall appoint unto them by my servant Joseph, and build up cities unto my name, that they may be prepared for that which is in store for a time to come."[36] Extending the sacred terrain of Zion to include Iowa made more choices possible and put more land within the reach of newcomers. William Clayton noted Joseph's subsequent exhortation to take the instruction seriously as the word of God, of which Joseph was the designated gatekeeper.[37]

The boundary between Joseph and his people was a permeable one, crossed literally as Joseph and Emma took guests, the ailing, and the orphaned into their home. When Lydia Walker died in mid-January 1842, at age forty-one, she left seven children, including a year-old baby, Mary. The Smiths took in three: Lucy, the oldest daughter, age fifteen and a half, nineteen-year-old William, and thirteen-year-old Catherine. "The Prophet and his wife introduced us as their sons and daughters," recalled Lucy, many years later. "Every privilege was acorded us in the home. Every privilege within reach

34. Ibid., 307-308 (Mar. 1, 1841).
35. Ibid., 362.
36. Ibid., 311 (Mar. 20, 1841).
37. William Clayton, Journal, Apr. 8, 1841, in George D. Smith, ed., *An Intimate Chronicle,* 86.

was ours." When eight-year-old Lydia was later "stricken with brain-fever," Joseph "told the boys to drive down to the Mississippi river, then took her in his arms and baptised her," then took her to Emma. "Here let me say," Lucy wrote, "that our own father and mother could scarsely have manifested greater solicitude … than did the Prophet and his wife–Emma."[38]

The malarial-type sickness that plagued the first Saints in Nauvoo made biblical tales of pestilence vividly believable. Although Joseph's proclamation referred glibly to draining the swamps (which was, in fact, efficacious) and quoted Bennett's optimistic assurances about the healthful climate, Joseph was still searching for answers about why so many fell ill in what should have been a city peculiarly blessed by the Lord. Joseph grieved terribly for those who were lost, and mournfully counted the loss to himself personally and the collective loss to the cause of Zion.

With so many apostles on missions in early 1841, it is no wonder that Joseph turned to Bennett. One of Bennett's biographers even asserts that the "power behind Bennett was Smith."[39] Ebenezer Robinson remembered Bennett as "a man of rather pleasing address, calculated to make a favorable impression on the minds of most people."[40] Even the Lord praised Bennett: "Again, let my servant John C. Bennett, help you in your labor, in sending my word to the Kings and people of the earth, and stand by you … and his reward shall not fail if he receive council; and for his love, he shall be great for he shall be mine if he does this, saith the Lord. I have seen the work he hath done, which I accept, if he continue; and will crown him with blessings and great glory."[41] Revelations like this legitimated Bennett's position and Joseph's trust in him.

In hindsight, Bennett emerged from virtually nowhere to become one of Joseph's trusted allies, confidantes, and friends. Many, including Hyrum and Sidney Rigdon, may have wondered why in view of Bennett's brief membership in the Church Joseph had, by the first week in February 1841, appointed Bennett chancellor of Nauvoo's barely authorized university.[42]

38. Lucy Walker Kimball, "A Brief Biographical Sketch, in the Life and Labors of Lucy Walker Smith"; William Holmes Walker, *The Life Incidents and Travels,* 10. On May 1, 1843, Lucy Walker would be drawn more closely into the Smith family when Joseph wed her as a plural wife, an event that resulted in her ejection from the Smith home when Emma found out.

39. Andrew F. Smith, *The Saintly Scoundrel,* 63.

40. Ebenezer Robinson, "Items of Personal History of the Editor," *The Return* 2 (June 1890): 285.

41. *History of the Church,* 4:275-76 (Jan. 19, 1841).

42. Ibid., 293.

Sometime in February, however, Joseph evidently began an investigation designed to put nagging rumors about Bennett's past to rest. At Joseph's request, George Miller, the forty-six-year-old bishop of the Nauvoo ward, traveled to Ohio to investigate Bennett's conduct there. Miller may have had his own reasons for being suspicious of Bennett and of how quickly and completely Joseph had embraced the newcomer. When Miller returned to Nauvoo, he brought troubling news. Bennett thinks he is "the smartest man in the nation," Miller reportedly claimed, "and if he cannot at once be placed at the head of the heap, he soon seeks a situation." He called Bennett "adulterous," and "an imposter, and unworthy of the confidence of all good men." Bennett was, in fact, still married, although estranged from his wife. Miller eventually left the Church himself, but would continue to insist that Bennett was "one of the most corrupt of corrupted men."[43]

Joseph evidently suppressed the results of Miller's investigation; in fact, no documentation exists that he discussed the report with Bennett, let alone took action on it. The reality was he needed Bennett. In 1843, Joseph preached a self-revealing sermon on friendship that explains something of his approach to interpersonal relationships: "If he's my friend–a true friend, I will be a friend to him, and preach the Gospel of salvation to him, and give him good counsel, helping him out of his difficulties."[44] "True," in Joseph's world, meant an almost-reflexive loyalty, not the more tempered relationship that appraised, evaluated, and even, when necessary, rebuked. After years of studying Joseph, LDS general authority B. H. Roberts observed that Joseph had "great tenacity in friendship for men he had once taken into his confidence after they had been proven unworthy of that friendship," as well as a "fierce disposition to give way to reckless denunciation when once he really broke the ties of friendship–his anger was terrible, all agree upon that."[45]

Conscious of his own vulnerability, or of his mounting fatigue, Joseph at various times designated successors to the prophet role. His choices reflect both his confidence in those around him and the Church's changing fortunes. By the time he died, each of his three earliest choices had either apostatized or distanced himself from the Church. Joseph first designated

43. George Miller, Letter to Joseph Smith, *Times and Seasons* 3 (July 1, 1842): 842; Smith, *Saintly Scoundrel,* 78-79. Miller's letter was not made public until after Bennett's public break with the Church.

44. *History of the Church,* 5:517 (July 23, 1843).

45. B. H. Roberts, *A Comprehensive History of the Church of Jesus Christ of Latter-day Saints,* 2:146, 358.

Sidney Rigdon as successor on April 19, 1834;[46] then David Whitmer on July 8, 1834;[47] Oliver Cowdery on December 5, 1834;[48] and finally Hyrum Smith on both January 19, 1841, and July 16, 1843.[49] Joseph would also sometimes say that his son Joseph III was his choice should anything happen to him.[50]

One element of the January 19, 1841, revelation that jump-started many temporal developments in Nauvoo was, as mentioned, the linked construction of the Nauvoo temple and Nauvoo House. In the revelation's language, the new hotel "shall be polished with the refinement which is after the similitude of a palace."[51] It is possible to see behind such language a yearning for gentility that Joseph never quite satisfied. The revelation continued, in stilted but specific terms: "My servant George [Miller], and my servant Lyman [Wight], and my servant John Snider, and others, [shall] build a house unto my name, such a one as my servant Joseph shall show unto them; upon the place which he shall show unto them also. And it shall be for a house of boarding, a house that strangers may come from afar to dwell therein; therefore let it be a good house, worthy of all acceptation, … and the cornerstone I have appointed for Zion." More than hotel, the Nauvoo House would thrive as long as it served the Lord's Church. "This house shall be a healthy habitation if it be built unto my name …"[52]

The revelation thus extended a temple-style sacralization process to the hotel because of the quality of persons, interactions, and activities it would contain.

> Let it be built unto my name, and let my name be named upon it, and let my servant Joseph, and his house have place therein, from generation to generation; For this anointing have I put upon his head, that his blessing shall also be upon the head of his prosperity after him.

46. *History of the Church,* 2:51 (Apr. 19, 1834). D. Michael Quinn, "The Mormon Succession Crisis of 1844," 1, describes eight possible scenarios that Joseph suggested at different points during his life: succession "1) by a counselor in the First Presidency, 2) by a special appointment, 3) through the office of Associate President, 4) by the Presiding Patriarch, 5) by the Council of Fifty, 6) by the Quorum of the Twelve Apostles, 7) by three priesthood councils, 8) by a descendant of Joseph Smith, Jr."

47. Far West Record, typescript, Mar. 15, 1838, 151; *History of the Church,* 3:32 (May 12, 1838; describing events of July 8, 1834).

48. Manuscript History of the Church, Book A-1, Dec. 5, 1834.

49. *History of the Church,* 4:284 (Jan. 19, 1841); 5:510 (July 16, 1843).

50. Ibid., 5:510. Although some interpreted Joseph's remarks to mean that he was resigning as president, he corrected the misconception the next Sunday. Ibid., 517-18.

51. Ibid., 4:274-75.

52. Ibid., 276.

> And as I said unto Abraham concerning the kindreds of the earth, even so I say unto my servant Joseph, in thee and in thy seed, shall the kindred of the earth be blessed.
>
> Therefore, let my servant Joseph and his seed after him have place in that house, from generation to generation, for ever and ever, saith the Lord.
>
> And let the name of that house be called the Nauvoo House, and let it be a delightful habitation for man, and a resting place for the weary traveler, that he may contemplate the glory of Zion, and the glory of this, the corner-stone thereof ...[53]

The revelation also included specific instructions about funding. Miller, Wight, Snider, and Peter Haws were instructed to "organize themselves, and appoint one of them to be president ... for the purpose of building that house. And they shall form a constitution whereby they may receive stock for the building of that house." Fifty-dollar shares would be sold up to a maximum of $15,000 per person. Moreover, the money could be used only for the hotel.

The final stipulation was that all stockholders should also believe in the Book of Mormon, "and the revelations which I have given you."[54] This revelation reflected Joseph's method of maintaining control over the venture, insuring that its proceeds would benefit the Church and individual members. Certain individuals were instructed to purchase stock, including Hyrum and Joseph, Vinson Knight, and Isaac Galland, whom the Lord specifically told: "I, the Lord, love him for the work he hath done, and will forgive all his sins."[55]

Two months later, another revelation returned to raising funds and mobilizing workmen for both structures so "that the poor of my people may have employment. ... for this purpose," the Lord closed, "let them devote all their properties, saith the Lord."[56]

On February 23, the Illinois State legislature incorporated the "Nauvoo House Association," the last of the three charters proposed the preceding year. The charter named the Lord's choices–Miller, Haws, Wight, and John Snider–as trustees to "erect and furnish a public house of entertainment to be called the 'Nauvoo House.'" The enabling legislation prohibited the sale or use of spirits and specified that "whereas Joseph Smith has furnished the

53. Ibid., 279.
54. Ibid., 279, 284.
55. Ibid., 281.
56. Ibid., 311 (Mar. 20, 1841).

... ground whereon to erect said house ... [he] and his heirs shall hold, by perpetual succession a suite of rooms ... to be set apart and conveyed in due form of law."[57] Thus, God's revelation passed into law.

Joseph solicited the help of Miller and Wight to manage the capital for the project during the fall of 1841. Miller helped to raise funds to purchase construction materials and pay salaries. Work stopped during the winter of 1841-42 because of the severe weather, although workers continued to receive housing and food.

Non-Mormon Lucien Woodworth, working as an architect/builder, designed the Nauvoo House as two rectangular wings that together formed an L, each wing 120 feet long, 40 feet deep, and three stories high. The basement and foundations were of stone, the rest of the building of brick. Limestone sills and lintels, shipped from St. Louis, demonstrated the best of local stonemasonry. Located kitty-corner from the Mansion House, the entrance to the hotel was on the Main Street elevation. This main section of the building was a central rectangular mass with an ample passageway running from the front to the back of the building where it opened onto a veranda. The original plan called for as many as seventy-five individual rooms, but the third floor never materialized.

The language of temple-building and hotel-building is a revelation in itself of Joseph's Zion-building abilities, and discloses both the mystical and secular realities of being a prophet. Cognizant that the building required a practiced and practical hand, and that actual cash needed to be turned into bricks and timbers, Joseph felt compelled to position the Nauvoo House metaphorically in the larger generational design that swept through time and space. Joseph's descendants would have a "place in that house" through their own faithfulness and the faith of those chosen to build it. It would form an anchor in the earthly world of Zion. The act of construction simultaneously became a sacred ritual of supplication and sacrifice. Revelation regulated the temporal affairs of the city.

Overlap in city and Church business sometimes surfaced in court proceedings. On February 5, 1841, the Nauvoo High Council tried Theodore Turley, then almost forty, for "unchristian conduct while on the sea [returning from England] for romping and kissing the females and dancing," and "for sleeping with two females coming up the Lakes and on the road to Dixons ferry." A repentant Turley, "in order to sustain his fellowship,"

57. Ibid., 302 (Feb. 23, 1841).

"acknowledge[d], both before the Council, and also, to a publick congregation, that he had acted unbecoming, and that he had set a bad example before his brethren and sisters as he was coming over from Europe."[58] Turley's behavior threatened not only his personal salvation, but also public order. His public repentance restored both.

The nearby *Sangamo Journal* published a sympathetic description of activities in Nauvoo on February 9, concluding that the people were "generally quiet, industrious and economical." The town "present[ed] a fine appearance for some miles above and below the town."

> Nauvoo is said to have a population of about 3,000 inhabitants, some 300 buildings, several small Traders, Tavern keepers, Physicians, and various kinds of mechanics and laborers; and some water craft, among which is a small steam boat called Nauvoo. The landing, soil and timber about the town, are favorable to the future growth of this interesting and growing town. … we may expect to see a very considerable city built up here–particularly as many of this sect in Europe are now known to be about removing to this country–and indeed some two hundred have already arrived at Nauvoo, and the vicinity. Mr. [Joseph] Smith is reported to have said that it is destined to be the largest city in the world.[59]

In February, Joseph, as committee chair, presented a bill to the city council outlawing liquor by the drink. Joseph argued that alcohol was "a poison." Nor did he make an exception for any medicinal use, since "roots and herbs can be found to effect all necessary purposes." The bill that passed prohibited the sale of "whisky in a less quantity than a gallon, or other spirituous liquors in less quantity than a quart … excepting on the recommendation of a physician, duly accredited in writing by the Chancellor [Bennett] and Regents of the University of the City of Nauvoo."[60]

Though the revelation Joseph presented in Kirtland in 1833, known as the Word of Wisdom (D&C 89), prohibited tobacco and "hot drinks" (usually understood to be tea and coffee), he seems to have been most concerned about liquor. On April 6, 1841, after the laying of the Nauvoo temple cornerstones, Joseph singled out the audience's sobriety as "add[ing] greatly to the happiness we experienced on this interesting occasion. … Thank God that the intoxicating beverage, the bane of humanity in these last days, is

58. Nauvoo High Council, Minutes, Feb. 6, 1841.
59. "Nauvoo," *Sangamo Journal,* Feb. 9, 1841, 2.
60. *History of the Church,* 4:299 (Feb. 15, 1841).

becoming a stranger in Nauvoo."[61] The *Times and Seasons* boasted the following August: "If you want to retire from the noise of the Bacchanalian's song, ... come to Nauvoo–No such proceedings are allowed."[62]

At the same time, Nauvoo was not only a religious center but a booming river town and a ready source of hard cash was visitors. In July 1841, Joseph successfully presented a motion to the city council that "any person in the City of Nauvoo be at liberty to sell vinous liquors in any quantity, subject to the city ordinances." Nine months later, the council began licensing taverns to sell beer–but not liquor.[63] The next year, Theodore Turley built a brewery. When Joseph opened the Nauvoo Mansion on October 3, 1843, he let Orrin Porter Rockwell establish a bar in the lobby. Emma objected,[64] and two months later, the city council passed an ordinance "for the health and convenience of travelers and other persons" that allowed Joseph, now mayor, to sell or distribute spirits from his home "in any quantity as he shall judge ... wisdom."[65] Nauvoo's ordinances assumed a peculiar moral stance.

By November 1841, a small grog shop operated behind a grocery store a block from the temple site, in violation of city law.[66] Salacious graffiti amplified the affront, and "the very sanctimonious" Mr. Kilbourne of Montrose soon criticized Joseph for allowing such a "nuesance."[67] On November 15, the city council agreed, despite Mayor Bennett's objections, and a Nauvoo Legion contingent pushed the small structure into a gully.[68]

Joseph reached out to form powerful alliances beyond the Church. In the First Presidency's proclamation of January 15, 1841, he dropped what he considered some heavy names who had become friends and allies: Sangamon County Judge of Probate General James Adams; Robert D. Foster, a physician from Nauvoo; and Isaac Galland, the land agent who moved in and out of the prophet's favor. "We make mention of them," commented Joseph, "that the Saints may be encouraged, and also that they may see that the persecutions we suffered in Missouri were but the prelude to a far more glorious display of the power of truth, of the religion we have espoused."[69] Joseph

61. Ibid., 330-31 (Apr. 6, 1841).

62. "City of Nauvoo," *Times and Seasons* 2, no. 19 (Aug. 2, 1841): 496.

63. *History of the Church,* 4:383 (July 12, 1841).

64. Mary Audentia Smith Anderson and Bertha A. Anderson Hulmes, eds., *Joseph Smith III and the Restoration,* 74-75.

65. *History of the Church,* 6:111 (Dec. 12, 1843).

66. Ibid., 4:442.

67. "City of Nauvoo," *Times and Seasons* 3, no. 2 (Nov. 15, 1841): 599-600.

68. Ibid.

69. *History of the Church,* 4:271.

entertained them enthusiastically, believing, naively, that their self-interests blended with the Church's.

Joseph's activities during the first quarter of 1841 were both ambitious and bold. His template for Zion included a blending of the executive, legislative, and judicial functions of civil government, and expanded to include a university, a hotel, and an agricultural association. Not looking like a place that Joseph might easily abandon, Nauvoo's dream was playing out in a real landscape of human beings, Saints and sinners, heaven and earth.

CHAPTER 7

"A Cheering Aspect"

The saints have a great and arduous work before them ... they will reap the full reward of their toil.

—*"Nauvoo Celebration of the 6th of April,"* Times and Seasons *2, no.11 (Apr. 1, 1841): 368*

On April 6, 1841, semi-annual Mormon general conference proved to be the perfect moment to rededicate Joseph's eleven-year-old church to its most important symbol. Workers dug a foundation and laid the cornerstone of the new temple. The Nauvoo Legion paraded in full dress review, led by Joseph resplendent in military costume.

More than anything else, the legion was motivated by the persistent Mormon fear of Missouri. Throughout the Nauvoo period, Joseph was a fugitive from Missouri justice, dodging a series of writs that often came without warning. Fear of extradition and certainty of prosecution and possibly death caused Joseph and others to take extreme precautions.

The military demonstrations were important ritualized morale boosters, convincing many that they were safe and would be protected. It was no accident that the temple's cornerstone ceremony followed a full military display. Early on the 6th, sixteen companies—Nauvoo's fourteen plus two volunteer Mormon cohorts from Iowa—assembled at assigned rendezvous points and marched to the temple grounds.

Artillery fire signaled the arrival of Brigadier Generals William Law and Don Carlos Smith at the forefront.[1] Both men cut impressive figures on horseback. Eunice Billings Snow, nine years old at the time, later recalled seeing Joseph with Emma beside him to review the legion, calling the experience one of the "most impressive moments" of her life. Sixty-nine years later, she remembered the "imposing sight": "He so fair, and she so dark, in

1. *History of the Church,* 4:327 (Apr. 6, 1841).

their beautiful riding-habits. He in full military suit, and she with her habit trimmed with gold buttons, a neat cap on her head, with a black plume in it, while the Prophet wore a red plume in his, and a red sash across his breast." Joseph wore a black coat with white pants, edged down the sides with red stripes. His favorite horse, Charlie, was a "big black steed."[2] Joseph's history notes: "The appearance, order, and movements of the Legion … reflected great credit upon the taste, skill, and tact of the men … We doubt whether the like can be presented in any other city in the western country."[3]

The spatial patterning of the legion's drill demonstrated a specific understanding of territoriality. The legion and the leaders of the Church marked off the Church's most sacred terrain–visible assurance that military strength would protect and ensure it.

Virtually every able-bodied man between eighteen and forty-five, including some adolescents, enlisted in the legion. By January 1842, only a year after its organization, the legion numbered 2,000. As quartermaster, John C. Bennett secured three cannons and 250 small arms. He also organized and drilled a corps of riflemen, rather than the more typical (but old-fashioned) units of swordsmen and musketeers.[4]

Although Bennett had initially envisioned how the Nauvoo Legion could enhance the city's power and included its authorization in the charters passed by the legislature, Joseph could not resist having first place in this unit. He requested–and Governor Thomas Carlin granted him–the commission of lieutenant general; Joseph ostensibly outranked every military officer in the United States. He was elected twice–both times, obviously, pro forma. The popular election occurred February 1 in the same citywide election that made him a member of the city council. The military election was by the "commissioned officers of the militia" at Joseph's office on February 4.[5] He was one of the "grandest samples of manhood that I ever saw walk or ride at the head of a legion," Angus Cannon would say long after Joseph's death.[6] Master of the grand gesture, Joseph would often wave his plumed hat in salute to the legion, filling the men with his sense of mission, devotion, and readiness to defend God's Zion.

Elam Cheney, a member of the legion, described Joseph as "sound bodied, very strong and quick–no breakage about his body. He most always wore

2. Hyrum L. Andrus and Helen Mae Andrus, eds., *They Knew the Prophet,* 153.
3. *History of the Church,* 4:326-27 (Apr. 7, 1841).
4. Thomas Ford, *History of Illinois …,* 2:184.
5. *History of the Church,* 4:287, 295-96 (Feb. 1 and 4, 1841).
6. Angus M. Cannon, "Joseph Smith, the Prophet," 546.

a silk stock, and was smooth faced. He was very sympathetic and would talk to children and they liked him."[7] Choreographed to display power to outsiders and to intimidate those likely to stir up trouble for the Saints, legion parades positioned Joseph at the center of nineteenth-century masculinity calculated to impress, bolstered by costume and ritual.

Children swarmed around the edges. As many as 600 dazzled boys formed a military unit of their own, parading and drilling alongside their fathers. Joseph III, who turned nine in 1841, marched in its wake, carrying a wooden sword and, sometimes, a banner reading, "Our fathers we respect; our mothers we'll protect."[8] He also remembered a raid the boys planned that was met with "resistance" from the legion itself. Rummaging through their mother's kitchens for pots, pans, and other noise-making utensils, the boys mustered in the woods, then stormed into the town. The startled horses panicked. Joseph, however, plunged forward on Charlie, frightening the boys who scattered in all directions.[9]

Although the Nauvoo Legion's roots were in the American tradition of local militias, it was also significant as a sign of the quasi-sovereignty of Nauvoo. Militias typically were formed within counties; but the Nauvoo Charter's inclusion of an "extraordinary militia clause" created a new type of organization–a semi-independent military force. The connection between the legion and the militia of the county and the state was less clearly defined. Although the legion accepted arms from the state like the other county militias, it reflected Joseph's conception of Nauvoo as an independent city in a federation of cities under Illinois's general umbrella, rather than as a subordinated entity.[10]

The legion was divided into two groups–foot soldiers and mounted troops. Bennett, the major general, was Joseph's second in command and the "secretary of the court-martial" and legion as well as "adjutant and inspector general." As lieutenant general, Joseph had a staff of three colonels and twelve captains. Bennett had "an adjutant, a surgeon in chief, a cornet," a quartermaster, a paymaster, a commissary, a chaplain, colonels according to the number of cavalry or infantry units, and surgeons assigned to one or the other groups with a quartermaster sergeant, sergeant major, chief musician

7. Elam Cheney Sr., "Joseph Smith, the Prophet," 339-40.
8. Roger Launius, *Joseph Smith III*, 6.
9. Joseph Smith III, "Memoirs of President Joseph Smith," 25.
10. Robert B. Flanders, *Nauvoo*, 109.

and others, and captains.[11] A brigadier captain and staff commanded the cohort. Officers of lesser rank could be nominated only by the court-martial. Many Mormons, Don Carlos Smith and Hosea Stout among them, were already officers in the Hancock County militia and moved easily up the ranks in the Mormon body. Position, rank, and a new set of honorific titles doubled the impact of priesthood identity. Enhancing male privilege and masculine power, identification with the Nauvoo Legion positioned Latter-day Saint men as protectors of the community of Saints.

Thirty minutes after the festivities commenced on April 6, Major General Bennett rode to his post near Joseph after the entrance of Don Carlos and William Law. Enhancing the sense of theater, in the distance, a cannon fired. Taking the stage at 9:30 a.m., Lieutenant General Joseph Smith made a dramatic entrance on horseback and proceeded across the grounds surrounded by guard, staff, and field officers, with Emma riding sidesaddle beside him. Trailing behind her was a number of women on horseback. It was Emma's role to present Joseph with a silk American flag. Afterwards, the crowd cheered, while men fired canons.[12]

These ceremonies took the entire morning. At the most public moment, noon, "the procession arrived upon the Temple ground inclosing the same in a hollow square, with Lieutenant General Smith, Major General Bennett, Brigadier Generals Law and Smith, their respective staffs, guard, field officers, distinguished visitors, choir, band, &c., in the centre, and the ladies and gentlemen, citizens surrounding in the interior. The superior officers, together with the banner, architects, principal speaker &c., were duly conducted to the stand at the [temple's] principal corner stone."[13] Religious services then began with public singing and a stirring speech by Sidney Rigdon that evoked poignant images of recent persecutions endured and hardships overcome.[14] This was the third time Rigdon had addressed a crowd at the laying of a temple cornerstone, and he declared that

> the Saints had assembled, not to violate law and trample upon equity and good social order; not to devastate and destroy; but to lift up the standard of liberty and law, to stand in defence of civil and religious rights, to protect the innocent, to save mankind, and to obey the will and mandate of

11. John C. Bennett, *The History of the Saints,* 214; "Court Martial of the Nauvoo Legion," *Times and Seasons* 3, no. 10 (Mar. 15, 1841): 733; *History of the Church,* 4:296.

12. *History of the Church,* 4:327 (Apr. 6, 1841).

13. Ibid., 327 (Apr. 7, 1841).

14. Ibid., 327-28.

> the Lord of glory; to call up to remembrance the once crucified, but now exalted and glorified savior … that he cannot be conquered–that he is working in the world to guide, to conquer, to subdue.

This address linked the temple to Jesus, to God's heaven and the divine message, not only before the assembled people but in a quasi-military setting. By literalizing the cornerstone of the temple as Jesus, Rigdon sanctified the day's events. The temple architects then lowered the "first (S.E. [southeast] corner) stone to its place." Joseph pronounced the benediction: "This principal corner stone, in representation of the First Presidency, is now duly laid in honor of the Great God; and may it there remain until the whole fabric is completed; and may the same be accomplished speedily that the Saints may have a place to worship God, and the Son of Man have where to lay his head."

Rigdon added a second blessing: "May the persons employed in the erection of this house be preserved from all harm while engaged in its construction, till the whole is completed; in the name of the Father and of the Son, and of the Holy Ghost; even so, Amen."[15] The ceremonies concluded with the military band crossing the field to join the choir in making music to fill the city streets.

The presence of the Nauvoo Legion projected in muscle, manpower, and munitions a layer of the political spanning the spiritual. Combining religious and temporal empire-building in the same gesture, it must have stirred feelings of patriotism, validation, and unity. Love of city, church, and each other would not have been distinguishable. All of these emotions were hallowed by the sacred sentiment of patriotism that defined Mormons against everyone who was not Mormon.

The powerful display inspired Eliza R. Snow, one of Joseph's future plural wives, to write a poem that framed the day's events with collective memory of the persecution in Missouri:

> … the Legion is form'd
> To oppose vile oppression, and nobly to stand
> In defense of the honor, and laws of the land.
> Base, illegal proscribers may tremble–'tis right
> That the lawless aggressor should shrink with affright,
> From a band that's united fell mobbers to chase,
> And protect our lov'd country from utter disgrace. …[16]

15. "Celebration of the Anniversary of the Church–Military Parade–Prest. Rigdon's Address–Laying the Corner Stones of the Temple," *Times and Seasons* 2, no. 12 (Apr. 15, 1841): 376.
16. Qtd. in Morris Robert Werner, *Brigham Young,* 121.

Later issues that would trigger suspicions included plurality, charges of financial mismanagement, and the city council's political power, but the Nauvoo Legion created a military atmosphere offensive to many city visitors. Two individuals, who played no formal role in the proceedings, dated changes in their life's directions as beginning at this celebration. Thomas C. Sharp, twenty-eight-year-old editor of the *Warsaw Signal,* present as a visiting dignitary, left Nauvoo that day as an enemy of Joseph and the Mormon people. According to historians John Hallwas and Roger Launius, Sharp began to view "the prophet's followers not as mistreated seekers of religious freedom but as threats to the established democratic order of the young American republic."[17]

Raised as a Jacksonian Democrat, Sharp saw Joseph's theocratic, militaristic community as a threat to American values. He editorialized on June 16, 1841, seven weeks after the glittering celebration in Nauvoo:

> Members of both parties unite cordially in battling with a power which threatens to deprive us of our dearest rights. Let the independent and unbought citizens throughout the county act with the same determination, and political leaders will soon learn to treat [Joseph Smith] as he deserves–namely, as an arrant knave and imposter, who has duped hundreds to follow his foul standard through rebellion and blood, and who now takes advantage of the misery and suffering which he himself has occasioned them, in order to arouse public sympathy in his behalf.–This is our position.

Sharp opposed Joseph's "religious despotism" and championed individual rights "in opposition to the dictates of a political and military church."[18] He would work to keep tensions taut between Mormons and non-Mormons until they erupted into assassination and expulsion.

The second person who watched the legion's pageantry with perhaps complex feelings was twenty-six-year-old Louisa Beaman. On the eve of this elaborate public ritual, Joseph had apparently married her in a secret ceremony as his first Nauvoo plural wife. Eventually no one in Nauvoo or the surrounding county would be left untouched by that small first step into plurality.

No project in Nauvoo generated as much interest as the temple construction. Hundreds of on-lookers, aware of the significance of the cornerstone

17. John E. Hallwas and Roger D. Launius, eds., *Cultures in Conflict,* 55. Sharp was born in Mount Holly, New Jersey, and became a lawyer in 1840. Before moving to Warsaw and editing the *Warsaw Signal,* he practiced law briefly in Quincy.

18. Thomas Sharp, "Our Position Again," *Warsaw Signal,* June 16, 1841, 2.

ceremony, watched as Joseph supervised the placement of a type of time capsule–sacred items in the hollow space carved in the cornerstone on the southeast edge of the temple. A woman in the audience described it as "cut out a square about a foot around and about as deep lined with zinc." In it, Joseph placed "a Bible, a Book of Mormon, hymn book, and other church works along with silver money that had been coined in that year."[19] William Cahoon, another observer, stated that the Bible was special: "It was thought necessary that it should be complete–containing the Apocrypha." Cahoon's brother, Reynolds, took the Apocrypha pages from his own family's Bible and inserted them into the Bible Joseph planned to put in the cavity.[20]

As often as not, the rhetorical position taken on kingdom-building relied on violent metaphors and hostile images of the world outside, followed by promises of peace and security within God's fold. The nation states of earlier generations were "raised to dignity amidst ... the din of war." Rigdon said, speaking at the conference's first day, while "the designs of God ... have been to promote the universal good of the universal world; to establish peace and good will among men ... to make the nations of the earth dwell in peace; and to bring about the millennial glory."[21] Joseph reiterated much the same message, emphasizing the centrality of the temple in the cause of Zion building; but this centrifugal focus was balanced by the centripetal influence of stressing the importance of constructing the Nauvoo House.[22] The Saints were building the city of God, but it was also going to be on display to the world.

When the First Presidency laid the temple cornerstone, Joseph prayed "that the building might soon be completed, that the saints might have an habitation to worship the God of their fathers" and where "the Son of Man [may] lay His head."[23] The Saints' millennial theology justified their removing themselves from society because God would eventually overturn an unjust social order, replacing it with the kingdom of God where men and women could become gods and goddesses. The temple made this ideal seem possible, and the tangible cornerstone was a promised step in that direction.

The day after the cornerstone ceremony, the Saints gathered at the temple site again. Bennett opened by reading revelations recorded in "The Book

---

19. Nancy Naomi Alexander Tracy, Autobiography, typescript, 26, http://www.boap.org/LDS/Early-Saints/NTtracy.html.

20. William Cahoon, in "Recollections of the Prophet Joseph Smith," 174.

21. Sidney Rigdon, "The Government of God," *Times and Seasons* 3 (July 15, 1842): 855.

22. Ibid.

23. "Laying the Corner Stone of the Temple," *Times and Seasons* 2, no. 12 (Apr. 15, 1841): 382; "Nauvoo Celebration of the 6th of April," *Times and Seasons* 2, no. 11 (Apr. 1, 1841): 376.

of the Law of the Lord." They included "a proclamation to the kings of the earth, building a Temple in Nauvoo, [and] the organization of the church," among other critical topics.[24]

Joseph's vision for Nauvoo swept farther than before when he rose as the second speaker. This time, he included the entire region in his purview: "we ... soon expect to see thousands of Israel flocking to this region in obedience to the heavenly command; numerous inhabitants–Saints–thickly studding the flowery and widespread prairies of Illinois; temples for the worship of our God being erected in various parts, and great peace resting upon Israel."[25] The temple was the centerpiece. "We would call attention of the Saints more particularly to the building of the Temple ... those who cannot contribute labor will bring their gold and their silver, their brass and their iron, with the pine tree and the box tree, to beautify the same."[26]

"Business begins to assume a cheering aspect in our city," Joseph wrote that evening:

> Notwithstanding the discouraging circumstances under which the saints were thrown, shipwrecked as it were, upon this shore, they have indeed wrought wonders. ... Though immigrants are flocking in multitudes, and have their homes and their wants to be supplied, yet all things move on in their accustomed order and with accelerating force. ... our city will present a scene of industry, beauty, and comfort, hardly equaled in any place in our country. The saints have a great and arduous work before them; but persevering industry and diligence, stimulated by a zeal for God and his cause, will surely accomplish it, and they will reap the full reward of their toil.[27]

Peter Berger suggests that the impact of such growth on the fertile minds of the newly converted may be seen in the growth of a sacred world.[28] Nauvoo's expansion proved the efficacy of Joseph's narrative. The everyday working world of farm land and town lot, of dry goods stores and boarding houses, became sacred, the manifestation of religious idea materializing under industrious hands. "Although the sacred is apprehended as other than man," Berger explains, "yet it refers to man, relating to him in a way in which other non-human phenomena (specifically, the phenomena of non-sacred

---

24. "Report of the Presidency," *Times and Seasons* 2, no. 12 (Apr. 15, 1841): 386.
25. Ibid.
26. Ibid.
27. "Nauvoo Celebration of the 6th of April," *Times and Seasons* 2, no. 11 (Apr. 1, 1841): 368.
28. Peter Berger, *The Sacred Canopy,* 19.

nature) do not. The cosmos posited by religion thus both transcends and includes man."[29]

For theorist Henri LeFebvre, creation of such sacred cosmos begins with representational space.[30] Typically, representational space has a strong "affective kernel or centre," LeFebvre writes. "It embraces the loci of passion, of action and of lived situations."[31] The images that Joseph spun of how the world would be once Zion was built were spatial in every way. He depicted in his verbal creations the way Zion would look, the way inhabitants would act, and what they would believe it meant.

Representational space objectifies ideas understood by the members of the group.[32] Heaven for some might be more difficult to imagine than Earth, but human industry and success translate heavenly images into real-life situations, concrete and understandable. Work becomes ritual, ordinary space becomes sacred.[33] A Latter-day Saint farming the earth was carving out a living for himself, but was also providing food for Saints gathered to Zion. His industry demonstrated faithfulness–and the sacred consecration of his life to God.

On Thursday, April 8, members of the Church's various all-male priesthood quorums took their seats at the temple grove with the First Presidency and quorum presidents on the stand, the Nauvoo High Council directly in front of the stand, high priests on the right with seventies behind them, elders in front to the left, and the "Lesser [or Aaronic] Priesthood" on the "extreme right."[34] Women, children, unordained men, and nonmembers filled in the rear. This arrangement of priesthood hierarchy communicated spatially the relationship of the Church leaders to each other and to the general membership. Joseph introduced the temple–which he called "The House of the Lord"–building committee. Bennett and Rigdon spoke about baptism for the dead, as did Joseph.[35]

That same day, Joseph appointed Bennett as "assistant [Church] president until Pres't Rigdon's health should be restored," which the congregation sanctioned.[36] Bennett had been in the city only seven months. Another title was also conferred–a master of arts from the barely existing University of the

29. Ibid., 26.

30. Henri LeFebvre, *The Production of Space,* 42.

31. Ibid., 42.

32. See Michel deCerteau, *The Practice of Everyday Life,* 187.

33. See LeFebvre, *The Production of Space,* 38; also Mike Crang and Nigel Thrift, *Thinking Space,* 174-75.

34. *History of the Church,* 4:340 (Apr. 8, 1841).

35. Ibid., 341.

36. Ibid., 339 (Apr. 7, 1841).

City of Nauvoo. Although not an ecclesiastic title, it communicated its own message about building Zion. Twenty-nine-year-old Apostle Orson Pratt was its recipient.

The next day, priesthood quorums met with Joseph at the temple site. Many members had served proselytizing missions, and Joseph drew on those experiences to assure them that volunteer labor on the temple was as "acceptable to the Lord as preaching in the world." He also announced that someone needed to collect funds for the temple construction but made no assignment.[37]

The First Presidency's report to the Church, appearing in the *Times and Seasons* on April 15, again rehearsed the pervasive Mormon myth of religious persecution. "Nor, have the flames of persecution, with all the influence of the mobs, been able to destroy it," the leaders insisted,

> We contemplate a people who have embraced a system of religion unpopular, and the adherence to which has brought upon them repeated persecutions–a people who for their love to God and attachment to his cause, have suffered hunger, nakedness, perils, and almost every privation–a people, who for the sake of their religion, have had to mourn the premature deaths of parents, husbands, wives, and children–a people who have preferred death to slavery and hypocrisy, and have honorably maintained their characters, and stood firm and immovable …[38]

Rhetorically, this litany of injustices justified a bright future for the Saints, because they had proven their faithfulness. "Stand fast, ye Saints of God," the Presidency encouraged. "[H]old on a little while longer, and the storms of life will be past, and you will be rewarded by that God whose servants you are …" At the moment, the situation in Illinois seemed especially propitious: "The citizens of Illinois have … given evident proof, that they are not only in the enjoyment of the privileges of freemen themselves, but, that they willingly and cheerfully extend that invaluable blessing to others, and that they freely award to faithfulness and virtue their due."[39]

Underneath the surface of community-building and neighborly relations, however, ran an undercurrent of secrecy, power, and eroticism, ready to manifest in ritual. Indeed, this underlayer would be positioned at the core of the experience of Nauvoo. Woven together from secrets, loyalties, alliances, kin, and coded behavior, it was intended to protect Joseph, to be

37. "Report of the First Presidency," *Times and Seasons* 2, no. 12 (Apr. 15, 1841): 388.
38. Ibid., 385.
39. Ibid.

sure, but, more importantly, the unfolding of sacred doctrine manifested in ritual and practice. What especially privileged members would experience, most others would not.

Thirty years after Joseph's death, his scribe William Clayton recorded that Joseph taught him the central importance of a plurality of wives at about this time. "I learned that the doctrine of plural and celestial marriage is the most holy and important doctrine ever revealed to man on the earth, and that without obedience to that principle no man can ever attain to the fullness of exaltation in Celestial glory," Clayton stated.[40] Essential to exaltation, plurality theoretically helped to insure the perpetuation of Church leadership and kinship networks, reduce promiscuity, and level yet another measure of obedience, conformity, and the desire for righteousness from men and women who believed Joseph was a true, living prophet.

Among the first in whom Joseph reportedly confided his still developing understanding of the unorthodox form of marriage in the fall of 1840, if not earlier, was Joseph Bates Noble, then age thirty. Twenty-nine years later, Noble stated, "Joseph [S]mith, taught [me] the principle of Celestial marriage or a 'plurality of wives', and that the said Joseph Smith declared that he had received a Revelation from God on the subject, and that the Angel of the Lord had commanded him, Joseph Smith, to move forward in the said order of marriage."[41] Joseph also told Noble that Louisa Beaman, Noble's sister-in-law, should become his first Nauvoo plural wife.

It is unclear who taught Louisa about the doctrine; but, according to Erastus Snow's account (Snow's civil wife was Louisa's sister), Louisa prayed for understanding: "The Lord heard her supplication and granted her request, and after being convinced that the principle had emanated from God, she accepted it, and was married to the Prophet Joseph Smith," apparently on April 5, 1841.[42] Louisa's acceptance of this radical doctrine moved her to the beginning point of Joseph's expansion of his family through plurality.

Joseph's selection of Louisa has no obvious logic behind it. The two families moved through the same social world and shared hospitality and friendship.

40. William Clayton, Affidavit, Feb. 16, 1874.

41. Joseph Bates Noble, Affidavit, June 26, 1869, in Joseph F. Smith, Affidavit Books, 1:3, 8, for Louisa Beaman's marriage. See also Joseph Noble, Affidavit, June 26, 1869, rpt. in Andrew Jenson, "Plural Marriage," 6:221.

42. Noble spoke freely to LDS audiences about officiating in this first plural marriage, but did not always give the same exact date. See the discussion in Gary James Bergera, "Memory as Evidence: Dating Joseph Smith's Plural Marriages to Louisa Beaman, Zina Jacobs, and Presendia Buell," *Journal of Mormon History* 41, no. 4 (Oct. 2015): 103-13.

Louisa was known as a talented singer, but nothing else distinguished her from other young Mormon women. Joseph was thirty-five, Louisa nine years his junior. Joseph had known Joseph Bates Noble since Kirtland, and probably had good reason to count on his ability to keep a secret. Understanding fully the trust he was displaying in Noble, Joseph reportedly asked him to perform the ritual, allegedly saying, "I have placed my life in your hands, therefore do not in an evil hour betray me to my enemies."[43]

According to much later accounts, in the early evening of April 5, Noble rowed across the river from Montrose to meet Joseph and Louisa in "a grove Near Main Street in the City of Nauvoo," with "the Prophet Joseph dictating the ceremony and Br Nobles repeating it after him."[44] The ceremony took place under an elm tree on the river bank; Louisa wore a man's hat and coat as a rough disguise.[45]

Plural marriage brought Louisa and Joseph into the performance of celestial identity–a ritual that transformed their lives, introduced them to the potentialities of heaven, and lifted them from the prohibitions placed by earthly religion and social mores. At the same time, plural marriage made them social pariahs. They could never be measured in Victorian American society as moral persons again. Instead, plurality brought them into a liminal religious state that was neither heaven nor earth, but somewhere in-between. It was true that both of them would immediately return to their normal lives. But for a brief moment, religious ritual, and in this case a plural marriage sealing that cast them forward beyond time and space, suspended them above the mundane tasks of domestic life and permitted them to glimpse heaven.

In 1892, when he was eighty-two, Noble testified that, after the ritual, and they had moved indoors, he said to Joseph, "Blow out the lights and get into bed, and you will be safer there, and he took my advice." Noble insisted in this same testimony that he did not see the couple get into bed, but that "[Smith] told me he did."[46] This earliest plural union may or may not have been consummated that night. But it would be unrealistic to ignore the sexual elements of plurality. Joseph was in the prime of his life, and Louisa was a gracious, warm-hearted woman. Surely, they must have been affected by

43. Noble, Affidavit, in Jenson, "Plural Marriage," 6:221.

44. For Beaman marriage date, see Erastus Snow, Speech, June 17, 1883, in Larson and Larson, *Diary of Charles Lowell Walker,* 2:610.

45. Some historians believe that Joseph married Fanny Alger in Kirtland and Lucinda Pendleton Harris in Missouri, but these marriages are undated and no officiator is identified.

46. *Reorganized Church vs. Church of Christ,* Deposition Testimony, Part 3, pp. 396, 426-27, questions 52-53, 681-704.

the splendor of what plurality represented. Despite their personal morality, in the ritual they became different–more–than their backgrounds. Consummating their sealing made it real on every level: spiritual, mythic, physical.

The unfolding of plurality ritual developed below view in a reality beyond what most Mormons knew. Even Emma was left in the dark, but it seems probable that Joseph confided something of its secrets in his new companion and lodger, John C. Bennett, who later innovated additional, unauthorized understandings of the practice.

Joseph forged new territory with plurality. Inevitably, he made mistakes. His humanity showed perhaps most conspicuously as he struggled with this new doctrine, which he seems to have seen as part of an eternal pattern established by Abraham and other Old Testament patriarchs. Within six and a half months, he would apparently marry again, and before his death, he had become the husband to thirty-plus celestial wives.

Among the range of doctrines that Joseph introduced to the Saints in Nauvoo, plurality stood to change the Church most. Sometime, during the beginning part of the summer of 1841, Joseph reportedly tried the doctrine out on an audience who caught the significance of his remarks without fully understanding them. In a weekly Sunday morning address, he began with the "restoration of all things" as in the times of Abraham, Isaac, and Jacob. Then he queried:

> Suppose we send one of our Elders to Turkey or India ... where they practiced polygamy and he would say to them, "Your laws are not good, you should put away your plural wives; what would they do to him?" They would [ask] ... "Elder, is there not a land of Zion, a place where the saints should gather to?" The Elder should not lie to him. He shall say, "Yes, Brother, there is a land of Zion where saints of God are required to gather to ... the laws in Zion are such that you can bring your wives and enjoy them here as well as there," the Elder shall say to that Brother.[47]

Joseph Lee Robinson, a thirty-year-old convert from Vermont, heard the speech and subsequently commented about it in his journal. "This was to me the first intimation that I ever received that polygamy would ever be practiced or lawful with this people," he later wrote.[48] His brother Ebenezer

47. Joseph Lee Robinson, Journal, typescript, 41-42. Helen Mar Whitney gives another account of the sermon in her 1882 pamphlet and provides an approximate date for the speech as "previous to the return of the Apostles from Europe in 1841."

48. Joseph Lee Robinson, Journal, 43.

described the shocked reaction of the prophet's brother Don Carlos, also in the audience: "Any man," Don Carlos was said to have vowed, "who will teach and practice the doctrine of spiritual wifery will go to hell, I don't care if it is my brother Joseph."[49] Robinson also added to his 1853 account that, during the dinner hour, "several of the first women of the church collected at the Prophet's house with his wife," saying, "Oh Mister Smith, you have done it now. ... You must take back what you have said today. ... It would ruin us as a people."[50]

Helen Mar Kimball, Heber and Vilate Kimball's daughter, who became Joseph's plural wife at age fourteen, defended the practice to Joseph's son, Joseph III, in 1882 and told a version of the same incident. According to her recollection, Joseph responded, "I will have to take that saying back and leave it as though there had been nothing said." He told the women that the time for plural wives lay far in the future. But tellingly, he also assured them that the Lord would help them understand if they were asked to live it.[51]

More immediately pressing than the demands of plurality, however, was the Church's financial situation. Kirtland's debts still plagued Joseph in Nauvoo, and the Kirtland temple was heavily mortgaged. On May 4, 1841, he wrote to Oliver Granger to straighten out financial affairs in Kirtland. He considered Granger, an ex-sheriff and militia officer, to be a man of integrity and ability. When he learned that Granger was ill, he encouraged him to solicit the help of Isaac Galland who was in the East. He said that if Granger could not retire the debts, he should find a Church member who might carry them instead. "This I must beg leave to urge upon you to do, for delays are dangerous ... I am very anxious indeed to have the matters which concern the First Presidency settled as soon as possible, for until they are I have to labor under a load that is impossible to bear."[52] Perhaps because he was ill, Granger failed to do everything that Joseph had asked, but did successfully negotiate the Kirtland temple out from the legal judgment before dying four months later.

Meanwhile, Nauvoo's community life continued. English Jew and Kabbalist Alexander Neibaur heard his first sermons since gathering on Sunday, April 25, in the "open air, a fine spot of land near the Temple." Given the

49. Don Carlos Smith, qtd. in Ebenezer Robinson, "Items of Personal History of the Editor," June 1890, 287.

50. Robinson, Journal, 43.

51. Helen Mar Kimball Whitney, "Why We Practice Plural Marriage," 56-58.

52. Joseph Smith, Letter to Oliver Granger, May 4, 1841, in Dean C. Jessee, ed., *The Personal Writings of Joseph Smith,* 527-28.

show of solidarity, community progress, and divine approval just three weeks earlier, the sermon texts had tantalizingly sinister themes. John Bennett claimed he had suffered character assassination from those who "prefesset to be Saints." William Law of the First Presidency followed, speaking about the "principles of righteousness & unrighteousness," which Neibaur interpreted as referring to "some depratations being committed by some that once had been Saints but was cut off from the Church for misconduct." Joseph closed the meeting with "very strong language determined to put down all iniquity."[53]

Despite the excitement of the first part of the month, April ended quietly. Joseph spent much of his time in meetings of the city council, organizing the first four-company cohort of the Nauvoo Legion, purchasing land for a graveyard, and speaking "at length on the rights and privileges of the owners of the ferry."[54]

Three weeks later on May 16, Joseph began a sermon by acknowledging the Lord's kindness and the error of blaming Satan for what human beings did by choice. "The devil cannot compel mankind to evil, all was voluntary," he insisted. "Those who resist the Spirit of God, are liable to be led into temptation, and then the association of heaven is withdrawn from those who refuse to be made partakers of such great glory."[55] In some ways, this was the most horrifying idea he could have proposed. Zion, the community of Saints, brought converts together into a sort of crucible. At the end of the process emerged God's chosen people. It was unbearable to endure the harsh realities of mortality without the promised bliss of heaven.

Joseph then picked up the text of election from Romans 9. Election pertained to the flesh, he stated, but the term also "had reference to the seed of Abraham, according to the promise God made to Abraham, saying, 'In thee and in thy seed all, the families of the earth shall be blessed.'" Moreover, Joseph continued, "to them belonged the adoption, and the covenants &c. Paul said, when he saw their unbelief, 'I wish myself accursed–according to the flesh–not according to the spirit.'"[56] "[A]ll the ordinances and duties that ever have been required by the Priesthood under the direction and commandments of the Almighty in any of the dispensations," Joseph had hinted

53. Alexander Neibaur, Journal, Apr. 25, 1841, qtd. in Ehat and Cook, *The Words of Joseph Smith,* 71.

54. *History of the Church,* 4:353 (May 1, 1841).

55. Ibid., 358 (May 16, 1841).

56. Ibid., 359-60.

the previous October, "shall be had in the last dispensation … bringing to pass the restoration spoken of by the mouth of all the Holy Prophets."[57]

Over the summer of 1841, the Twelve Apostles enlarged their administrative duties to include publishing the Church's newspaper, the *Times and Seasons.* This paper had begun as a quasi-private enterprise, publishing its first issue under the editorship of Robert Thompson and Ebenezer Robinson in February 1840. After Thompson's death in August 1841, Gustavus Hills assumed the editorial chair, but the Twelve in Nauvoo were dissatisfied with the results.[58]

Joseph's concentration on doctrine was broken on June 5 when a Missouri sheriff with a writ for his arrest, this time with a posse, appeared in Nauvoo. It had been only eight months since the first unsuccessful attempt to extradite him. The Mormons believed that Illinois Governor Carlin knew about the plan and conspired with the men. Joseph had been visiting Bear Creek, Illinois, twenty-eight miles away. Thomas King, sheriff of Adams County, moved quickly from Nauvoo to Bear Creek and arrested him at the Heberlin Hotel on June 5.[59] The officers took Joseph before Charles Warren, an official of Quincy's equity court, who issued a writ of habeas corpus which returned Joseph to Nauvoo.[60]

On June 7, Joseph left his home early in the morning for Monmouth, Illinois, where his hearing before Stephen A. Douglas, a justice in the Illinois Supreme Court, would be held.[61] Douglas agreed to test the validity of the Missouri writ. Douglas, an ambitious Democrat who was building a political presence in Illinois, was known as the "Little Giant" (he was five feet tall) and as a man of considerable integrity. Still, three Whig lawyers suspected Douglas's motives to be prompted primarily by politics. Orville H. Browning was one of the three who offered their services to defend the Mormon prophet. The hearing commenced on Wednesday, June 9, in a courtroom packed with curious bystanders, government officials, and Joseph's entourage.

Browning's defense was an eloquent two-hour plea to the constitutional guarantee of freedom of religion.[62] On June 10, Douglas ruled that the writ

57. Ibid., 210-11 (Oct. 3, 1840).

58. See Robinson, "Items of Personal History of the Editor," 324.

59. *History of the Church,* 4:364 (June 5, 1841).

60. Ibid., 365 (June 6, 1841); "The Late Proceedings," *Times and Seasons* 2, no. 16 (June 15, 1841): 448.

61. *History of the Church,* 4:370-71 (June 10, 1841).

62. Ibid., 369 (June 9, 1841).

was "dead" because it had been returned to Carlin in September 1840 and thus the arrest had been illegal. He discharged Joseph and declined to judge the case further, maintaining that interstate extradition, which would have "great and important considerations relative to the future conduct of the different states," lacked precedent.[63] In September, Joseph invoiced the sheriff of Adams County $685 for the costs he had incurred.[64]

As Nauvoo's crops and gardens thrived in June's heat, Joseph fended off another assault from Missouri, weaving his people's story of commitment despite persecution, and also took his first secret plural wife. He must have been gratified when he entertained a visitor in June 1841 who described his stay in Nauvoo pseudonymously in the *Joliet Courier.* He praised both "the plain hospitality of the Prophet" and "his excellent wife, a woman of superior ability." Joseph's followers

> appear to be honest and industrious ... On Sunday I attended one of their meetings, in front of the Temple [they are] now building, and one of the largest buildings in the state. There could not have been less than 2,500 people present, and as well appearing as this or any number that could be found in this or any state. Mr. Smith preached in the morning, and one could have readily learned then, the magic by which he has built up this society, as we say in Illinois, "they believe in him," and in his honesty. It is a matter of astonishment to me ... why so many ... have slandered and persecuted this sect of Christians.[65]

John C. Bennett might have supplied an answer.

---

63. Ibid., 370 (June 10, 1841).
64. Ibid., 420 (Sept. 30, 1841).
65. "My Dear Sir," *Joliet Courier,* June 22, 1841, qtd. in B. H. Roberts, *A Comprehensive History of the Church,* 2:82.

CHAPTER 8

A New Design for Heaven

... therefore shall they be from everlasting to everlasting, because they continue.

–Doctrine and Covenants 132:20

While seven of his Twelve Apostles proselytized in the British Isles, Joseph stepped across a liminal threshold and onto another stage of restorationist religion with his plural marriage to Louisa Beaman. It took him beyond contemporary mores and family traditions to experience what he saw as the eternal potentialities of heaven. By July 1842, fifteen months later, he had reportedly married an additional eleven women, a year and a half later at least seventeen more.

Joseph evidently could not wait to tell the apostles about this new design for heaven. On July 1, 1841, the very night that Brigham Young, Heber C. Kimball, and John Taylor returned, he apparently first broached–at least in general terms, if not in specifics–with them his doctrine of plurality. George A. Smith returned to Nauvoo twelve days later, Orson Pratt two days after that.

By then, Joseph's longing to enlighten his inner circle knitted their stories with his. Although Kimball did not narrate the event, his daughter Helen Mar did–forty years later. She painted a scene of Joseph anxiously waiting on the riverfront landing accompanied by some horsemen to escort the three returning missionaries to his home. There Emma had prepared a celebratory dinner, not knowing the true significance of the moment. After the meal, Joseph took the group to Kimball's house. According to Helen, who was then thirteen, he seemed "unwilling to part with my father and from that time kept the Twelve in Council early and late." She added that her mother, Vilate, "never dreamed that he was during those times revealing to them the principles of Celestial Marriage" or that "her trials ... had scarcely begun."[1]

1. Helen Mar Whitney, "Life Incidents," *Woman's Exponent* 15, no. 16 (Aug. 15, 1882): 42.

As participants later narrated, the moment when Joseph first taught them the doctrine was a landmark event. Taylor later said that he learned about the principle in the brick store: "He [Joseph] has told us about our associations hereafter. He has told us about our wives and our children being sealed to us, that we might have a claim on them in eternity. He has revealed unto us the law of celestial marriage, associated with which is the principle of plural marriage." Taylor believed the doctrine came from God: "It was the Prophet of God who revealed that to us in Nauvoo," he told an audience in Utah, "and I bear witness of this solemn fact before God … that it is the will and law of God."[2] Important to Taylor's ability to find a way to follow what he considered a sacred commandment, Joseph's influence was profound on his life.

> [On another occasion] I was riding out of Nauvoo on horseback, and met Joseph Smith coming in, he, too, being on horseback. … I bowed to Brother Joseph, and having done the same to me he said; "Stop;" and he looked at me very intently. "Look here," said he, "those things that have been spoken of must be fulfilled, and if they are not entered into right away, the keys will be turned." Well, what did I do? Did I feel to stand in the way of this great, eternal principle, and treat lightly the things of God? No. I replied: "Brother Joseph, I will try and carry these things out," and afterwards I did, and I have done it more times than once …[3]

Brigham Young's oft-quoted initial reaction was revulsion: "It was the first time in my life that I had desired the grave, and I could hardly get over it for a long time."[4] In 1874, he described receiving in England a premonition of a new revelation that would impact his life. "The Lord manifested to me by visions and his Spirit, things that I did not then understand," he told a Utah congregation. "I never opened my mouth to any person concerning them, until I returned to Nauvoo … when I told Joseph what I understood, … he turned round and looked me in the eyes, and says he–'Brother Brigham, you are speaking what you understand,–are you in earnest?' Says I–'I speak just as the Spirit manifests to me.' Says he–'God bless you, the Lord has opened your mind,' and he turned and went off."[5]

It is likely that Joseph taught the doctrine of celestial marriage, or what would more popularly be known as plural marriage after his lifetime, privately but, as quickly as he felt safe, gradually expanded the small group

2. John Taylor, Feb. 11, 1883, JD 24:230.
3. Ibid., 232.
4. Brigham Young, July 14, 1855, JD 3:266.
5. Brigham Young, June 23, 1874, JD 18:241.

of trusted confidants throughout the second half of 1841. Some accepted the teaching more quickly than others. Nevertheless, it caused opposition, despite Joseph's positioning of the doctrine both in the ancient order of things and in his prophetic narrative. The doctrine would cause deep, lasting schisms between Joseph and some of his long-time friends, including family members.[6] He never directly broached the topic with younger brother Don Carlos because of his objections.[7]

Joseph's devotees stood by him in private as they struggled to embrace the new doctrine. Like others, Wilford Woodruff knew of plural marriage long before he entered it himself. His wife, Phoebe Carter Woodruff, later confessed: "I thought it was the most wicked thing I ever heard of; consequently I opposed it to the best of my ability, until I became sick and wretched." After serious thought, she came to understand that it was a principle of God's gospel.[8] Still, Wilford did not take his first plural wife until after Joseph's death.[9]

For Joseph's clerk and British convert, William Clayton, the secret teaching became personal on March 7, 1843. That night, he wrote in a coded way about the day's events. He had spent some time at Joseph's with other men to settle some "claims on city Lots." Brigham Young pulled aside twenty-nine-year-old Clayton and said "the prophet had told him to do so and give me a favor which I have long desire." The "favor" was the privilege of entering plural marriage. "I feel grateful to God and his servant," Clayton wrote, "and the desire of my heart is to do right and be saved."[10] Clearly, Clayton had by this time not only accepted the doctrine but believed it was essential to exaltation.

Joseph had first told Clayton earlier that year that "he had other wives living besides his first wife Emma, and in particular gave me to understand that Eliza R. Snow, Louisa Be[a]man, Desdemona W. Fullmer and others were his lawful wives in the sight of heaven."[11]

6. George D. Smith, *Nauvoo Polygamy.*

7. Ebenezer Robinson, "Items of Personal History of the Editor," July 1890, 302; also June 1890, 287. Robinson wrote that Don Carlos "was a bitter opposer of the 'spiritual wife' doctrine which was being talked quite freely, in private circles, in his lifetime."

8. Phoebe W. Carter Woodruff, "Autobiography," in Edward Tullidge, *The Women of Mormondom,* 413. See also Stanley B. Kimball, *Heber C. Kimball,* 95.

9. Thomas G. Alexander, *Things in Heaven and Earth,* 128.

10. George D. Smith, ed., *An Intimate Chronicle,* 94, xxvii.

11. "William Clayton's Testimony," Feb. 16, 1874, in Andrew Jenson, *Historical Record* 6 (May 1887): 224-26; Smith, *An Intimate Chronicle,* 557. Since Joseph's death in June 1844, successive generations of historians have attempted to identify the women who married the prophet, as

The arch of Joseph's Nauvoo marriages seems to have commenced in the spring of 1841 and concluded two years later in the fall. Joseph's interpretation of the role of men and women in marriage shattered what any of them had known before. Between his marriage with Beaman in April 1841 and his (apparently) final plural marriage to Fanny Young in November 1843, Joseph recorded the date of his now-famous revelation on plural marriage in his journal on July 12, 1843.[12] In those thirty-one months, Joseph married more than thirty women (the exact number may be impossible to fix). Linda King Newell and Valeen Tippetts Avery, Emma's biographers, note that by the end of 1843, the majority of the women around the prophet's wife, including the young women, often orphans, who boarded under her roof in exchange for housework and childcare, and many of her closest, most trusted friends, had married her husband or had allowed their daughters to marry him without Emma's knowledge.[13]

One of these girls was Zina Diantha Huntington, whom Emma brought into her home and nursed while she was ill during the winter of 1839-40. Mourning the loss of her mother, who had died from malaria not long after they had reached Nauvoo, eighteen-year-old Zina asked Joseph if she would ever see her mother again. Joseph reportedly told her that she would. In fact, "more than that you will meet and become acquainted with your eternal Mother, the wife of your Father in Heaven." Never having previously considered the idea of a heavenly mother, Zina asked: "[H]ave I then a Mother in Heaven?" You most certainly do, he replied. "How could a Father claim His title unless there were also a Mother to share that parenthood?"[14] Joseph and Zina talked more about a Mother in Heaven that winter. Their conversations may have even touched upon another mystery: plural marriage. For

---

well as the other men and women who were participants in plural marriages during his lifetime. See especially Danel W. Bachman, "A Study of the Mormon Practice of Plural Marriage Before the Death of Joseph Smith"; Todd Compton, *In Sacred Loneliness;* George D. Smith, "Nauvoo Roots of Mormon Polygamy, 1841-46"; and George D. Smith, *Nauvoo Polygamy*.

12. "Received a Revelation in the office in presence of Hyrum and W[illia]m Clayton," in Scott H. Faulring, ed., *An American Prophet's Record,* 396. The official Church history, written after Joseph's death but phrased in first person, states: "I received the following revelation in the presence of my brother Hyrum and Elder William Clayton." It gives the title as "Revelation on the Eternity of the Marriage Covenant, including the Plurality of Wives; Given through Joseph, the Seer, in Nauvoo, Hancock County, Illinois, July 12th, 1843." *History of the Church,* 5:501. Clayton confirmed this report in a letter to Madison M. Scott, Nov. 11, 1871, William Clayton Letterbooks, Marriott Library.

13. Linda King Newell and Valeen Tippets Avery, *Mormon Enigma,* 147.

14. Zina Huntington Jacobs Smith Young, qtd. in Susa Young Gates, *History of the Young Ladies' Mutual Improvement Association,* 16.

at some point before October 1841, Joseph entreated Zina to join him in plural marriage.[15] "O dear Heaven, grant me wisdom! Help me to know the way," she allegedly prayed. "O Lord, my god, let thy will be done and with thine arm around about to guide, shield and direct. Illuminate our minds with intelligence as you do bless the earth with light and warmth."[16] She finally consented, reportedly on October 27, 1841.[17] As of this date, Zina was civilly married to Henry Bailey Jacobs and was seven months pregnant with their first child.

After his marriages to Louisa and to Zina, Joseph must have formulated the components of the discourse by which he would present the idea to prospective wives. For women who had been raised in Christian monogamy, the mere whiff of plurality must have been shocking. Their identity as Christian women defined virtue for them. For these women, such a presentation had to be anchored in doctrine. Over time, Joseph's presentation became religious ritual presented on a platform of biblical references and Joseph's interpretation of God's instructions to him about ordered relations on the earth. He taught that God's "new and everlasting covenant" promised Mormons who complied that their posterity "both in the world and out of the world … [would be] as innumerable as the stars" (D&C 132:19-20). Couples sealed by proper priesthood authority in the "new and everlasting covenant" had the potential of receiving "an exceeding and an eternal weight of glory, thrones, kingdoms, principalities, and powers."[18] The reward for righteous obedience

---

15. Mary Firmage Woodward, Interviewed by Martha Bradley, Jan. 6, 1996.

16. Qtd. in Martha Sonntag Bradley and Mary Brown Firmage Woodward, *Four Zinas,* 111.

17. See Bradley and Woodward, *Four Zinas,* 114. Zina and Henry Jacobs's son, Zebulon, was born on January 2, 1842. On October 27, 1887, Zina attended a family gathering at the home of her brother Oliver where she told his children it was the anniversary of her marriage to Joseph Smith. Oliver Huntington, Journal, Oct. 27, 1887, 17. In Zina Young, "Joseph, the Prophet His Life and Mission as Viewed by Intimate Acquaintances," 212: "He [Joseph] sent word to me by my brother, saying, 'Tell Zina, I put it off and put it off till an angel with a drawn sword stood by me and told me if I did not establish that principle upon the earth I would lose my position and my life.'" According to John Wight, "Evidence from Zina D. Huntington-Young," 29, Zina told him: "Joseph Smith sent my brother Dimick to explain it to me. … My brother Dimick told me what Joseph had told him. I knew it was from the Lord, and I received it. Joseph did not come until afterward." For Zina, the key issue was that the commandment came from God: "The Lord told him to take me and he did so."

Though tradition assigns October 27, 1841, as the date of Zina's plural marriage to Joseph, there is some question about the reliability of Zina's and others' memories. See the discussion in Gary James Bergera, "Memory as Evidence: Dating Joseph Smith's Plural Marriages to Louisa Beaman, Zina Jacobs, and Presendia Buell," *Journal of Mormon History* 41, no. 4 (Oct. 2015): 95-131.

18. See Bradley and Woodward, *Four Zinas,* 107-16, for a discussion of the ways Joseph presented the idea of plurality to some of the women he married.

guaranteed them a "fullness and a continuation of the seeds [offspring] forever and ever." In doing so, they became "gods, because they have no end; therefore shall they be from everlasting to everlasting, because they continue." It was a heady proposition for the Saints–this dazzling promise that they could become gods through the ordinance of celestial marriage.

Future plural wives like Zina Huntington, Eliza and Emily Partridge, Eliza R. Snow, and Sarah Cleveland experienced considerable additional conflict because of their relationship with Emma. They had shared the same house in times of need. They had worked together at household chores, falling into a rhythm of exchanged confidences that willingly sacrificed comfort and reputation. They had nursed each other when ill or pregnant, lifted their voices in hymns, and knelt together for prayer. However honored they may have felt by a proposal from the Lord's mouthpiece, these women also suffered at the disloyalty their obedience inflicted, whether known or not, on the prophet's wife.

Why did Joseph choose this one and not the other? Surely some measure of spiritual attraction and affinity must have formed part of the appeal. Some of these women must have impressed Joseph with their commitment to the gospel in ways that distinguished them in groups and in private, that made them more susceptible to his overtures, more likely to accept, more prone to a faithful obedience. Joseph was not always the best judge of character, and he misjudged some of the women he courted. Records exist of two notable cases (Sarah Pratt and Jane Law) in which he got to the point of an unmistakable proposal, although there may have been others whose recipients carried the knowledge to their graves, and possibly others who did not recognize the first faint hint for what it was and from whose pursuit Joseph withdrew. But he was successful in thirty-plus other instances. Many women, who repelled his first proposal, found their way to acceptance through prayer, fasting, or confirmation. Such experiences helped them to frame Joseph's story of plurality in the context of their own religious lives until they stitched this new teaching into the spiritual world they wove.

Zina's stepsisters, Eliza and Emily Partridge (their widowed mother had married Zina's grieving father), also moved into Joseph and Emma's home to help care for the prophet's children in the spring of 1840. Joseph introduced both sisters separately to the doctrine of plural marriage in the spring of 1842, slowly and in secret.

In 1841, when Lucy Walker and her three fatherless siblings moved into the Smith household, Joseph beckoned her aside for a private conversation.

She was astonished but listened as he reportedly told her that the principle would benefit the human family, but more importantly that "it would be an everlasting blessing to my father's house, and form a chain that could never be broken, worlds without end."[19] Joseph told her to pray "for light and understanding," which she did. Trying to ease her agony, he told her that he "can not under existing circumstances, acknowledge you as my wife, the time is near when we will go beyond the Rocky Mountains and then you will be acknowledged and honored as my wife." (Walker's reminiscence of Joseph's words seem to have been influenced by later events in Mormon history.) Joseph expressed concern for her emotional state, but, he stated, "I have no flattering words to offer. It is a command of God to you. I will give you until tomorrow to decide this matter. If you reject this message the gate will be closed forever against you."[20] (For more on Joseph's marriage to Walker, see chap. 19.)

In a similar exchange with Mary Elizabeth Rollins Lightner, married to a non-Mormon, Joseph promised her, according to Lightner's later accounts, that an "angel of the Lord" would teach her it was right.[21] Later, Lightner recalled having dreamed for years that she was the prophet's wife but had considered it a sin on her part. She later insisted that Joseph had broached the subject to her while she was still young; but only in retrospect and after she was already married to Adam Lightner did she realize that he was talking about plurality.

Like other prospective wives, Zina was confused by Joseph's teaching. After Zina moved out of the Smith home, Henry Jacobs courted her and proposed marriage, which she accepted. When they married on March 7, 1841, Zina was twenty, and perhaps felt that she had now made Joseph's proposals moot. Joseph did not perform the ceremony; John C. Bennett officiated instead. When asked why he had not been there, Joseph reportedly said that "the [Lord] made it known to him that she [Zina] was to be his

19. Lucy Walker Kimball, "A Brief But Intensely Interesting Sketch of Her Experience Written by Herself," 12.

20. Ibid., 47.

21. Mary Elizabeth Rollins Lightner, "Remarks at Brigham Young University at age 87, April 14, 1905," LDS Church History Library. Rex Eugene Cooper, *Promises Made to the Fathers,* 140, suggests that Lightner interpreted her sealing to mean that she shared Joseph's salvation in the celestial kingdom. According to George D. Smith, "Nauvoo Roots of Mormon Polygamy, 1841-46," 1-72, the average age of new polygamist men was thirty-six and had been married an average of ten years before their plural marriage. The mean age of the second wife was twenty-five. At that time, the men's civil wives averaged age thirty-two. The civil wives were, on average, four years younger than their husbands, and seven years older than the first plural wife, a reality that may point to a focus on reproduction and child rearing.

Celestial wife," and that "he couldn't give to one man [a woman] who had been given him by the Lord."[22]

Zina prayed that summer for understanding. She had accepted Joseph's authority over her life and was confused by the implications of her failure to obey. "I received a testimony for myself from the Lord of his work, and that Joseph Smith was a prophet of God before I ever saw him," she told an audience years later, "I knew him in his lifetime and know him to have been a great true man and a servant of God."[23]

It would be easy to line up the events of the summer of 1841 in a neat row if the cause-and-effect relationships were clear, but they are not. There is apparently a gap of six months between Joseph's marriages to Beaman and to Huntington. These months were characterized by doctrinal evolution, personal struggle, and the drama that played out in the lives of women who wondered what was happening to them. Eternal marriage sealed a woman to a man for eternity, a space and time in which they could become gods. Celestial marriage, also known as the law of Abraham, was mandatory for gaining the highest degree of exaltation in the afterlife. Both kinds of marriages depended on Joseph's authority. As lawgiver, Joseph occupied the pinnacle in priesthood hierarchy for Mormon males. Joseph's choice of mates–including the wives of other members and of non-Mormons–was the penultimate expression of male priesthood.

During 1842, at least three other men joined Joseph in plurality. Young, Kimball, and Reynolds Cahoon each evidently married a plural wife. Only Young and Kimball were apostles. By Joseph's death in mid-1844, according to one knowledgeable estimate, thirty-three men (including Joseph) were practicing polygamists, for a total of some ninety plural marriages (including Joseph's) in all.[24]

As Joseph's apostles began to accept their prophet's doctrine, for Orson Pratt the matter was cruelly complicated. While Pratt left for his mission in England in August 1839, his thirty-four-year-old wife, Sarah Bates Pratt, and their three-year-old son, Orson Jr., lodged off and on with Stephen and Zeruiah Goddard, and Sarah supported herself taking in laundry and sewing. In 1842, when charges and countercharges were exploding in the wreckage of Bennett's downfall (see chap. 11), the Goddards asserted that

22. Oa J. Cannon, "History of Henry Jacobs," Oa J. Cannon Collections, LDS Church History Library.

23. Zina D. H. Young, Address in the Tabernacle, n.d., 1.

24. George D. Smith, *Nauvoo Polygamy,* 311-12; Jenson, "Plural Marriage," 6:219-40.

Bennett had regularly visited Sarah during this time, sometimes lingering until midnight. They also said that Sarah moved in November 1840 to a different house but moved back with them in June 1841. But, implying that Sarah and Bennett were having an affair, they said Bennett continued to visit her.[25] After two of Bennett's inflammatory letters appeared in the *Sangamo Journal* in 1842, Stephen Goddard claimed that during the time that Sarah had stayed with them in October 1840, "from the first night until the last, with the exception of one night, it being nearly a month, the Dr. was there as sure as the night came." Zeruiah described their conduct as "anything but virtuous, and I know Mrs. Pratt is not a woman of truth …"[26]

Bennett's version of events appeared in his second letter published after his departure from the Church. "Joe Smith stated to me at an early day in the history of that city that he intended to make that amiable and accomplished lady [i.e., Sarah Pratt] one of his spiritual wives, for the Lord had given her to him, and he requested me to assist him in consummating his hellish purposes, but I told him that I would not do it–that she had been much neglected and abused by the church during the absence of her husband in Europe, and that if the Lord had given her to him he must attend to it himself." Bennett thus presented himself as a hero, resistant to temptation where Joseph was not.

"I will do it," Joseph replied, in Bennett's version, "for there is no harm in it if her husband should never find it out. I called upon Mrs. Pratt and told her that Joe contemplated an attack on her virtue, *in the name of the Lord,* and that she must prepare to repulse him in so infamous an assault." Her reaction was flat denial: "'Joseph cannot be such a man; I cannot believe it until I know it for myself or have it from his own lips; he cannot be so corrupt.' Well, I [Bennett] replied, you will see unless he changes his mind."[27]

Joseph did not change his mind. A few days later, according to Bennett, Joseph launched his campaign. Together they went to Pratt's house where, in front of Bennett, Joseph made his proposal: "'Sister Pratt, the Lord has given you to me as one of my spiritual wives. I have the blessings of Jacob

25. The Goddards made these affidavits in August 1842 when Bennett's reputation was unraveling. Stephen and Zeruiah Goddard, *Affidavits and Certificates, Disproving the Statements and Affidavits Contained in John C. Bennett's Letters.* Later, however, Sarah Pratt maintained that the Goddards confessed that they had been pressured into this character-blackening testimony. Sarah Pratt, qtd. in Wilhelm Wyl (pseud. Wilhelm Ritter von Wymetal), *Mormon Portraits,* 62-63. See also Andrew F. Smith, *Saintly Scoundrel,* 81.

26. Goddard and Goddard, *Affidavits and Certificates.*

27. John C. Bennett, Letter 2, July 2, 1842, *Sangamo Journal,* rpt. in his *The History of the Saints,* 228-29; and John C. Hallwas and Roger D. Launius, eds., *Cultures in Conflict,* 119.

granted me, as he granted holy men of old, and I have long looked upon you with favor, and hope you will not deny me.' She replied: 'I care not for the blessings of Jacob, and I believe in no such revelations, neither will I consent under any circumstances. I have one good husband, and that is enough for me.'" In his later *History of the Saints,* Bennett wove a more intricate narrative, attempting to implicate Joseph as an aggressor. "He remained with her an hour or two and then returned … to Carthage that night …"

The next day, they returned to Nauvoo where Bennett reported that he called privately upon Sarah to find out how she had reacted to Joseph's proposition. She replied, "He is a bad man beyond a doubt." Bennett continued to speak as an alleged eyewitness, claiming that "three times afterward [Joseph] tried to convince Mrs. Pratt of the propriety of his doctrine, and she at last told him: 'Joseph, if you ever attempt any thing of the kind with me again, I will tell Mr. Pratt on his return home. I will certainly do it.' Joseph replied, 'Sister Pratt, I hope you will not expose me; if I am to suffer, all suffer; so do not expose me. Will you agree not to do so?' 'If,' said she, 'you will never insult me again, I will not expose you unless strong circumstances require it.'"[28]

It is unlikely that any of the three participants were as innocent as they claimed to be. There is much in both Sarah's and Bennett's accounts that parallels the experience of other women Joseph approached. Sarah told her own story in Utah, more than forty years later; but the writer to whom she related it may have had his own reasons for shaping the story: "When Bennett came to Nauvoo Joseph brought him to my house, stating that Bennett wanted some sewing done, and that I should do it for the doctor. I assented and Bennett gave me a great deal of work to do. He knew that Joseph had plans set on me; Joseph made no secret of them before Bennett, and went so far in his impudence as to make propositions to me in the presence of Bennett, his bosom friend. Bennett, who was of a sarcastic turn of mind, used to come and tell me about Joseph to tease and irritate me."[29]

Regardless of elements that have the ring of truth, Bennett's account

28. Joseph's response to this rejection may have been to revive another ancient Israelite custom. In Bennett's description, it tips over into the unbelievable: "'General, if you are my friend I wish you to procure a lamb, and have it slain, and sprinkle the door posts and gate with its blood, and take the kidneys and the entrails and offer them upon an altar of twelve stones that have not been touched with a hammer, as a burnt offering, and it will save me and my priesthood. Will you do it?' I will, I replied. So I procured the lamb … and it was slain … and I offered the kidneys and entrails in sacrifice for Joe, as he desired; and Joe said, 'all is now safe–the destroying angel will pass over, without harming any of us'" (John C. Bennett, July 2, 1842, Letter, *Sangamo Journal,* also in Hallwas and Launius, *Cultures in Conflict,* 118-19; Bennett, *History of the Saints,* 229).

29. Sarah Pratt, qtd. in Wyl, *Mormon Portraits,* 61.

must be contextualized by his angry exit from the Church and Nauvoo. Once friends, and then bitter enemies, he intentionally shaped his narrative to damage Joseph's reputation and prophet role.

In mid-July 1841, Orson returned home. "Times passed on in apparent friendship," according to Bennett, until sometime in early 1842 when "Joe grossly insulted Mrs. Pratt again … by approaching and kissing her. This highly offended her, and she told Mr. Pratt, who was much enraged and went [and] told Joe never to offer an insult of the like again.–Joe replied, 'I did not desire to kiss her. Bennett made me do it!' …"[30]

Orson subsequently fell into a dark, perhaps suicidal, despair. According to Ebenezer Robinson, Orson was told that Joseph wanted Sarah as a plural wife and that Bennett had committed adultery with her. Both Bennett and Joseph denied the stories, but "it was too much for him [Pratt] … his mind temporarily gave way, and he wandered away, no one knew where."[31] Corroboration comes in a letter from Brigham Young to Orson's brother Parley, then in England: "Br Orson Pratt is in trubble in consequence of his wife [Sarah], hir feelings are so rought up that he dos not know whether his wife is wrong, or whether Josephs testimony and others are wrong and due L[ie] and he [has been] dec[e]ived for 12 years or not." Orson was, as a result, "all but crazy about matters, you may aske what the matter is concerning Sister P– it is enoph, and doct. J. C. Bennett could tell all about [it]."[32]

Orson's story evokes a sense of pathos at the damage plurality sometimes created in the lives of those around Joseph. Orson had shaped his entire life around Joseph's prophet-narrative and had relinquished his sense of self for an identification with the Church and Joseph's leadership. Throughout the summer of 1842, Orson was in "open, if anguished conflict with the prophet,"[33] a "sullen rebel," in the words of one biographer.[34] Most notably,

30. John C. Bennett, Letter 2, *Sangamo Journal,* Jul. 15, 1842; see also Andrew F. Smith, *The Saintly Scoundrel,* 82. Although neither Orson nor Joseph recorded his response to these events, a possible, pro-Church reference to Bennett appeared in the *Times and Seasons* a year later almost to the day. It accused Bennett of having "professed to be virtuous and chaste, yet he did pierce the heart of the innocent, introduce misery and infamy into families, reveled in voluptuousness and crime, and led the youth that he had influence over to tread in his unhallowed steps; he professed to fear God, yet did he desecrate His name, and prostitute his authority to the most unhallowed and diabolic purposes; even to the defiling of his neighbor's bed." "John C. Bennett," *Times and Seasons* 3, no. 19 (July 22, 1842): 869.

31. Ebenezer Robinson, "Items of Personal History of the Editor," *The Return* 2 (Nov. 1890): 363.

32. Brigham Young, Letter to Parley P. Pratt, July 17, 1842.

33. Gary James Bergera, *Conflict in the Quorum,* 21.

34. Breck England, *Life and Thought of Orson Pratt,* 78.

he stepped out of the circle of faithful who joined Masonry, the Quorum of the Anointed, and the important temple rituals Joseph began instituting.[35]

Pratt spent three agonizing days in August 1842 with Young, Kimball, and George A. Smith who tried to convince him to reconcile with Joseph. Reportedly, he would not, choosing to believe his wife instead. Not long after, on August 20, they "cut [Pratt] off from the church, and according to the Prophet's direction, … ordained bro. Amasa Lyman in his stead."[36]

Five months later, Joseph and Hyrum, meeting with Young, Kimball, and others of the Twelve, determined that the actions expelling Pratt from the Church had been illegal since there had not been a majority of the Twelve present at the time. As a consequence, they reinstated Pratt on January 20, 1843, as a member of the Twelve.[37] That same afternoon, Orson and Sarah were rebaptized, a symbolic ritual indicating their willingness to follow Joseph once again.[38] After Joseph's death, Orson himself entered plurality in the fall of 1844.[39] For the next three decades, he remained a faithful member of the Church. Sarah, however, was excommunicated in Utah in 1868, in part because she objected to Orson's marriages to young women.[40]

Joseph, Bennett, Sarah, and the Goddards all told different stories. The accounts by Sarah and Bennett should be weighed carefully, for both left the Church in considerable anger (though not at the same time). Those by Joseph and the Goddards are also colored by their own biases. All of them agree, however, that Joseph visited Sarah at the Goddards' in Orson's absence and made overtures that may initially have confused her but which, within a few months, she interpreted as proposals of adultery or plurality.

---

35. Heber C. Kimball, Letter to Parley P. Pratt, June 17, 1842; Brigham Young, Letter to Parley P. Pratt, July 17, 1842, cited in Bergera, *Conflict in the Quorum,* 21n46.

36. "History of Brigham Young," Deseret News, March 17, 1858, 1. According to Bergera, *Conflict in the Quorum,* 31, Orson did not function as an apostle for the rest of 1842 but did "not consider himself excommunicated." He wrote in his own behalf: "Neither have I renounced the Church of Jesus Christ of Latter Day Saints, but believe that its doctrine … is pure and according to the scriptures [and] of eternal truth." Dismissing the "petty difficulties" that divided him from Joseph, he maintained that the Church's "course is onward to accomplish the purposes of its great Author in relation to the happiness and salvation of the human family." Orson Pratt, "Mr. Editor," *The Wasp,* Sept. 2, 1842.

37. Minutes of the Quorum of the Twelve Apostles, Jan. 20, 1843, Brigham Young Papers, LDS Church History Library; Faulring, *An American Prophet's Record,* 294-95; Scott G. Kenney, ed., *Wilford Woodruff's Journal, 1833-1898,* 2:212-3 (Jan. 20, 1843); "History of Brigham Young," *Deseret News,* Mar. 17, 1858, 1; Bergera, *Conflict in the Quorum,* 33.

38. Bergera, *Conflict in the Quorum,* 36. T. Edgar Lyon, "Orson Pratt," 160-62, argues that Pratt did not necessarily have to be rebaptized because he had not been excommunicated.

39. Bergera, *Conflict in the Quorum,* 47-48.

40. Ibid., 223. See also D. Michael Quinn, "The Practice of Rebaptism at Nauvoo."

Further complicating our ability to evaluate these early, reminiscent, and often defensive/hostile accounts is the fact that the secrecy worked hand-in-glove with the code of unity developed over the past years of ostracism and persecution. But the core of the problem was each person's relationship to Joseph. If he was a prophet, how could one contradict him and be right? If they had an incomplete understanding of plurality, how could they make a decision to change their life in such a dramatic way? And standing against Joseph in a community that revered him triggered psychological and social vulnerability. The inevitable (and logical) reaction of one's neighbors was mistrust, suspicion, and reputation-damaging gossip.

Joseph's self-presentation does not seem to be a smooth-talking, beguiling argument. In fact, that approach seems to have been Bennett's. Instead, Joseph relied on his prophetic identity. When he proposed to Mary Lightner, she recalled asking, "If God told you that why does he not tell me?" Joseph did not respond directly, but simply wondered if she was "going to be a traitor."[41] When Joseph reportedly informed Lucy Walker that she had twenty-four hours before "the gate will be closed forever against you," or words to that effect, she had a spiritual manifestation that settled the question for her.[42]

According to Sarah Kimball (no relation to Heber), Joseph "realized that he jeopardized his life" in teaching the radical doctrine, "but God had revealed it to him many years before as a privilege with a blessing, now God had revealed it again and instructed him to teach it with commandment ..."[43] Attempting to persuade Nancy Rigdon, Sidney's nineteen-year-old daughter, to consider his proposal, Joseph insisted, "Whatever God requires is right, no matter what it is, although we may not see the reason thereof till long after the events transpire."[44] (See chap. 12.)

When June 1841 began, Joseph may have harbored suspicions that Bennett was less than he represented, and asked Hyrum and William Law to probe Bennett's story, following up on George Miller's earlier report, which Joseph seems to have tabled. Two weeks later on June 14, they confirmed that Bennett "had a wife and children living and that she had left him because of his ill-treatment towards her." This time, Joseph confronted Bennett

41. "Remarks by Sister Mary E. Lightner Who Was Sealed to Joseph Smith in 1842. She is 87 Years of Age," at Brigham Young University, Apr. 14, 1905, LDS Church History Library, rpt. in Thomas Milton Tinney, *The Royal Family of the Prophet Joseph Smith, Junior,* 255-56.

42. "Statement of L[ucy] W[alker]. [Smith] Kimball," 13-14.

43. Sarah M. Kimball, qtd. in Augusta J. Crocheron, *Representative Women of Deseret,* 26.

44. Qtd. in *The Essential Joseph Smith,* 158.

who reportedly "acknowledged the fact."[45] Three years later, Brigham Young asserted that, throughout these weeks, Bennett "cried and begged of us to forgive him, and said if he could be permitted to stay in the city as a private individual he should be happy."[46] Apparently distressed over his conversation with Joseph, Bennett allegedly attempted suicide–or feigned doing so–sometime mid-July by drinking poison.[47] After having lived in the Smith home for thirty-nine weeks, Bennett moved out, possibly at Joseph's insistence.[48]

Ironically, some time later, Bennett attended a Nauvoo City Council meeting. Although many members would have been unaware of Bennett's plunge into disfavor, others must have voted for him as mayor but with misgivings.[49] It seems apparent that, at this point, Joseph was trying to plaster over the cracks in their crumbling relationship to assure his good behavior. Bennett still held his position as mayor and as major general in the Nauvoo Legion.[50] Apparently the uneasy truce held during the fall and winter; but by May 1842, he would withdraw from the Church, then be expelled, and eventually become the Church's most dangerous enemy (see chap. 12).

Retrospective accounts look back on Bennett as a viper unwittingly harbored on the Mormon hearth. Speaking decades later, Joseph Smith III offered his opinion: "it was ambition which had brought [Bennett] there, which caused him to join the church and accept office therein which stimulated and motivated most of his activity, and which finally led him into immorality and transgression resulting in his leaving the church in disgrace."[51]

Although plurality would continue to roil irrepressibly to the surface, during the summer of 1841 events in Nauvoo were still relatively progressive and confident. In July, Joseph linked natural disasters to political disasters, suggesting that the attitude of the federal government toward the Mormons somehow affected extreme weather or criminal behavior. "[T]he Lord has begun to vex this nation. … A hailstorm has visited South Carolina … which

45. "City of Nauvoo," *Times and Seasons* 3, no. 17 (July 1, 1842): 840.

46. Brigham Young, "State of Illinois, Hancock, County; City of Nauvoo," *Times and Seasons* 5, no. 10 (May 15, 1844): 539. The article deals primarily with Joseph's petition for a writ of habeas corpus before the municipal court.

47. *History of the Church,* 5:37 (July 23, 1841). Ebenezer Robinson noted that "it required quite an effort on the part of the physicians to save his life, as he strenuously resisted their efforts to save him." Robinson, "Items of Personal History," Nov. 1890, 362.

48. Smith, *Saintly Scoundrel,* 80.

49. Gary James Bergera, "John C. Bennett, Joseph Smith, and the Beginnings of Mormon Plural Marriage in Nauvoo," 65.

50. *History of the Church,* 4:550-52.

51. Mary Audentia Smith Anderson and Bertha A. Anderson Hulmes, eds., *Joseph Smith III and the Restoration,* 59.

swept crops, killing some cattle. Insects are devouring crops on the high lands, where the floods of the country have not reached, and great commercial distress prevails everywhere. … [God] will continue except they repent; for they now stand guilty of murder, robbery, and plunder, as a nation, because they have refused to protect their citizens, and execute justice according to their own constitution."[52]

Although seeing natural calamities as signs of the last days had long been a delight to millennialists, it is clear that Joseph connected them to his personal narrative. God's willingness to express divine displeasure with the nation could comfort the Saints, who were the beneficiaries of his favor. In retrospect, it also becomes clear that such "signs" were Joseph's way of externalizing the turmoil that disrupted his secrets-ridden private life. Furthermore, the city's growth seemed to be evidence that the Saints' faithfulness had paid off. Joseph dedicated the temple baptismal font, scene of many baptisms for the dead, on July 11. Brigham Young had the honor of officiating with Reuben McBride standing as proxy for a deceased relative.

The seven members of the Twelve who had served missions in England reported on their experiences on August 1.[53] Joseph's younger brother, Don Carlos, died six days later from malaria.[54] Only twenty-five, he was buried the next day with military honors, while a group of friends, family, and associates gathered at the graveside.[55] On the 11th, Joseph wrote an announcement for the Nauvoo Legion that entered the Zionic narrative in which even grief and loss became part of the ultimate triumph: "It becomes our painful duty to officially notify the troops of our command of the untimely decease of that noble chief, Brigadier-General Don Carlos Smith–he fell, but not in battle–he perished, but not by weapons of war– … he is gathered to his fathers to receive greater honor."[56]

Joseph's millennial convictions may have been exacerbated by his brother's death. On August 10, he wrote with what can be read only as gloomy satisfaction: "shipwrecks, floods, houses and workshops failing, great and destructive fires, sudden deaths, banks breaking, men's hearts failing them for fear, shop-keepers and manufacturers failing … many accidents on the railways, etc., betoken the coming of the Son of Man." He also laced subsequent

52. *History of the Church,* 4:145 (July 3, 1841).
53. Ibid., 390 (Aug. 1, 1841).
54. Ibid., 393 (Aug. 7, 1841).
55. Ibid., 399.
56. Ibid., 400 (Aug. 10, 1841).

speeches with similar references. For example, a month later, he referenced an account in the *New York Sun,* a sign of the times, to an attentive congregation: "wars and rumors of wars, earthquakes, tempests, pestilence, and great fires, connected with every kind of wickedness, distress, and destruction of property are heard in almost every land and nation."[57]

On the same busy August 10, Joseph assigned missionaries to go to New Orleans, Charleston, Salem, Massachusetts, Baltimore, and Washington, D.C. He also met with some of the Twelve to plan future missionary work. The gathering became the mantra for new members. Gathering to Zion was the way to build strong members, while fleeing the destruction that would soon fall on Babylon.[58]

Two days later, Joseph spoke to more than a hundred Native Americans from the "Kis-ku-kosh" and "Appanoose" tribes encamped at Montrose. His remarks ranged from the Book of Mormon to the relationship between the living and the dead, with emphasis on the Lord's promises to the "Lamanites" in the context of Mormon scripture.[59] According to his record, "I … instructed them in many things which the Lord had revealed unto me concerning their fathers … I advised them to cease killing each other and warring with other tribes; also to keep peace with the whites; all of which was interpreted to them."[60]

On Sunday, August 15, the Saints assembled for their meeting in the prophet's absence. He was home, counting out the brief life of his youngest son, also named Don Carlos: "14 months, 2 days."[61] Thirty-seven-year-old Willard Richards, who had been presiding over the British Mission, reached Nauvoo on August 16.[62] That same day, Joseph asked the Twelve "to assist emigrants who may arrived at the place of gathering." The overburdened prophet begged them to "stand in their place next to the First Presidency, and attend to the settling of emigrants and the business of the Church, at the stakes, and assist and at the same time relieve him, so that he might attend to the business of translating [presumably the Book of Abraham]."[63]

Joseph was disheartened by the deaths in quick succession of his brother and son, but it is also true that he had not achieved any notable success in

57. Ibid., 401, 405, 414 (Aug. 10, 1841).
58. Ibid., 400 (Aug. 10, 1841).
59. Ibid., 401-402 (Aug. 12, 1841).
60. Ibid.
61. Ibid., 402 (Aug. 15, 1841).
62. Ibid., 402 (Aug. 16, 1841).
63. Ibid., 403.

business. Horace Hotchkiss drafted a letter to Joseph on July 24 that he "had much reason to be dissatisfied at this silence and apparent neglect."[64] Hotchkiss demanded that the Church pay the interest owed to him on the notes and threatened to reverse the title-swap agreement. Joseph had managed to pay the first two notes, but the next two would present the same challenge and the deadline was looming. By then Joseph had fixed on using the gathering as a way to fund the debt. New converts in the East would turn over their real estate titles to Church agents (Isaac Galland and Joseph's brother William Smith), who either sold it and paid Hotchkiss or transferred the title to Hotchkiss. The converts would receive their Nauvoo inheritances, and Joseph could breathe a little easier. It seemed a workable scheme, and Joseph sent his brothers Hyrum and William as well as Galland to represent him in continuing negotiations with Hotchkiss. Although Hotchkiss seemed interested, Hyrum let Joseph know in August 1841 that Galland had told Hotchkiss that he was headed West and that Nauvoo, and meeting Joseph, was not on his itinerary.

The news triggered Joseph's reflexes to tell once more his tale of God's persecuted people:

> You are aware that we came from Missouri destitute of everything but physical force ... Have you no feelings of Commiseration[?] Or is it your design to crush us with a ponderous load before we can walk? ... We have been making every exertion, and used all the means at our command to lay a foundation that will enable us now to begin to meet our pecuniary engagements, and no doubt in our minds to the entire satisfaction of all those concerned, if they will but exercise a small degree of patience, and stay a resort to coercive measures which would kill us in the germ, even before we can (by reason of the season) begin to bud and blossom in order to bring forth a plentiful yield of fruit.[65]

Worrying about their prophet's seemingly unsufferable burdens, the Twelve gathered at Young's house on August 21. They considered their future role in the Church and their commitment to support Joseph's prophethood, and to set goals about the missionary work they had launched in Europe. They unanimously resolved to aid "the Trustee in Trust in his arduous duties, attend to the settling of immigrants, &c."[66] This meant helping immigrants

64. Ibid., 406 (July 24, 1841).
65. Ibid., 407.
66. Ibid., 412 (Aug. 21, 1841).

get situated–finding and purchasing land, and insuring appropriate pricing and funding.

The Twelve expressed concern about the precarious financial position Joseph had put himself in. "We deeply feel for our beloved President Joseph Smith & his fathers family on account of the great losses they have sustained in their properties by the unparalleled persecutions in Missouri, … which has brought them to their present destitute situation." Joseph had been accorded the right to deed Church property to himself and to his family ever since October 1839, and the Twelve validated these transactions by "approv[ing] … the proceedings of President Smith, so far as he has gone, … & that He continue to deed & make over certain portions of church property which now exist, or which may be obtained by exchange as in his wisdom he shall judge expedient, till his own & his fathers household shall have an inheritance secured to them in our midst." But regardless of their concern, they did not vote to remove Joseph from the task. Instead, they pointed out that, given the complicated deeds and loan arrangements, Joseph needed to remain as "trustee in trust."[67]

A related measure was care of the poor. Again the Twelve institutionalized Joseph's private efforts. "In view of the poverty & distress of many who had been robbed of all by unrelenting mobbers, and of others who had sacrificed all they possessed to assist those who had thus been robbed," they voted unanimously "that President Smith, as trustee-in-trust, be requested and instructed by this conference in behalf of the Church, to extend relief to such indigent suffering brethren, either by land or goods, as the properties of the Church would admit, and his wisdom shall judge expedient …"[68]

A third death of someone close to Joseph followed on August 27, only two days after this letter. It was Joseph's clerk, Robert B. Thompson, whose wife, Mercy, was the sister of Hyrum's wife, Mary Fielding Smith. Burdened by sorrow and clerical labors, Joseph replaced him with the diligent, if also occasionally erratic, W. W. Phelps.[69]

By September 11, Bennett was still in Nauvoo but was regarded with suspicion by an increasing number around Joseph. Hosea Stout, clerk of the Nauvoo Legion, recorded on that date's muster that its two cohorts included

67. Ibid., 412-13.

68. Ibid.

69. Ibid., 411 (Aug. 25, 1841); see also Bruce Van Orden, "William W. Phelps's Service in Nauvoo as Joseph Smith's Political Clerk," 81-94.

1,490 men and described Joseph's speech "in his usual energetic style."[70] Three days later, Joseph traveled to Montrose, to attend a military parade by the Lee County militia. General Ezekiel Swazey, his officers, and the militia welcomed him as a visiting dignitary. Even though Joseph and his entourage were not in uniform, he recorded with that they were "treated" with all the respect that "visiting officers of our rank could be, through the entire day."[71]

On October 9, Joseph responded to a letter from one of Hotchkiss's partners complaining about Galland's failure to represent the Church's interests. Although the letter is not extant, we know about it from Joseph's response. Joseph wrote with sympathy, joining in at least an emotional alliance against Galland as a common enemy: "My feelings are changed, and I think you all had cause for complaining. … Why he has not done according to my instructions, God only knows."[72]

In the Church's growing centralization and unification, Sunday sermons at the temple site, patriotic addresses to the Nauvoo Legion, or even simple conversation in the homes of Saints were important in Joseph's efforts to build a Zion people. In almost every setting, Joseph introduced them to ever-expanding doctrinal vistas and the possibilities that lay before them, reminding them that what made them Saints was their love of truth and obedience to God's will. He narrated the history of persecution that defined their identity as a church and as a people. In this narrative, it was inconsequential whether new converts settled in Nauvoo or across the river. They were settling in Zion and participating as equal partners in building God's new kingdom.

70. *History of the Church,* 4:415 (Sept. 11, 1841).

71. Ibid., 416-17 (Sept. 14, 1841).

72. Ibid., 431 (Oct. 9, 1841). See also Dean C. Jessee, ed., *The Personal Papers of Joseph Smith,* 530.

CHAPTER 9

"Our God Will Not Wait Always"

The Twelve or a part of them spent the day with Joseph the Seer & he unfolded unto them many glorious things of the kingdom of God the privileges & blessings of the priesthood &c.
–Wilford Woodruff, Journal, *2:144 (Dec. 27, 1841)*

The authority that Mormonism promised did not rest on the subtlety of its theology. It rested on an appeal to fresh experience: a set of golden tablets "seen" and "hefted" by "witnesses" that had been translated into a book whose language sounded authoritatively biblical. Joseph knew instinctively what all other founders of new American religions in the nineteenth century knew. Many Americans in that period, in part because of popular enthusiasm for science, were ready to listen to any claim that appealed to "empirical evidence."[1]

The discourse presented at the Church's semi-annual general conference in October 1841 merged the concerns of earth and heaven in a characteristically Mormon way. Joseph's people gathered in the field in the cool autumn air, listening as he described the burden of debt that was crushing him. Tested throughout 1841 by land transactions that stretched deals made in good faith to the breaking point, Joseph made his complicated finances one of the topics of his address, but it is doubtful if anyone found it strange. Indeed, he often blurred the line between the sacred and the profane. For Joseph, his life in the world was enriched by his prophetic role; but that role did not include automatic resources to provide land, feed families, and build businesses.

The confusion over faulty titles to the Half-Breed Tract lands and Joseph's debt overload made it difficult to meet the payments on land purchased from Horace Hotchkiss. Joseph proposed that "the Twelve write an epistle to the Saints abroad, to use their influence and exertions to secure by exchange,

1. R. Laurence Moore, *Religious Outsiders and the Making of Americans*, 40.

purchase, donation, etc., a title to the Hotchkiss purchase."[2] From that point, the Twelve were charged with acquiring eastern lands for the Church's creditors. It would be left to Joseph to figure out how this would work.

Apostle Lyman Wight proposed that "the trustee-in-trust be instructed not to appropriate Church property to liquidate old claims that may be brought forward from Kirtland and Missouri,"[3] and the conference unanimously endorsed the proposal. The measure brought a sort of legitimacy to the repudiation of old debts that had, in fact, become one of Joseph's methods for dealing with debt when no other remedies seemed possible. Hyrum Smith admitted embarrassment since he had signed "as security, a certain obligation in Kirtland in favor of Mr. Easton."[4] The conference relieved him of the mortification by resolving "that Church property here not be appropriated to liquidate such claim."[5] It is a small but significant example of the end seeming to justify the means–in this case, asserting a rule that abrogated another rule.

Six months later, the Twelve would backtrack on this policy, writing to "the Saints in America": "Let nothing in this epistle be so construed as to destroy the validity of contracts, or give anyone license not to pay his debts. The commandment is to pay every man his dues, and no man can get to heaven who justly owes his brother or his neighbor, who has or can get the means and will not pay it; it is dishonest, and no dishonest man can enter where God is."[6]

By definition, an epistle is nothing more than a letter, but when signed by the Christ's apostles, the instructions carry additional weight. Settling the convoluted legal and financial issues of moving into an already occupied space and engaging as representatives of the Church in real estate transactions tried even the most financially adept members of Joseph's church. But at the end of the day, fairness, honesty, and equity not only needed to prevail but were critical to Joseph's version of the good society.

Taking advantage of the crowd assembled for conference, on its opening day, October 2, 1841, Joseph laid the cornerstone for the Nauvoo House, placing a square wooden box in the carved-out cornerstone. It contained the

2. "Minutes of the General Conference of the Church–held at Nauvoo, October, 1841," *History of the Church*, 4:428 (Oct. 2, 1841).

3. Ibid., 427.

4. Ibid.

5. Ibid.

6. "An Epistle of the Twelve to the Saints in America, Greeting," *History of the Church*, 4:593 (Apr. 12, 1842).

original manuscript of the Book of Mormon.[7] This placement–preserving a sacred relic at the foundation of a secular, money-making institution–perfectly captured the Mormon blend of the work of God and the earth.

At the second day of conference on Sunday morning, October 3, Joseph also expounded on both baptism for the dead and completing the temple, "which was listened to with intense interest by the large assembly" and reported in detail by the *Times and Seasons*.[8] Joseph portrayed baptism for the dead as "the only way that men can appear as saviors on mount Zion."[9] To the faithful, the doctrine "appears glorious, inasmuch as it exhibits the greatness of divine compassion and benevolence in the extent of the plan of human salvation."[10] Joseph used his listeners' love for their dead kin to prod them into greater exertions on the temple: "There shall be no more baptisms for the dead, until the ordinance can be attended to in the font of the Lord's House; and the church shall not hold another general conference, until they can meet in said house," Joseph announced, adding: *"For thus saith the Lord!"*[11] At virtually all successive conferences, Joseph spoke strongly about the need to concentrate on the temple construction.

On the third day of conference, Joseph again took as his text the Church's business affairs. Running quickly down a list of contemporary issues, he explained the "manner that he had discharged the duties involved … and the condition of the lands and other property of the church."[12] Joseph often reminded his audience of his authority and responsibility as he did in this moment. At the same time, he demonstrated his particular power and instructed them with a prophet's voice.

A year before, Joseph had alluded to his role as a modern prophet: "God purposed in himself that there should not be an eternal fullness until every dispensation should be fulfilled and gathered together in one[,] and that all things whatsoever that should be gathered together in one in those dispensations unto the same fullness and eternal glory should be in Christ Jesus, therefore he set the ordinances to be the same for Ever and ever."[13] Joseph ushered followers through ritual and gathered them with him in his version of Zion.

---

7. *History of the Church*, 4:423 (Oct. 2, 1841).
8. "Minutes of a Conference," *Times and Seasons* 2, no. 24 (Oct. 15, 1841): 577.
9. Ibid.
10. Ibid., 578.
11. Ibid.; emphasis in original.
12. "Minutes of a Conference," *Times and Seasons* 2, no. 24 (Oct. 15, 1841): 579.
13. Robert Thompson, October 5, 1840, "Original Manuscript," at http://www.boap.org/LDS/Parallel/1840/5Oct40.html; June 26, 2013.

When Hotchkiss's business partner had complained to Joseph in September about Isaac Galland, Joseph had blamed Galland. Now, on October 9, armed with the conference action, Joseph responded with a letter aimed at mollifying Hotchkiss's agent, asking how he might remedy the situation. "I must plead innocent," Joseph wrote, "I have done all that I could on my part. I will still do all that I can. I will not leave one stone unturned."

Joseph's negotiating approach in these tricky situations was sometimes huffy and slightly self-righteous, as he found himself pressed to address disputes he had hoped to avoid. At the same time, he was frustrated at being duped or seduced into ill-advised deals that left him limited choices at resolution. Joseph noted that he had been imprisoned "by sickness & various other things that were beyond my control" for part of the summer (an exaggeration–he had been arrested but released on a writ of habeas corpus the same day), which presumably made business more difficult to complete. He wrote, "I find that I am under the necessity of asking a little further indulgence–say, till next spring, so that I may be able to recover myself, and then, if God spares my life … I will … never cease my labors until the whole matter is completely adjusted to the full satisfaction of all of you. … We are very sensitive as a people; we confess it; but we want to be pardoned for our sins, if any we have committed."[14]

Fretting, Joseph also wrote directly, again blaming Galland for the Mormons' failures in financial dealings.[15] He described how Hyrum had traveled with Galland to search for property to "fulfill the contract" with Hotchkiss. Hyrum had returned early because of illness, leaving Galland with instructions that he should turn over property or money to Hotchkiss to "make every thing square." The debt itself amounted to $53,000 at that point, and the interest to $6,000.[16] As far as Joseph knew, Galland had the means to pay the interest and why he had not, Joseph did not know but promised to investigate.[17] What was more, he had "fairly presented [the matter] before our general conference … of ten thousand people [asking] for the wisest and best course in relation to meeting your demands."[18] Meanwhile, the Twelve were spread throughout the "eastern branches of the Church, ordering them to go

---

14. Ibid., 532-33.

15. *History of the Church*, 4:431 (Dec. 9, 1841).

16. Ibid., 430 (Oct. 12, 1841).

17. Joseph Smith, Letter to Smith Tuttle, Oct. 9, 1841, in Dean C. Jessee, ed., *The Personal Writings of Joseph Smith*, 530.

18. Ibid., 531.

to you & turn over their property as you & they could agree." The property that new converts brought with them into the Church would become collateral on Illinois land. With such promising prospects, Joseph could persuade debtors to wait until they could finish making payments on already-secured land and, on the strength of this arrangement, asked that the interest on the loan no longer accumulate.[19]

This simple solution, in Joseph's mind, promised to solve the Church's problems with the land debt, at least for the moment. The "Epistle of the Twelve Apostles, to the Brethren Scattered Abroad on the Continent of America," written on October 12, spelled out the gathering as part of the dramatic exodus from Missouri: "Whippings, imprisonments, tortures, and death stared them in the face, and they were compelled to seek asylum in a land of strangers. … In this state, … the Saints have found a resting place … freed from tyranny and mobs." Land was key to the fulfillment of prophecy. Nauvoo "have been laid out in city lots, a part of which have been sold, a part has been distributed to the widow and orphan, and a part remains for sale. These lots are for the inheritance of the Saints … for here He has commanded a house to built unto His name where He may manifest Himself unto His people as in former time." It was a simple matter, the Twelve explained: "Thus your property will prove to you as good as money, inasmuch as you desire to emigrate; and you will no longer be obliged to tarry afar off because that money is so scarce you cannot sell to get your pay."[20]

The epistle also had a sub-theme: defending Joseph against charges of personal financial gain:

> When Brother Joseph stated to the general conference the amount and situation of the property of the Church … he also stated the amount of his own possessions on earth; and what do you think it was? We will tell you: his old Charley (a horse) given him in Kirtland, two pet deer, two old turkeys and four young ones, the old cow given him by a brother in Missouri, his old Major (a dog), his wife, children, and a little household furniture; and this is the amount of the great estates, the splendid mansions and noble living of him who has spent a life of toil and suffering, of privation and hardships, of imprisonments and chains, of dungeons and vexatious lawsuits, and every kind of contumely and contempt ungodly men could heap upon him, and last of all report him as rolling in wealth

19. Ibid.
20. *History of the Church*, 4:434, 436 (Oct. 12, 1843).

> and luxury which he had plundered from the spoils of those for whose good he has thus toiled and suffered.[21]

This defense was critical as the epistle moved on to emphasize the importance of gathering to Zion in Illinois.[22] The land-swapping scheme looked commonsensical on paper, especially as Nauvoo's population doubled each year between 1839 and the beginning of 1842. Despite these complications, Apostle Parley P. Pratt, while on his 1841 mission in Great Britain, portrayed Zion as a refuge: "Millions on millions of acres lie before them unoccupied, with a soil as rich as Eden," he promised,

> and a surface as smooth, clear, and ready for the plow as the park scenery of England. Instead of a lonely swamp or dense forest filled with savages, wild beasts, and serpents, large cities and villages are springing up in their midst, with schools, colleges, and temples. The mingled noises of mechanism, the bustle of trade, the song of devotion, are heard in the distance, while thousands of flocks and herds are seen grazing peacefully on the plains, and the fields and gardens smile with plenty, and the wild red men of the forest are only seen as they come on a friendly visit to the Saints, and to learn the way of the Lord.[23]

By October 1841, Joseph had negotiated scores of land deals. He was constantly arranging for transfers of property, loans from new converts, or potential donations to the Church. Such conspicuous speculation gave the impression that he was a wealthy man, but Joseph was quick to point out that his chronic poverty was proof of his good intentions. Thus, he did not hesitate to use his prophetic position to enhance such deals and to persuade participants. Those around him were also often required to defend an extraordinary amount of wheeling and dealing–that it was the only way the Church could build the kingdom of God on earth.[24]

Hotchkiss and his partners opted for patience. But Galland proved to be another matter altogether. Historian Lyndon W. Cook makes the case that Joseph did not pay Galland cash for the properties he sold the

21. Ibid., 437-38.

22. Ibid., 437, 434.

23. Parley P. Pratt, "Emigration," *Millennial Star* 2 (Feb. 1, 1841): 154; see also *History of the Church*, 4:510-13 (Feb. 1, 1841).

24. His defense was usually taken up by members of the Twelve. Indeed, the "Epistle of the Twelve Apostles, to the Brethren Scattered Abroad on the Continent of America," is an elaborately drawn statement of Joseph's efforts to purchase, fund, and sell land for what they interpreted was the well-being of the Church.

Mormons in Illinois or Iowa. Rather Galland assumed title to lands they had owned in Missouri, an arrangement that made the land exchanges incredibly tangled.[25] Cook also tracks Galland's activities as a land agent for the Church, identifying Pennsylvania and New Jersey as the two locations where he most likely worked.[26] Even though Joseph believed Galland had money sufficient to pay Hotchkiss, it is unclear how he acquired it. He likely gathered donations from the Saints devoted to the Nauvoo House and the Nauvoo temple projects.

Joseph was irritated to learn that Galland had stayed during July in Ohio[27] and then proceeded to Keokuk but without coming upriver to Nauvoo.[28] During December 1841 and January 1842, Joseph and Galland sent duelling demands. Joseph wrote first, a letter that is no longer in existence, but Galland responded on December 11. He was waiting for the arrival of "a Gentleman from St. Louis … on very important business," but promised: "I … shall certainly give myself the pleasure in a few days of … an immediate interview with you."[29] The month passed, and Galland did not appear. Joseph, impatient, wrote on January 14: "if you can make it convenient to call on me within two or three days I shall be much pleased, if not you would send by the bearer of all the funds you possibly can as my wants are verry great."[30] Galland responded across the bottom portion of Joseph's page: "On the receipt of the above note I am at a loss to determine whether you intended it as an absolute dun [i.e., demand for payment] or as an appeal to my liberality to advance funds for your relief, but let it be either case, I assure you sir, it is not in my power to advance at this time 5 dollars until I obtain it from my creditors or in some other way."[31]

Angered, Joseph revoked the power of attorney he had given Galland in 1839 to negotiate land deals for the Church and cancelled his powers of attorney, posting a notice to that effect in the *Times and Seasons* on January

25. Lyndon W. Cook, "Isaac Galland–Mormon Benefactor," 277.

26. Ibid., 279. Cook cites *History of the Church*, 4:391-92, and finds that Galland did secure land titles in Joseph's name from some members of the Church.

27. See William Smith, Letter to Joseph Smith, Aug. 5, 1841, in *History of the Church*, 4:391-92. William thought Galland was headed directly to Iowa, but he stopped first in Ohio and then in Iowa.

28. Cook, "Isaac Galland–Mormon Benefactor," 280, dates his arrival as some time before December 10, 1841.

29. Isaac Galland, Letter to Joseph Smith, Dec. 11, 1841, Joseph Smith Collection.

30. Joseph Smith, Letter to Isaac Galland, Jan. 14, 1842, in *History of the Church*, 4:499 (Galland reply, Jan. 18, 1842).

31. Joseph Smith, Letter to Isaac Galland, Jan. 19, 1842, in Joseph Smith Collection.

18, 1842. The very next day, perhaps trying to soften his earlier reaction, Joseph wrote:

> I am led to conclude that you received my communication in a manner altogether unintended by me, and that there may be no misunderstanding between us, and that you may be satisfied that I did not intend, and that I do not now intend anything, only upon principles of the strictest integrity and uprightness before God, and to do as I would be done unto. … With this view of the matter, I would request you to call as soon as you possibly can make it convenient and compare accounts.[32]

Exacerbating an already tense situation, two more weeks passed, and Galland still had not appeared. Pushed to the limit, Joseph asked Brigham Young and James Ivins to travel to Keokuk to confiscate the power of attorney papers Galland had used.[33] On February 2, 1842, Joseph and Galland finally "councilled" in person; and two days later, Joseph "instructed that an invoice of Dr. Galland's scrip be made."[34] It was the last time Joseph mentioned Galland in his journal. Not long after, Galland ceased his association with the Church and eventually, according to historians Nelson C. Roberts and Samuel W. Moorehead, "he came to the conclusion that the prophet's claim to supernatural powers was a fraud [and] therefore gave up on the Mormons."[35] Joseph could not have been surprised to learn in the spring of 1842 that the titles to land in the Half-Breed Tract, purchased from Galland, were invalid and that the Saints who had purchased land there in good faith would be forced to leave.

As Joseph expounded on new growth, he still faced complications from the past. Briefly mentioned in Joseph's revelation about the temple and the Nauvoo House was the touchy subject of Kirtland, which promised more problems. Ten months earlier in January 1841, he had revealed, "I the Lord will build up Kirtland, but I, the Lord have a scourge prepared for

32. *History of the Church*, 4:499-500.

33. Ibid., 503.

34. Ibid., 513.

35. Robert B. Flanders, *Nauvoo,* 134, assesses Galland's exit from the Church: "It is scarcely accurate to say that he 'fell from favor'; rather he seems to have been dropped from official cognizance. At the same time there was increasing attention being given to the problem of General [John C.] Bennett, whose 'fall' was to be spectacular and soon; and trouble with Galland was to be avoided. Probably the Saints' dealings with him, and the heavy costs they entailed, were charged to experience. Perhaps Galland had been recognized from the beginning as a 'temporal' Latter-day Saint to be concerned with business rather than religious matters." Nelson C. Roberts and Samuel W. Moorehead, *History of Lee County, Iowa*, 308.

the inhabitants thereof." The leaders there, Almon W. Babbitt in particular, seemed to be leading the Saints away from Joseph's leadership. "And with my servant Almon Babbitt," the revelation continued, "there are many things with which I am not pleased; behold, he aspireth to establish his council instead of the council which I have ordained … and he setteth up a golden calf for the worship of my people."[36]

Seeing Kirtland as competition for Nauvoo, Hyrum Smith addressed the Saints in his general conference address on October 2, 1841, criticizing "the course pursued by some Elders in counteracting the efforts of the presidency to gather the Saints, and enticing them to stop in places not appointed for the gathering." The conference clerk spelled it out: "particularly referring to the conduct of Elder Almon W. Babbitt of Kirtland."[37]

The independence of the elders in Kirtland challenged not only the "spirit of unity" that dominated Nauvoo, but also Joseph. Joseph had shut down the Kirtland Stake in 1838. But while Hyrum was scolding Babbitt at October 1841's general conference, Babbitt was speaking at Kirtland's semi-annual conference. Rather than gather to Nauvoo, he proposed a community-building project–publication of a stake newspaper called *The Olive Leaf*.[38] The news earned him a swift rebuke. On October 31, Hyrum wrote to "the Saints in Kirtland," instructing the members to stop investing in Ohio enterprises. The press, Babbitt's practice of "ordaining of Elders, and sending out Elders to beg for the poor, are not according to the will of God." Furthermore, they were diverting funds that should be used to support the Nauvoo temple's baptismal font.

Nauvoo was in 1841 the epicenter of Church activity and focus, and embodied in physical form what Joseph believed was possible. Regardless of the patchwork of land schemes and entrepreneurial efforts, the force of the Saints who gathered to Zion at Nauvoo was immense. Thousands of converts left the lives they had known because they believed Joseph's narrative. Joseph reinforced their belief by ordering Church priorities and focusing on the work at hand: he warned that Kirtland would not be "polished and refined according to my word" until the Nauvoo temple was finished and Nauvoo itself was "filled up, and polished, and sanctified."[39] In response, the Kirtland Saints and Babbitt wrote to Joseph, asking him to modify his vision. Joseph

36. *History of the Church*, 4:281 (Jan. 19, 1841).
37. Ibid., 424 (Oct. 2, 1841).
38. Ibid., 443 (Oct. 31, 1841).
39. Ibid., 444.

responded on December 15, 1841, stressing that Nauvoo and only Nauvoo was the official gathering place.[40]

Despite the clarity of this response, some confusion was inevitable. Joseph had commanded the Saints to settle Kirtland and Missouri in the name of the Lord; now he was invoking the same authority to shut the Church down in what once had been Zion. Naturally the Saints were bewildered. Joseph constructed a new narrative for them: A father might "command his son to dig potatoes and saddle his horse, but before he had done either," he would "to tell him to do something else." A note of self-pity accompanied this anecdote. No one thought the father was at fault, "but as soon as the Lord gives a commandment and revokes that decree and commands something else, then the Prophet is considered fallen." Because the Saints' obedience was lagging, "the Lord chastiseth us with sickness and death."[41]

Wilford Woodruff took notes on Joseph's construction of this narrative: "Some people say Joseph is a fallen prophet because he does not bring forth more of the word of the Lord. Why does he not do it? Are we able to receive it? No! (says he) not one in this room." He included supporters and critics both when "he then chastened the congregation for their wickedness and unbelief knowing that whom the Lord loveth he Chasteneth, & Scourgeth evry son & daughter whom He receiveth, & if we do not receive chastisements then we are Bastards and not Sons. … The reason we do not have the Secrets of the Lord revealed unto us is because we do not keep them but reveal our difficulties to the world even to our enemies. Then how would we keep the secrets of the Lord?"[42] It was, tellingly, Joseph's third public reference to secret-keeping in less than two months, and it was not lost on Woodruff.

A potter himself, Heber Kimball followed Joseph in speaking to the congregation and added his own interpretation to the biblical parable of the potter's clay: "When it marred in the hands of the potter it was cut off the wheel and then thrown back into the mill, to go into the next batch, and was a vessel of honor; and thus it was with the human family, and ever will be: all that are pliable in the hands of God and are obedient to His commands, are vessels of honor, and God will receive them."[43] Brigham Young reinforced the message: "we should be prepared to keep each commandment as it came

40. Ibid., 476 (Dec. 15, 1841).

41. Ibid., 478-79 (Dec. 19, 1841).

42. Scott G. Kenney, ed., *Wilford Woodruff's Journal, 1833-1898*, 2:142-43 (Dec. 19, 1841); hereafter Woodruff, *Journal*.

43. *History of the Church*, 4:478 (Dec. 19, 1841).

from the Lord by the mouth of the prophet."[44] These two apostles were expressing unqualified public support for Joseph's new emphasis–not only for shutting down Kirtland but also, by implication, for the doctrine of plurality where secrecy was a life-and-death matter.

On many points, Joseph seemed oblivious to the ways his actions threatened all he had built. His life, to be sure, was always in danger, but so were the lives of his followers. Each doctrinal concept also had a social and political component that took it far beyond theology. The simple myth of persecution could not have sustained itself if Joseph had not also eventually organized the Council of Fifty with an overtly political message, announced his candidacy for the presidency of the United States, and expounded freely on the problems with the sacred U.S. Constitution. Joseph designed these innovations to sustain the Church, but all brought with them dangers and potential destruction to that same church. Nervous neighbors saw each new development, not as a distant idiosyncracy, but as a direct challenge to their voting rights, property rights, faith, and even their families.

However tempting it may be to brand Mormonism an "American" religion, it should be noted that Mormon doctrines did not mirror the American experience or somehow emerge from American values or constitutional government. Rather, as Lawrence Moore suggests, "Mormons followed a lesson, already by their time well established in American experience, that one way of becoming American was to invent oneself out of a sense of 'opposition.'" He continues, "It was the impulse which the Mormons represented that made their story important. … American religious experience began as dissent, and invented oppositions remained the major source of liveliness in American religion both in the nineteenth and twentieth century."[45]

Originally, Mormonism positioned itself on ancient foundations as a restoration religion; but in Nauvoo, the people who became Mormons forged a social identity as "other." More important, Mormon otherness stood in opposition, even defiance, to all that "polite society" despised.[46] Seeming to transform the individualism, independence, and rationality of the American frontier to cooperation, obedience, and spiritual inspiration, Joseph's Zion and its human community desired a new type of social responsibility. Allegiance opened the way to social mobility through the ranks; and for men, an ever more elaborate system of hierarchies and priesthood gave evidence of

44. Ibid., 479.
45. R. Laurence Moore, *Religious Outsiders and the Making of Americans*, 45-46.
46. Ibid.

their upward spiritual mobility. Simultaneously, the priority given to diligent labor and cooperativeness greatly solidified their political and social power in the world.

It seems likely that the Saints did not understand their own otherness. In their October 1841 epistle, the Twelve portrayed Illinois as "a state whose citizens" were inspired by a "love of liberty" and "whose souls were endowed with charity and benevolence." Desiring it to be true, the apostles affirmed that the Church in this location was "beginning to realize the fulfillment of the ancient prophets ..." Nauvoo was thus the Land of Promise (1 Nephi), a place set apart by God for the Elect.[47]

In adopting Joseph's narrative, the Twelve compared the Saints to other covenant people who wandered in search of a place to establish Zion. Here is where Joseph's power as a storyteller shines. Rhetorically positioning the story of the Saints in parallel to that of the Bible's holy people, he combined biblical traditions and recent history into a unified identity of promise and power. "The journeyings, the gatherings, and buildings of the Saints are nothing new," reminded the Twelve, "and as they are expecting, looking, and praying for the completion of the dispensation of the fulness of times ... can you believe that God will hear your prayers and bring you on your journey, gather you and build your houses, and you not put forth your hand ... to help yourself?"[48]

Enjoining listeners to dismiss all other cares to build Zion, the Twelve, without explicitly saying so, positioned Joseph beside ancient prophets like Abraham and Moses. Seizing the opportunity to reiterate the importance of the temple in the context of their restorationist gospel, they explained: "The people of God were commanded to build a house where the Son of Man might have a place to lay his head ... and if these things are not in this generation, then we have not arrived at the dispensation of the fullness of times ... and our faith and prayers are vain."[49] The temple stood increasingly at the heart of Joseph's narrative. It was both foundation and capstone to his assertion of prophetic power.

As Joseph had stressed in his closing address at October 1841 general conference, the core of his authority was the ordinances and rituals unfolding in Nauvoo. Only those conducted with his imprimatur had eternal significance, both for the living and the dead (D&C 22). Civil marriages

47. *History of the Church*, 4:434 (Oct. 12, 1841).

48. Ibid., 436.

49. Ibid., 436-37.

performed before the sealing had been established in Nauvoo were essentially invalid, superseded by the eternal contracts formed through sealing ordinances (though Joseph and Church officials continued to approve and perform civil marriages in Nauvoo).[50] Joseph would announce in mid-1843: "All covenants, oaths, vows, performances, connections, associations, or expectations that are not made and entered into and sealed by the Holy Spirit of promise, of him who is anointed," meaning himself or his authorized agent, "are of no efficacy, virtue, or force in and after the resurrection from the dead." Crucial among those covenants was the power to bind partners in plurality, and that revelation, when it was finally written down, stated flatly: "if a man marry him a wife in the world, and he marry her not by me nor by my word, ... they are not bound by any law when they are out of the world" (D&C 132:7, 15). Hyrum preached the same gospel in an April 1844 address, "[W]hat is done by the Lord has an endless duration." If a husband wife hope to be together forever, he said, "the marriage covenant [must] be sealed on earth by one having the keys and power from the Almighty God."[51] Just as Joseph could seal a couple up to heaven, he could render a civil marriage invalid. Both depended on his authority as God's prophet/lawgiver.

Secretly, the doctrine of plurality was slowly making its way as 1842 dawned. As Joseph drew the Twelve closer together, he obligated them to enter this clandestine world. His trusted confidants learned to elaborate on Joseph's story, adding their own interpretations and inhabiting the liminal space between the mundane and celestial worlds. Joseph's network of priesthood leaders created new levels of intimacy among those who accepted the bonds of secrecy and ritual–the equivalent of Victor Turner's *communitas*–as well as new forms of exclusion and suspicion.[52]

The supremacy of Nauvoo rested on the temple. It centered the rituals and relationships of covenants Joseph expanded in that city. The otherwise perplexing doctrine of plurality may be best understood in the context of the expansive ritual embedded in the temple and the sanctification of the sacred space that composed Zion. Plural kinship networks spread horizontally to tie men and women together in new ways and created a new context of loyalty, meaning, intimacy, and, ultimately, secrecy. For men who willingly

50. See Danel W. Bachman, "A Study of the Mormon Practice of Plural Marriage before the Death of Joseph Smith," 124-36; and Todd Compton, *In Sacred Loneliness*, 17-18.

51. Hyrum Smith, Discourse, Apr. 8, 1844.

52. Lawrence Foster, in *Religion and Sexuality*, 166-69, first developed the connection between Victor Turner's concepts of liminality, ritual, *communitas*, and the Latter-day Saints. My study ties these more specifically to plurality, prophethood, and the persecution narrative.

yielded their lives in obedience to Joseph, plural marriage became a test of their commitment and proof of their righteousness.[53]

Joseph did not have the luxury of preaching plurality openly, so he presented plurality as a privilege for the very elect. Joseph's cousin George A. Smith reported that at one of the first conversations about plural marriage after they had returned from England, Joseph extended this privilege to those around him according to the measurement he used for himself. "The Lord had given him the keys of this sealing ordinance," George wrote, and "he felt as liberal to others as he did to himself … and said to me 'You should not be behind your privileges.'"[54] Despite contemporary frames that make Joseph's marriages seem a promiscuous reflection of male ego, it seems clear that Joseph insisted he felt a responsibility to engage in the ritual out of a fear that he would be removed from God's presence if he did not. Joseph "found no one any more willing to lead out in this matter in righteousness than he was himself," his nephew Joseph F. Smith said in 1878. "Many could see it–nearly all to whom he revealed it believed it, and received the witness of the Holy Spirit that it was of God; but none … matched the courage of the Prophet himself."[55]

Despite limited documentation, Lucinda Harris is recognized as one of Joseph's plural wives.[56] Like two of Joseph's 1841 marriages, hers was a polyandrous-like arrangement, for she continued to cohabit with her civil husband, George Washington Harris, between 1840 and their divorce in 1853.[57] Joseph had known the Harrises in Missouri,[58] and when the Church moved to Illinois, he located a lot for them "just across the street from my own,"[59]

53. See, for example, George Smith, ed., *An Intimate Chronicle*, 102: "He also said that in the celestial glory there was three heavens or degrees, and in order to obtain the highest a man must enter into this order of the priesthood and if he don't he can't obtain it." For an opposing view, see http://www.josephsmithspolygamy.com/MISCFiles/PMRequiredForExaltation.html (accessed Aug. 2, 2011).

54. George A. Smith, Letter to Joseph Smith III, Oct. 9, 1869, Journal History. "It is an additional privilege for that same man and wife to re-enter the Temple of God to receive another wife in the manner if they are worthy. … It is a glorious privilege to go into a Temple of God and be united as man and wife in the bonds of holy wedlock for time and all eternity by the authority of the Holy Priesthood."

55. Joseph F. Smith, July 7, 1878, JD 20:29-30.

56. Andrew Jenson lists no date for this marriage or source for the information. Andrew Jenson, "Plural Marriage," 6:233. Harris was sealed to Joseph by proxy in Nauvoo on January 22, 1846, reinforcing the probability that she was his plural wife. Devery S. Anderson and Gary James Bergera, eds., *The Nauvoo Endowment Companies*, 1845-1846, 464.

57. Compton, *In Sacred Loneliness*, 53.

58. Donna Hill, *Joseph Smith*, 221-22.

59. Joseph Smith, Letter to E. W. Harris, May 24, 1839, in *History of the Church*, 3:362, mentions "Mr. G. W. Harris." See also Compton, *In Sacred Loneliness*, 50.

not far from the home of another pair of new friends, John and Sarah Cleveland. (Sarah would also become a plural wife of Joseph.) Joseph's diaries locate George and Lucinda both in Nauvoo and in Joseph's social circles. George was a faithful Saint, serving on the Nauvoo High Council and with Joseph in various business transactions.

It is impossible to know how Joseph justified to himself these marriages with the wives of some of his friends. Although later accounts portray some of these marriages as unhappy at the time, this was not always the case. Instead, Joseph created a new type of family that trumped prior commitments. In what is on some levels an enormous expression of entitlement, he chose women in ways that made sense only to himself. Those around him or those impacted most by his choices had to find a way to reconcile his decisions or to fall from faith. If the proposition of a secret ritual that involved the restoration of an ancient biblical practice proved impossible to accept, resisters slid away from Joseph's charismatic hold and, usually, away from the identity required of them as Mormons. As a result, this type of member lived outside the liminal space that proved dominant in the lives of those who both believed and participated.

Moreover, it is clear that Joseph believed plurality benefitted those he married and their families. Speaking in the voice of God, he reassured the father of one of his young wives: "The thing that my servant Joseph Smith has made known unto you and your Family and which you have agreed upon, is right in mine eyes and shall be rewarded upon your heads with honor and immortality and eternal life to all your house both old & young."[60] It was also true that, if a woman failed to obey this commandment from God, she and her family might be deprived eternally of God's fullest blessings (see D&C 132:3-4).[61]

On October 27, 1841, the same day that a delegation left Nauvoo to present grievances to the federal government for the second time, Joseph

60. "A Revelation to N[ewel] K. Whitney," in *The Essential Joseph Smith*, 165. For Rex Eugene Cooper, *Promises Made to the Fathers*, 140: "A main motive of some plural marriages seems to have been to extend this saving power through the sealed woman to members of her family."

61. Kathryn M. Daynes, *More Wives Than One*, 26, points to the power this doctrine gave Joseph as he taught it to members: "Believing that one's eternal exaltation depended on Joseph Smith ensured loyalty to him, especially when his power extended not only to his plural wives but also to their families." Compton, *In Sacred Loneliness*, 456, also underscores the theological centrality of plurality: "the principle was not just an optional revelation–they viewed it as the most important revelation in Joseph Smith's life, which is what he undoubtedly taught them. If they accepted him as an infallible prophet, and if they wanted full exaltation, they had no recourse but to marry many plural wives."

was reportedly sealed to Zina Jacobs, her capitulation to the will of his claim on her, even though she was seven months pregnant with her civil husband's son, Zebulon. In the layering of experience so typical of the Nauvoo period, Joseph bade the group of men an enthusiastic goodbye, conducted some business, and before dinner sent for Dimick Huntington who would perform this sealing, with Dimick's wife, Fanny, as a witness. Five years later, Zina entered a second polyandrous union by marrying Brigham Young after Joseph's death. This time the witness was her civil husband, Henry Jacobs.[62] Much later, Zina interpreted the meaning of this sacred ritual as she had come to understand it:

> When I heard that God had revealed the law of celestial marriage that we would have the privilege of associating in family relationships in the worlds to come I searched the scripture and by humble prayer to my Heavenly Father I obtained a testimony for myself that God had required that order to be established in this church. I made a greater sacrifice than to give my life for I never anticipated again to be looked uppon as an honorable woman by those I dearly loved. Could I compremise [sic] conscience lay aside the sure testimony of the spiret [sic] of God for the Glory of this world after having been baptized by one having authority and covenanting at the waters edge to live the life of a saint[?][63]

Laying the groundwork for another polyandrous union, Joseph himself taught Zina's and Dimick's older sister, Presendia, about the new order of marriage. Presendia had visited Joseph in Liberty Jail, Missouri, in the winter of 1838-39, and the letter he wrote in response suggests that a tender relationship already existed between them, even though she had married to non-Mormon Norman Buell in 1827. A later account interpreted Presendia's rationale for entering plurality as spiritual: "She knew Joseph to be a man of God, and she had received many manifestations in proof of this, and consequently when he explained to her clearly the knowledge which he had obtained from the Lord, she accepted the sealing ordinance with Joseph as a sacred and holy confirmation."[64] Presendia and Joseph were reortedly married on December 11, 1841, two months after Zina; again, Dimick officiated.[65]

62. Oa Cannon, "Autobiography of Zina Diantha Huntington Young," n.d., typescript, 23: "Feb. 2, 1846, Brigham Young married Zina–they recorded it 'sealed for time.' Henry is listed as a witness in the record with Dimick C. Huntington performing the marriage." See also Oa Cannon, "Henry Bailey Jacobs," n.d., typescript, 7.

63. Zina Diantha Young, Autobiography, 1.

64. Emmeline B. Wells, "A Venerable Woman: Presendia Lathrop Kimball," 163.

65. Presendia Lathrop Huntington Smith Kimball, Autobiographical Sketch, Apr. 1, 1881, 1.

One wonders why Joseph did not call on his apostles to perform these early marriages, since they had returned from the British Mission. Eventually they would. Typically in this first group of marriages, Joseph relied on trusted friends and close relatives of the women, often having them present the initial teachings as well as arranging and performing the secret sealings. Rather than moving vertically down the hierarchy, plurality initially spread laterally to involve individuals who had proved loyal enough to take this deeper step into what Susan Staker called a "cultural landscape articulated around a dense labyrinth of secrets especially secrets about plural marriage." These men had sisters or wives whom Joseph desired to marry, and who could facilitate the private rituals.[66]

It must have been an exhilarating experience for a Dimick Huntington or a Joseph Bates Noble, sworn to secrecy by a man he revered, to be drawn across a threshold into that shared secret, treasuring in his heart the knowledge that Joseph trusted him with potentially ruinous knowledge of a doctrine that most did not even know existed. In saying yes to his request, they put their eternal life into his hands, and perhaps their mortal lives as well. This elitism had an enormous appeal, and each may have thought at least for a while that he enjoyed an especially privileged relationship with Joseph.[67]

As members of an elite sisterhood, Joseph's wives, despite fears of scandal and social isolation, must also have felt set apart from others because of their secret knowledge and destiny. The ritual they had performed–and continued to perform with their lives of obedience–marked them as a class apart, requiring of them different loyalties and behaviors than ordinary Church members.[68]

Half of Joseph's plural wives[69] joined, or would eventually join, Nauvoo's

66. Susan Staker, "'The Lord Said, Thy Wife is a Very Fair Woman to Look Upon,'" 290. "Early Mormonism was steeped in secrecy," maintains Danel Bachman, "A Study of the Mormon Practice of Plural Marriage," 192.

67. According to Oliver Huntington, Dimick's younger brother, Joseph asked Dimick how he could reward his loyalty. Dimick reportedly answered, "[W]here you and your fathers family are, there I and my fathers family may also be." Dimick Huntington, qtd. in Oliver B. Huntington, Journal 2:202 (Feb. 18, 1883). Evidently, Dimick–or Oliver–believed that the whole family, not just Presendia and Zina, would be guaranteed a place in heaven because of their acceptance of plurality.

68. Emmeline B. Wells, "A Venerable Woman," 163, assessed this self-awareness: "Their minds were more expanded, new light had burst in upon them, and they were buoyed up by a spirit which they scarcely understood." But the women also became the subject of gossip: "No tongue can describe, or pen portray the peculiar situation of these noble, self-sacrificing women who through the providence of God helped to establish the principle of celestial marriage."

69. Gary James Bergera, "Identifying the Earliest Mormon Polygamists, 1841-44," 50.

all-female Relief Society, when it was organized in the spring of 1842. Part of its purpose, Joseph explained, was to teach members to keep secrets and to establish networks of loyalties. Emma noted that "each member should be ambitious to do good–that the members should deal frankly with each other–to watch over the morals–and be very careful of the character and reputation–of the members of the Institution."[70] John Bennett sensationally described the Relief Society as a sisterhood composed of Joseph's "harem."[71] Presendia Buell became a member of the Relief Society at its fifth meeting on April 19, 1842,[72] even though she and her civil husband lived in Lima, twenty-nine miles southeast of Nauvoo.

In an atmosphere of secrecy, it is irresistible to speculate why Joseph instructed an audience of Saints on November 7, 1841, "If you do not accuse each other, God will not accuse you. … If you will not accuse me, I will not accuse you. If you will throw a cloak of charity over my sins, I will over yours–for charity covereth a multitude of sins. What many people call sin is not sin; I do many things to break down superstition, and I will break it down."[73] At least one man in the audience, Ebenezer Robinson, later reported seeing this instruction for mutually concealed guilt as predicting things to come: "The foregoing, and kindred doctrine … could not fail to bear evil fruit, as is evidenced by the subsequent course pursued by the Church. It began to be frequently talked by the people, that what was formerly considered sin was not sin."[74]

At that point, Robinson may have been embittered because the *Times and Seasons* had been taken from his control on January 28, 1842, and assigned to the Twelve, a change that required him to leave his home in the same building as the printing office.[75] The situation was complicated by an earlier revelation involving the Robinsons. A month after his "cloak of charity" speech, on December 2, Joseph instructed: "Behold it is my will that she [Marinda Hyde, Apostle Orson Hyde's civil wife] should have a better place prepared for her than that in which she now lives, in order that her life may be spared." Stories told by Marinda's descendants portray her

70. Relief Society, Minutes, Mar. 17, 1842. In early 2016, the LDS Church published a variety of Relief Society original documents, including the important Nauvoo minutes. See Jill Mulvay Derr, Carol Cornwall Madsen, Kate Holbrook, and Matthew J. Grow, eds., *The First Fifty Years of Relief Society: Key Documents in Latter-day Saint Women's History* (Salt Lake City: The Church Historian's Press, 2016).

71. John C. Bennett, *History of the Saints,* 219.

72. Relief Society, Minutes, Apr. 19, 1842.

73. *History of the Church*, 4:445 (Nov. 7, 1841).

74. Ebenezer Robinson, "Discourse by Joseph Smith," 323.

75. *History of the Church*, 4:503 (Jan. 28, 1842).

life in Orson's absence–he was on a Church mission–as marked by privation, sickness, and loneliness:

> … she had to live in a little log house whose windows had no glass but in place of which were pieces of greased paper. … A little cornmeal and a few groceries were all the provisions remaining to sustain her and the little ones. Had she been well and strong this might not have been so dreadful, but she was just able to move about after having been confined to her room with ague. She took in knitting, taught a little school, and by the dim light of a candle at night did what little sewing she could.[76]

Marinda's situation was distressing but not so different from that experienced by other wives of apostles. The Lord's solution, through Joseph, was to instruct Ebenezer and Angeline Robinson to "open their doors and take her and her [two] children into their house and take care of them faithfully and kindly" until Orson's return. The revelation continued, tellingly, with directions to twenty-six-year-old Marinda to "hearken to the counsel of my servant Joseph in all things whatsoever he shall teach unto her, and it shall be a blessing upon her and upon her children after her, unto her Justification saith the Lord."[77] It is not clear how long the merged households lived together before the revelation came unhousing the Robinsons, but it apparently did not apply to Marinda. According to Robinson, the same day as their departure, "that evening Willard Richards nailed down the windows, and fired off his revolver in the street after dark [presumably in celebration], and commenced living with Mrs. Nancy Marinda Hyde, in the rooms we had vacated in the printing office building, where they lived through the winter. His family [civil wife Jennetta Richards] was residing at the time in Massachusetts, and Elder Orson Hyde was absent on his mission to Palestine."[78] Clearly, Robinson implies some kind of plural relationship between Richards and Marinda.

Orson Hyde had been sent to Jerusalem on a mission to dedicate the Holy Land for the return of the Jews.[79] He had performed that dedication on October 24, 1841, and was on his way home; but according to accounts

76. Florence M. Susser, "Life of Nancy Marinda Hyde," qtd. in Compton, *In Sacred Loneliness*, 235.

77. *History of the Church*, 4:467 (Dec. 2, 1841).

78. Ebenezer Robinson, "Items of Personal History of the Editor," *The Return* 2 (Oct. 1890): 346. Robinson's response should be contextualized by all he had lost: his livelihood, his home, and perhaps an intact ego.

79. *History of the Church*, 4:113 (Apr. 8, 1841). Joseph wrote, "We have by the counsel of the Holy Spirit, appointed Elder Orson Hyde … to be our agent and representative in foreign lands,

by men who later left the Church, Joseph allegedly also displayed an interest in Marinda during Orson's absence.[80] The precise nature of that relationship is open to interpretation.

Willard Richards's and others' diaries place him in social situations in Marinda's company: "Christmas eve [1841] visited & dined at Hiram Kimballs with Nancy M. Hyde. B. Young. H. C. Kimball O. Pratt, W. Woodruff, J. Taylor & wives …" On February 7, 1842, William Clayton wrote, "I dined at Sister Hydes with Brother Joseph Smith, H Kimball, W Woodruff, B Young and Willard Richards." Joseph noted yet another meeting on February 24: "P.M. was explaining the Records of Abraham To the Recorder [Willard Richards]. Sisters Marinda Mary and others present. to hear the Explanations." Thus one is left with two piles of reports: one produced by men who sought to destroy the Church, the other descriptions of what might–or might not–have been ordinary social events. The conflicting evidence makes it possible only to say that Richards and Marinda might have lived for a time in the same small building, but the exact nature of their relationship is unclear. Todd Compton, pointing to the "code of silence" that those involved in plurality maintained, finds Robinson's allegation that Richards shot a gun at night in celebration and treated Marinda as a "wife" questionable.[81]

Possibly troubling rumors reached Jennetta Richards on June 23, 1842, when she was still in Richmond, Massachusetts, with her parents. Joseph wrote a letter assuring her of Willard's continued loyalty and integrity, "a man in whom" he had "the most implicit confidence and trust." He wrote, "You say I have got him; so I have, in the which I rejoice for he has done me great good and taken a great burden off my shoulders since his arrival in Nauvoo never did I have a greater intimacy with any man than with him." This letter also prepared the ground for Richards to teach his wife the principle of plurality: Richards would join her soon, "and I want you, beloved Sister," Joseph stated, "to be a Genral [sic] in this matter, in helping him along, which I know you will he will be able to teach you many things which you have never heard you may have implicit confidence in the same. … I hope that you may be steadfast in the faith, even unto the end."[82]

to visit the cities of London, Amsterdam, Constantinople and Jerusalem." "Communications," *Times and Seasons* 1, no. 6 (Apr. 1840): 86.

80. Compton, *In Sacred Loneliness*, 237, summarizes these accusations.

81. Ibid., 238.

82. Joseph Smith, Letter to Jennetta Richards, June 23, 1842, in Jessee, *The Personal Writings of Joseph Smith*, 552. See also Devery S. Anderson, "'I Could Love Them All': Nauvoo Polygamy in the Marries of Willard and Jennetta Richards," *Sunstone*, June 7, 2013, at https://www.

As Willard Richards's domestic relations unfolded, Joseph pushed for completion of the temple. A month after he suspended baptisms for the dead until a time when they could be performed in the temple, construction workers finished the baptismal font in the basement. Joseph dedicated the font with the promise it held for temple ritual on November 8, 1841.[83] As always, Joseph moved facilely between his private and public personas, addressing a range of doctrinal issues. Five weeks after the dedication, on December 13, in his new role as temple recorder, Willard Richards opened "an office in the small counting room in Joseph's store. Donations were entered into 'The Book of the Law of the Lord.' The first recorded donation was by John Sanders, who contributed $5.00. The Temple Committee was no longer to receive contributions."[84] As a sign of renewed urgency, a small army of 200-300 elders who had previously been called on missions were reassigned to work on the temple.[85] By the month's end, the stone for the basement wall on the south side had been laid up to the water table. On the north, the wall was about two feet high when work halted until the next spring.[86]

A temporary frame structure of oak clapboard enclosed the temple's baptismal font until a more durable stone structure could replace it. The font was

> oval shaped, sixteen feet long east and west, and twelve feet wide, seven feet high from the foundation, the basin four feet deep, the molding of the cap and base are formed of beautiful carved work. A flight of stairs in the north and south side leads up and down into the basin, guarded by a side railing. The font stands upon twelve oxen, for on each side and two at each end, their heads, shoulders, and fore legs projecting out from under the font; they are carved out of pine plank, glued together ...[87]

Water came from a well in the east end of the basement dug by Hiram Oaks and Jess McCarrol.[88]

---

sunstonemagazine.com/i-could-love-them-all-nauvoo-polygamy-in-the-marriage-of-willard-and-jennetta-richards/ (accessed July 26, 2015).

83. *History of the Church*, 4:446-47 (Nov. 8, 1841).

84. William Clayton, "Nauvoo Temple History Journal," 8-9.

85. Journal History, Dec. 13, 1841.

86. William Clayton, "Nauvoo Temple History Journal," 8. The Twelve's November 14, 1841, epistle reported that the temple's foundation was laid and the walls of the basement were nearly completed. "An Epistle of the Twelve," *Times and Seasons* 3, no. 2 (Nov. 15, 1841): 601.

87. *History of the Church*, 4:446.

88. Ibid. By Oaks's report, they "lost the drill" when they "struck water," but the stream "spirted up with great force." Oaks clapped "his hat over the hole until McCarrol stopped the

Baptisms for the dead did not resume until November 21, when Apostles "Brigham Young, Heber C. Kimball, and John Taylor baptized about forty [members] for the dead."[89] Completing the second part of the holy ritual, Willard Richards, George A. Smith, and Wilford Woodruff "confirmed" them, laying hands on the proxies' heads and giving the gift of the Holy Ghost. Its significance was not lost on Woodruff, who noted: "It was the first FONT erected for this glorious purpose in this last dispensation."[90] Joseph's record shows that, on December 28, he "baptized Sidney Rigdon in the font, for and in behalf of his parents; also baptized Reynolds Cahoon and others."[91] Many Saints absorbed Joseph's energy for completing the temple. According to Ebenezer Robinson, "The brethren seemed to vie with each other in their diligence, as many of them felt … if they failed to have the work accomplished by the time appointed, they lost not only their own souls' salvation, but also that of their dead friends, for whom they had been baptized."[92]

On November 14, Joseph met with nine members of the Twelve to follow up October's epistle with another to the European Saints on the gathering–the third in 1841 alone.[93] Such epistles were critical. Not only were they news bulletins, informing the Saints about Church policies and doctrines, but they generated enthusiasm for the gathering, reminded the faithful of what they shared as a church, and shaped the identity of even the most distant members.

The epistle began with assurances that Church leaders were thinking of them constantly: "We rejoice and thank our Heavenly Father daily" at reports "of your faithfulness and diligence in the great work unto which you have been called, by the Holy Spirit." Members should heed the missionaries who instructed them in principles "calculated to prepare the children of men for … the restitution of all things spoken by the Prophets."

The Church's central mission was building the temple and the Nauvoo House so as "to secure the salvation of the Church in the last days." In the

---

flow with a wooden plug." Phoebe Swain and Lizzie Anderson, "History of Hiram Oaks," cited in Virginia C. Harrington and J. C. Harrington, *Rediscovery of the Nauvoo Temple*, 29.

89. *History of the Church*, 4:454 (Nov. 21, 1841).

90. Woodruff, *Journal*, 2:138 (Nov. 21, 1841).

91. *History of the Church*, 4:486 (Dec. 28, 1841).

92. Ebenezer Robinson, "Items of Personal History of the Editor," *The Return* 3 (Jan. 1891): 12-13.

93. "To the Saints Scattered Abroad in England, Scotland, Ireland, Wales, the Isle of Man, and the Eastern Continent," *History of the Church*, 4:448-53 (Nov. 15, 1841).

temple, "His servants may be ... endowed with power from on high, to prepare them to go forth among the nations, and proclaim the fullness of the Gospel for the last time, and bind up the law, and seal up the testimony, leaving this generation without excuse ..."[94] The epistle painted a glowing picture of political power: "Soon the kings and the queens, the princes and the nobles, the rich and the honorable of the earth will come up hither to visit the Temple of our God ..." But this future teetered in the balance if the Saints faltered in faithfulness. "[A]ll are under equal obligations to do all in their power to complete the buildings by their faith, and by their prayers."[95]

The epistle closed with general exhortations: "[E]ver be as unwilling to believe an evil report about a brother or a sister as if it were about yourself, and as you dislike to be accused, be slow to accuse the brethren." This direction, echoing Joseph's "cloak of charity" speech, seems telling.[96] In conclusion, the Saints should "pray for us and the First Presidency," and particularly "that his [Joseph's] life and health may be precious in the sight of heaven, till he has finished the work which he has commenced."[97]

On November 28, Joseph addressed the Twelve, rhetorically sweeping them toward ultimates of perfection: "Joseph Said the Book of Mormon was the most correct of any Book on Earth & the key stone of our religion & a man would get nearer to God by abiding by its precepts than any other Book," recorded Woodruff.[98] The promise inherent in this statement was that mere mortals could, by prayerfully studying the Book of Mormon, understand the mind of God. Most important, by ordering their lives according to its precepts, it would bring them salvation.

Three weeks later, on December 21, Joseph expressed pressing practical concerns about Nauvoo's need for industry. He wrote to Edward Hunter, a convert in Pennsylvania who was poised to move to Nauvoo: "As respects steam engines and mills ... we cannot have too many..." Revealing his understanding of the economic and social systems required to make a successful city, Joseph simultaneously revealed how far Nauvoo had come:

> There is scarcely any limits which can be imagined to the mills and machinery and manufacturing of all kinds which might be put into profitable operation in this city, and even if others should raise a mill before you get

94. *History of the Church*, 4:449 (Nov. 15, 1841).
95. Ibid., 450.
96. Ibid.
97. Ibid., 453.
98. Woodruff, *Journal*, 2:139 (Nov. 28, 1841).

> here, it need be no discouragement ... for it will be difficult for the mills to keep pace with the growth of the place, and you will do well to bring the engine. If you can persuade any of the brethren who are manufacturers of woolens or cottons to come on and establish their business, do so.[99]

What was limitless was Joseph's ambition for the place; still, Nauvoo remained pre-industrial and home manufacturing was much more common than factory work. Understandably, the industry that employed the most men and used the most capital was construction.

Joseph gave Nauvoo's business high priority during most of December. On the 5th, he proofed the Book of Mormon before it was stereotyped (having previously commented on the text's correctness),[100] he corresponded with two attorneys, Nehemiah Browning and Orville H. Bushnell, soliciting their help on the unpaid debts remaining from Kirtland.[101] He made Willard Richards his personal scribe, a position of great confidence since it exposed him to Joseph's most private experiences.[102] Joseph wrote to James Gordon Bennett, editor of the *New York Herald,* on the 18th, thanking him for what his unbiased description of Nauvoo.[103] Joseph wrote a letter for the *Times and Seasons* endorsing Democrat Adam Snyder, candidate for Illinois governor, along with his running mate, Richard Moore, as "sterling men ..." Joseph continued, "We care not a fig for Whig or Democrat; they are both alike to us; but we shall go for our friends, our TRIED FRIENDS, and the cause of human liberty which is the cause of God. We are aware that 'divide and conquer' is the watchword with man, but with us it cannot be done.–We have suffered too much to be daily duped–we have no cat's paws amongst us."[104]

"States goods" arrived in Nauvoo for Joseph's red brick store, completed in December 1841 at the corner of Granger and Water Streets. Joseph greeted the shipments enthusiastically at the dock and unpacked some of the crates himself on December 14, perhaps anticipating the security the new

---

99. Joseph Smith, Letter to Edward Hunter, in *History of the Church,* 4:482 (Dec. 21, 1841).

100. *History of the Church,* 4:468 (Dec. 5, 1841).

101. Joseph Smith, Diary, Dec. 7, 1841, in Jessee, *The Personal Writings of Joseph Smith,* 535-36.

102. *History of the Church,* 4:470 (Dec. 13, 1841); Howard Searle, "Willard Richards as Historian," 41-62.

103. *History of the Church,* 4:477-79 (Dec. 18, 1841).

104. Joseph Smith, "State Gubernatorial Convention," 651. Snyder was elected but died in May 1842, to be replaced by Thomas Ford, the governor who would subsequently vote to repeal the Nauvoo Charter.

commercial venture might bring his family.[105] A shipment of groceries for the store, delayed at St. Louis, arrived a week later.[106]

Work on the temple continued. Joseph managed its construction carefully, was suspicious of others who took ownership of the project from him, and was not averse to involving the Twelve in enforcing his regulations. On December 11, for example, he "directed Brigham Young ... to go immediately and instruct the building committee in their duty, and forbid them receiving any more property for the building of the temple, until they received it from the Trustee-in-Trust, and if the committee did not give heed to the instruction, and attend to their duty, to put them in the way so to do."[107]

Repeatedly, Joseph predicted that Saints who failed to contribute to the building of the temple would not receive the blessings tied to it, jeopardizing their eternal salvation. On December 13, the Twelve stressed the same theme in another epistle to the Church. Mentioning enthusiasm for the baptismal font, they described its second role in baptizing "the sick" who "have been made whole" by this ordinance, in addition to conferring baptism on the worthy dead. The next theme, however, was a threat. Was it proper to baptize "those who have not been obedient and assisted to build the place for baptism[s?]. ... [I]t seems unreasonable to us that the Great Jehovah will approbate such ... for if the Church must be brought under condemnation and rejected with her dead, .. why should not individuals, who thus neglect, come under the same condemnation?"

More than a year before, the apostles elaborated, the conference had established that tithing would be the temple's funding source:

> [T]he tithings [sic] required, is one-tenth of all anyone possessed at the commencement of the building, and one-tenth part of all his increase from that time until the completion of the same, whether it be money, or whatever he be blessed with. Many in this place are laboring every tenth day for the house, and this is the tithing of their income, for they have nothing else; others would labor the same, but they are sick, therefore excusable; when they get well, let them begin; while there are others who appear to think their business of more importance than the Lord's.

They concluded with another threat: "We hope this gentle hint will suffice, that we may not be compelled to publish the names of those referred to."[108]

105. *History of the Church*, 4:476 (Dec. 14, 1841).
106. Ibid., 483 (Dec. 22, 1841).
107. Ibid., 470 (Dec. 11, 1841).
108. Ibid., 473-74 (Dec. 13, 1841).

Men in and near Nauvoo were required to devote one day out of ten to full-time work on the temple. Young was particularly vigilant in monitoring these commitments. In the same letter, he reminded Saints who had volunteered to lodge the laborers, "we expect soon to send someone to your table ..."[109]

As many as a hundred men may have worked on the project at any given moment–quarrying stone, doing carpentry, carving or laying stone, and dealing with the dozens of other required tasks. Organizing local resources was a monumental task, demanding compelling arguments and motivation. Most members were also building their own houses or businesses. Nearly everyone from Joseph on down was strapped for supplies and funds.

Recruiting laborers beyond Nauvoo's borders, the Twelve had "invite[d] the brethren for many miles distant around us, to send in their teams for drawing stone, lumber, and materials for the building ... that the laborer faint not, and the teams be made strong ..." Everyone contributed. Women knitted stockings and sweaters, quilted bedding, and sewed "clothing of every description."[110] Each donation, whether hours or labor or material objects, was recorded in the "Book of the Law of the Lord."

Business did not slacken as Christmas 1841 approached. On Christmas Eve day, Joseph consulted with Brigham Young and Newel K. Whitney about establishing a central agency to manage the immigration of converts and "for the[ir] cheap and expeditious" transport to Nauvoo.[111]

The evening after Christmas, the Twelve gathered in Joseph's home to hear Hyrum and Joseph speak about "good principles." They advised that "When devout men from every nation shall assemble to hear the things of God, let the Elders speak to them in their native tongue, ... and let those interpret who understood the language spoken, in their own mother tongue."[112]

The Twelve met again the next night at Joseph's house where he explained the significance, according to Young, of "the Urim and Thummim which he found with the [golden] plates, called in the Book of Mormon the Interpreters. He said that every man who lived on the earth was entitled to a seerstone, and should have one, but they are kept from them in consequence of their wickedness, and most of those who do find one make an evil use of

109. Ibid.
110. Ibid., 434 (Oct. 12, 1841).
111. Ibid., 484 (Dec. 24, 1841).
112. Ibid., 486 (Dec. 26, 1841).

it; he showed us his seerstone."[113] Woodruff added: "I had the privilege of seeing for the first time in my day the URIM & THUMMIM."[114]

By the end of 1841, the contours of mythic Mormonism had clarified. The Saints saw themselves as players in a cosmic drama, determined to obey God's will as an evil world worked against them. Joseph directed the elite of his Saints to enter plurality, to keep the sacred secret, to seek justice, to execute his designs for a holy city, and to build a temple. These were deliberate, calculated moves, notes in a symphony to unite Saint and heaven.

113. Elden J. Watson, ed., *Manuscript History of Brigham Young*, 1801-1844, 112. Urim and Thummim was the term commonly used to describe one of Joseph's seer stones.

114. Woodruff, *Journal*, 2:144 (Dec. 27, 1841).

CHAPTER 10

Revelations from the Lord

> *My Son Joseph Smith has recently received a revelation from the Lord in regard to these people and times–and he has told all these things to me.*
>
> *–Lucy Mack Smith, qtd. in John E. Hallwas and Roger D. Launius,* Cultures in Conflict, *32*

Joseph's prophet-narrative was grounded in one blunt reality: He was a human being first, a prophet second. The expectations of masculinity that permeated much of early-to-mid-nineteenth-century America informed Joseph's humanity. His was, in part, a gendered experience, tinted by Jacksonian expectations about what men were supposed to be. Historian Mark C. Carnes's work helps to position Joseph's membership in Nauvoo's Masonic lodge (March 15, 1842) and establishment of temple ritual (May 4-5, 1842) in the gendered experience of nineteenth-century manhood. However extraordinary many of Joseph's experiences may have been, much of his life was impacted by the same forces that other men around him experienced.

During Joseph's lifetime, Alexis de Toqueville observed that America was a nation devoid of the social hierarchies and expectations that stimulated men to form associations in a search for greater personal strength.[1] Men clamored for membership in clubs which substituted for earlier cohesive social networks. Historian Lynn Dumenil argues that, among other types of social association, Freemasonry provided a type of "spiritual renewal" and "mystic tie."[2] Dumenil's analysis of ritual locates Masonry as yet another agent that catapulted the Latter-day Saints into a liminal state. Such rituals separated Mormon men from the world outside the lodge, strengthening bonds of friendship in a separate world. Masonic ritual compounded the

1. Alexis de Toqueville, *Democracy in America*, 129.
2. Lynn Dumenil, *Freemasonry and American Culture*, 1880-1939, 42, 38.

effect of the Mormon temple ritual on the men to whom Joseph taught his heavenly secrets.

Sociologist Emile Durkheim suggests that such forms of ritual appear in response to specific social phenomena–in this case, the social dislocation caused by transformations in the social structure of mid-century America.[3] Carnes argues that rituals like those of the Masons were, significantly, *masculine* institutions, "closely linked to issues of gender." They were a way for men to relate to each other directly in arrangements unaffected by women. "Fraternal ritual provided solace and psychological guidance during young men's troubled passage to manhood in Victorian America."[4] In Mormon Nauvoo, Masonry, plurality, and temple ritual combined to usher Mormon men through disruptions and social chaos, empowering them with new identities and grounding them, and their loved ones, in hopes of a bright future.

What is more, Masonry, temple ritual, and plurality transformed the world Joseph inhabited. Plural marriage became more meaningful because of its juxtaposition within the sacred cosmos. Joseph spent much of 1842 arranging new marriages, forming alliances necessary to assure their secrecy, and arguing for the necessity of such an exotic shift of marriage affairs. In 1841, he married three plural wives. Between January and August 1842–seven months–he apparently added at least eleven more, six of them to women who had living husbands, three to widows, and two to women who had never been married before. Despite the messiness, when Joseph was sealed to his sister-in-law, Agnes Moulton Coolbrith Smith, wife of his deceased brother Don Carlos, on January 6, 1842, or to Adam Lightner's wife, Mary Elizabeth Rollins Lightner, at the end of February or to Eliza R. Snow on June 29, 1842, heaven and earth formed, under Joseph's supervision, a new relationship.

Because Joseph was both prophet and man, masculinity complicated his arguments about plurality. Permutations, self-understandings, and theologies multiplied in ways that the sketchy, retrospective records only make more complex. A growing group of men and women wrestled with what they understood to be appropriate or not, sacred or not, what were or were not proper gender roles in marriage, and the demands this new requirement placed on them. Individuals introduced to plurality stood at a moral and ethical crossroads. Plurality taught them new personal realities

3. Emile Durkheim and Marcel Mauss, *Primitive Classification*, trans. Rodney Needham (Chicago: University of Chicago Press, 1963), 88.

4. Mark C. Carnes, *Secret Ritual and Manhood in Victorian America*, 14.

and understandings of significant others in their lives, including whom they could or could not trust. It tested their willingness to stand loyal to Joseph and his desires.

Joseph's new marriages in 1842 apparently began with a daughter and a month later her mother: Sylvia Sessions Lyon and Patty Bartlett Sessions. Patty and David Sessions joined the Saints in Nauvoo on May 2, 1840, living in a log cabin and enduring the malaria meted out by Zion's swamps. Following her parents not long after, twenty-one-year old Sylvia (b. July 31, 1818) and her husband, Windsor P. Lyon, moved to the new Mormon town as well. Within two years, their lives went through a spectacular shift, when, on February 8, 1842, Sylvia and Joseph Smith were apparently sealed in celestial marriage.[5] Capitalizing on the gathering of the Saints, Windsor set up a mercantile and drug business, the first of many businesses he would try in Nauvoo.[6] Patty was herself sealed to Joseph a month later in Sylvia's presence.[7]

Because these two wives were a mother-daughter pair, a unique set of emotional and psychological issues was involved, even though neither woman left a contemporary record of her response to this challenging situation. Patty married Joseph at age forty-seven when she was probably menopausal and after she had spent thirty years married to David. Sylvia had given birth to two of Windsor's children and bore another four after her plural marriage to Joseph (one of whom may have been Joseph's progeny).

Patty was evidently the oldest woman to marry Joseph up to that time, but she seems to have been loyal, both to him personally and to the practice of plural marriage. Joseph Jackson, a hostile witness who was briefly Joseph's confidant in the fall 1842, commented in his published exposé: "Joe had in his employ certain old women, called 'Mothers in Israel,' such as ... old

5. The date for Sylvia Sessions Lyon's marriage to Joseph is only partly recorded in Joseph F. Smith, Affidavit Books, which sometimes meant that the affiant was willing to give information about her sealing to Church authorities but did not want to acknowledge the marriage publicly. Andrew Jenson, "Plural Marriage," 6:234, lists Sylvia as a wife but does not date the marriage. Sylvia's daughter, Josephine Lyon Fisher, said that Sylvia was sealed to Joseph Smith "at a time when [Windsor] Lyon was out of fellowship with the church." Josephine Lyon Fisher, Feb. 24, 1915, typescript statement. However, Compton, *In Sacred Loneliness*, 682, points to the Angus M. Cannon, Statement of interview with Joseph Smith III, Oct. 12, 1905, 25-26, that describes Lyon as being in good standing at the time. Compare Hales, *Joseph Smith's Polygamy*, 1:449.

6. Emmeline B. Wells, "Patty Sessions," *Woman's Exponent* 13 (Sept. 15, 1884): 63; 13 (Nov. 1, 1884): 86.

7. Patty Sessions, Diary, on the page after June 16, 1860, entry. A note most likely added in 1867 clarified the earlier (1860) note. Sylvia's sealing to Joseph Smith was recorded on January 26, 1846, after Joseph's death, with Heber C. Kimball standing as proxy. See Stanley B. Kimball, *Heber C. Kimball*, 313; Donna T. Smart, ed., *Mormon Midwife*, 276-77; John C. Bennett, *History of the Saints*, 256, lists Mrs. S******* as one of Joseph's wives.

Madam [Patty] Sessions, in whom the people have great confidence, but in fact, they are the most depraved hypocrites on Earth. If Joe wishes to make a spiritual wife of a certain young lady, he would send one of these women to her. The old woman, would tell the young lady, that she had, had a vision, in which it was revealed to her that she was to be sealed up to Joe, (or his friend as the case might be) as a spiritual wife, to be his in time and eternity."[8]

If Jackson is accurate, Joseph's elder plural wives understood the duty of "mothering" younger women through their plural marriages, impressing upon them its divine origin, negotiating in Joseph's behalf, and providing a cover of secrecy. Presumably, Patty carried messages secretly for him, pleaded with Joseph's potential wives, and was absolutely devoted to him as prophet, friend, and husband.[9] Patty never claimed that she cohabited with Joseph, which is consistent with the lack of evidence about the nonconnubial pattern of his sealings to older women.[10]

Patty's marriage established the range of possibilities which the ritual of plural unions provided. More than a potential mother or sexual companion, she became a sort of undercover diplomat, representing Joseph in sensitive situations, traveling where he could not in the female world of kitchens, quilting bees, or Relief Society gatherings, and speaking for him, both in his defense and as his representative. Occasionally, she even witnessed the marriages that she had helped to bring about. While contemporary accounts would help to illuminate the way these marriages were argued for and maintained, it must have been an inspiring, flattering proposition for older and younger women alike. Sealed to God's prophet, they must have considered their exaltation guaranteed.

Both Sessions women participated in Emma Smith's all-female Relief Society. On March 24, 1842, Sylvia joined the society. With Patty, she attended several meetings over the following weeks.[11] Their names surface

8. Joseph Jackson, *A Narrative of the Adventures and Experience of Joseph H. Jackson in Nauvoo*, 13-14. Elizabeth Davis Durfee was also an older plural wife, like Patty.

9. Smart, *Mormon Midwife*, 22-23.

10. Patty and Sylvia are the only mother-daughter pair for which documented sealings exist, although there is circumstantial evidence that Phoebe Watrous Woodworth and her daughter, Flora, may have formed another pair. Flora's sealing occurred sometime during the spring of 1843; Phoebe's is less documented. Gary James Bergera, "Identifying the Earliest Mormon Polygamists, 1841-44," 30-31, points to Phoebe's possible status as a plural wife based on her posthumous sealing to Joseph on January 17, 1846. Todd Compton, *In Sacred Loneliness*, 8, 171, 391, points out the absence of contemporary evidence for a marriage during Joseph's lifetime. See also Smith, *Nauvoo Polygamy*, 168-72; compare Hales, *Joseph Smith's Polygamy*, 1:331, for Flora Ann Woodworth.

11. Relief Society, Minutes, Mar. 24, 1842.

occasionally in the minutes. On April 19, for instance, one of the sisters spoke in tongues, while Patty translated.[12] Like Zina and Presendia, they were prepared to live in radically altered ways to conform to the directives of God through his prophet Joseph.

Relief Society validated the collective efforts of women to contribute to the building of community and the sharing of spiritual gifts. For more than ten years, they had watched their husbands gather for priesthood councils. Relief Society gave women the same chance for the performance of gendered religious identity. For women like Sylvia and Patty, the opportunity must have satisfied their hunger for a tangible expression of their faith. Patty's journal attests to her engagement in Mormonism, an activity level that typified the life practices of the women Joseph married. On June 23, 1842, Patty attended Relief Society and the next day visited a public meeting of Masons. The following day, she visited Lucy Mack Smith, her unknowing mother-in-law, then heard Brigham Young preach in the morning and Reynolds Cahoon in the afternoon. With her family, she attended the 4th of July parade, Relief Society on the 7th, and, on the 10th, went again to the grove for instruction from Wilford Woodruff. This two-week round summed up the mix of the sacred and profane that was typical for citizens of the Mormon kingdom on the Mississippi River.[13]

When David Sessions was called on a proselytizing mission on June 11, 1842, Patty recorded, "He left me alone, and I am very lonesome."[14] Visits from Joseph cheered her up, and she was active as a midwife. At the epicenter of the female community at Nauvoo, Patty often saw Church leaders or other elite members.[15] Patty referred to Joseph or to members of his family twenty-six times between August 1842 and February 1844.[16] She recorded on August 12 that she was "making shirts for Bro. Joseph."[17] On one occasion Joseph blessed her, placing his hands on her head to pray. "From that time she speaks of Joseph having visited at her house almost daily," according to Emmeline B. Wells, "on the 12th of February she says Brother Joseph was at her house, and Mr. Lyons, Sylvia's husband, lent him five hundred

12. Ibid., Apr. 19, 1842.

13. Wells, "Patty Sessions," Nov. 1, 1884, 86.

14. Ibid. Patty's diary for some of this period is not extant, but Emmeline B. Wells had access to it for this *Woman's Exponent* article.

15. Smart, *Mormon Midwife*, 22.

16. Ibid., 23.

17. Wells, "Patty Sessions," Nov. 15, 1884, 94.

dollars."[18] This was five days before the birth of Sylvia's daughter, Josephine, apparently named for the prophet. Patty's midwife services were in demand at birthings or to prepare the dead, and she regularly attended weekday prayer meetings and Sunday preaching services.

On March 20, 1842, Joseph spoke at the grove near the Nauvoo temple construction site at Marian Lyon's funeral, Sylvia and Windsor's two-year-old daughter. In this sermon, he preached the view that children who died "will be enthroned in the presence of God and the Lamb with bodies of the same stature that they had on earth."[19] Only a handful of people knew that the dead child was, in a doctrinal sense, sealed to him in the afterlife by virtue of his and Sylvia's sealing. Such relationships added a poignancy even to the most ordinary occasion.

Moving in Joseph's visionary world required faith. A glimpse of the possible demands made on that faith comes from the account of Eudocia Baldwin Marsh, age thirteen in 1842, who visited Nauvoo occasionally during the early 1840s with her family. Curiosity motivated their brief passage into the Mormon world, as it did other tourists. When they dined at the Mansion House where Joseph and his family were living, Joseph's mother took them, for a small fee, on a guided tour of the room where the Kirtland Egyptian mummies were displayed. Eudocia recalled Mother Smith as possessing a tendency toward dramatics: "With a long wand she pointed out to us the old King Pharaoh of the Exodus himself, with wife and daughter, and gave us a detailed account of their lives and doings three thousand years before." When Eudocia asked her how she knew this, "she replied in a severely virtuous tone and manner calculated to repress all doubt and further question–'My Son Joseph Smith has recently received a revelation from the Lord in regard to these people and times–and he has told all these things to me.'" Eudocia and her family were unpersuaded: "We left the house without faith in these revelations–neither did we believe in the old ladies faith in them which seemed hard on the mother of the 'Prophet.'"[20]

Joseph's performance of religious identity captivated some with deathless loyalty and left others repelled. Grand, outlandish rumors sometimes swirled around the Mormon city, drawing in the curious and the converted alike. But for male converts, at least, nothing they could imagine surpassed

18. Ibid., 95.

19. *History of the Church*, 4:555-56 (Mar. 20, 1842).

20. Lucy Mack Smith, qtd. in Marsh, "Reminiscences," in Hallwas and Launius, *Cultures in Conflict*, 32.

what Joseph promised. Patriarchs each who passed their mortal test would preside eternally over a family kingdom with wives and children. Celestial glory was reserved for the married, and the much-married extended their kingdom dramatically.

Joseph dictated a revelation on priesthood quorums and baptism for the dead on January 1, 1842. The revelation positions Hyrum with Joseph as members of a kind of joint presidency over the Church. It also made provision for a bishop to serve churchwide: "his reward shall not fail, if he receive counsel; and for his love he shall be great, for he shall be mine if he do this, saith the Lord" (D&C 124:92-96).

Three months later, Joseph released for the first time ever an account for widespread public consumption of his first vision, publishing a narrative in the April 1, 1842, issue of the *Times and Seasons.* Joseph candidly described himself as an adolescent "frequently [falling] into many foolish errors and display[ing] the weakness of youth and the corruption of human nature, which I am sorry to say led me into divers temptations, to the gratification of many appetites offensive in the sight of God. In consequence of these things I often felt condemned for my weakness, and imperfections."[21]

Also in early 1842, Joseph picked up his Book of Abraham translation after some six years. The stories this text added to the Bible's fleshed out a vision of heaven, premortal existence, and the role of human beings in kingdom building. Equally important were the relationships between Abraham and Sarah and those around them in modeling the relationships that Joseph himself created during the Nauvoo years–including plurality. He positioned this practice in both the ancient Abrahamic tradition and in a vision of prophets, God, and men and what they can and cannot do. The narrative in the Book of Abraham differs subtly from the biblical account. According to Joseph's translation, God instructs Abraham to lie to the Pharaoh about Sarah's marital status with Abraham coaching Sarah. The measure of what was true and good became a sort of amorphous web instead of a set of absolutes. The story of Abraham helped Joseph justify what he did with his own prophet-narrative.[22]

Joseph saw the priesthood as the means of "accomplishing all things." And he saw the organization of the priesthood as a means for preparing or "ordering" the Church through instructions, though the endowment, and

21. "History of Joseph Smith," 3, no. 11:749.

22. Susan Staker, "'The Lord Said, Thy Wife Is a Very Fair Woman to Look Upon,'" 291.

through special blessings of authority, including the receipt of spiritual authority and power. As Church president, Joseph "ordered" the First Presidency, which in turn "ordered" the Twelve, who then ordered the Seventies, and so forth. Joseph's narrative often incorporated creation stories, which explains why he may have felt a special affinity for the Masonic ritual and the creation accounts that appear in the temple endowment and in the Book of Abraham. Demonstrating that the creation of the earth had been an orderly, rational process, these stories embodied hierarchical sequences and the place of human and divine beings in it. It was only one additional step more to add the same hierarchy to the narrative of Joseph's story and the potential godhood narrative that each individual could script through obedience and ritual.

Priesthood keys justified and empowered Joseph. Understanding this authority explains Joseph's belief in the superiority of God's law over civil law, including marriage laws. Joseph saw marriage as part of a celestial design. This attitude had begun as early as November 23, 1835, when he performed the marriage of Lydia Goldthwait Bailey, abandoned by her first husband but not divorced, to Newel K. Knight. According to Knight, "President Smith said many things relative to marriages anciently, which were yet to be revealed."[23] This frame anchored marriage in the world of ancient prophets. Because "marriage was an institution of heaven … it was necessary it should be solemnized by the authority of the everlasting Priesthood."[24]

Joseph continued to reflect throughout the first half of 1842 on his role as a prophet. Periodically, he became weary with the prophet's mantle and sometimes insisted instead that a prophet is a prophet "only when he is acting as such."[25] His self-reflection was stimulated by his own desire to reconcile his role with his perception of God and by a stream of reactions to his "prophethood" from others. Both skeptics and admirers found it impossible to avoid measuring his every word, expression, act against their own sense of what a prophet should be. Joseph also found himself reflecting on the prophet's role in society at large. Coupled with his experience at seeing the government fail to protect his kingdom-building efforts, Joseph's thoughts began to include musings on a more appropriate government structure.

Giving special weight to Joseph's positioning of the prophet role was his view of the end times. His view of the world was apocalyptic, a world

23. Newel Knight, "Autobiography Sketch," 5.

24. *History of the Church*, 2:320.

25. Joseph Smith, Diary, Feb. 8, 1842, in Scott H. Faulring, ed., *An American Prophet's Record*, 299.

reeling in sin and ready to collapse. Brooding, he announced to a congregation of Saints gathered on a hot, muggy Friday afternoon in July 1842: "The great and wise of ancient days have failed in all their attempts to promote eternal power, peace, and happiness. Their nations have crumbled to pieces … Where is there a man that can step forth and alter the destiny of nations and promote the happiness of the world?" Standing now before them, he might have answered. Indeed, Nauvoo's *raison d'être* was that as "God's people, under His direction, and obedient to His law, we may grow up in righteousness and truth; that when His purposes shall be accomplished, we may receive an inheritance among those that are sanctified."[26] For Joseph, the ideal government was a theocracy led by a prophet, advised by good, intelligent counselors and keenly alive to the laws of both God and man.[27]

Closer to home, Joseph managed the fortunes of his own family as well as, when needed, those of others. Soon after the death of baby Don Carlos on September 15, 1841, Joseph brokered, in January 1842, an arrangement that would help Emma move through her grief: Emma would tend one of William and Anna McIntire's twins during the day. Both Joseph and Emma became attached to little Mary. Emma stopped tending the baby when her grief eased. Eventually, Mary stayed home with her mother, and when Mary unexpectedly died the next year, Emma again had to face the sadness of losing a child she had loved.[28] Meanwhile, Joseph expanded Emma's activities. She had his power of attorney in ordering, receiving, and paying for the "states' goods" he would sell in his planned mercantile establishment.[29] Joseph additionally asked for Emma's help in appraising tithing donations of city lots, acreage, and goods of various types for sale.

For a time during early 1842, the Mormon prophet enjoyed standing personally behind the counter of his new mercantile store. It is easy to imagine Joseph as a merchant, a social role that provided him an opportunity to visit with neighbors and friends, to chat about the goods he had for sale and the news about town. The store was located where Granger and Water Streets intersected, not far from Joseph's house. A two-story red brick building, it was a vernacular, but proud structure, the backdrop to sacred ritual on the second floor and temporal exchange in goods on the first.

26. *History of the Church*, 5:64 (June 15, 1842).

27. Ibid.

28. Linda King Newell and Valeen Tippets Avery, Mormon Enigma, 103-104.

29. Joseph Smith, Letter to Edward Hunter, Jan. 5, 1842, in Dean C. Jessee, ed., *Personal Writings of Joseph Smith*, 541-44.

"The painting of the store," Joseph proudly wrote on opening day, "has [been] executed by some of our English brethren; . . and the counters, drawers– & pillars present a very respectable representation of oak, mahogany & marble for a back woods establishment."[30] By this he meant that, in the main room with its ten-foot ceilings, the counters were marbleized; and the pillars, which stood every twelve feet or so, were paint-grained with a feather to look like mahogany and maple.[31]

Joseph continued:

> ... we have been enabled to secure goods ... sufficient to fill all the shelves as soon as they were completed, and have some in reserve, both in loft and cellar. ... [T]he hearts of many of the poor brethren and sisters will be made glad with those comforts which are now within their reach. ... I have stood behind the counter all day, dealing out goods as steady as any cleark you ever saw ... I love to wait upon the Saints, and be a servant to all, hoping that I may be exalted in the due time of the Lord.[32]

Although the store brought "states' goods" to Nauvoo, it operated on a liberal credit policy, suggesting prosperity even as it also eroded its own foundations. Joseph's objectives were more about stocking the temporal kingdom than drawing a strong cash profit.

A small hall gave access to the staircase leading to the upper floor. A cellar was downstairs on the left, and a private room to the right could be used as an office. Counters lined the walls. Before one came to the bottom of the stairs, Joseph's private office door opened across from a window to the south which provided a view of the river. Joseph kept his sacred writings there and spent countless hours contemplating the view of the river, which "constitutes a peculiarly interesting situation, in prospect & no less interesting from its retirement from the bustle & confusion of the neighborhood & city, and altogether is a place the Lord is pleased to bless."[33]

Whatever commerce was taking place in Joseph's red brick store, even more important for the Church was the activity upstairs. Positioned over the main room, it could hold some thirty people seated comfortably, more if they stood. It rapidly became a central meeting place for Church officers, and Joseph sat in council with city government or Church officials virtually

30. Ibid., 542-43.
31. Ibid., 543.
32. Ibid.
33. Ibid., 542.

every evening in this room. Here doctrine was expounded, revelations dictated, rituals performed, and unique bonds formed among male leaders and between husbands and wives.

In addition to Joseph's store, the temple and the Nauvoo House also competed for stock, cash, materials, and other limited resources. "The eight hundred dollars for the Temple and Nauvoo House, I wish you to bring in goods," Joseph wrote to Edward Hunter in March 1842, for "which I will give you stock & credit as soon as Received." He warned that there was virtually no paper money in the city, and even bank loans could not be depended on. "I would say that Gold and Silver is the only safe money a man can keep these times." If Hunter could bring hard currency, he could command a return disproportionate to what it might earn in interest at a bank.[34] In letters on both March 9 and 11, Joseph told Hunter he had purchased the lands Hunter had asked for and would make sure that needed improvements were made. As for Joseph himself, he had a new interest: "I am now very busily engaged in Translating [the Book of Abraham], and therefore cannot give as much time to Public matters as I could wish, but will nevertheless do what I can to forward your affairs."[35]

After being in the mercantile business for less than three months, Joseph had already lost interest in it and was hoping, pending a mutually beneficial arrangement, to turn its management over to the more solvent Hunter. "You can have my new brick store to rent," he wrote expansively. "… [I]t is a very fine house, and cost me a handsome sum."[36]

By the end of March 1842, references to the store disappear from Joseph's journal. The Church was absorbing his time and energy. Moreover, even during his period of greatest involvement–January through March 1842–Joseph never devoted his full attention to the store's daily operation. In May 1844, two years after Joseph established the business, the *Nauvoo Neighbor* announced that non-Mormon Hiram Kimball had purchased the building and was opening a "general dry goods store."[37] Being a storekeeper required more skill and attention than Joseph possessed or could devote. If little else, the store gave Joseph the opportunity to visit with friends and strangers, thus showcasing his interpersonal strengths.

The weather during that January 1842 was usually severe. Instead of

34. Smith, Letter to Hunter, Mar. 9, 1842, in Jesse, *Personal Writings of Joseph Smith*, 549-50.
35. Ibid., 550.
36. Ibid.
37. Qtd. in Roger D. Launius and F. Mark McKiernen, *Joseph Smith, Jr.'s Red Brick Store*, 18.

taking the stand outdoors, Joseph preached in more intimate settings, including the Homestead during both the morning and evening of Sunday, January 16, "illustrating the nature of Sin and shewing that it is not right to sin that grace may abound."[38] The Smiths opened their home to Saints who craved spiritual guidance. Joseph "engaged in Counselling the Saints" in his home on January 30 "concerning the different Spirits, their operations, [and] designs," then again on February 27.[39] He spoke at Orson Spencer's home near the temple site on March 6 and in other indoors locations wherever a crowd gathered.[40] His followers never tired of hearing him weave a story about heaven and their place in it. Joseph, for his part, never seemed to tire of drawing an image of what was possible.

Later in Utah, Jedediah M. Grant commented that "in his [Joseph's] day the brethren would not build a log cabin till they went to Joseph to ask counsel how they should set it whare they should put the door &c."[41] Grant may have exaggerated for effect, but his comments capture a vignette of eager followers seeking every possible occasion to approach Joseph and of Joseph reciprocating for the sheer pleasure of the warm interaction. As Joseph moved through Nauvoo, he was organizing the business of a city, the affairs of a church, and forging eternally lasting relationships.

Regional newspapers, in contrast, seem to have blasted Joseph's every move. The *Sangamo Journal,* for one, regularly attacked Joseph's rule until his death. The *Peoria [Illinois] Register* and *Northwestern Gazetteer* editorialized on January 21, 1842, against the Mormons' political position:

> As we at various times expressed ourselves pretty decidedly against political tendencies of this sect, ... we cannot be charged with sudden hostility now that their leader has gone over, horse, foot, and dragoons, to our opponents. This is probably the first time that a public manifesto of this sort has been issued by a religious leader of this country. ... we have no recollection anywhere of a movement similar to that of the Mormon prophet. We trust that all parties will see its dangerous tendency, and at once rebuke it.[42]

---

38. Joseph Smith, Diary, Jan. 16, 1842, in Scott H. Faulring, ed., *An American Prophet's Record*, 244.

39. Ibid.

40. Joseph Smith, Diary, Mar. 6, 1842, in ibid., 244.

41. Jedediah M. Grant, qtd. in Scott G. Kenney, ed., *Wilford Woodruff's Journal, 1833-1898*, 4:193 (Feb. 13, 1853); hereafter Woodruff, *Journal.*

42. "Remarks," *Peoria Register,* Jan. 21, 1842, www.sidneyrigdon.com/dbroadhu/IL/peor1838.htm#012142 (accessed Nov. 20, 2008).

James Arlington Bennet in New York City published both Mormon apologetics and, simultaneously, stories of the misuse of power and scandalous behavior in Nauvoo. He was attempting to achieve some measure of balance in depicting the Mormon prophet's life, a fairly unusual stance for nineteenth-century journalists. On January 15, 1842, for example, he editorialized: "The Mormons under the guidance of their great prophet and seer, the famous Joe Smith, are organizing a religious empire in the far west that will astonish the world in these latter days. Civil, religious, military, judicial, social, moral, advertising, commercial organization, are all embraced within the comprehensiveness of their new system ..." Recognizing that Joseph's bustling city was not just another Midwestern river town but the genesis of a religious movement, he continued: "The astonishing mixture of world prudence and religious enthusiasm ... is without parallel in the history of nations since the time of Mahomet. The model of Joe Smith, the Mormon Prophet seems to be great Jewish legislator, Moses."[43]

The national press often remarked on the kingdom-building efforts of the Mormons. The allusion to "kingdom" was powerful and surely influenced Joseph's own thinking on his role. The pomp and circumstance surrounding parades of the Nauvoo Legion bolstered the image he held in his own mind. He had to walk a fine line between impressing outsiders and offending them by such displays of power and force. It seems likely that he felt expansive when he read admiring reports and took a more temperate approach when he read skeptical ones. For example, the editor of the *Sangamo Journal* wrote on January 21, 1842: "If he would take friendly advice, we would say, ... let him [Joseph] stick to interpretation and prophecy,–and for we do assure him upon an honest belief, that his situation in Illinois is far more dangerous than ever it was in Missouri if he undertakes to take Mahomet's part."[44]

On January 13, 1842, Willard Richards moved into Joseph's home. Joseph trusted Richards with a knowledge of his plural relationships, and Richards, as his secretary, provided the aura of respectability as Joseph socialized with plural–or soon-to-be plural–wives. Such contacts helped to strengthen the affective bonds that connected them.

Helen Mar Kimball told how her parents' loyalty was subjected to the supreme test when Joseph informed Heber that the Lord told him, Joseph,

43. James Arlington Bennet, "Highly Important from the Mormon Country on the Mississippi," *New York Herald*, Jan. 15, 1842, www.sidneyrigdon.com/dbroadhu/NY/NYherld0.htm#011542 (accessed Dec. 2008).

44. "Citizens of Illinois–Read and Consider," *Sangamo Journal*, Jan. 21, 1842, 3.

to marry Vilate, Heber's civil wife, to keep this request a secret–including from Vilate. According to Heber's son-in-law, James Lawson, as reported to Orson F. Whitney, Heber's grandson, Heber was "paralyzed" by the idea.[45] Kimball was tormented by doubt.

Vilate could see that Heber was troubled and soon had to confront her own test of faith. Perplexed about Heber's grief, Vilate prayed to know what was troubling him and came to her own understanding of plurality, even as Heber continued to wrestle with Joseph's command to relinquish her.[46] According to Helen Mar, "Before her was illustrated the order of Celestial Marriage, in all its beauty and glory, together with the great exaltation and honor it would confer upon her in that immortal and celestial sphere, if she would accept it … as well as the increase of her husband's kingdoms, and power and glory extending throughout the eternities, worlds without end."[47] According to Helen Mar's son, Orson, after three days of praying and fasting, Heber took Vilate to Joseph's house. Joseph wept, told them he had only been testing them, and then sealed the couple "for all eternity."[48]

Regardless of–or perhaps because of–its Old Testament parallel, this episode seems like an extraordinary exercise of both Joseph's power and his willingness to strain the obedience of others in the name of a religious doctrine. Nevertheless, it demonstrates how badly he needed the support of those around him to complete his narrative of plurality. These Kimball family accounts show the agonizing threshold that believers had to cross to accept the doctrine. Even the most faithful, as Vilate and Heber were, were tested beyond what they had previously known. Plurality would color their lives from that point forward, providing a "before-and-after" benchmark in their lives.

Helen Mar, at age fourteen, followed her parents into plurality, becoming Joseph's wife not quite a year and a half later in May 1843.[49] Heber told his daughter to keep her marriage secret: "you see others walking through trouble and sorrow, because those who have covenanted to be their friends

---

45. Orson F. Whitney, *Life of Heber C. Kimball*, 323.

46. Ibid., 334-35. Helen Mar Whitney included a letter from her father to her mother, June 12, 1844, indicating the great anguish they both felt. Helen Mar Whitney, "Scenes and Incidents in Nauvoo," *Woman's Exponent* 11 (Jan. 1, 1883): 114.

47. Helen Mar Whitney, "Scenes and Incidents in Nauvoo," *Woman's Exponent* 10, no. 10 (Oct. 15, 1881): 74.

48. Orson Whitney, *Life of Heber C. Kimball*, 324.

49. Andrew Jenson, "Plural Marriage," 6:234. Helen Mar Kimball Whitney comments on her marriage to Joseph in her "Scenes and Incidents in Nauvoo," *Woman's Exponent* 10, nos. 9-12 and 19, in Jeni Brobert Holzapfel and Richard Neitzel Holzapfel, eds., *A Woman's View*.

have betrayed them."[50] The decision for the daughter had been no less anguishing than the parents'. Viewing the marriage almost forty years later, Helen Mar believed that her father had wanted to cement a kinship connection to Joseph. "My father had but one Eue lamb, but willingly laid her upon the altar." For Vilate, accepting this decision for her daughter was even harder than accepting Heber's plural marriages. "How cruel this seemed to the mother," recalled Helen Mar, "whose heartstrings were already stretched until they were ready to snap asunder … but the Lord required more."

After Joseph proposed the union to Helen Mar, she struggled for a day and a night, measuring her hoped-for monogamous future against her faith in Joseph. The next day, Joseph assured her: "If you will take this step, it will insure your eternal salvation & exaltation and that of your father's household & all of your kindred." This argument proved decisive: "This promise was so great, that I willingly gave myself to purchase so glorious a reward. None but God & his angels could see my mother's bleeding heart." When Joseph asked for Vilate's consent, the mother reportedly responded: "If Helen is willing I have nothing more to say."[51]

In early 1842, Joseph's marriage to Helen Mar was still more than a year away. On January 21, 1842, Joseph spent the day reading the Book of Mormon, transacting business in both his store and the city, and in the evening was "in the office with Elders John Taylor and Willard Richards interpreting dreams."[52] The next day at the meeting of the Nauvoo City Council, Joseph worked to revise the rules of the council.[53] Although religion permeated all that he did, most of his days passed in relatively common chores. January 27 shows a blend of mundane and ecclesiastical: Joseph "attended to baptism in general," addressed the most pressing business matters, put a new carpet on the floor of his office, and "spent the evening in council."[54] On January 28, he received a revelation to tell the Twelve: "It is my will to have them take in hand the editorial department of the *Times and Seasons* …"[55]

On February 3, Joseph issued a follow-up revelation: "Elder Woodruff took the superintendence of the printing office, and Elder Taylor the

50. Helen Mar Kimball Whitney, Mar. 30, 1881, Autobiography, in Holzapfel and Holzapfel, *A Woman's View*, 482, 486.

51. Ibid.

52. *History of the Church*, 4:501 (Jan. 21, 1842).

53. Ibid., 501 (Jan. 22, 1842).

54. Ibid., 502-503 (Jan. 27, 1842).

55. Ibid., 503 (Jan. 28, 1842).

editorial department ... under the direction of Joseph the Seer."[56] The revelation contained no new assignment for or appreciation of the displaced editor, Ebenezer Robinson. The change became effective with the February 15 issue of the *Times and Seasons.*[57]

The day after the revelation, February 4, Joseph closed the deal with Robinson for the paper inventory, the furniture, the bookbindery, and the stereotype foundry for the price of $7,000 to $8,000.[58] It presumably included the *Times and Seasons* and the building located on the corner of Bain and Water Streets. The printing industry was vitally important to the Church's effort to promulgate its story, publish its scripture, and conduct missionary work. The *Times and Seasons* helped Joseph to craft his prophet-narrative and to create a forum where he could defend policy and practice as his Church faced their enemies.

On February 6, Emma delivered a stillborn son, the sixth of seven children the couple would lose to death. They buried him unnamed.

Joseph became the editor and publisher of the *Times and Seasons* on February 15 and called by the office on the 23rd, stimulated by his new interest–a translation of the Book of Abraham. He instructed engraver Reuben Hedlock about "the cut for the altar and gods in the Record of Abraham, as designed for the *Times and Seasons.*"[59] Apparently John Taylor and Wilford Woodruff had not yet installed themselves as publishers since Joseph gave instructions to Hedlock, not them, about publishing Abraham's record.

56. Ibid., 513 (Feb. 3, 1842). See also Ebenezer Robinson, "Items of Personal History of the Editor," May 1890, 257-62; Hugh Grant Stocks, "The Book of Mormon, 1830-1879," 51-65.

57. Robinson had learned the printing trade in Kirtland, and had been involved in most of the Church's printing ventures since. When the Church press that had printed the *Evening and Morning Star* in Missouri was rescued and brought to Illinois, Joseph assigned his brother, Don Carlos, and Robinson to publish the *Times and Seasons*, using the proceeds to support their families. In 1840, Robinson traveled to Cincinnati, Ohio, to negotiate with a publishing company to stereotype plates for a new edition of the Book of Mormon. Developed during the late eighteenth century, a stereotype plate was more durable than a more traditionally composed page of type, made by locking the type columns and illustration plates for a full page into a form. Then, using papier-mâché or something like it, a matrix or mat would be molded, then dried. It could then be used as a mold so that the stereotype could be cast with hot metal. When Don Carlos died in August 1841, Robinson agreed to sell the printing business to the Church with the understanding, concluded on February 24, 1842, that Robinson had permission to use the stereotype plates to produce a new Book of Mormon edition of 1,500 copies. See Robinson, "Items of Personal History of the Editor," May 1890, 257-62; *History of the Church*, 4:239; Stocks, "The Book of Mormon, 1830-1879," 651. Joseph recorded on February 24, 1842: "Ebenezer Robinson is intitled to the use of the sterotipe plates and Coppy right for the print[in]g [of] fifteen Hundred Books of Mormon." In Jessee, *Personal Writings of Joseph Smith*, 545.

58. *History of the Church*, 4:513-14 (Feb. 4, 1842).

59. Ibid., 518 (Feb. 23, 1842).

Four days earlier, on February 19, Joseph had shown his Book of Abraham manuscript to the Twelve. Woodruff noted that the Old Testament patriarch had "written [it] by his own hand but hid from the knowledge of man for the last four thousand years ... Joseph has had these records in his possession for several years but has never presented them before the world in the English language until now ..." Woodruff continued: "I have had the privilege this day of assisting in setting the TIPE for printing of the first piece of the BOOK OF ABRAHAM ..."[60] Woodruff was no typesetter, and his role must have been largely ceremonial, but it was a way of participating in Joseph's production of new scripture.

February 1842 also saw Joseph's efforts to organize temple crews for maximum productivity,[61] and to improve the city council's operational efficiency. In fact, nothing seemed too insignificant for Joseph's attention. On March 5, he proposed a resolution to "keep [the city's] children at home (except on lawful business) on sundays and from skayting on the ice and from marauding upon their neighbours property and any persons refusing to do the same shall pay five dollars fine for every offence for the same &c."[62] The proposal passed.

60. Woodruff, *Journal*, 2:155 (Feb. 19, 1842).

61. *History of the Church*, 4:517 (Feb. 21, 1842).

62. "A Record of the Proceedings of the City Council," 62, in Jessee, *Personal Writings of Joseph Smith*, 547.

CHAPTER 11

"A Traitor or a True Man"

> *... should the time ever come that I may have the opportunity to test my faith, it will then be known whether I am a traitor or a true man.*
>
> –*John C. Bennett, qtd. in* History of the Church, *5:13 (May 19, 1842)*

Much of the first half of 1842 was marked by a series of explosions forming three intertwined narratives occurring almost simultaneously. Joseph entered more deeply into plurality, only to have the secrecy he imposed on its practice begin to crack. His reliance on John C. Bennett backfired spectacularly as Bennett's own sexual practices contaminated the city. And Joseph's political aspirations led him into meddling in Illinois state politics. As a further catastrophe, an attempt in early May on the life of former Missouri Governor Lilburn Boggs became linked to Joseph through the efforts of Bennett. Although all of these Gorgon's serpents hissed in concert, the Bennett saga links them together, since he launched his next career–that of an energetic anti-Mormon–even before leaving Nauvoo in mid-1842.

Bennett's trajectory through Mormonism was brief, forceful, conflicted. In his wake, he left mangled relationships, demolished trust, political intrigue, and layers of truths and lies. Perhaps any man with equal ambition, charm, and intelligence could have entered the Mormon world as abruptly and advanced as quickly to a position of power and trust. He was arguably one of Joseph's closest confidantes for a period of time. Joseph shared the public stage with Bennett, bestowing on him opportunities to lead. Bennett's influence challenged Joseph's while also supporting it. Before Bennett left Nauvoo, he had held offices in most of the major institutions established in the city. He served as mayor before his fall, as chancellor of the University of Nauvoo and as major general of the Nauvoo Legion. Engendering Joseph's trust as a man of spirit and intellect, he was a member of the First Presidency, master in chancery, secretary of the Masonic lodge, entrepreneur, physician, politician, and president of the Agriculture and Manufacturing Association.[1]

The university Bennett proposed for Nauvoo was not his first creative educational effort. Before coming to Nauvoo, he had campaigned for the incorporation of Indiana University, of Christian College in Albany, Ohio, and tried to raise money by selling diplomas in Indiana and Ohio, among other programs in different locales. Because he was articulate and clever, he built a convincing case for his ideas, persuading a range of persons to support his programs.[2]

Bennett brought energetic vision to Nauvoo, a different angle on the challenges presented in building Zion. He almost single-handedly drafted the city charter which enabled the Mormon prophet in expanding his power, and ushered it through the state legislature. More importantly, he helped to craft the notion of the Mormon kingdom alongside Joseph himself.[3] During the eighteen months that Joseph and Bennett worked more or less together, they publicly praised each other with affectionate, admiring rhetoric. Once Bennett fell from favor, each man hurled accusations to damage or destroy his former boon companion. While it may be impossible to sort fully truth from fiction in the debris left by this warfare, enough moments of enlightenment survive to illuminate what may have been one of Joseph's most significant friendships. Bennett helped Joseph make Mormonism something it was not before he arrived: a stratified and hierarchical landscape of institutions, alliances, intrigues, and plots designed to bolster the kingdom of God, a more economically and politically viable Mormon presence, and a community whose lifestyle mirrored the heaven Joseph portrayed in increasing detail.

Ironically, given the sexual histories of both men, Bennett had evidently drawn a less-than-honest picture of his past when he met Joseph.[4] Behind him in Ohio were children and a wife who reportedly had been unable to tolerate marriage with him any longer. Instead, he had depicted himself as

---

1. "John C. Bennett," *Times and Seasons* 3, no. 19 (Aug. 1, 1842): 868-76. See also Gary James Bergera, "John C. Bennett, Joseph Smith, and the Beginnings of Mormon Plural Marriage in Nauvoo."

2. Andrew F. Smith, *The Saintly Scoundrel,* 13-24.

3. See Leonard J. Arrington, "Centrifugal Tendencies in Mormon History," 168; Andrew C. Skinner, "John C. Bennett: For Prophet or Profit?," 249-85. For a believer's critique of Bennett, see Brian C. Hales, "John C. Bennett and Joseph Smith's Polygamy: Addressing the Question of Reliability," *Journal of Mormon History* 41 (April 2015), no. 2:131-81.

4. Bergera, "John C. Bennett, Joseph Smith, and the Beginnings of Mormon Plural Marriage in Nauvoo," 51, 64.

free of familial responsibilities and seems to have entered with gusto into his own particular interpretation of spiritual wifery.

Once Joseph had confirmed reports regarding Bennett's past, he confronted but continued to depend on him. Thus, Bennett enjoyed access to Joseph and his teachings for almost two years. This continued friendship positioned Bennett to observe Joseph's comings and goings, including his entry into plurality. Bennett knew of the practice and, after he left Nauvoo at the end of June 1842, used this knowledge to challenge Joseph's reputation and the Church's.

In January 1841, Joseph described Bennett as among the "principal men in Illinois, who have listened to the doctrines we promulgate, have become obedient to the faith, and are rejoicing in the same."[5] Thus, it seems certain that Bennett knew something of plurality, whether first-hand or through informed rumors. Reliable stories about plurality encouraged Bennett in increasingly scandalous behavior and, importantly, divided him from Joseph's other trusted leaders. As Bennett accumulated increasing numbers of enemies, his exit from the Church accelerated.

Reacting to being marginalized by Brigham Young, Willard Richards, George Miller, and others, Bennett withdrew into a group of his own devotees. Younger men and women such as Darwin Chase, Mary Clift, Lysander Davis, Chauncey Higbee, Gustavus Hills, Lyman Littlefield, Joel Miles, Sarah Miller, Justus Morse, sisters Margaret and Matilda Nyman, George Thatcher, and Catherine Warren, and especially Joseph's own younger brother William clustered around Bennett, drawn by the allure of the male-centered ritualized domain.[6] Relationships in the Church could be described as concentric circles that spread out from the center of Joseph's charismatic leadership, then moved on to his family, friends, apostles, and those whom they taught. Lyman Littlefield "was taught that doctrine or principle [of plural wives], and conversed upon it with different parties," he remembered, "but I was never taught that doctrine from Joseph Smith, himself personally, but the doctrine was talked of between myself and a great many other

5. *History of the Church*, 4:270 (Jan. 8, 1841).

6. Bergera, "John C. Bennett, Joseph Smith, and the Beginnings of Mormon Plural Marriage in Nauvoo," 77; Danel W. Bachman "A Study of the Mormon Practice of Plural Marriage before the Death of Joseph Smith," 130-33. "Many even of the 'good Mormons' have always believed that Joseph taught Bennett of the proposed introduction of polygamy," wrote T. B. H. Stenhouse, who originally converted to the LDS Church and later left it, "but that Bennett ran ahead of his teacher, and introduced free-loveism in its broadest sense." T. B. H. Stenhouse, *The Rocky Mountain Saints*, 184. See also Gary James Bergera, "'Illicit Intercourse,' Plural Marriage, and the Nauvoo Stake High Council," 67-73.

parties, and always with the understanding that it had its origin with Joseph Smith the Prophet, himself."[7]

Joseph's and Bennett's involvements with Sarah Pratt, Marinda Hyde, and Nancy Rigdon (see chap. 12) bubbled just beneath the surface during these months. Bennett had access to young men and women who were most likely intrigued by the implications of plurality. They hung on his and William Smith's hints about Joseph's proposals, his courting, and the implications of both. But the rules of Bennett and Joseph's relationship ultimately drove a wedge between them. Why was Joseph free to enter plurality, but Bennett not? Why did Joseph's proposals to young women hold the promise of heaven, but Bennett's a future of certain ruin?

Joseph fell back on the Nauvoo High Council to shine a light on the sordid truths and half-truths that made many believe they were free to enter illicit sexual relationships. Joseph told the council only as much as he thought they needed to know, keeping most of his teachings regarding plurality a secret (at least until August 1843). Joseph adopted this same strategy with the Church generally. During the first half of 1842, rumors circulated that some of the Twelve Apostles were "very intimate with females." Hyrum, himself still oblivious to the full meaning of Joseph's teachings, publicly repudiated the stories "alleging [that] a sister ... had been shut in a room for several days, and that they had endeavored to induce her to believe in having two wives" (see chap. 12). Joseph added that no one who was "acquainted with our principles who would believe such lies."[8] Three days later, Joseph "pronounced a curse upon all adulterers, and fornicators, and unvirtuous persons" who had utilized his "name to carry on their iniquitous designs." These statements did not explicitly name Bennett or his followers, but the implication was clear.[9]

On April 28, 1842, speaking to the Relief Society sisters, Joseph lashed out at his opponents and complained about "the difficulties he had to

7. Lyman O. Littlefield, Testimony, 149, question 19, in Temple Lot Case, Respondents' Testimony. The knowledge impacted Littlefield. "It is well known to yourself as to me," he wrote to Joseph Smith in 1844, "that there has a difference existed between us for sometime. ... I have, at times, been very weak in the faith, but I thank my God that I have never lifted my voice or pen in denunciations of Mormonism. ... I close by saying it is human to err, but magnanimous to forgive." Littlefield, Letter to Joseph Smith, Feb. 10, 1844. Littlefield talked carefully about his involvement with Bennett and those who grouped around him in his memoirs: Lyman Omer Littlefield, *Reminiscences of Latter-day Saints*, 157-59.

8. Smith, *Saintly Scoundrel*, 85, quoting Oliver Olney. *History of the Church*, 4:111 (Apr. 7, 1842).

9. *History of the Church*, 4:589 (Apr. 10, 1842).

surmount ever since the commencement of the work in consequence of aspiring men '[g]reat big Elders' as he called them, who had caused him much trouble, to whom he had taught the things of the kingdom in the private council; and they would go forth into the world and proclaim the things he had taught them; as their own revelations."[10] Joseph's complaint reads as another veiled reference to Bennett.

Joseph continued his mixed message, praising the women's virtuous activities but reminding them of their subordinate roles: "He said if one member becomes corrupt, and you know it you must immediately put it away. … [P]ut down iniquity and by your good example provoke the Elders to good works,–if you do right, no danger of going too fast." Yet he also checked them. The Relief Society must receive instruction "through the order which God has established thro' the medium of those appointed to lead"–namely, Joseph himself.[11]

Virtually everywhere he went, Joseph was asked to speak. When he did, he framed the experience of the Church in the larger drama of his prophet-narrative of villains determined to ruin to the Saints. Told with the same literary devices as the most gripping novel, the plots and subplots were sometimes obvious and sometimes subtle, but always tied to the lived experiences of the Mormons on the earth and their future lives in heaven. Like a complicated code, the layered stories told at least two tales, one public, one private, clarifying and confusing simultaneously. He seemed compelled, even obsessed, to talk through his perplexing relationships. Bennett was one.

When Joseph spoke on May 1, 1842, to a gathering of Saints, it was nothing new. His words, however, again held hidden meaning for those whom he had drawn into his inner circle. There were "certain signs and words by which false spirits and personages may be detected from true, which cannot be revealed to the Elders till the Temple is completed. … The Elders must know them all to be endowed with power," he announced. "… No one can truly say he knows God until he has handled something, and this can only be in the Holiest of Holies."[12] For those who shared a secret knowledge of plurality, the prophet warned them to follow him because he

10. Relief Society, Minutes, Apr. 28, 1842, 37. Also in *History of the Church*, 4:604 (Apr. 28, 1842).

11. Relief Society, Minutes, Apr. 28, 1842, 37. Also in *History of the Church*, 4:607 (Apr. 28, 1842).

12. Joseph Smith, Diary, May 1, 1842, in Scott H. Faulring, ed., *An American Prophet's Record*, 245.

not only spoke with God but also knew the truth and had the power to discern who did not.

Joseph struggled to keep his people's loyalty during that spring, both praising them and invoking the authority that set him apart and above them all. On May 2, the day after this sermon, he published an editorial in the *Times and Seasons,* reminding the Saints that "the building up of Zion is as much one's business as another. The only difference is that one is called to fulfil one duty and another another duty; ... party feelings, separate interests, exclusive designs should be lost sight [of] in the one common cause, in the interest of the whole."[13]

Military display helped to rally Nauvoo's citizenry through community theater performed on the fields of God's city. On May 7, the Nauvoo Legion held a day-long muster as part of a "Programme Militaire," complete with "an animated sham battle." Joseph made an "appropriate" address in which he asserted "that his soul was never better satisfied than on this occasion." He was particularly flattered that Judge Stephen Douglas attended "the splendid military parade of the Legion."[14] At the end of the day, Joseph invited Bennett to join Douglas and other special guests for dinner in Joseph's home. Later, however, Joseph turned paranoid, convincing himself that Bennett had been plotting his death, and that only the watchfulness of the captain of his bodyguards had kept him safe.[15]

At the time, relations between Joseph and Bennett looked more like the chaos produced by a dysfunctional family, but others impacted by Bennett worked to reign him in. On the same day, the Nauvoo Masonic Lodge held a special meeting. Grandmaster Abraham Jonas had a letter from "a valued and esteemed Brother" read to the group. Echoing the earlier message about Bennett's scandalous behavior, the letter claimed that Bennett was "any thing but a good and true Mason."[16] The mounting evidence against Bennett–including the claim that a lodge in Ohio had disqualified him for

13. "The Temple," *Times and Seasons* 3, no. 13 (May 1, 1842): 776.

14. *History of the Church*, 5:3 (May 7, 1842).

15. Ibid. Joseph's suspicions–or perhaps his scribe's–emerge in the May 7 entry in *History of the Church*: "If General Bennett's true feelings toward me are not made manifest to the world in a very short time, then it may be possible that the gentle breathings of that Spirit, which whispered me on parade, that there was mischief concealed in that sham battle, were false ..." Bennett's biographer notes that the "*History of the Church* was compiled after Joseph's death and was probably written by Willard Richards, who was extremely anti-Bennett. No collaborative support for the assassination attempt has been located in Joseph Smith's writings." Smith, *The Saintly Scoundrel*, 85.

16. Joseph King, Letter to M. Helm, May 17,1842, LDS Church History Library.

cause–made it increasingly difficult for Joseph to hope for his reformation. Twelve days later on May 19, Thomas Grover, a Mason and member of the Nauvoo High Council, formally charged Bennett for violating Masonic regulations; Bennet had thirteen days to respond.[17]

This independent corroboration pushed Joseph into action. He decided that Bennett posed a threat.[18] On May 16, Joseph met with Brigham Young, Heber C. Kimball, Willard Richards, and others to discuss how to force Bennett to leave the Church while avoiding public embarrassment by formally excommunicating him. Possibly they planned for a worst-case scenario and drafted documents, if needed, for Bennett's excommunication.[19]

A common challenge with narratives like Joseph's is that imposing a single plot on the historical process excludes stories of the "Other," as Bennett became, while privileging the stories of powerful insiders. Ten days after the ill-fated muster and Masonic meeting, Bennett met with the city council and resigned as mayor on May 17.[20] He also signed an affidavit that exonerated Joseph from accusations that had not yet been made. Bennett asserted that he "was never taught anything in the least contrary to the strictest principles of the Gospel, or of virtue or of the laws of God or man, under any circumstances, or upon any occasion, either directly or indirectly, in word or deed, by Joseph Smith, and that he never knew the said Smith to countenance any improper conduct whatever either in public or private … that an illegal, illicit intercourse justifiable, and that I never knew him to so teach others."[21]

The meeting concluded with Joseph's instructions to the Church's

17. Because the lodge had no evidence to support the charges against Bennett on June 2, the investigation was postponed. On June 16, Bennett presented "various documents from men of high standing in Society in the Willoughby, and some from brethren of the Fraternity in the same neighborhood … showing the high estimation in which he was held by those gentlemen." He also showed them another "communication … breathing the most friendly feelings, and in the strongest language soliciting the continuance of former friendship, and further in consequence of his still urging that if he had been so expelled he never had been informed of the circumstance until the same was read in a communication from Grand Master A. Jonas." Mervin B. Hogan, "The Confrontation of Grand Master Abraham Jonas and John Cook Bennett at Nauvoo," qtd. in Andrew F. Smith, *Saintly Scoundrel*, 77. The case was once again put off, this time for July. By that time, Bennett was no longer in the city.

18. Bergera, "John C. Bennett, Joseph Smith, and the Beginnings of Plural Marriage in Nauvoo," 83n189, suggests another scenario–that Joseph would denounce Bennett publicly and excommunicate him, but then reinstate him. Bergera bases this on Joseph's statement to William Clayton on October 19, 1843: If Clayton's plural marriage caused any public difficulty, he would give Clayton "an awful scourging & probably cut you off from the church and then I will baptize you & set you ahead as good as ever" (quoting George D. Smith, ed., *An Intimate Chronicle*, 122).

19. *History of the Church*, 5:11 (May 16, 1842).

20. Ibid., 12 (May 19, 1842).

21. Ibid., 11 (May 17, 1842).

general recorder: "You will be so good as to permit Gen[eral] Bennett to withdraw his Name from the Church Records, if he desires to do so, and this with the best of feelings towards you and General Bennett." The recorder duly noted Bennett's withdrawal with "the best of feelings Subsisting between all Parties."[22]

The city council soon met again and elected Joseph as mayor, Hyrum as vice-mayor, and William Smith as city councilman, erasing Bennett from the public record.[23] (William's status as Joseph's brother trumped any taint of his association with Bennett.) It was a carefully staged occasion. Joseph addressed the council "at some length concerning the evil reports which were abroad in the city concerning himself–& the necessity of counteracting the designs of our enemies."[24] Already in possession of Bennett's affidavit, he asked Bennett "if he had aught against me." Bennett stood, faced the room, and delivered his assigned lines:

> I publicly avow that any one who has said that I have stated that General Joseph Smith has given me authority to hold illicit intercourse with women is a liar in the face of God. Those who have said it are damned liars; they are infernal liars. He never either in public or private gave me any such authority or license, and any person who states it is a scoundrel and a liar. I have heard it said … that I was at variance with the heads, and would use an influence against them, because I resigned the office of mayor. This is false … and I intend to continue with you, and hope the time may come when I may be restored to full confidence, fellowship, and my former standing in the Church …

Joseph pushed with increasingly aggressive questions. Did Bennett have any accusations about Joseph's behavior "in public or private?" Bennett did not: "In all my intercourse with General Smith, in public and private, he has been strictly virtuous." Joseph then hammered away at the rumor-mongers: "If they will not repent and stop their lyings and surmisings, let God curse them …"[25]

During the next few weeks, more details emerged of Bennett's private teachings about spiritual wives. The Nauvoo High Council determined that Bennett had caused sufficient harm to justify his expulsion, even though he had already resigned. Would they have taken this public action without Joseph's permission–even his encouragement? It seems unlikely.

22. John C. Bennett, *History of the Saints*, 41.
23. *History of the Church*, 5:12 (May 19, 1842).
24. Dean C. Jessee, ed., *The Papers of Joseph Smith*, 2:384.
25. *History of the Church*, 5:13-14 (May 19, 1842).

Furthermore, Joseph attended the next high council meeting after becoming mayor, and was present when they began the hearing to expel Chauncey Higbee, brother of Francis Higbee, and colonel in the Nauvoo Legion, because of "unchaste and unvirtuous conduct with the widow Miller and others."[26] Higbee denied the charges and asked that the trial be continued so that he could better defend himself.[27] The high council proceeded regardless. Margaret J. Nyman, Matilda Nyman, and Sarah Miller herself testified that Higbee "had seduced them, and at different times been guilty of unchaste and unvirtuous conduct with them and taught them, the doctrine that it was right to have free intercourse with women if it was kept secret &c and also taught that Joseph Smith authorized him to practise these things."[28]

The case was widely publicized and must have been a final nail in the coffin of Bennett's reputation. Emma Smith, addressing the Relief Society the same day, lamented: "[T]his day was an evil day–that there is as much evil in this as in any other place–said she would that this Society were pure before God–that she was afraid that under existing circumstances, the sisters were not careful enough to expose iniquity–the time had been when charity had covered a multitude of sins–but now it is necessary that sin should be expos'd–that heinous sins were among us–that much of this iniquity was practiced by some in authority, pretending to be sanction'd by Prest. Smith." Eliza R. Snow's minutes continue: "Mrs. Prest. .... exhort[ed] all who had err'd to repent and forsake their sins–said that Satan's forces were against this church. that every saint should be at the post."[29] A month later, Eliza would be sealed to Joseph as his newest plural wife.

Stories about plurality oozed through Nauvoo's streets and alleys. What would follow? On May 24, Sarah Miller, Margaret Nyman, and Matilda Nyman testified again, each adding more scandalous detail to her stories.[30]

The parade continued when the high council heard testimony from Catherine Fuller Warren about her "unchaste and unvirtuous conduct with John C. Bennett and others." She made a tearful confession, giving

> the names of several others who had been guilty of having unlawful intercourse with her stated that they taught the doctrine that it was right to

26. Ibid., 14-18 (May 22-24, 1842); Nauvoo High Council, Minutes, May 20, 1842. Sarah Searcy Miller was born on March 15, 1815, and had married James Miller.

27. Nauvoo High Council, Minutes, May 20, 1842.

28. Ibid.

29. Relief Society, Minutes, May 19, 1842.

30. Nauvoo High Council, Minutes, May 24, 1842.

> have free intercourse with women and that the heads of the Church also taught and practised it, which things caused her to be led away thinking it to be right but becoming convinced that it was not right and learning that the heads of the church did not believe nor practise such things she was willing to confess her sins and did repent before God for what she had done and desired earnestly that the Council would forgive her and covenanted that she would hence forth do so no more.[31]

The high council "by unanimous vote … restored [Fuller] to fellowship" and then excommunicated Bennett for "his wicked and licentious conduct."[32] The next day, Bennett, informed "that the First Presidency, Twelve, and Bishops had withdrawn fellowship from him … acknowledged his sins," reportedly confessed that "he was worthy of the severest chastisements, and cried like a child, and begged that he might be spared, in any possible way; so deep was his apparent sense of guilt … so deeply did he feign, or really feel contrition, that he was forgiven still."[33] His only request was to keep the news out of the paper "for his mother's sake."[34]

Later, the Nauvoo High Council issued a public statement that Bennett had been excommunicated on May 11–before he had resigned. This ex post facto punishment served the council's need for retribution but did not necessarily reflect the true sequence of events.[35] The excommunication was not, however, publicly announced until the June 15 issue of the *Times and Seasons.*[36] It was signed by Joseph among others with the prominent exception of Orson Pratt (who was probably still struggling over reports that Joseph had tried to seduce his wife).

After Bennett's capitulation, he met with Brigham Young and Wilson Law, asking their help in recovering his position with Joseph. He also begged Sidney Rigdon for help. But the stories of his seductions, the lies about his former life, and allegations of abortion and even prostitution were simply too shocking.[37]

---

31. Ibid., May 25, 1842.
32. *History of the Church*, 5:18 (May 26, 1842).
33. Ibid., 19 (May 26, 1842).
34. Ibid., 18-19 (May 25, 1842); see also Brigham Young, qtd. in "Notice," *Times and Seasons* 3, no. 16 (May 11, 1842): 830; Hyrum Smith, "Notice," *Times and Seasons* 3, no. 19 (Aug. 1, 1842): 872.
35. William Law made an affidavit that was published in the *Times and Seasons* that Bennett's excommunication preceded his resignation. It is unclear if he witnessed the deliberations or if his testimony was based on hearsay. "Notice," *Times and Seasons* 3 no. 19 (Aug. 1, 1842): 872.
36. "Notice," *Times and Seasons* 3, no. 16 (June 15, 1842): 830.
37. Smith, *Saintly Scoundrel*, 90.

On May 26, Bennett, standing before a hundred men in the Masonic Hall, reportedly told much of his story of sin and seduction through tears.[38] Joseph was so moved that he asked for forbearance for his former friend and trusted counselor. However, the majority seem to have felt that such sin merited punishment, not mercy. Among those who came down on the side of justice were several of the women of the Relief Society when they heard the story.[39]

It is easy to imagine Joseph's fear. He had trusted Bennett when he should not. His actions over the next few days show a pattern of defending Bennett even as he wove Bennett's betrayal into his prophet-narrative. He spoke to the Relief Society the same day that Bennett spoke to the Masons, May 26. Emma and Joseph arrived late in the overflowing room. Emma sat down, but Joseph immediately took the floor. "There is another error which opens a door for the adversary to enter," Eliza R. Snow recorded. "As females possess refined feelings and sensitiveness, they are also subject to an overmuch zeal which must ever prove dangerous, and cause them to be rigid in a religious capacity. [You] should be arme'd with mercy notwithstanding the iniquity among us. … Put a double watch over the tongue. … [You] should chasten and reprove and keep it all in silence, not even mention them again."

Joseph turned to address Emma then. "One request to the Prest. and society, that you search yourselves–the tongue is an unruly member–hold your tongues about things of no moment." Although Joseph knew he could sway followers, this approach was an unfortunate attempt to minimize immorality on the part of a close friend:

> At this time the truth on the guilty should not be told openly, strange as this may seem, yet this is policy. We must use precaution in bringing sinners to justice, lest in exposing these heinous sins we draw the indignation of a Gentile world upon us (and to their imagination, justly, too). It is necessary to hold an influence in the world and thus spare ourselves an extermination; … [B]eware, be still, be prudent, repent, reform, but do it in a way not to destroy all around you.

He did not mention Bennett's name, but almost every woman must have been thinking it. Joseph added, "I do not want to cloak iniquity–all things contrary to the will of God, should be cast from us, but don't do more hurt than good with your tongues." Joseph warned the women that they "should chasten and reprove and keep it all in silence, not even mention them again,

38. *History of the Church*, 5:18 (May 26, 1842).
39. "Notice," *Times and Seasons* 3, no. 19 (Aug. 1, 1842): 872.

then you will be established in power, virtue and holiness and the wrath of God will be turn'd away."[40] These instructions seemed to contradict his earlier statement that the women should watch over the community's morals.

Emma had the last word: "All idle rumors and idle talk must be laid aside yet sin must not be covered, especially those sins which are against the law of God, and the laws of the country." She spelled out her position: "All who walk disorderly must reform, and any of you knowing of heinous sins against the law of God, and refuse to expose them, becomes the offender–I want none in this society who have violated the laws of virtue!" She then ended the meeting.[41]

Emma must have heard the same rumors as the other women. She must have been troubled at what they clearly implied about her husband. And his attempts to impose silence and secrecy could not have been reassuring. Her message was as much to Joseph as to the other women in the room, a coded but heavy warning of consequences for the violation of moral law.

In the most painful position of all must have been those women who had already entered the morally contested realm of plural marriage. Some had been taught plurality by Joseph himself, but those who had been taught by others must have wondered about authority. Bennett had been mayor, regent, member of the First Presidency. Whose practice of plurality was sanctioned by God and who was deceiving the faithful? Emma contributed to their confusion because of her own hatred of the doctrine. As president of the Relief Society, she used her influence to erect obstacles to Joseph's teaching of plurality.

A third meeting–after those of the Masonic lodge and Relief Society–convened on May 26. At 1:00 p.m. after the Masonic lodge meeting, Joseph attended a gathering of "citizens" near the temple. There, he instructed them on "principles of government, ... showing that I did not intend to vote the Whig or Democratic ticket as such, but would go for those who would support good order, ... The meeting nominated candidates for senators, representatives, and other officers."[42]

The next day, the Relief Society, whose membership now counted more than 600, met in the grove near the temple site. Emma herself offered the opening prayer, then welcomed 200 new members and extolled the virtues of

40. Relief Society, Minutes, May 26, 1842; also in *History of the Church*, 5:20 (May 26, 1842).
41. Relief Society Minutes, May 26, 1842.
42. *History of the Church*, 5:19 (May 26, 1842).

helping the needy.[43] Joseph and Church Bishop Newel K. Whitney arrived and mounted the stand. Whitney spoke first, complimenting the Society on its lofty purposes: "without the female all things cannot be restor'd to the earth–it takes all to restore the Priesthood. ... God has many precious things to bestow, even to our astonishment if we are faithful." The Church's bishop consoled the confused, "If we are striving to do right, altho' we may err in judgment many times yet we are justified in the sight of God if we do the best we can." Then he developed a theme that would thread through meetings held that week: "Far be it from me to harbor iniquity and outbreaking sins. We may have different views of things, still there is some criterion which all may come to, and by bringing our minds and wills into subjection to the law of the Lord, may come to unity." Leaving a message Joseph might have wished to deliver himself, he concluded, "I tell you, there are blessings before to be confer'd as soon as our hearts are prepar'd to receive them." Joseph elected not to speak, and the women adjourned.[44]

The high council, the Quorum of the Twelve, and other ecclesiastical officers joined Joseph in trying to impose order on Bennett's growing catastrophe. Wilford Woodruff summarized in his journal on May 27 the high council's charges of "unchaste and virtuous conduct" on many of Bennett's followers: "The first Presidency & The High Council & virtuous part of the Church are making an exhertion abot these days to clense the Church from Adulterors fornicators & evil persons ... The high council have held a number of meeting of late & their researches have disclosed much iniquity & a number been Cut off from the church." Despite the chastisement, Church leaders did not want the young men to abandon the Church, and may have also felt, at this stage, that Bennett himself could be redeemed.[45]

Joseph apparently did. Speaking to the Relief Society on June 9, he declared, again without mentioning names, "The pow'r and glory of Godliness is spread out on a broad principle to throw out the mantle of charity. God does not look on sin with allowance, but when men have sin'd there must be allowance made for them."[46]

But events had gone beyond Joseph's ability to manage successfully. A week later, the Nauvoo Masonic Lodge published a notice that Bennett could

43. Relief Society, Minutes, May 27, 1842.

44. Ibid.

45. Scott G. Kenney, ed., *Wilford Woodruff's Journal, 1833-1898*, 2:177 (May 27, 1842); hereafter Woodruff, *Journal*.

46. Relief Society, Minutes, June 9, 1842.

not represent himself as being in the "fraternity of masons" in the future.[47] The June 15 edition of the *Times and Seasons* (it is not clear if the issue appeared on time) carried the May 11 official announcement of Bennett's excommunication. Perhaps trying to salvage his own reputation and to appease Emma, who must have been humiliated by the growing tide of innuendo, Joseph on June 18 spoke "his mind in great plainness concerning the iniquity & wickedness of Gen[eral] John Cook Bennet, & exposed him before the public."[48] This was the earliest criticism Joseph had made of Bennett before the body of the Church, sealing what had already happened in private.

Bennett lingered in Nauvoo for three days. On June 21, he finally left, plotting revenge on the prophet he had once pledged to defend. Joseph followed up on June 23 with the publication of his June 21 address and made public Bennett's edict of excommunication:

> He [Bennett] went to some of the females in the city who knew nothing of him but as an honorable man, and began to teach them that promiscuous intercourse between the sexes was a doctrine believed in by the latter-day Saints, and that there was no harm in it, but this failing, he had recourse to a more influential and desperately wicked course, and that was to persuade them that myself and others of the authorities of the Church, not only sanctioned but practiced the same wicked acts, and when asked why I publicly preached so much against it, said that it was because of the prejudice of the public, and that it would cause trouble in my own house.

Joseph's outrage reveals his fear of the impact Bennett's actions would have. He described Bennett as

> well aware of the consequences of such wilful and base falsehoods, if they should come to my knowledge, and consequently endeavored to persuade his dupes to keep it a matter of secrecy, persuading them there would be no harm if they did not make it known. This proceeding on his part answered the desired end; he accomplished his wicked purposes; he seduced an innocent female by his lying, and subjected her character to public disgrace, should it ever be known. But his depraved heart would not suffer him to stop here. . . . We also ascertained . . . that others had been led by his conduct to pursue the same adulterous practice, and in order to accomplish their detestible designs made use of the same language insinuated

47. *History of the Church*, 5:32 (June 16, 1842).

48. Woodruff, *Journal*, 2:179 (June 18, 1842); see also *History of the Church*, 5:35 (June 18, 1842).

by Bennett, with this difference, that they did not hear me say anything of the kind, but Bennett was one of the heads of the Church, and he had informed them that such was the fact and they credited his testimony.[49]

Then, making certain his version prevailed, Joseph wrote to Illinois Governor Thomas Carlin while George Miller wrote to Missouri Governor Thomas Reynolds, reporting that Bennett had been expelled from the Church.[50] Bennett returned briefly to Nauvoo, staying with George W. Robinson (Sidney Rigdon's son-in-law), to gather evidence to use against the Mormon prophet.[51] Joseph met with the Rigdons, then convened a meeting of his elite Anointed Quorum (see chap. 12). There he prayed that "God … would deliver His anointed, His people, from all the evil designs of … John C. Bennett."[52] At this time, Bennett, according to his own account, left Nauvoo for good, claiming that his life was in danger.[53]

On June 23, the same day that Joseph wrote his detailed denunciation of Bennett for publication, Sarah Cleveland, Emma's counselor in the Relief Society, warned the sisters to be respectful of Church authorities, "especially those persons objected to by some, yet considered virtuous … [W]e would have none among us who would speak against the prophet of the Lord, or the authorities of the Church." Emma added that the sisters should issue "a Circular … expressive of our feeling in reference to Dr. Bennett's character … said we had nothing to do but to fear God and keep the commandments, and in doing so we shall prosper."[54] Like Joseph's published address, the Relief Society's circular would validate the official stance of supporting Joseph and spurning Bennett.[55]

---

49. *History of the Church*, 5:37 (June 23, 1842); "To the Church of Jesus Christ of Latter Day Saints, and to all the Honorable Part of the Community," *Wasp* 1 (June 25, 1842): [42]-[43]; (reprint) "To the Church of Jesus Christ of Latter Day Saints, and to all the Honorable Part of the Community," *Times and Seasons* 3, no. 7 (July 1, 1842): 839-42.

50. *History of the Church*, 5:42-44 (June 24, 1842).

51. Andrew F. Smith, *The Saintly Scoundrel*, 93.

52. *History of the Church*, 5:45 (June 26, 1842).

53. John C. Bennett, *History of the Saints*, 290-91.

54. Relief Society, Minutes, June 23, 1842.

55. Joseph Grafton Hovey, a thirty-year-old blacksmith and farmer, writing his autobiography twenty years later, captured the view of the prophet's supporters:

> All things were in a prosperous condition … when the aforesaid Bennett, C[hauncey]. Higbee, and others did go about our city insulting our wives and our daughters, telling them that it was right to have free intercourse with the fair sex. They said that the Prophet Joseph taught that it was the word of the Lord. … However, he [Bennett] was brought before the authorities and cut off from the Church. … He then went into the other cities [bringing] … persecution on us [by] telling that we believed in more than one wife and having all things

In retrospect, the Bennett episode is another demonstration of Joseph's occasional lack of judgment in determining his friends. In his polarized world of extremes, he placed his highest hopes in Bennett, trusted his judgment and loyalty, and was devastated by Bennett's perfidy, faulty judgment, and aberrant behavior.

For his part, Bennett began a sort of holy war against Joseph, using the press to wreak vengeance on his former friend. Joseph was dealing simultaneously with the fallout from his political policy and was in genuine danger of extradition for the attempted murder of Lilburn Boggs. He spent part of the summer in hiding, while Bennett exercised his talents as a crusading anti-Mormon.

On June 30, Bennett opened with a salvo to the *Sangamo Journal*: "I had been threatened with death by the Holy Joe and his Danite band of murderers, in case *I dare make any disclosures* prejudicial to that polluted mass of corruption, iniquity, and fraud,–that King of Impostors–the holy and immaculate Joe Smith."[56] He wrote letters to editors of local papers, and arranged personally with the editor of Springfield's *Sangamo Journal,* Simeon Francis, to run a multi-part exposé. Francis introduced the series by taking the position that he had solicited the report from a courageous patriot:

> We call upon Gen. Bennett, to come out NOW. … Such an exposure may save life–may expose corruption–may avert consequences which no man can contemplate without fearful apprehensions. We call upon Gen. Bennett to produce documentary evidence, that the public may form opinions that cannot be gainsayed–that they may understand the entire character, as it stands naked before his God, of a long successful religious impostor.[57]

Not surprisingly, Francis did not appeal in vain. The *Sangamo Journal* published, beginning on July 8, the sensational story of Bennett's expulsion from Nauvoo. Bennett's letters appeared at intervals between July and September when Bennett gathered them into a book: *The History of the Saints: or, An Exposé of Joe Smith and Mormonism.* On January 10, 1843, he wrote to Sidney Rigdon and Orson Pratt to tell them he planned to work for

---

> in common; everything the devil could invent to destroy our Prophet Joseph. Hovey, "Autobiography," 15-16, at http://www.boap.org/LDS Early-Saints/JHovey.html (June 13, 2013).

Hovey's version fit neatly into the narrative of persecution that the Saints had been constructing since New York.

56. In John C. Bennett, *History of the Saints*, 290.

57. Simeon Francis, "The Mormons," *Sangamo Journal*, July 1, 1842.

Joseph's extradition to Missouri. "The war goes bravely on; and, although Smith thinks he is now safe, the enemy is near, even at the door. He has awoke the wrong passenger," presumably himself.[58] He then began a national speaking tour, beginning first in nearby Carthage, Warsaw, and Springfield where he attempted to organize anti-Mormon associations, then went on to New York, Boston, Salem, Philadelphia, Buffalo, Kalamazoo, Chicago, and St. Louis. Thereafter, he gradually faded from the Mormon scene.[59]

For the most part, the national press feasted on Bennett's story, reprinting it widely, although some Democrat papers refrained and accused the Whigs of descending to a low point for publicity. The range of opinions was wide. The *Quincy Whig* on July 16, expressed skepticism: "We can hardly put reliance upon the statements of Bennett, they disclose so much wickedness."[60] The *Missouri Reporter* viewed Bennett's account as tainted by his need for revenge.[61] "The whole thing," wrote the *New York Herald* on July 24, "is full of philosophy, fun, roguery, religion, truth, falsehood, fanaticism, and philosophy."[62] James Gordon Bennett, editor of the *New York Herald,* discounted Bennett's account as the effort of a bitter man trying to wreak vengeance.[63] "The whole of this muss is only extending your fame, and will increase your numbers tenfold," he wrote reassuringly to Joseph.[64] The *Herald* described the book as "obscene and licentious in the highest degree."[65] Loyal to Joseph, Wilford Woodruff characterized John C. Bennett as "base wicked & corrupt."[66] Similarly, Thomas Ford dismissed him as "probably the greatest scamp in the western country."[67]

Because Bennett had been Joseph's second in command and for a period one of his trusted confidantes, Bennett's story was effective in stirring up animosity against Joseph and his people. Bennett slandered Joseph freely

58. *History of the Church*, 5:251 (Jan. 10, 1843). The letter published on this date is one Bennett wrote the day he left and dated January 10, 1843.

59. Smith, *Saintly Scoundrel*, 107-33.

60. "The Difficulties at Nauvoo–The Other Side of the Story–John C. Bennett–Spiritual Wives,– &c, &c," *Quincy Whig*, July 16, 1842.

61. *Missouri Reporter*, qtd. in *Illinois Register*, July 29, 1842, and *Wasp* 1(July 30, 1842):3.

62. "The Terrible Trouble in the Mormon Country–More Disclosures Relative to the Alleged Seduction and Adulteries of Joe Smith and Others–Crimination and Re-crimination," *New York Herald*, July 24, 1842.

63. *History of the Church*, 5:113 (Aug. 16, 1842).

64. Ibid.

65. "The Mormons," *New York Herald*, Oct. 21, 1842.

66. Woodruff, *Journal*, July 21, 1842 (2:182).

67. Thomas Ford, qtd. in Harry M. Beardley, *Joseph Smith and His Mormon Empire*, 207-208.

as "the notorious Mormon Prophet and swindler,"[68] as an ambitious despot intent on seizing power over the entire western United States.

Bennett claimed he had joined the Mormons only to expose them. This altruism fell short of explaining why Bennett spent his first fifty pages praising his own character. The Nauvoo Legion was a key element in Bennett's alarmist prose. According to Bennett, the Mormons were fully armed and ready for combat. But more important was the loyalty of the troops to their prophet, having sworn an oath "to regard Joe Smith as the supreme head of the church, and to obey him, as the 'Supreme God.'"[69] Bennett luridly announced that some "would kill any person, if the presidency would say it was the will of God."[70] Ironically, the legion had achieved its prominent position, in large part because of Bennett's own performance of military and masculine power, costume, and title. He had helped in every way to design the military stage on which Mormon townsmen could stand with Joseph and feel secure.

Certainly the most scandalous element in Bennett's narrative was sexual–an elaborate tale of immorality which included a system of religious prostitution. He classified the women into three groups: (1) "Cyprean maids and maidens," who had been lured into promiscuity and who "lapsed from the straight path of virtue" simply because they were warm hearted and easily seduced; (2) "Chambered Sisters of Charity" or "Saints of the Green Veil," who are "at the service of … each and all of the Apostles, High Priests, and Elders of Israel";[71] and (3) "Cloistered Saints, or Saints of the Black Veil," who became spiritual wives through a marriage ritual,[72] seven, by Bennett's tabulation, whom he listed by their initials.[73] Bennett's fantasy of women's categories[74] made it easy to discount other sensational claims; but most of the seven "Cloistered Saints" were, in fact, genuine plural wives. Bennett's Joseph is uniformly a cad, a master manipulator, and definitely false prophet. His letters may contain accurate elements, but they are too exaggerated to measure as entirely true. "In this, as in almost all cases," Lawrence Foster

---

68. John C. Bennett, "For the Sangamo Journal," *Sangamo Journal*, July 8, 1842, 2.

69. John C. Bennett, *History of the Saints*, 149.

70. John C. Bennett, "Bennett's Second and Third Letters," *Sangamo Journal*, July 15, 1842, www.sidneyrigdon.com/dbroadhu/IL/sang1842.htm#0715 (Jan. 20, 2009).

71. John C. Bennett, *History of the Saints*, 222.

72. Ibid., 223.

73. Ibid., 256: Mrs. A**** S**** [Agnes Smith], Miss L***** B ***** [Louisa Beaman], Mrs. B**** [Buell], Mrs. D***** [Durfee], Mrs. S******* [Sessions], Mrs. G***** [?], and Miss B***** [?].

74. Cyprian referred specifically to prostitutes; Green Veil was probably meant "naive," "new," "fresh," etc. ; and Black Veil "tarnished," "stained," "dirty/filthy," etc.

suggests, "the tangle of allegation and counter-allegation is so complex that one cannot reliably determine exactly what did happen."[75] Regardless of their accuracy, Bennett's stories impacted Nauvoo and complicated Joseph's ability to continue to teach and to practice the doctrine.

For example, and willing to damage the reputations of more than Joseph's own, Bennett charged that "the great Mormon seducer" had laid siege to "Miss Nancy Rigdon … to submit to his hellish purposes, and become one of his clandestine wives." Although the exaggerated rhetoric is easy to discount, it is true that Joseph approached Nancy (see chap. 12). Bennett stripped this encounter of its ritualistic intent, rendering it devoid of actual meaning.

Bennett named Martha Brotherton (see chap. 12) as another attempted target–true–but also claimed that a certain "Miss Mitchell," who was herself "one of the most chaste and spotless females in the west," had shocking information about "the PROPHET'S SECRET WIVES."[76] Mitchell has never been identified, despite Bennett's allegation that she was "one of Joe's most notorious Cyprian Saints."[77]

Emma must have been particularly hurt by Bennett's stories. There is no record of whether she ever trusted him, and certainly one would not need to be highly skeptical to be cautious about embracing a stranger into her home. However, Emma had apparently exerted herself to make Bennett comfortable and no doubt saw his efforts in winning passage of the Nauvoo charter as making the Saints feel more secure. But with his exposé, Bennett rubbed Emma's rawest nerve and dragged into daylight her most nightmarish fears.

Later, as he reworked his story, Bennett claimed that he had been under duress when he told the Nauvoo City Council in tears on May 19 that Joseph's behavior had been impeccable while his own was contaminated by sin. To counter his retraction, the city council on July 20 swore a joint affidavit: "There was no excitement at the time, nor was he in anywise threatened, menaced, or intimidated. His appearance … was voluntary … and [he] went … as free as any member of the Council."[78]

On July 22, Bennett's incendiary fourth letter appeared in the *Sangamo Journal* with a reprint of Martha Brotherton's affidavit regarding Brigham Young's overtures to her (see chap. 12) taken from the *St. Louis Bulletin* and introduced as: "Can men who have a just sense of honor, and their duty to

75. Lawrence Foster, *Religion and Sexuality*, 159.
76. "For the Sangamo Journal," *Sangamo Journal*, July 8, 1842.
77. Ibid.
78. *History of the Church*, 5:68 (July 22, 1842).

themselves and their families, longer follow a base deceiver and teacher of such a system of licentiousness and debauchery, such as is Joe Smith? They cannot without being partakers with him in his hellish deeds."

Also on the 22nd, thousands at a Nauvoo mass meeting adopted a resolution stating that Joseph was a "good, moral, virtuous, peaceable and patriotic man."[79] Orson Pratt cast one of only a very few negative votes.[80] Annoyed at the implication, Joseph demanded: "Have you personally a knowledge of any immoral act in [by] me toward the female sex, or in any other way?" Pratt answered carefully, "Personally, toward the female sex, I have not." After this, Hyrum Smith, George Miller, Daniel Wells, and others signed affidavits they published in the *Times and Seasons.*[81] J. B. Backenstos also publicly testified that Bennett and Sarah Pratt's "illicit intercourse" was known.[82]

On August 4, the non-Mormon Grand Master of Illinois sent the Nauvoo Masonic Lodge a letter ordering it to expel Bennett "for his conduct." The lodge read the letter on the 8th and issued six indictments against Bennett for seducing "certain previously respectable females of our city by using Joseph Smith's name as one who sanctioned such conduct."[83] The absent Bennett was found guilty and cast out as "one of the most base and infamous adulterers, liars, and a general plunderer of female chastity."[84] According to Bennett's biographer, Bennett had no further association with Masonry.[85]

A measure of Joseph's fear is that he asked Illinois Governor Thomas Carlin if the state would help to defend against a possible "attack upon the peaceable inhabitants of the city of Nauvoo and vicinity, through the intrigues and false representations of John C. Bennett and others."[86] Carlin responded on July 27–ironically, the day Joseph would die two years later. He acknowledged his authority to mobilize the militia but scoffed: "I must say that I cannot conceive of the least probability, or scarcely possibility, of an attack … [on] Nauvoo from any quarter whatever …" He scolded: The

79. *History of the Church*, 5:70 (July 22, 1842).

80. Bergera, *Conflict in the Quorum*, 24.

81. "Notice," *Times and Seasons* 3 no. 19 (Aug. 1, 1842): 869.

82. J. B. Backenstos, Affidavit, July 28, 1842.

83. Mervin B. Hogan, "The Involvement of John Cook Bennett with Mormonism and Freemasonry at Nauvoo," 20.

84. Ibid.

85. Andrew F. Smith, *Saintly Scoundrel*, 111.

86. Joseph's letter is quoted in Carlin's response dated July 27, 1842. *History of the Church*, 5:82 (July 27, 1842).

"excitement is confined to the Mormons themselves, and only extends to the community at large as a matter of curiosity and wonder."[87]

While Carlin was penning this letter, Joseph married Sarah Ann Whitney, with her father officiating and her mother witnessing. By any measure, the timing was reckless. Joseph also took the defensive measure on July 27 of authorizing *The Wasp* to publish an extra edition containing affidavits by Stephen Markham and Stephen Goddard accusing Nancy Rigdon and Sarah Pratt of "anything but virtuous" conduct with Bennett,[88] and described Bennett as a "spoiler of character and virtue, and a living pestilence, walking in darkness to fester in his own infamy."[89] (The *Wasp* was published by Joseph's brother William, whose own involvement with Bennett had been officially hushed up.)

Markham's and Goddard's affidavits marked the beginning of a flood of salvos attacking Bennett. A two-page broadside followed on August 31 titled: *Affidavits and Certificates Disproving the Statements and Affidavits Contained in John C. Bennett's Letters.* In it appeared testimonies by Stephen Goddard, Zeruiah Goddard, Jacob B. Backenstos, John McIlwrick, Mary McIlwrick, Elizabeth Brotherton, Heber C. Kimball, Brigham Young, Vilate Kimball, Stephen Markham, Sidney Rigdon, and others. They aligned their stories with Joseph's, accusing Bennett of seduction, pandering, and abortion.[90]

In September, Sidney Rigdon, George W. Robinson, and others rallied to Nancy Rigdon's defense (see chap. 12). Robinson, for example, charged Markham with crafting a fantasy–that Robinson had been with Nancy when Bennett had attended her as a physician. Sidney Rigdon hired an attorney to defend his daughter's virtue.[91]

The *Sangamo Journal* announced the resignation of apostate Mormons from the Church in what became a sort of parade of horrors through the summer and fall of 1842. On October 7, it published a letter by Oliver Olney, "another seceding Mormon": "… Stephen Markham's affidavit was for the express purpose and design of helping the elders who (were going out to

87. *History of the Church*, 5:83 (July 27, 1842).

88. Stephen Markham, "Affidavit," *Wasp*, July 27, 1842.

89. "More Disclosures," *Wasp*, July 27, 1842.

90. "Affidavits and Certificates Disproving the Statements and Affidavits Contained in John C. Bennett's Letters."

91. Richard S. Van Wagoner, *Sidney Rigdon*, 301; Sidney Rigdon, Letter to the *Wasp*, rpt., *Sangamo Journal*, Sept. 23, 1842, 2; Sidney Rigdon, Letter to the "Editor of the Wasp," *Wasp*, extra edition, July 27, 1842, 2.

preach) to refute the statements of Gen. Bennett which statements I believe to be true ..."[92] Continuing his diatribe against Joseph's leadership, Bennett published his fifth and sixth letters in the *Sangamo Journal,* dated July 23 and August 3, but published on August 19. In the sixth letter, Bennett published Joseph's proposal to Nancy Rigdon, since dubbed the "Happiness Letter" (which Francis Higbee had given to him): "Whatever God requires is right, NO MATTER WHAT IT IS, although we may not see the reason thereof till long after the events transpire."[93] (See chap. 12.)

While hiding during the summer to avoid extradition to Missouri, Joseph addressed the closed meetings of the Nauvoo High Council or Quorum of the Twelve. He also answered correspondence and received occasional visits from Emma. On August 29, however, he surprised the Saints when he took to the public stand. He expressed his joy to be with them and his pleasure at having successfully evaded the Missourians. Behind him was Orson Pratt, who had been ostensibly excommunicated nine days earlier. Joseph charged: "O. Pratt and others of the same class caused trouble by telling stories to people who would betray me ... I will live to trample on their ashes with the soles of my feet. I prophesy in the name of Jesus Christ that such shall not prosper, they shall be cut down in their own plans. ... I can kick them off my heels, as many as you can name, I know what will become of them."[94] Thus Joseph positioned these episodes in the on-going prophet-narrative of the battle between good and evil. Joseph ended by calling for volunteers to travel through the country to contradict Bennett's lies.

Hyrum spoke in the afternoon session, also asking for elders to canvass "every part of the United States" in Joseph's defense. "They must ... humbly [set] forth the truth as it is in God, and our persecutions, by which the tide

---

92. "A Communication from Another Seceding Mormon," *Sangamo Journal*, Oct. 7, 1842. Six months earlier, Bennett himself had accused Olney of improper conduct for setting himself up as a prophet and revelator in the Church. *History of the Church*, 4:552 (Mar. 17, 1842). The next year, Olney was charged with "Grand Larceny and Burglary," and jailed at Carthage. "Effects of Apostasy," *Times and Seasons* 4, no. 6 (Feb. 1, 1843): 89.

93. John C. Bennett, "To the Editor of the Journal," *Sangamo Journal*, Aug. 19, 1842. According to Dan Vogel (statement to Bradley Evans, June 15, 2011, in author's possession): the "earliest known copy of Joseph Smith to Nancy Rigdon, ca. Apr. 1842, is *Sangamo Journal*, 19 Aug. 1842 ..., which was reprinted in J. C. Bennett's 1842 book *History of the Saints*, 243-45, ... which was apparently copied [into the *History of the Church*] from Bennett's 1842 book ca. 1869-70. Bennett claimed that the original letter in his possession was written by W[illard] R[ichards] at J[oseph] S[mith's] dictation, and that it was given to him by Francis M. Higbee in the presence of George W. Robinson, S[idney] R[igdon's] son-in-law (Bennett 1842, 243, 245)."

94. Joseph Smith, Diary, Aug. 29, 1842, in Faulring, *An American Prophet's Record*, 253.

of public feelings will be turned."[95] According to Joseph's account, there was "an indescribable transport of good feeling" among the audience, and on the spot 380 elders "volunteered to go immediately on the proposed mission."[96]

Two days later, Joseph again ventured out to tell the Relief Society that "the Missourians shall not get me into their power," and challenged anyone to prove his pronouncements false.[97] He was reinvigorating himself through his own rhetoric. "I shall triumph over my enemies. I have begun to triumph over them at home, and I shall do it abroad. … Although I do wrong, I do not the wrongs that I am charg'd with doing … the wrong that I do is thro' the frailty of human nature like other men. No man lives without fault. Do you think that even Jesus, if he were here would be without fault in your eyes?"[98]

He then warned the sisters: "If you have evil feelings and speak of them to one another, it has a tendency to do mischief–these things result in those evils which are calculated to cut the throats of the heads of the church," he stated. "… I now counsel you, if you know anything, hold your tongues, and the least harm will be done."[99]

The *Times and Seasons* published on October 1 an excerpt from the Doctrine and Covenants to show that "Bennett's 'secret wife system' is a matter of his own manufacture": "All legal contracts of marriage made before a person is baptized into this church, should be held sacred and fulfilled. Inasmuch as this church of Christ has been reproached with the crime of fornication, and polygamy: we declare that we believe, that one man should have one wife; and one woman, but one husband, except in the case of death, when either is at liberty to marry again. It is not right to persuade a woman to be baptized contrary to the will of her husband neither is it lawful to influence her to leave her husband."[100]

It was an obvious answer to Bennett, but how did Church members like Newel and Elizabeth Whitney read the statement? What did their daughter (Sarah Ann) or Benjamin Johnson's sisters (Delcena and Almera) or the poetess teaching Joseph's children in his own home (Eliza R. Snow) think when they read the denial that they were plural wives? Even today

95. *History of the Church*, 5:136 (Aug. 29, 1842).

96. Ibid., 139.

97. Ibid., 140.

98. Ibid., 140; Relief Society, Minutes, Aug. 31, 1842.

99. Relief Society, Minutes, Aug. 31, 1842.

100. "On Marriage," *Times and Seasons* 3, no. 23 (Oct. 1, 1842): 939. In the same issue, two disclaimers carried thirty-one signatures, including twelve men and nineteen women of the Relief Society (all married).

the statement jars, leaving readers to account for what seems like blatant dishonesty. Through most of 1842, Joseph maneuvered between truth and subterfuge. Ultimately confusing, damaging to the lives and reputations of members and to Joseph's own personal peace, it was a risky course to pursue.

In the fall of 1842, James Gordon Bennett expressed regrets in his *New York Herald* that the Bennett affair had cast such aspersions on Joseph's character. "Smith, I conceive," he wrote, "has just as good a right to establish a church, if he can do it, as Luther, Calvin, Wesley, Fox, or even King Henry the Eighth. … I fully believe that all the real, sincere Mormons would die sooner than abandon their faith and their religion. … It is the best policy, both of Missouri and Illinois, to let them alone."[101]

Unbelievable though it may seem, before the end of October, Joseph thought it was safe enough to float a thirty-seven-page trial balloon on the topic of plural marriage. *An Extract, From a Manuscript Entitled The Peace Maker, of the Doctrines of the Millennium,* authored by a non-Mormon (at the time), Udney Hay Jacob (1791-1860), appeared on October 28 with Joseph identified as the "Printer."[102] According to Jacob, polygamy was a solution for marital incompatibility. "What, although a woman is not known to be an adulteress, yet she may be a perfect devil to her husband, train him in the most imperious manner, despise him in her heart, abuse him before his children, drive him like a menial slave where she pleases; and he must tamely submit to the ungodly law of his wife, must hug the serpent to his bosom, and love her as he does his own body!"[103] At least three of Joseph's wives had troubled marriages before his marriages to them. And while divorce may not be permitted in the scriptures,[104] any woman who continued to have sexual relations with a husband she no longer loved committed "fornication." Jacob described a world where men were superior to women. "[T]he man marries the woman; and the woman is given in marriage. … When God made the woman he gave her to the man; but he never gave the man to the woman."[105]

Contemporary documents are silent about the pamphlet, but the shock must have been severe. A month later on December 1, Joseph issued an equivocal repudiation. The pamphlet, he claimed, had been published "without my knowledge; and … I do not wish to have my name associated with

101. "Gen. J. G. Bennett," *New York Herald*, Oct. 23, 1842.
102. Udney Hay Jacob, *An Extract, From a Manuscript Entitled The Peace Maker …*, 1.
103. Ibid., 15.
104. Ibid.
105. Ibid., 16.

the author's, in such an unmeaning rigmarole of nonsence, folly, and trash."[106] Joseph may have separated himself rhetorically from the pamphlet, but his disclaimer denied and affirmed simultaneously in a curious dance between the two extremes of truth. Lawrence Foster argues that the pamphlet was "a brilliant and often highly unorthodox intellectual and social argument for the 'Biblical' basis of divorce and polygamous marriage."[107] Jacob's justification of the rearrangement of marriage relationships in the context of religious belief recalled arguments Joseph was then also formulating for plurality.

By the time he left Nauvoo, Bennett had burned every bridge he ever had to the Mormons. But he would also say in 1846, two years after Joseph's death: "All I ever said against any members of the church was in self defense ... I have loved the church for many years; I love it now!"[108] Although sorting the lies from the truth is no easy task, one hears–albeit with difficulty–a note of wistfulness in Bennett's protestations.

106. "Notice," *Times and Seasons* 4, no. 2 (Dec. 1, 1842): 32.
107. Lawrence Foster, *Religion and Sexuality*, 174-75.
108. John C. Bennett, Letter to James Strang, June 2, 1846.

CHAPTER 12

Interlude: Plurality and the Experience of Religious Ecstasy

Marginal situations are characterized by the experience of "ecstasy" ... [of] standing or stepping, outside reality as commonly defined.

–Peter Berger, The Sacred Canopy, *43*

Joseph's relationship with John C. Bennett and its crashing debacle showed the vulnerability of plurality to sexual exploitation. It also showed the political dangers of trying to manage such a system by requiring oaths of secrecy. This kind of secret, especially when known cases had to be punished as sexual transgression, simply could not be kept. In retrospect, the mere idea that damage control was a viable option seems naively optimistic. Yet Joseph devoted a major portion of his time and energy during the last three years of his life not only to practicing plurality but in trying to win adherents to it. Obviously, more was at stake for him than boredom with his civil wife or a mid-life crisis that took the form of testing his virility with young women. For Joseph, plurality was religious ritual. Mormon historian Marvin Hill argues: "polygamy may provide further proof of Smith's early and complete absorption in his prophetic role."[1]

No understanding of plurality can be complete without first understanding Joseph's vision of human destiny. Increasingly, he situated his prophet-narrative in a religious kingdom, a "role" that promised to free him and others from the "social restraints which customarily control sexual behavior."[2] In that drama, Joseph was the key figure, placing the meaning of his experience in the context of restoring ancient times. In the materialization of this kingdom, plurality stimulated the experience of religious ecstasy, in

1. Marvin Hill, "Secular or Sectarian History?," 94.
2. Ibid.

which men and women stepped outside the confines of conventional morals to engage in sacred ritual.[3] Plurality helped them, in part, to forge new identities as well as to rededicate themselves to the work at hand.

Joseph was not oblivious to plurality's potential impact, even if he sometimes seemed overly confident in his ability to control its repercussions. Indeed, according to Nauvoo Stake president-turned-dissident William Marks, before he died, Joseph reportedly predicted that plurality "eventually would prove the overthrow of the church and we should be obliged to leave the United States, unless it could be speedily put down."[4]

Plurality could proceed only within the confines of the political kingdom that framed it and gave it a particular meaning. It helped to order relationships. It created networks in temporal and eternal family kingdoms.[5] It tested loyalty and unified the Saints. It marked the citizens of God's kingdom with a distinctive set of rituals, beliefs, and theology.

Sacred ritual occurs in temples, meetinghouses, or ordinary homes; the place does not matter, because ritual sacralizes the locale. What matters is the way ritual contributes to religious world-building. For sociologist Peter Berger, "Religion is the human enterprise by which a sacred cosmos is established"–where "sacred" means "a quality of mysterious and awesome power, other than man and yet related to him, which is believed to reside in certain objects of experience."[6] For Joseph and the other men and women who entered plurality, the sacred could be found on the banks of the river, the back rooms of brick houses, behind windows framed by wooden shutters, or buggies traveling across a prairie. Plurality, the temple, the kingdom of God, and Zion were all linked through the sacralization process that occurred through religious ritual.

Because plurality was available only to the most faithful, it was a ritual with immense transformative power. "The cosmos posited by religion," Berger explains, "thus both transcends and includes man. The sacred cosmos is confronted by man as an immensely powerful reality other than himself. Yet this reality addresses itself to him and locates his life in an ultimately meaningful order."[7] By entering plurality and teaching it to others, Joseph

3. Berger, *The Sacred Canopy*, 43.

4. Qtd. in *Saints Herald* 1:22, 23.

5. Samuel Morris Brown refers to this as the Mormon "Great Chain of Belonging." See his *In Heaven as It Is on Earth: Joseph Smith and the Early Mormon Conquest of Death* (New York: Oxford University Press, 2012).

6. Berger, *The Sacred Canopy*, 25.

7. Ibid., 26.

expressed his belief in the transformative power of the doctrine and ritual it required. Through it, the potentialities of heaven were revealed. The difference between celestial and civil marriage expressed the dichotomy between the sacred and profane, making it palpable. Civil marriage in Nauvoo was, doctrinally, the antonym to the sacred. Plurality imposed a new order on the Mormon world. "To be in a 'right' relationship with the sacred cosmos is to be protected against the nightmare threats of chaos."[8] Mormon plurality was patriarchal, a social ordering that rewarded faithful men with "privileges"[9] and women with positions next to their husbands in the upper reaches of the celestial kingdom. Joseph's movement into plurality created a new cosmos that transcended the ordinary space of human beings.

Sources

Just how broadly that new space spread, how many marriages Joseph and others entered into during his lifetime, are matters of conjecture. The effort to identify Joseph's marriages requires piecing together evidence from a number of sources created mainly by those who attempted to prove (or to deny) the reality of Joseph's plural families. In Nauvoo, plural marriage sealings forged by God's restored priesthood authority were described as celestial marriages and were considered the highest order of marriage. Monogamous marriages performed for time and eternity would also last beyond life on the earth but would not afford the spouses the same exalted blessings. These terms, "celestial" and "eternal" marriages, had particular meanings in Nauvoo; but after the Latter-day Saints stopped practicing plurality after about 1890, the terms began to be used synonymously, describing LDS temple marriage more broadly.

What information we have about Joseph's marriages comes not from Joseph–whose public statements deny his involvement[10]–but from several of his wives, some of whom left first-person accounts. Others confided in their sisters or friends, or were observed by persons who saw them with Joseph,

---

8. Ibid.

9. See Lucy Walker Smith Kimball, qtd. in Lyman Omer Littlefield, *Reminiscences of Latter-day Saints*, 45-46; Sarah M. Kimball, qtd. in Augusta J. Crocheron, *Representative Women of Deseret*, 26; "William Clayton's Testimony," Feb. 16, 1874, in George D. Smith, ed., *An Intimate Chronicle*, 557.

10. For example, on May 26, 1844, Joseph asserted, "What a thing it is for a man to be accused of committing adultery, and having seven wives, when I can only find one" (*History of the Church*, 6:411 [May 26, 1844]). As historian George D. Smith observes, "If we are left with the prophet's own words, he never married plural wives" (Smith, "How Joseph Smith Cultivated Thirty to Forty Young Women for Plural Marriage in Nauvoo, Illinois," 14).

performed their marriages, or made conclusions based on circumstantial evidence. After Joseph's martyrdom and while still in Nauvoo, dozens of women were sealed "for eternity" or "for time" to Joseph by proxy. Many, if not most, of these women had apparently become his wives while he lived. There is evidence that Joseph entered at least thirty plural marriages in Nauvoo. The main lists, in chronological order, follow:

1. John C. Bennett listed seven plural wives in his 1842 *The History of the Saints* as well as four women to whom Joseph allegedly proposed but did not necessarily marry.[11] The wives are: Mrs. A**** S**** (Agnes Smith), Miss L***** B***** (Louisa Beaman), Mrs. B**** (Presendia Buell), Mrs. D***** (Elizabeth Durfee), Mrs. S******* (Patty Sessions), Mrs. G***** (unidentified), and Miss B***** (unidentified).[12]

2. Following the LDS Church's public announcement of plural marriage in 1852, Joseph Smith III, head of the Reorganized Church of Jesus Christ of Latter Day Saints, tried to disprove his father's involvement. Countering to prove that Joseph had indeed taught and practiced plurality, in 1869 Joseph F. Smith began to collect affidavits on his own.[13] The LDS Church History Library has the originals of these materials.[14]

---

11. John C. Bennett, *The History of the Saints*, 256. Todd Compton claims that Joseph proposed to at least five women who refused his proposal of marriage: Sarah Melissa Granger (Kimball), Rachel Ivins (Grant), Lydia Moon, Cordelia C. Morley (Cox), and Esther Johnson. Compton, "Trajectory of Plurality," 7.

12. Ibid.

13. Joseph F. Smith, comp., Affidavit Books, 1869; listed, briefly summarized, and analyzed in Danel W. Bachman, "A Study of the Mormon Practice of Plural Marriage before the Death of Joseph Smith." See also Brian C. Hales, *Joseph Smith's Polygamy*, 2:343-51.Twenty-three of the affidavits are also quoted in Joseph Fielding Smith, *Blood Atonement and the Origin of Plural Marriage*. Joseph F. Smith included the following plural wives: Zina and Presendia Huntington, Sylvia Sessions Lyon, Elvira Annie Cowles, Martha McBride, Marinda Nancy Johnson Hyde. See also the discussion in George D. Smith, *Nauvoo Polygamy: "... But We Called It Celestial Marriage,"* 454-64; Brian C. Hales, *Joseph Smith's Polygamy*, 1:7-9.

14. Another list came from George A. Smith, LDS Church Historian and Joseph's cousin. On October 9, 1869, he wrote to Joseph III, identifying nine wives, apparently based on Joseph F.'s list. George A. also explained: "At one of the first interviews thereafter with your father (after the return of Joseph Smith's twelve apostles from England in 1841), I was greatly astonished at hearing from his lips that doctrine of Patriarchal marriage, which he continued to preach to me from time to time." He continued:

> My last conversation on this subject just previous to my departure from Nauvoo [was May 9, 1844]. ... he administered a little chastisement to me for not stepping forward as he had indicated in patriarchal marriage. He assured me that the man who had many virtuous wives had many great prizes. He testified to me ... that the Lord had given him the keys of this sealing ordinance, and that he felt as liberal to others as he did to himself. He ... said to me "you should not be behind in your privileges." George A. Smith, Letter to Joseph Smith III, Oct. 9, 1869, 2.

3. In 1887, LDS historian Andrew Jenson created a list of twenty-seven women for an article, "Plural Marriage," he published in his *Historical Record.*[15]

4. This basic list created by Joseph F. Smith, George A. Smith, Andrew Jenson, and a few others was expanded by twentieth-century historians. These include Danel W. Bachman, Gary James Bergera, Lisle G Brown, Todd Compton, Brigham C. Hales, Stanley Ivins, H. Michael Marquardt, D. Michael Quinn, and George D. Smith, who have, since Fawn M. Brodie's influential 1945 *No Man Knows My History: The Life of Joseph Smith,* worked to correct the list. Brodie posited that Joseph married close to fifty women, possibly more.[16] Although her numbers are probably inflated, she accurately identified thirty women who were sealed to Joseph by proxy in the Nauvoo temple in early 1846. At least two-thirds of these women can be documented as having married Joseph during his lifetime. Thus, there is some reason for Brodie's hypothesis that temple marriage sealings lacking evidence for a marriage sealing during Joseph's life may have been, in actuality, plural marriages. Others of Brodie's names remain doubtful. Because of this, an early proxy marriage may be read as evidence when it confirms other evidence in support of a plural marriage.[17]

My story of the many-layered narrative of Joseph's movement into plurality agrees generally with the list of marriages produced by Todd Compton in 2001. There is "strong" evidence for twenty-eight plural wives: Louisa Beaman, Zina Huntington Jacobs, Presendia Huntington Buell, Agnes Coolbrith Smith, Sylvia and Patty Sessions, Mary Elizabeth Rollins Lightner, Marinda Hyde, Eliza R. Snow, Sarah Ann Whitney, Martha McBride, Ruth Vose Sayers, Flora Ann Woodworth, Helen Mar Kimball, Almera and Delcena Johnson, Lucy Walker, Desdemona Fullmer, Emily and Eliza

15. Andrew Jenson, "Plural Marriage," 6:219-40; also Hales, *Joseph Smith's Polygamy,* 1:10-12. There are some problems with Jenson's list. He does not always record where he got his information or whom he had hoped to interview but did not. For example, Nancy Maria Winchester and Sarah Kingsley Cleveland were both sealed to Joseph by proxy after his death and before the Saints' exodus to the West but left no personal records to verify the marriages (see Lisle G Brown, comp., *Nauvoo Sealings, Adoptions, and Anointings,* 284, 282). Jenson's list includes the names that appear on both Joseph F.'s and George A.'s lists but also women whom William Clayton mentioned as wives (see George D. Smith, *An Intimate Chronicle,* 93-198; Jenson, "Plural Marriage," 219-40). By the time the nineteenth-century practice of plurality came to a close, some thirty wives had been attributed to Joseph.

16. Fawn Brodie, *No Man Knows My History,* 457-88.

17. For years, the premier scholar on Nauvoo plurality was Danel W. Bachman, an employee of the LDS Church's educational program. His 1975 master's thesis for Purdue University, "A Study of the Mormon Practice of Plural Marriage," provided the most thorough and carefully argued analysis of Joseph's plural marriage to date. Bachman's analysis of Brodie's list of forty-eight wives found convincing evidence for thirty-one (112).

Partridge, Maria and Sarah Lawrence, Melissa Lott, Rhoda Richards, Elvira Holmes, Fanny Young, and Lucinda Harris.[18]

The evidence is less strong but still compelling for another five probable plural marriages. The names of Sarah Cleveland, Nancy Winchester,[19] and Parley P. Pratt's sister-in-law, Olive Frost, appeared on Jenson's list, and each also was sealed by proxy to Joseph.[20] Two later sources mention Frost as a wife.[21] The elderly Elizabeth Durfee's marriage was alleged by Bennett;[22] and when combined with a proxy marriage to Joseph on January 22, 1846, it suggests an in-life sealing.[23] Hannah Ells appears on Jenson's list, and John Benbow testified that she cohabited with Joseph at his home.[24] Ells accompanied Eliza Snow to a dinner party hosted by Emma and Joseph,[25] was a Relief Society member, and participated in a "grand annual parade" of the Nauvoo Legion on May 6, 1842.[26] Ells and her alleged marriage to Joseph is suggested through second-hand testimony but it seems sufficiently detailed that I tend to accept her as a probable wife. At the very least, her case demonstrates the complexities of piecing together a puzzle composed largely outside public view. Caution must be exercised in concluding that all of these women were Joseph's wives, but their situation is similar enough to that of other wives that the marriages make a certain sense.[27]

---

18. Compton dates Lucinda Harris's marriage to Joseph as possibly occurring in 1838, though this early of a date is open to question. Jenson includes her as an early wife, and she was sealed by proxy to Joseph in the Nauvoo temple on January 22, 1846 (Brown, *Nauvoo Sealings, Adoptions, and Anointings*, 282). Gary James Bergera writes that this particular plural marriage may be better situated in the "context of Smith's pattern of contracting plural marriages ca. 1841-42 with married or widowed women than it does to the late 1830s" (Bergera, "Identifying the Earliest Mormon Polygamists, 1841-44," 30n75).

19. Nancy Winchester was married to Heber C. Kimball as proxy for Joseph Smith on October 10, 1844, in the Nauvoo temple. Brown, *Nauvoo Sealings, Adoptions, and Anointings*, 284.

20. Olive Frost, proxy marriage to Joseph Smith, Nov. 7, 1844, Brigham Young as proxy. Brown, *Nauvoo Sealings, Adoptions, and Anointings*, 286.

21. See www.josephsmithspolygamy.com/JSPSexuality/OliveFrostSRhtml.html (July 4, 2011); courtesy of Brian C. Hales.

22. Bennett, *History of the Saints*, 256.

23. Brown, *Nauvoo Sealings, Adoptions, and Anointings*, 282.

24. Benbow testified, "Hannah Ells Smith, a wife of the Prophet, boarded at his [Benbow] house two months during the summer of the same year [1843]; and the said Hannah E. Smith also lived at his [Benbow's] house several months in 1844, after the Prophet's death. And further, that President Smith frequently visited his wife Hannah at his (J. B.'s) house" (John Benbow, Affidavit, in Jenson, "Plural Marriage," 6:222-23).

25. *History of the Church*, 5:248 (Jan. 11, 1843).

26. Charlotte Haven, "A Girl's Letters from Nauvoo," 629.

27. These candidates make a total of thirty-three Nauvoo marriages with combinations of the following evidence: fifteen alleged wives of Joseph who left affidavits with Joseph F. Smith, Andrew Jenson, and others; three fist-hand accounts by women who wrote about their marriages in reminiscences or statements; thirteen second-hand accounts of two wives, including statements

There is considerable agreement among twenty-first-century historians about a second category–"possible wives"–that includes women who were sealed to Joseph posthumously but for whom there is no additional corroborating evidence of a plural marriage. Mary Huston,[28] Phebe Woodworth,[29] and Mary Ann Pratt[30] were sealed to Joseph in proxy marriages in the Nauvoo temple. The case for these women may some day be strengthened, but I consider them as "possible," not "probable" or "certain," wives and take a more skeptical interpretation of the available evidence.[31]

Although Joseph's plural marriage to Ruth Vose Sayers may have been for "eternity" only (a controversial assertion), there is some evidence that a few of his other plural marriages may have been intended for time only, while a third–the largest–category combined both. This third category would have included, as it came to mean in Utah, connubial privileges. Affidavits and other statements sworn later by some of Joseph's remaining wives verify this fact. Marvin Hill's work posits that Joseph probably had conjugal

---

by those who witnessed the alleged marriages; eleven others who were identified as wives by persons who would have been privy to this secret knowledge; and two wives for whom the most convincing evidence is that they were sealed by proxy to Joseph in the Nauvoo temple. Bachman, "A Study of the Mormon Practice of Plural Marriage," 112. The adjustment in these figures from those recommended by Bachman include the adjustment made for the Nauvoo marriages only (excluding Fanny Alger and Lucinda Morgan) and include four additional names: Mary Huston, Sarah Scott Mulholland, Mary Ann Frost Stearns Pratt, and Phebe Watrous Woodworth. They were sealed by proxy, a privilege reserved for the most part for known wives of the prophet. Heber C. Kimball said that, during Joseph's lifetime, Sarah Scott and Mary Huston were widely considered to be plural wives of Joseph Smith. Orson F. Whitney, *Life of Heber C. Kimball*, 419. See also Bergera, "Identifying the Earliest Mormon Polygamists, 1841-44," 30.

28. With seven other widows of Joseph Smith, Mary Huston "Smith" was sealed in the Nauvoo temple with Heber C. Kimball as proxy, Feb. 3, 1846. Brown, *Nauvoo Sealings, Adoptions, and Anointings*, 284.

29. There is no contemporary evidence for Phebe Woodworth's marriage to Joseph. Her husband worked for Joseph on the Nauvoo House, and her daughter Flora Woodworth was sealed to Joseph on March 4, 1843. Todd Compton, *In Sacred Loneliness*, 388, 393, describes Phebe Woodworth as a "posthumous" wife. D. Michael Quinn, *The Mormon Hierarchy: Origins of Power*, 399, says it is "only a possibility" she married Joseph before he died in June 1844. I accept George D. Smith's argument that Phebe Woodworth and Flora Woodworth are a probable mother/daughter pair of marriages because of Phebe's sealing to Joseph in the Nauvoo temple on January 17, 1846–evidence that "is tenuous but strongly suggests a marriage to Smith when he was alive." George D. Smith, *Nauvoo Polygamy*, 171. See also Lyndon W. Cook, *Nauvoo Marriages, Proxy Sealings: 1843-1846*, 85n3. Phebe Watrous Woodworth, proxy marriage to Joseph Smith, Jan. 17, 1846, Brigham Young as proxy. Brown, *Nauvoo Sealings, Adoptions, and Anointings*, 282.

30. Mary Ann Frost (Pratt), proxy marriage to Joseph Smith, Feb. 6, 1846, Heber C. Kimball as proxy. Brown, *Nauvoo Sealings, Adoptions, and Anointings*, 285.

31. George D. Smith and Gary James Bergera include as a possible wife Sarah Scott Mulholland, the wife of one of Joseph's scribes. See Smith, *Nauvoo Polygamy*, 218; Bergera, "Identifying the Earliest Mormon Polygamists," 31. Brian C. Hales adds two more possibilities: Esther Dutcher and Mary Heron. Hales, *Joseph Smith's Polygamy*, 1:401, 424, 449, 464.

relations with fewer than fifteen of the total thirty-some wives.[32] However, it is impossible to assert such a conclusion with complete certainty because Victorian sensibilities would have made these women reluctant to talk about their sexual experience, even using veiled or coded language. Emily Partridge Smith Young is unusual in saying, in response to questioning under oath, that the night after her marriage with Joseph, she "roomed" with him and had "carnal intercourse with him."[33] Another plural wife of Joseph, Melissa Lott Willes, testified in 1893 that she was Joseph's wife for "time and eternity" "in very deed."[34] But such admissions are among the exceptions.

Lucy Meserve Smith, wife of George A. Smith, claimed that Emma told her Joseph's wives "were sealed for eternity they were not to live with him and have children." Emma clearly meant that Joseph did not have sexual relations with them, a comment that expresses her hope but which cannot be supported completely by the evidence. Lucy herself countered by adding that George A. told her about "calling on Joseph late one evening and he was just taking a wash and Joseph told him that one of his wives had just been confined and Emma was the Midwife and he had been assisting her. He [George A.] told me [Lucy] this to prove to me that the women were married for time [and eternity], as Emma had told me that Joseph never taught any such thing."[35] Recognizing that even though Emma could have chosen not to know the reality of some of Joseph's unions, there was enough confusion about the nature of such marriages to leave many in the dark.

In 1905, when Joseph Smith III was trying to sort out his father's involvement in plural marriage, Salt Lake Stake President Angus M. Cannon visited with him in the Midwest. Joseph III asked a logical question: If his father truly had other wives, why there was "no issue from them." Cannon replied, "All I knew was that which Lucy Walker herself contends. They were so nervous and lived in such constant fear that they could not conceive. He made light of my reply. He said, 'I am informed that Eliza Snow was a virgin at the time of her death.' I in turn said, 'Brother Heber C. Kimball, I am informed, asked her the question if she was not a virgin although married

32. Marvin S. Hill, "Secular or Sectarian History," 95.

33. Emily Dow Partridge Young, in Temple Lot Case, Deposition Testimony, questions 310-11, 480-84, 747, 762.

34. Melissa Willes, Affidavit, Aug. 3, 1893, qtd. in Raymond Bailey, "Emma Hale," 99; see also Temple Lot Case, Complainant's Testimony, Deposition Testimony, questions 17, 227-31, 237-38, 255; Lawrence Foster, *Religion and Sexuality*, 156.

35. Lucy Meserve Smith, "Statement," May 18, 1892.

to Joseph Smith and afterward, to Brigham Young, when she replied in a private gathering, "I thought you knew Joseph Smith better than that.'"[36]

The memory of Joseph's plural wife Lucy Walker regarding the way Joseph talked about the gendered role of women in marriage is consistent with how later LDS prophets framed the subject. As he proposed the idea of celestial marriage, Joseph wove plurality into his narrative of salvation, life after death, and the difference between men and women. In marriage, according to Walker, a wife

> should be his bosom companions, the nearest and dearest objects on earth in every sense of the word. He [Joseph] said men must beware how they treat their wives. They are given them for a holy purpose that the myriads of spirits waiting for tabernacles might have pure healthy bodies. He also said many would awake in the morning of the resurrection sadly disappointed; for they, by transgression would have neither wives or children, for they surely would be taken from them, and given to those who should prove themselves worthy.[37]

Compton's tabulations create a demographic profile of the thirty-three women he identified as Joseph's wives. The largest group, eleven (33 percent) were either teenagers or young adults between the ages of fourteen and twenty. The next largest group was nine wives (27 percent), ages twenty-one to thirty. Thus, twenty of the thirty-three wives (60 percent) were in prime fertility years. Twenty-four percent (eight wives) were ages thirty-one to forty. Another 6 percent (two) were between forty-one and fifty, with a final three (9 percent) between ages fifty-one and sixty.[38] Fifty-five percent of these women were single when Joseph married them, 33 percent were living with civil husbands, and the remainder (12 percent) were widows.[39] The range of ages and circumstances of these marriages suggest the complexity of plural marriage in Nauvoo. There is no simple explanation for why Joseph married any of these women or when the sealings occurred.

Plural marriage in Nauvoo was more expansive and widely practiced than has been previously understood. George D. Smith's work demonstrates that, in addition to Joseph, some apostles and other Nauvoo men–close to

36. Angus M. Cannon, Statement of Interview with Joseph Smith III, 23.

37. Lucy Walker, in Lyman O. Littlefield, "*Reminiscences of Latter-day Saints*," www.boap.org/LDS/Early-Saints/LLittlefield.html (July 4, 2011).

38. Todd Compton, *In Sacred Loneliness*, 11-12.

39. Ibid., 12-23.

200 in all–began practicing plurality in Nauvoo. By the time they left Nauvoo, these men each had anywhere between one and thirty additional wives.[40] Smith argues for thirty-eight marriages, including Joseph's marriage to Emma Hale, or an average of one new wife each month between April 1841 and November 1843.[41] Smith distinguishes his study from Compton's by focusing on Joseph's marriages as part of his daily routines, thereby capturing a sense of the layering of Joseph's life. His work also provides an invaluable analysis of the patterns in Joseph's choices: he had been acquainted with most of his plural wives for at least a year, some for as many as eleven years, as the children of friends and associates, the widows of contemporaries or Church members, or the wives of men with whom he conducted business. Six of Joseph's wives had lived in his family home, helping and supporting Emma in a variety of ways.[42]

Of course, Joseph was not alone among American religious leaders in teaching the concept of plurality. Some nineteenth-century religious figures taught that affinity between spiritually attentive persons arose instinctively.[43] When men and women were stimulated by an awareness of their spiritual natures, they became spiritual husbands and wives. The spiritual sensitivity that led to spiritual unions was achieved through a lifelong movement toward perfection. Such behaviors as repentance, belief, and prayer prepared one for a spiritual union. Some groups such as John Humphrey Noyes's Oneida Colony embraced sexual intercourse as a manifestation of spiritual unions, but not all groups did.[44] Mormon plurality proposed a new paradigm that reflected Joseph's evolving concept of heaven.[45]

---

40. George D. Smith, *Nauvoo Polygamy*, 574-639.

41. Ibid.

42. According to Smith, rather than follow the attraction of a turn of a head or a winsome smile, Joseph seems to have mused deeply on the meaning of plurality and how it extended theologically throughout Mormonism. He likely chose marriage partners based on his understanding of plurality itself. As Joseph sought to understand his life as a prophet, his plural relations enhanced his knowledge of that role, his connections to others, and the significance of the sacrifices plurality demanded.

43. Bachman, "A Study of the Mormon Practice of Plural Marriage," 21.

44. For histories of some of these experimental marriage systems, see Erik Achorn, "Mary Cragin, Perfectionist Saint"; Maren L. Carden, Oneida; Sidney Ditzion, *Marriage, Morals, and Sex in America*; William Hepworth Dixon, *Spiritual Wifery*; John B. Ellis, *Free Love and Its Votaries*; William M. Kephart, "Experimental Family Organization"; Robert A. Parker, *A Yankee Saint*; Lawrence Foster, *Religion and Sexuality*; and Ernest R. Sandeen, "John Humphrey Noyes as the New Adam."

45. For a general discussion of the marriage customs and mores of nineteenth-century America, see Whitney R. Cross, *The Burned-Over District*, 238-51.

Evolution

In Kirtland, Ohio, during the 1830s, Joseph received some sixty-four revelations in seven years. Although he did not announce plurality publicly, there is some later evidence that plurality was in his mind even this early.[46] The ideas that framed polygamy may have evolved from 1831, foreshadowing the full expansion of the doctrine in Nauvoo.[47] In Joseph's thinking, the restoration of ancient religion must have included God's promise to Abraham that he would have posterity as plentiful as the dust of the earth (Gen. 13:16, 16:10, 17:6, 18:18, 22:17). When Joseph revised the Book of Genesis ("translating" it, as he said) in February 1831, he reportedly prayed for answers about plurality. Danel Bachman believes the Abraham passages sparked Joseph's imagination and made him curious about how plurality fit into the restoration religion of his day.[48] In fact, Joseph's 1843 revelation on celestial marriage links Abraham, the Abrahamic promise, marriage, and exaltation (D&C 132:30-37). Clearly American Christian primitivism helped to shape both Joseph's query about marriage and the way plurality evolved.[49] Faithfulness would be measured, in part, by the size of one's "earthly kingdom." Plural marriage and the increased number of children that might result was the surest method of expanding one's family, or kingdom, on the earth and an equally certain way to add to one's exaltation in the afterlife. For Joseph, Compton writes, "a fullness of salvation depended on the *quantity* of family members sealed to a man in this life."[50]

Orson Pratt, at October 1869's LDS general conference in Salt Lake City, asserted that early convert and apostle Lyman Johnson told him that Joseph "had made known to [Johnson] as early as 1831 that plural marriage was a correct principle" but it was not yet the right time to practice it. Pratt continued: "In the fore part of the year 1832, Joseph told individuals ... that the principle of taking more wives than one is a true principle, but the time had not yet come for it to be practiced."[51] Pratt also insisted that Joseph took "no license" as far as he knew.[52]

---

46. Bachman, "A Study of the Mormon Practice of Plural Marriage," 56.

47. Ibid., 54-59, discusses Joseph's relationship with Fanny Alger, a relationship that Compton, *In Sacred Loneliness*, 33, argues was Joseph's first plural marriage. See also Danel Bachman, "New Light on an Old Hypothesis," 19-33.

48. Bachman, "A Study of the Mormon Practice of Plural Marriage," 67-68n53; see also Robert J. Matthews, *A Plainer Translation*, 64-67.

49. Hill, "The Role of Christian Primitivism in the Origin and Development of the Mormon Kingdom, 1830-1844," chap.1.

50. Compton, *In Sacred Loneliness*, 11.

51. Orson Pratt, Oct. 7, 1869, JD 13:193; *History of the Church*, 5:xxxi.

52. Ibid.

Joseph reportedly told Joseph Bates Noble, who reportedly performed the first recognized plural marriage in Nauvoo, about a "revelation" regarding plural marriage during the fall of 1840, three years before he dictated the revelation that became Doctrine and Covenants 132. According to Noble, an angel instructed Joseph to "move forward in the said order [of marriage]."[53] For women and men who believed in angels, this potent image compelled them to act. Benjamin F. Johnson, whose two sisters married Joseph, reported, "The Lord revealed this to Brother Joseph long ago," but Joseph waited "until the Angel of the Lord came to him with a drawn sword and told him that he would be slain if he did not go forth and fulfill this law."[54]

Plurality, like much of Joseph's vision for the world, hinged on the use of priesthood keys–that is, power and authority. Moses, Elias, and Elijah reportedly visited him in the sacred space of the Kirtland temple in March 1836 to expand–if not always to clarify–his understanding of priesthood power, prophetic power, and the authority they evoked. Each ostensibly represented a different type of power and authority, rooted in a narrative that tied the Latter-day Saint experience to a larger course of religious history (D&C 110).[55] As religious motifs, the Saints' persecution narrative, doctrine of restoration, and interpretation of marriage and religious authority pulled nineteenth-century Mormons toward Old Testament predecessors and the roots of their religious belief.[56]

During the 1830s, ambiguity regarding the new knowledge and the lack of clarity in interpretation, combined with confusion about its actual practice, led to conflict and rumor. Moreover, it created an atmosphere of anomie where, as a result, others moved into unorthodox, unauthorized sexual relationships.[57] After his entrance into plurality, Joseph fought unauthorized polygamy to his death. "Satan," he said in 1839, inspired the idea but it was "licentiousness, such as a community of wives, which is an abomination in the sight of God." He used an easily understood analogy: "When a man consecrates or dedicates his wife and children, he does not give them to his brother, or his neighbor, for there is no such law: for the law of God is, Thou

53. Joseph B. Noble, Affidavit in Jenson, "Plural Marriage," 6:221.

54. Benjamin F. Johnson, *My Life's Review*, 85.

55. Jonathan A. Stapley refers to this as "cosmological priesthood." See his "Adoptive Sealing Ritual in Mormonism," *Journal of Mormon History* 37, no. 2 (Summer 2011): 53-117(esp. 57).

56. Bachman, "A Study of the Mormon Practice of Plural Marriage," 97.

57. Benjamin F. Johnson contends that Oliver Cowdery, Jared Carter, and Warren Parrish became the equivalent of a law unto themselves in their practice of plurality. In Dean R. Zimmerman, ed., *I Knew the Prophets*, 38.

shalt not commit adultery."[58] This early public reference to spiritual wives was ambiguous but laden with veiled references that could be interpreted in many ways, according to the listener's degree of inside knowledge.

The precedent for Joseph's right to enter plurality was set, at least in theory, in Kirtland, based on his position as prophet and the primacy of religious doctrine over secular law. Joseph addressed his right to perform marriage ceremonies on November 24, 1835, remarking that they should be solemnized "by the authority of the everlasting priesthood."[59] An 1841 document titled, "Words of the Prophets, Sprictural [sic] Items," quotes Hyrum Smith on the issue: "He that is called of God is not only a minister of the Law given by God but is also anointed to make Law according to their Authority."[60] Indeed, the LDS edition of the Doctrine and Covenants positions celestial marriage in the context of religious rather than civil law: "All covenants, oaths, vows, performances, connections, associations, or expectations, that are not made and entered into and sealed by the Holy Spirit of promise, of him who is anointed, both as well as for time and for all eternity, ... are of no efficacy, virtue, or force in and after the resurrection from the dead; for all contracts that are not made unto this end have an end when men are dead" (D&C 132:7).

Despite statements suggesting that Joseph received a revelation about plurality as early as 1831, that it was part of the "restoration of all things," and that it shaped his understanding of godliness and the afterlife, there are no records of contemporary conversations that demonstrate such early knowledge. Throughout these years, Joseph continued in his marriage to Emma, leaving hints in his correspondence about the evolution of his understanding of the possibly eternal nature of their relationship. He signed some of his early correspondence to her: "your husband until death." By 1842, he was closing: "through all eternity forevermore" and "through all eternity."[61] When one of his other wives brought stories to him about Emma, he reportedly rebuked her: "If you desire my love you must never speak evil

58. *History of the Church*, 3:230 (Dec. 16, 1839).

59. Ibid., 2:320 (Mar. 24, 1835).

60. Hyrum Smith, in "Words of the Prophets, Sprictural [sic] Items," qtd. in Bachman, "A Study of the Mormon Practice of Plural Marriage," 125-26.

61. Joseph Smith, Letter to Emma Smith, Oct. 13, 1832, in Dean C. Jessee, ed., *Personal Writings of Joseph Smith*, 277-83; May 18, 1834, 340-43; June 4, 1834, 344-46; Aug. 19, 1836, 389-90; Nov. 4, 1838, 398-404; Dec. 1, 1838, 415-22; Mar. 21, 1839, 448-53; Apr. 4, 1839, 463-69; Nov. 9, 1839, 483-84; Jan. 20, 1840, 489-92; Aug. 16, 1842, 553-56; June 23, 1844, 615-16; June 25, 1844, 620-23; June 27, 1844, 643-36.

of Emma."[62] When Emma fell seriously ill in October 1842, he hovered anxiously over her. She was some seven months pregnant with a son who did not survive birth, and the illness, probably typhoid or malaria, no doubt contributed to the baby's demise.

Confiding the Secret

Even before plurality was known by some of those surrounding him, Joseph occasionally alluded to arcane doctrines that he withheld out of fear they would be rejected, or worse. "[I]f I should make known what God has made known to me," Joseph reportedly told Levi Hancock in Kirtland, "they would seek my life."[63] In 1852, Brigham Young commented that Joseph had said to him in Kirtland, "If I was to reveal to this people what the Lord has revealed to me, there is not a man or woman who would stay with me."[64] In fact, rumors would run rampant in Nauvoo,[65] and plurality would eventually divide Joseph from some of his most trusted friends.

Despite Joseph's emphasis on the necessity for secrecy, his fear about the consequences to the Church of public disclosure, and his equally obvious misery caused by Emma's suspicions, there is considerable evidence that he longed to move fast, share more, and publicly proclaim the new doctrine of plural marriage. As he often did, Joseph combined venting with sermonizing when he spoke to the women of the Relief Society on April 29, 1842: "The Lord makes manifest to me many things, which it is not wisdom for me to make public."[66] Again to the Relief Society on June 9, he criticized those who claimed to be loyal but questioned his judgment. "How oft have wise men and women sought to dictate Brother Joseph by saying, 'O, if I were Brother Joseph, I would do this and that;' but if they were in Brother Joseph's shoes they would find that men or women could not be compelled into the kingdom of God, but must be dealt with in long suffering, and at last we shall save them."[67]

These references could have referred both to Joseph's vision of the political kingdom of God and to plurality. Not everyone embraced all of Joseph's teachings. The *History of the Church* quotes Joseph as saying in 1844, "I have

62. Lucy M. Wright, "Emma Hale Smith," *Woman's Exponent* 30, no. 8 (Dec. 15, 1901): 59.

63. Levi Hancock, qtd. in Mosiah Hancock, "The Prophet Joseph–Some of His Sayings," *Deseret News*, Feb. 21, 1884.

64. Brigham Young, May 25, 1852, JD 9:294.

65. See Oliver Olney, *The Absurdities of Mormonism Portrayed*, 5.

66. *History of the Church*, 4:608 (Apr. 29, 1842).

67. Ibid., 5:24 (June 9, 1842).

tried for a number of years to get the minds of the Saints prepared to receive the things of God; but we frequently see some of them, after suffering all they have for the work of God, will fly to pieces like glass as soon as anything comes that is contrary to their traditions; they cannot stand the fire at all."[68]

After Brigham Young and the Twelve Apostles returned to Nauvoo from England in mid-1841, Joseph began to introduce them to plural marriage, also known as celestial and/or patriarchal marriage, as well as to eternal marriage. "Spiritual wives" seems not to have been the preferred term. Heber C. Kimball was instructed not to tell his wife, Vilate, "for fear that she would not receive it." Reportedly, Joseph reasoned that "his life was in constant jeopardy, ... [including] from false brethren who had crept like snakes into his bosom and then betrayed him."[69]

Nor was secrecy the only demand. Joseph told Kimball he wanted Vilate for himself. It is impossible to know for certain what Joseph hoped to accomplish with these stunning simultaneous requests; but it is easy to imagine how disturbing this must have been for Kimball. Kimball fasted and prayed for understanding, and afterwards took the unknowing Vilate to Joseph's home. As it turned out, Joseph was only testing Kimball, who passed the Abrahamic test and, as a reward, was sealed to Vilate–who remained in the dark–for eternity.[70] When Joseph next instructed Kimball to take a plural wife, still without Vilate's knowledge, Kimball pled to be excused from the requirement. Joseph was unpersuaded and insisted he marry Sarah Noon, an Englishwoman with two small daughters who had left her husband.[71] According to Kimball's daughter, "sometimes the agony of his mind was so terrible that he would wring his hands and weep like a child, and beseech the Lord to be merciful and reveal to her this principle, for he himself could not break his vow of secrecy."[72] Eventually, Vilate guessed what was happening. In her 1881 reminiscence, she reportedly told her husband, "Heber, what you kept from me the Lord has shown me."[73]

68. Ibid., 6:185 (Jan. 21, 1844). According to Lawrence Foster, almost all of those who first heard about the doctrine of plurality reacted with "shock, horror, disbelief, or general emotional confusion," trailed by a "period of inner turmoil lasting from several days to several months." Praying, fasting, and testifying of a transformative "personal experience" left them with a changed mind about the doctrine. Foster, *Religion and Sexuality*, 153.

69. Helen Mar Whitney, "Scenes in Nauvoo," *Woman's Exponent* 10, no. 10 (Oct. 15, 1881), 74.

70. Stanley B. Kimball, *Heber C. Kimball*, 93.

71. Helen Mar Whitney, "Scenes and Incidents in Nauvoo," *Woman's Exponent* 10 (Oct. 15, 1881): 74.

72. Ibid.

73. Ibid.

Parley P. Pratt developed an understanding of the nature of eternal marriage before Joseph introduced the subject of plural marriage.[74] Prior to Joseph's teachings, Pratt had believed that close affections were "something from which the heart must be entirely weaned" before one entered heaven. However, Joseph taught, Pratt stated, "that the wife of my bosom might be secured to me for time and all eternity, ... while the result of our endless union would be an offspring as numerous as the stars of heaven, or the sands of the sea shore." He added, "Joseph Smith ... lifted a corner of the veil and [gave] me a single glance into eternity."[75] Pratt's first wife, Thankful, died before he learned about celestial marriage. He married Mary Ann Frost in 1837. Before teaching him about plurality, Joseph first assured him that he would have both wives in eternity. Later, in 1843, both Parley and Mary Ann accepted plurality (though Mary Ann first had to work through her objections).[76]

Hyrum Smith was not one of the first to learn about plural marriage. After Kimball and Young had been brought into Joseph's confidence, Hyrum confronted Young, saying, "I am convinced that there is something that has not been told me." Young denied knowing what he meant. Hyrum pushed harder: "I have mistrusted for a long time that Joseph has received a revelation that a man should have more than one wife, and he has hinted as much to me, but I would not bear it." Young told him that Joseph would tell him if he could, then agreed to tell Hyrum provided that he "never say another word against Joseph, and his doings, and the doctrines he is preaching to the people." Hyrum agreed, and Young laid out the new doctrine. Hyrum "bowed to it and wept like a child and said 'God be praised.'" Hyrum then told Joseph what he had learned, and "they went heart and hand together while they lived." Young framed the story around the martyrdom: "and they were together when they died, and they are together now defending Israel."[77]

It is interesting that Hyrum reconciled himself to Joseph's teaching as yet another covenant made sacred through God's authority. Hyrum apparently accepted plurality as a moral imperative and entered the ritual in 1843 when he married Robert B. Thompson's widow, Mercy Fielding Thompson,

74. Terry L. Givens and Matthew J. Grow, *Parley P. Pratt: The Apostle Paul of Mormonism* (New York: Oxford University Press, 2011), 174.

75. Parley P. Pratt, *Autobiography*, 297-98.

76. Vilate Kimball, Letter to Heber C. Kimball, June 24, 1843, Winslow Whitney Smith Collection, LDS Church History Library. Also printed with some modification in Helen Mar Whitney, "Scenes and Incidents in Nauvoo," *Woman's Exponent* 11, no. 8 (Sept. 15, 1882): 57.

77. Brigham Young, Oct. 8, 1866, General Conference Addresses, LDS Church History Library, qtd. in Driscoll, *Hyrum Smith*, 290n30.

the sister of his own civil wife, Mary Fielding. According to Mercy, Hyrum made "a covenant to deliver me up in the morning of the resurrection to Robert Blashel Thompson, with whatever offspring should be of that union,"[78] suggesting a form of levirate marriage. Joseph sealed Hyrum to his second plural wife in August 1843.[79]

When Joseph's male friends told the story of their introduction to polygamy, they recounted the anguish they felt at first hearing the doctrine, noting the time it took them to adjust mentally to it. Their narratives portray the power of Joseph's arguments, the persuasive rhetoric he used to convince them to comply. Kimball begged Joseph to remove the mandate, and "not till he commanded him [Kimball] in the name of the Lord did he obey."[80] Young said "it was the first time in my life that I desired the grave."[81] John Taylor "felt as a married man that this was to me … an appalling thing to do." He continued: "Joseph Smith told the Twelve that if this law was not practiced … then the Kingdom of God could not go one step further." Taylor, among others, "did not feel like putting ourselves in a position to retard the progress of the kingdom of God."[82]

But the challenge to their moral scruples went farther. Loyalty to Joseph obligated them publicly to deny plurality and to argue convincingly that the Church was not engaged in its practice. Public denials became a point of honor. Consequently, Hyrum taught those around him to do what they could to inhibit the doctrine, while, simultaneously, as many as thirty-three men and 124 women were sealed in plural unions before Joseph's death.[83]

Like other Saints when they first heard what must have seemed like an outrageous proposition, twenty-five-year-old Benjamin Johnson recoiled in disbelief. "Brother Joseph, this is all new to me," he said in April 1843, "it may all be true–you know, but I do not [know]. To my education it is all wrong." Joseph assured him that God commanded it, then asked for Almera, Johnson's sister. "His words astonished me," recorded Johnson,

But I am going, with the help of the Lord with the promise to you–to

78. Mercy Thompson, Letter to Joseph Smith III, Sept. 5, 1883; and Mercy R. Thompson, "An Important Testimony," *Deseret News*, Feb. 17, 1886, 15.

79. Catherine Phillips Smith, Affidavit, Jan. 28, 1903, in Joseph Fielding Smith, *Blood Atonement and the Origin of Plural Marriage*, 70.

80. Orson F. Whitney, *Life of Heber C. Kimball*, 325.

81. Brigham Young, July 14, 1855, JD 3:266.

82. John Taylor, qtd. in B. H. Roberts, *The Life of John Taylor*, 99.

83. George D. Smith, *Nauvoo Polygamy*, 353. Brian C. Hales postulates thirty men and 85 women. See www.josephsmithspolygamy.com/MISCFiles/JSPOverview.html (July 4, 2011).

> you–to do just what you say, if I [ever] should Know that you do this to degrade my sister I will kill you as the Lord lives. He looked at me, oh so calmly, and said "Br. Benjamin you will never see that day, but you shall see the day you will know it is true, and you will fulfill the law and greatly rejoice in it. … I promise you that when you open your mouth to your sister, it shall be filled."[84]

The young man, struggling to get his bearings, deferred to his prophet's judgment. He did what Joseph asked out of obedience; but when he began to talk to his sister about the doctrine, understanding swept over him. "I opened my mouth and my heart opened to the Light of the Lord my tongue was loosened and I was filled with the Holy Ghost."[85] Johnson's understanding deepened when he later heard Joseph's assurances that he never would have asked his people to embrace this principle if an angel of the Lord had not ordered it.[86]

Erastus Snow also learned about plurality from Joseph privately, confessing that Emma opposed the practice. "Emma believed that there could not be a Holy Alliance between the man and the woman unless the woman consented to it with all her heart." Snow told this heart-wrenching story five years before he died in 1888. "Emma used her womanly nature to teas[e] and annoy Joseph and went so far as to threaten Joseph that she would leave Him and cohabit with another man and the Lord forbade her in the Revelation."[87] In another account, Snow said the revelation came from the Lord and "requir[ed] his chosen and proved servants to take unto themselves wives," adding that Joseph had "introduced several of those who had been sealed to himself and others of the first elders of the Church."[88]

Justification

Joseph's justifications for plurality were varied–strategically so. They included the need for the restoration of "all things," the need to multiply one's offspring, and the centrality of positioning one–and one's kin–for celestial glory. Opponents, of course, had other explanations.[89] Five decades after his conversations with Joseph when Benjamin Johnson was in his seventies, he

84. Johnson, *My Life in Review*, 84.

85. Ibid.

86. Johnson, in Zimmerman, *I Knew the Prophets*, 44.

87. Erastus Snow, qtd. in "A Sinopsas of Remarks made by Apostle E[rastus] Snow July 22 [1883] at Nephi [Utah] Sunday evening."

88. Franklin R. Snow, "Autobiography of Erastus Snow," 109.

89. See, for example, John C. Bennett, *The History of the Saints*; Fanny Stenhouse, *Exposé*

recorded his understanding of the way plurality was best justified: "The First Command was to 'Multiply' and the Prophet taught us that Dominion & power in the great Future would be Commensurate with the no [number] of 'Wives Children & Friends' that we inherit here and that our great mission to earth was to organize a Neculi of Heaven to take with us. To the increase of which there would be no end."[90] Since Joseph evidently consummated at least some marriages and apparently continued the sexual relationship beyond initial intercourse, he seems to have accepted the desirability that these unions would produce offspring, though there is, admittedly, no actual proof yet that pregnancies resulted.[91]

Doctrine and Covenants 49:8 offers an interesting angle from which to consider plurality: "Wherefore, I will that all men shall repent, for all are under sin, except those which I have reserved unto myself, holy men that ye know not of." Joseph's teaching about lineage suggests that the spiritual elite might do more than simply multiply. They could create a special lineage. These elites, inducted privately into the mysteries of God, had been endowed with priesthood powers, practiced God's rituals without the constraints of sin and repentance, and were prepared to build the kingdom of God on the earth and in heaven. What could their children not accomplish?

Less esoterically, marriages that seem to have been motivated primarily by dynastic considerations extended beyond young women capable of bearing children (Helen Mar Kimball, Sarah Ann Whitney, and Flora Ann Woodworth) whose fathers were Church leaders. In the case of two older women, Fanny Young and Rhoda Richards, their brothers were well-regarded apostles who were close to Joseph and who, thanks to their sisters' plural marriage sealings, would remain so in the next life.

Although Joseph left no direct accounts of how he understood plurality, second-hand reports are steeped in Old Testament rhetoric about multiplying and replenishing. Logically, wives of child-bearing age would be at a premium. The average age of wives in Danel Bachman's list of thirty-one probable wives is 29.4, with twenty-five out of thirty-one wives younger than

---

of Polygamy in Utah and *"Tell It All"*; Increase McGee Van Dusen, *The Mormon Endowment*; and Oliver Olney, *The Absurdities of Mormonism Portrayed.*

90. Johnson, in Zimmerman, *I Knew the Prophets*, 47.

91. Brian C. Hales argues for two pregnancies: a daughter born to Sylvia Sessions in 1844 and a son either miscarried or stillborn to Olive Frost. See www.josephsmithspolygamy.com/JSPSexuality/MASTERJSPSexuality.html (July 4, 2011). According to Lawrence Foster, "evidence for children Smith may have had by plural wives in based largely on oral and family traditions" (Foster, *Religion and Sexuality*, 157).

forty at the time of their marriages to Joseph. Of Todd Compton's list of thirty-three wives, 84 percent were under forty.[92] Excluding the alleged offspring of Joseph, only four children are known to have been born in plurality before Joseph's death.[93] Even recognizing the difficulty of reconstructing an accurate record, this small number suggests that acceptance of the doctrine may have spread carefully through the most tightly knit circle of Saints but that the actual practice was more cautiously undertaken. Periods of improvisation and experimentation were followed, during which some men and women conducted makeshift marriages while others waited to observe the model or to receive additional instructions.[94]

Plurality cemented social and familial relationships with kinship bonds that wove new family networks through the Mormon community. Emily and Eliza Partridge, Sarah Ann Whitney, and Helen Mar Kimball were the daughters of Joseph's closest colleagues. According to Elizabeth Ann Whitney, her daughter, Sarah, was the "first woman ever given in plural marriage by or with the consent of both parents."[95] Joseph's proposed marriage to Nancy Rigdon makes sense in this same context, as a powerful way for Joseph to connect Sidney Rigdon and his family to him. Helen Kimball understood that her father's motivation in offering her to Joseph as a plural wife was his "great desire to be connected with the Prophet."[96]

Not the least of the many conundrums roused by plural marriage are the questions it poses about gendered understandings in Nauvoo.[97] Gender

92. Bachman, "A Study of the Mormon Practice of Plural Marriage," 104-43; Compton, *In Sacred Loneliness*, 11.

93. Bergera, "Identifying the Earliest Mormon Polygamists, 1841-44," 50.

94. Young married his first plural wife, Lucy Ann Decker Seeley, in mid-1842; August Adams Cobb and Harriett Cook in November 1843; and Lucy's cousin, Clarissa Decker, in May 1844. Besides these women, Young courted Martha Brotherton who turned eighteen in 1842. After she rebuffed his proposal, she published a description of the episode in the *American Bulletin* (St. Louis) and in the *Warsaw Signal*.

95. Elizabeth Ann Whitney, qtd. in Carol Cornwall Madsen, ed., *In Their Own Words*, 202.

96. Helen Mar Kimball Smith Whitney, "Autobiography to Her Children," Mar. 30, 1881 in Jeni Brobert Holzapfel and Richard Neitzel Holzapfel, eds., *A Woman's View*, 482. According to Bergera, "Identifying the Earliest Mormon Polygamists," 48: "The majority of plural husbands were members of an elite class of LDS priesthood holders. All of them had been ordained to the Melchizedek Priesthood and all held the office of Seventy or higher. Just being practicing polygamists prior to Joseph Smith's death put them in a select category. But all of them were also members of either Smith's Quorum of the Anointed (early temple endowment initiates) or of the Council of Fifty (political kingdom of God), or had received their second anointings. One-third of plural husbands received all of these privileges prior to Smith's death; but more than a third of plural husbands received none of these blessings before Smith died."

97. As sociologist Michael S. Kimmel notes: "Gender is a central, primordial experience, one that permeates every aspect of social life, constructing the values, attitudes, and behaviors

implies socially constructed meanings. It is a process, in that it is negotiated, renegotiated, and contested over time. Gendering processes are simultaneously inclusive and exclusive by nature. In plural marriage, gender roles put women in vulnerable, essentially powerless positions. Faced with an impossibly loaded request, some women found a way to reconcile the gap between what they believed was righteous behavior while others could not find a way to accommodate this new understanding.

Furthermore, since Joseph spoke for God in every one of these encounters, the weight of his pronouncements was enormous. A conversation with William Clayton in July 1842 reveals a disquieting look at Joseph's view of himself as gatekeeper:

> This A.M. President Joseph took me and conversed considerable concerning some delicate matters. Said [Emma] wanted to lay a snare for me. He told me last night of this and said he had felt troubled. He said [Emma] had treated him coldly and badly since I came … and he knew she was disposed to be revenged on him for some things. … He said [Robert] Thompson professed great friendship for him but he gave away to temptation and he had to die. Also Brother [Newel] Knight he gave him one but he went to loose conduct and he could not save him. Also B[righam] Y[oung] had transgressed his covenant and he pled with the Lord to spare him this end and he did so, otherwise he would have died. B[righam] denied having transgressed He said if I would do right by him and abide his council he could save my life while he lived. I feel desirous to do right and would rather die than to loose my interest in the celestial kingdom.[98]

These musings, if Clayton recorded them accurately, show Joseph struggling for ways to emphasize the seriousness of God's instruction about this radical reordering of human life. For Joseph, agreeing to plurality became a line in the sand. Those who failed to step across it into a new life would surely suffer dire consequences. The men he named were literally dead, but the metaphoric threat was eternal damnation. "For Smith," Gary James Bergera writes, "plural marriage represented the pinnacle of his theology of exaltation: the husband as king and priest, surrounded by queens and priestesses eternally procreating spirit children. As these spirit offspring enter mortality, they, by their obedience, accrue both to themselves, through their

---

that constitute cultural experience" (Kimmel, "Introduction: The Power of Gender and the Gender of Power," 1).

98. Clayton, Journal, July 23, 1842, in George D. Smith, *An Intimate Chronicle*, 108.

own children, and to their eternal parents additional glory, power, and exaltation–the entire process of exaltation cycling forever worlds without end."[99]

Joseph's Plural Wives, 1841-42

As 1842 began, Joseph had already married three plural wives in Nauvoo: Louisa Beaman, Zina Huntington Jacobs, and Presendia Huntington Buell. Before the end of that year, he would reportedly marry at least ten more: Agnes Coolbrith Smith, Mary Elizabeth Rollins Lightner, Patty Bartlett Sessions, Marinda Johnson Hyde, Elizabeth Davis Durfee, Sarah Cleveland, Delcena Johnson Sherman, Eliza R. Snow, Sarah Ann Whitney, and Martha McBride.[100] Of these 1841-42 marriages, three involved widows, seven were polyandrous, and three were to single women. Eventually, three pairs of sisters would account for 16 percent of Joseph's plural wives: Eliza and Emily Partridge, Maria and Sarah Lawrence, and Zina and Presendia Huntington. Half of his wives were members of the Nauvoo Female Relief Society and had heard his instructions about secret-keeping.[101]

Without duplicating previous studies of Joseph's wives, including my own, a closer look at some of these women provides insights into how Joseph taught polygamy, won acquiescence, and ushered the women into the life-changing practice.

The Huntington Sisters

Daughters of William Huntington and Zina Baker Huntington, Zina and Presendia Huntington were converts from upstate New York who sold their family farm, left their extended families behind, and exchanged one plan for life for another. (See also chap. 9.) In Kirtland, the girls became known for their spiritual sensitivity, defined by their spiritual gifts.[102]

When Zina Baker died in 1839, Emma Smith nursed the teenage Zina Diantha, also seriously ill, back to health in the Smith home. It was about

99. Bergera, "Identifying the Earliest Mormon Polygamists, 1841-44," 4.

100. There is some conflicting evidence about the dating of Joseph's sealing to Sylvia Sessions Lyon (either in early 1842, a month before her mother's marriage to Joseph, or in February 1843). Brian Hales believes that Sylvia and Joseph were sealed in 1843, when Sylvia was possibly separated from her husband, Windsor Lyon. See Brian C. Hales, "The Joseph Smith-Sylvia Sessions Plural Sealing: Polyandry or Polygyny?" *Mormon Historical Studies* 9, no. 1 (2008): 41-57. However, that Sylvia was present for her mother's sealing to Joseph and also soon thereafter was admitted into the Relief Society may suggest that she knew about plurality in 1842 but gave uncertain data about the date of her own marriage to Joseph.

101. See Bergera, "Identifying the Earliest Mormon Polygamists, 1841-44," 47-48, 50.

102. See Presendia Huntington Buell Smith Kimball, in Edward W. Tullidge, *Women of Mormondom*, 207-208.

that time that Joseph, then thirty-four, reportedly taught Zina about the celestial dimensions of the afterlife.[103] He positioned plural marriage as central to God's "new and everlasting covenant." Couples sealed through priesthood authority would receive "an exceeding and an eternal weight of glory, thrones, kingdoms, principalities, and powers." For persecuted, poverty-stricken men and women struggling to get a foothold in a new life, the promise of a "fullness and a continuation of the seeds forever and ever" was compelling. Through plurality, they could become "gods, because they have no end; therefore shall they be from everlasting to everlasting, because they continue" (D&C 132:19-20).

Weighing against Zina's repulsion was her deference to Joseph. She considered him God's spokesman and the embodiment of male priesthood power. On the one hand, she must have been flattered that the prophet–a charismatic, powerful male–found her desirable, however she understood that complicated proposition. But she also felt loyalty to Emma. Even in the series of short autobiographies that Zina would write, she was reserved and circumspect about her reaction. Praying continuously for understanding, she focused on what she believed was true about Joseph's role as prophet and restoration of ancient religion.[104]

No record exists of how Zina explained her decision to accept Joseph's marriage proposal to her new husband, Henry Jacobs, or how Henry responded. Jacobs was a faithful Mormon who served several missions during the Nauvoo years. Because he was devoted to Joseph, his faith likely bound him to accept his prophet's instruction. Whether Zina presented this new demand as securing her place in heaven, tying her fortune to the life of an individual with higher status in the priesthood hierarchy, or something else, she "made a greater sacrifice than to give my life for I never anticipated again to be looked upon as an honorable woman by those I dearly loved."[105]

As an elderly woman, Zina described her marriage to Jacobs as "unhappy," cryptically telling an interviewer in 1898 that "we parted"; other records suggest a more complex situation. Her conversation with the interviewer leaves readers unclear about the nature of her marriage to Joseph–was it for eternity only, or for time and eternity?[106] If for eternity only, then perhaps there was not a sexual aspect to it. However, in an affidavit Zina signed,

103. Zina Diantha [Huntington Jacobs Smith] Young, Autobiography, n.d. [ca. 1890].

104. See Zina D. H. Young, Address in the Tabernacle, n.d., 1.

105. Zina D. H. Young, Autobiography, n.d., typescript.

106. John W. Wight, "Evidence from Zina D. Huntington-Young," Oct. 1, 1898, 28-30.

she asserted that she had been "married or sealed to Joseph Smith, ... according to the laws of the same, regulating marriage," a contract that seems to imply marital relations.[107]

Six weeks after Zina's marriage to Joseph, reportedly on October 27, 1841, the same message was delivered to her older sister, Presendia. Years after the fact, Presendia would write, "In 1841 I entered into the New Everlasting Covenant–was sealed to Joseph Smith the Prophet and Seer, and to the best of my ability I have honored plural marriage, never speaking one word against the principle. ... Never in my life, in this kingdom, which is 44 years, have I doubted the truth of this great work."[108] Presendia described her civil husband, Norman Buell, as an apostate; and it is true that he was not actively Mormon after leaving Missouri.[109] Still, she remained his wife and continued to bear his children. If the two sisters discussed their entrance into plural marriage, they left no records of it. Still, their special status must have provided a measure of support as they negotiated the complications of a split commitment between their two husbands.

The third of Joseph's unions that were polyandrous are puzzling because they represent an innovation that the apostles who perpetuated polygamy did not continue, with the possible exception of Brigham Young. Perhaps Joseph's main motive was dynastic, for new and powerful family relationships were created or enforced. Like twenty-first century scholars, mid-twentieth-century LDS Apostle John A. Widstoe examined the varieties of plural unions in the 1840s. During Joseph's life, there was not a single template for plural marriages. Instead, various combinations created new types of familial connections for this and the next life: "Zealous women, some of them married as well as unmarried, loving the cause of the restored gospel, considered

107. Zina D. H. Young, Affidavit, in Joseph F. Smith, Affidavit Books, May 1, 1869. Probing such intimate issues was difficult for Zina, "It was something too sacred to be talked about," she confessed. "It was more to me than life or death. I never breathed it for years" (Zina D. H. Young, qtd. in Wight, "Evidence from Zina D. Huntington-Young").

108. Presendia Lathrop Huntington Smith Kimball, Autobiographical Sketch, Apr. 1, 1881, typescript, 1.

109. Bachman, "A Study of the Mormon Practice of Plural Marriage," 134, claims: "Three of Smith's wives experienced marital difficulties in their first marriage, and it appears that he [Joseph] wed them out of concern for both their earthly and eternal welfare." But Compton, "Trajectory of Plurality," 22, counters: "Such an interpretation is not supported by the totality of the evidence. Of the twelve certain polyandrous marriages (counting Sarah Ann Whitney), only three had non-member husbands: Mary Rollins (Lightner), Ruth Vose (Sayers), and Sarah Kingsley (Cleveland). And only one first husband was disaffected from the church when Joseph married the wife–Norman Buell, husband of Presendia Huntington." All the other husbands were active members of the Church at the time of their wives' marriages to Joseph.

their condition in the hereafter and asked that they might be sealed to the Prophet for eternity. They were not to be his wives on earth, in mortality, but only after death, in the eternities. Such marriages led to much misunderstanding by those not of the Church and unfamiliar with its doctrines and practices."[110] Although Widtsoe does not differentiate between wives who were single and those who were already married, framing such marriages in the context of eternal progression suggests a reason–though somewhat self-serving–why some women consented to a kind of polyandry.

Women married to nonmembers were not likely to confide their new status to their husbands, no matter how sympathetic. Those wives married to member-husbands, on the other hand, would no doubt have been cruelly burdened by secrecy. The result was a hierarchy of relationships that created mental compartmentalizations that must have been psychologically challenging in the extreme.

Sylvia Sessions Lyon and Patty Bartlett Sessions

A unique mother-daughter bond connected Sylvia Sessions Lyon and her mother, Patty Barlett Sessions. Both were married to faithful Latter-day Saint men. Patty was forty-seven and married to David Sessions when she was sealed to Joseph by Willard Richards on March 9, 1842.[111] Sylvia, twenty-three, married to Windsor Lyon and herself a mother, witnessed her mother's plural marriage.[112]

Older women like Patty Sessions and Elizabeth Durfee acted as instructors and go-betweens in negotiating Joseph's plural unions and provided social cover for his meetings with young wives. Although it may be challenging to understand the motivation behind Patty's activity, it is fair to say that it demonstrated her obedience to Joseph's prophetic role. But why these two women, who seem to have had good marriages to righteous men, linked their futures to Joseph is more complicated. Windsor Lyon's temporary departure–or excommunication–from the Church may explain Sylvia's choice, in part. Nearly a decade after polygamy had been publicly announced, Brigham Young stated: "Also there was another way–in which a

110. John A. Widtsoe, *Joseph Smith*, 240.

111. Patty Bartlett Sessions, Journal, page after June 16, 1860, in Donna Toland Smart, ed., *Mormon Midwife*, 276.

112. Sylvia Sessions Lyon, Affidavit, 1869, Joseph F. Smith, Affidavit Books. Bergera wonders if Sylvia would have been permitted to be present if she herself had not already been sealed to Joseph as a plural wife. See Gary James Bergera, review of Newell G. Bringhurst and Craig L. Foster, eds. *The Persistence of Polygamy: Joseph Smith and the Origins of Polygamy*, 111.

woman could leave [a] man–if the woman Preferred–another man higher in authority & he is willing to take her & her husband gives her up–there is no Bill of divorce required in the case it is right in the sight of God."[113] Young said that he received this directly from Joseph. If Patty and David, and Sylvia and Windsor all agreed, these sealings tied their family to Joseph with a unique, powerful bond.

Sylvia's daughter, Marian, died on March 19, 1842. The grieving mother may not have known it, but she was either newly pregnant or would become pregnant within days. The childbirth was tortuous. Sylvia survived, but the baby boy died. In about May 1842, she became pregnant with her fourth child, daughter Josephine. On January 27, 1844, three-year-old Philofreen died. Joseph and Willard Richards paid a condolence call that evening. Nineteenth-century parents faced the death of a children more frequently than twentieth-first-century parents. Still, Sylvia's sadness may have been immense. Complicating matters, Windsor had suffered significant financial setbacks in August 1842, almost six months after his wife's sealing to Joseph. After bringing a lawsuit against Nauvoo Stake President William Marks for conflicted interests, Lyon was "cut off" from the Church but was rebaptized in 1846.

On February 8, 1843, Sylvia gave birth to Josephine Rosetta Lyon, who evidently came to believe she had been fathered by Joseph. In 1915, Josephine attested: "Just prior to my mothers death in 1882 she called me to her bedside … to tell me something which she had kept as an entire secret from me and from all others … She then told me that I was the daughter of the Prophet Joseph Smith, she having been sealed to the Prophet at the time that her husband Mr. Lyon was out of fellowship with the Church."[114] It is unclear how Sylvia suspected that Josephine was Joseph's child (though Josephine's name may indicate a certain inclination on Sylvia's part); impossible to know the state of Sylvia's marriage to Windsor; and if, in fact, she felt Windsor's

113. Brigham Young, qtd. in James Beck, Notebooks, 1859-65, Vol. 1, Oct. 8, 1861, LDS Church History Library, qtd. in Foster, *Religion and Sexuality*, 162. See also Frederick Kessler, Diary, Oct. 8, 1861.

114. Sylvia Sessions Lyon, Affidavit, 1869, in Joseph F. Smith Affidavit Books, 1:60 (the affidavit is unfinished). See Bachman, "A Study of the Mormon Practice of Plural Marriage," 108n10, which could indicate her reticence at giving specific information about such private matters. According to Compton, *In Sacred Loneliness*, 681-82: "One possible interpretation of an unfinished affidavit is that the woman gave the information about her marriage to church authorities, but was unwilling to publicly admit it." Josephine Rosetta Lyon Fisher, certificate, Feb. 24, 1915, original in LDS Church History Library, qtd. in Bachman, "A Study of the Mormon Practice of Plural Marriage," 141n76.

temporary excommunication had effectively nullified their union.[115] LDS historian Kathryn Daynes notes that "nothing is less understood than Joseph Smith's sealings to women already married, because the evidence supports conflicting interpretations."[116]

It is consistent with the LDS doctrine of "higher law"–for example, a priesthood-sanctioned marriage sealing–to imagine that Sylvia and Windsor's civil marriage was superceded by a sealing between Sylvia and Joseph, one that trumped civil marriage without a legal divorce. Apostle Orson Pratt denounced civil law in 1847: "As all the ordinances of the gospel Administered by the world since the Apostícy of the church was illegal, in like manner was the marriage Cerimony illegal." The children of such "illegal" unions were effectively "bastards," requiring adoption into the Mormon priesthood to "become sons and legal heirs to salvation."[117] More than three decades after Sylvia and Joseph's marriage, early Mormon stalwart-turned-dissident John D. Lee recalled Nauvoo's fluid relationships: "If a [couple's] marriage relations had not been productive of blessings and peace, and they felt it oppressive to remain together, they were at liberty to make their own choice, as much as if they had not been married."[118] Worthy priesthood holders could assure prospective wives of the correctness of their union.[119]

At Joseph's death, most of his plural wives were sealed to members of the Twelve.[120] In the Mormon cosmos, these men were kings, the pinnacle of priesthood hierarchy. After her sealing to Brigham Young as proxy for Joseph on February 2, 1846, Zina Huntington Jacobs Smith received her second anointing as a queen and priestess, the Church's highest temple ordinance. A month earlier, Presendia was sealed to Heber Kimball as proxy for Joseph.[121] Effectively released from their civil marriages to their civil husbands, Zina and Presendia were married for time to Young and to Kimball, respectively, but for eternity to Joseph. No formal divorces (from Jacobs or

---

115. See Brian C. Hales, "The Joseph Smith-Sylvia Sessions Plural Sealing," 48, 50, 53; also Kathryn M. Daynes, *More Wives Than One: Transformation of the Mormon Marriage System, 1840-1910*, 29-30, for a discussion of sexuality in Joseph's plural marriages.

116. Kathryn M. Daynes, *More Wives Than One*, 29.

117. Orson Pratt, qtd. in Scott G. Kenney, ed., *Wilford Woodruff's Journal, 1833-1898*, 3:260. It is important to note that Church leaders continued to sanction and perform civil marriages in Nauvoo.

118. John D. Lee, *Mormonism Unveiled*, 151.

119. See Rex E.. Cooper, *Promises Made to the Fathers*, 142.

120. Oa Cannon, untitled narrative, 23.

121. Martha Sonntag Bradley and Mary Firmage Woodword, *The Four Zinas*, 132.

Buell) ever occurred, and both women continued to live with their civil husbands for a time thereafter.

According to Victor Turner, ritual enacts multiple processes as an individual transitions from one state to another.[122] Participants in LDS marriage sealing ceremonies spent some time in a liminal state, as "liminal" persons who expressed with their lives the ambiguities of that state.[123] Sylvia's entrance into plurality introduced her to sacred, coded meanings that set her apart from others as one of her Church's most elite members, gifted with sacred knowledge. Women like Sylvia, Patty, and other wives no doubt reflected on the meaning and values of their new spiritual, social, and cosmological order. In the liminal state created by ritual, relations made different sense, earthly norms became irrelevant, and authority flowed through priesthood figures. The "sameness" of "liminal" persons created "a community of comrades and not a structure of hierarchically arrayed positions."[124]

Mary Elizabeth Rollins Lightner

Probably in February 1842–the exact day is not known–Joseph was sealed to Mary Elizabeth Rollins Lightner, perhaps his eighth plural wife.[125] At the time she was in her mid-twenties and had known Joseph since Kirtland. In 1905, when she was eighty-seven, she related her cherished–probably embellished–memories of 1842 to a sympathetic audience at LDS Church-owned Brigham Young University. Her narrative illuminates what she remembered of her courtship: how Joseph presented plural marriage, positioned the doctrine in the Mormon plan of salvation, and justified his request by invoking divine confirmation, including angelic ministrations. Mary's own dreams of being Joseph's wife had foreshadowed the proposal. As she recalled them, the dreams distressed her. "I thought I was a great sinner. I prayed to God to take it from me."[126] Mary does not say if the dreams continued after August

122. Victor Turner, *The Forest of Symbols*, 93-103; Victor Turner, *The Ritual Process*, 94-96, 102-106.

123. Turner, *The Ritual Process*, 95.

124. Turner, *The Forest of Symbols*, 100.

125. Lightner's own accounts differ. See her "Statement," Feb. 8, 1902: "Brigham Young sealed me to him, for time and all eternity–Feb. 1842"; her letter to A. M. Chase, Apr. 20, 1904, qtd. in J.D. Stead, *Doctrines and Dogmas of Brighamism Exposed*, 218-19: "I was sealed to him the fore part of February 1842"; her "Mary Elizabeth Rollins," photocopy of holograph, Susa Young Gates Papers: "After receiving other testimoies, I felt I could no longer disbelieve and in the month of March [1842], Brigham Young sealed us for time and all eternity."

126. Mary Elizabeth Rollins Lightner, "Remarks at Brigham Young University ... April 14, 1905." Mary sometimes gave her sealing date as February 1841 but more frequently as February

11, 1835, when, at age seventeen, she married Adam Lightner, a twenty-five-year-old non-Mormon. For an impressionable young woman, Joseph's masculinity and spiritual charisma, combined with these dreams, made her ripe for what followed despite her efforts to resist it. Her response was gendered, impossibly entangled with her faith in Joseph as a prophet and a man, but also in the sense that a male exercise of power was something to which a young woman would submit.

Like Zina and Presendia, Mary continued to cohabit with her husband after being sealed to Joseph. Asked later in life why she stayed married to Adam, she replied, "I did just as Joseph told me to do for he knew what troubles I would have to contend with."[127] During the Nauvoo period, Adam and Mary moved three times in and around Nauvoo.[128] She taught painting for a while and, with her earnings, bought a lot not far from the Smith home where she and Adam planned their fourth move. Among her students were Julia Murdock Smith, the adopted daughter of Joseph and Emma, and Sarah Ann Whitney, the daughter of Elizabeth Ann and Newel K. Whitney and future plural wife of Joseph Smith.[129]

According to Mary's autobiographical account, recorded in her seventies, Joseph first approached her about plurality in February 1842, accompanied by Brigham Young. She married Joseph that same month. Adam was struggling to find a job in Farmington, fifty miles east of Nauvoo, and Mary was pregnant with their third child. Joseph reportedly told Mary that she was predestined to belong to him: "[Joseph said] I was his before I came here. … I was created for him before the foundation of the Earth was laid." Joseph's reference to a premortal existence and to the continuation of their union after death placed plurality in a grand eternal context. Because civil marriage was of the earth, and therefore momentary, it was overridden by the sacred bond of celestial marriage which united man and woman for eternity.

Mary apparently resisted. She had, after all, been raised in a monogamous family, had been in a committed marriage for six years, and–except for her guilty dreams–had never considered plurality. She recalled questioning Joseph almost sarcastically:

1842. Thomas Milton Tinney, "The Royal Family of the Prophet Joseph Smith," 254-58; "The Life and Testimony of Mary E. Lightner," 1-44.

127. Mary Elizabeth Rollins Lightner Smith Young, Letter to Emmeline B. Wells, Nov. 21, 1880, qtd. in Richard S. Van Wagoner, *Mormon Polygamy*, 43.

128. Mary Elizabeth Lightner, "Autobiography."

129. Compton, *In Sacred Loneliness*, 211.

> "Well" said I, "don't you think it was an angel of the Devil that told you these things?"
>
> Said he "No. It was an angel of God. God Almighty showed me the difference between an angel of Light and Satan's angels. The angel came to me three times between the years of '34 and '42 and said I was to obey the principle or he would slay me."

Joseph's answer exerted his authority in two ways: he could tell the difference between an angel and a devil, and he had received the commandment three separate times, the last time with a death threat attached. He told Mary that their marriage would guarantee Mary's salvation, making her part of his own eternal dynasty: "I know that I shall be saved in the Kingdom of God," she reported him as saying. "All that he gives me I shall take with me for I have that authority and that power conferred upon me."

Even after a "long" conversation, Mary insisted: "I would have a witness." Joseph asked if she "was going to be a traitor." Mary responded, "I have never told a mortal and shall never tell a mortal I had such a talk from a married man." Joseph then assured her: "Pray earnestly for the angel said to me you should have a witness."

She continued:

> I went out and got between three hay-stacks where no one could see me.... I knelt down and if ever a poor mortal prayed I did. A few nights after that an angel of the Lord came to me and if ever a thrill went through a mortal it went through me. I gazed upon the clothes and figure but the eyes were like lightening. They pierced me from the crown of my head to the soles of my feet. I was frightened almost to death for a moment. ... The angel leaned over me and the light was very great although it was night....

Mary recalled Joseph seeking her out the next Sunday and asking if she had received her "witness." Perhaps taken aback when she said, "No." He rejoined, "The angel expressly told me you should have." Mary then confessed:

> "I have not had a witness, but I have seen something I have never seen before. I saw an angel and I was frightened almost to death. I did not speak." He studied awhile and put his elbows on his knees and his face in his hands. He looked up and said, "How could you have been such a coward?" Said I, "I was weak." ... "[T]hat was an angel of the living God. He came to you with more knowledge, intelligence, and light than I ever dared to reveal." ... Said I, "will it ever come again?" He thought a moment and then said, "No. Not the same one, but if you are faithful

> you shall see greater things than that." And then he gave me three signs of what would take place in my own family, although my husband was far away from me at that time. Every word came true. I went forward and was sealed to him. Brigham Young performed the sealing, and Heber C. Kimball the blessing.[130]

As Mary's account makes plain, even after sixty years, these confrontations with ultimate demands were anguishing. Torn by the question of whether Joseph talked with God or was misguided, the women struggled to understand, to consider how their response would change their lives.

Marinda Nancy Johnson Hyde

Twenty-seven-year-old Marinda Johnson Hyde was part of the initial group of women who joined the Relief Society on March 17, 1842. In April, she was sealed to Joseph, ten years her senior. They had known each other for eleven years. In a coded list of Joseph's marriages that a scribe later wrote in Joseph's diary appears this entry: "Apr[il] [18]42 Marinda Johnson [Hyde] to Joseph Smith."[131] The marriage probably occurred by the end of the first week in April since, on April 9, Joseph solicited Marinda's help in approaching nineteen-year-old Nancy Rigdon as another potential plural wife.

It is impossible to reconstruct Marinda's motivation, but her cooperation points to his power over those around him. In situations like this, Joseph's charisma drew people like Marinda out of their ordinary lives and into a new reality which they believed could bring them into the presence of God.

Orson Hyde, who had left Nauvoo on April 15, 1840, to dedicate the land of Palestine in anticipation of the return of the Jews, returned to his young wife and his prophet on December 7, 1842. The very same day, Joseph dined with Orson and Marinda. "His [Orson's] presence was gratifying,"

130. "Remarks by Sister Mary E. Lightner Who Was Sealed to Joseph Smith in 1842, She is 87 Years of Age," at Brigham Young University, April 14, 1905, LDS Church History Library. In 1892, Mary commented: "I could explain some things in regard to my living with Mr. L. after becoming the Wife of another, which would throw light, on what now seems mysterious–and you would be perfectly satisfied with me. I write this; because I have heard that it had been commented on to my injury." Mary E. Lightner, Letter to John R. Young, Jan. 25, 1892. For Lightner, this marriage seemed to guarantee her salvation.

131. *History of the Church*, 5:200 (Dec. 7, 1842). For other references to this marriage, see "W.," "Communication Mr. Editor," *Warsaw Signal*, June 11, 1845, 2; William Hall, *The Abominations of Mormonism Exposed*, 113; John D. Lee, *Mormonism Unveiled*, 147; Ann Eliza Webb Young, *Wife Number 19*, 324-26. In May 1843, Joseph and Marinda may have been sealed a second time. See Marinda Hyde, Affidavit, May 1, 1869, Joseph F. Smith, Affidavit Books, 1:15. Orson and Marinda subsequently received their temple endowments as a reward for their faithfulness. Orson continued to cohabit with Marinda, and the couple's last child was born in 1858.

Joseph wrote. "[S]pent the day with E[lde]r Hyde & drawing wood."[132] This terse note truly understates the interaction so charged with sexual or, in the case of an eternity sealing, spiritual overtones, and illustrates how free plurality was from guilt, regret, or remorse. For Joseph, it seems to have been simply a ritual required by God, regardless of the complexities it introduced into his life.

It is unclear when Orson learned that Marinda had been sealed to Joseph. But by February or March 1843, Joseph had evidently taught the doctrine to Orson. According to twenty-seven-year-old convert Mary Ann Price,

> On the return of Orson Hyde from his mission to Palestine, he carried letters of introduction to me and invited me to visit his wife. I was there met by Joseph Smith, the Prophet, who, after an interesting conversation introduced the subject of plural marriage and endeavored to teach me that principle. I resisted it with every argument I could command … as I could not reconcile it with the purity of the Gospel of Christ. Mr. Hyde took me home in a carriage and asked me what I thought of it and if I would consent to enter his family? I replied that I could not think of it for a moment. Thus it rested for awhile and Mr. Hyde married another young lady [Martha Rebecca Browett[133]]. In the mean time I was trying to learn the character of the leading men … I soon learned to my satisfaction, that Mr. Orson Hyde was a conscientious, upright[,] and noble man and became his third wife. Mrs. Hyde had two sweet little girls and I soon learned to love them and their dear mother who in the Spring of 1842 [actually, July 20, 1843] received me into her house as her husband's wife. Sealed to him by Joseph the Prophet in her presence.[134]

Nancy Rigdon's Refusal

Regardless of Joseph's enhanced masculinity and spiritual role in Nauvoo, not every woman or man who heard the story of plurality responded obediently. Mary Ann Price flatly refused Orson Hyde's first proposal but yielded months later. Sidney Rigdon's daughter Nancy, however, did not relent. Three accounts exist of Joseph's unsuccessful marriage proposal to her. One is given by John C. Bennett. The second is by Nancy's brother-in-law,

132. Dean C. Jessee, *Papers of Joseph Smith*, 2:497.

133. In 1869, Hyde described his plural marriage to Browett. "In the month of February or March, 1843, I was marriage to Miss Martha R. Browitt, by Joseph Smith, the martyred prophet, and by him she was sealed to me for time and all eternity in Nauvoo, Illinois." Myrtle Stevens Hyde, *Orson Hyde*, 160.

134. Mary Ann Price Hyde, "Autobiography," Written Aug. 20, 1888, 2-3.

George W. Robinson, who later turned away from Joseph's leadership. The third is by Nancy's brother John W. Rigdon.[135] Biases color each.

Marinda Hyde talked briefly with Nancy on April 9, 1842, at the funeral of eighteen-year-old Ephraim Marks, son of William Marks. At the time, Nancy was apparently seeing Francis Higbee, who might have been present as well. Joseph spoke at the services. Marinda took Nancy aside and told her that Joseph wanted to talk to her privately. At first intrigued by the implied layers of trust, Nancy accompanied her. Then, at the last minute, Willard Richards told them Joseph was unable to come and proposed another rendezvous the following Thursday. Nancy told Higbee about the upcoming meeting. Bennett also claims that he told Higbee to warn Nancy of Joseph's intentions.[136]

It is difficult to know why Marinda shared her experience with Joseph's avowed enemies, but, by Bennett's and Robinson's accounts, she did. In John W. Rigdon's ex post facto account, an identified "old lady friend" (perhaps his memory of Marinda) arranged the meeting.

> It happened in this way: Nancy had gone to Church, meeting being held in the grove near the temple lot on which the "Mormons" were then erecting a temple, an old lady friend who lived alone invited her to go home with her, which Nancy did. When they got to the house … the old lady began to talk to her about the new doctrine of polygamy which was then being taught, telling Nancy, during the conversation, that it was a surprise to her when she first heard it, but that she had since come to believe it to be true. While they were talking Joseph Smith the Prophet came into the house, and joined them, and the old lady immediately left the room. It was then that Joseph made the proposal of marriage to my sister. Nancy flatly refused him, saying if she ever got married she would marry a single man or none at all, and thereupon took her bonnet and went home, leaving Joseph at the old lady's house. Nancy told father [Sidney Rigdon] and mother [Phebe Rigdon] of it.[137]

---

135. Robinson wrote his letter to James Arlington Bennet on July 27, 1842. John C. Bennett traveled to Brooklyn to ask Bennet to co-publish his book. Bennet declined but gave Bennett the Robinson letter and another. Andrew F. Smith, *Saintly Scoundrel*, 108-109; Bennett, *History of the Saints*, 241-45; George W. Robinson, Letter to James Arlington Bennet, July 27, 1842, qtd. in John C. Bennett, *History of the Saints*, 245-47; John Wickliffe Rigdon, Affidavit, June 18, 1882, in Joseph Fielding Smith, *Blood Atonement and the Origin of Plural Marriage*, 83-84.

136. Bennett, *The History of the Saints*, 242.

137. John Wickliff Rigdon, Affidavit, July 28, 1905, in Joseph Fielding Smith, *Blood Atonement and the Origin of Plural Marriage*, 83-84.

Joseph's proposal and Nancy's disclosure complicated the already strained relationship between Joseph and Sidney. Her brother John W. continues: "A few days after the occurrence Joseph Smith came to my father's house and talked the matter over with the family, my sister, Mrs. Athalia Robinson [wife of George W. Robinson] also being present ... The feelings manifested by our family on this occasion were anything but brotherly or sisterly, more especially on the part of Nancy, as she felt that she had been insulted. A day or two later Joseph Smith returned to my father's house, when matters were satisfactorily adjusted between them, and there the matter ended."[138]

In late 1842, George Robinson's version was published in Bennett's *History of the Saints,* a venue that taints it with potential bias. Bennett described Nancy as a "beautiful girl, of irreproachable fame, great moral excellence, and superior intellectual endowments."[139] She was "buxom and Winsome," according to another description.[140] Joseph reportedly assumed she would welcome the proposal. Instead, she was outraged. John W. stated that Joseph then called the old lady into the room to persuade Nancy that the teaching was from God. She assured Nancy that she also had been dismayed at first but now believed that "great exaltation would come to those who received and embraced it."[141]

Nancy's rejection did not sit well with Joseph, and he stewed over how to respond during the next few days. Rather recklessly, he dictated a letter to Willard Richards, who hand-delivered it to Nancy. Joseph chose a tone of sermonizing that takes on shocking meanings in the context of plurality:

> Happiness is the object and design of our existence; and will be the end thereof, if we pursue the path that leads to it; and this path is virtue, uprightness, faithfulness, holiness, and keeping all the commandments of God. ... That which is wrong under one circumstance, may be, and often is, right under another. ... Whatever God requires is right, no matter

138. Ibid. The variations between John W. Rigdon's and John C. Bennett's accounts–Nancy's visit with an "old lady" when Marinda was, in fact, twenty-seven years old–may be partly accounted for by John W.'s only being twelve years old at the time of the proposal. He undoubtedly heard the story countless times over the next decade when its details evolved.

139. Bennett, *The History of the Saints*, 241.

140. William H. Whitsett, "Sidney Rigdon," 3:1233.

141. John Wickliffe Rigdon, "Life Story of Sidney Rigdon," 1654. Wickliffe made at least two formal accounts of the Nancy Rigdon incident. The first was an interview with the *Salt Lake Tribune* that appeared on May 20, 1900, 3; second, he made an affidavit dated July 28, 1905, in LDS Church History Library.

> what it is, although we may not see the reason thereof till long after the events transpire.
>
> Every thing that God gives us is lawful and right, and it is proper that we should enjoy His gifts and blessings whenever and wherever He is disposed to bestow; but if we should seize upon those same blessings and enjoyments without law, without revelation, without commandment, those blessings and enjoyments would prove cursings and vexations in the end, and we should have to go down in sorrow and wailings of everlasting regret. … [God] never has, He never will institute an ordinance or give a commandment to His people that is not calculated in its nature to promote that happiness which He has designed, and which will not end in the greatest amount of good and glory to those who become the recipients of his laws and ordinances.

Although the letter did not explicitly propose marriage–and failed to persuade Nancy–Joseph here compares himself to God, an authoritative stance that framed his request. His overture is not all that different from that of a loving parent who gives "privileges" to certain of his children. "A parent may whip a child, and justly, too, because he stole an apple; whereas if the child had asked for the apple, and the parent had given it, the child would have eaten it with a better appetite; there would have been no stripes; all the pleasure of the apple would have been secured, all the misery of stealing lost." The argument of "privilege" is steeped in patriarchy, and assumes a hierarchy of both persons and righteousness. It places Joseph above Nancy, as God was above him, a position that obligates him to guide her. God gave Solomon all the "desires of his heart," Joseph explained, "even things which might be considered abominable to all who understand the order of heaven only in part, but which in reality were right because God gave and sanctioned by special revelation."[142]

Joseph must have realized that his argument required more justification, so he added a subtle threat: "Our heavenly father is more liberal in his views, and boundless in his mercies and blessings, than we are ready to believe or receive, and at the same time is as terrible to the workers of iniquity, more awful in the executions of his punishments, and more ready to detect every false way than we are apt to suppose him to be."[143] It is one of Joseph's only

142. *History of the Church*, 5:135 (Aug. 27, 1842). Joseph's letter to Nancy was probably written and delivered in late April or early May 1842.

143. Nancy gave the letter to Francis Higbee, who gave it to Bennett, who published it in the *Sangamo Journal* and then in his *History of the Saints*, 243-45. Joseph did not sign it. Later it appeared in *History of the Church*, 5:134-36, as an essay on "Happiness," dated Aug. 11, 1842.

recorded comments, though veiled, to emphasize his authority and to focus on the demands of obedience to plurality.

News of the missive spread through a small group of close associates, including Bennett. John W. Rigdon later commented, "The story got out and it became the talk of the town that Joseph had made a proposition to Nancy to become his wife, and that she refused him."[144]

Sidney Rigdon, enraged, confronted Joseph during the second week of April. Sidney and Joseph were already estranged over a number of issues, including Rigdon's management of the Nauvoo post office and his alleged relationship with Bennett the previous year. According to Robinson, Joseph "attempted to deny it at first, and face [Nancy] down with the lie." He was not convincing, especially in view of Nancy's "earnestness" in reporting "the facts" of the "attempt made on her virtue."[145] Sidney and Phebe Rigdon were infuriated, both by Joseph's audacity and the fact that Joseph had apparently hoped Nancy would keep the matter a secret from them until he could introduce them to the doctrine himself.

Joseph attempted to reinterpret the event, drawing on his experience with Heber C. Kimball: He had merely been testing Nancy's virtue "and took that course to learn the facts!"[146] He "then and there acknowledged that every word of Miss Rigdon's testimony was true," according to Robinson's account, which John W. confirmed. After Joseph left, Sidney tried to reassure his family that Joseph "could never be sealed to one of his daughters with his consent as he did not believe in the doctrine."[147]

Obviously, an angelic confirmation of the belief typically produced a more favorable result; but in cases like this one, when the individuals Joseph taught rejected the doctrine wholesale, ruined relationships followed in its wake. Even as a young man, John W. was aware that a "bad feeling exist[ed] between Joseph Smith and Sidney Rigdon[;] they did not often meet although they lived within a few rods of each other[;] they did not seem to be on Verry friendly terms."[148]

On May 12, Joseph dictated another letter, this time "to Elder Rigdon

---

See also Devery S. Anderson's discussion in his "'I Could Love Them All': Nauvoo Polygamy in the Marriage of Willard and Jennetta Richards," *Sunstone*, June 7, 2013, at https://www.sunstonemagazine.com/i-could-love-them-all-nauvoo-polygamy-in-the-marriage-of-willard-and-jennetta-richards (Aug. 7, 2015).

144. John Wickliffe Rigdon, Statement, July 28, 1905, 83-84.

145. Robinson, Letter to James Arlington Bennet, July 27, 1842, 246.

146. Ibid.

147. Rigdon, "Life of Sidney Rigdon," 166.

148. Ibid., 175.

concerning certain difficulties, or surmises which existed." Rigdon wrote back immediately, a letter which has apparently not survived. On May 14, Joseph and Willard Richards visited Rigdon "concerning certain evil reports put in circulation by Francis M. Higbee, about some of Elder Rigdon's family, and others."[149] It is not clear how Joseph managed to blame Higbee for the rumors, and evidently the explanation was not completely satisfactory. Probably threatened by Joseph's approach to the woman he was courting, Higbee, who had previously had his own run-ins with the prophet, had given Joseph's letter to Bennett and perhaps had helped to spread the rumors that led to the confrontation between Rigdon and Joseph.

May 19 brought rain, an atmosphere of gloom that characterized what was transpiring in the councils of city and church. Joseph stayed at home until 1:00 p.m, Bennett resigned as mayor, and Joseph was elected mayor by the city council.[150] There is a sort of crescendo in these days, an intensifying rhythm that presages a climatic result.

On June 28, Joseph made another attempt to restore peace. "I visited Elder Rigdon and his family, and had much conversation about John C. Bennett, and others, much unpleasant feeling was manifested by Elder Rigdon's family, who were confounded and put to silence by truth."[151] This conclusion may have been wishful thinking. Joseph needed Rigdon's solidarity, but the angry father felt betrayed, apparently unwilling to accept a facile explanation that scapegoated Bennett.

Rigdon wrote to Joseph on July 1, expressing his hope that the two men could talk about the conflict: "I write this in the greatest confidence to yourself and for your own eye and no other. … I am your friend and not your enemy as I am afraid you suppose. I want you to take your horse and carriage on tomorrow and take a ride with me out to the Prairie." He repeated the strictures on privacy: "Say not a word to any person living but to Hiram [Smith] only. [A]nd no man shall know it from me."[152]

The only record of the meeting is Robinson's, who said that Rigdon asked Joseph to stop slandering Nancy. Joseph reportedly agreed to "take back what was said."[153] But only two days later, he criticized Rigdon and Robinson in sermon: "Any man that would suffer Bennett to come into their

149. *History of the Church*, 5:8 (May 13, 1842).
150. Ibid., 12 (May 19, 1842).
151. Ibid., 46 (June 28, 1842).
152. Sidney Rigdon, Letter to Joseph Smith, July 1, 1842.
153. Robinson, Letter to John C. Bennett, July 3, 1842, qtd. in Bennett, *The History of the Saints*, 45.

houses, was just as bad as he."[154] In the same way that conversion to plurality was the greatest show of loyalty, association with Bennett was now emblematic of treason. Rigdon planned to write a response, but fell ill.

Another attempt to paper over the Rigdon affair was a move to assert Joseph's "high moral character." *The Wasp* published a petition signed by well-known local citizens testifying to their knowledge of the prophet's reputation. Notably absent were the names of Orson Pratt, Sidney Rigdon, and George Robinson.[155]

During that summer of Bennett's scandalous letters, Rigdon wrestled with his own demons, unable to stand against the prophet but angered by Joseph's proposition to Nancy. In August, a miracle involving another of his daughters resolved his indecision and bound him anew to the Church. Sixteen-year-old Eliza, who had become ill with typhoid pneumonia, slipped into a coma so deep that a visiting physician had pronounced her dead.[156] Then, in a dramatic development, she reportedly rose on her deathbed to warn Nancy: "It is in your heart to deny this work; and if you do, the Lord says it will be the damnation of your soul." Bennett was a wicked man, Eliza insisted, and "the Lord would tread him under his feet." But if Nancy "continued in the faith," she would be showered with "great blessings."[157]

For hours, as Eliza moved in and out of consciousness, Rigdon prayed at her bedside for forgiveness. As a result, he felt bound to deny the "many idle tales and reports abroad concerning him," assuring her that he did not consider Joseph a "fallen prophet." He is said to have testified to his ailing daughter that "he had no controversy with the world," and that "through the obedience to the ordinances of the religion he now believes, the Lord had actually given back his daughter from the dead."[158] Eliza's recovery was sufficiently complete that she did not die until April 1846.[159] Relations between Joseph and the Rigdons remained fragile.[160] For his part, Robinson moved his family to La Harpe in McDonough County and, within a year, left the Church.[161]

154. Ibid., 45.

155. *Wasp*, July 27, 1842, 1.

156. Van Wagoner, *Sidney Rigdon*, 300.

157. *History of the Church*, 5:121 (Aug. 21, 1842). See also "Elder Rigdon, &C.," *Times and Seasons* 3, no. 22 (Sept. 15, 1842): 922-23.

158. "Rigdon &C.," 922.

159. Van Wagoner, *Sidney Rigdon*, 380.

160. F. Mark McKiernan, *The Voice of One Crying in the Wilderness: Sidney Rigdon, Religious Reformer 1793-1876*, 115-24.

161. Van Wagoner, *Sidney Rigdon*, 298.

Rigdon, absent from the stand for weeks because of ill health, read a letter to the Saints on August 20. He promised that he was "not upon the stand to renounce his faith in Mormonism." Instead, he hoped to "bear his testimony of its truth, and add another to the many miraculous evidences of the power of God." As he told his miracle story, Eliza had assured him that since he had "dedicated her to God, and prayed to him for her, that he [God] would give her back again." He had never lost his faith, he testified.[162]

Rigdon subsequently issued a statement of remarkable support, considering Joseph's attack on Nancy's reputation. In a letter dated August 27, published in the *Wasp*'s September 3 issue, he insisted that Bennett's publication of Joseph's "happiness" letter was

> unauthorized by her, and that she never said to Gen. Bennett or any other person, that said letter was written by said Mr. Smith, nor in his hand writing, but by another person, and in another person's hand writing. She further wishes me to say, that she never at any time authorized Gen Bennett to use her name in the public papers as he has done, which has been greatly to the wounding of her feelings, and she considers that the obtruding of her name before the public in the manner in which it has been done, to say the best of it, is a flagrant violation of the rules of gallantry, and cannot avoid to insult her feelings, which she wishes the public to know. I would further state that Mr. Smith denied to me the authorship of that letter.[163]

Apparently this expression of loyalty was not sufficient. Two days later on August 29, Joseph lumped Rigdon with Orson Pratt and Robinson, claiming, "I can kick them off my heels, as many as you can name." He told his audience that he would "give a lashing every opportunity [to] apostates and enemies" and "curse them."[164]

Although Rigdon was delighted when Joseph, as candidate for U.S.

162. "Rigdon, &C.," 923; *History of the Church*, 5:122 (Aug. 20, 1843).

163. Sidney Rigdon, "[Letter to the] Editor of the Wasp, Nauvoo, August 27, 1842," *The Wasp*, Sept. 3, 1842.

164. *History of the Church*, 5:139 (Aug. 29, 1842); also quoted in "Manuscript History, August 29, 1842," in Andrew F. Ehat and Lyndon W. Cooks, eds., *The Words of Joseph Smith*, 129. The *Sangamo Journal* reprinted Rigdon's letter on September 16, with the comment, "we never supposed Joe Smith the *writer* of the communication sent to Miss Rigdon. It was unquestionably written by some of his numerous assistants who minister to his depravity. Joe Smith has not sufficient talent to write such a letter. Nevertheless it was written to accomplish his purpose. Of this, there is no denial." This entry follows Joseph's journal closely (Jessee, *Papers of Joseph Smith*, 2:444-47), with some editing and, in particular, a change of language to the first person. "Another Abortive Attempt to Arrest Joe Smith," *Sangamo Journal*, Sept. 16, 1842, 3.

president, later named him as his vice-presidential running mate in 1844, Rigdon's refusal to embrace plurality left him outside accelerating events.[165] After Joseph's death in late June 1844, Rigdon offered to serve as the Church's guardian; but in early August 1844, a Church conference rejected the offer and instead sustained the Twelve Apostles. Rigdon was excommunicated the next month.[166] Sidney, Phebe, and their ten unmarried children moved to Pennsylvania, where, with a small group of followers, Rigdon organized another Church of Christ.[167]

After Joseph's death, Orson Hyde publicly claimed that Nancy Rigdon was "regarded generally, little, if any better, than a public prostitute," and that Joseph had merely attempted to "reprove and reclaim her if possible."[168] He continued: "Miss Nancy, I presume, considered her dignity highly insulted … She ran home and told her father that Mr. Smith wanted her for a spiritual wife, and that he employed my wife [Marinda] to assist him in obtaining her."[169] Whether a gesture of loyalty or an effort at asserting the Twelve's authority, Hyde's remarks represented the response of the apostles at the time.

Sarah Kimball's Refusal

Nancy Rigdon was not the only woman to rebuff Joseph. The Relief Society was a training ground for secret-keeping as well as for leadership development. Sarah Melissa Granger Kimball, married to non-Mormon Hiram Kimball since 1840 (no known relation to Heber C. Kimball), would later become a prominent leader in the 13th Ward Relief Society in Salt Lake City. Sarah remembered that "Joseph Smith taught me the principle of marriage for eternity, and the doctrine of plural marriage. He said that in teaching this he realized that he jeopardized his life; but God had revealed it to him many years before as a privilege with blessings, now God had revealed it again and instructed him to teach with commandment, as the Church could travel [progress] no further without the introduction of this principle."[170] Like Nancy, Sarah declined, reportedly telling Joseph to "teach it to someone else." But unlike Nancy, Saran elected to stay with the Church.

165. *History of the Church*, 6:356 (May 6, 1844).

166. "Continuation of Elder Sidney Rigdon's Trial," *Times and Seasons* 5, no. 18 (Oct. 1, 1844): 666-67.

167. Van Wagoner, *Sidney Rigdon*, 388.

168. Orson Hyde, *Speech of Elder Orson Hyde, Delivered Before the High Priests' Quorum, in Nauvoo, April 27th, 1845 …*, 27-28.

169. Ibid., 28.

170. Sarah M. Kimball, Affidavit, in Jenson, "Plural Marriage," 232; Joseph F. Smith, Affidavit Books, 1:76.

Because she was in a committed and happy marriage, Sarah may have confided in her husband; regardless, she did not spread gossip about Joseph's new doctrine. Evidently Hiram was less reticent. During the uncertainties caused by the Nancy Rigdon affair, Joseph at one point hastily wrote down a "revelation" and "threw [it] across the room" to Kimball during a stormy Nauvoo City Council meeting on May 19, 1842. It accused: "Hiram Kimball has been insinuating evil, and forming evil opinions against you, with others; and if he continue in them, he and they shall be accursed, for I am the Lord thy God, and will stand by thee and bless thee." The minutes do not report how Kimball reacted, but Joseph addressed the council about the "evil reports which were abroad in the city concerning myself, and the necessity of counteracting the designs of our enemies."[171] Despite these complications, Sarah remained simultaneously faithful to Joseph's narrative, her marriage vows, and her baptismal covenant to the end of her long life.[172]

Martha Brotherton's Refusal

A third failed proposal was not Joseph's, although the fall-out implicated him. Sometime during the spring of 1842, Brigham Young approached young English convert Martha Brotherton about becoming his plural wife. Brotherton signed an affidavit on July 13, 1842, describing how Heber Kimball first broached the offer, as Young's intermediary. Young then took her to the meeting room over Joseph's store. As she recalled it, Young's proposal was neither subtle nor persuasive: "Brother Joseph has had a revelation from God that it is lawful and right for a man to have two wives. ... If you will accept of me I will take you straight to the celestial kingdom, and if you will have me in this world, I will have you in that which is to come, and brother Joseph will marry us here today, and you can go home this evening, and your parents will not know anything about it."

When Martha asked for time to think about it, Young called in Joseph, who urged, "He is the best man in the world, except me. ... If you will accept of Brigham, you shall be blessed–God shall bless you, and my blessing shall rest upon you ... and if you do not like it in a month or two, come to me, and I will make you free again; and if he turns you off, I will take you on."

Martha repeated that she wanted to think about it and promised not to tell anyone. She did not tell her parents in words, but wrote out an account for them, complete with dialogue. Her horrified parents promptly took Martha

171. *History of the Church*, 5:12-13 (May 19, 1842).

172. Van Wagoner, "Mormon Polyandry in Nauvoo," 77.

to St. Louis. Joseph and Young defended themselves by attempting to ruin Martha's reputation. Martha's statement subsequently appeared in Bennett's exposés.[173] Her two sisters, Mary and Elizabeth, stayed in Nauvoo; both sisters and Mary's husband, John McIlwrick, publicly asserted that Martha was immoral, dishonest, a liar, and, by implication, unchaste.[174] A year later, Elizabeth Brotherton married Parley P. Pratt. After Martha Brotherton's death, Brigham Young had her sealed by proxy to him on August 1, 1870.

Elizabeth Durfee and Sarah Cleveland

Sometime before June 1842, Joseph married Elizabeth Davis Durfee, a woman born on March 11, 1791, and hence fifteen years his senior.[175] Functioning as a sort of matchmaker like Patty Sessions, Durfee taught potential wives about plurality and arranged private meetings with the prophet.

Another woman who performed this function was Sarah Maryetta Kingsley Cleveland, Emma's counselor in the Relief Society. Sarah, age fifty-four in 1842 and almost twenty years Joseph's senior, was born in Massachusetts on October 20, 1788. Sarah and her non-Mormon husband, John, had opened their home to Emma and her children when they arrived from Missouri in February 1839, taking in Joseph after his escape from Liberty Jail in April. Sarah was a respected community matron. On June 29, 1842, she witnessed Brigham Young seal Joseph to Eliza Snow. Her own sealing to Joseph seems to have occurred on, if not shortly before, the same day.

The sealing may have been a reward for Sarah's loyalty. Two and a half months earlier on April 14, Clarissa Marvel had spread rumors that Joseph had married Agnes Coolbrith Smith. According to the Relief Society minutes, Sarah warned members of the group "against speaking evil of Prest. J[oseph]. Smith and his companion [Emma Smith] … and the case of C. M. [Clarissa Marvel] should be a warning, how we hear and how we speak … the Lord would cut off those who will not take counsel &C."

Emma was in full agreement, but while Sarah was urging silence, Emma kept the door open for legitimate investigation. Secretary Eliza Snow noted Emma's comment: "[T]he disagreeable busines of searching out those that

173. Bennett, *The History of the Saints*, 238-39.

174. Elizabeth Brotherton, John McIlwrick, Mary McIlwrick, Affidavits, Aug. 27, 1842, in *Affidavits and Certificates*, qtd. in Hales, *Joseph Smith's Polygamy*, 1:493.

175. Andrew Jenson, "Plural Marriage," does not include Durfee in his list of Joseph's wives, but John C. Bennett, *History of the Saints*, 256, lists a "Mrs. D*****" among Joseph's alleged wives. Sarah Pratt, qtd. in Wyl, *Mormon Portraits*, 54, in 1886 said she had heard "Mrs. Durfee" say she was a wife of Joseph. See also Compton, *In Sacred Loneliness*, 254.

were iniquitous, seem'd to fall on her–said it was an unpleasant task, but her desire was to do good–wish'd all the members of the Society to assist her–said it was necessary [to] begin at home–eradicate all evil from our own hearts–and warn those who wish to join with us to come calculating to divest themselves of every thing wrong and write to expose iniquity, to search it out and put it away."[176] Emma's reference to her own marriage ("begins at home") is impossible to miss.

As was true of so many of the characters in Joseph's narrative, the Clevelands disappear for a period of time only later to reappear. Sarah and John left Nauvoo in April 1843 because of business difficulties,[177] but were back by late December. Six months later, Joseph was dead. John never joined the Church.

Where marriage on earth was rooted in sexuality, child-bearing, and family-rearing, celestial marriage between an older woman and a much younger, virile man took on different meanings. Separated in literal as well as psychological ways from the complications of sexuality, this type of marriage stressed other interactions and emphasized other privileges a woman might provide to and receive from her husband (see D&C 132:16-17).

Eliza Roxcy Snow

During the summer of 1842, Joseph married at least four additional women. Arguably the best-known was Eliza Roxcy Snow, sealed to Joseph on June 29, 1842. A former Campbellite baptized in 1835 who first learned about Joseph from Sidney Rigdon, Eliza must have seen the irony in her position as founding member of and secretary to the Relief Society as she listened to Emma explain the necessity for morality among the sisters. Eliza had personal knowledge of the deception that lay behind decorum and was an inevitable candidate for plural marriage, despite her initial reaction to the whispers. She wrote in 1886, "The subject was very repugnant to my feelings so directly was it in opposition to my educated prepossessions, that it seemed as though all the prejudices of my ancestors for generations past congregated around me."[178]

Over time, Eliza came to accept plurality because she identified so fully with Joseph's prophet-narrative: "When I reflected that I was living in the

176. Relief Society, Minutes, Apr. 14, 1842.

177. Sarah Cleveland, "To the Presidency, and Ladies of the Female Relief Society of Nauvoo," *Times and Seasons* 4, no. 2 (May 1, 1843): 187, bade farewell to her friends.

178. Eliza R. Snow, "Sketch of My Life," in Maureen Ursenbach Beecher, ed., *The Personal Writings of Eliza Roxcy Snow*, 16.

Dispensation of the fullness of times, embracing all other Dispensations, surely Plural Marriage must necessarily be included." For Eliza, plurality was a practice of ancient prophets waiting to be restored. "I consoled myself," she wrote, "with the idea that it [polygamy] was far in the distance, and beyond the period of my mortal existence."[179]

Eliza passes silently over how Joseph first made his approach to her, explaining only the foundation of her commitment: "I had covenanted in the waters of baptism to live by every word He should communicate, and my heart was firmly set to do His bidding." She then pronounced, from the distance of more than forty-three years and her subsequent plural marriage sealing to Brigham Young: "As I increased in knowledge concerning the principle and design of Plural Marriage, I grew in love with it, and to-day esteem it a precious, sacred principle necessary in the elevation and salvation of the human family in redeeming woman from the curse, and the world from corruption."[180] She carefully described her entry into the sacred ritual that was the Latter-day Saint centerpiece of heaven and salvation: "From personal knowledge I bear my testimony that Plural Celestial Marriage is a pure and holy principle, not only tending to individual purity and elevation of character, but also instrumental in producing a more perfect type of manhood mentally and physically, as well as in restoring human life to its former longevity."[181]

Eliza had heard others talking about plurality in hushed conversations and received her own "first intimation, before the announcement reached me," she wrote, "that the 'set time' had come–that God had commanded His servants to establish the order, by taking additional wives–I knew that God, who had kept silence for centuries was speaking."[182] This "intimation" was most likely Joseph's proposal. Nine days before she married Joseph, her parents left both Nauvoo and Mormonism.

Brigham Young performed the ritual on June 29, 1842, with Sarah Cleveland as witness.[183] That night, Eliza made the first entry in a diary she

179. Ibid.

180. Ibid., 17.

181. Ibid.

182. Ibid.

183. Eliza R. Snow, Affidavit, June 7, 1869, in Joseph F. Smith, Affidavit Books, 1:25; see also Jenson, "Plural Marriage," 6:233. Eliza R. Snow, *Biography and Family Record of Lorenzo Snow*, 68, tells yet another version of another faithful woman who developed the rationale for following his instructions. For female friendships in nineteenth-century America, see Carroll Smith-Rosenberg, *Disorderly Conduct*, 53-76, and her "The Female World of Love and Ritual";

kept from June 1842 to April 1844. The need for secrecy would not allow her to describe what she veiled in generalities:

> This is a day of much interest to my feelings. Reflecting on past occurrences, a variety of thoughts have presented themselves to my mind with regard to events which have chas'd each other in rapid succession in the scenery of human life. As an individual, I have not passed altogether unnoticed by Change, in reference to present circumstances and future prospects. ... While I am contemplating the present state of society the powers of darkness, and the prejudices of the human mind which stand array'd like an impregnable barrier against the work of God. ... I will not fear. I will put my trust in Him who is mighty to save; rejoicing in his goodness and determin'd to live by every word that proceedeth out of his mouth.[184]

A month and a half after Eliza's and Sarah's plural marriages, Sarah and John Cleveland moved across the river. The day before, ironically, Emma had asked Eliza, who had been lodging with the Clevelands, to move in with Joseph and her and teach their children. At that point, Emma did not know she was extending hospitality to yet another of Joseph's secret wives. Eliza wrote: "This sudden, unexpected change in my location, I trust is for good; it seem'd to come in answer to my petitions to God."[185]

Eliza's identity throughout her life from that point forward was tied with a Gordian knot to her marriage to Joseph. Even after she became a plural wife to Brigham Young in 1844, she signed her name Eliza Snow Smith. Her brief diary narrated in veiled language her understanding of Joseph's prophetic world and her role in it: "[T]hough I rejoice in the blessings of the society of the Saints, and the approbation of God; a lonely feeling will steal over me before I am aware, while I am contemplating the present state of society–the powers of darkness, the prejudice of the human mind which stand array'd like an impregnable barrier against the work of God. ..." Certain of impending hardship, she resolved, nevertheless, to "live by every word that preceedeth out of his [God's] mouth," including plurality.[186]

Mary Ryan, "The Power of Female Networks," 66-86; and Jill Mulvay Derr, "'Strength in Our Union,'" 153-207.

184. Eliza R. Snow, Journal, June 29, 1842, in Beecher, *The Personal Writings of Eliza Roxcy Snow*, 52.

185. Eliza R. Snow, Journal, in Beecher, *The Personal Writings of Eliza Roxcy Snow*, 54.

186. Eliza Snow, Journal, in Beecher, *The Personal Writings of Eliza Roxcy Snow*, 52.

Sarah Ann Whitney

Both Elizabeth Ann and Newel K. Whitney witnessed their seventeen-year-old daughter Sarah Ann's sealing to Joseph on July 27, 1842. Longtime friends, the Whitneys had joined the Church in Kirtland and shared Joseph's vision of Zion. Newel had served as the Church's second bishop (presiding over Nauvoo's "Middle" Ward) beginning in 1839 and became a founding member of the Holy Order on May 4, 1842.[187] He performed the sealing between his daughter and his prophet, using words that Joseph dictated according to revelation. The wording itself alludes to dynastic implications:

> ... They shall take each other by the hand and you shall say, "You both mutually agree," calling them by name, "to be each other's companion so long as you both shall live, preserving yourselves for each other and from all others and also throughout all eternity, reserving only those rights which have been given to my servant Joseph by revelation and commandment and by legal Authority in times passed . If you both agree to covenant and do this, I then give you, S[arah]. A[nn]. Whitney, my daughter, to Joseph Smith, to be his wife, to observe all the rights between you both that belong to that condition. I do it in my own name and in the name of my wife, your mother, and in the name of my Holy Progenitors, by the right of birth which is of priesthood, vested in me by revelation and commandment and promise of the living God, obtained by the Holy Melchisedeck Gethrow [Jethro] and others of the Holy Fathers, commanding in the name of the Lord all those powers to concentrate in you and through you to your posterity forever. All these things I do in the name of the Lord Jesus Christ, and through this order he may be glorified and that through the power of anointing David may reign King over Israel, which shall hereafter be revealed Let immortality and eternal life hereafter be sealed upon your heads forever and ever.["]][188]

Importantly, the sealing ritual begins by distinguishing it from civil marriage and invoking the authoritative priesthood power of Joseph the prophet. The language of covenants was already familiar in the Church; this covenant bound both parties to certain behaviors and rewards and linked them to

187. Anderson and Bergera, *Joseph Smith's Quorum of the Anointed*, 4.

188. Joseph Smith, Revelation, June 27, 1842, in *The Essential Joseph Smith*, 165-66. See also Bachman, "A Study of the Mormon Practice of Plural Marriage," 121-22; Kenneth W. Godfrey, "Causes of Mormon/Non-Mormon Conflict in Hancock County, Illinois, 1839-1846," 99n27; H. Michael Marquardt, *The Strange Marriages of Sarah Ann Whitney to Joseph Smith the Mormon Prophet, Joseph C. Kingsbury, and Heber C. Kimball*, 23.

Jesus' ancient church and the prophets. The ritual forged a holy bond, linked plurality to eternal life, and guaranteed salvation for Sarah and her parents. Sarah's marriage was intended to produce children who would be connected to their parents eternally. The reference to "posterity" and "rights" of marriage clearly indicates a spiritual/sexual union.

Twenty-seven years later, Sarah Ann's mother described her feelings at the marriage–both confused and exhilarated, one suspects, because of the clandestine nature of the union:

> He [Joseph Smith] had been strictly charged by the angel ... that the most profound secrecy must be maintained. ... He ... confided to him [Newel] the principles [of polygamy]. ... My husband revealed these things to me. ... We pondered upon them continually, and our prayers were unceasing that the Lord would grant us some special manifestation concerning this new and strange doctrine. The Lord was very merciful to us; He revealed unto us His power and glory. We were seemingly wrapt in a heavenly vision, a halo of light encircled us, and we were convinced in our own minds that God heard and approved our prayers ... Our hearts were comforted and our faith made so perfect that we were willing to give our eldest daughter, then only seventeen years of age, to Joseph, in the holy order of plural marriage ... laying aside all our traditions and former notions in regard to marriage, we gave her with our mutual consent.[189]

Knowing Newel and Elizabeth were obedient, God through Joseph assured them of their place in heaven: "[T]he thing that my servant Joseph Smith has made known unto you and your family and which you have agreed upon is right in mine eyes and shall be rewarded upon your heads with honor and immortality and eternal life to all your house, both old and young because of the lineage of my Priesthood, saith the Lord, it shall be upon you and upon your children after you from generation to generation, by virtue of the holy promise which I now make unto you, saith the Lord."[190] A month later, Joseph confirmed the significance of their bond when Elizabeth

---

189. Elizabeth Whitney, in Lyndon Cook, *The Revelations of the Prophet Joseph Smith*, 102; Elizabeth Whitney, Affidavit, June 19, 1869, in Joseph Fielding Smith, *Blood Atonement and the Origin of Plural Marriage*, 74. See also Joseph F. Smith, comp., Affidavit Books, 1:36; Sarah Ann Whitney, Affidavit, 1869, in *Blood Atonement and the Origin of Plural Marriage*, 73. Helen Mar Whitney, "Scenes from Nauvoo," *Woman's Exponent* 11, no. 19 (Mar. 1, 1883): 146, told the same story: "They willingly gave to him [Joseph Smith] their daughter, which was the strongest proof that they could possibly give of their faith and confidence in him as a true Prophet of God."

190. Qtd. in Marquardt, *The Strange Marriages of Sarah Ann Whitney*, 23; *The Essential Joseph Smith*, 165.

and Newel were rebaptized and reconfirmed as members of the Church, and then were sealed together for eternity.[191]

During most of August 1842, Joseph was hiding from Missouri officers seeking to extradite him, but he nurtured his union with Sarah Ann in both literal and figurative ways. Joseph wrote to the Whitneys on August 18, lamenting his loneliness: "Dear, and Beloved, Brother and Sister, Whitney, and &c.," he began, "I take this oppertunity to communi[c]ate, some of my feelings, privetely at this time, which I want you three Eternaly to keep in your own bosams; for my feelings are so strong for you since what has passed lately between us ..."

This letter, to a couple who had been loyal friends for a decade, acquires a new layer of meaning when the unaddressed but obviously present Sarah Ann is factored into the audience: "it would afford me great relief, of mind[,] if those with whom I am alied, do love me, now is the time to afford me succour. ... the nights are very pleasant, indeed, [and] all three of you can come and See me in the fore part of the night."

With a mixture of fear but also, perhaps, a thrill from the risk, he instructed them: "let Brother Whitney come a little a head, and nock at the south East corner of the house at the window; it is next to the cornfield; I have a room intirely by myself, the whole matter can be attended to with most perfect saf[e]ty."

Clearly, he assumed that they would come. "[B]e careful to escape observation, as much as possible[.] I know it is a heroick undertakeing; but so much the greater friendship, and the more Joy[.] ... burn this letter as soon as you read it; keep all locked up in your breasts, my life depends upon it."

Emma was visiting her sequestered husband almost daily, and he warned at another point in this urgent but rambling letter: "The only thing to be careful of; is to find out when Emma comes [because] then you cannot be safe, but when she is not here, there is the most perfect saf[e]ty. ... I think Emma wont come tonight[.] if she don't[,] dont fail to come

191. Andrew F. Ehat, "Joseph Smith's Introduction to Temple Ordinances and the 1844 Mormon Succession Question," 102, Table 2. Orson F. Whitney's account of Joseph and Sarah's marriage highlights the distinctiveness of this union in the context of 1842. He writes, "This bond of affection [between Joseph and the Whitneys] was strengthened and intensified by the giving in marriage to the former of the Bishop's eldest daughter, Sarah, in obedience to a revelation from God." Moreover, her parents were the first to consent to their daughter's marriage. Also important to Orson F. Whitney, son of Helen Mar Kimball and Horace Whitney: "The revelation commanding and consecrating this union, is in existence." Orson F. Whitney, "*Life of Heber C. Kimball*," *The Contributor* 6, no. 4 (Jan. 1885): 131.

tonight."[192] The trusting parents obeyed the instructions–all except the order to burn the letter.

As for Sarah Ann, no record or reminiscence captures her own feelings.[193] Described by close friend Helen Mar Kimball as "proud and somewhat eccentric," Sarah's effect on others could be "almost magnetic." The two girls had become friends in Nauvoo, and Helen warmly described them like "the two halves of one soul." Helen added that Sarah Ann was "incapable of professing anything which she did not feel," and considered her "a most pure-minded, conscientious and God-fearing girl."[194] Sarah joined the Relief Society at the April 28, 1842, meeting.

At Joseph's request, Sarah also entered a "pretend" polyandrous marriage with Joseph C. Kingsbury, as a cover for her relationship with Joseph. Joseph Smith performed the marriage on April 29, 1843. Kingsbury had frequent opportunities for getting to know Sarah. He stood behind the counter in Newel Whitney's store and served on high councils in Kirtland and in Iowa. In fact, he was Whitney's brother-in-law, having married Newel's younger sister Caroline, who died in October 1841. He recorded his version of obeying Joseph's counsel

> to Stand by Sarah Ann Whitney as Supposed to be her husband & had a pretended marriage for the purpose of Bringing about the purposes of God in these last days as spoken by the mouth of the Prophits Isiah Jeremiah Ezekiel and also Joseph Smith, & Sarah Ann Should Recd a Great Glory Honner & Eternal Lives and I Also Should Recd a Great Glory Honner & Eternal lives to the full desire of my heart in having my Companion Caroline in the first Reserection to Icaim [claim] her & no one to have power to take her from me & we Both shall be Crowned & Enthroned together in the Celestial Kingdom.[195]

This "pretended marriage" did not involve cohabitation or connubial relationships but was a shield–perhaps in the event of a pregnancy–for the sacred ritual Sarah had engaged in with Joseph.

After Joseph's death, twenty-year-old Sarah married Helen Mar's father,

---

192. Joseph Smith, Letter to "Dear, and Beloved, Brother and Sister Whitney, and &c.," Aug. 18, 1842.

193. The only record is her spare 1869 affidavit: "on the twenty-seventy day of July, A.D. 1842, at the city of Nauvoo ... she was married or sealed to Joseph Smith ... by Newel K. Whitney, Presiding Bishop of said Church, according to the laws of the same regulating marriage, in the presence of Elizabeth Ann Whitney her mother." Joseph F. Smith, Affidavit Books, June 19, 1869.

194. Helen Mar Whitney, "Scenes in Nauvoo," Mar. 1, 1883, 146.

195. Joseph C. Kingsbury, "The History of Joseph C. Kingsbury," 13.

Heber Kimball, and Helen Mar married Sarah's brother, Horace, for time rather than eternity, binding them in a new familial bond. The layering of family relationships and understandings seemed to grow increasingly complex.

Martha McBride Knight

In August (day not known) 1842, Heber Kimball sealed Joseph to thirty-seven-year-old Martha McBride Knight, Vinson Knight's recent widow.[196] City councilor Knight had been a presiding bishop, a member of the Board of Regents of the University of Nauvoo, and a farmer and livestock man.[197] Vinson and Martha had seven children, and were loyal followers of Joseph. Vinson may have learned about plurality in September 1841.[198] He died on July 31, 1842. Within the month, Martha was sealed to Joseph. Acquainted with Emma and others of Joseph's plural wives, Martha was present at the organizational meeting of the Nauvoo Female Relief Society.

The Johnson Sisters

It is not surprising that Benjamin Johnson's sisters, Delcena and Almera, became plural wives of Joseph. Benjamin had been close to the prophet since Kirtland. At twenty-nine, Almera had never been married when she was sealed to Joseph; Delcena Johnson Sherman was the thirty-five-year-old widow of Lyman Sherman and was living with Louisa Beaman.[199] If one imagined the landscape of plurality as a series of moments of potential encounter, Almera and Delcena were as perfectly placed as could be envisioned. As described above, Benjamin taught Almera about plurality, but Delcena's marriage "to the Prophet was before my Return to Nauvoo [from a mission in July 1842], and it being <u>Tasitly admitted</u> I asked no questions."[200]

The uneven distribution of power in such relations made women vulnerable to the lessons preached by their fathers or brothers. Joseph used these men as spokespersons because of the influence they already had over their sisters or for the same reason Marinda Hyde helped Nancy Rigdon. The

---

196. Martha McBride Kimball, Affidavit, July 8, 1869, qtd. in Joseph Fielding Smith, *Blood Atonement and the Origin of Plural Marriage*, 72; see also Joseph F. Smith, Affidavit Books, July 8, 1869, and Sarah Ann Kimball, Affidavit, June 19, 1869.

197. Compton, *In Sacred Loneliness*, 369.

198. Ibid.

199. Ibid., 289, 295.

200. Benjamin noted that Delcena had been sealed to Joseph by "proxy." It is uncertain whether Joseph stood in for Lyman Sherman or not. Benjamin Johnson, in Zimmerman, *I Knew the Prophets*, 45; emphasis his. Delcena was sealed in the Nauvoo temple on January 24, 1846, to Lyman Sherman for eternity.

technique of weaving family loyalties with loyalty to Joseph made refusal even more difficult for these women. Angels and brothers, flaming swords and Old Testament precedents pulled women into plural marriage, made them believe they were carrying their families with them toward celestial glory, and sealed their destiny with that of the prophet.

Regardless of the transformation that overcame Benjamin as he spoke with Almera (see chap. 10), she was less convinced. A few days after the conversation with Joseph on April 3, 1843, Benjamin took her to Nauvoo where they met Joseph, William Clayton, and Hyrum Smith.[201] Hyrum admitted his own hesitation and said that it was not until God had shown him it was true that he accepted it. He testified that his brother "was commanded to take more wives and he waited until an Angel with drawn Sword Stood before him and declared that if he longer delayed fulfilling that Command he would Slay him."[202]

Hyrum next shared his testimony with Almera: "The Lord has revealed the principle of plural marriage to me, and I know for myself that it is true."[203] Almera also remembered that Hyrum assured her that she "need not be afraid. I had been fearing and doubting about the principle and so had he, but he now knew it was true."[204] She talked with other women who had been sealed to Joseph, and found a way to accept the belief.

Almera was thirty, Joseph thirty-eight. According to Benjamin, Clayton performed the sealing and Louisa Beaman witnessed it, after which Joseph asked Benjamin to take Almera to a room in the Smith family's Mansion House.[205] In the affidavit Almera made in 1883 at age seventy, she described her sealing day as "on a certain occasion in the spring of the year 1843, the exact date of which I do not now recollect."[206] Such forgetfulness was not unique and may indicate, in part, how these women incorporated the injunction to secrecy. Other women besides Almera were fuzzy on the dates of their weddings. Elderly, reticent, trained in silence, they remembered the year, sometimes the season, but in some affidavits, no specific date at all.

201. Ibid., 43.

202. Ibid.

203. Almera Johnson, Affidavit, in Jenson, "Plural Marriage," 6:236

204. Almera Johnson, Affidavit, Aug. 1, 1883, in Joseph Fielding Smith, *Blood Atonement and the Origin of Plural Marriage*, 70-71.

205. Benjamin Johnson, in Zimmerman, *I Knew the Prophets*, 44; Benjamin Johnson, Affidavit, in Jenson, "Plural Marriage," 6:222.

206. Almera Johnson, Affidavit, Aug. 1, 1883, in Joseph Fielding Smith, *Blood Atonement and the Origin of Plural Marriage*, 70-71. Her obituary gives an incorrect marriage year of 1842. Benjamin F. Johnson, Affidavit, in Jenson, "Plural Marriage," 6:221, gives the incorrect date of August 1843.

Denials and Defenses

Jedediah M. Grant, a counselor to Brigham Young in pioneer Utah, defended Joseph's expansion of plurality and the demands he placed on participants' loyalty. "Did the Prophet Joseph want every man's wife he asked for?" Grant asked rhetorically. "He did not. … The grand object in view was to try the people of God to see what was in them."[207] This exchange speaks volumes about the necessary "freeing" from conventional mores. It was one thing for Joseph to keep his own secrets from Emma–it was more complicated when he asked others to act similarly.

Surrounding plurality was a complex web of code words and phrases to shroud the doctrine with secrecy and protect the ritual it engaged. Terms like "sealings," "the order of the priesthood," "eternal marriage," and "new and everlasting covenant of marriage"[208] described what contemporaries might call spiritual wifery. Such language made holy sense to those who accepted the doctrine but retained sinister meanings for outsiders.[209] Speaking in coded language to newspaper reporters, to audiences of Saints or strangers, Church leaders wove plurality into the Mormon concept of salvation, knowingly misleading those who quizzed them about allegations regarding polygamy.

Victor Turner's concept of *communitas* captures the result of the surrender that Joseph required of those who joined him in plurality. *Communitas* "puts all social structural rules in question and suggests new possibilities."[210] *Communitas* is, for Turner, that which "liberates … from conformity to general norms."[211] Joseph painted an image of heaven and earth that opened his Saints' lives to new possibilities and invited them to participate in new relationships, to forge new meanings and understandings, and to practice a new version of an ancient religion.

The circle of loyal men surrounding Joseph tightened, not only to protect him, but also to safeguard themselves. During the six months he taught them–August 1842 to February 1843–Joseph evidently did not enter any new marriages.[212] Twenty-five years after Joseph's death, George A. Smith

207. Jedediah M. Grant, Feb. 19, 1854, JD 2:14.

208. See Hales, *Joseph Smith's Polygamy*, 1:213, 369-70.

209. For some of those viewing Mormon plurality as corrupt and licentious, see John H. Beadle, *Polygamy, or the Mysteries and Crimes of Mormonism;* John Bowes, *Mormonism Exposed, in Its Swindling and Licentious Abominations …;* John Hyde, Mormonism; Wyl, *Mormon Portraits;* and Catherine V. Waite, *The Mormon Prophet and His Harem.*

210. Turner, *Dramas, Fields, and Metaphors,* 202; see also Turner, *The Ritual Process*, 127.

211. Turner, *Dramas, Fields, and Metaphors,* 274; see also Victor Turner, "Frame, Flow and Reflection," 474.

212. George D. Smith, *Nauvoo Polygamy*, 159.

explained the logic of the shielding language: "Anyone who will read carefully the denials, as they are termed, … will see clearly that they denounce adultery, fornication, brutal lust and the teaching of plurality of wives by those who were not commanded to do so …"[213] In March 1844, Hyrum Smith denounced as "false doctrines" the idea that "a man having a certain priesthood, may have as many wives as he pleases." He emphasized, "[T]here is no such doctrine taught here; neither is there any such thing practiced here."[214] By this point, Hyrum had two plural wives.[215]

At April 1842 general conference, before he had embraced the doctrine, Hyrum expressed dismay about rumors of a spiritual wife doctrine: "I am authorized to tell you from henceforth, that any man who comes in and tells you such damn fool doctrine to tell him to give up his [preaching] license."[216] Speaking at the same conference, Joseph flatly denied plurality: No one who "is acquainted with our principles would believe such lies."[217] The next day, he pronounced "a curse upon all adulterers, fornicators, and unvirtuous persons, and those who have made use of my name to carry on their iniquitous designs."[218] The same day Marinda Hyde, acting on Joseph's behalf, took Nancy Rigdon to meet privately with him.

Two years later, still publicly denying the plurality he now practiced, Hyrum constructed a coded explanation relying on Joseph's prophetic role: "I read, that what God joins together let no man put asunder[.] … [A]ll the old covenants made by the authority of man are only made to be in force during the natural life and end there … No marriage is valid in the morn of the resurrection unless the marriage covenant be sealed on earth by one having the keys and power from Almighty God to seal on earth as it shall be bound in heaven."[219]

"Keys and power." That was Joseph's authority. Brigham Young testified that all Joseph knew had been "received from the hand of the Lord."[220] Men and women like the Whitneys or the Kimballs would have heard Joseph say

213. George A. Smith, Letter to Joseph Smith III, Oct. 9, 1869, 8.

214. Hyrum Smith, "Nauvoo, March 15, 1844," rptd. in "Our City, and the Present Aspect of Affairs," *Times and Seasons* 5, no. 6 (Mar. 15, 1844): 474.

215. Catherine Phillips gave her sealing date to Hyrum as "August, 1843." Affidavit, in Joseph Fielding Smith, *Blood Atonement and the Origin of Plural Marriage*, 70.

216. Hyrum Smith, qtd. in Bachman, "A Study of the Mormon Practice of Plural Marriage," 201-202.

217. *History of the Church*, 4:586 (Apr. 8, 1842).

218. Ibid., 587-88 (Apr. 9, 1842).

219. Hyrum Smith, Discourse, Apr. 8, 1844.

220. Joseph Smith, qtd. by Brigham Young, Sept. 11, 1853, JD 1:78.

such things often enough. Their faith compelled them to integrate plurality as one more of God's revelations that they were obliged to obey.

On April 28, 1842, Joseph stressed to the Relief Society the importance of following his leadership. "He said he had been trampled under foot by aspiring Elders ... They could not be patted but must run away as tho' the care and authority of the church were vested with them." He then hinted darkly: "they would not long have him [Joseph] to instruct them[.] ... According to his [Joseph's] prayers God had appointed him elsewhere."[221] It reads as a subtle threat.

Joseph was speaking not only to Emma but to at least three plural wives (Louisa Beaman, Presendia Buell, and Zina Jacobs) and to at least six future wives (Martha Knight, Elvira Cowles, Eliza Snow, Eliza Partridge, Desdemona Fullmer, and Sarah Ann Whitney). Joseph positioned opposition as resistance to his prophetic mission. On April 29, his journal noted: "A conspiracy against the peace of my household was made manifest, and it gave me some trouble to counteract the design of certain base individuals, and restore peace. The Lord makes manifest to me many things, which it is not wisdom for me to make public, until others can witness the proof of them."[222] The "conspiracy" no doubt related to some conflict with Emma over plurality; and peace was not as easily "restore[d]" as Joseph suggests.

---

221. Relief Society, Minutes, Apr. 28, 1842. See also Joseph Smith, Diary, Apr. 28, 1842, in Faulring, *An American Prophet's Record*, 244).

222. *History of the Church*, 4:607-608 (Apr. 29, 1842). "J. C. B."–for John C. Bennett–is written in the margin of Joseph Smith's journal by Willard Richards.

CHAPTER 13

"To Keep a Secret"

... there may be some among you who are not sufficiently skill'd in masonry as to keep a secret.
–Joseph Smith et al., in Relief Society, Minutes, Sept. 28, 1842

In Nauvoo, the spring of 1842 looked idyllic with the city government functioning well, the Bennett scandal yet to explode fully, and former Missouri Governor Lilburn W. Boggs not yet obsessed with Joseph as his would-be assassin. True, Joseph was investing major efforts in practicing and preaching plurality, but the teaching was still secret enough. During this brief respite, Joseph poured new revelation, new emphasis on the construction of the temple and the Nauvoo House, and two important innovations that were a prelude to the Quorum of the Anointed and the distinctive Mormon temple endowment ceremonies.

The city thrived. Ebenezer Robinson predicted in a *Times and Seasons* article in February: "Nauvoo in a few years may be made almost a paradise," he said. "Let each citizen fill his spare ground with fruit trees, shub[b]ery, vines, etc., tastefully arranged and properly cultivated, and in a short time we may each sit under his own vine and fig tree. ... and we shall soon have formed some idea of how Eden looked."[1] Robinson praised the work of horticulturist Edward Sayers (husband of Ruth Vose Sayers), who was busy "pruning trees, laying out gardens, grafting, inoculating of trees, etc."[2]

Steamboats churning up the Mississippi River stopped at Nauvoo's western shore to deposit curious tourists whom Joseph proudly conducted around the city. Attractions included the Ohio Egyptian mummies, the temple baptismal font, and the temple building site. He bore these visits good-humoredly. James Arlington Bennet described Joseph's appeal: "Joe is

1. Ebenezer Robinson, "Horticulture," *Times and Seasons* 3, no. 7 (Feb. 1, 1842): 678.
2. Ibid., 686.

a magnet in a large way, which he calls a power or spirit from heaven." Most important, "Joe is a mighty man of God–possessing large stores of human nature–great shrewdness, and as he has taken the management of the Mormon newspaper organ, the 'Times and Seasons' into his hand, we look for many revelations ..."[3] One visitor saw him as countering modern materialism: "Joe Smith is creating a spiritual system, combined also with morals and industry, that may change the destiny of the race."[4]

Another found Joseph's power "over his followers ... unlimited ... [H]is declarations are as the authority and influence of the word of God himself." On the other hand, this commentator added: "He is a complete despot ... Some people consider him a great man; I do not. He is not possessed of a single element of greatness, unless it be in vice and blasphemy. He is a compound of ignorance, vanity, arrogance, coarseness and stupidity and vulgarity."[5]

People frequently saw what they came prepared to see; but one visitor, who had expected "an impoverished, ignorant and bigoted population, completely priest-ridden, and tyrannized over by Joseph Smith, the great prophet of these people," instead saw "no idleness, no intemperance, no noise, no riot." He added, "With the religion of these people I have nothing to do; if they can be satisfied with the doctrines of their new revelation, they have a right to be so." He specifically praised the private installation of Masonic officers: "Never in my life did I witness a better-dressed or a more orderly and well-behaved assemblage." Joseph also challenged his stereotype: "[J]udge my surprise at finding him a sensible, intelligent, companionable and gentlemanly man."[6]

On March 1, the *Times and Seasons* published Joseph's letter to John Wentworth, a Chicago newsman, describing the early history of the Church. Important as one of the first widely published accounts of the Church's history, it positioned Joseph's story in a world where the line between heaven and earth was drawn through faith.[7] In the next issue, Joseph began publication of what would eventually become the multi-volume *History of the Church:* "Owing to the many reports which have been put in circulation by

3. James Arlington Bennet, "The Mormons–A Leaf from Joe Smith," *New York Herald*, Apr. 3, 1842.

4. Ibid.

5. Benjamin F. Morris, qtd. in John E. Hallwas and Roger D. Launius, eds., *Cultures in Conflict*, 34.

6. "An Observer," Mar. 22, 1842, qtd. in *History of the Church*, 4:566.

7. Joseph Smith, Letter to John Wentworth, in *History of the Church*, 4:536-41 (Mar. 1, 1842); Joseph Smith, "Wentworth Letter," 296.

evil designing persons in relation to the rise and progress of the Church of Jesus Christ of Latter-day Saints, all of which have been designed by the authors thereof to militate against its character as a church, and its progress in the world, I have been induced to write this history, so as to disabuse the public mind, and put all enquirers after truth in possession of the facts as they have transpired in relation both to myself and the church, so far as I have such facts in possession."[8]

Joseph spent the first week of March preaching, preparing to publish his translation of the Book of Abraham, settling business matters, writing correspondence, and drafting resolutions for the Nauvoo City Council.[9] It was a busy, productive time; and he experienced a flowering of creative action, driving forward the further organization of the Church and the "ordering" of its people. Just what this concept meant became clearer as, within two days, he organized both the Masonic Lodge and the Female Relief Society of Nauvoo.

Masonry

The number of Masonic lodges nationwide had decreased during the decades before the Mormon advent in Illinois, and the number of members nationally was about 2,000. In New York state, an area that historically had embraced Masonry, the number dropped from 500 to fewer than 100.[10] Despite national shifts in membership, Masonry continued to be popular enough in the Midwest to inspire the creation of new lodges. Although there were fewer than a hundred interested men in Illinois in the late 1830s, the Masons chartered a new Grand Lodge two years before the organization of the Nauvoo Lodge in 1839.[11] In Nauvoo, the first slate of officers on April 6, 1840, combined non-Mormon and Mormon Masons: friend to Joseph Smith and Mormon convert Judge James Adams, as Deputy Grand Master, and non-Mormon Abraham Jonas, as Grand Master.[12]

As was true of the drafting of the city charter and the organization of the Nauvoo Legion, John C. Bennett was instrumental in the formation of a Masonic order. In his leadership role, Adams may have encouraged Bennett

8. "Church History," *Times and Seasons* 3, no. 9 (Mar. 1, 1842): 706.

9. *History of the Church*, 4:535-43 (Mar. 1, 1842).

10. Michael W. Homer, "'Similarity of Priesthood in Masonry,'" 26-27; Michael W. Homer, *Joseph's Temple: The Dynamic Relationship Between Freemasonry and Mormonism* (Salt Lake city: University of Utah Press, 2014), 140.

11. Homer, "'Similarity of Priesthood in Masonry,'" 27.

12. *The Proceedings of the Grand Lodge of Illinois, from its Organization in 1840-1850 Inclusive,* 1-5.

to request permission from the Bodley Lodge No. 1 in Quincy for the launch of a Masonic lodge in the new Mormon town.[13] Although the response has not survived, it must have been a refusal, as the minutes record only that the Mormons were "unknown to this lodge as Masons."[14] But then Grand Master Jonas subsequently "issued a dispensation authorizing the organization of a Lodge in Nauvoo."[15]

Nineteenth-century fraternal organizations attracted men, in part, because they "underscored a more fundamental opposition in the minds of mid-Victorian men: a tension between men and women," according to historian Mark Carnes.[16] Such organizations assessed the needs of industrial society, provided networking and mentoring for rising young men to affiliate with a "brotherhood" that also had commercial and business advantages. Such groups offered "a source of stability amidst the social chaos of modern life." Carnes also suggests that key elements in the success of such organizations–Masonic and other–were gender segregation, secrecy, and ritual.[17] Albert C. Stevens, writing in the 1897 *Cyclopaedia of Fraternities,* reported that 6 million Americans belonged to 300 such organizations.[18] Members were primarily white, middle-class, and male from a range of religious affiliations.

According to Barbara Franco, director of the Historical Society of Washington, D.C., fraternal organizations reinforced the notion of separate spheres and gender differences. In fraternal organizations, members "form[ed] friendships and practice[d] virtues when they left the moral female sanctuary of home."[19] She continues: "Manliness in the nineteenth-century division of gender roles was associated with an aggressive individualism that placed a man's value on his competitiveness and success as the breadwinner of the family."[20]

Carnes analyzes the appeal of secret rituals, which he finds were "closely linked to issues of gender. Farmers, industrial workers, and veterans practiced the rituals, not because they aspired to the way of life of the urban

13. James J. Tyler, *John Cook Bennett* (n.p., n.d.), qtd in Kenneth W. Godfrey, "Joseph Smith and the Masons," 83. See also Homer, *Joseph's Temple*, 144.

14. John C. Reynolds, *History of the M. W. Grand Lodge of Illinois*, 154.

15. Homer, "'Similarity of Priesthood in Masonry,'" 28.

16. Mark C. Carnes, *Secret Ritual and Manhood in Victorian America*, 90.

17. Ibid., 89, 2, 14.

18. Albert C. Stevens, qtd. in ibid., 1n1.

19. Barbara Franco, "The Ritualization of Male Friendship and Virtue in Nineteenth-Century Fraternal Organizations," 287.

20. Ibid., 291.

middle classes, but because they shared with them similar concerns about gender."[21] Ritual forged identity and connections to others where they could express paternal emotions. He writes, "Initiates could not acquire manhood and gain entry into the masculine family of the lodge until they had won the approval of patriarchs." Mirroring familial relationships, ritual "made it possible to approach manhood with greater self-assurance."[22]

Typically lodge rooms were equipped with period revival decor, places where "men could create a pseudodomestic environment that offered relief from the competitiveness of public life but was not dominated by wives and female relatives."[23] Like a theatrical set, the lodge room formed the backdrop for the articulation of masculine roles and associations. For men dissatisfied or uncomfortable with Victorian family relationships and traditions, the lodge provided a new source of identity, power, and emotional support. Franco asserts, "Masonic ritual created a safe haven for the expression of brotherhood beyond the more petty concerns of business or politics."[24]

Many of Freemasonry's devices such as secrecy, signs, ritual gestures, passwords, and methods of teaching through dramatizations and rituals may date back as far as the sixteenth century, though not, as claimed, to the days of Solomon's temple. Carnes focuses on the role of ritual in lodges like that in Nauvoo. Masonic ritual intended to "provide solace and psychological guidance during young men's passage to manhood in Victorian America."[25] What is more, Carnes argues, "many men were deeply troubled by the gender bifurcations of Victorian society, which deprived them of a religious experience with which they could identify and of a family environment in which they could freely express nurturing and paternal emotions." Masonic ritual challenged the message they heard from the modern world "that men were innately impure, aggressive, and unemotional. By affirming that men possessed traits socially defined as female, the symbols conveyed a message expressed nowhere else in Victorian America."[26] Accompanying the potentialities suggested by the Mormon temple endowment, Masonic ritual rendered men more powerful than they had been before, with brotherhood, a strong fraternal and personal identification with sound values and a sense of history.

21. Carnes, *Secret Ritual and Manhood in Victorian America*, 14.

22. Ibid., 121, 123.

23. Franco, "The Ritualization of Male Friendship and Virtue," 292.

24. Ibid.

25. Carnes, *Secret Ritual and Manhood in Victorian America*, 14

26. Ibid., 149.

On March 15, 1842, Grand Master Jonas came to Nauvoo, stood at the outdoor stand next to the temple site, and officially established the Nauvoo Masonic Lodge with eighteen Mormon members. By the end of the day, Joseph and Sidney Rigdon had become Entered Apprentices.[27] Following established procedures, they became Fellow Craft and finally Master Masons by passing the "three several degrees of ancient York Masonry,"[28] an inordinately rapid series of promotions.[29] The circle most closely associated with Joseph–Brigham Young, Willard Richards, Wilford Woodruff, and John Taylor–had submitted petitions for membership two months earlier on January 3.[30] Other officers included George D. Miller as Grand Master, John D. Parker as Grand Warden, and Lucius Scovil as Junior Warden.[31]

Following Joseph's lead, Mormon men flocked into Masonry. Writing to Parley P. Pratt on June 17, 1842, Heber C. Kimball noted: "Thare was near two hundred been made Masons [here] .... All of the Twelve apostles have become members Except Orson Pratt ... There is a similarity of preas[t] Hood in Masonry. Bro. Joseph Ses Masonry was taken from preasthood, but has become degenerated. But menny things are perfect."[32] Some months later, the lodge was suspended, but by then it had initiated 286 candidates and raised "almost as many" to Master Masons.[33] This was "six times as many initiations and elevations as all the other lodges in the state combined."[34] Like Mormon priesthood, Masonry afforded potent means of association with the Latter-day Saint hierarchy. In fact, such rapid increase in membership drew the ire of non-Mormon Illinois lodges, fearing that official standards regarding admission had been compromised and that this new Mormon lodge might weaken the state's Grand Lodge.[35]

Despite the enthusiastic start, and within four months of its organization, questions about the Nauvoo Lodge inspired the state leadership to call for the reevaluation of its official status. On July 16, Grand Master Jonas

27. *History of the Church*, 4:551, 566 (Mar. 15, 1842).

28. Hogan, *Founding Minutes of the Nauvoo Lodge*, 8.

29. *History of the Church*, 4:552 (Mar. 16, 1842).

30. Hogan, *Founding Minutes of the Nauvoo Lodge*, 8; *History of the Church*, 4:550, 556 (Mar. 15, 1842).

31. A special committee of the Grand Lodge approved Nauvoo's petition on February 3, 1842, and issued a charter. Mervin B. Hogan, ed., *Founding Minutes of the Nauvoo Lodge*, U.D. [Under Dispensation], 8, 10.

32. Heber C. Kimball, Letter to Parley P. Pratt, June 17, 1842.

33. Samuel H. Goodwin, *Mormonism and Masonry*, 28; Homer, "'Similarity of Priesthood in Masonry,'" 30.

34. Godfrey, "Joseph Smith and the Masons," 85.

35. Ibid.

received instruction from the Bodley Lodge No. 1 that the dispensation of the Nauvoo Lodge should be suspended until the Grand Lodge had time to examine the appropriateness of the procedures used for initiation and advancement in the Nauvoo Lodge.[36] Specifically, the Bodley Lodge questioned the unorthodox ways "officers of the Nauvoo Lodge were installed," including the dizzying speed to "initiate, pass, and raise Joseph Smith and Sidney Rigdon at the same meeting, at one and the same time."[37]

In October 1842, the Grand Lodge finally began the investigation of the Nauvoo Lodge's practices. The report expressed concern about "the practice of balloting for more than one applicant at one and the same time" and "an applicant of at least doubtful character was received on a promise of reformation and restitution."[38] Despite reservations, the Grand Lodge ended the suspension but warned Nauvoo's Masons that their procedures were incorrect and urged them to be more careful in the future.

Generally, most Mormon historians have been somewhat reluctant to discuss the similarities between the Mormon temple ceremony and Masonic ritual. "The best history of the Mormon church, written by Mormons, skirts this issue," Carnes writes, referring to Leonard J. Arrington and Davis Bitton's 1979 *The Mormon Experience.* "The authors ... note that Mormons recognized that there were 'similarities as well as differences' in the rituals; there is no further elaboration." Carnes stresses: it "cannot be disputed that quasi-Masonic ritual figured prominently in the lives of most Mormon men."[39] Mormon sociologist Armand Mauss's suggestion that "even the most original revelations have to be expressed in the idioms of the culture and biography of the revelator" places Joseph's emerging temple ritual in the context of a larger cultural expression.[40] Masonry foregrounded a rich web of terminology, imagery, and meanings about temple building, ancient scripture, and ritual that were easily transferable to the restored Mormon gospel.

Relief Society

Two days after Mormon elders formed their new all-male, secret organization, Nauvoo's women established an organization of their own, with Joseph stepping in at almost the last moment to be sure that it had a clearly

36. Goodwin, *Mormonism and Masonry*, 26-27; also Homer, *Joseph's Temple*, 160.
37. Ibid., 175.
38. Ibid., 172-73.
39. Carnes, *Secret Ritual and Manhood in Victorian America*, 173n22, 6-7.
40. Armand L. Mauss, "Culture, Charisma, and Change," 79-80.

defined place within the Church's priesthood "order." Although the best context of the Relief Society may be the creations of the Masonic Lodge and the Quorum of the Anointed, it also leagued Mormon women with American women who more broadly sought association in the context of service. In Sarah Kimball's home, a small group of friends decided to found a sewing society to produce clothing for laborers on the Nauvoo temple. They drew up a brief "constitution" which they submitted to Joseph. He praised the effort but stated that he would "organize the sisters under the priesthood after a pattern of the priesthood."[41] Twenty women met with Joseph on March 17.

The setting was the upper floor of Joseph's red brick store. Joseph was accompanied by John Taylor, who gave the opening prayer, and Willard Richards.[42] Presciently, the sisters sang the anthem from the Kirtland temple's dedication: "The Spirit of God Like a Fire Is Burning." Joseph moved and Sarah Cleveland seconded that the women show by vote whether they were willing to be accepted into full fellowship in the new institution "and admit them to the privileges of the Institution about to be formed."[43] All did so. Joseph then lectured the women on the necessity of keeping secrets, also a major emphasis to new Masons two days earlier. "[I]f members of the Society shall conduct themselves improperly deal with them, and keep all your doings within your own bosoms, and hold all characters sacred."[44]

Joseph told the sisters to elect their officers, including a president or "Elect Lady." The term had previously been applied to Emma in a revelation dated July 1830 that authorized her to compile the Church's first hymnal. Joseph read this revelation, including instructions that Emma was "to expound scriptures, and to exhort the church according as it shall be given thee by my Spirit" (D&C 25:3, 7; see also 2 John 1). But the term "Elect Lady" was also the name of a woman's degree in Masonry's French Adoptive Rite.[45] Adoptive Lodges were activated during the Napoleonic era; in fact, Empress

41. Sarah M. Granger Kimball, "Auto-biography," 51.

42. *History of the Church*, 4:552-53 (Mar. 17, 1842).

43. Relief Society, Minutes, Mar. 17, 1842. Those present included Emma Smith, Sarah M. Cleveland, Bathsheba W. Smith, Phebe Ann Hawkes, Phebe M. Wheeler, Elizabeth Jones, Elvira A. Coles, Sophia Packard, Margaret A. Cook, Philinda Merrick, Athalia Robinson (name crossed out), Martha Knights, Sarah M. Kimball, Desdemona Fulmer, Eliza R. Snow, Elizabeth Ann Whitney, Sophia Robinson, Leonora Taylor, Nancy Rigdon (name crossed out), Sophia R. Marks.

44. Ibid.

45. As Michael Homer points out (p. 29), the French Adoptive Rite admitted women and was recognized by the Grand Orient in 1774. "The Elect Lady" would be used as the name for the 5th degree in the adoptive ritual of the Eastern Star in 1868; also Linda King Newell and Valeen Tippetts Avery, *Mormon Enigma*, 105. Henry Wilson Coil, *Coil's Masonic Encyclopedia*, 9, 123, 130. See also F. A. Bell, comp., *Order of the Eastern Star*, 20-22, 88-93.

Josephine was the Grand Master of one.[46] Joseph's scribe recorded that "the elect meant to be elected to a certain work &c and that the revelation [D&C 25] was then fulfilled by Sister Emma's election to the Presidency of the [Relief] Society."[47] Following her election, Emma chose two counselors. Joseph, Taylor, and Richards set each apart for her new calling with a priesthood blessing by the laying on of hands. Joseph told his wife that she would be "a pattern of virtue; and possess all the qualifications necessary for her to stand and preside and dignify her Office to teach the females those principles requisite for their future usefulness."[48]

The women wondered about a name for their group–whether "Benevolent" or "Relief" better captured the essence of what they hoped to accomplish. Elizabeth Ann Whitney proposed the name Nauvoo Female Relief Society. John Taylor suggested the Nauvoo Female Benevolent Society. Joseph disagreed: "[T]he term Relief is more extended in its signification than Benevolent." Eliza Snow agreed. Emma added, "[W]hen a boat is stuck on the rapids, with a multitude of Mormons on board we shall consider <u>that</u> a loud call for <u>relief</u>. ... [W]e expect extraordinary occasions and pressing calls." Snow formally proposed the Female Relief Society of Nauvoo. The motion carried. Emma then issued her own mission statement: "[E]ach member should be ambitious to do good ... members should deal frankly with each other–to watch over the morals–and be very careful of the character and reputation of the members of the Institution."[49] In conclusion, the members sang, "Come, Let Us Rejoice in the Day of Salvation."

Between March and the end of August 1842, the Relief Society met fourteen times. Joseph frequently attended, and often spoke. He sometimes used Masonic language as a code to communicate the significance both organizations represented for the Church,[50] but also to indicate how he saw the Relief Society as fitting into the layered understandings of doctrine and

46. "History of Women's Freemasonry," www.womenfreemasonsusa.com/history.html (Nov. 13, 2007). The rituals performed by women in the Adoptive Lodges were "allegorical rather than symbolic. They evoked qualities such as modest, candor, faithfulness and chastity. Their main activities were social and philanthropic."

47. Manuscript *History of the Church*, Mar. 17, 1842, qtd. in Andrew F. Ehat and Lyndon W. Cook, eds., *The Words of Joseph Smith*, 106.

48. Relief Society, Minutes, Mar. 17, 1842.

49. Ibid.

50. Homer has identified as Masonic borrowings the terms and phrases: "institution," that "the society should grow up by degrees," that "the society should move according to the ancient Priesthood ... said he was going to make this society a kingdom of priests as in Enoch's day–as in Paul's day"; and, finally, his instruction that the sisters needed to be "sufficiently skill'd in Masonry as to keep a secret" and to be "good masons." Homer, "'Similarity of Priesthood in Masonry,'" 29.

ritual. Masonry, Relief Society, and temple ritual created a set of thresholds over which the most faithful crossed to draw closer to Joseph, sharing his secret understandings, and forging unity and identity that would carry them into the future.[51]

As men had flocked to Masonry, women gathered to participate in this first Mormon organization devoted to women and having community-spirited purposes. But the organization existed on two levels, one of public goodwill and another of private tensions. It was during the second meeting on March 24, for example, that Emma scolded twenty-year-old Clarissa Marvel for gossiping about Joseph, who was present, and Agnes Coolbrith Smith.[52] Emma said she "intended … to shun the appearance of evil–all are required to be very careful in their words and actions at all times."[53] By that time, Joseph had secretly married nine women, at least some of whom were present at the meeting.

Relief Society meetings also became the place for the manifestation of spiritual gifts. Sarah Cleveland commented on April 19: "As the Prophet had given us liberty to improve the Gifts of the gospel … [she] desired to speak in the gift of tongues, which she did in a powerful manner"; another woman interpreted. In the minutes, Eliza Snow described the display as "interesting."[54]

On April 28, Joseph told the women that he "now turn[s] the key to you in the name of God and this Society shall rejoice and knowledge and intelligence shall flow down from this time."[55] Years later, exercising some editorial liberty, George A. Smith, in assembling documents for the *History of the Church,* silently adjusted Joseph's words "I now turn the key to you" to "I turn the key in your behalf,"[56] both rhetorically and practically distancing women from any implicit priesthood power the key might give them. Joseph's language could be read to suggest that the women held a special type of priesthood, although there is no evidence that anything like ordination or

51. By 1844, the Relief Society would number 1,341 members, significantly more than the Masonic lodge.

52. Relief Society, Minutes, Mar. 24, 1842. Agnes Smith said that Marvel had lived with her for nearly a year. Emma added, "She has no parents–she is under our care and observation–she needs friends."

53. Ibid.

54. Relief Society, Minutes, Apr. 19, 1842.

55. Ibid.

56. For the debate over this wording and what it implied, see Linda King Newell, "Gifts of the Spirit," 112-17. *History of the Church*, 4:607 (Apr. 28, 1842).

special empowerment came of it. If it had, it would have been one of Joseph's more radical moves.

Also at the April 28 meeting, Joseph defended women's exercise of spiritual gifts, pointing to the way women could invoke the power of God to enhance healing: "If the sisters should have faith to heal the sick let all hold their tongues, and let every thing roll on. ... there would be no more sin in any female laying hands on the sick than in wetting the face with water."[57] When it came to speaking in tongues, however, he was more restrictive: "If any have a matter to reveal, let it be in your own tongue. ... I lay this down for a rule that if any thing is taught by this gift of tongues, it is not to be received for doctrine."[58]

When Joseph and Emma entered the Relief Society's meeting room on May 26, the tension between them was masked by the decorum required of the Church president and his wife. Joseph began with a scoulding couched in the language of scripture. He began by quoting from Ezekiel 14, saying that the people should stand firm in their faith. Making veiled reference to rumors circulating among the Church's women, he said: "As females possess refin'd feelings and sensitivenes, they are also subject to an over much zeal which must ever prove dangerous ... [they] should be arm'd with mercy notwithstanding the iniquity among us." Some of the women had already entered plurality, and despite careful efforts to keep it secret, rumors created a secret reality. Joseph had two recommendations: "put a double watch over the tonge" and "chasten and reprove and keep it all in silence, ... then you be established in power, virtue and holiness and the wrath of God will be turn'd away." Emma followed and emphasized the seriousness of Joseph's exhortation while adding her own injunction. "All idle rumor and idle talk," she said, "must be laid aside yet sin must not be covered, especially those sins which are against the law of God." The verbal jousting that proceeded in private between Joseph and Emma over the subject of plurality lay partially exposed in such public gatherings as this.

Emma was absent from the July 7 meeting but conducted the next two on July 14 and August 4. A proposed "Mrs. Brown" was rejected, tainted by scandal. Emma supported Joseph's prophetic role even in his absence, urging the women to live righteous lives. "God knows we have a work to do in this place," she said, "we have got to watch and pray and be careful not to excite

57. Relief Society, Minutes, Apr. 28, 1842.

58. Ibid.

feelings–not make enemies of one another." One woman moved to extend a vote of thanks to Emma, but she said, "I do not want the thanks but the pray'rs of the Society."[59]

Perhaps the most explosive meeting occurred two and a half months later when John C. Bennett was publishing his inflammatory exposé. On September 28, Joseph wrote out a defensive document that he had Emma read to the group, which now numbered about 1,100. In it, he asserted that some men sought to "deceive and debauch the innocent," claiming they had authority from Joseph or others. "We do not mention their names, not knowing but what there may be some among you who are not sufficiently skill'd in Masonry as to keep a secret," he wrote. "Let this epistle be had as a private matter in your Society, and then we shall learn whether you are good masons." In addition to Joseph, signing the document were Hyrum Smith, Heber Kimball, Willard Richards, Vinson Knight, and Brigham Young.[60]

Emma must have longed to find refuge in shared good works, hoping she could trust the women in Relief Society. Whether she knew the extent of what she could only have considered a betrayal, she soon must have suspected much; and her suspicions, whether confirmed or not, must have gnawed at her relentlessly, even as she alternately gave way to them or battered them back. It must have been an agonizing position for her in almost every way. Her lifelong silence thereafter was her own attempt to create a reality in which plurality had never happened or had, at worst, been only a momentary aberration.

The Quorum of the Anointed

Both new organizations–the Masonic Lodge and the Female Relief Society–were still finding their way when on May 4-5, a select group of seven men, in addition to Joseph and Hyrum, learned about the endowment ceremony. Intrigued by Masonic ritual and its allusions to ancient power, Joseph was also interested in the ancient architecture that was rhetorically, at least, at the heart of Masonry. One of those present in that first Mormon endowment gathering was Masonic Grand Master James Adams. In instructing the men in "the principles and order of the Priesthood," Joseph attended to special "washings, anointings, endowments and the communication of keys." This council, also known as the Holy Order and Quorum of the Anointed, was, Joseph informed them, "instituted [according to] the ancient order of

59. Ibid., July 14, Aug. 4, 1842.

60. Ibid., Sept. 28, 1842.

things for the first time in the last days."[61] His topics "were of things spiritual, and to be received only by the spiritual minded." Available "even to the weakest of Saints" in the "proper place," these new teachings became another reason to "be diligent in building the Temple."[62]

Joseph's statement to the men lays out his understanding of the hierarchy of individuals, rituals, and ideas that he believed prepared the way for Christ's second coming. Ritual provided a threshold for revelation, deeper and more meaningful knowledge, and a *communitas* created through secret-keeping, through faith and belief, and a framework of the "ancient order of things." Joseph's priesthood-centered, biblically-infused ritual eventually became the LDS temple endowment ceremony, the ritual that embodies beliefs about the Creation, the Fall, the Atonement, salvation, special signs, tokens, and punishments, and the importance of safeguarding secret knowledge. Its ceremonies were reserved for the most faithful, who, when endowed, believed that the rituals were essential to their exaltation.

Through the summer of 1842, only men were admitted to the Quorum of the Anointed. Membership expanded in September 1843 to include women. If Joseph had seen the endowment initially as a companion to Masonry, Emma's focus on community service and the lack of enforceable secrecy made such an approach impossible. On September 28, 1843, Emma and a few other women–mostly civil wives of the men in the group–received their endowments. ("Being endowed" and "receiving one's endowment" are terms describing the process of passing through the endowment ritual.) By his death in June 1844, Joseph had admitted more than sixty-six men and women into this elite group.[63] The endowment and the Masonic ritual were both exclusive, intended for trusted insiders only. Each brought initiates out of their ordinary world and into a symbolic life of ritual. Donning priestly vestments, they moved into a mysterious better place.[64] The requirement of secrecy connected them to each other and to Joseph himself. Ritual became a mechanism for identity building, loyalty maintenance, and secret keeping.

---

61. *History of the Church*, 5:2 (May 4, 1842); see also Devery S. Anderson and Gary James Bergera, eds., *Joseph Smith's Quorum of the Anointed*, 5.

62. *History of the Church*, 5:2 (May 4, 1842).

63. Anderson and Bergera, *Joseph Smith's Quorum of the Anointed*, xxxiii.

64. Initiates laid aside their everyday clothing, washed and anointed with perfumed oil, and dressed in special "garments" as they did for Masonic ritual. Bennett described the outer garment as a shirt, the "robe of the order." The novice was told the shirt should "be sacredly preserved, to keep the Destroying Angel from them and their families ... They believe that these shirts will preserve them from death, and secure to them an earthly immortality." Bennett, *History of the Saints*, 277.

Some of the endowment resembled Masonic ritual. But the endowment's essence and purpose were different. Masonry was primarily a mechanism for forging fraternal bonds that unified men with common values and beliefs. The endowment ushered individuals into sacred space, not only literal and physical, but a space of the imagination that transformed their ordinary lives and helped them see what was possible in the hereafter.[65] Those potentialities promised them lives beyond what they imagined on earth–lives beyond the conventions of society, law, and even traditional religion.

Certain Masonic symbols figured prominently in the endowment ceremony and eventually in the Nauvoo temple's design. Such elements as the beehive, the all-seeing eye, special hand shakes, and the compass and square were familiar iconography from both Masonry and American religious symbolism.[66] Prayer circles appeared in each, as well. The endowment scenario recalled the Masonic drama of Hiram Abiff, using many of the same Old Testament passages.[67] Even as the endowment was being introduced, some recognized similarities but believed the Masonic ritual distorted the original, ancient Solomonic ritual. Regardless of the borrowings, LDS temple ritual and masonic ritual are not the same. For Latter-day Saints, temple ritual moves them through a contemplation of their relationship with God, the eventuality of heaven, and their connection with those who have died. Participation forms a boundary between insiders and outsiders, those who believed Joseph's prophet narrative and those who did not. Brigham Young, for one, later told the story, drawing on Masonic legend, of how "Solomon built a Temple for the purpose of giving endowments," although not many were given, because "one of the high priests was murdered by wicked and corrupt men … because he would not reveal those things appertaining to the Priesthood that were forbidden him to reveal until he came to the proper

65. According to historian Richard Bushman, "The use of the word 'endowment' in Nauvoo implied that the goal of coming into God's presence would be realized now through ritual rather than a transcendent vision. This transition gave Mormonism's search for direct access to God an enduring form" (Richard Lyman Bushman, *Joseph Smith*, 451). Noah Webster's 1828 *American Dictionary of the English Language* defined "endowment" as "That which is given or bestowed on the person or mind by the creator; a gift of nature; any quality or faculty bestowed by the creator" (s.v. "ENDOWMENT"). Samuel Johnson's *A Dictionary of the English Language* (1755) defined "to endue" (variant of "to endow") as "to supply with mental excellencies; to invest with intellectual powers," and illustrated this usage with the following quotation from the *Book of Common Prayer:* "*Endue* them with thy holy spirit" (s.v. "To Endue").

66. Andrew, *Early Temples of the Mormons*, 84-85. See also Alan Gowans, "Freemasonry and the Neoclassic Style in America."

67. David John Buerger, *The Mysteries of Godliness*, 53-55.

place."[68] Both Masonry and the endowment maintained Mormon identity, pulling men–and, in the temple, eventually women–into a community forged through ritual.

Organizations and Secrecy

It is the case that the truth or dishonesty of a personal narrative is a matter of supreme consequence for the individual. Those who study narrative theory may argue over whether individuals are ever the authors of their own stories in any real sense, or if they are instead only the protagonists. Do such narratives reflect or unfold inner character, or even actively mold identity? Is the interpreted life something we create? Something that has its own reality? These questions are critical in understanding Joseph's life as a prophet.

Joseph's prophet-narrative reflects normative and behavioral implications in the ways he measured his own life and how others might have as well. This interpretive process on both conscious and unconscious levels, transformed his life from a chronicle into a series of cause-and-effect relations that formed a coherent whole. His life story became a core source of identity for the Church, a central defining myth that unified a people who looked to the same prophet.

A prophet sometimes steps out of the role to behave as a mere man, complicating the story of his life and creating a layering effect of moral roles. The secrets which concealed this step between moral roles and the consequences for Joseph and others around him were immense. Joseph tested the loyalty of his people with secrets imbedded in temple ritual, in expectations about membership or priesthood, in the practice of plurality, and even exhortations to unity in the face of the world's threats.

Sometimes these secrets looked like lies, and those trying to understand Joseph look for models in a variety of places. Contemporary world history is replete with examples of chief executives who lied. Some such lies are perhaps forgivable or tolerable, and others not. But all have consequences. Tracing the consequences of Joseph's statements in the narrative of his prophethood is a complicated task. Sometimes ambiguous, sometimes laced with double or triple entendres, they were meant to obscure a view of the truth. Once a lie was formed to protect a sacred ritual or belief, it took on a life of its own and often became dogmatic in its structure, the discourse it created, and the way it perpetuated limited knowledge of the truth. The lie

68. Brigham Young, Jan. 1, 1877, JD 18:305.

complicated Joseph's ability to modify, reinterpret, or dismantle the original story. It is also true that, regardless of the context in which such lies occurred–whether as part of the beginnings of plurality or as a shield against Joseph's enemies–they all became self-destructive on some level.

On numerous occasions, Joseph denied his involvement with plurality. For example, in early October 1843, he noted, "Gave instructions to try those persons who were preaching, teaching, or practicing the doctrine of plurality of wives: for, according to the law, I hold the keys of this power in the last days; for there is never one on earth at a time on whom the power and its keys are conferred; and I have constantly said no man shall have but one wife at a time, unless the Lord directs otherwise."[69] The following May, he testified in front of the Nauvoo City Council: "I had not been married scarcely five minutes, and made one proclamation of the Gospel, before it was reported that I had seven wives. … This spiritual wifeism! Why, a man dares not speak or wink, for fear of being accused of this."[70] While at first glance, passages such as these express a denial of plurality, they also left room for escape. The first quietly suggests that a man should have only one wife, while specifying an exemption to make possible a plurality of wives. The second is not really a denial so much as a statement, placing some distance between himself and the practice and making light of the accusation.

Joseph kept secrets from almost everyone. A shared secret marked Joseph's assessment of those around him–not always accurately. Non-Mormon historian Laurence Moore generously suggests that secrecy protected "infant, half-formulated ideas from persecution by keeping them hidden from public knowledge."[71] This method worked when Joseph's followers were loyal to his prophethood. But when they saw a more complicated picture, the shadow of secret doctrines and practices sprang into harsh relief. Inevitably, opposition surrounded Joseph's secret practices to create trouble for the Church. Smith "used secrecy for another reason, as part of his effort to give his followers a sense of distinct identity," continues Moore. "Those who knew the secret, or those to whom it was promised, were joined together. Those who were excluded from the secret were invited to regard the Mormons as mysteriously different."[72]

Nor did the secrets stop with Joseph but engaged a larger community

69. *History of the Church*, 6:46 (Oct. 5, 1843).
70. Ibid., 410 (May 26, 1844).
71. R. Laurence Moore, *Religious Outsiders and the Making of Americans*, 36.
72. Ibid., 37.

in the protection of religious practice. On October 1, 1842, the *Times and Seasons* reprinted the statement on marriage from 1835 affirming marriage as "one man" and "one wife." It was signed by Church leaders including some who had already entered plurality. A companion statement was signed by women, including plural wives Eliza Snow, Sarah Cleveland, and Sarah Ann Whitney.[73] Eliza Snow later made her own careful differentiation that allowed her misrepresentation to be not-quite-a-lie.[74] For Charles W. Penrose, the distinction was justified by religious ritual which God had instituted through his prophet: "[W]hen assailed by their enemies and accused of practising things which were really not countenanced in the Church they were justified in denying those imputations and at the same time avoiding avowal of such doctrines as were not yet intended for the world."[75] Clearly, lying became part of the ritual of plurality in Nauvoo, not embedded in the sealing ceremony but in the lived behavior of those involved who took on the burden of concealing it.[76]

Other New Revelations

The emergence of these new organizations occurred during a period of theological innovation. But a month before he began to teach the endowment ritual, Joseph delved into government. On April 7, 1842, according to retrospective accounts, he reportedly received a revelation regarding theocratic government which expanded his reach and the boundaries of the Kingdom of God. "Verily thus saith the Lord, this is the name by which you shall be called, the kingdom of God and his law with the keys and powers thereof and judgments in the hands of his servants Ahman Christ."[77] (This concept of God's kingdom would lie largely dormant until the spring of 1844; see chap. 24.)

Early that same month, James Arlington Bennet published in the *New York Herald:* "While modern philosophy, which believes in nothing, but what you can touch, is overspreading the Atlantic States, Joe Smith is creating a

73. "On Marriage," *Times and Seasons* 3, no. 24 (Oct. 15, 1842): 939. In February 1891, Ebenezer Robinson claimed that he and others had signed the statement in genuine innocence: "[W]e had no knowledge of such a ceremony, or that 'spiritual wifery,' or 'polygamy,' was taught by the heads of the church, as they had not up to that time taught it to us. …" (Ebenezer Robinson, "Items of Personal History," *The Return* [Feb. 1891]: 29-30).

74. Eliza R. Snow, Letter to Joseph F. Smith, n.d.

75. Charles W. Penrose, "Joseph Smith and Celestial Marriage."

76. B. Carmon Hardy, *Solemn Covenant*, 363-426.

77. In H. Michael Marquardt, ed., *The Joseph Smith Revelations*, 314.

spiritual system, combined also with morals and industry, that may change the destiny of the race."[78] Recognizing that Joseph's doctrines informed virtually every element of secular and spiritual life, Bennet portrayed Mormon kingdom-building as an all-encompassing life course that built towns as well as temples and destined persons for political life, success in commerce or industry, and salvation. A grateful Joseph promptly responded by bestowing on Bennet an honorary degree from the University of Nauvoo, a brigadier-generalship in the Nauvoo Legion, and the keys to the city.

Willard Richards met Bennet during the summer of 1842, at his home on Long Island, New York, and was impressed: "His mansion is of the first order, surpassed by none in New York and few in England. … He is a gentleman and stands at the head of the elite of New York. He is a scholar and believing that every man should be the creator of himself, or the originator of his own resources, has applied himself with unremitting diligence to all the arts and sciences and subjects within his reach, and those not a few. His mind is of the highest order and stoops not to notice those little broils which distract the human family."[79]

Also by April, Joseph had given final approval for the second "facsimile" illustration (the first had been published on March 1) from his Book of Abraham translation, with accompanying text.[80] Joseph must have identified with Abraham, a fellow prophet, when the "Lord" showed him how "the intelligences that were organized before the world was; and among these there were many of the noble and great ones, and God saw these souls that they were good … and he said, These, I will make my rulers … and he said unto me, Abraham, thou art one of them" (Abr. 3:22).

Another of Joseph's revelations that spring included the ambitious project of reaching beyond death to assure salvation through priesthood ritual. On March 20, Joseph preached a sermon "to a large assembly in the grove" about death and resurrection, prompted by the death of Windsor and Sylvia Lyon's child. Why, Joseph reflected, would God take an innocent child who had not yet had the privilege of receiving the necessary ordinances of salvation?[81] Framing his comments with his own acute memories of his dead children, he opined, "The Lord takes many away, even in infancy, that they may escape the envy of man, and the sorrows and evils of this present world;

78. James Arlington Bennet, "The Mormons: A Leaf from Joe Smith," 2.
79. Willard Richard, qtd. in Dean C. Jessee, ed., *The Personal Writings of Joseph Smith*, 574.
80. "The Book of Abraham," *Times and Seasons* 3, no. 10 (Mar. 15, 1842): 720.
81. *History of the Church*, 4:553 (Mar. 20, 1842).

they were too pure, too lively, to live on earth; therefore, if rigidly considered, instead of mourning we have reason to rejoice as they are delivered from evil, and we shall soon have them again."[82]

Joseph also spoke about priesthood keys as the authority by which binding ordinances, including baptism, were performed on earth: "there is no other way beneath the heavens whereby God hath ordained for man to come [to Him] … & any other course is in vain."[83] That afternoon, "a multitude of people" lined the banks, as Joseph walked into the shallow riverbank to baptize some eighty persons for the remission of sins. The first person baptized was one of Emma's nephews, Lorenzo Wasson, "the first of her kindred that has embraced the fullness of the Gospel." In a gesture both dramatic and emotional, Joseph raised his hands "toward heaven, and implored the blessing of God to rest upon the people"; those there felt that the "Spirit of God did rest upon the multitude, to the joy and consolation of our hearts."[84] Afterward, the group moved to the temple grove where Joseph confirmed the newly baptized, giving them the gift of the Holy Ghost.

Later that week, Joseph spoke again, this time in metaphors that revealed the need for a hierarchical and highly ordered church. God created "the sun, the moon, the stars in the heavens," giving them "their laws conditions, & bounds which they cannot pass except by his command." In the same way, the Church and its members needed to reflect divine order in their obedience.[85] The perfect metaphor for the religious community and the doctrine that Joseph constructed around his person, the imagery of the centrality of the sun exemplified proper relations established by ritual, righteous living, and belief.[86]

On April 1, Joseph published a lengthy editorial in the *Times and Seasons* which instructed the Saints on the power of discernment and how to identify good spirits from demonic ones by offering a homely handshake.[87] It was a small example of his larger agenda of drawing all aspects of life, both natural and supernatural, into ritual. He also struck back at rumors of apostasies, intrigues, and transgressions. Priesthood leaders tempted by vanity

82. Ibid.

83. Ehat and Cook, *The Words of Joseph Smith*, 108.

84. *History of the Church*, 4:556 (Mar. 20, 1842).

85. Scott G. Kenney, ed., *Wilford Woodruff's Journal, 1833-1898*, 2:161 (Mar. 20, 1842); "We Have Again the Warning Voice Sounded in Our Midst," in *The Essential Joseph Smith*, 155.

86. *History of the Church*, 4:553-58 (Mar. 20, 1842).

87. Joseph Smith, "Try the Spirits," in *History of the Church*, 4:571-81 (Apr. 1, 1842). The idea of hand-clasps as passports would figure in the temple ceremony.

or pride should, he had charged earlier, pull "the beam out of their eye, that they may see more clearly the mote that is in their brother's eye."[88]

Gathered in general conference on the afternoon of April 7 near the temple site, Joseph "put in order" the various priesthood quorums, then instructed them on the "duties of the church, the necessity of unity of purpose" in "the blessings connected with doing the will of God; and the inconsistency folly and danger of murmuring against the dispensation of Jehovah."[89]

Two days later, he preached at a funeral in the grove, and on April 10 he continued the same theme. "A man is saved no faster than he gets knowledge," he said, "for if he does not get knowledge, he will be brought into captivity by some evil power in the other world, as evil spirits will have more knowledge, and consequently more power than many men who are on the earth. Hence it needs revelation to assist us, and give us knowledge of the things of God."[90] Articulating his own anxieties, Joseph positioned himself as the conduit for revelation and as the only key to salvation.

This largely routine, representative round of weekly activities was Joseph's reality, requiring that he always be in peak form, always articulate and charismatic, always able at a moment's notice to mine a seemingly endless vein of wisdom, folk charm, and wit. It must have been exhausting but exhilarating, fatiguing but addictive. The Saints' constant need to draw nourishment from Joseph gave him–and them–a profoundly meaningful existence.

---

88. *History of the Church*, 4:571, 105.
89. Ibid., 555.
90. Ibid., 588 (Apr. 10, 1842).

CHAPTER 14

The Imagined Space of Heaven

I deign to reveal … things which have been kept hid from before the foundation of the world …

–Joseph Smith, qtd. in History of the Church, *4:278 (Jan. 19, 1841)*

For Joseph, the temple existed both as idea and object. Carving out sacred space for holy rituals, he used various physical locales, notably the upstairs room of his red brick store, as temple-related space where he administered the endowment ceremony rituals and ordinances. While a physical temple structure may have been ideal, under Joseph's plenary priesthood power, temple ordinances could be performed in any place designated by him as temple-sacred. Thus, the term "temple," as employed during Joseph's Nauvoo years, may be best understood as both the locus of activity of any sacred-oriented space and the under-construction Nauvoo temple or House of the Lord. Indeed, Joseph died before the temple was completed.

Conceived first as the backdrop to ritual and worship, the temple created a landscape of the imagination where the journey a human being makes from birth to the ascent to heaven was expressed through both architectural forms and imagined space. Liminal in every way, the spaces of the temple exposed heaven's potentialities. The experience of the temple was not available to non-Mormons but was reserved for the faithful, believers in Joseph's prophetic mission and message about heaven. The ordinances performed there ushered Mormons into a particular heaven. In the symbolic and liminal environment of the temple, access to heaven was negotiated by space, controlled by physical and tangible thresholds and markers. More importantly, it required a radically changed mind, or consciousness. Movement literally and figuratively through the spaces of the temple constructed the celestial realm of heaven. Temple ritual mirrored the experience that Mormons believed was their future when death ushered them into the afterlife. The temple for Church members was at once a place and an idea that concealed both a desire for heaven and a fear of the alternative.

For Nauvoo's Saints, the temple site was especially sacred, imbued with spiritual content. Rudolf Otto in his exploration of the "sacred" explains how an individual "finds the feeling of terror before the sacred, before the awe-inspiring mystery, the majesty that emanates an overwhelming superiority of power; he finds religious fear before the fascinating mystery in which perfect fullness of being flowers." Otto characterizes these experiences as numinous (Latin *numen,* god), for they are induced by the revelation of an aspect of divine power. The numinous presents itself as something "wholly other," as nothing human. Confronted with it, human beings sense their profound nothingness, feel that they are infinitely fragile creatures, or, in the words Abraham used to address the Lord, are "but dust and ashes" (Gen. 18:27).[1]

As Joseph taught, the temple was exclusive, sacred, pure. Its precincts would be polluted by the presence of any but the most faithful. It revealed social hierarchies that distinguished between insiders and outsiders, between priesthood hierarchies, between gendered relations. Its ceremonies guaranteed certain conditions in the afterlife for the chosen. The temple became a sort of affront to the world outside Mormonism, a claim to truth, access to God, and boundary around the Mormon vision of heaven and life on the earth. The temple became the sacred landscape where ideas about heaven and earth were performed and lines were drawn–not just between the faithful and the faithless, but between the most faithful and the not-as-faithful. Temple worship played out beyond public view, accompanied by special gestures, passwords, and new names. It required the utmost faith, including the suspension of disbelief and the deliberate crossing into the numinous, the acceptance of one's holiness. Faith centered on Joseph's ability to confer that holiness as a messenger of God.

Moreover, the temple created liminal space, where "novel configurations of ideas and relations may arise."[2] Liminality presents "a formulable domain in which all that is not manifest in the normal day-to-day operation of social structures … can be studied."[3] The space of the temple was hierarchical. Each threshold that participants crossed moved them upward as well as onward, ascending to the pinnacle.

1. Rudolf Ott, qtd. in Mircea Eliade, *The Sacred and the Profane*, 9-10.
2. Victor Turner, *The Forest of Symbols*, 97.
3. Victor Turner and Edith L. B. Turner, *Image and Pilgrimage in Christian Culture*, 3.

Human structures, whether homes or churches, are attempts to reshape the world and its meaning. Much of this achievement involves the creation of physical things as symbols, representing "man's attempt at 'orienting' in the given unknown environment," according to Christian Norberg-Shultz.[4] Conceptualization results in the concretization of intangibles. Nauvoo's nineteenth-century citizens sought to make their ideas about religion and community tangible. In each case, again largely unconsciously, they sought to make their lives understandable by creating spaces that kept and transmitted meanings.

That a building like a temple may gather "to itself in *its own* way earth and sky, divinities and mortals,"[5] acknowledges how objects, buildings, and cities become culture barriers/transmitters, collecting and carrying meanings. "Man dwells when he can orientate himself within and identify himself with an environment," Norberg-Schultz continues, "or, in short, when he experiences the environment as meaningful. Dwelling therefore implies something more than 'shelter.' It implies that the spaces where life occurs are *places,* in the true sense of the word. A place is a space which has a distinct character."[6]

The Romans spoke of *genius loci*–the power of a particular place or environment. They did so in religious terms, invoking its spirit or character. In Roman religion, human beings have a "genius" or a guardian spirit who gives life to people and the places they inhabit.[7] This spirit, or genius, produces the character of a place they share and determines its essence. "The genius thus denotes what a thing is, or what it 'wants to be,'" according to architect Louis Kahn.[8] Architecture and cities exhibit the *genius loci* of an environment and are concrete manifestations of both identity and presence. A river town like Nauvoo may have represented a frontier vision of future growth and economic prosperity, but beneath the bustling facade moved the mystery and power of the kingdom of God. Its *genius loci* was of a millennial centerpiece, a holy place and a holy people in a world about to become new.

Nauvoo functioned as a liminal threshold, gathering people as well as their ideas and aspirations. Its brick buildings and streets imposed order on what had been a bluff and a swamp, but it also created meaning and new bounded spaces. For some, boundaries are not endings but beginnings, the

4. Christian Norberg-Schultz, *Genius Loci*, 9.

5. See Martin Heidegger, "Building Dwelling Thinking," http://acnet.pratt/edu/-arch43/readings/Heidegger.html (February 10, 2005).

6. Christian Norberg-Schultz, *Genius Loci*, 23.

7. Ibid., 18.

8. Louis Kahn, qtd. in ibid.

places "from which something begins its presencing."[9] In this way, character may be understood by focusing on the ways centralization is created. What forms are repeated? What spaces become the backdrop to significant religious activities? How does the building relate to the site? Each of these questions takes on heightened significance when we consider the Nauvoo temple and the way it located the interaction between believers and God, expressing that centrality of that interaction to the believer's experience.

For human beings to find meaning in their world, they must be able to orient themselves in it. Kevin Lynch, an urban planning theorist, suggests: "A good environmental image gives its possessor an important sense of emotional security."[10] Norberg-Schultz adds, "The world may be organized around a set of focal points, or be broken into named regions, or be linked by remembered routes."[11] Objects of identification and image have concrete environmental qualities that tell the story of a people and a place.

One's memory of place, or place-memory, is the "container of experiences that contribute so powerfully to its [i.e., the place's] intrinsic memorability."[12] Memory is both place oriented and place supported. Place triggers memories for insiders who share common pasts. In some places, public memories are embedded with narrative elements that evoke visual signifiers, social memory, and shared authority. Places offer the power to communities to define their collective pasts and also to tell them what they may forget. The temple site/place reminded Joseph's followers of what to remember, ordered those memories by what was most significant, and fit them into a relationship with God.

The power that comes with place is a sort of cultural citizenship. It reaches beyond individual identities to encompass larger common themes such as persecution, restoration, truth, and the kingdom of God. Identity is intimately tied to memory, to the interconnections of collective or social memories.[13] A society's memory "goes back only as far as it can," notes French philosopher Maurice Halbwachs, "that is, it goes back as far as the memory of its constituent groups." Information may be forgotten when "the groups which used to remember them have disappeared." The memories of another group may aid our own by not only providing "testimony and evidence" but

9. Martin Heidegger, "Language," 154.
10. Kevin Lynch, *The Image of the City*, 4.
11. Ibid., 7.
12. Edward Casey, qtd. in Dolores Hayden, *Power of Place*, 46.
13. Hayden, *Power of Place*, 8-9.

also when ours remains "in harmony with theirs." Memory starts from "shared data or conceptions," which are present in our and their minds "because they are continually being passed back and forth. This process occurs only because all have been and still are members of the same group."[14]

The Nauvoo Temple

The Nauvoo temple was the centerpiece of the Saints' Zion-building efforts. Excavation began in the fall of 1840, followed by a series of dedications starting with the laying of the cornerstone on April 6, 1841, the dedication of the basement and baptismal font on November 8, 1841, and finally the public dedication of the temple proper four and a half years later on May 1-3, 1846, when most of the Saints were already on the Iowa prairies on their way to the Rocky Mountains.[15] Joseph never participated in any ordinances inside the temple except baptisms for the dead, which moved from the river to the font when it was finished and dedicated in November 1841. Brigham Young's resolve to continue Joseph's works–both plurality and temple worship–would be decisions of considerable significance in establishing continuity and binding thousands of Saints to him at a time when the Church was fragmenting in the aftermath of Joseph's death.

As earlier noted, the same revelation dated January 19, 1841, detailed instructions for both the temple and the Nauvoo House. Laced throughout with the argument of the gathering, the Saints were instructed to bring their wealth to the building up of Zion. "Come ye, with all your gold, and your silver, and your precious stones, and with all your antiquities; and with all who have knowledge of antiquities, that will come, may come, and bring the box-tree, and the fir-tree, and the pine-tree, together with all the precious trees of the earth," instructed the divine message, "… and build a house to my name for the Most High to dwell therein."

But the temple would be more than a church or a meetinghouse for Sunday services. It was intended to be the scene of rituals by which the Saints conferred salvation on themselves and on their dead ancestors. "For the baptismal font there is not upon the earth, that they, my Saints, may be baptised for those who are dead," the revelation continued; "For this

14. Maurice Halbwachs, *The Collective Memory*, 18, 31.

15. After Joseph's death, the construction on the temple took on new meaning. The capstone was laid on the southeast corner by Brigham Young, then acting president of the Church, on May 24, 1845 (*History of the Church*, 7:417-18). Young dedicated the altar on January 7, 1846, located in the southeast corner of the attic (ibid., 566). Before the Saints left Nauvoo, Young dedicated the temple as far as it was completed on February 8, 1846 (ibid., 580).

ordinance belongeth to my house, and cannot be acceptable to me, only in the days of your poverty, wherein ye are not able to build a house unto me." Then the voice of Jesus Christ shifted to the subject of ritual itself: "[Y]our anointings, and your washings, and your baptisms for the dead, and your solemn assemblies, and your memorials for your sacrifices, by the sons of Levi [the priesthood] and for your oracles in your most high places, wherein you receive conversations, and your statutes and judgments, for the beginning of the revelations and foundations of Zion ... are ordained by the ordinance of my holy house which my people are always commanded to build unto my holy name." In the temple, the heavens would open, the Lord through Joseph continued, for "I deign to reveal ... things which have been kept hid from before the foundation of the world, things that pertain to the dispensation of the fullness of times."[16]

Even more important than lists of materials with which the Saints would build the temple were the sacred rituals that they would perform inside: "I will show unto my servant Joseph all things pertaining unto this house, and the Priesthood thereof; and the place whereon it shall be built; And ye shall build it on the place where you have contemplated building it"–the temple had been underway for six months when the revelation was given–"for that is the spot which I have chosen for you to build it. If ye labor with all your might, I will consecrate that spot and make it holy."[17]

Over the course of the next four months, Joseph set in place the resources, leadership, and framework required to materialize this important building. The site for the temple was dramatic, on a bluff facing west so that it overlooked the city and the Mississippi River. Originally a farm owned by Daniel H. Wells, then a non-Mormon friendly to the Church, the land was annexed to Nauvoo as part of the Wells Addition, eighteen four-acre blocks and six two-acre blocks.[18] Joseph first announced the need for the temple at the Church's October conference in 1840. By the end of the meeting, the congregation had voted to form "a committee to build the same." Reynolds Cahoon, Elias Higbee, and Alpheus Cutler accepted the assignment, and the adult men present pledged to "tithe" their labor to work at the temple site.[19] Joseph charged the temple committee to oversee the entire operation,

16. *History of the Church*, 4:277 (Jan. 19, 1841).

17. Ibid.

18. George D. Smith, ed., *An Intimate Chronicle*, 527; David E. Miller and Della S. Miller, Nauvoo, 36, 38; Gustavus Hills, *Map of the City of Nauvoo*, 1842.

19. *History of the Church*, 4:205 (Oct. 3, 1840); see also Smith, *An Intimate Chronicle*, 526.

donations came in on the spot, and Higbee wrote out careful receipts.[20] Within the week, a stone quarry was opened west of Main Street between Hyrum and Joseph Streets. Albert P. Rockwood, with assistant Charles Drury, supervised crews that cut the limestone for the temple walls.[21] Joseph issued a notice soliciting architectural drawings for the temple and eventually selected William Weeks as architect.[22]

Even though Joseph began working with Weeks much earlier, the appointment did not become formal until 1843. He broadened Weeks's control "in consequence of misunderstanding on the part of the Temple committee, and their interference with the business of the architect, … no person, or persons shall interfere with him or his plans in the building of the Temple."[23] A carpenter-builder, Weeks was familiar with the Classical idioms that passed through frontier towns in popular architectural handbooks.[24] There is no one prototypical building that influenced the Nauvoo temple design–indeed Joseph attributed the design to revelation–but the temple motifs come from its American cultural milieu.

On January 8, 1841, Joseph distinguished the unique function of the temple in the hierarchy of Mormon worship in a First Presidency epistle: "The temple of the Lord is in process of erection here … and will be so constructed as to enable all the functions of the Priesthood, to be duly exercised, and where instructions from the Most High will be received and will go forth to distant lands."[25] As Peter Berger notes, "The performances of the ritual are closely linked to the reiteration of the sacred formulas that 'make present' once more the names and deeds of the gods."[26] The grand scope of Joseph's temple vision may have been breathtaking, but the building itself was a bootstrapped operation, funded by donated time, materials, and labor, unlike many public projects of similar size that were funded by borrowed money.

The legitimacy of the building's construction was anchored in religious belief. From that point and until the Saints left Nauvoo five years later, the temple became the city's religious centerpiece. Long before it was actually finished, it was physically visible from just about any point in town.

20. See Smith, *An Intimate Chronicle*, 526.

21. *History of the Church*, 4:229 (Oct. 19, 1840).

22. J. Earl Arrington, "William Weeks, Architect of the Nauvoo Temple," 13n97; see also Smith, *An Intimate Chronicle*, 526.

23. *History of the Church*, 5:353 (Apr. 12, 1843); also Smith, *An Intimate Chronicle*, 526.

24. Laruel B. Andrew, *The Early Temples of the Mormons*, 62.

25. "A Proclamation of the First Presidency of the Church to the Saints Scattered Abroad," *History of the Church*, 4:269 (Jan. 8, 1841).

26. Peter Berger, *The Sacred Canopy*, 40.

Emotionally, it dominated the energies of the city. Even before construction, the Saints gathered in its shadow in the nearby grove for preaching services. It would be also physically imposing, standing 165 feet high and measuring 88 by 128 feet. By the time it was finished, it had cost almost a million dollars, a huge sum for the time.

In its form, the Nauvoo temple corresponded to the revelation Joseph received about the Kirtland (Ohio) House of the Lord, or temple. But the "shape of content" that the temple enclosed, in the language of Lithuanian artist Ben Shahn, was the body of ideas contained and embodied within ritual.[27] Rectangular like congregational churches throughout the Northeast and like churches built in Great Britain during the same era, the shape itself was anything but original. The interior configuration, however, carved out sacred space distinct to Mormon ritual and practice. Both the Nauvoo temple and the Kirtland temple featured spacious meeting rooms on both the first and second floors. Connecting this level to the next and marking a hierarchy of spaces and sacred uses, staircases to the second level were built into the corners. Proportionally, the two temples were also similar. They differed in subtle ways–the Kirtland building sat directly on a foundation without a basement level or a baptismal font. Also, reflecting context as much as preference, the Kirtland temple was built of wood, while the Nauvoo temple was to be made of stone. Locating the forms of the temple in precedent is complicated by Joseph's claim to revelation. "The appearance of these buildings, however," comment architectural historians David S. Andrew and Laurel B. Blank, in describing early LDS temples, "makes it clear that they are the result of a complex evolution of architectural ideas and forms–a process which began at Kirtland and Nauvoo."[28]

What might be described as a nave in a more traditional basilica form was conceptualized in Nauvoo as the "Solomonic idea that regarded the temple as an enclosure for the Holy of Holies."[29] A place of assembly of the faithful, the room enveloped the contemplation of God and heaven and what was possible for human beings. Like the Kirtland temple, the eclectic design of the Nauvoo temple freely blended historic style elements. Growing out of a particular architectural and cultural milieu, it was nevertheless unique to the Latter-day Saints. Its low attic story replaced a more traditional pediment. The use of astronomical symbols to suggest theological

27. Ben Shann, *The Shape of Content* (Cambridge, Mass.: Harvard University Press, 1992).
28. David S. Andrew and Laurel B. Blank, "The Four Mormon Temples in Utah," 54.
29. Ibid., 53.

teachings reach their most unusual expression in the sunstones–where the "sun's face [is] encircled by stylized rays and surmounted by two disembodied heavenly hands clutching trumpets."[30]

The *History of the Church,* citing an entry dated February 5, 1844, suggests inspiration for the Nauvoo temple design was Joseph's. "In the afternoon, Elder William Weeks … came in to me for instruction," the *History* reads:

> I instructed him in relation to the circular windows designed to light the offices in the dead work of the arch between stories. He said that round windows in the broad side of a building were a violation of all the known rules of architecture, and contended that they should be semicircular–that the building was too low for round windows. I told him I would have the circles, if he had to make the Temple ten feet higher than it was originally calculated; that one light at the centre of each circular window would be sufficient to light the whole room, that when the whole building was thus illuminated, the effect would be remarkably grand. "I wish you to carry out my designs. I have seen the vision the splendid appearance of that building illuminated, and will have it built according to the pattern shown me."[31]

However, caution is advised since the alleged conversation took place two years after Weeks made his first drawings of the temple, complete with round windows.[32] Moreover, Joseph's journal entry dated February 5, 1844, does not mention any conversation about temple design.[33]

The design further developed, as demonstrated in Gustavus Hills's 1842 engraving of the Nauvoo plat, which included the first known sketch of the Nauvoo temple in its margin by Weeks. His drawing portrays a building with classical proportions, roof pitch, and detailing familiar to a Greek temple such as pilasters and a triangular pediment. Although the design continued to evolve, it expressed allegiance to nineteenth-century New England meetinghouse design. The central tower on the facade reflects the influence of the Georgian style.

Three months after construction had started, Joseph preached "the doctrine of baptism for the dead" in the temple grove on October 2, 1841.[34]

---

30. Ibid., 57.

31. *History of the Church*, 6:196-97 (Feb. 5, 1844).

32. Andrew and Blank suggest, "The most plausible assessment of each man's part in the building is to assign to Weeks those elements which are purely architectural, while crediting the determination of functional and symbolic requirements to the president himself" (62-63).

33. Faulring, *An American Prophet's Record*, Feb. 4, 1844, 445; a slip of paper with the anecdote is found between pages 7-8 of the Rough Draft, 1838-44, LDS Church History Library.

34. *History of the Church*, 4:424 (Oct. 2, 1841). The previous year, Joseph had instructed the

Although 1 Corinthians 15:29 ambiguously refers to baptism for the dead, and Joseph rhetorically connected baptism to the temple in 1839, by October 1841, Mormons had already performed dozens of proxy baptisms, usually in the Mississippi River, with enthusiasm. Empowered by his followers' esteem, Joseph's enunciation of baptism for the dead by the immersion of living proxies brought redemption to those who had never heard Joseph's word, extending his prophetic scope both forward and backward. He depicted baptism for the dead as a sort of threshold to a new power by which human beings could be "as saviours on Mount Zion." By revelation, however, he announced that "there shall be no more baptisms for the dead, until the ordinance can be attended to in the Lord's House; and the church shall not hold another General Conference until they can meet in said house. *For thus saith the Lord!*"[35]

Joseph dedicated the baptismal font after workers completed it a month later, on November 8. Reuben McBride was the first to be baptized in the font.[36] This new ritual was launched with forty baptisms for the dead on November 21 by Brigham Young, Heber C. Kimball, and John Taylor. Willard Richards, George A. Smith, and Wilford Woodruff performed the confirmations, laying their hands on the heads of the faithful and calling down the gift of the Holy Ghost.[37]

Managing the temple construction project was like running a small business. During the winter of 1841-42, Joseph created an organizational structure to systematize resources and labor. On February 10, 1842, he mobilized men he believed he could trust and asked William Clayton to assist Willard Richards in recording the transactions related to the project.[38] The work had "increased so rapidly he could not keep pace with the work."[39] The following September, revelatory instructions established the requirement of a witness and record keeper "that ... it may be recorded in heaven: that whosoever you bind on earth, may be bound in heaven" (D&C 127:7). For a headquarters, the temple workmen built a modest brick building near the construction site for the recorder and his assistants. Known as the temple store, it housed the records and the contributed goods that temple workers

Saints about the doctrine's consistency and "reasonableness; and [that] it presents the Gospel of Christ in probably a more enlarged scale than some have imagined it" (ibid., 231 [Oct. 19, 1840]).

35. Ibid., 426 (Oct. 2, 1841); emphasis in original.

36. Smith, *An Intimate Chronicle*, 532.

37. *History of the Church*, 4:454 (Nov. 21, 1841).

38. Journal History, Feb. 14, 1842; William Clayton, "History of the Nauvoo Temple," qtd. in Allen, *No Toil Nor Labor Fear*, 419.

39. Smith, *An Intimate Chronicle*, 531.

could claim as their wages. Richards and Clayton moved to the site on November 2, 1842, and worked out of the small office for the next two years.

Baptism was essential to the unfolding of the new dispensation and to ushering in the last days.[40] All men and women would be rendered perfect, cleansed by baptism either in person or by proxy, and organized into family units. For "the earth will be smitten with a curse unless there is a welding link of some kind or other between the fathers and the children." Joseph envisioned nothing less than an endless chain, that began with Adam and continued to the present, making a "whole and complete and perfect union" (D&C 128:18). Baptism for the dead pulled the living and the dead into a continuous current of humankind, forging a link between ancient and modern times. "In addition," comments Laurel Andrew, "baptism for the dead was, in Smith's eyes, more authentic than baptism practiced by the other churches and provided an opportunity to redo history, to eradicate past evil, and to prepare for the recreation of the American Eden, populated by Adam and his resurrected descendants, all of whom would, through baptism for the dead, be incorporated into the new society."[41]

Although eventually a series of sacred ordinances would be performed in temples, in Nauvoo, baptism for the dead was the only ordinance performed regularly before Joseph's death. The Twelve issued an epistle on October 12, 1841, that described baptism as a primary purpose for which the temple was built. It would be a place "where the Saints may enter the baptismal font for their dead relatives, so that they [the dead] may be judged according to men in the flesh, and live according to God in the spirit, and come forth in the celestial kingdom; a place over which the heavenly messengers may watch and trouble the waters as in days of old, so that when the sick are put therein, they shall be made whole: a place wherein all the ordinances may be made manifest."[42]

Through the winter of 1841-42, Joseph voiced the centrality of temple construction. Inspired to work by direct admonition as well as by the religious framework that Joseph reiterated in sermons and private conversations, as many as a hundred men worked at the quarry. The stones they cut would

---

40. "From the beginning, the Mormons had designated their temples as 'Houses of the Lord'–a common enough way of expressing the metaphoric function of churches, until one recalls that the Mormons were anticipating an imminent visit of Christ in the flesh," note Andrew and Blank. "He was to come again not only to ensure the salvation of the good, but also to reign, in the fullest sense of the word, and he would therefore need a house–a temple–from which to perform these services"(Andrew and Blank, "The Four Mormon Temples in Utah," 63).

41. Andrew, *The Early Temples of the Mormons*, 80.

42. *History of the Church*, 4:437 (Oct. 12, 1841).

be laid up in the temple walls during the summer, materializing a religious ideal and, more practically, driving toward the goal of an enclosed space by the fall.[43] Joseph gave the project steadfast attention. Rather than depending on an announcement to the more limited audience that might gather for his Sunday sermon during the bitter winter months, in February 1842, Joseph issued a general letter, scolding the workers for a lack of organization. On some days, too many men showed up; on other days, there were not enough. He asked that each ward organize volunteers, assigning them to particular days and instructing them to come with the appropriate tools.[44]

Rough stones were produced at the quarry, but the finishing work was done at the temple site itself.[45] Joseph Smith III remembered seeing rough-cut stones brought up the hill to the temple, "the ox teams dragging them along the roads between the quarries and the temple block."[46]

Much of the Nauvoo temple's distinctiveness is related to its stonework, largely because of the work of William W. Player, a master stone mason from England.[47] A convert to the Church, Player arrived in Nauvoo in early June 1842 and began work shortly afterwards. Despite frustrating setbacks over the summer months, sometimes working with less than cooperative teams of workers, he made progress in the rock work for the walls until the fall when weather forced the project to stop. During the winter months, Player "nearly lost the use of his hands and feet, and several times he fell, through weakness while on his way home," according to William Clayton. Player assumed his illness was related to contaminated water that he had drunk from the river or to the "change in climate."[48]

By October 11, 1842, construction workers were ready to position the first plinth or moonstone at the southeast corner.[49] Because the project gave the citizens of Nauvoo cause to rally, each advancement of the construction was met with celebration. Stonemason William Jones cut the moonstone,

---

43. "City of Nauvoo," *Times and Seasons* 3, no. 13 (May 1, 1842): 775. It optimistically predicted that the temple would be enclosed by fall or at least that the stones at the top would be laid.

44. *History of the Church*, 4:517 (Feb. 21, 1842).

45. "Saturday, Apr. 23, 1842," *The Wasp*, Apr. 23, 1842, 2.

46. Richard P. Howard, ed., *The Memoirs of President Joseph Smith III: 1832-1914*, 44 (Feb. 5, 1935), 178. Ephraim J. Pearson's teams hauled the stone to the temple site most of the time. He was replaced by Alma N. Shennan. When a second team was added, William H. Dame was the teamster, according to William Clayton, Journal, Journal History, Dec. 31, 1844.

47. Journal History, Oct. 11, 1842; Clayton, "History of the Nauvoo Temple," 11; Smith, *An Intimate Chronicle*, 532.

48. Smith, *An Intimate Chronicle*, 533.

49. Journal History, Oct. 11, 1842; Clayton, "History of the Nauvoo Temple," 19; also Smith, *An Intimate Chronicle*, 533.

a deeply carved bas-relief crescent moon, turned downward, complete with the profile of a man's face.[50]

For architectural historian Laurel Andrew, "The most intriguing aspect of the Nauvoo Temple was certainly the new order which it displayed–the first appearance of an architectural symbolism with a basis in Mormon theology."[51] Joseph did not interpret the symbolism of the images that spread across the temple walls like a text, but a revelation he received ten years earlier in February 1832 may hold clues to the relationship he saw between the temple and salvation. Joseph's theology divided the world's people into a tightly structured hierarchy. Righteous men and women could progress to greater authority through their good work. In the same way, those who had died could go on, through the work of earthly proxies, to earn rewards. Three graded levels of heavenly glory–celestial, terrestrial, and telestial–were symbolized by the sun, moon, and stars, as mentioned in 1 Corinthians 15:40. "The symbols on the new architectural order of the Nauvoo Temple thus indicated the purpose of the building–the gaining of one of the kingdoms of heaven," comments Andrew.[52]

The temple came to symbolize the rapidly developing separation between Mormonism and American Christianity and, in the context of sacred architecture, created a new typology. The Latter-day Saints practiced religion in ways distinctive to their body of scripture, revelatory tradition, and connection to community. Based in part on biblical tradition aligned with the Book of Mormon, Mormonism was nevertheless a radical interpretation of scripture, a different understanding of the role of Jesus Christ, and a body of ritual that revealed a new understanding of the potential of human beings to become Gods themselves and their relationship to their dead ancestors. For the Saints, the temple was a miraculous setting. Samuel Rolfe injured his hand while building the baptismal font for the temple. Joseph told him to dip his hand in its water and he would be healed. He did and, according to William Clayton, a week later Rolfe was healed, evidence that baptisms in the font would hold "great blessings, both spiritually and bodily."[53]

Although temple finances were not a public matter, they created considerable controversy just below the surface of the construction project. On October 1, 1842, Clayton noted: "Some reports had been circulated that the

50. William Clayton, Journal, qtd. in Journal History, Dec. 31, 1844.
51. Andrew, *The Early Temples of the Mormons*, 82.
52. Ibid., 83.
53. William Clayton, "History of the Nauvoo Temple," 21.

committee was not making a righteous disposition of property consecrated for the building of the Temple, and there appeared to be some dissatisfaction amongst the laborers." Joseph, with Bishop Newel K. Whitney, the temple recorders, and members of the temple committee, reviewed disputes from workers. Joseph went over the accounts, announced his satisfaction with the finances, and declared that the committee members were accountable to no one but himself.[54] Joseph established the daily wage at $2.00 and instructed Clayton to summarize the meeting for the *Times and Seasons.*[55]

However, not quite two months later, on November 28, problems erupted again and Joseph intervened. Furious about the way resources had been distributed, temple stone cutters accused Cahoon and Higbee of making "unequal distribution of provisions, giving more iron and steel tools to Reynolds Cahoon's sons than to others, giving short measure of wood to father [William] Huntington, also letting the first course of stone around the Temple to the man who would do it for the least price," among other issues. Despite the projects' sacred nature, uncertainty and irregularity in salaries and payment schedules turned laborers against leaders and threatened to stall the work. The stone cutters accused them of "oppressive and unchristian conduct," words that suggest the complicated mix of work and religion.[56] Trying to calm the situation, Joseph invited the men to meet with him to discuss the complaints in a mock trial with Hyrum, who represented the committee as defendants, and Henry G. Sherwood who acted as counsel for the stone cutters. Giving time to resolve the most pressing issue, the hearing ran from 11:00 a.m. until about 9:00 p.m. Hyrum, according to Joseph's account, spoke of "the important responsibility of the committee, also the many difficulties they have to contend with," he encouraged them to exercise "charity one with another, and be united." At the end, Joseph gave his "decision, which was that the committee stand in their place as before. … [They] were responsible to me."[57]

Joseph was realistic about the sacrifice required to construct the temple. He frequently acknowledged the burden as he preached. Such meetings as those with the temple workers were complicated. In some ways, he was the client, the boss, and the judge of the matter. In each role, he had different agendas, rendering an impartial judgment impossible. "[G]reat exertions will be required on the part of the Saints, so that they may build a house

54. *History of the Church*, 5:166 (Oct. 1, 1842).
55. Clayton, "History of the Nauvoo Temple," 19; Smith, *An Intimate Chronicle*, 537.
56. Smith, *An Intimate Chronicle*, 537.
57. *History of the Church*, 5:196-97 (Nov. 28, 1842).

which shall be accepted by the Almighty, and in which His power and glory shall be manifested," he wrote in a January 1841 proclamation. "Therefore let those who can freely make a sacrifice of their time, their talents, and their property, for the prosperity of the kingdom, and for the love they have to the cause of truth, bid adieu to their homes and pleasant places of abode, and unite with us in the great work of the last days, and share in the tribulation, that they may ultimately share in the glory and triumph."[58]

Although it was modest progress, after the summer of 1842 and by the early fall, the temple walls reached the window sills and fenestration patterns began to emerge. Cognizant of the sacred nature of their efforts, workers carefully leveled and positioned window sills. Before winter, two courses of stone lined the plinths.[59] Two of Reynold Cahoon's sons, Daniel and Andrew, cut the remaining plinths. The men used a single crane to move the heavy stones into place.[60] It was the promise of a temple anchored firmly in the earth but stretching toward heaven.

On October 23, 1842, the temple committee placed a temporary floor over the basement level to provide a more sheltered meeting space than the grove.[61] Five days later, the "seats were fixed for meetings."[62] With Joseph ill, John Taylor became the first Church leader to preach in the unfinished temple. The meeting site added a new stimulus to the Saints, and "every heart seem to be filled with joy for this privilege."[63] For Joseph, the temple was the reason new converts should come to Zion, the vehicle for returning to God, and the scene of the most important rituals yet performed by the Church.[64]

The Temple and Masonry

As noted in chapter 13, Joseph embraced Masonry's symbolism and ideology, and relished the attendant fellowship. Such images were already part of the cultural milieu in which Mormonism emerged, but Joseph soon wove them into his language. William Weeks's drawing of the temple on the

58. "Proclamation of the First Presidency of the Church to the Saints Scattered Abroad," in *History of the Church*, 4:273 (Jan. 8, 1841).

59. Journal History, Oct. 11, 1842; Clayton, "History of the Nauvoo Temple," 23; Smith, *An Intimate Chronicle*, 533.

60. Clayton, "History of the Nauvoo Temple," 22.

61. Dean C. Jessee, ed., *The Papers of Joseph Smith*, 2:488; *History of the Church*, 4:180 (Oct. 23, 1842).

62. Smith, *An Intimate Chronicle*, 536.

63. *History of the Church*, 4:180 (Oct. 23, 1842); Allen, *No Toil Nor Labor Fear*, 423; Jessee, *The Papers of Joseph Smith*, 2:490. See also Clayton, "History of the Nauvoo Temple," 32.

64. See *History of the Church*, 4:269 (Jan. 8, 1841).

Gustavus Hills map reflects symbols familiar to men who had been initiated to the Masonic order, located in readily available Masonic handbooks, and found decorating Masonic halls throughout the Midwest or on the East Coast. The most familiar would have been the Bible, the compass, and the square–the "three great lights" of Freemasonry.[65] Joseph used the Masonic elements that applied to Mormonism and its theology.

In the temple, the Saints believed they could become gods and belong to a religious hierarchy that had cosmic meaning and powerfully shaped their identity. "Temple ritual, as a consequence of all these new doctrines, took on an overwhelming importance in the Mormon theological system," observes Laurel Andrew. "It was no longer sufficient to live according to the precepts of the Bible alone, but the rewards which were to come with the fulfillment of very specific and carefully defined rites were staggering. It is no wonder, then, that the temple, the only place where these ceremonies could take place properly, played such a significant part in Mormon life."[66] The Saints' Nauvoo temple was a religiously sacred structure, a scene of sacred ritual, and a sacred threshold between heaven and earth.

The temple was a novelty for outsiders, but it was also an innovation for those inside the faith. Despite its familiar architectural forms and idioms, its meaning for Mormons was profoundly different from any building that had proceeded it and from any fraternal organization that influenced it. Placed in the course of western architecture that began with the Christian basilica and traveled to this fledgling town in the American Midwest, the building was legible as a church but exhibited additional meanings as the restoration of ancient religion, as a complex vision of the afterlife, and as a mechanism for uniting the living and the dead.

The culmination of Nauvoo's elaborate theology, the temple separated Joseph from his contemporaries, anchored the endowment and other rituals in a sacred place, and provided the Saints with a moment when the heavens appeared open to them. Claiming the rise overlooking the vista of the town, the Nauvoo temple expressed religious authority, branded Latter-day Saint identity, and alerted visitors and insiders alike to the claim to revelation from God. The temple announced Joseph's presence and demanded that the world take notice.

65. Andrew, *Early Temples of the Mormons*, 85.
66. Ibid., 92.

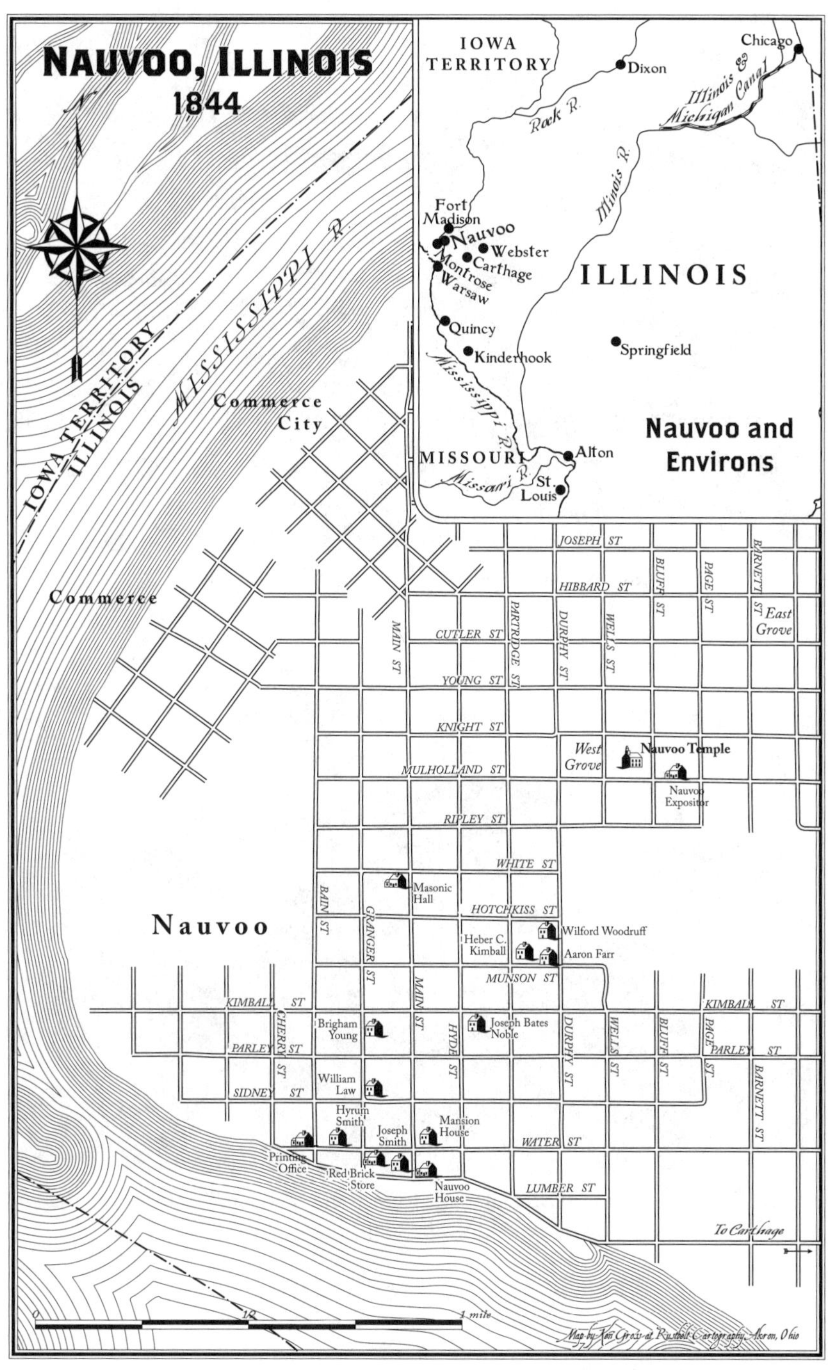

Joseph Smith's Nauvoo, 1844. (Map by Ken Gross, Rustbelt Cartography, Akron, Ohio; appreciation to Joseph Johnstun.)

Joseph Smith Homestead, from the front, ca. 1886.

The Mansion House, ca. 1904. Joseph, Emma, and their family moved into this structure in mid-1843. A wing to the south served as a hotel.

The red brick store. Scene of Joseph's entrepreneurial commercial activity, the store's upper story hosted meetings of both the all-female Relief Society and the Anointed Quorum.

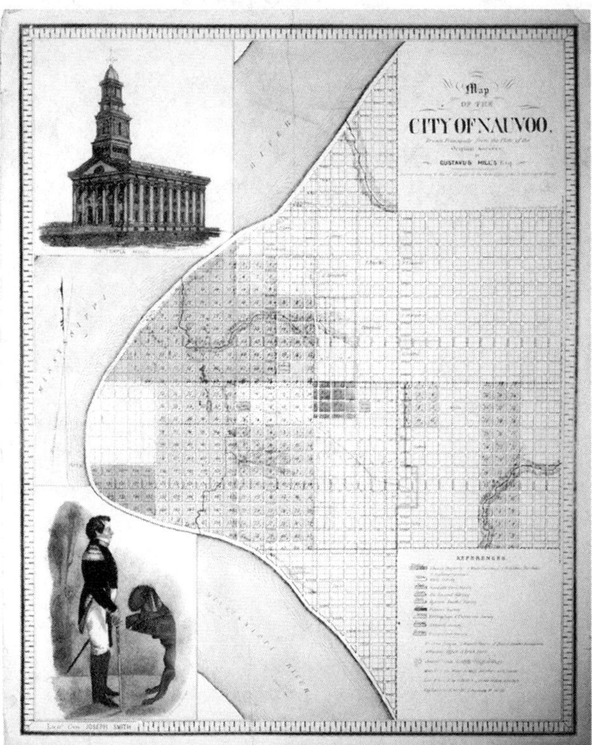

"Map of the City of Nauvoo," 1844; street map by Gustavus Hills, portrait of Joseph Smith by Sutcliffe Maudsley; rendering of Nauvoo temple by William Weeks.

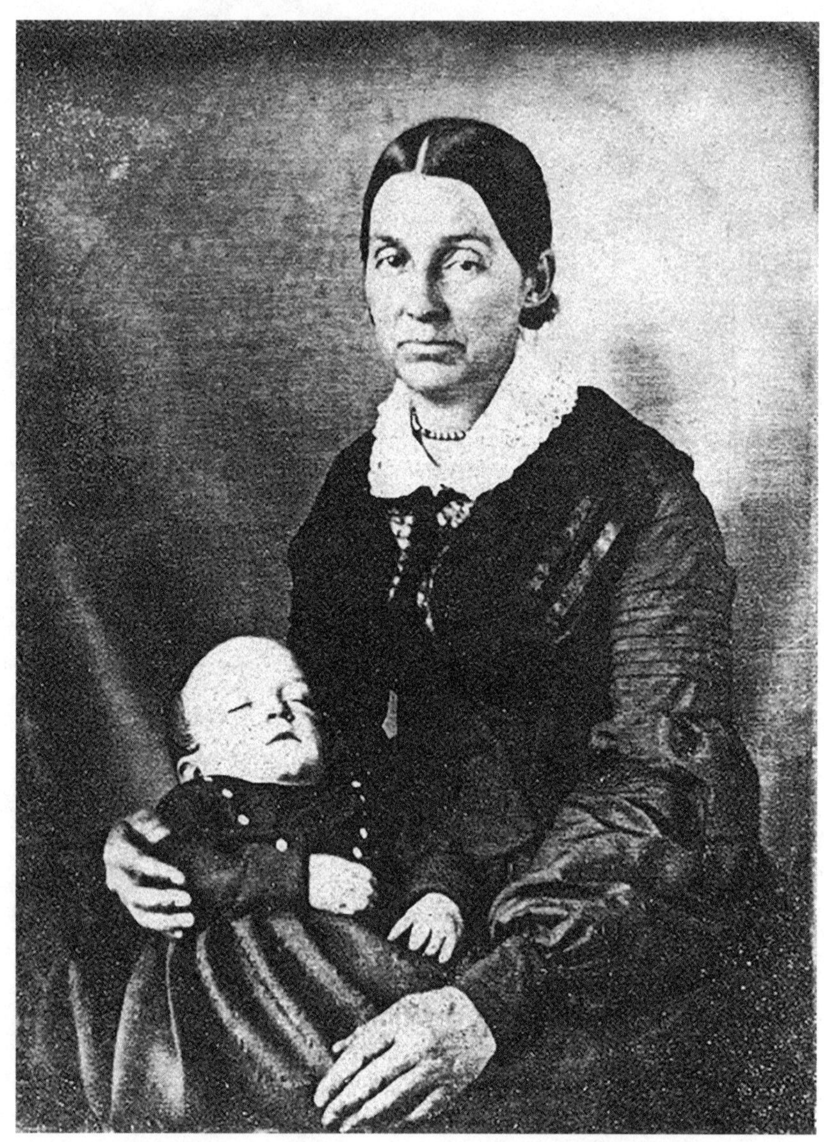

Emma Smith, with newborn David Hyrum Smith, ca. 1845-46.

Joseph's older brother, Hyrum, holding a copy of the Doctrine and Covenants, by Sutcliffe Maudsley, ca. 1845.

Brigham Young, ca. 1846.

Heber C. Kimball, ca. 1850s.

Wilford Woodruff, ca. 1850s.

Orson Pratt, ca. 1850s.

Sarah M. Pratt, 1867.

Orson Hyde, ca. 1850s.

Marinda Nancy Hyde, ca. 1850s.

Willard Richards family, ca. 1844; left to right: Heber John, Willard, and Jennetta.

Sidney Rigdon.

Joseph Bates Noble.

William Clayton.

Zina Diantha Huntington Jacobs Smith Young, ca. 1856.

Presendia Huntington Buell Smith Kimball, ca. 1860s.

Emily Dow Partridge Smith Young, ca. 1851.

Eliza Maria Partridge Lyman, with Don Carlos Lyman and, on lap, Caroline Maria Lyman, ca. 1852.

Helen Mar Kimball Smith Whitney.

Patty Bartlett Sessions
Smith Parry, ca. 1880s.

Eliza R. Snow Smith Young.

Elizabeth Ann Whitney, ca. 1870.

John C. Bennett, 1842, from his memoir, *The History of the Saints; or, an Exposé.*

Stephen A. Douglas, Illinois politician (Secretary of State, 1840-41; U.S. representative, 1843-47; U.S. senator, 1847-61).

Thomas Ford, Illinois governor, 1842-46.

"Joseph Smith Mustering the Nauvoo Legion," by C. C. A. Christensen, ca. 1870s.

"Joseph and His Friends," 1843-44, by William W. Major; left to right: Hyrum Smith, Willard Richards, Joseph Smith (standing), Orson Pratt, Parley P. Pratt, Heber C. Kimball, and Brigham Young.

Nauvoo temple architectural drawing, by William Weeks.

Nauvoo temple, ca. late 1840s.

"Joseph the Prophet Addressing the Lamanites," ca. 1844.

Masonic apron, ca. 1840s; note the square, compass, and all-seeing eye.

TIMES AND SEASONS.

"Truth will prevail."

Vol. III. No. 9.] CITY OF NAUVOO, ILL. MARCH, 1, 1842. [Whole No. 45.

A FAC-SIMILE FROM THE BOOK OF ABRAHAM.
NO. 1.

EXPLANATION OF THE ABOVE CUT.

FIG. 1,—The Angel of the Lord.
2. Abraham, fastened upon an Altar.
3. The Idolatrous Priest of Elkenah attempting to offer up Abraham as a sacrifice.
4. The Altar for sacrifice, by the Idolatrous Priests, standing before the Gods of Elkenah, Libnah, Mahmachrah, Korash, and Pharaoh.
5. The Idolatrous God of Elkenah.
6. The " " " Libnah.
7. The " " " Mahmachrah.
8. The " " " Korash.
9. The " " " Pharaoh.
10. Abraham in Egypt.
11. Designed to represent the pillars of Heaven, as understood by the Egyptians.
12. Raukeeyang, signifying expanse, or the firmament, over our heads; but in this case, in relation to this subject, the Egyptians meant it to signify Shamau, to be high, or the heavens: answering to the Hebrew word, Shaumahyeem.

"The Book of Abraham," as first published in the *Times and Seasons,* 1842.

One of the Kinderhook plates, later shown to have been a forgery.

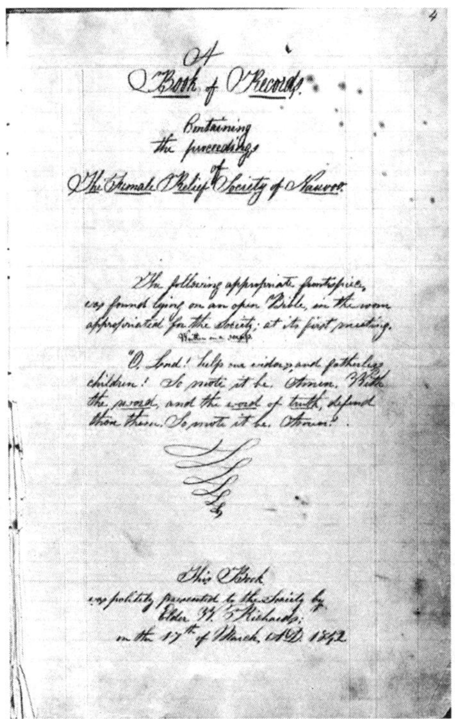

4

A Book of Records.
Containing the proceedings of
The Female Relief Society of Nauvoo.

The following appropriate frontispiece, was found lying on an open Bible, in the room appropriated for the Society; at its first meeting.
[illegible]

"O, Lord! help our widows, and fatherless children! So mote it be. Amen. With the sword, and the word of truth, defend thou them. So mote it be. Amen."

This Book
was politely presented to the Society by
Elder W. Richards;
on the 17th of March, A.D. 1842

Title page from the record book of the Female Relief Society of Nauvoo.

Joseph Smith's last conference address, April 6, 1844.

PROSPECTUS

OF THE

NAUVOO EXPOSITOR.

The "NAUVOO EXPOSITOR" will be issued on Friday of each week, on an Imperial sheet, with a new Press and materials of the best quality, and rendered worthy of the patronage of a discerning and an enlightened public.

The Expositor will be devoted to a general diffusion of useful knowledge, and its columns open for the admission of all courteous Communications of a Religious, Moral, Social, Literary, or Political character, without taking a decided stand in favor of either of the great Political Parties of the country. A few of its columns will be devoted to a few primary objects, which the Publishers deem of vital importance to the public welfare. Their particular locality gives them a knowledge of the many **Gross abuses exercised under the "pretended" authorities of the Charter of the City of Nauvoo,** by the Legislative authorities of said city; and the *Insupportable OPPRESSIONS of the MINISTERIAL powers, in carrying out the* Unjust, Illegal, *and* Unconstitutional *Ordinances of the same.* The Publishers, therefore, deem it a sacred duty they owe to their country and their fellow citizens, to advocate, through the columns of the EXPOSITOR, the **Unconditional REPEAL of the NAUVOO CITY CHARTER**—to restrain and correct the abuses of the UNIT POWER—to ward off the Iron Rod which is held over the devoted heads of the citizens of Nauvoo and the surrounding country—to advocate unmitigated *DISOBEDIENCE to POLITICAL REVELATIONS*, and to censure and decry gross moral imperfections wherever found, either in the Plebian, Patrician, or SELF-CONSTITUTED MONARCH—to advocate the pure principles of morality, the pure principles of truth, designed not to destroy, but strengthen the main-spring of God's moral government—to advocate, and exercise; the freedom of speech in Nauvoo, independent of the ordinances abridging the same—to give *free toleration to every man's Religious sentiments*, and sustain ALL in worshiping their God according to the monitions of their consciences, as guarantied by the Constitution of our country, and to oppose, with uncompromising hostility, any ☞Union of CHURCH and STATE☜ or any preliminary step tending to the same—to *sustain ALL, however humble*, in their equal and Constitutional RIGHTS—and oppose the sacrifice of the Liberty, the Property, and the Happiness of the *MANY*, to the *Pride* and *Ambition* of the *FEW*. In a word, to give a full, candid, and succinct statement of FACTS, AS THEY REALLY EXIST IN THE CITY OF NAUVOO—*Fearless of whose particular case the facts may apply*—being governed by the laws of Editorial courtesy and the inherent dignity which is inseparable from honorable minds, at the same time exercising their own judgment in cases of flagrant abuses, or moral delinquencies—to use such terms and names as they deem proper, when the object is of such high importance that the end will justify the means. In this great and indispensable work, we confidently look to an enlightened public to aid us in our laudable effort.

The columns of the Expositor will be open to the discussion of all matters of public interest, the productions of all correspondents subject to the decision of the Editor alone, who shall receive or reject at his option. National questions will be in place—but no preference given to either of the political parties. The Editorial department will contain the political news of the day, proceedings of Congress, election returns, &c., &c. Room will be given for articles on Agriculture, the Mechanic Arts, Commercial transactions, &c.

The first number of the Expositor will be issued on Friday, the 7th day of June 1844. The publishers bind themselves to issue the paper weekly for one year, and forward 52 copies to each subscriber during the year. Orders should be forwarded as soon as possible, that the publishers may know what number of copies to issue.

The publishers take pleasure in announcing to the public, that they have engaged the services of SYLVESTER EMMANS, Esq., who will have entire charge and supervision of the Editorial department. From an acquaintance with the dignity of character, and literary qualifications of this gentleman, they feel assured that the "Nauvoo Expositor" must and will sustain a high and honorable reputation.

TERMS of the "NAUVOO EXPOSITOR."

The TERMS of the paper will be
$2,00 per annum, in advance.
$2,50 at the expiration of six months.
$3,00 at the end of the year.

Six copies will be forwarded to one address for $10,00 in advance—Thirteen copies for $20,00, &c., &c.

☞All Letters and Communications must be addressed to "CHARLES A. FOSTER, Nauvoo, Ill.," *post paid*, in order to insure attention.☜

WILLIAM LAW,
WILSON LAW,
CHARLES IVINS,
FRANCIS M. HIGBEE,
CHAUNCEY L. HIGBEE,
ROBERT D. FOSTER,
CHARLES A. FOSTER.
} PUBLISHERS.

Nauvoo, Ill, May 10th, 1844.

SUBSCRIBER'S NAMES.	POST OFFICE.	NUMBER OF COPIES.

The "Prospectus" for the *Nauvoo Expositor*.

The office of the *Nauvoo Expositor*.

SUPER HANC PETRAM ÆDIFICABO.

FOR PRESIDENT,

GEN. JOSEPH SMITH,

OF NAUVOO, ILLINOIS.

FOR VICE PRESIDENT,

SIDNEY RIGDON,

OF PENNSYLVANIA.

Broadside announcing Joseph Smith's candidacy for the U.S. presidency, 1844.

"Last Public Address of Lieut.-Gen. Joseph Smith," by John Hafen, ca. 1888.

Carthage Jail, scene of the violent deaths of Joseph and Hyrum Smith, June 27, 1844.

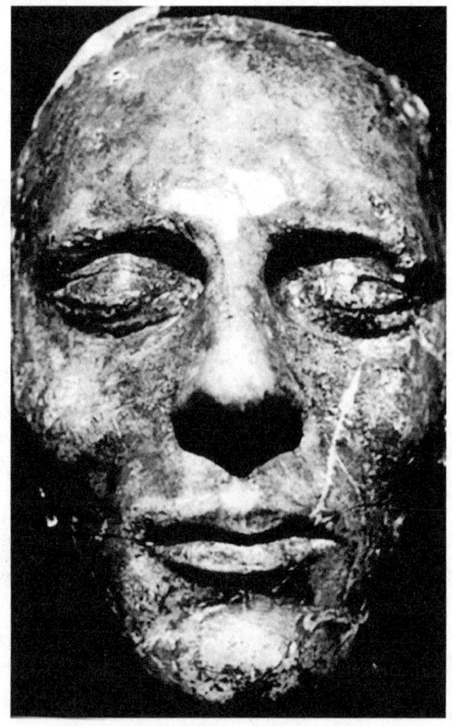

The death mask of Joseph Smith.

CHAPTER 15

God's Kingdom

The kingdoms of this world are become the kingdoms of our Lord, and of His Christ. … And the Saints of the Most High shall possess the greatness of the Kingdom under the whole heaven.
–Joseph Smith, "Government and Institutions of Nauvoo," Millennial Star *3 (Aug. 1842): 69*

Joseph's role as prophet functioned as a magnet, holding in place multiple roles that threatened to fragment his identity. During the spring of 1842, he became mayor, chief magistrate, then, on May 19, register of deeds.[1] These political roles were layered against a demanding theology, economic, and social life. Engaged in producing the Book of Abraham, Joseph was distracted by land deals, family tensions, escalating conflict with John C. Bennett, and demands for payment from land speculators Isaac Galland and Horace Hotchkiss. He also oversaw the construction of both the temple and the Nauvoo Mansion, despite delegating both resource-draining projects to committees.

Still, Joseph remained proud of his city. By April 1842, the *Times and Seasons* reported, Nauvoo's 7,000 inhabitants were "fast increasing." Indeed, "the city of Nauvoo will be the largest and most beautiful city of the west, provided the Mormons are un-molested in the peaceable enjoyment of their rights and privileges." Apart from the optimistic comparison, the town showed progress. Two years later, the number of citizens had more than tripled.[2]

Joseph's stamp is evident–not always consistently–in virtually every aspect of the city's growth. Although as mayor he controlled liquor licensing and distribution, Joseph would briefly open a bar in the Mansion House. He

1. *History of the Church*, 5:12 (May 19, 1842).
2. "Nauvoo and the Mormons," *Times and Seasons* 3, no. 11 (Apr. 1, 1842): 750.

managed the sale of liquor sternly, yet seemed unwilling to cooperate with temperance crusaders: "It was reported to me," his journal recorded, "that some of the brethren had been drinking whisky that day in violation of the Word of Wisdom [the Church's dietary code]. I called the brethren in and investigated the case, and was satisfied that no evil had been done, and gave them a couple of dollars with directions to replenish the bottle to stimulate them in the fatigues of their sleepless journey."[3]

Joseph's complicated real estate transactions and debt-juggling did not provide a secure cash flow. Applying a convoluted logic, he decided to repudiate some debts to non-members and had the faithful forgive him of still others. The next step was bankruptcy which, under a law passed by Congress in August 1841, effective February 1, 1842, promised to wipe out debt all together. Even before the bill was passed, Joseph hired attorney Calvin Warren to begin "an investigation of the principles of general insolvency in my behalf according to the statutes."[4] He justified his avoidance of paying his debts by citing a litany of good deals he had made for others, coupled with his standard narrative of persecution.

> … I was forced into the measure by having been robbed, mobbed, plundered, and wasted of all my property, time after time, in various places, by the very ones who made the law [i.e., bankruptcy], namely the people of the United States, thereby having been obliged to contract heavy debts to prevent the utter destruction of myself, family and friends, and by those who were justly and legally owing me, taking advantage of the same act of bankruptcy, so that I could not collect my just dues, thus leaving me no alternative but to become subject again to stripping, wasting, and destitution, by vexatious writs, and law suits, and imprisonments, or take that course to extricate myself, which the law has pointed out.[5]

Bankruptcy offered a fresh start, after which "the individual was at liberty to start anew in the world …"[6]

On April 18, 1842, Joseph and Hyrum filed petitions for bankruptcy with the U.S. District Court for Illinois.[7] Several other Church leaders followed suit: Sidney Rigdon, Vinson Knight, Elias Higbee, Reynolds Cahoon,

3. "History of Joseph Smith," *Millennial Star* 21, no. 18 (Apr. 30, 1859): 283. The last phrase, starting with "and gave them …" was deleted when the passage appeared in *History of the Church*, 5:450 (June 27, 1843).

4. *History of the Church*, 4:594 (Apr. 14, 1842).

5. Ibid.

6. Ibid.

7. Ibid., 600 (Apr. 18, 1842).

Henry Sherwood, John Green, Arthur Morrison, George Morey, Jared Carter, Amos Davis, Charles Warner, William Lyon, William Niswanger, and John Fullmer.[8] Joseph's petition was denied, in part because a trustee-in-trust was not eligible for bankruptcy and in part because the U.S. government insisted on payment for the *Nauvoo,* a steamboat that Joseph had purchased from the government with four partners in 1840 and which had run around after only a couple of months.[9]

Joseph notified Hotchkiss on May 13, a month after filing for bankruptcy, assuming that, if his petition were granted, it would relieve the Hotchkiss debt. He again appealed to the scenario of persecution, specifically the story of Missouri.[10] Joseph felt that he and the Saints had been taken advantage of because of their inexperience and desperation. He described the Saints' delays in paying as honorable, based in the hope "that something would turn in our favor," and reassured Hotchkiss that the Mormons still intended to pay, even though, paradoxically, a successful petition would wipe out the debt:

> ... there is property in the inventory sufficient to pay every debt, and some to spare, according to the testimony of our solicitors, and the good judgment of others; and if the court will allow us someone for assignee, who will do justice to the cause, we confidently believe that yourself and all others will get their compensation in full ... I have no doubt you will ... have your pay in full, in the way I have before proposed, or some other equally advantageous, but money is out of sight, it might as well be out of mind, for it cannot be had. .... I will seek the earliest moment to acquaint you with anything new in this matter.[11]

Joseph included the Hotchkiss purchase in his list of assets.

The U.S. Attorney for Illinois, Justin Butterfield, objected to the bankruptcy application, in part, because of an outstanding judgment against Joseph. Moreover, according to biographer Donna Hill, Butterfield said that Joseph "had made improper transfers of property and had concealed assets in order to benefit from the bankruptcy act."[12]

8. *The Wasp,* June 7, 14, and 18, 1842: see also *History of the Church,* 4:600 (Apr. 18, 1842).

9. *The Public Statutes at Large of the United States of America, 1789-1845* (Boston, 1848); Joseph I. Bentley, "In the Wake of the Steamboat *Nauvoo.*" This debt was still being adjudicated after Joseph's assassination.

10. *History of the Church,* 4:600 (Apr. 18, 1842).

11. Ibid., 5:6-7 (May 13, 1842).

12. Donna Hill, *Joseph Smith,* 318.

Then summer erupted, bringing crises that pushed these financial problems into the background. In his memoirs, Illinois Governor Thomas Ford summed them up: "in some respects the Mormons were rogues who had taken refuge in Nauvoo as a convenient place for the headquarters of their villany; and others were good, honest, industrious people, who were the sincere victims of an artful delusion."[13] Nauvoo's neighbor to the south, Warsaw, vied with the Mormon town to capitalize on the Mississippi River trade. Thomas Sharp, editor of the *Warsaw Signal,* picked at the Mormons, criticizing their every move. Others like Galland or Hotchkiss saw the Mormons as partners, gambling that they would prosper. "Of course I feel an interest in the prosperity of Nauvoo," Hotchkiss told Joseph, "the more so, certainly, as their pecuniary interest is identified with my own."[14]

Although in 1841 only about 800 people lived in Warsaw, the town that most strenuously opposed the Mormons, one author described it as "among the best locations on the Mississippi."[15] Capitalizing on the prime location, streets spread outward from the river after 1834 to feature businesses that maximized the easy transport of goods. Founded in 1834 as a shipping and commerce center, it was the perfect contrast to Nauvoo. Pluralistic in contrast to the monoculture developing under the Saints, secular in contrast to Mormon theocracy, it was peopled by staunchly Jacksonian Americans, republican citizens steeped in individualism. The residents of Warsaw objected passionately to Joseph's dominance over Nauvoo's voting practices, political philosophy, and social behavior. Some of Joseph's critics thought that the civil rights of outsiders were at risk, but more important was the growing power of the un-American Mormon world which seemed to threaten other Midwest communities. The rumors that drove apostates out of fellowship in Nauvoo filtered through surrounding towns and planted seeds of persecution.

When the Saints arrived in Illinois, like many new western states, it was deeply in debt after years of depression, land speculation, and the massive costs of internal improvements.[16] In the recent past, the Whigs had prevailed in Hancock County. The Church was welcomed in part because of its political power, but the promise of votes was also a risky one. Governor Ford,

---

13. Thomas Ford, *History of Illinois . . .*, 2:215.
14. Horace Hotchkiss, qtd. in *History of the Church*, 6:55 (Sept. 27, 1843).
15. "Our Town and Country," *Westernworld* (Warsaw, Illinois), May 13, 1840, 1.
16. Robert B. Flanders, *Nauvoo*, 19.

reporting to the legislature five months after the Smith brothers' murders in Carthage, analyzed Joseph's bargaining with the Mormon vote:

> The great cause of popular fury was, that the Mormons … cast their vote as a unit; thereby making the fact apparent that no one could aspire to office … without their approbation and votes. It appears to be one of the principles by which they insist on being governed as a community to act as a unit in all matters of government and religion. They express themselves to be fearful that if division should be encouraged in politics, it would soon extend to their religion, and rend their church with schism, and into sects.[17]

Stephen Douglas had visited Nauvoo in the spring of 1841 when he was justice of the Supreme Court of Illinois and judge of the Fifth Judicial Court. Impressed, Douglas praised their industriousness.[18] Joseph responded in kind. More than any other politician, Douglas actively courted Joseph's favor. Ambitious for national office, cognizant of the Church's potential bloc voting, he visited Nauvoo repeatedly and used his influence to support Joseph when he could. In 1842 and looking toward the Congressional election in 1843, Douglas was gracious, accommodating, and earnest in his pursuit of the Mormon vote.

Mormon historian Glen M. Leonard describes Illinois as a "proving ground for national issues."[19] Historically, Mormons had voted for Democrats in both Ohio and Missouri, but in Illinois it seemed that Whigs offered more likely protection for the Church. Mormons voted Whig in both 1840 and 1841, although "the two parties claimed nearly equal support in Hancock and Adams Counties."[20] Ironically, Whigs campaigned for the repeal of the Nauvoo Charter in 1842, among other anti-Mormon ploys.[21] But the Saints often switched votes, perhaps confused by the double dealing techniques of both parties. Understandably, Joseph's clearest objective was the Church's security. Missouri's extradition efforts pulled Joseph into trading political power for votes; in 1841, the Church voted for Whig candidate John T. Stuart in appreciation for helping Joseph to thwart an extradition

17. Thomas Ford, "Message of the Governor of Illinois in Relation to the Disturbances in Hancock County, December 21, 1844," 7.

18. Stephen A. Douglas, qtd. in *History of the Church*, 4:357 (May 6, 1841).

19. Glen M. Leonard, *Nauvoo*, 289.

20. Ibid., 291.

21. Ibid., 296.

order from Missouri. Stephen Douglas, the judge in the case, was himself anxious to gain the Mormon vote.

Nationally, Whigs and Democrats faced off about power and where it should be located. Both parties rallied around national politicians. The Whig Party sought to counterbalance Andrew Jackson and the Democrats who favored Congress over the executive branch. Well-known Whigs like Daniel Webster, William Henry Harrison, and Henry Clay campaigned for the growth of federal power in the 1840s. Before the Republican Party was formed, Abraham Lincoln was also a Whig Party leader in Illinois. Divided over whether to expand slavery into the territories, other key issues included internal improvements, state rights, and banking.[22] The Whig Party disappeared after a resounding defeat in the presidential election of 1852. Although Whigs did not publish a formal platform, Democrats did in the 1840 election. It reads, in part, "Resolved. That the federal government is one of limited powers, derived solely from the constitution, and the grants of power shown therein, ought to be strictly *construed* (interpreted) by all the departments and agents of the government, and that it is *inexpedient* (not advantageous) and dangerous to exercise doubtful constitutional powers."[23] Besides Douglas, the Democratic gubernatorial candidate, Ford, who originally opposed the Nauvoo charter, courted the Mormon electorate and won.[24]

Whigs and Democrats in Warsaw had organized an Anti-Mormon Party in the summer of 1841. According to Thomas Gregg, the convention decided to elect candidates from both parties, and was "the first organized attempt to oppose the encroachments of Mormonism."[25] Gregg described this party's rise as responding solely to Mormon politics: "The old citizens of the county, becoming alarmed at the increasing power and tyranny of Smith, began to enquire as to the best mode of counteracting them. … It was decided to nominate candidates to office equally from both parties, to be run as Anti-Mormon candidates, and who were pledged to use their influence against the political corruption which had become so prevalent." The convention resolved, "[W]e are guided only by a desire to defend ourselves

22. John M. Blum, Edmund S. Morgan, Willie Lee Rose, Arthur M. Schlesinger Jr., Kenneth M. Stampp, and C. Vann Woodward, *The National Experience*, 230, 243.

23. "Democratic Platform of 1840," http://edsitement.neh.gov/view_lesson_plan.asp?id=554. (Nov. 20, 2007).

24. Annette Hampshire, "Nauvoo Politics," 3:1000.

25. Thomas Gregg, "A Descriptive, Statistical, and Historical Chart of the County of Hancock," in John E. Hallwas and Roger D. Launius, eds., *Cultures in Conflict*, 82.

against a despotism, the extent and consequences of which we have no means of ascertaining."[26] George Gayler claims that Hancock County politics were as much divided along Mormon and Anti-Mormon lines as political affiliation in 1841 and 1842.[27]

Joseph responded to the growing anti-Mormon sentiment by digging in his heels. When the Democrats decided to propose Adam W. Snyder and John Moore as candidates for Illinois governor and lieutenant-governor, respectively (both men had actively supported the Nauvoo charter through the legislature), Joseph decided to swing the vote to Synder and, in the process, to the Democrats. He did so with a proclamation on December 20, 1841, that was shocking to the Whigs who had planned on his support.[28]

Joseph's proclamation was addressed as an open letter to "my friends in Illinois" and was titled, "The Prophet on the Attitude of the Saints in Politics." After noting that Snyder and Moore were "sterling men, and friends of equal rights" and had greatly assisted in securing the Nauvoo Charter, Joseph boasted that he could throw the Mormon vote in one direction or another: "We are aware that 'divide and conquer' is the watchword with many, but with us it cannot be done–we love liberty too well–we have suffered too much to be easily duped–we have no catspaws amongst us." He then reminded readers of the friendship he and the Church had established with Stephen Douglas, a Democrat and a man he described in the most enthusiastic terms. "His friends are our friends. Snyder and Moore are his friends–they are ours. … such men will ever receive our support … We will never be justly charged with THE SIN OF INGRATITUDE–they have served us, and we will serve them."[29] In case anyone missed the point, he stressed, "[W]e care not a fig for Whig or Democrat; they are both alike to us, but we shall go for our friends, our tried friends, and the cause of human liberty, which is the cause of God."[30]

The editor of the *Quincy Whig,* Sylvester M. Bartlett, voiced strong opposition on January 22, 1842, to Joseph's power to direct his followers and denounced Joseph's effort to receive restitution from the federal government:

26. Ibid. Gregg would later write *The History of Hancock County, Illinois* and *The Prophet of Palmyra*, both volumes paying considerable attention to the Mormons.

27. George R. Gayler, "The Mormons and Politics in Illinois: 1839-1844," 51.

28. "State Gubernatorial Convention," *Times and Seasons* 3 (Jan. 1, 1842): 651; *History of the Church*, 4:479-80 (Dec. 20, 1841).

29. Ibid.

30. *History of the Church*, 4:480 (Dec. 20, 1841).

> This is, indeed, a highminded attempt to usurp power and to tyrannize over the minds of men. … [I]t will have a tendency to widen the breach which already exists between this people [and] those who are not of their faith, and as a consequence create difficulties and disturbances growing out of an unsettled state of feeling in the community. … Why not allow [his people] the exercise of their own best judgments in the choice of civil rulers?

Bartlett then expressed uneasiness with Joseph, "whose mysteries and awful claims to divine inspiration make his voice to believers like the voice of God, trained to sacrifice their individuality, to utter one cry; and to think and act in crowds; with minds that seem to have been struck from the sphere of reason on one subject."[31]

William Smith, Joseph's headstrong younger brother and editor of the *Wasp* in Nauvoo, launched his first issue on April 16, 1842, by attacking "the public press" as "daily teaming with slanders, foul calumnies, and base misrepresentations," intended to "misconstrue our movements and desecrate our characters." William announced: "In our editorial labours we shall endeavor to manifest that decision of character, and speak with that simplicity and plainness …"[32] William coined the jeering pet name "Thom-ASS" for Thomas Sharp, editor of the *Warsaw Signal*,[33] and he lost no time in attacking Sharp for his politics, editorial approach, and anti-Mormonism.

In ways, Joseph's response to the anti-Mormonism of Missouri had been spatial–removing the Church to Illinois. Not surprisingly, he made his next move just beneath the surface. When he began to conceptualize the political kingdom of God, he did it in private. He reportedly received the name of the new theocracy–the Kingdom of God and His Laws–on April 7, 1842, but delayed putting it in operation until March 11, 1844, under the name Council of Fifty.[34] Joseph described its purpose in familiar New Testament forms in an 1842 editorial: "[T]he purposes of God shall be accomplished; when 'the Lord shall be king over the whole earth' and 'Jerusalem his throne.' … As God governed Abraham, Isaac and Jacob, as families, and the children of Israel as a nation, so we, as a church, must be under his guidance if we are prospered, preserved, and sustained … and he alone must be our protector and safeguard, spiritually and temporally, or we fall."[35]

31. Sylvester Bartlett, *Quincy Whig*, Oct. 17, 1840, in Hallwas and Launius, *Cultures in Conflict*, 79.
32. William Smith, "Introduction," *The Wasp*, Apr. 16, 1842, 2.
33. "Pluto" (pseud.), "Mr. Editor," *The Wasp*, Apr. 16, 1842, 3.
34. Leonard, *Nauvoo*, 326.
35. "The Government of God," *Times and Seasons* 3, no. 11 (July 15, 1842): 857.

This treatise on government intensified the anti-Mormon sentiment, as events of the next year and a half would show: "The government of the Almighty, has always been very dissimilar to the government of men ... The government of God has always tended to promote peace, unity, harmony, strength and happiness; while that of man has been productive of confusion, disorder, weakness and misery."[36] This layering of law gave easy room for exploration and innovation, including, as one example, the practice of plurality.

The timing of this new organization is interesting. Positioned in the wake of increasing apostasy and dissension in the Church leadership, a widening circle of plurality, the secrecy required to sustain its subterranean practice, and growing external criticism of the Church's growth, economic strength, and political aspirations, the political kingdom of God propelled the Saints, not only into an uncertain future in 1842, but eventually into the distant West in 1847.

On May 14, 1842, gubernatorial candidate Snyder died. Into his place stepped Thomas Ford, then a justice of the state supreme court. Ford knew the Mormon vote was critical, despite the furor then raging over Bennett's allegations. Up to that point, Ford had tended to distance himself from the religious issue.[37] The Mormons found this neutrality acceptable. Ford received 1,748 votes in Hancock County, Joseph Duncan, a Whig, 711.[38]

On May 26, Joseph referred obliquely to his January political declaration[39] with the announcement at a "large and respectable meeting of the citizens of Nauvoo": "I did not intend to vote the Whig or Democratic ticket as such, but would go for those who would support good order, &c."[40] Alarmed, both sides adjusted their campaign strategies to accommodate Joseph's local power. The gathering of Nauvoo's citizens nominated candidates and passed a resolution expressing "disapprobation" of the *Quincy Whig*, which had suggested Joseph's culpability in the assassination attempt on Lilburn Boggs (discussed below).[41] The *Alton Telegraph* editorialized on June 4: "This issuing a proclamation ... commanding [Joseph's] followers to vote for this or that candidate, is too bold a stride towards despotism ever to be long countenanced by a free and intelligent people."[42]

36. Ibid., 856.
37. Ford, *History of Illinois*, 269.
38. Gayler, "The Mormons in Western Illinois," 167.
39. *History of the Church*, 4:479 (May 20, 1841).
40. Ibid., 5:19 (May 26, 1842).
41. Ibid.
42. "The State Register and the Mormons," *Alton Telegraph*, June 4, 1842, www.sidneyrigdon.com/dbroadh/IL/aHn1838.htm#060442 (Nov. 20, 2007).

For the Mormons, a separation between temporal and spiritual was impossible. To Joseph, the "kingdom of God" and "Zion" were synonyms. Both represented the fulfillment of prophecy and his people's devotion. In Missouri, Joseph spoke about Zion in literal and geographical terms. By Nauvoo, "Zion" represented any place where the faithful gathered. The stakes of Zion expanded, transforming both the concept and the rhetoric.

Reflecting on the way Joseph had built his prophetic narrative, Brigham Young recalled in 1874 how Joseph had defined the kingdom of God on earth in 1842: "Here is the Church of Jesus Christ of Latter-day Saints, organized with its rules and regulations and degrees, with the quorums of the holy Priesthood, from the First Presidency to the teachers and deacons; here we are; an organization. … This is what we are in the habit of calling the kingdom of God."[43] Joseph's life held meaning in the context of kingdom building and rendered the lives of Brigham and others around him sacred and profound.

Zion and the kingdom were, for the time being, Nauvoo. The apostles interpreted the work they did for the Church as important. In Nauvoo was a meaningful center place, according to Parley P. Pratt writing in the *Millennial Star*'s May-April 1842 issue, "the nucleus of a glorious dominion of universal liberty, peace and plenty; it is an organization of that government of which there shall be no end of that kingdom of Messiah, which shall roll forth, from conquering and to conquer until it shall be said, that *'the kingdoms of this world are become the kingdoms of our Lord, and of His Christ.'* … AND THE SAINTS OF THE MOST HIGH SHALL POSSESS THE GREATNESS OF THE KINGDOM UNDER THE WHOLE HEAVEN."[44]

In an understated paragraph, the *History of the Church* describes Sunday services on May 15, 1842, as the moment when "News of the attempted assassination of [former Missouri] Governor [Lilburn W.] Boggs was confirmed by general report, and was mentioned on the stand." Considering the impact this event would have on his life, one wonders how Joseph reacted. What was his tone as he delivered the news to the congregation? Did whispers roll across the crowd with concern? With satisfaction? Boggs had been shot three times in his home in Independence, Missouri, on May 6, but had

43. Brigham Young, Aug. 9, 1874, JD 17:156.

44. Parley P. Pratt, "Government and Institutions of Nauvoo," *Millennial Star* 3, no. 4 (Aug. 1842): 69; emphasis in original.

survived.[45] The *Quincy Whig* published the story on May 6, and followed up on May 21 with an editorial note, quick to link Joseph to the attack: "[A]s we understand, [Joseph Smith] prohesied a year or so ago, his death by violent means. Hence there is plenty of foundation for rumor."[46]

Joseph defended himself in a letter to his brother's *Wasp* on May 22: The *Whig* had done a "manifest injustice in ascribing to me a prediction of the demise of Lilburn W. Boggs." He found it likely that Boggs had been attacked by a political opponent, stressing that his own "hands are clean, and my heart pure, from the blood of all men. I am tired of the misrepresentation, calumny and detraction, heaped upon me by wicked men ..."[47]

Predictably, Missourians pointed at Joseph as instigator and his occasional bodyguard Orrin Porter Rockwell as the trigger. A month later, the prophet's six-year-old son, Frederick, announced to his family that he had dreamed that the "Missourians had got their heads knocked off." The child had internalized the story being passed around town like a package.[48] Rockwell, rough and uncouth, was devoted to Joseph. Known for his temper, Rockwell was short and small boned, with long brown hair that he sometimes wore in braids. Rockwell had been in Missouri in May 1842 but returned to Nauvoo on May 14, the day before the Boggs's shooting was announced to the Saints.[49] He left his wife, Luana, behind in Independence.[50]

Still bitter about his treatment by Joseph, John C. Bennett immediately claimed that he had heard Joseph offer a $500 reward for Boggs's death. He was certain Rockwell was the assassin because the long-haired disciple had left Missouri poor but had resurfaced in Illinois with pockets "filled with gold."[51] After Boggs partly recovered, Bennett visited him the first week in July and laid out his suspicions.[52] As a result, Boggs swore an affidavit July 20, 1842, that Joseph was "an accessory before the fact," and asked Thomas

45. *History of the Church*, 5:9 (May 15, 1842).

46. "Assassination of Ex-Governor of Missouri, Lilburn Boggs," *Quincy Whig*, May 21, 1842, 1.

47. Joseph Smith, "Mr. Bartlett," *The Wasp*, May 28, 1842, 2, also qtd. in *History of the Church*, 5:15 (May 22, 1842).

48. *History of the Church*, 5:45 (June 27, 1842).

49. John C. Bennett claimed that Rockwell admitted to being in Missouri at the time of the shooting but denied shooting Boggs himself. Bennett, *History of the Saints*, 285. Harold Schindler, *Orrin Porter Rockwell*, 69.

50. Schindler, *Orrin Porter Rockwell*, 80.

51. "Disclosures–the Attempted MURDER OF BOGGS! To the Editors of the St. Louis Bulletin," *Sangamo Journal*, July 22, 1842, 2. See also Andrew F. Smith, *The Saintly Scoundrel*, 103-104.

52. "More Disclosures," *Sangamo Journal*, July 8, 1842, 2.

Reynolds, governor of Missouri, to issue warrants for Rockwell's arrest as principal and Joseph as accessory and to seek Joseph's extradition.[53]

Meanwhile, in a swift but dubious move, the Nauvoo City Council on July 5 passed an ordinance giving the Nauvoo municipal court the power to test the legality of writs or processes served on Nauvoo citizens. Moreover, it empowered the court in Nauvoo, when such processes were found to have "private pique, malicious intent, or religious persecution,"[54] to dismiss them.[55] Designed to protect Joseph, the law was an extraordinary expression of Mormon entitlement. The Missouri writ, according to the Nauvoo court, "is another Missouri farce … [is] beneath the dignity of the Sons of Liberty, and would be a blot on our judicial escutcheon."[56]

On July 29, Emma, four months pregnant, set out for Quincy to defend her husband. She brought with her Eliza Snow and Amanda Barnes Smith. Carlin welcomed the women into his office. Amanda sat and listened as Emma pled for Thomas Carlin's protection. Emma's story had particular poignancy for Amanda, who had lost her own husband in one of Missouri's especially bloody tragedies. Emma feared for her husband's life. Joseph would be a ready target if arrested and placed in jail, the enmity towards the Mormons made it impossible for him to be treated fairly. Carlin admitted that he would not advise Joseph to trust himself to Missouri, but answered Emma's pleas in generalities, "saying that the laws and Constitution of our country shall be his polar star in case of any difficulty." Eliza, who recorded the meeting in her journal, commented skeptically, "It remains for time and circumstance to prove the sincerity of his professions."[57]

Eliza's fears were well founded. Joseph was arrested on August 8 on two charges: complicity in the Boggs assassination attempt and the old treason charge.[58] The deputy sheriff of Adams County and two other men held a writ and warrant issued by Carlin but based on a requisition from Missouri Governor Reynolds, which, in turn, was based on Boggs's affidavit. The warrant claimed that Joseph was "an accessory before the fact, to an assault with

53. *History of the Church*, 5:67 (July 20, 1842); Schindler, *Orrin Porter Rockwell*, 134-35; "Boggs'd," *Sangamo Journal*, July 8, 1842, 2; "John C. Bennett, Affidavit," *Sangamo Journal*, July 5, 1842, 2.

54. *History of the Church*, 5:88 (Aug. 8, 1842).

55. Edwin Brown Firmage and Richard Collin Mangrum, *Zion in the Courts*, 93.

56. *History of the Church*, 5:86-87 (July 20, 1842).

57. Maureen Ursenbach Beecher, ed., *The Personal Writings of Eliza Roxcy Snow*, 54.

58. *History of the Church*, 5:86 (Aug. 8, 1842).

intent to kill made by one Owen Porter Rockwell."[59] Joseph and Rockwell both submitted to arrest but were promptly released on a writ of habeas corpus from Nauvoo's municipal court.[60]

Months after he had left Nauvoo, John Bennett continued to create controversy for Joseph. In the exposé he promoted across the country, he charged that Rockwell, without confessing to the attempted murder, had bragged on July 5, 1842: "If I shot Boggs they have got to prove it–I never done an act in my life that I was ashamed of, and I do not fear to go anywhere that I have ever been, for I have done nothing criminal."[61] As to his own involvement, Joseph claimed that thousands of witnesses had seen him and could testify that he had been in Nauvoo at the time of the attack. Even so, he went into hiding on August 11 to avoid a kidnap attempt to return him to Missouri, while Rockwell left for Philadelphia.[62]

For the next three weeks, Joseph made no public appearances and stayed in the homes of friends. It was a fitting metaphor for the hidden nature of much that was transpiring during this threatening but productive time. He stayed the first night across the river in Zarahemla, Iowa, with his uncle John Smith.[63] Desiring the comfort of some of those dearest to him, he sent a secret message to Emma, Hyrum, and William Law to meet him on the island in the Mississippi between Nauvoo and Montrose. Emma's hurt at the Bennett episode had been great, and Joseph must have wondered if she would forgive him. He need not have worried. After dark, they came with George Miller, William Clayton, and Dimick Huntington. Erastus H. Derby rowed Joseph to the rendezvous from the other direction. Joseph learned that the governor of Iowa had issued a warrant for his arrest so the Lee County sheriff was also hunting him.[64] Still, it was Emma's loyalty that drew his most emotional response five days later when he reflected on the week's events:

> ... with what unspeakable delight, and what transports of joy swelled my bosom, when I took by the hand, on that night, my beloved Emma–she that was my wife, even the wife of my youth, and the choice of my heart. Many were the reverberations of my mind when I contemplated for a moment the many scenes we had been called to pass through, the fatigues

59. Ibid., 86.
60. Ibid., 87.
61. Bennett, *History of the Saints*, 285.
62. *History of the Church*, 5:90 (Aug. 11, 1842).
63. Ibid., 89-90 (Aug. 11 and 16, 1842).
64. Ibid., 89-90 (Aug. 11, 1842).

and the toils, the sorrows and sufferings, and the joys and consolations, from time to time, which had strewed our paths and crowned our board. Oh what a commingling of thought filled my mind for the moment, again she is here, even in the seventh trouble–undaunted, firm, and unwavering–unchangeable, affectionate Emma![65]

The group agreed that Joseph should go next to Edward Sayers's house, traveling on the river, and then to a farm located near the northeast boundary of Nauvoo.[66] Summing up his response to this latest pressure, Joseph commented: "[T]he whole business is another glaring instance of the effects of prejudice against me as a religious teacher, and that it proceeds from a persecuting spirit."[67]

On August 12, William Law updated Emma about Joseph's legal situation. William Walker, whose sister Lucy would marry Joseph nine months later, traversed the river from Nauvoo, pretending to be the prophet by riding Joseph's horse, while Joseph stayed with the Sayerses.[68] On August 13, creating a false trail for four strangers waiting outside town, Emma visited Elizabeth Durfee, Joseph's plural wife of two months. Contributing to the ruse, William Clayton and Lorin Walker picked her up in a carriage with "raised windows" that had already driven once past the four watchers. They led her out to the Sayers farm, and Emma surprised her husband. "I was in good spirits," Joseph later said, "and was much rejoiced to meet my dear wife once more." She stayed with him that night, talking and reading the history he was writing of his life. "[We] both felt in good spirits and very cheerful," he said.[69]

The two also spent August 14 together. The hunt was still actively underway.[70] On the 16th, Wilson Law (William's brother) wrote, encouraging Joseph to come home and wait until a new governor took office who would treat him more fairly. Law declared himself ready "in a moment's warning to defend the rights of man, both civil and religious."[71] Joseph was less ready.

---

65. Ibid., 107 (Aug. 16, 1842).

66. Ibid., 90 (Aug. 11, 1842). See also Monte McLaws, "The Attempted Assassination of Missouri's Ex-Governor, Lilburn W. Boggs," 50-62; and Warren A. Jennings, "Two Iowa Postmasters View Nauvoo," 275-92. U.S. District Attorney Justin Butterfield's opinion on the legality of attempting to arrest Joseph on the Boggs charge is in Butterfield, Letter to Sidney Rigdon, Oct. 20, 1842, in *History of the Church*, 5:173-79.

67. *History of the Church*, 5:90 (Aug. 11, 1842).

68. Ibid., 91-92 (Aug. 13, 1842).

69. Ibid., 92.

70. Ibid., 92 (Aug. 13 and 15, 1842).

71. Wilson Law, Letter to Joseph Smith, *History of the Church*, 5:96 (Aug. 15, 1842); *History*

He responded to Law's letter, dictated reflections to Willard Richards, and wrote a letter to Emma that a vision convinced him to stay in Illinois rather than seek refuge in Wisconsin's "Pine Country" where lumber was being milled for the temple and the Nauvoo House.[72]

On the same day, Emma wrote a businesslike missive:

> Dear Husband–I am ready to go with you if you are obliged to leave; and Hyrum says he will go with me. I shall make the best arrangements I can and be as well prepared as possible. But still I feel good confidence that you can be protected without leaving this country. There are more ways than one to take care of you, and I believe that you can still direct in your business concerns if we are all of us prudent in the matter.
>
> If it was pleasant weather I should contrive to see you this evening, but I dare not run too much of a risk, on account of so many going to see you.[73]

Emma's letter also passed on proposed terms for a real estate transaction and confirmation that the Iowa warrant was a rumor. Late that evening, Erastus Derby delivered a letter from Joseph dashed off after he had received hers: "… I take the liberty to tender you my sincere thanks for the two interesting and consoling visits that you have made me during my almost exiled situation. Tongue cannot express the gratitude of my heart, for the warm and true-hearted friendship you have manifested in these things towards me." He gave her blanket authorization to "write to him [Thomas Carlin] whatever you see proper."

As for leaving Illinois, he seemed to waver: "If I go to the Pine country, you shall go along with me, and the children; and if you and the children go not with me, I don't go. … It is for your sakes, therefore, that I would do such a thing. … I am not willing to trust you in the hands of those who cannot feel the same interest for you that I feel."

He then indulged in a bit of romanticism:

> Let all the goods, household furniture, clothes, and store goods that can be procured be put on the Boat; and let 20 or 30 of the best men that we can find be on board to man it, and let them meet us at Prairie-Du-Chien;

of the Church, 5:110-12 (Aug. 16, 1842); see also Dean C. Jessee, ed., *The Personal Writings of Joseph Smith*, 557-58.

72. Jessee, *Personal Writings of Joseph Smith*, 553-58, 559-65; *History of the Church*, 5:104, 110-12.

73. *History of the Church*, 5:110 (Aug. 16, 1842).

> and from thence we will wend our way like larks up the Mississippi untill the towering mountains and rocks shall remind us of the places of our nativity and shall look like safety and home; and then we will bid defiance to the world, to Carlin, Boggs, Bennett and all their whorish whores and motly clan, that follow their wake, Missouri not excepted, and until the damnation of hell rolls upon them, by the voice, and dread thunders, and trump of the eternal God.

He signed the letter, "Yours in haste, your affectionate husband until death, through all eternity; for evermore."[74]

The same day, August 16, Joseph also wrote an outpouring of appreciation to Wilson Law, whom he addressed as "Beloved brother and friend": "I love that soul that is so nobly entabernacled in that clay of yours." He prayed: "May we be able to triumph gloriously over those who seek our destruction and overthrow, which I believe we shall."[75] Away from the complexity of life as a prophet, bombarded by a excess of persons and troubles, Joseph had time to think.

About this same time, Joseph began recording a combination blessing-musing about the faithfulness of his friends. He mentions Erastus Derby, Hyrum, William Law, Newel Whitney, Dimick Huntington, George Miller, and William Clayton among others, all by name: "These I have met in prosperity and they were my friends, I now meet them in adversity, and they are still my warmer friends," he said tenderly. "They love the truths that I promulg[at]e. They love those virtuous, and those holy doctrines that I cherish in my bosom with the warmest feelings of my heart, and with that zeal which cannot be denied. I love friendship and truth." Individually and as a group, they "are men … possessing noble and daring, and giant hearts and souls." He specifically singled out "brother Hyrum" to praise the "faithful heart you have got."[76]

The next day, Emma wrote to Carlin to insist that Joseph had been in Nauvoo at the time of the attack on Boggs. She again challenged Carlin to "consider our claims upon your protection … as we always have been, still

74. Joseph Smith, Letter to Emma Smith, Aug. 16, 1842, in Jessee, *Personal Writings of Joseph Smith*, 555-56.

75. Joseph Smith, Letter to Wilson Law, Aug. 16, 1842, in Jessee, *Personal Writings of Joseph Smith*, 557-58.

76. Joseph Smith, Diary, Aug. 16, 1842, in Scott H. Faulring, ed., *An American Prophet's Record*, 246, 247.

are, and are determined always to be a law-abiding people."[77] Emma made an emotional entreaty, appealing to Carlin's head and heart to let Joseph's "aged mother" see her son live.[78] Her words engaged the convention of the pleading woman, conscious of the difference in power and position between her and the letter's male recipient: "I find myself almost destitute of that confidence, necessary to address a person holding the authority of your dignified and responsible office." In Joseph's absence, Emma pled his case:

> Need I say he is not guilty of the crime alleged against him by Governor Boggs? ... When I reflect upon the many cruel and illegal operations of Lilburn W. Boggs, and the consequent suffering of myself and family, and the incalculable losses and sufferings of many hundreds who survived, and the many precious lives that were lost,–all the effect of unjust prejudice and misguided ambition, produced by misrepresentation and calumny, ... my bosom heaves with unutterable anguish.[79]

Emma entrusted William Clayton with delivery of the letter.

Throughout this difficult week, Emma controlled the exchange of messages and worked for Joseph's safety. After night fall, and accompanied by Erastus Derby, Emma herself brought Joseph the message that he still was not safe and that Harmon T. Wilson, Hancock County Sheriff, had come to Nauvoo secretly to arrest Joseph. Even more alarming, Carlin had not been persuaded by her arguments, knew where Joseph was hiding, and planned to issue another writ. Joseph, Emma, and Derby left to avoid detection and sought refuge at Carlos Granger's house in Nauvoo.[80] The next three days were crisis free, and Joseph conducted a meeting on August 20 in the "council chamber" over his store.[81]

Emm's determination had impressed the Illinois governor. Carlin "expressed astonishment at the judgement and talent manifest in the manner of her address," but waited until August 24 to respond. His duty, Carlin said, was to honor requests from other states to extradite fugitives. This task left him "no discretion or adjudication as to the innocence or guilt of persons as demanded and charged with crime." If Joseph were indeed innocent, his friends should not be alarmed. He made certain to correct misunderstanding

77. *History of the Church*, 5:117 (Aug. 17, 1842).
78. Ibid., 116-17 (Aug. 17, 19, 1842).
79. Ibid., 115-16.
80. Ibid., 118 (Aug. 17, 1842).
81. Ibid., 119 (Aug. 20, 1842).

he may have caused, insisting that he meant mobs, not Missouri's officials or the legal system in general, could not be trusted.[82] Once again, Missouri defined what happened in Joseph's life in Illinois.

As Joseph moved among hiding places in and around Nauvoo, he periodically sank into a seeming depression, entering a death image in his journal and elaborating a plan for a family sepulchre to be known as "the tomb of Joseph, a descendant of Jacob."[83] That same day, he recommenced the blessing-musing he had begun dictating on the 16th: "I contemplate the virtues and the good qualifications and characteristics of the faithful few."[84] He listed Joseph Knight and his sons, two more brothers, Samuel and Don Carlos, his parents, and twenty-eight-year-old Orrin Porter Rockwell. "He is an innocent and a noble boy," Joseph concluded. "May God Almighty deliver him from the hands of his pursuers."[85]

Joseph then turned to prayer: "O Lord, God, my heavenly Father, shall it be vain, that Thy servant must needs be exiled from the midst of his friends, or be dragged from their bosoms, to clank in cold and iron chains; to be thrust within the dreary prison walls; to spend days of sorrow, and of grief, and misery there, by the hands of an infuriated, incensed, and infatuated foe; to glut their infernal and insatiable desire upon innocent blood; and for no other cause on the part of Thy servant, than for the defense of innocence; and Thou a just God will not hear his cry? Oh, Thou wilt hear me–a child of woe ... mine enemies shall not prevail; they all shalt melt like wax before Thy face."[86]

Along with safety, Joseph pled for "grace, glory, and honor," perhaps knowing that the outcome of the arrest could be interpreted in his favor. These passages can be interpreted as both a musing on friends and family and as a sort of performance of religious authority. Joseph's role was that of God's suffering but faithful servant, surrounded by enemies who threatened his efforts to obey God's will. At the end of this day's entry in the Book of the Law of the Lord, he jotted, with a return to the prosaic, "This afternoon received a few lines from Emma, informing me that she would expect me home this evening, believing that she could take care of me better at home

82. Thomas Carlin, Letter to Emma Smith, in *History of the Church*, 5:130 (Aug. 24, 1842).
83. Joseph Smith, Diary, Aug. 23, 1842, in Faulring, *An American Prophet's Record*, 251.
84. Joseph Smith, Diary, Aug. 23, 1842, in Faulring, *An American Prophet's Record*, 248.
85. Joseph Smith, Diary, Aug. 23, 1842, in Faulring, *An American Prophet's Record*, 249.
86. *History of the Church*, 5:128 (Aug. 22, 1842).

than elsewhere. Accordingly, soon after dark, I started for home, and arrived safe, without being noticed by any person."[87]

On August 27, Eliza Snow drafted another letter for Emma's signature to Carlin: "[I] still hope you will avail yourself of sufficient time to investigate our cause, ... We do believe that it is your duty to allow us in this place, the privileges and advantages guaranteed to us by the laws of this State and the United States. This is all we ask." She quoted the Nauvoo charter that allowed the city council to make ordinances not conflicting with state laws. Her letter argued that the writ of habeas corpus was issued according to the charter's provisions. She continued, "What good can accrue to this State or the United States, or to yourself, or any other individual, to continue this persecution upon this people, or upon Mr. Smith–a persecution that you are well aware, is entirely without any foundation or excuse." She invited Carlin and his family to stay with them in Nauvoo.[88]

William Clayton wrote in Joseph's journal, later that day, "In the assembly room [over Joseph's store] with some of the Twelve and others, who were preparing affidavits for the press."[89] The affidavits, published four days later, testified to Joseph's good character, affirmed that he had been in Nauvoo during the attack on Boggs, and insisted that he was not involved in the conspiracy. It remained unclear whether they would make a difference.

When Joseph stepped to the stand on August 29, he had been away from Nauvoo for nearly a month. The congregation seemed newly energized by his presence. His high spirits led straight to grandiosity, drawing his people into his own feat by congratulating the "brethren and Sisters on the victory I had once more gained over the Missourians." He told them that he had not fought with "carnal weapons," but with "stratagem, by outwitting them, and there had been no lives lost, and there would be no lives lost if they would hearken to my Council." He predicted "in the name of Jesus Christ" that the arresting officers "shall be cut down in their plans. ... We don't want or mean to fight with the sword of the flesh, but we will fight with the broad Sword of the Spirit." He bragged that he would show his enemies that there was a "Moses and a Joshua amongst us; and I will fight them, if they don't take off oppression from me."[90]

87. Ibid., 128-29.

88. Emma Smith, Letter to Thomas Carlin, Aug. 27, 1842, photocopy of holograph in Linda King Newell Collection, Special Collections, Marriott Library. *History of the Church*, 5:132-33 (Aug. 27, 1842).

89. *History of the Church*, 5:132 (Aug. 27, 1842).

90. Ibid., 137-39 (Aug. 29, 1842).

Then Joseph vanished, reappearing two days later to address the Relief Society on August 31. He began by expressing his happiness at being with them. "God had enabled him [Joseph] to keep out of their hands," according to the minutes. Joseph was still in an exalted mood: "I shall triumph over my enemies, I have begun to triumph over them at home and I shall do it abroad. All those that rise up against me will feel the weight of their iniquity upon their own heads. Those that speak evil are abominable characters and full of iniquity. All the fuss and all the stir against me, is like the jack in the lantern, it cannot be found. Altho' I do wrong, I do not the wrongs that I am charg'd with doing. The wrong that I do is thro' the frailty of human nature like other men. No man lives without fault."[91]

Joseph measured the degree of persecution against the degree of good he was accomplishing. "When I do the best I can," he continued, "... then the most evils are got up against me. I would to God that you would be wise. I now counsel you, if you know any thing, hold your tongues, and the least harm will be done."[92]

Learning on September 2 that Missouri sheriffs were coming again to Nauvoo,[93] he returned to hiding while the governors of Missouri and Illinois posted rewards of $300 and $500, respectively, for his arrest. In exile, Joseph wrote further instructions about the doctrine of baptism for the dead and its meaning–instructions that later would be canonized as LDS Doctrine and Covenants 128.[94] He filled a few hours with a lengthy letter to James Arlington Bennet, bemoaning his current plight.[95] He testified that Mormonism was "the pure doctrine of Jesus Christ; of which I myself am not ashamed." His letter reveals the burden the business affairs of the Church placed on him, compounding his feelings of persecution. "I am this time," he wrote, "persecuted the worst of any man on the earth ... all our sacred rights, are trampled under the feet of the mob. I am now hunted as an hart by the mob, under the pretense, or shadow of law, to cover their abominable deeds."[96] For Joseph, the worst possible punishment was to be separated from his people.

91. Relief Society, Minutes, Aug. 31, 1842.

92. Ibid.

93. *History of the Church*, 5:144 (Sept. 2, 1842).

94. Ibid., 148-53 (Sept. 6, 1842).

95. Ibid., 156-59; Jessee, *Personal Writings of Joseph Smith*, 574-79. When Willard Richards returned to Massachusetts to bring his wife, Jennetta, and their son to Nauvoo, he visited the Bennet home and reported that Bennet regarded Joseph as "great a prophet as Moses and a better man. But he does not believe in special revelation in any period of time. He belongs to no sect or party ... he hates persecution with a perfect hatred." Ibid., 574.

96. Ibid.

Emma again leaped to Joseph's defense, soliciting the women of the Relief Society to sign a petition to Carlin, dated September 5. More than a thousand women conceded that "it would be more consistent with the delicacy of the female character to be silent," and asked for protection from the Missouri mobs. They affirmed their belief in the "integrity, honesty, truth and patriotism" of Joseph Smith and begged that he not be extradited.[97] Although Carlin, by authorizing the reward, had clearly come down on Missouri's side, the women seem to have felt some lingering hope that Illinois would protect their religious rights.

Two days later, Carlin responded to Emma. "Every word of [your letter] evinces your devotedness to the interest of your husband, and pouring forth the effusions of a heart wholly his." He repeated that habeas corpus gave the citizens of Nauvoo the right to face the court in Nauvoo regardless of where they were arrested, but denied that the municipal court had power over writs issued by other courts or other states. He thought any other interpretation was "absurd and ridiculous" and asserted that "to attempt to exercise it is a gross usurpation of power that cannot be tolerated."[98] He was clearly distancing himself from any defense that depended on Nauvoo's charter. The stage was set for a power struggle, and the only wonder is that it was two years off instead of two weeks.

Through the *Times and Seasons*, Joseph published a flat denial of plurality as well as a letter to the "Saints in Nauvoo," informing them he would be away until the "storm is fully blown ... And as for the perils which I am called to pass through they seem but a small thing to me, as the envy and wrath of man has been my common lot all the days of my life and for what cause it seems mysterious." Joseph encouraged them to continue the work, especially construction of the temple.[99]

While Joseph was in hiding, Eliza Snow published a coded message to her plural husband in the *Wasp* of September 10, phrasing it as though she spoke for the community:

I feel thy woes–my bosom shares,
Thy spirit's agony:
How can I love a heart that dares
Suspect thy purity?

97. Emma Smith, Letter to Thomas Carlin, Sept. 5, 1842, in *History of the Church*, 5:146.

98. *History of the Church*, 5:154 (Sept. 7, 1842).

99. Joseph Smith, "To All the Saints," Sept. 1, 1842, in Jessee, *Personal Writings of Joseph Smith*, 571.

I'll smile on all, that smile on thee
As angels do above–
All who in pure sincerity
Will love thee, I will love.[100]

Before the end of the month, Joseph was "safely home undiscovered."[101]

Joseph reappeared to preach on persecution on September 25 passionately enough to evoke a strong response from the audience. He repeated the theme over the ensuing weeks.[102] "Carlin is determined to have me taken to Missouri, if he can. But may the Almighty Jehovah shield and defend me from all their power, and prolong my days in peace, that I may guide the people in righteousness, until my head is white with old age."[103] Despite the bravado, Joseph stayed close to home; in fact on September 29, he spent the day nursing Emma who, in addition to being six months pregnant, was ill with malaria or typhoid fever.[104] During the first few days of October, he fretted: "Emma sick as usual. … Emma a little better, I was with her all day. … Emma is very sick again. I attended with her all day …"[105] Vilate Kimball noticed the same: "Emma was brought down nigh unto death; Bro. Joseph dispaired of her life, he mourned over her and refused to be comforted."[106] Frantic with worry, he tried the remedy of faith: "[Emma] was baptized twice in the river, which evidently did her much good. … She grew worse again at night and continued very sick indeed. I was unwell and much troubled on account of Emma's sickness."[107]

On October 6, he again went into hiding, avoiding two sheriffs who had arrived on the 8th. The next day, Eliza Snow recorded: "Sister Emma had been sick eleven days,–still confined to her bed–but he [Joseph] must go or be expose'd to the fury of the merciless!"[108] The same day, Eliza sent Joseph a cheering report in verse:

Sir, for your consolation permit me to tell

100. Eliza R. Snow, "To Who Needs Consolation," 1.

101. *History of the Church*, 5:161 (Sept. 10, 1842).

102. Ibid., 165 (Sept. 25, 1842).

103. Ibid., 168 (Oct. 5, 1842).

104. Joseph's history mentions that October 5 was the day "Emma was worse," suggesting an intermittent fever, like malaria. *History of the Church*, 5:166-67, 168 (Oct. 6, 1842).

105. *History of the Church*, 5:166-67 (Oct. 5, 1842).

106. Vilate Kimball, Letter to Heber C. Kimball, Oct. 16, 1842. in Helen Mar Whitney, "Scenes and Incidents in Nauvoo," 1-2.

107. *History of the Church*, 5:167 (Oct. 5, 1842).

108. Eliza R. Snow, Journal, Oct. 9, 1842, in Beecher, *Personal Writings of Eliza Roxcy Snow*, 57.

That your Emma is better–she soon will be well;
Mrs. Durfee[109] stands by her, night & day like a friend
And is promt every call–every wish to attend;
Then pray for your Emma, but indulge not a fear
For the god of our forefathers, smiles on us here.[110]

Three weeks later, Joseph returned to the city after staying in the homes of various friends. After residing with his family overnight, he went into hiding for another week. He reappeared off and on through the successive weeks, taking Emma on carriage rides to the temple site or in the countryside, to every appearance a solicitous, loving husband. Their relationship was layered with heartache, but also with a shared history of warmth and love.

When disgruntled apostates warned off immigrants, Joseph spoke to a group of newcomers on October 29, "showing them … how to act in regard to making purchases of land, etc. I showed them it was generally in consequence of the brethren disregarding or disobeying counsel that they became dissatisfied and murmured; … I told them I was but a man, and they must not expect me to be perfect … if they would bear with my infirmities and the infirmities of the brethren, I would likewise bear with their infirmities."[111]

Thomas Ford was elected that fall as Illinois governor. Capitalizing on the inclement weather to stay indoors, Joseph attended to business during several days in November, clearing up irregularities in the Nauvoo Post Office. He also resigned as editor of the *Times and Seasons,* appointing in his place John Taylor, "who is less encumbered and fully competent …"[112] On November 21, the Twelve Apostles met in Heber C. Kimball's house to vote to suspend publication of the *Millennial Star* upon Parley P. Pratt's return from England.[113] The Church published both the *Wasp* and the *Times and Seasons,* which remained the most important public relations voice in the Church, in the same building and on the same press, and "through their content … helped define the Nauvoo-era Saints as a people of faith and destiny."[114]

As Joseph straightened out the Church's print media issues, the lingering messiness of his real estate dealings continued to plague him, and

109. Elizabeth Durfee, another of Joseph's plural wives.

110. Eliza R. Snow, Journal, Oct. 9, 1842, in Beecher, *Personal Writings of Eliza Roxcy Snow*, 58.

111. *History of the Church*, 5:181 (Oct. 29, 1842).

112. Ibid., 193 (Nov. 15, 1842); "Valdictory," *Times and Seasons* 4, no. 1 (Nov. 15, 1842): 8.

113. *History of the Church*, 5:194 (Nov. 21, 1842).

114. Leonard, *Nauvoo*, 219.

on November 26, he begged long-suffering Horace Hotchkiss for more patience: "When I found it necessary to avail myself of the benefits of the bankruptcy law, I knew not but what the law required of me to include you amongst the list of my creditors, notwithstanding the nature of the contract between us."[115] Hotchkiss was far from satisfied and questioned Joseph about the inventory he presented in the bankruptcy proceedings, while Joseph justified his decision and added excuses to his defense.

Raising the issue of the "extreme hardness of the times" and "the great scarcity of money," Joseph asked Hotchkiss to "offer a lenity equivalent to the state of the times. … I shall yet endeavor to make the payments as fast as possible."[116] But Joseph had not even managed to pay the taxes on the land the Saints occupied. His best strategy at the moment was to stall.

As Joseph juggled business transactions, plural marriages, doctrinal innovations, and complications with the law, a special delegation traveled in mid-December to Springfield to register their affidavits that Joseph was in Illinois on the day of the attack on Boggs.[117] The remainder of the month, Joseph mostly worked at home. He appointed Willard Richards as his official secretary and made him responsible for gathering materials for the Church's history.[118] Joseph also sometimes practiced his German by reciting passages to Orson Hyde, and talked doctrine with visitors who came to his house.[119]

The day after Christmas, Emma, still sick, went into labor. Joseph, accompanied by Willard Richards, attended a court held at the city council. En route, they met a Brother Tully whom, Joseph asked, "if he had ought against him?" Tully answered, "I have not." At the court, a Brother Morey gave Joseph an ivory-handled walking stick, the staff made of a sperm-whale's tooth with a mahogany insert.[120] Joseph also consulted briefly with Wilson Law, whom Thomas Carlin had assigned to arrest Joseph for extradition to Missouri.[121] Weary by his insecure existence, Joseph decided to trust the city charter's provisions and arranged with Law to arrest him on December 26, the same day that Emma gave birth to a stillborn son. Only three of Emma's eight children lived beyond infancy, nor would this child be the last of their losses.

115. Joseph Smith, Letter to Horace R. Hotchkiss, Nov. 26, 1842, in *History of the Church*, 5:195.

116. Ibid.

117. *History of the Church*, 5:204-205 (Dec. 14, 1842).

118. Faulring, *An American Prophet's Record*, 257.

119. Ibid.

120. Ibid., 258.

121. Ibid.

Joseph must have traveled with a heavy heart the twenty-nine miles to Springfield on December 29.[122] Governor Ford had denied Joseph's request for protection while he traveled to court,[123] so friends accompanied him instead: Wilson Law, Hyrum, John Taylor, William Marks, Levi Moffitt, Peter Hawes, Lorin Walker, Willard Richards, and Orson Hyde. Halfway to Carthage, they met Willam Clayton and Henry G. Sherwood who had secured an order for habeas corpus. But because the court clerk was not available, they had not been able to obtain the actual writ.[124] By nightfall, the group, arrived at Plymouth where they were soon joined by Edward Hunter, Theodore Turley, a Dr. Tate, and Shadrach Roundy as well as by Elizabeth Durfee and her daughter.[125]

Joseph slept that night with Willard Richards on a buffalo skin laid out on the floor. Richards recalled Joseph's musings: "the purifying of the sons of Levi was by giving unto them intel[l]igence that we are not capable of mediating [on] and receiving all the intel[l]igence which belongs to an immortal state. It is to[o] powerful for our faculties."[126] Joseph dreamed that he was by a "beautiful stream of water." He saw "noble handsome fish," which he caught and threw out on the bank. More fish swarmed in the clear water, but he scooped threw them all out and "sent for salt to salt them down and salted them."[127] He did not interpret the dream in his journal.

After traveling another twenty miles, the party dined at the Rushville Bell Tavern. In no hurry to retire, they engaged in lively conversation, visited a Mrs. Brown, and measured each other. Joseph and Hyrum both stood six feet. The next morning, they were on the frosty road at 9:00 a.m.[128]

When one of the carriages broke down, the remainder continued. The first group arrived in Springfield at Judge James Adams's house at about 2:30 p.m. During the conversation with their host, Joseph told Adams that he would never vote for a slaveholder. "[I]f they could obtain sufficient power and get a religious peak [pique] against any religionists they would

122. *History of the Church*, 5:210-13 (Dec. 29, 1842).

123. Ibid., 205-206 (Dec. 17, 1842).

124. Joseph Smith, Diary, Dec. 29, 1842, in Faulring, *An American Prophet's Record*, 258.

125. Ibid.

126. Joseph Smith, Diary, Dec. 29, 1842, in Faulring, *An American Prophet's Record*, 259; see also *History of the Church*, 5:210-11 (Dec. 29, 1842).

127. Joseph Smith, Diary, Dec. 29, 1842, in Faulring, *An American Prophet's Record*, 259; see also *History of the Church*, 5:210-11 (Dec. 29, 1842).

128. Faulring, *An American Prophet's Record*, 259.

subdue them and compel our children to mix with their Slaves."[129] The second group arrived about an hour later.

In the hearing, Joseph appeared and presented bail.[130] Justin Butterfield, U.S. District Attorney for Illinois, Judge James Adams, James Pittman, and the sheriff of Adams County discussed whether Joseph's writ had been secured. "It was decided by the council that the old writ should be had if possible in the morning by some one beside Pittman [and] Joseph be arrested thereon and by Habeus Corpus brought before Judge [Nathaniel] Pope in the morning and he would go clear, and Said Joseph, 'Let me have a happy new years.'"[131]

Joseph then drew these outsiders into his persecution narrative. He denied that he had ever done military service in Missouri, and described how he had been "taken prisoner of war at Far West in his own door yard," court-martialed, condemned, and imprisoned. He told them about his trial, the prisoners' escape, and his arrival at Quincy, and then testified of Christ's imminent millennial reign and that "heathen nations who will not come up to worship will be destroyed."[132]

During the morning of December 31, Butterfield announced that a court officer had the governor's writ and Joseph signed a petition to Ford requesting a new writ. In his office, Butterfield read the petition to Judge Pope of the U.S. Circuit Court. According to Joseph's account, Pope read a variety of documents showing that "Reynolds (with all defference to the Gov[ernor] of M[iss]o[uri]) has made a false statement as nothing appears in the affidavit to show that said Smith ever was in M[iss]o[uri during the attempt on Governor Boggs's life or that Joseph had attempted to flee justice."[133]

The court rituals continued, channeling hopes, fears, and disappointments into predictable patterns. Butterfield asked for a new habeus corpus, which was granted, and moved that the court accept bail from Joseph until the case could be heard, which was again granted. The trial date was set for Monday. As the participants left the courtroom, someone on the staircase exclaimed, "There goes Smith the Prophet and a great looking man he is." Another added, "As damned a rascal as ever lived." Hyrum retorted, "And a good many [others]," at which the first man rejoined: "God Damn you

129. Ibid., 260.
130. Ibid., 261.
131. Ibid.
132. Ibid.
133. Joseph Smith, Diary, Dec. 31, 1842, Faulring, *An American Prophet's Record*, 263.

and any one that takes his part is as damned a rascal as he is." The marshal calmed the crowd. Joseph called on the governor, who was ill, dined with Butterfield at the American House, then called again on Ford, who commented good-naturedly: "we had reason to think the Mormons were a peculiar people. Different from other people having horns or something of the kind, but I find they look like other people. Indeed I think Mr. Smith is a very good looking man."[134] Their conversation ranged across many subjects, including the provisions of Nauvoo Charter. Joseph argued that, as a perpetual charter, it could not be revoked. Ford, an attorney, probably was not convinced.

On Sunday, they held a preaching service in the chamber of the state House of Representatives, a location that provided a perfect opportunity for the performance of religious identity. Before the service began, Joseph "explained the nature of a prophet":

> If any person should ask me if I were a prophet, I should not deny it, as that would give me the lie; for, according to John, the testimony of Jesus is the spirit of prophecy; therefore, if I profess to be a witness or teacher, and have not the spirit of prophecy, which is the testimony of Jesus, I must be a false witness; but if I be a true teacher and witness, I must possess the spirit of prophecy, and that constitutes a prophet ...[135]

After the service, the Mormons dined with Judge Adams, then heard an afternoon sermon from John Taylor.[136] Demonstrating a range of Mormon oratory, the men laid out their best religious insights for the citizens of Illinois. Feeling optimistic, Joseph boasted after breakfast Monday morning that he would not go to Missouri "dead or alive."[137] Joseph commented confidently about the outcome of the trial. It was easy to do so, given his network of devoted disciples and how he was deferentially treated by the state's most important officials.

All in all, the experience had been filled with paradox. Surrounded by friends, Joseph had been threatened and mocked; relying on the law, he had been delivered, but its provisions were being scrutinized. Joseph had seized the opportunity to teach–his presentation had been praised, but some townsfolk had cursed the Mormons.

---

134. Ibid., 264.
135. *History of the Church*, 5:215-16 (Jan. 1, 1843).
136. Faulring, *An American Prophet's Record*, 266-67.
137. *History of the Church*, 5:216 (Jan. 2, 1843).

In a touching finale to the year, Joseph visited the McIntire family, where twin daughters had recently been born. He asked Sister McIntire if he could share one of her babies, hoping the infant would comfort Emma.[138] Having the new baby from morning until dusk, together with Joseph's sensitivity, helped Emma move through her grief.

138. Linda King Newell and Valeen Tippetts Avery, *Mormon Enigma*, 103.

CHAPTER 16

"Dead or Alive"

> *... the civil magistrate should restrain crime, but never control conscience; should punish guilt, but never suppress the freedom of the soul.*
>
> *–Doctrine and Covenants 134:4*

Joseph lived on the edge of danger, much of it real, some of it imagined. Predictable attacks came from political opponents, merchants threatened by the economic growth of the Church, neighbors and clerics uneasy with Mormonism's expansion. For them, Joseph was the head to be removed, after which the body would die. But blows came from within as well. When friends and associates fell from the faith, Joseph nearly always experienced it as a personal injury.

The year 1843 began with a legal threat successfully surmounted, one that got the year off to an optimistic start. But Joseph's appearance before the court was framed by the larger narrative built around Missouri's persecutions. Joseph expected that the government would unjustly pursue him for his confrontations with Missouri officials. This new development would be a continuation of the story begun years before, the denouement of a tale told through the life experiences of this chosen people. Therefore, Joseph's performance before the court and the crowd of curious bystanders was like high theater, a prophet playing his role as one who speaks with God, has been treated unjustly by the state, and who has powers even the skeptical do not fully understand. He was worth watching.

The trial forged tight bonds among the Mormons involved, contributing to their collective narrative. In Nauvoo, religious identity was measurable experientially. Those who survived the travails of Missouri, who entered the secretive practice of plurality, and who joined Joseph in the Anointed Quorum were tied to Joseph individually and to Mormonism in profound ways. This multidimensionality motivated a particular response to crises. Perceived or actual threats triggered reactions linked to the Saints' defensive experience. There was a multidimensional motivation for Joseph's religious behavior throughout the complications of 1843.

Why did Joseph respond to the trial the way that he did? What motivated the individuals around him to behave the ways they did? Their religious identity provides insight into Joseph's response to Missouri's repeated efforts to extradite him and into his performance of his prophetic identity before the court and the American public.[1] As was true of the Nauvoo period generally, Missouri provided a core narrative of Joseph's prophethood, creating bonds among the survivors. Their sufferings rendered them martyrs, justified their stretching of the Nauvoo Charter for their own safety, and colored every interaction with outsiders. Joseph's performance of religious identity displayed indignation and outrage, flaunted authority, and disarmed even his worst enemies with characteristic jocularity.

On Wednesday, January 4, the procedure began. Judge Nathaniel Pope entered the courtroom with five women on each arm, mocking perhaps, the allegations of Joseph's many wives. Most likely, they were curious about the Mormon prophet. The first day's outcome was setting a date for the trial. However, before the session closed, attorney Justin Butterfield filed objections to the habeas corpus itself. As Joseph's lawyer, he argued that Joseph was not a fugitive from the law, had not been in Missouri for three years, and had not been in Missouri when Boggs was shot.[2] The critical issue in the case, clearly stated by Pope the next day, was "whether a citizen of the state of Illinois can be transported from his own state to the state of Missouri, to be there tried for a crime, which, if he ever committed, was committed in the state of Illinois; whether he can be transported to Missouri, as a fugitive from justice, when he has never fled from that state."[3] Arguments centered on the Lilburn Boggs affidavit.

During the next several days, a parade of senators, barristers, and

1. Aryeh Lazar, Shlomo Kravetz, and Peri Frederich-Kedem, "The Multidimensionality of Motivation for Jewish Religious Behavior," 509-19. This study posits five factors in the relationship between religious motivation and religious identity: "belief in a divine order, ethnic identity, social activity, family activity, and upbringing. … Persons with different religious identities were found to attribute their performance of religious ritual to different motives, providing a partial explanation for the apparent anomaly of the performance of religious ritual by persons who identify themselves as secular."

2. *History of the Church*, 5:220-22 (Jan. 4, 1843).

3. Ibid., 224 (Jan. 5, 1843).

observers came to meet and converse with the Mormon prophet during the proceedings. Some wanted to see what he looked like and pass judgment on his character, measuring the threat he posed to Illinois. Some invited him to dine with them; others spoke with him in the hall. Whenever possible, Joseph bore his testimony that God spoke to modern man through prophets and that his teachings would save them all.

As they would have done daily at home, Joseph and his group gathered at the end of each day to sing and pray together, an important means of keeping their spirits high before they arranged their blankets on the floor as beds.

The case itself covered a range of issues: habeas corpus, jurisdiction, contradictions in the writ, and evidence demonstrating that Joseph had been in Nauvoo at the time of the shooting. Butterfield found the charges ludicrous, and let it be known in elaborate argumentation that he would prove that the case was shaky. "That an attempt should be made to deliver up a man who has never been out of the State strikes at all the liberty of our institutions. His fate to day may be yours tomorrow."[4] His arguments hit at the heart of the matter: "It is a matter of history that he and his people have been murdered and driven from the state ... He is an innocent and unoffending man, if there is a difference between him and other men, it is this people believe in prophecy and others do not."[5]

During a recess, Joseph went into the judge's chambers where he was introduced to a senator and more women, including the governor's wife. The courtroom was crowded, but "the utmost decorum and good feeling prevailed," according to Willard Richards, who judged Butterfield's handling as "very learned."[6] A crowd gathered to "behold the Prophet" and, importantly, to see how Pope decided.[7]

Pope ruled that Joseph was discharged from all "prosecution on the case." The governor later certified the court's decision but, in passing, warned Joseph to "refrain from all political electioneering."[8] Pope also ordered that Joseph make good on what he owed Butterfield: two notes of $230 each.

4. Ibid., 222 (Jan. 4, 1843).

5. Ibid.

6. Richards was the scribe for the journal notations during the trial. Joseph Smith, Diary, Jan. 5, 1843, in Scott H. Faulring, ed., *An American Prophet's Record*, 279. The record that appears in the *History of the Church* version of the same proceedings includes bracketed notations that might have been copied from the *Sangamo Journal.*

7. *History of the Church*, 5:223 (Jan. 5, 1843).

8. Joseph Smith, Diary, Jan. 6, 1843, in Faulring, *An American Prophet's Record*, 284.

The party went to the courtroom where they secured copies of the many relevant affidavits, requisitions, writs, proclamations, orders, and a summary of the proceedings.[9]

Feeling vindicated, Joseph's party left Springfield on Saturday, January 7. Despite the all-day snowstorm, William Law's voice rolled out "The Mormon Jubilee." The song captured the men's collective sentiment: The Lord had intervened to assure the outcome of a righteous cause.

And are you sure the news is true?
And are you sure he's free?
Then let us join with one accord,
And have a Jubilee[.]

Chorus:

We'll have a Jubilee, My Friend
We'll have a Jubilee
With heart and voice we'll all rejoice
In that our Prophet's free

Paying tribute to their attorneys, to Governor Ford, and to Judge Pope, the song framed the victory as stemming from the provisions of the Nauvoo Charter:

Our Charter'd rights she has Maintained
Through opposition great
Long may her charter champions live
Still to protect the State.[10]

The lyric narrative positioned those who had experienced this most recent crisis on common ground, a rhetorical sameness that framed their experience. They would tell the story upon their return, drawing yet another group into the expanding circle.

Whether in the form of an orally transmitted narrative or, as in this example, a song, the narrative contributes to the formation of collective identity and is a core element of religious community. Identity is created in stories in conscious and unconscious processes. For clinician and pastor Andrew Lester, "The core narratives communicate a person's values, purposes,

9. Ibid., 285-86.
10. Ibid., 287-89.

and unique characteristics, which allow us to imagine an identity."[11] A core narrative is an overarching theme that runs through an individual's story and interprets life. For Joseph and his companions, the core story was of persecution–endured, resisted, overthrown.

Community identity is tied to what is assumed will happen next to the group. For the Latter-day Saints, the assumption of their collective future was the hope of heaven. This shared prospect was made certain by the way they reacted to persecution. Theologian John Navone speaks to this community interconnectedness: Stories "of a self cannot be told without the stories of other selves."[12] Theologian George Stroup places a community's religious identity in the context of narrative: "The identity of Christian individuals and communities is finally rooted in and dependent on the yet unfinished narrative … on the expectation of a future in which God's promises in the past will be consummated in new and unexpected ways."[13]

As Joseph, William Law, Willard Richards, and the others slogged over the muddy roads toward Nauvoo, their own lives made sense in context of one another. Despite the emphasis on personal salvation, on the importance of one's personal choices, this experience was one with a group, structured by the assumptions they shared. They must have talked endlessly on that journey about what had transpired in Springfield, the justice that tasted so sweet.

The snow delayed them. On January 9, one carriage fell off the edge of a bridge and was damaged; fortunately, no one was hurt. The men stayed that night in Plymouth at the home of Joseph's brother Samuel, where Joseph spoke fondly about family, and how close they had come to being deterred from their mission of preaching God's message.[14]

The party reached Nauvoo on Tuesday, January 10, in the mid-afternoon. They entered the city on a wave of melody, triumphantly singing "The Mormon Jubilee." Relieved to have her prophet-son home, Joseph's mother, Lucy, seized his arm and pulled him to her, "overjoyed to behold her son free once again." Joseph took Emma out sleigh riding the next day and again four days later, compensating partially for his absence and enjoying her company in this relaxed setting.

Seizing the opportunity for celebration, on January 10, Eliza Snow and William Law distributed copies of the Jubilee song to more than fifty men

11. Andrew Lester, *Hope in Pastoral Care and Counseling*, 30.
12. John Navone, *Toward a Theology of Story*, 78.
13. George Stroup, *Promise of Narrative Theology*, 258.
14. *History of the Church*, 5:246 (Jan. 9, 1843).

and women invited to attend a party at Joseph and Emma's house.[15] The dinner was not only to celebrate Joseph's release, but also to recognize the couple's sixteenth wedding anniversary.[16] Publicly acknowledged for her support, Emma must have been flooded by emotions both sweet and bitter. Joseph spoke freely about his favorite theme, the kingdom of God, and diverged into an exposition of John the Baptist and baptism by immersion.[17] Like so much of Joseph's narrative, even this welcome home was layered. As Emma's heart filled with relief, two pairs of young sisters–Sarah and Maria Lawrence and Eliza and Emily Partridge–who may have helped to prepare the meal, were soon to become secret wives of Joseph. A couple of long rectangular tables supported an assortment of sumptuous foods for Joseph's friends. Children and household servants sat at a separate table nearby enough to share the excitement of Joseph's return.

Despite the joyous occasion–but perhaps underscoring the persecution theme–Joseph read aloud a letter that John C. Bennett addressed to Orson Pratt and Sidney Rigdon, written in Springfield on January 10. Bennett claimed that Hancock County Sheriff "Jacob B. Backenstows [Backenstos]" would arrange to have Joseph rearrested on the old Missouri writ for murder, even though it had been ruled invalid. Pratt had loyally shown Joseph the letter, while Rigdon did not want it "known that he had any hand in showing the letter."[18] Joseph said he had already sent a message to Governor Ford that he would fight any further Missouri accusations.[19]

Joseph's dreams were particularly vivid during these tense days, and his fears were partly grounded in fact. In one, he dreamed he was being attacked in the lobby of the House of Representatives: "Some of the members who did not like my being there began to mar and cut and pound my shins with pieces of Iron. I bore it as long as I could, then Jumped over the rail into the hall, caught a rod of Iron and went at them cursing and swearing at them in the most awful manner and drove them all out of the house." Outside was "quite a collection … trying to raise an army to take me … I thought they would not have the privilege of getting me so I took a rod of Iron and mowed my way through." He interpreted its meaning at a council meeting

15. Joseph Smith, Diary, Jan. 18, 1843, in Faulring, *An American Prophet's Record*, 291.

16. Ibid., 292-93.

17. Scott G. Kenney, ed., *Wilford Woodruff's Journal, 1833-1898*, 2:212 (Jan. 17, 1843); hereafter Woodruff, *Journal*.

18. *History of the Church*, 5:252 (Jan. 18, 1843).

19. Faulring, *An American Prophet's Record*, 293.

on January 20: "To dream of flying signifies prosperity and deliverance from Enemies. Swimming in deep water signifies success among Many people. The word will be accompanied with power."[20] As his dreams reveal, Joseph's life was marked by dichotomies–anxiety was matched with certitude, pressure with the promise of release, depression with hope for a life beyond that of the earth.

On January 20, Joseph reinstated Orson Pratt in the Quorum of the Twelve at a meeting held at Brigham Young's home. The minutes reveal the Twelve's maneuvering for position among themselves, Pratt's personal humiliation, and Joseph's attempt to rewrite the story involving Pratt's wife with a scriptural parallel, comparing Pratt to Old Testament king David. Joseph argued that a majority of quorum members had not been present for Pratt's trial the previous August, so the action against him was not valid. Pratt testified that "he had rather die then go to preach in any other standing than I had before."[21] Young said that the only thing Pratt did wrong was love his wife more than "David" (presumably Joseph). Positioning this difficult present against a glorious future to diminish the current pain, Joseph said: "Orson I prophesy in the name of the Lord Jesus Christ that it will not be 6 month before you learn things whi[c]h will make you glad you have not left us. ... The latter part of your life shall be more Joyful than the former."[22] Although alluding to the privileges of plurality seems like ironic comfort, Joseph's instinct was correct that Pratt would respond favorably to the promise of reconnection through religious ritual.

Even more complicated was Joseph's assertion that Sarah Pratt had lied to Orson about Joseph's offering her a plural sealing. He insisted that his story was accurate–Orson had to believe Sarah lied–but he left Orson the loophole of not acting on it. "I will not advise you to break up you[r] family–unless it were asked of me [T]hen I would council you to [get] a bill [of divorce] from you[r] wife & marry a virtuous woman & raise a new family[,] but if you do not do it [I] shall never throw it in your teeth."[23] Did Joseph want to reestablish his reputation with his former friend? Was he genuinely outraged at Sarah's claims? If he had, in fact, made such overtures to Sarah in Orson's absence, had he now reconstructed a new version of reality? It is

20. Ibid., 293-94.

21. Quorum of the Twelve, Minutes, Jan. 20, 1843.

22. Ibid. See also Woodruff, *Journal*, 2:213 (Jan. 20, 1843): "Joseph confirmed them & ordained Orson Pratt to the Apostleship & his former standing which caused joy to our hearts."

23. Joseph Smith, qtd. in Gary James Bergera, *Conflict in the Quorum*, 35.

impossible to know for sure. But, contemporaneously, Joseph was proposing sealings with women in both direct and nuanced conversations. It was confusing since what women–or men–heard and thought they heard could produce other levels of potentially problematic understandings.

At 4:00 p.m. that same day, Joseph rebaptized Orson and Sarah in the icy river. They were reconfirmed as members of the Church, Orson's priesthood was restored, as were his apostleship and standing in the quorum. The turn of events, Wilford Woodruff wrote, "caused Joy to our hearts."[24] Amasa Lyman, who had been called to the Twelve to replace Pratt but had never been sustained by a conference vote, was made a member of the First Presidency so that Pratt could return to the Twelve as though he had never left.[25]

Above and beyond their spiritual mission, the members of the Twelve Apostles protected their prophet's interests. The alarming costs incurred during Joseph's recent legal affairs were compounded by unresolved debts related to real estate. Not long after the trial, the Twelve intervened, soliciting Church members to help clear their prophet's debts. Joseph had, they noted, "been … obliged to expend large sums of money in procuring his release from unjust persecution, leaving him destitute of the necessaries. … We therefore recommend that collections be taken at the various meetings for his benefits …"[26] Further, for his civic role as mayor, Joseph received $500 annually and a daily rate of $3 as court justice.[27]

It is impossible to know exactly when Joseph acted as prophet, as businessman/entrepreneur, or as an authorized agent for the Church, but dealing endlessly with real estate and business matters wore increasingly on him. Yet he was also exhilarated by the possibilities. "Nauvoo is the hub: we will drive the first spoke in Ramus, second in La Harpe, third Shokoquon, fourth in Lima: that is half the wheel," he said on March 4. "The other half is over the river: we will let that alone at present. We will call the Saints from Iowa to these [Illinois] spokes, then send elders over to convert the whole people."[28] Four days later, he rode eagerly into the countryside with a New York land agent.[29]

---

24. Woodruff, *Journal*, 2:212-23 (Jan. 20, 1843); see also Joseph Smith, Diary, Jan. 20, 1843, in Faulring, *An American Prophet's Record*, 294. Lydia Granger was also rebaptized that day and confirmed.

25. Bergera, *Conflict in the Quorum*, 34.

26. *History of the Church*, 5:249 (Feb. 11, 1843).

27. "An Ordinance Regulating the Fees, and Compensation of the Several Offices, and Persons Therein Mentioned," *The Wasp*, Jan. 28, 1843, 4.

28. *History of the Church*, 5:296 (Mar. 4, 1843).

29. Ibid., 299 (Mar. 8, 1843).

In Nauvoo, when the lines between Joseph's secular and spiritual activities were confusing at best, he functioned in an organizational hierarchy that located decision-making power in the group of men around him. The First Presidency and the Twelve shared his management of the city, of the Church, and the complicated relationships with outsiders. The next level included the Nauvoo City Council, the Nauvoo High Council, and the various local officers. These groups' memberships overlapped, with the same men frequently holding Church or civic positions simultaneously. But however organizational charts may have looked on paper, leadership stemmed from and revolved around the person of the Prophet Joseph.

Different from the skepticism that characterized the relationship between citizens and their government leaders so key to democratic processes, in Mormon Nauvoo, a certain level of trust ruled the day. For historian Timothy Wood, "Good secular leadership was not authoritarian; rather, it concerned itself with meeting the people's needs and protecting their rights. Indeed, Mormonism also affirmed much of the natural rights theory which undergirded the United States Constitution and Bill of Rights."[30] For Joseph, the most important functions of government were to protect individual freedom of conscience, to protect the lives of citizens, and to protect their property. The same was true of the laws of God. "We believe that religion is instituted of God; and that men are amenable to him, … unless their religious opinions prompt them to infringe upon the rights and liberties of others; but we do not believe that human law has a right to interfere in prescribing rules of worship to bind the consciences of men, nor dictate forms for public or private devotion …" (D&C 134:4). Scripture for Latter-day Saints, this declaration might have been a manifesto of government. Religion, like government, exists in part to secure rights and liberties, and to ensure the freedom of both person and soul. Thus, according to Wood, "implicit in LDS theology was the necessity for the religion to exist within a free society. If one was ultimately to be saved by their works in this life, one must be allowed the opportunity to perform those works. Existing alongside the church's more authoritarian tendencies, then, was also the expectation that Mormonism could only flourish in a society that was free."[31]

Joseph had already distanced himself somewhat from the Whig Party before 1843 began. The Democrats still saw use in courting his favor,

30. Timothy Wood, "The Prophet and the Presidency," 176.
31. Ibid., 177.

knowing the potential force in Mormon bloc voting. No one was more cognizant of this possibility than Joseph himself. Addressing a broad audience, Joseph penned a January 23 letter to the Nauvoo *Wasp* that seemed to contradict his earlier position on political involvement: "[A]s my feeling revolt at the idea of having anything to do with politics, I have declined, in every instance, having anything to do on the subject. I think it would be well for politicians to regulate their own affairs. I wish to be let alone, that I may attend strictly to the spiritual welfare of the Church."[32] Joseph's reversals could be dizzying in their speed and totality.

The *Quincy Whig* lamented Joseph's influence: "[T]his man who has acquired an influence over the minds of his people through the peculiar religious creed which he promulgates, is so repugnant to the principles of our Republican form of Government, that its consequences ... will be disagreeable to think of–bitter hatred and unrelenting hostility will spring up, where before peace and good will had an abiding place."[33] The congressional election that would be held in August 1843 promised to be a show down between those whom Joseph favored and those whom he opposed. His power in the election was as yet unknown, but a possibility to be taken seriously.

Joseph's resolution to stay out of politics lasted only a month. Speaking to workmen at the Nauvoo temple on February 21, he asserted, "'Tis right, politically, for a man who has influence to use it ..." Joseph saw this an obligation, "It is our duty," he said, "to concentrate all our influence to make popular that which is sound and good, and unpopular that which is unsound. ... From henceforth I will maintain all the influence I can get."[34] Overtly, Joseph was trying to keep the workmen focused on the temple and the Nauvoo House, but he applied the same logic to politics. Furthering the Lord's work was the core criterion for political involvement, the only persuasive argument for one political alliance over another.

Since 1841, Stephen Douglas had worked at a diplomatic relationship with Joseph. Douglas visited Nauvoo in May 1843 and dined with Joseph on May 18 in Carthage. Joseph found this audience irresistible, perhaps impressed both by Douglas's stature and willingness to deal fairly with the Church. William Clayton recorded the conversation of these two men, each powerful in his own way. Joseph returned to his familiar narrative

32. *History of the Church*, 5:259 (Jan. 23, 1843).
33. *Quincy Whig*, Jan. 22, 1842.
34. *History of the Church*, 5:286 (Feb. 21, 1843).

and delivered a three-hour history of the Missouri persecutions, including his journey to Washington, D.C., and his disappointment with President Martin Van Buren. Joseph deplored the "cold, unfeeling manner in which he was treated by most of the senators and representatives in relation to the subject."[35]

Clayton was also captivated by Douglas's persona and ability to echo Joseph's telling of the story of the Latter-day Saints. He described how the statesman listened carefully, perhaps gauging his response to his audience, then spoke "warmly in depreciation of the conduct of … the authorities of Missouri … and said that any people that would do as the mobs of Missouri had done ought to be … punished." Seizing the opportunity to plead his case to a sympathetic politician, Joseph issued a prophetic warning, according to Clayton's journal: "I prophecy in the name of the Lord God that in a few years this government will be utterly overthrown and wasted so that there will not be a potsherd left for their wickedness in conniving at the Missouri mobocracy."[36]

Nor was that Joseph's only prophecy. "Judge," he told Douglas, "you will aspire to the presidency of the United States; and if ever you turn your hand against me or the Latter-day Saints, you will feel the weight of the hand of Almighty upon you; and you will live to see and know that I have testified the truth to you; for the conversation of this day will stick to you through life."[37] Whether Douglas accepted the warning or not, Joseph made sure his implication was clear.

Historian George Gayler argues that Douglas, who surfaced repeatedly during the Nauvoo period, influenced Joseph's political thinking more than another contemporary figure.[38] When Douglas was justice of the Supreme Court of Illinois in 1841, he blocked Missouri's effort to extradite the Mormon prophet. Thomas Ford argued that Joseph was "inclined to esteem his discharge as a great favor from the democratic party."[39] If true, then Ford personally benefitted from Douglas's influence on Joseph, since he won the gubernatorial race of November 1842 by a margin of more than two to one.[40] The *Sangamo Journal* accused Joseph of collusion with the Democrats in its

35. Ibid., 393 (May 18, 1843).
36. Qtd. in Smith, *An Intimate Chronicle*, 104 (May 18, 1843).
37. *History of the Church*, 5:393-94.
38. George R. Gayler, "The Mormons and Politics in Illinois, 1839-1844."
39. Thomas Ford, *History of Illinois …*, 2:69.
40. Ibid., 70-71.

June 10, 1842, issue, and the *Warsaw Signal* on August 6, 1842, deplored the election: "The whole ticket was a mongrel affair, made up by agreement between Joe Smith and some anxious office-seekers, of one of the political parties [the Democrats]."[41] Joseph's power to persuade his followers to vote at will for the candidates of his choice seemed un-American to many, an unsavory misuse of religious power.

A second and equality problematic issue was the continuing debate over the legality of the Nauvoo Charter. Although it was modeled after the Springfield charter and other cities held similar powers, Ford's predecessor, Thomas Carlin, expressed alarm at the potential misuse the charter afforded Joseph.[42] Ford, too, had challenged the Mormon interpretation of the charter, favoring change by legislative repeal.[43] When Ford became governor in November 1842, the anti-Mormon party was ramping up efforts to repeal the charter. But in his December 1842 inauguration address, Ford met with resistance from his own party when he requested special powers to change the charter.[44]

Not long after Missouri Governor Thomas Reynolds visited Ford in St. Louis in June 1843, Sheriff Jacob Backenstos sent a secret missive to Joseph that Ford had no intention of arresting the Mormon leader if he could be guaranteed the Mormon vote.[45] Regardless of the faith the Saints may have placed in the misinformation, Missouri officers and a Hancock County constable arrested Joseph not long after on June 23 (see chap. 21). Cyrus Walker of Macomb was on the campaign trail as a candidate for Congress from the nearby Sixth District when the arrest occurred and seized the moment to offer Joseph his help. By Joseph's account, Walker "told me that he could not find time to be my lawyer unless I could promise him my vote. ... I determined to secure his aid, and promised him my vote."[46]

The Congressional election of August 7, 1843, demonstrated the danger

41. "Let Him that Readeth Understand," *Sangamo Journal*, June 10, 1842; www.sidneyrigdon.com/dbroadhu/IL/sang1842.htm#0610; 12/20/2009; "Election," *Warsaw Signal*, Aug. 6, 1843, www.sidneyrigdon.com/dbroadhu/IL/sign1842.htm#0806 (Dec. 20, 2008).

42. Thomas Carlin, Letter to Emma Smith, Sept. 7, 1842.

43. Robert B. Flanders, *Nauvoo*, 230.

44. Ibid., 233; John E. Hallwas and Roger C. Launius, eds., *Cultures in Conflict*, 83; Glen M. Leonard, *Nauvoo*, 307.

45. Gayler, "The Mormons and Politics in Illinois," 55. Ford, *History of Illinois*, 317-18, later claimed that this pledge originated with an unnamed Democratic leader without his approval. Ford, *History of Illinois*, 2:151, claimed that the offer "produced a total change" among Mormon voters from Whigs to Democrats.

46. Flanders, *Nauvoo*, 233.

in attempting to wield such blatant political control. Walker assumed he had Joseph's support. The Democratic candidate, Joseph P. Hoge, knew of Walker's claim.[47] However, with the election heating up, Joseph gave a rousing 4th of July address that deepened the ambiguity: "With regard to elections, some say all the Latter-day Saints were together, and vote as I say. But I never tell any men how to vote or whom to vote for."[48]

Both Walker and Hoge campaigned actively in Nauvoo between July 29 and August 1, 1843. The last day he was in town, Hoge and Hyrum Smith "called at the office, when Hoge acknowledged the power of the Nauvoo Charter habeas corpus. Esquire Walker gave a stump speech at the stand until dusk, and was immediately replied to by Esquire Hoge for over two hours, having lit candles for the purpose to hear them politically castigate each other."[49] The habeas corpus had been key in Joseph's avoiding extradition, so Mormon voters approved Hoge's position.

As editor, John Taylor used the *Nauvoo Neighbor* as a platform to come out in favor of Hoge: "It can answer no good purpose that half the citizens should disfranchise the other half, thus rendering Nauvoo powerless as far as politics are concerned."[50] The election was five days later.

On Sunday, August 6, the day before the election, Joseph began his Sunday sermon by asserting, "I am not come to tell you to vote this way, that way, or the other. In relation to national matters, I want it to go abroad unto the whole world that every man should stand on his own merits." But after the disavowal of partisanship, he hinted that he had decided to vote for Walker. "The Lord has not given me a revelation concerning politics," he insisted. "I am a third party, and stand independent and alone." He then differentiated his personal political views from divine revelation, but the distinction was probably lost on most of his listeners. He said that Hyrum had a "testimony to the effect it would be better for the people to vote for Hoge." When Joseph added, "and I never knew Hyrum to say he ever had a revelation and it failed," the intent of his message was unmistakable.[51] Despite the coyness, Joseph could not have been surprised when critics concluded he was trying to play it both ways.

Obviously not a neutral bystander, William Law, according to Ford,

47. Ibid., 235.

48. *History of the Church*, 5:490 (July 4, 1843).

49. Joseph Smith, Diary, Aug. 1, 1843, in Faulring, *An American Prophet's Record*, 401.

50. "For the Neighbor," *Nauvoo Neighbor*, Aug. 2, 1843, 2.

51. Ibid.; *History of the Church*, 5:526 (Aug. 5, 1843).

challenged the validity of the revelation publicly. Others may have done so in private.[52] Law, claiming that Joseph had promised Walker as many as nine out of every ten LDS votes, denounced Joseph's actions as "trickery."[53] However, Hyrum's "revelation" was enough to sway the Mormon vote, and Hoge defeated Walker in Hancock County, 2,088 to 733.[54] The result was devastating for Democrats and, over time, for Mormons as well because of the enmity created on both sides of the political spectrum. The Mormon vote was not an expression of individual preferences but of collective will. Both parties would try to use Joseph, but neither would ever trust the Mormon prophet again.

52. Ford, *History of Illinois*, 2:161.
53. Lyndon W. Cook, "William Law, Nauvoo Dissenter," 58.
54. Gayler, "Mormons and Politics in Illinois," 57.

CHAPTER 17

"The Long-Looked-for Place"

When within five or six miles of this place, we heard the agreeable cry, "Nauvoo to be seen," the long-looked-for place; every eye was stretched toward the place, as you may be sure our eyes gazed with delight, but astonishment, to see the great extent of it.

–John Needham, "Letter from Nauvoo,"
Millennial Star *4, no. 6 (Oct. 1843): 87*

For the thousands of eager new Mormon converts, like John Needham, who crossed the Atlantic Ocean then traveled by wagon and river boat to Nauvoo, the Mormon boomtown was the "long-looked-for place." As Needham wrote to his family after arriving in 1843:

> The extent of the city is four miles, laid out in lots and streets in nice order; I mean that each house has a piece of land attached to it, either a quarter, half, or whole acre … and some more, which makes the houses appear scattered. For two miles square the city is covered that way, but in the center, near the temple, they are quite close like other towns. If all the houses were put together like other places, they would make a large place; I should think twice or thrice the size of Warrington.[1]

Nauvoo's growth was a constant source of pride to Joseph. Settlement stretched in each direction and leaped across the river to Iowa. Expansively, he welcomed converts flooding into the city–nearly 1,614 through 1842 and, during the early months of 1843, another 769.[2] Each boatload of converts that arrived at Nauvoo's docks enlarged this Illinois branch of Zion. Joseph's advice to them was practical and theological, as he interpreted Zion and their place in it.

Each convert proved the efficacy of the Church's message, and Joseph

1. John Needham, "Letter from Nauvoo," *Millennial Star* 4, no. 6 (Oct. 1843): 87-88.
2. Robert B. Flanders, *Nauvoo*, 58.

welcomed them with warmth and enthusiasm. On April 12, 1843, he cheered the arrival of Parley P. Pratt and his family–wife Mary Ann and a daughter, born just days before–as well as several new members from England,[3] and could not refrain from shedding tears.[4] Pratt had arrived with his family at New Orleans early in January 1843 after completing his mission in England and after ten weeks at sea on the *Emerald.*[5] They traveled upriver for a week until Chester, Illinois, eighty miles from St. Louis.[6] The only news Pratt had heard of Nauvoo was reports that Joseph had been honorably discharged in Springfield. The incident, Pratt wrote, was but "one more malicious lawsuit … in which the rulers have been disappointed and bloodthirsty men have lost their prey …"[7] He had also heard that William Smith, the prophet's younger brother, was a state legislator, and that two bills proposing to revoke the Nauvoo City Charter had failed. "It grieves the enemies of the Saints very much," Pratt concluded, "to see them enjoying political privileges in common with others, and every exertion is made to hinder the progress of a people and of principles which they consider as already becoming too formidable to be easily trampled under foot."[8]

Pratt left his family in Chester and traveled the 280 miles to Nauvoo on horseback, riding eight days in winter weather. "I was astonished to see so large a city all created during my absence," he remembered, "and I felt to rejoice."[9] He brought his family to Nauvoo when the weather improved in April.

Joseph's remarks at the landing that day characterized his mythic vision of Zion. "I most heartily congratulate you on your safe arrival at Nauvoo," he said in his cheery way, "your safe deliverance from all the dangers & difficulties you have had to encounter but you must not think your tribulations are ended." He advised incoming Saints how to get situated, what to seek or avoid, and reminded them to turn to God for help. He highlighted the significance of this sacred place "appointed for the oracles of God to be revealed."[10] Recorded by Willard Richards, the speech combines secular and sacred themes in ways that typified how converts blended into the existing community. Like Pratt's interpretation of local events, Richards emphasized

3. *History of the Church*, 5:354 (Apr. 12, 1843).
4. Ibid.
5. Parley P. Pratt, *Autobiography*, 326.
6. Ibid.
7. Ibid.
8. Ibid., 327.
9. Ibid.
10. Joseph Smith, Diary, Apr. 13, 1843, in Scott H. Faulring, ed., *An American Prophet's Record*, 361, 362.

the sacredness of place, the positioning of Nauvoo in a larger religious drama, and the thin line between God's heaven and Joseph's earth.

Key to the way Joseph framed the Saints' experience as he welcomed each boatload, the city was central to the way they assimilated. Nauvoo was a place, he said, where "a crowd is flocking from all parts of the world of different minds, religions, &c. there will be some who do not live up to the commandments; & there will be designing characters who would turn you aside & lead you astray." Unscrupulous speculators would be ready to bilk them of their property. He counseled them to get advice from Church leaders, not outsiders. "Some start on the revelations to come here & get turned away & loose all, & then come, and enter their complaints, to us when it is too late to do any thing for them." Be careful at first, he advised. Our object in asking you to come to Nauvoo, he reminded them, "has been to bring you from Sectarian bondage." "We have brought you into a free government"–"free from Bondage. taxation–oppression. free in every thing if he [his listeners] conduct himself honestly & circumspectly with his neighbor–free in a Spiritual capacity."[11] This is where God's kingdom was being built.

New members must learn to put ego and selfishness aside for the benefit of the group. The quintessential tension of the American experience between individualism and community had a unique Latter-day Saint coloration here. "You must have a oneness of heart in all things," Joseph instructed. "You shall be satisfied one way or the other with us before you have done with us! ... We have been praying for you all winter, from the bottom of our hearts. We are glad to see you. We are poor and cannot do by you as we would, but will do all we can."[12]

Then turning to matters of business, Joseph navigated his audience toward practical considerations of where they would live: "'Tis not to be expected that all can locate in the city. There are some who have money and who will build and hire others. Those who cannot purchase lots can go out in the cou[n]try. The farmers want your labor. No industrious man need suffer in this land."[13] Implying that hard work was both a guarantee of success and proof of righteousness, Joseph gave them the chance to dig in and do the Lord's work as well.

Regarding the stickier issue of land purchase for an audience of poverty-stricken newcomers, he said, "Suppose I sell you land for $10 per acre and

11. Ibid., 361.
12. Ibid., 362.
13. Ibid.

I gave $3.45 per acre then you are speculating [says one]. Yes, I will tell you how. I buy other lands and give them to the widow and the fatherless. … I speak to you as one having authority that you may know when it comes and that you may have faith and know that God has sent me."[14] The mundane, sometimes messy, work of a prophet (he called himself "the buckler of Jehovah") was tied unavoidably to the exigencies of the modern world.

Real Estate

Land deals continued to complicate Joseph's daily round of work in 1843. In part a methodology for growing the Church and constructing Zion, such activities also gave Joseph the chance to narrate the Church. Shokoquon resident John B. Cowan offered Joseph another chance for land speculation on February 10 in a series of negotiations that suggest how such deals could be reciprocal. Cowan asked Joseph to send a "talented Mormon preacher" to come to their town twenty miles to the north in Henderson County, offering a house and promising to "accord him liberty." Joseph set out for Shokoquon on February 15 with two apostles–Orson Hyde and Parley P. Pratt–and Cowan to look at the available land. They bundled up with blankets and jackets to travel by sleigh in the "extremely cold" winter. Over dinner that night, Joseph made a lengthy "exposition of Millerism" and bunked with Cowan. Despite the fact that Hyde and Pratt's sleigh apparently turned over and Hyde "hurt his hand," they viewed the available lots. Joseph, who had not seen the site, said it was "a very desirable location for a city," but nothing ever came of the offer.[15] While there, Joseph preached to a "large and attentive audience" for two hours, "and proved to the people that any man that denied himself as being a prophet was not a preacher of righteousness."[16]

Converts looking for farms were particularly interested in tracts outside Nauvoo's limits. However, Joseph discouraged settling in Iowa, urging new arrivals to locate in Illinois. His motivations were partly political. At April 1843 general conference, Joseph reminded the Saints that Iowa's writ for his extradition still hung "as a cudgel [i.e., club] over my head. … I will therefore advise you to … come away and leave them, come into Illinois, and let the Iowegians take their own course." He disclaimed any "wish to control you; but if you wish for my advice, I would say, let every man, as soon as he conveniently can, come over here; for you can live in peace with us. We are

14. Ibid., 363.
15. *History of the Church*, 5:277 (Feb. 15, 1843).
16. Ibid., 278.

all green mountain boys–Southerners, Northerners, Westerners, and every other kind of 'ers,' and will treat you well: and let that governor know that we don't like to be imposed upon." He insisted, "I would not buy property in Iowa territory: I consider it stooping to accept it as a gift."[17]

In addition to his grudge against Iowa, Joseph had also been burned in a bad land deal. In August 1842, James Remick, described by Joseph as a "stranger in this city," claimed that Isaac Galland had transferred to him the Church's deeds. Remick tried to trade favors with Joseph for the land he had bought from Galland. "You paid Galland the notes," he said, "and ought to have them; they are in my hands as his agent, and I will give them up."[18] It is likely that Remick's true motive was to get Joseph to endorse Keokuk, Iowa, as a location for Mormon converts to purchase land. He promised to transfer the papers to Joseph in exchange. But by April 1843's general conference, half a year later, "I have since found that he is swindling," Joseph reported, "there is no prospect of getting anything from him."[19]

Joseph fumed over Galland's fraudulent titles in the "Half-Breed Tract" and announced that "every wise and judicious person as soon as he can dispose of his effects, if he is not a half-breed, will come away. I wish we could exchange some half-breeds and let them go over the river. If there are any that are not good citizens, they will be finding fault tomorrow with my remarks. … I do not wish for the Saints to have a quarrel there."[20]

Joseph's business affairs with Horace Hotchkiss had deteriorated as well and were threatening to implode. On February 23, 1843, Joseph instructed his clerk to stop paying taxes on the Hotchkiss purchase, described in 1841 as "the most sickly part of Nauvoo"[21] but also featured the "best steamboat land." In fact, by the end of the summer of 1843, Joseph's records no longer mentioned Hotchkiss and Joseph had obviously given up on leveraging real estate brought into the Church by new members to satisfy the debt. Despite his efforts to distance himself from the land trade, Joseph contradictorily wanted to keep his monopoly on land purchases by newcomers. "We have claim on your good feelings for your money, to help the poor," he asserted, "and the church debts also have their demands to save the credit of

17. Ibid., 334 (Apr. 6, 1843). By "Green Mountain Boys," Joseph was alluding to his Vermont birthplace and the Revolutionary War unit led by the legendary Ethan Allen (1738-89).

18. Ibid., 335 (Apr. 6, 1843).

19. Ibid.

20. Ibid., 336.

21. Ibid., 4:408 (Aug. 25, 1841).

the church. ... We have the highest prices, [the] best lands, and do the most good with the money we get."[22]

Inexperience and poor management ran parallel to revelation, theological development, and the social evolution of the Church. Joseph's efforts to build Zion were both strengthened and sabotaged by the roles he played. Being prophet did not protect him from ordinary reversals but compounded his confusion over his own judgment.

According to LDS historian Glen Leonard, the members of the Church who built their homes on the Hotchkiss syndicate land filed deeds with the county. But because Joseph had been unable to pay off the debt, Hotchkiss still held the deed. Choosing to be flexible rather than to foreclose on the land and push the settlers out of their new homes, Hotchkiss offered them the option of leasing the land. "Joseph Smith left the matter with the Twelve," according to Leonard. "Financially strapped, in a depressed national economy, the optimistic hopes of paying the debt fell far short. The investors in the Hotchkiss syndicate trusted their buyers but failed to realize the anticipated profit on their initial investment."[23]

Instead, Joseph turned his attention to finishing the building projects he had begun besides the temple: the Mansion House and the Nauvoo House, the hotel he envisioned would be "a delightful habitation for man, and a resting place for the weary traveler" (D&C 124:60). Since 1839, the Smith family had lived in the Homestead, a log-and-frame house on the west side of Main Street and south of the intersection with Water Street. It must have been crowded with Joseph and Emma, their four children, usually two or more hired girls, and almost always a stream of visitors: sick and ailing Saints, curiosity seekers, and individuals queuing up to meet the prophet.

South of the Smith home, the Mississippi flowed, and across the street was the site of the Nauvoo House hotel. Joseph donated the land himself, established the Nauvoo House Association, and issued stock certificates that the Saints could purchase in minimum amounts of fifty dollars. Reflecting the structure's importance to the spiritual and temporal mission of the Church, Lucien Woodworth and William Weeks (the Nauvoo temple architect) designed the three-story building with two wings intersecting at a right angle, while maximizing the street elevation on Main Street and at the edge of the Mississippi River. Construction began in the spring of 1841,

22. Ibid., 5:356.
23. Glen M. Leonard, *Nauvoo*, 167. See also Flanders, *Nauvoo*, 128-36, 171-75.

progressed slowly in fits and starts, and remained unfinished at Joseph's death. Positioned strategically in front of a steamship port, the Nauvoo House had a rusticated stone foundation level and more finished red-brick upper levels. Like so many other buildings of the period, finishing details included brick pilasters, elaborate lintels over windows and doors, and the formality of a building influenced by the popular Greek Revival style. Joseph repeatedly coupled the Nauvoo Hotel with the temple in sermons, seeing support for both as a sort of loyalty test that divided the faithful from the lackluster.

Both a money-making scheme and a symbol of the need to engage with the world, the Nauvoo House became emblematic of waning enthusiasm for certain of Joseph's ambitious projects requiring sacrifice in a financially strained environment. For historian William Mulder, the "twin symbols of [Nauvoo's] sacred and secular character were the temple and a hostelry." Joseph, "in his usual combination of the visionary and the practical, gave the enterprise the twin force of revelation and incorporation," as he organized the construction project and its financial support.[24] However, despite the force of revelatory mandate, the Nauvoo House lagged as money, time, and manpower consistently drained off to the temple. The Nauvoo House only reached the foundation walls when the Mormons evacuated Nauvoo in 1846.[25]

That summer of 1843, Joseph added a large two-story wing to the east end of the Mansion House to serve as the family home, and the Smiths moved in at the end of August.[26] Anticipating the increased scale of entertaining that Joseph and Emma were called upon to host, the new wing comprised on the main floor a new dining room and kitchen. The couple had always seemed to have had Saints living with them, for various reasons. The Mansion House expanded their capacity to host guests. Visitors and boarders were offered six single sleeping rooms on the second level and four double rooms on the next. Pending completion of the Nauvoo House, this larger home also functioned as a small hotel. Over the next several months, boarders included Eliza Snow, Eliza and Emily Partridge, and Maria and Sarah Lawrence; the latter four worked for their board and were quasi-hired girls and quasi-family members. Beneath the kitchen were a storage room, cellar space, and a second stove. The dining room could seat as many as fifty persons for special dinners

---

24. William Mulder, "Nauvoo Observed," 95.

25. David E. Miller and Della S. Miller, *Nauvoo*, 136. The cornerstone was laid on October 2, 1841, and pine for the project was harvested in Wisconsin. But competition with the temple and other local projects meant that it was definitely the less successful of the two projects.

26. *History of the Church*, 5:556.

such as that held to welcome Joseph back from Springfield after his trial. The Mansion House's stable could reportedly accommodate seventy-five horses.[27] Frequently, family and guests pushed the chairs and tables against the walls to make a space "for four sets of dancers in the old fashioned square dances," remembered Joseph III.[28] Emma loved to host such gatherings and had shopped in St. Louis for hotel furnishings and for dishes, table linens, and other accoutrements appropriate to the family's elite status.

As Church president and prophet, Joseph was sometimes required to rally forces impoverished by financial straits and weary with Zion-building efforts. More cheerleader than spiritual leader at such times, he strained for new arguments, shaming temple workers who resisted working on the Nauvoo House and who complained about limited pay. Joseph promised everyone who worked on either the temple or the Nauvoo House that they would eventually be paid for what they did despite his own poverty. His determination was fierce to finish the two projects as instructed, "for I began it & will finish it," he said, according to Willard Richards's notes.[29] Joseph had 300 men working primarily on the temple but sometimes also on the Nauvoo House.[30]

When critics questioned building a hotel when poor people were living down on the flats, Joseph indulged in a bitter outburst against "speculators" who say "how the Nauvoo house cheats this man & that man. … they are fools [who] ought to hide their heads in a hollow pumpkin & never take it out." Defensively, he asserted that "Bro Joseph in the name of the Lord [is engaged in these projects] not for his aggrandizement but for the good of the whole. … [E]very thing God does is to aggrandize his kingdom how does he lay the foundation? build a temple to my great name. and call the attention of the great. but where shall we lay our heads–an old log cabin."[31] Not finishing the hotel, Joseph predicted, would be the ruin of Nauvoo.[32] According to Wilford Woodruff, Joseph added: "If we did not build those buildings we might as well leave the place & that it was as necessary to build one as the other."[33] Critics of the Nauvoo House were probably in the audience, and included entrepreneurial competitors Robert Foster and Chauncey

27. Ibid., 6:33 (Sept. 15, 1843).

28. Mary A. Smith Anderson and Bertha A. Anderson Hulmes, eds., *Joseph Smith III and the Restoration*, 73.

29. Joseph Smith, Diary, Feb. 21, 1843, in Faulring, *An American Prophet's Record*, 308.

30. Ibid.

31. Ibid.

32. Joseph Smith, qtd. in Scott G. Kenney, ed., *Wilford Woodruff's Journal, 1833-1898*, 2:218 (Feb. 21, 1843).

33. Ibid.

and Francis Higbee, who by next spring would join dissidents in challenging Joseph's overall leadership. More than a demanding, expensive construction project, the Nauvoo House became a dividing point for those beginning to question Joseph's prophethood.

The hotel, the development of the waterfront, and even the purchase of a steamboat–the *Maid of Iowa*–demonstrate Joseph's understanding of the opportunity posed by the river. Historian Dennis Rowley places Nauvoo's development in the context of the American transportation revolution that opened the West to settlement and tied national and local economies into a connected whole. The opportunities afforded by the river were immense. In fact, according to Rowley, when "Nauvoo was founded, the steamboat industry of the Mississippi Valley was at the threshold of its golden era." On average, ten steamboats a week passed Nauvoo during spring, summer, and fall. By 1843, four or five boats stopped daily at Nauvoo.[34] Smaller boats brought an array of commercial goods as well as visitors and immigrants. On July 4, three separate steam boats docked, carrying between 800 and 1,000 visitors from St. Louis, Quincy, and Burlington.[35] On May 3, Joseph had ordered that the *Maid of Iowa* be converted to a ferry, carrying passengers between Nauvoo and Montrose.[36] The river also brought down rafts of cut timber for both the temple and Nauvoo House from the Wisconsin forests. In November 1843, Joseph proposed a petition to Congress for funds to excavate a canal around the Des Moines Rapids or over "the falls, or a dam to turn the water to city, so that we might erect mills and other machinery."[37] The city council voted to give Joseph as mayor and his "successors" power to build a dam, docks, wharves, and landings, and whatever associated structures were needed "for the purpose of propelling mills."[38] Its only attempt to fund the project was to allow an exchange of fees between the mill operation and the tolls/fees charged for the use of the water itself.

By May 1843, Joseph was sending conflicted messages, insisting that the temple be built while challenging members of the temple committee who protested Joseph's diversion of funds for his personal use. The responsibilities of providing for his family, promoting the Church, and constructing sacred architecture posed contradictions, difficult to resolve. "Told the Temple committee that I had a right to take away any property I chose from the Temple

34. Dennis Rowley, "Nauvoo: A River Town," 255.
35. *History of the Church*, 5:491 (July 4, 1843).
36. Ibid., 380 (May 3, 1843).
37. Ibid., 6:80 (Nov. 23, 1843).
38. Ibid., 106; see also Rowley, "Nauvoo: A River Town," 264.

office or store, and they had no right to stand in the way. It is the people who are to dictate me, and not the committee. All the property I have belongs to the Temple; and you have no authority only as you receive it from me."[39]

According to the instructions in Joseph's revelation of 1833 about the layout of the sacred city of Zion, the temple site was off center.[40] However, according to the sweep of Nauvoo's geography, it was in the center, rising from the bluff to overlook the city. Central also to the unfolding of revelation that seemed to pour from Joseph like a river, the temple symbolized how Joseph led his followers to turn their attention to heaven and to their future lives as gods. The city did not have the feeling of a riverfront foothold creeping up the bluff but a series of concentric circles moving outward from the temple. The temple illustrated its "primacy as the major architectural endeavor of the new Zion." In fact, architectural historian Laurel B. Andrew asserts, "much less attention was given to domestic buildings, which were small and quite primitive."[41]

By early 1843, the walls of the temple reached only twenty feet into the air but were still high enough to suggest the space they would eventually contain.[42] The building's design articulated Joseph's hierarchical system of priesthood authority and ordering of heaven into celestial, terrestrial, and telestial kingdoms. This ordering spoke to a particular understanding about heaven, the relationship of human beings to God, and Joseph's role in the last days. The carved images of sun, moon, and stars appeared elsewhere on tombstones and other religious architecture; on the Nauvoo temple facade, they assumed a particularly potent restoration meaning.

Masonic Hall

Nauvoo's Masons began by meeting in the upper chamber of Joseph's red brick store before they had a building of their own. A notable achievement in the growing city was the construction of a building reserved for Masonic ritual. Hyrum Smith presided at the cornerstone ceremony in June 1843.[43] A special committee, chaired by Lucius Scovil, managed construction, and the building, designed by William Weeks, was completed ten months later. At the dedication on April 5, 1844, Joseph boasted to the more

39. *History of the Church*, 5:382 (May 5, 1843).

40. "An explanation of the plot of the city of Zion, sent to the brethren in Zion, the 25th of June, 1833," *Times and Seasons* 6, no. 2 (Feb. 1, 1845): 786-87.

41. Laurel Blank Andrew, *The Early Temples of the Mormons*, 59.

42. Ibid., 82.

43. *History of the Church*, 5:446 (June 25, 1843).

than 550 Masons present that there were visitors with them "from various parts of the world." When he finished, "a procession was formed, which was accompanied by the Nauvoo brass band."[44] Mark Carnes suggests the fanfare that accompanied Masonic activities marked a search for meaning and unity. Regardless of whether the ceremony was performed in front of an altar or as a procession through the center of town, Masons "were convinced that the yearning to search was widespread and profound, and … conveyed through successions of religious ceremonies and mystical symbols."[45] The Church's patriarch and brother to the prophet, Hyrum, as worshipful Master, conducted the ceremonies.

Afterwards the group met at the Masonic Hall.[46] Ebenezer Robinson later described one of the hall's main-floor chambers as a theater. Undoubtedly, the performance element in Masonry was part of its appeal for Joseph, with others attracted to the chance for male friendship and the performance of male values. But Robinson was offended by the secret ritual: "Heretofore, the church had strenuously opposed secret societies," he lamented. But "after Dr. [John C.] Bennett came into the Church a great change of sentiment seemed to take place."[47] True, Bennett had demonstrated a proclivity for the theatrical before he came to Nauvoo. But he was not the only man in Nauvoo attracted to Masonry's blend of myth and brotherhood. In the face of poverty and the displacement the Saints felt from mainstream society, Masonry promised men a chance to taste hierarchy, to rise through the ranks of Masonic ritual, and to step from the world that was visible into one that was not. Heady, irresistible, the seeming complement to the religious rites that Joseph was introducing in Nauvoo, the Masonic lodge joined men in yet another type of bond that stretched beyond family to a larger community.

The Pineries

Complicating Joseph's campaign to finish the Nauvoo House was the failed effort to establish a business in the Wisconsin "pineries." Ironically, the pinery, not the hotel, was, for a time, the most productive enterprise sponsored by the Nauvoo House Association.[48] Despite difficulties experienced by the second company to travel to Wisconsin, on July 18, 1843, George

44. Ibid., 6:287 (Apr. 5, 1844).

45. Mark Carnes, *Secret Ritual and Manhood in Victorian America*, 31.

46. Samuel H. Goodwin, *Mormonism and Masonry*, 34.

47. Ebenezer Robinson, "Items of Personal History of the Editor," *The Return* 2, no. 6 (June 1890): 287.

48. Flanders, *Nauvoo*, 183.

Miller "arrived [in Nauvoo] with 157,000 feet of lumber, sawed shingles, ... about 170,000 feet in all," and other material for the temple and Nauvoo House. Miller reported that he had met with success: signed contracts. Until 1846, the Church could purchase claims against the company for their value in lumber. "All that is wanting," Miller said, "is hands."[49] But while Miller engineered the pineries to the point of potential success, Lyman Wight jeopardized the association by mismanaging its finances in Nauvoo. Miller questioned Wight's judgement, which he considered tainted by drink. Critical Nauvoo House documents had gone missing while Wight traveled to the East. "No investigations of Nauvoo House books yet," Willard Richards wrote sourly to Brigham Young in July 1843, "Joseph says little about it."[50] Joseph and Hyrum recommended that Miller take Wight back to Wisconsin and away from worldly temptations.[51]

Wight soon rallied, however. He expanded the community of Saints working at the pineries, making room for women and children. By the end of the year, new houses and plowed fields exhibited their industry. Still, the savage winter of 1843-44 drained their resources and will. Miller, Wight, and the other leaders promoted the idea of closing the pineries.[52] Despite the high hopes, the project was more difficult, costly, and challenging than anyone anticipated.

Governing Zion

The building of Zion was the Mormon version of the good society. Brokering real estate deals, controlling crime, and exercising spiritual gifts were all elements. On February 6, 1843, Nauvoo's voters unanimously reelected Joseph mayor of Nauvoo.[53] Five days later, Joseph made his inaugural address after nine city councilors were first sworn in: Hyrum Smith, John Taylor, Orson Hyde, Orson Pratt, Sylvester Emmons, Heber C. Kimball, Benjamin Warrington, Daniel Spencer, and Brigham Young.[54] Joseph instructed the council to relieve "the city from all unnecessary expenses and burdens, and

49. George Miller, qtd. in Willard Richards, Letter to Brigham Young, July 18, 1843, in *History of the Church*, 5:512.

50. Ibid.

51. Ibid.

52. *History of the Church*, 6:255-57.

53. Ibid., 5:264 (Feb. 6, 1843). The Nauvoo City Charter stipulated: "All free white male inhabitants who are of the age of twenty one years, who are entitled to vote for state officers, and who shall have been actual residents of said city sixty days next preceding said election shall be entitled to vote for city officers." "Nauvoo City Charter," in John E. Hallwas and Roger D. Launius, eds., *Cultures in Conflict*, 22.

54. *History of the Church*, 5:270 (Feb. 11, 1843).

not attempt to improve the city, but enact such ordinances as would promote peace and good order; and the people will improve the city ... and Nauvoo would become a great city."[55] Joseph predicted that "if the council would be liberal in their proceedings they would become rich."[56] Joseph's faith in government was immense. Clever about influencing the system to his own benefit, he saw the advantage of the rule of law in creating the good society.

Joseph again insisted on Nauvoo's autonomy: "We stand in the same relation to the state as the state does to the union ...," he told the city council on February 25. "Shall we be such fools as to be governed by its [Illinois] laws, which are unconstitutional?"[57] In this extraordinary speech, Joseph, asserting his unique vantage point as prophet, re-interpreted the U.S. Constitution as a threshold or mediator between church and state. "The Constitution acknowledges that the people have all power not reserved to itself. I am a lawyer"–he was speaking hyperbolically–"I am a big lawyer and comprehend heaven, earth and hell, to bring forth knowledge that shall cover up all lawyers, doctors and other big bodies. This is the doctrine of the Constitution, so help me God."[58] Simultaneously claiming a law and a prophetic credential doubled his authority, but only for those who already saw him as a prophet.

Outsiders, who did not view Joseph as a prophet, pointed to Church dominance in all city offices–aldermen, councilors, and judges. In 1842, the *Times and Seasons* had claimed, "A large number of the officers of the *Nauvoo Legion;* several members of the *City Council,* both *Aldermen* and *Councillors;* and a large portion of the *Regents of the University;* are not members of any church–many of them are old citizens who resided here long before we were driven from Missouri." Outsiders had every opportunity, they insisted: "men of sterling worth and integrity," who did not "believe in our religion," could be elected to office in Nauvoo and make a contribution to the building of this new river town.[59] However, the day-to-day reality only a year later belied this claim.

As mayor, Joseph ran up against regulating the sale of liquor to reveal the inconsistencies of building a city and a religious community. While he openly preached against both the sale and production of liquor, he was Nauvoo's booster and advertisements ran regularly in the *Nauvoo Neighbor* for both beer and ale. Mayor John C. Bennett called a meeting charged by Joseph to propose regulating the sale of liquor by the drink except that prescribed by

55. Ibid.

56. Joseph Smith, Diary, Feb. 11, 1843, in Faulring, *An American Prophet's Record*, 302.

57. *History of the Church*, 5:289 (Feb. 25, 1843).

58. Ibid.

59. "Officers," *Times and Seasons* 3, no. 5 (Jan. 1, 1842): 646; see list of officers (638).

physicians.[60] Joseph's diary recorded a gift of wine from Jennetta Richards, the wife of Willard Richards; her mother had made it in England. Regardless of the Word of Wisdom, she considered the gift appropriate, perhaps because of Joseph's public ambivalence.[61]

Oliver Huntington reported another incident which reveals Joseph's attitudes toward liquor: "Robert Thompson was a faithful, just clerk for Joseph Smith the Prophet in Nauvoo, and had been in his office steady near or quite two years. Joseph said to brother Thompson one day, 'Robert I want you to go and get on a buss [bust],[62] go and get drunk and have a good spree. If you don't you will die.'" Huntington continued, "Robert did not do it. He was a very pious exemplary man and never guilty of such an impropriety as he thought that to be. In less than two weeks he was dead and buried."[63]

Joseph also had to confront other, less controversial issues of city governance. For example, on April 18, Joseph conversed with three Pottawattamie tribal chiefs who visited the city from across the river in Iowa.[64] They were upset because their livestock and other possessions had been stolen by local settlers, although the identity of the thieves was not apparent. "They had borne their grievances patiently," Joseph praised.[65] The next day, eight members of the Quorum of the Twelve met in Joseph's office. Among other items of business, Joseph "identified a site for a future music hall,"[66] which was subsequently constructed at the intersection of Woodruff and Young Streets.

Sidney Rigdon

Soon after John Bennett left Nauvoo, Joseph came to believe that Sidney Rigdon, Nauvoo's postmaster, was sharing the contents of his private correspondence with his enemies. "Few if any letters for me can get through the post office in this place, more particularly letters containing money, and matters of much importance," he had written to Horace Hotchkiss in November 1842. "I am satisfied that Sidney Rigdon and others connected with him have been the means of doing incalculable injury, not only to myself, but to the citizens in general."[67] On November 8, 1842, lining up support to call

60. *History of the Church*, 4:298, 299 (Feb. 15, 1841); Leonard, *Nauvoo*, 148.

61. Joseph Smith, Diary, May 3, 1843, in Faulring, *An American Prophet's Record*, 375.

62. Bust: "2.a. a drinking spree" (*Random House Historical Dictionary of American Slang*, vol. 1, s.v. "bust")

63. Oliver B. Huntington, "History of the Life of Oliver B. Huntington," 10.

64. *History of the Church*, 5:365 (Apr. 18, 1843).

65. Ibid., 365 (Apr. 18, 1843).

66. Ibid., 368 (Apr. 19, 1843).

67. Joseph Smith, Letter to Horace Hotchkiss, *History of the Church*, 5:195 (Nov. 26, 1842).

for Rigdon's removal, Joseph instructed Windsor P. Lyon to "make affidavits concerning the frauds and irregularities practiced in the post office in Nauvoo." Lyon gathered signatures in support of Joseph's interpretation of recent history to bring before U.S. Senator Richard Young.[68] Joseph made other attempts to have Rigdon dismissed in 1842 and 1843. On February 9, 1843, he wrote to Senator Young himself, claiming that "letters had frequently been broken open, money detained, and letters charged twice over, etc., etc." He urged the senator to "use his influence to have the present postmaster removed, and a new one appointed." And should the senator be casting about for a replacement, Joseph suggested: "I can only say that, if I receive the appointment, I will do my utmost to give satisfaction."[69]

Only two days later, on February 11, Joseph decided to reconcile with Rigdon, although his reasons for doing so are unclear. The two chatted briefly at the city council meeting, with Rigdon commenting ambiguously that he and his family were "willing to be saved." "Good feelings prevailed," Joseph wrote, "and we have shaken hands together."[70] Understandably, Rigdon's family would interpret the significance of this encounter differently. His son John W. later remembered: "Joseph Smith came to my fathers house a crying and wanted to shake hands with all the family and be good friends as they used to be he shook hands with all the family that was present."[71] Whatever good feelings emerged were temporary.

Richard Van Wagoner, Rigdon's biographer, argues that Rigdon was a key in preventing Missouri's proposed extradition of Joseph, while Joseph suspected Rigdon of colluding with Bennett's exposés.[72] Only six weeks later on March 27, Joseph again attacked Rigdon, claiming to act with "deep regret and poignant grief" since "it is again[s]t my principles to act the part of a hypocrite, or to dissemble in any wise whatever, with any man." Joseph said that he had "tried for a long time to smother my feelings, and not let you know, that I thought, that you were secretly and underhandedly, doing all you could, to take the advantage and injure me: but, whether my feelings are right or wrong, remains for Eternity to reveal." He accused Rigdon of cooperating with Bennett in "secret plottings & conniving." He again brought up the post office, and hinted darkly at "many other things which I have

68. *History of the Church*, 5:184 (Nov. 8, 1842).

69. Ibid., 266-67 (Feb. 9, 1843).

70. Joseph Smith, Diary, Feb. 11, 1843, in Faulring, *An American Prophet's Record*, 302.

71. John W. Rigdon, qtd. in Richard S. Van Wagoner, *Sidney Rigdon*, 316.

72. "Letter to Sidney Ridgon, Esq.," *Times and Seasons* 4, no. 3 (Dec. 15, 1842): 33-36, qtd. in Van Wagoner, *Sidney Rigdon*, 317-19.

kept locked up in my own bosom."[73] Amazingly, considering the breadth of the accusations, he also suggested mending the conflict, while simultaneously threatening, if Rigdon's response was unsatisfactory, to "publish my withdrawal of my fellowship from you to the Church … and demand of the conference a hearing concerning your case [on conviction of which] they will demand your [preaching] license."[74]

Willard Richards delivered the letter to Rigdon who immediately denied all charges.[75] In fact, Rigdon countered, Bennett had threatened him "severely," claiming that he "could do with me as he pleased, and that if I did not cease to aid you and quit trying to save 'my Prophet' as he calls you, from the punishment of the law, he would turn against me; and … in one of his speeches, made a violent attack on myself, all predicated on the fact that I would not aid him."[76] "I had hoped," Rigdon wrote, "that all former difficulties had ceased forever. On my part they were never mentioned to any person, nor a subject of discourse at any time or any place. I was tired of hearing of them."[77]

Joseph and Sidney briefly reconciled and arrived "arm in arm" at April's "special" conference, which was celebrating a metaphoric "Jubilee."[78] The Saints were seated on a platform built over the "rough" floor of the temple basement. The sun poured down "very warm and pleasant" into the roofless structure.[79] As usual, the Saints' officers were sustained, including Rigdon as Joseph's first counselor. The next day, Joseph, speaking privately to Rigdon, during a choir hymn, assured him: "This day is a Millennium. It is a millen[n]ium within these walls. There is nothing but peace."[80] Rigdon must have breathed more easily.

---

73. Joseph Smith, Letter to Sidney Rigdon, Mar. 26, 1843, in Dean C. Jessee, ed., *The Personal Writings of Joseph Smith*, 580-81.

74. *History of the Church*, 5:313-14 (Mar. 26, 1843).

75. A serialization of this material continued in the *Times and Seasons*, May 15, 1843 (193-94), June 1, 1843 (209-10), Aug. 15, 1843 (289-90), and Sept. 15, 1843 (320-21).

76. *History of the Church*, 5:313-14 (Mar. 26, 1843)

77. Ibid., 315-16 (Mar. 27, 1843).

78. Van Wagoner, *Sidney Rigdon*, 319.

79. Joseph Smith, Diary, Apr. 6, 1843, in Faulring, *An American Prophet's Record*, 342.

80. Joseph Smith, Diary, Apr. 7, 1843, in Faulring, *An American Prophet's Record*, 353.

CHAPTER 18

Narratives for a New Zion

God Almighty is my shield; and what can man do if God is my friend? I shall not be sacrificed until my time comes; then I shall be offered freely.
–Joseph Smith, History of the Church, *5:259 (Jan. 22, 1843)*

Regardless of the weight bearing down upon Joseph because of land speculation, the necessity of providing for newcomers flooding into his city, and other pressing business, it was the seemingly endless round of Church meetings–Sundays as well as the rest of the week–that most energized the Mormon prophet. These addresses provided the platform from which he developed his narrative of Zion and all that was required of the Saints to build the kingdom of God on Earth.

Those who believed in Joseph heard him differently from outsiders. Tied to their own identity, they interpreted his stories in ways that strengthened their own beliefs and that unified them as a church body. William Mulder notes, "Visitors were not prepared for a populist prophet whose vernacular speech differed strikingly from the formal eloquence of his published revelations."[1]

An "Observer" from Adams County, writing for the *Advocate* of Columbus, Ohio, witnessed the installation of new officers at Nauvoo's Masonic Lodge: "Never in my life did I witness a better-dressed or a more orderly and well-behaved assemblage." Contrary to his expectation that Joseph would be an "ignorant and tyrannical upstart," the reporter continued, he is a "sensible, intelligent, companionable and gentlemanly man … and has an interesting family."[2]

Reverend Samuel A. Prior, a Methodist minister, had reached Nauvoo

1. William Mulder, "Nauvoo Observed," 100.
2. *History of the Church*, 4:566 (Mar. 22, 1842).

with "no very favorable opinions of the Latter-day Saints" and had expected to "witness many scenes detrimental to the Christian character, if not offensive to society." There he listened to a sermon by Joseph, "that truly singular personage," delivered to an audience sitting in "breathless silence," hanging on his every word. In his use of scripture, Joseph "glided along through a very interesting and elaborate discourse, with all the care and happy facility of one who was well aware of his important station, and his duty to God and man, and evidencing to me, that he was well worthy to be styled 'a workman rightly dividing the word of truth.'"[3] Prior preached that evening with Joseph in the audience. Afterward, Joseph and he debated doctrine. Joseph did so "mildly, politely, and affectingly; like one who was more desirous to disseminate truth and expose error, than to live the malicious triumph of debate over me," Prior observed.[4] Prior left with a changed mind.

However, other outsiders could be harsher judges. A young, non-Mormon lawyer, Edwin de Leon, visited Nauvoo as a student during the summer. He was not impressed with the Mormon prophet, and noted that Joseph's "education was very limited. He was an awkward but vehement speaker. In conversation he was slow, and used too many words to express his ideas, and would not generally go directly to a point."[5] Later, de Leon wrote a story about Joseph for *Harper's* magazine. He remembered that Joseph "spoke very fluently, but ungrammatically, like an uneducated man; but he possessed the gift of a rough eloquence, and could be most persuasive when he tried."[6]

Not surprisingly, Parley P. Pratt disagreed:

> [It] abound[ing] in original eloquence peculiar to himself–not polished–not studied–not smoothed and softened by education and refined by art; but flowing forth in its own native simplicity, and profusely abounding in variety of subject and manner. He interested and edified, while, at the same time, he amused and entertained his audience; and none listened to him that were ever weary with his discourse. I have even known him to retain a congregation of willing and anxious listeners for many hours together, in the midst of cold or sunshine, rain or wind, while they were laughing at one moment and weeping the next.[7]

3. Samuel A. Prior, "A Visit to Nauvoo," *Times and Seasons* 4, no. 15 (May 15, 1843): 198.
4. Ibid.
5. Peter H. Burnett, *Recollections and Opinions of an Old Pioneer*, 66. Burnett would become California's first governor.
6. Edwin de Leon, *Thirty Years of My Life on Three Continents*, 57.
7. Parley P. Pratt, *Autobiography*, 46.

Brigham Young compared Joseph to "all the priests of the day," whom he found as "blind as Egyptian darkness." They "could not tell me anything correct about heaven, hell, God, angels, or devils." In contrast, Joseph "took heaven, figuratively speaking, and brought it down to earth; and he took the earth, brought it up, and opened up, in plainness and simplicity, the things of God; and that is the beauty of his mission."[8] Joseph stirred believers spiritually and made them believe anything was possible. Jared Carter acknowledged Joseph's sometimes awkward delivery, but emphasized the impact of his words: the "Holy Ghost Spoke in him and marvelous was the displays of the power of the Spirit."[9]

Sometimes when Joseph spoke, he built an argument for why those who heard him should believe him. At other times, he wove stories, helping the Saints to see that his narrative was theirs too. Both methods shared the purpose of convincing his audience, but argument depended on logic while story depended on verisimilitude. Both were positioned in religious historical time and space; both were particular to their shared experience. Joseph constructed the discourse that the Saints adopted to talk about religion but also about community, city-building, politics and government, and relationships among members, between members and outsiders, with God, and with Joseph himself. "Narrativity," R. Ruard Ganzevoort, explains, is "the story-like structure through which summoned authors experience and understand their lives, and by which they try to make, shape or break relationships, with the purpose of maximizing significance."[10] Joseph told his story to a particular audience, with a specific purpose.

Joseph's speeches and the discourse they established illuminate four components of religious narratives: (1) As author, Joseph was responsible for their construction; (2) He was also an actor in them; (3) He altered his stories "in such a way that the factual actions" of his life became acceptable; and (4) His narratives were characterized by hope and trust in God, a belief in continuing messages from deity. "Openness for transcendence is a fundamental element and a necessary substrate for a religious story," Ganzevoort notes. Joseph's audience judged "every story told, forcing the author [in this case, Joseph himself] to tell the story so that it is accepted as legitimate and plausible."[11] Finally, Joseph's purpose was sometimes to enhance social

8. Brigham Young, Oct. 7, 1857, JD 5:332.
9. Jared Carter, Autobiography, 17.
10. R. Ruard Ganzevoort, "Religious Coping Reconsidered," 262.
11. Ibid.

identity for members, but at other moments he wanted to convince his audience of the legitimacy of his story.

Philosopher Paul Ricoeur's notion of the "summoned self" captures the essence of Joseph's positioning himself as one who addresses God in response to a specific mission.[12] Joseph portrayed himself as God-summoned to restore an ancient religion and to marshal a chosen people to usher in the last days. In important ways, the religious story voices the prophet's response to God's demands. As Ganzevoort summaries: an "awareness of playing a role in the story of God marks the religious author … Awareness of God as part of the audience marks the religious audience and purpose."[13] Mormon convert Joseph L. Robinson identified just such elements: "There is a power and magesty that attends his [Joseph's] words and Preaching that we never beheld in any man before."[14] Zilpha Williams agreed: "Could you have seen him [Joseph] as I did, standing before the great congregation with a frank, open countenance beaming with intelligence, while his whole frame seemed animated with it and filled with love to his flock who hung with intense interest upon all he had to say to them."[15] Often rapt while listening to Joseph, Wilford Woodruff wrote, "There was more light made manifest at that meeting respecting the gospel and Kingdom of God than I had ever received from the whole Sectarian world."[16]

On Sunday, January 22, 1843, Joseph spoke at the temple stand on the relationship between prophets and the kingdom of God. "What Constitutes the kingdom of God?" he queried, apparently speaking without notes or outline. "Whare there is … an administrator who has the power of calling down the oracles of God, and subjects to receive those oracles no matter if there are but 3, 4, or 6 there is the kingdom of God."[17] Explaining the role of John the Baptist, Jesus Christ, and other prophets, Joseph differentiated the kingdom from "the fruits & blessings that flow from that kingdom; because their was more miracles, gifts, visions, healings, tongues &c in the days of Jesus Christ & the Apostles."[18] These understandings helped Joseph to comprehend his own role.

12. Paul Ricoeur, *Figuring the Sacred*, 262.

13. Ganzevoort, "Religious Coping Reconsidered."

14. Joseph L. Robinson, Journal, 22.

15. Qtd. in Mark L. McConkie, ed., *Remembering Joseph*, 208.

16. Scott G. Kenney, ed., *Wilford Woodruff's Journal, 1833–1898*, 1:9 (Apr. 27, 1834); hereafter Woodruff, *Journal*.

17. Franklin D. Richards, "Scriptural Items," at http://www.boap.org/LDSParallel/1843/27Aug43.html (June 1, 2013).

18. *History of the Church*, 5:258 (Jan. 22, 1843).

A week later, Joseph used the parable of the prodigal son to illustrate the consequences of a life of sin: "Servants of God of the last days myself & those I have ordained, have the priesthood & a mission–to the publicans & sinners–& if ... they are sinners & if they reject our voice they shall be damnded."[19]

Although Joseph spent the greatest amount of time in Nauvoo, he often met with the Saints in nearby towns, usually accompanied by parties of close companions. These meetings were critical in terms of unifying the Church, solidifying the loyalty of members, and expanding doctrine.

On February 16, Joseph spoke to a small group of family members and friends who dined in his home. In this informal discourse, he waxed metaphoric about the earth and its history, saying that it would some day become a "urim and thummin," a source of enlightenment regarding both past and present meanings and interpretations.[20]

At any given moment, Joseph juggled myriad social, religious, and political issues, matters of great importance to those involved, but priorities that challenged him both to set and manage. On Sunday morning, March 12, Joseph preached from John 14, directing the attention of the Church toward the dead: "in my fathers house are many mansions," he said, reminding his audience of the thin line between heaven and Earth and the work they had to bring the gospel message to all of God's children. The necessity of turning the hearts of the children to their fathers would be the Saints' great achievement in the temple.[21] Despite the need to speak, Joseph was not feeling well that day; but, according to Brigham Young, "he taut menne [many] grait [great] and glorious things."[22]

As he spoke in such settings, in what sociologists K. I. Pargament and C. L. Park term the "search for the sacred," Joseph's motives, as far as he evidently was concerned, were spiritual. But his speaking was accompanied by the "search for intimacy." He pulled audiences near, wrapping language around them like an affectionate embrace.[23] There must have been a parallel non-prophetic discourse for dealing with, say, planting gardens, tending livestock, or conversing with children. The fact that no record describes in any significant detail this mundane discourse suggests that, even in informal settings,

19. Franklin D. Richards, "Scriptural Items."

20. *History of the Church*, 5:279 (Feb. 16, 1843); D&C 130.

21. Joseph Smith, Diary, Mar. 12, 1843, in Scott H. Faulring, ed., *An American Prophet's Record*, 332.

22. Brigham Young, Diary, Mar. 12, 1843, in Ehat and Cook, *Words of Joseph Smith*, 168.

23. K. I. Pargament and C. L. Park, "Merely a Defense?," 13-32.

listeners must have sensed when Joseph was speaking in the prophetic mode. A formal setting would, of course, have been its own signal of authoritative discourse. Certainly, Saints in later reminiscences had a tendency to endow even slight matters communicated by their martyred prophet with significance. But perhaps it is also true that, in each encounter, Joseph sought to construct a coherent, consistent interpretation of his own experience to order that of the Saints and to remind them of their common purpose.

William Clayton accompanied Joseph to a worship service on Sunday, April 2, in Ramus, Illinois, and opened the meeting with prayer. As was true when Joseph visited surrounding branches, the room was packed. Joseph spoke from Revelation 5, which describes events to occur "rapidly" near the end of times. John's vision proposes that decisions made in heaven determine the course of human history. For Joseph, such events as the rise and fall of human government, the destiny of the world and humanity, and in particular the future of the Church seemed illumed by the text. This discourse continued in an evening session as well. So much of Mormonism was millennial in its rhetoric and expectations that the prophet's remarks necessarily had an apocalyptic immediacy: "I earnestly desired to know concerning the coming of the Son of Man and prayed, when a voice Said to me, 'Joseph my son, if thou livest until thou art 85 years old thou shall see the face of the Son of Man. Therefore let this suffice and trouble me no more on this matter.'" More important, for Joseph, he observed, "When he shall appear we shall see him as he is. We shall see that he is a Man like ourselves. And that same sociality which exists amongst us here will exist among us there only it will be coupled with eternal glory which glory we do not now enjoy." He denounced with conviction the idea that God and Christ dwell only in the human heart as "Sectarian" and "false."[24]

In both addresses, Joseph elaborated on his understanding of obscure scriptural concepts: "There are no angels who administer to this earth but who belong or have belonged to this earth. The angels do not reside on a planet" but in God's presence. God lives on a Urim and Thummin, which when purified will become like crystal, to be used to reveal "all things below it in the scale of creation, but not above it." The white stone mentioned in Revelation is a Urim and Thummin given to those who stand exalted in the Celestial Kingdom. He added descriptive details. The stone "is a small representation of this globe" upon which is written "a new name … which no

24. Joseph Smith, Diary, Apr. 2, 1843, in Faulring, *An American Prophet's Record*, 340, 339.

man knoweth save he that receiveth it. The new name is the key word."[25] For listeners, every sentence contained a new theological insight into heaven, a new understanding of a scripture. No wonder they hung on each word.

Parley P. Pratt, recalling one of Joseph's 1839 sermons, wrote that he spoke "in great power, bearing testimony of the visions he had seen, the ministering of angels which he had enjoyed; and how he had found the plates of the Book of Mormon, and translated them by the gift and power of God. ... The entire congregation were astounded; electrified, as it were, and overwhelmed with the sense of the truth and power of which he spoke, and the wonders which he related."[26] On another occasion, William Rowley wrote of Joseph: "We soon felt and knew we were listening to one that had not been taught of men–so different were all his thoughts and language."[27] "[A]ll ears were opened and the most profound silence was *observed,*" James Palmer added. "On *reflection* one would think [Joseph had] always [k]new *it,* [and] he ... *had* the appearance of *one* ... sent from the heavenly worlds on some divine miss[i]on."[28] Ricoeur describes the language Joseph used in these types of religious narrative as lying on the border between ordinary life and the spiritual realm.[29]

For Joseph, this kind of intelligence was at the heart of an individual's life on Earth. Indeed, he reiterated, "Whatever principle of intelligence we obtain in this life will rise with us in the resurrection; and if a person gains more knowledge in this life through his diligence & obedience than another, he will have so much the advantage in the world to come."[30] Knowledge, obedience, and action created an order that guaranteed salvation, laid out a consistent and purposeful movement through life, and imposed an obligation to those who desired faith. "There is a law irrevocably decreed in heaven," he taught, "before the foundation of this world upon which all blessings are predicated; and when we obtain any blessing from God, it is by obedience to that law upon which it is predicated."[31] God's grace blessed the lives of the Saints but did not erase how they actually lived their lives. Instead, they had to learn through their prophet what God wanted them to do.

25. William Clayton, Journal, Apr. 2, 1843, in George D. Smith, ed., *An Intimate Chronicle*, 96.

26. Pratt, *Autobiography*, 298-99.

27. William Rowley, Diary, Nov. 12, 1843, Special Collections, Marriott Library, University of Utah, Salt Lake City.

28. James Palmer, Reminiscences, 69; emphasis his.

29. Ricoeur, *Figuring the Sacred*, 262.

30. Clayton, Journal, Apr. 2, 1843, in Smith, *An Intimate Chronicle*, 96.

31. Ibid.

This knowledge–and obedience–were the only guarantees of celestial glory, and Joseph positioned himself as essential to their salvation.

Religious stories are laced with symbolic and metaphorical language, designed to help individuals access the transcendent. In Ramus, some twenty miles east of Nauvoo, Joseph related a dream that the government would ask him for aid, and from the western regions, he would lead a large force into battle. This dream led to a prophecy "in the Name of the Lord God that the commencement of bloodshed as preparatory to the coming of the son of man will commence in South Carolina,–(it probably may come through the slave trade.)–This the voice declared to me. while I was praying earnestly on the subject 25 December 1832."[32] In Ramus, the same day he spoke to a substantial group interested in his ability to inspire, Joseph listened to Orson Hyde preach on the Second Coming, privately correcting some doctrinal misunderstandings.[33] These corrections and a fuller exposition of the topic were later canonized as what is now LDS Doctrine and Covenants Section 130.

When crises hit Joseph, they occurred in a particular frame of reference that had evolved through multiple experiences and interpretations. His prophet-narrative helped to produce his response, reinforcing the ongoing construction of his identity as a modern prophet. Joseph situated each new crisis according to the defining stories of his life. Whether consciously or not, this device had the same intent: to produce coherence that would provide meaning.

At April 1843's "special" conference, Joseph switched from the Apocalypse to hostelry as the "the most important matter for the time being." Constructing the Nauvoo House was faltering under the "prejudice which exists against building it, in favor of the Temple. The church must build it or abide the result of not obeying the commandment." Tired of the criticism and lack of support, Joseph asked, "Are you satisfied with the first presidency, so far as I am concerned, or will you choose another? If I have done any thing to injure my character in the sight of men & angels–or men & women, come forward tell of it & if not ever after hold your peace."[34] Brigham Young leaped to his feet, nominating Joseph to continue in his role as president of the Church. Orson Hyde, seconded the nomination, and the group supported it with "such a show of hands [as] was never seen before in the church."[35]

32. Joseph Smith, Diary, Apr. 2, 1843, in Faulring, *An American Prophet's Record*, 340.
33. *History of the Church*, 5:323 (Apr. 2, 1843).
34. Joseph Smith, Diary, Apr. 6, 1843, in Faulring, *An American Prophet's Record*, 343.
35. Ibid.

In the afternoon session on April 6, Hyrum spoke first. Joseph followed, again delivering a litany of frustrations. "I despise a thief above ground," he said, without being more specific. "I'll wring a thief's neck off if I can find him, if I cannot bring him to Justice any other way." He talked about disputed land sales and about dishonest land traders, advising the Saints, "who have deeds & possessions, … [to] fight it out. you who have no deeds or possessions let them alone.–touch not a stick of their timber. … In the name of the Lord God, I forbid any man from using any observations of mine, to rob the land of wood."[36] His vernacular speech was perhaps more characteristic of a farmer than an Isaiah or a Jeremiah. But both were accurate descriptors of Joseph.

Before he sat down, Joseph switched topics again, whetting his listeners' millennial appetites with a typical blending of the spiritual and the profane. According to James Burgess, a recently arrived British convert, Joseph said that "no man knoweth the day or the hour when the Son of Man cometh." But that when he does come, it will be possible to see the sign in the "clouds of Heaven. … [As] the lighting up of the morning or the dawning of the morning cometh from the east and shineth unto the west–So also is the comeing of the Son of Man." In a metaphor that mixed the image of Jesus' coming with more generalized enlightenment, Joseph added, "It will be small at first and will grow larger and larger until it will be all in a blaze so that every eye shall see it."[37]

Joseph dated Jesus' second coming with a more concrete hint than was typical: "There are those of the rising generation who shall not taste death till Christ comes. … I prophesy in the name of the Lord God, and let it be written–the Son of Man will not come in the clouds of heaven till I am eight-five years old." Exposing the weight that prophethood placed on his life, Joseph concluded, "If I had not actually got into this work, and been called of God, I would back out. But I cannot back out, I have no doubt of the truth."[38]

On Friday morning, April 7, Joseph was hoarse from speaking too long the previous day. Vexed by people who had left the lengthy conference sessions early, Joseph announced: "It is an insult to the meeting."[39] In the afternoon session, Orson Pratt picked up on Joseph's theme of the Second Coming, resurrection, and transition of matter. Joseph, hoarse or not,

36. Ibid., 347.

37. James Burgess, Notebook, [n.d.], at http://www.boap.org/LDSParallel/1843/6Apr43(2).html (June 1, 2013).

38. *History of the Church*, 5:336 (Apr. 6, 1843).

39. Joseph Smith, Diary, Apr. 7, 1843, in Faulring, *An American Prophet's Record*, 352.

followed, correcting doctrinal errors. "If any one supposes that any part of our bodies, that is the fundamental parts thereof, ever goes into another body he is mistaken."[40] Using conference to elaborate on doctrine and clarify specifics, Joseph exhausted himself in the effort, pouring himself into the performance of his identity as a prophet.

As conference continued, high winds buffeted the Saints. Saturday morning, Joseph asked the choir to repeat its opening number, saying that the "tenor charms the ear–bass the heart." He then made "three requests" of listeners: "that all who have faith will exercise it, that the Lord may be willing to calm the wind." The second and third were for God to "strengthen my lungs" and "have the Holy Ghost to rest upon me."[41] Franklin D. Richards summarized Joseph's remarks but added his own response: "The reason why God is greater than all others IS He knows how to subject all things to himself Knowledge is Power."[42] The wind did not abate, and speakers shifted from "the East end of the temple walls to a temporary (and momentary) stand near the west end."[43] By then, the walls of the temple had risen to twelve feet above the floor.[44]

At regular Sunday morning services, April 16, Joseph again preached on the unity that should prevail and the importance of the gathering. It was a privilege to be "buried on the land where God has appointed to gather his saints together. Where there will be nothing but saints. [It is] where the Son will make his appearance and where they may hear the sound of the trump that shall call them to behold him. that the morn of the resurrection they may come forth in a body and come right out of their graves and strike hands /immediately in eternal glory/ and felicity rather/ than to be scattered thousands of miles apart.["][45]

Joseph revealed an intimate, domestic heaven: "if we learn how to live and how we die, when we lie down we contemplate how we may rise up in the morning. /It is/ pleasing for friends to lie down together locked in the arms of love, to sleep, and [awake] locked in each others embrace & renew their conversation." All who worship Jesus will be saved, he promised. "Those who have died in Jesus Christ, may expect to enter in to all that fruition of Joy when they come forth, which they have pursued here. So plain

40. Ibid., 355.
41. *History of the Church*, 5:339 (Apr. 8, 1843).
42. Franklin D. Richards, "Scriptural Items."
43. Joseph Smith, Diary, Apr. 8, 1843, in Faulring, *An American Prophet's Record*, 358.
44. Smith, *An Intimate Chronicle*, 538.
45. Joseph Smith, Diary, Apr. 16, 1843, in Faulring, *An American Prophet's Record*, 365.

was the vision I actually saw men, before they had ascended from the tomb, as though they were getting up slowly, they took each other by the hand. It was my father and my son, my Mother and my daughter, /my brother and my sister when the voice calls suppose I am laid by the side of my father. What would be the first joy of my heart?"[46]

For Joseph, this was the most important of meditations: "all the day & more than my meat & drink to know how I shall make the Saints of God to comprehend the visions that roll like an overflowing surge, before my mind." Joseph's desire that those around him understand him, and particularly this important truth, pressed heavily on his heart and mind. "O how I wo[u]ld delight to bring before you things which you never thought of, but poverty and the cares of the world prevent. But I am glad I have the privilege of communicating to you some things, which if grasped closely will be a help to you when the clouds /are/ gathering and the storms /are/ ready to burst upon you like peals of thunder. lay hold of these things & let not your knees tremble. Nor your hearts faint."[47]

A month later, on Sunday, May 14, Joseph expounded on knowledge and its relationship to salvation. According to Wilford Woodruff: "Knowledge through our Lord & savior Jesus Christ is the grand Key that unlocks the glories & misteries of the Kingdom of heaven."[48] Joseph condemned those who rejected a knowledge of the truth or who falsely professed to understand heaven. Instead, he exhorted his audience to "continue to call upon God until you make your Calling & election sure for yourselves by obtaining this more sure word of Prophesey & wait patiently for the promise until you obtain it."[49]

William Clayton's interpretation of the sermon positioned Joseph as heaven's gatekeeper because of the knowledge he received from God. "He shewed that knowledge is power & the man who has the most knowledge has the greatest power. Also that salvation means a man being placed beyond the powers of all his enemies. He said the more sure word of prophecy meant a mans knowing that he is sealed up unto eternal life by revelation & the spirit of prophecy through the power of the Holy priesthood."[50] This positioning strengthened Joseph's efforts to negotiate financial deals like those to fund the temple, while assuring compliance from followers.

46. Ibid., 366.
47. Ibid.
48. Woodruff, *Journal*, 2:231 (May 14, 1843).
49. Ibid.
50. Clayton, Journal, May 17, 1843, in Smith, *An Intimate Chronicle*, 103.

On May 16, Joseph returned to Ramus, accompanied by new plural wife Eliza Partridge with whom he spent the night at Benjamin Johnson's.[51] Eliza was again in the party that returned to Ramus later in May, but that night, Joseph slept with Benjamin's sister Almera.[52] In his sermon to the Saints, Joseph addressed the doctrine and practice of celestial marriage as well as other clandestine ordinances, with meanings clearer to some than to others:

> Except a man and his wife enter into an everlasting covenant and be married for eternity, while in this probation [life], by the power and authority of the Holy priesthood, they will cease to increase [propagate] when they die; that is, they will have no children after the resurrection. But those who are [so] married and continue without committing the sin against the Holy Ghost, will continue to increase and have children in the celestial glory. … In the celestial glory there are three heavens or degrees; and in order to obtain the highest, he must enter into this order of priesthood. … He may enter into the other, but that is the end of his kingdom: he cannot have an increase.[53]

Joseph was, in some ways, creating a stronger platform from which to expand the doctrine of plurality. But at the same time, he was making himself considerably more vulnerable to attack.

On May 21, Joseph spoke at the temple stand, pressing through the throng to reach the dias. He began with humor: "[T]here were some people who thought it a terrible thing that any body should exercise a little power." For his part, he thought it was terrible that anyone would make exercising power necessary.[54] He half-lamented: "I find my lungs failing–it has always been my fortune almost to speak in the open air to large assemblies."[55] Howard and Martha Coray's reported Joseph's definition of salvation as "for a man to be Saved from all his enemies even our last enemy which is death."[56] James Burgess added that Joseph used three grand keys to "unlock the whole subject. First what is the knowledge of God, Second what is it to make our calling and election sure. Third and last is how to make our calling and election sure."[57] According to Willard Richards, Joseph also returned to the

51. Smith, *An Intimate Chronicle*, 101.

52. Benjamin F. Johnson, Letter to George Gibbs, in Dean R. Zimmerman, ed., *I Knew the Prophets*, 40-44.

53. *History of the Church*, 5:391-92 (May 16, 1843).

54. Ibid., 400.

55. Joseph Smith, Diary, May 21, 1843, in Faulring, *An American Prophet's Record*, 378.

56. Howard and Martha Coray Notebook, 12, LDS Church History Library; *History of the Church*, 5:403 (May 21, 1843).

57. James Burgess, Notebook, qtd. in Ehat and Cook, *Words of Joseph Smith*, 209.

theme of his role as prophet. "Many think a prophet must be a great deal better than any body else." In reality, Joseph explained, "I love that man better who swears a stream as long as my arm, and administering to the poor & dividing his substance, than the long smoothed faced hypocrites."[58]

The next month, Joseph spoke autobiographically, comparing himself to the stones produced for the temple. "I [am] a rough stone," he claimed, "the sound of the hammer and chisel was never heard on me."[59] He also elaborated on the gathering, interpreting passages from the scriptures that spoke of postmortal life and Godhead.[60] Then he touched on other familiar topics: baptism for the dead, washings and anointings, the importance of the temple. "If a man gets the fullness of God he has to get [it] in the same way that Jesus Christ obtain[ed] it & that was by keeping all the ordinances of the house of the Lord."[61] He brought his remarks to a conclusion by tying the temple's construction to the establishment of Zion. "[W]hy gather the people together in this place For the same purpose that Jesus wanted to gather the Jews, to receive the ordinances the blessings & the glories that God has in store for his Saints. And I would now ask this assembly and all the Saints if they will now build this house & receive the ordinances & Blessings which God has in store for you, or will you not build unto the Lord this house & let him pass by & bestow these blessings upon another."[62] Eliza R. Snow said Joseph spoke "beautifully and in a most powerful manner," exhorting his people "to be diligent–to be up and doing lest the tabernacle pass over to another people and we lose the blessing."[63]

On July 15, Joseph took on a pleasure ride to Quincy on board the *Maid*

58. Joseph Smith, Diary, May 21, 1843, in Faulring, *An American Prophet's Record*, 378.

59. Joseph Smith, Diary, June 11, 1843, in Faulring, *An American Prophet's Record*, 383.

60. *History of the Church*, 5:423-27 (June 11, 1843).

61. Woodruff, *Journal*, 2:240 (June 11, 1843).

62. Ibid., 240. Joseph had said in an earlier discourse, "I have no enmity. I have no desire but to do all men good. I feel to pray for all men. We don't ask any people to throw away any good they have got. We only ask them to come and get more." Qtd. in Woodruff, *Journal*, 2:217 (Jan. 22, 1843). Preferring to avoid bitter disagreements, he said in June 1844: "When things that are great are passed over with[ou]t. even a tho[ugh]t, I want to see all in all its bearings & hug it to my bosom–I bel[ieve]. all that God ever rev[eale]d. & I never hear of a man being d[amne]d for bel[ieve]g. too much but they are d----d for unbel[ief]." Thomas Bullock, Report, June 16, 1844, in Ehat and Cook, *Words of Joseph Smith*, 381. Heber C. Kimball elaborated in December 1845: "Those who come in here and have received their washing & anointing will l[ater] be ordained Kings & Priests, and will then have received the fullness of the Priesthood, all that can be given on earth. For Brother Joseph said he had given us all that could be given to man on the earth." Heber C. Kimball, Journal, Dec. 26, 1845, qtd., in Andrew F. Ehat, "Joseph Smith's Introduction of Temple Ordinances and the 1844 Mormon Succession Question," 147.

63. Eliza R. Snow, Journal, June 11, 1843, in Beecher, *The Personal Writings of Eliza R. Snow*, 76.

of Iowa with his family and perhaps another hundred friends.[64] On June 2, he had paid Dan Jones "two notes for $1,375" to purchase half ownership in the boat. They moved slowly downstream, accompanied by a band.[65] It was on days like this that Nauvoo seemed most beautiful, an ideal home to the Saints and the location of Zion. The gentle slope reaching to the bluff where Joseph could imagine the temple's finished profile, a view he would never see in life. The town's straight streets and sturdy homes promised security, prosperity, and righteous lives. The Mississippi itself promised growth and fecundity. Success in this most recent venture at kingdom building seemed guaranteed.

The next day, Sunday, Joseph was in a contrary mood. According to Willard Richards, Joseph "said he would not prophesy any more; Hyrum should be the prophet; (did not tell them he was going to be a priest now, or a king by and by;) told the elders not to prophesy when they go out preaching."[66] To Brigham Young, Richards added a few details: Joseph preached "all day" from Matthew 27 using it to hint about "secret enemies in the city–intermingling with the Saints &c."[67]

Charlotte Haven, a bright and skeptical non-Mormon visiting Mormon relatives, saw this sermon as primarily a political ploy: "Our Gentile friends say that this falling of the prophetic mantle on to Hyrum is a political ruse. Last winter when Joseph was in the clutches of the law, he was assisted by some politicians of the Whig party, to whom he pledged himself in the coming elections. Now he wants the Democratic party to win, so Hyrum is of that party, and as it is revealed to him to vote, so go over all the Mormons like sheep following the bell sheep over the wall."[68]

Joseph waited a week, then again switched signals. "Last Monday morning," he said, "certain brethren came to me and said they could hardly consent to receive Hyrum as prophet, [or] for me to resign." He scoffed, "But I told them, I only said it to try your faith; and it is strange, brethren, that you have been in the Church so long, and not yet understand the Melchizedek Priesthood." He left this last enigmatic and presumably guilt-producing comment without elaboration but intensified the confused Saints' discomfort by complaining about his burdens as their leader:

---

64. *History of the Church*, 5:510.

65. Ibid., 417-18 (June 2, 1843).

66. Ibid., 512 (July 16, 1843).

67. Willard Richards, Letter to Brigham Young, July 16, 1843, qtd. in *History of the Church*, 5:512 (July 18, 1843).

68. Charlotte Haven, "A Girl's Letters from Nauvoo," *Overland Monthly*, 2d ser., 16, no. 96 (Dec. 1890): 636.

> It has gone abroad that I proclaimed myself no longer a prophet. I said it last Sabbath ironically; I supposed you would all understand. It was not that I would renounce the idea of being a prophet, but that I had no disposition to proclaim myself such. But I do say that I bear the testimony of Jesus, which is the spirit of prophecy. … I am under the necessity of bearing the infirmities of others, who, when they get into difficulty, hang on to me tenaciously to get them out, and wish me to cover their faults. On the other hand, the same characters, when they discover a weakness in Brother Joseph, endeavor to blast his character. … Men often come to me with their troubles, and seek my will, crying, Oh, Brother Joseph, help me! help me! But when I am in trouble, few of them sympathize with me, or extend to me relief. I believe in the principle of reciprocity, if we do live in a devilish and wicked world where men busy themselves in watching for iniquity, and lay snares for those who reprove in the gate. … Friendship is the grand fundamental principle of Mormonism, to revolution[ize and] civilize the world, … [to] pour forth love. Friendship is like [the metals bonded by] Brother [Theodore] Turley in his Blacksmith shop welding iron to iron; it unites the human family with its happy influence. I do not dwell upon your faults, and you shall not upon mine.[69]

At this point, he had talked himself into a better mood. Moved by the devotion of those who stood by him, he said, "No greater love than that a man lay down his life for his friends. I discover 100s & 1000s–ready to do it for me." The unity he felt with the Church was strong. "Let me be resurrected with the Saints whether to heaven or hell or any other good place–good society."[70]

Joseph next spoke at the funeral of Judge Elias Higbee on August 13.[71] Higbee's funeral pulled from Joseph a sketch of the world's end and the Church's future, articulating one of the most important doctrinal developments of the Nauvoo period. Willard Richards noted: "Elijah the prophet … shall reveal the covenants of the fathers in relation to the children, and the covenants of the children in relation to the fathers." Joseph described four "destroying angels holding power over the four quarters of the earth until the servants of God are sealed in their foreheads, which signifies sealing the blessing upon their heads, meaning the everlasting covenant, thereby making their calling and election sure. When a seal is put upon the father

69. *History of the Church*, 5:516-17 (July 23, 1843).
70. Ibid.
71. Ibid., 529-31 (Aug. 13, 1843).

and mother, it secures their posterity, so that they cannot be lost, but will be saved by virtue of the covenant of their father and mother."[72] Richards added a vivid comment about Joseph's intensity on this topic: "The president was much exhausted."[73]

As was his usual practice, Joseph spoke freely and extemporaneously that day. He told his audience, "I am not like other men, my mind is continually occupied with the business of the day, and I have to depend entirely upon the living God for everything I say on such occasions as these."[74]

Important to the way Joseph taught plurality and wove it into the generational theology was the relationship between generations. He suggested in this discourse, in veiled ways, the promise of innumerable, faithful progeny in relationships bound by sacred covenants. Repeatedly, Joseph reiterated the importance of sealing, of the connection between children and their fathers/parents, an order that would eventually be reflected in the celestial kingdom after the Millennium had begun. Hierarchical in every way, with the Father and Jesus at the pinnacle, Joseph positioned himself as next in authority and responsibility, thereby implying parallel positions as possible for the faithful who participated in the necessary ordinances. Israel Barlow spoke to what he understood to be the family component at the heart of plurality:

> In all the Kingdoms of the world you will find that there will be only one King. All will be governed as one great family; and every man will preside over his own family. ...You and your children will rise up and administer to your children and children's children, and you will rule over your posterity, and they may increase into tens, hundreds, thousands, and millions. Yet all will finally join with Adam, who will be King of all under Christ. ... This is the order of the Kingdom of Heaven, that men shall rise up as Kings and Priests of God. We must have posterity to rule over.[75]

Joseph seems to have promised that blessings passed through the sealing ordinance between parents and children were guaranteed unconditionally.

But Joseph communicated homey concerns as well. He berated some

---

72. Ibid., 530 (Aug. 13, 1843). Elias Higbee was the father of Chauncey and Francis Higbee, who, the previous year, had fomented problems for Joseph over his plural marriage teachings. Joseph seems to be saying here that the faithfulness of parents may trump, in some ways, the sins of their children.

73. Joseph Smith, Diary, Aug. 13, 1843, in Faulring, *An American Prophet's Record*, 405.

74. The language of this comment does not appear in Joseph Smith, Diary, Aug. 13, 1842, in Faulring, *An American Prophet's Record*, 403, but is in *History of the Church*, 5:529.

75. Ora H. Barlow, *The Israel Barlow Story and Mormon Mores* (Salt Lake City: Author, 1968), 212.

young men who had sat on the ground reserved for the sisters and who "laughed and mocked during meeting."[76] He criticized recent election results, then inexplicably lashed out once more at Sidney Rigdon. The good feeling of April 1843's conference when he had shared a "millennial" feeling of peace with Rigdon (see chap. 17) had not lasted long. Now, in August, he completed his sermon but, reminded in some unspecified way of what he saw as Rigdon's failings, stood back up and charged: "[T]here is a certain man in this city who has made a covenant to betray and give me up to the Missourians, and that, too, before Governor Carlin commenced his persecutions. That man is no other than Sidney Rigdon. This testimony I have from gentlemen from abroad, whose names I do not wish to give. I most solemnly proclaim the withdrawal of my fellowship from this man, on condition that the foregoing be true; and let the Saints proclaim it abroad, that he may no longer be acknowledged as my counselor; and all who feel to sanction my proceedings and views will manifest it by uplifted hands."[77] According to Rigdon's biographer, Richard S. Van Wagoner, Joseph was reacting to a false report by Orson Hyde. Already suspicious about Rigdon, Joseph too readily believed what he heard, even though Van Wagoner makes the case that Rigdon "was innocent."[78]

Rigdon responded by showing Joseph a letter dated August 20, 1843, from Carlin demonstrating Carlin's understanding that Rigdon was loyal to Joseph.[79] Unconvinced, Joseph scoffed at the letter during his sermon the next day: "The letter … is one of the most evasive things, and carries with it a design to hide the truth." Rigdon himself spoke that same day in response: "I never … exchanged a word with any man living on the subject [of betraying Joseph]. I ask pardon for having done anything which should give occasion to make you think so."[80]

The public record of this all-too-public drama gives an impression of swift stroke and counter-stroke; but Mormon historian Dean Jessee warns that, regardless of Joseph's careful scribes, in reality "the records do not

76. Clayton, Journal, Aug. 13, 1843, in Smith, *An Intimate Chronicle*, 116.

77. *History of the Church*, 5:531-32 (Aug. 13, 1843). According to Clayton, Journal, Aug. 13, 1843, in Smith, *An Intimate Chronicle*, 116: "He then showed that Sidney Rigdon had bound himself by an oath to Governor Carlin to deliver J[oseph] into the hands of the Missourians if he could & finally in the name of the Lord withdrew the hand of fellowship from him and put it to the vote of the people."

78. Richard S. Van Wagoner, *Sidney Rigdon*, 320-21.

79. Thomas Carlin, Letter to Sidney Rigdon, Aug. 20, 1843, qtd. in ibid.

80. *History of the Church*, 5:554, 556 (Aug. 27, 1843). Joseph Smith, Diary, Aug. 27, 1843, in Faulring, *An American Prophet's Record*, 409.

measure up to the stature of the life they chronicle, and only a fraction of the Prophet's discourses was preserved." According to Jessee, between January 1843 and June 1844, Joseph delivered seventy-eight public addresses, at least one a week. Over his lifetime, he most likely gave 450-plus sermons, but "the lack of reported speeches by Joseph Smith prior to 1842 illustrates the dictum 'No records, no history.' Without question," Jessee concludes, "this lack limits our understanding of the development of his thought."[81] Jessee's observation is a sobering reminder of the tentativeness of our interpretations.

81. Dean C. Jessee, "Priceless Words and Fallible Memories," 22, 23.

CHAPTER 19

Interlude: An Indispensable Doctrine

> *... those who are married by the power & authority of the priesthood in this life and continue without committing the sin against the Holy Ghost will continue to increase and have children in the celestial glory.*
>
> *–Joseph Smith, qtd., in William Clayton, Journal, May 16, 1843, in George D. Smith,* An Intimate Chronicle, *102*

As Joseph continued in 1842-43 to introduce plurality to an expanding circle of men and women, he coupled it with the practice of "sealing": worthy Latter-day Saint husbands and wives could be married, or sealed, for eternity by proper priesthood authority, a radical rethinking of the marriage relationship. These "eternal marriage sealings" could be performed for couples who were alive as well as for those whose spouse had died.[1]

Much of plurality's discourse was veiled in coded language. Key words like "new and everlasting covenant of marriage" shielded the movement into ritualized plural relationships and permitted Church leaders to tell a sort of "truth" about it while denying that polygamy existed. This clarification was understood by some but certainly not by everyone in the 1840s. Later accounts draw a distinction. "Polygamy, in the ordinary and Asiatic sense of the term, never was then and is not now a tenet of the Latter-day Saints. That which Joseph and Hyrum denounced ... was altogether different to the order of celestial marriage including a plurality of wives. ... Joseph and Hyrum were consistent in their action against the false doctrines of polygamy and spiritual wifeism ..."[2]

1. See Andrew F. Ehat, "Joseph Smith's Introduction of Temple Ordinances and the 1844 Succession Question," 59-62. It should be pointed out that Joseph continued to approve the performance of strictly civil marriages in Nauvoo even as he broadened the scope of eternal and celestial marriages.

2. "Joseph Smith and Celestial Marriage," *Deseret News*, May 20, 1866, rptd. in *Woman's Exponent* 15 (June 15, 1886): 10.

Joseph had learned from the Bennett affair the importance of secrecy. Indeed, the blanket of secrecy Joseph threw over the practice of plurality and the explanations he devised to convince the faithful of its importance created a matrix of meanings. Anthropologist Clifford Geertz describes culture as a type of matrix: "an historically transmitted pattern of meaning embodied in symbols."[3] In this context, Joseph as prophet symbolized what was possible for others as well as human communication with God. In fact, Joseph's claim as the sole source of authority placed him indisputably at the center of the Mormon endeavor. Anyone who threatened his authority, ultimately, moved to the edge and possibly out of fellowship. The Saints' belief in Joseph's authority demarcated the boundary between the righteous and the apostate.

However clear this line may have been to insiders, the purpose was equally apparent: to conceal, obscure, and provide plausible deniability. The circumlocutions were heroic, if also tangled. Until 1852, when the practice was publicly announced in Salt Lake City by Orson Pratt, on Brigham Young's authorization, plurality was hidden by language that meant a variety of things but rarely the full truth. Once Joseph had taught supporters the "patriarchal order of marriage" or "celestial order of plurality of wives," plurality existed among and was practiced by the Saints. To say anything otherwise was less than the truth. The consequences of this word game were costly, resulting in a loss of trust from the American public, the disillusionment of formerly devoted followers, and complex familial networks struggling to make sense of parsed meanings and complications in the decades after the prophet's death.

Joseph had apparently taken his next most recent plural wife, Martha McBride, in August 1842.[4] Then the furor caused by Bennett's defection made the subject even more explosive. For the next six months, the prophet evidently did not venture again into plurality. That changed in early 1843, when he resumed his master-ritual; and before the year's end, he married at least seventeen more women, one in February, eight in the spring, five in the summer, and three in the fall.[5] Two were already married, adding to the number of putative polyandrous unions. The other fifteen women were never-married between ages fourteen and fifty-eight.

With plurality discussed in private, it was perhaps inevitable that the

---

3. George Geertz, *The Interpretation of Cultures* (New York: Basic Books, 1973), 89.

4. Martha McBride Kimball, Affidavit, July 8, 1869, Joseph F. Smith Affidavits Books, 2:36; 3:36

5. Todd Compton, *In Sacred Loneliness*, 6.

doctrine would take strange shapes in the minds of those who depended on gossip for information. Joseph himself, some members of the Nauvoo High Council, and other leaders who had been personally introduced to the doctrine worked to untangle truth from fiction, navigating seas of lies designed to hide the practice.

Emma's Dilemma

Emma was in an impossible dilemma. Her prophet-husband taught her that plurality was essential for salvation, but she could not, as a wife and a believer, accept Joseph's revelation as divine. Non-Mormon outsider from New Hampshire, Charlotte Haven spent a year in Nauvoo with her brother and his wife, writing letters home about the many curiosities of the city and her time spent with Joseph and Emma Smith. Haven described Emma as subordinating her sense of self to Joseph:

> Sister Emma … is very plain in her personal appearance, though we hear she is very intelligent and benevolent, has great influence with her husband, and is generally beloved. She said very little to us, her whole attention being absorbed in what Joseph was saying. He talked incessantly about himself, what he had done and could do more than other mortals, and remarked that he was a "giant, physically and mentally." In fact, he seemed to forget that he was a man. I … suppose he has good traits. They say he is very kind-hearted, and always ready to give shelter and help to the needy.[6]

Regardless of the trouble plurality caused, Joseph defended Emma and stayed loyal to her. Brigham Young was not so magnanimous, and years later told a Utah audience: Emma "will be damned as sure as she is a living woman. Joseph used to say that he would have her hereafter, if he had to go to hell for her, and he will have to go to hell for her as sure as he ever gets her."[7]

Orson Pratt also remembered Emma seeming to rage against Joseph as he pushed against the limits of traditional marriage: "at times [she] fought against him with all her heart; and then again she would break down in her feelings … and would then lead forth ladies and place their hands in the hands of Joseph."[8] Emma found a confidante in William Law, for a time Joseph's counselor in the First Presidency, with whom she shared her distress.

6. Charlotte Haven, "A Girl's Letters from Nauvoo," *Overland Monthly*, Dec. 16, 1890: 623; http://olivercowdery.com/smithhome/1880s-1890s/havn1890.html (Jan. 29, 2009).

7. Brigham Young, Aug. 9, 1874, JD 17:159.

8. Orson Pratt, Oct. 7, 1869, JD 13:194.

As more and more of Joseph's inner circle became polygamy insiders, Emma's circle of friends grew increasingly compromised.[9] Law, who did not share Joseph's enthusiasm for the doctrine, later alleged that Emma would sometimes complain about Joseph keeping "young wives in her house and elsewhere, and his neglect of her." Law claimed she "spoke freely about the revelation and its threats against her life. … She seemed to have no faith in it whatever." He also reported Joseph "said his wife Emma had annoyed him very much about it, but he thought the revelation would cause her to submit peacefully, as it threatened her removal if she did not." Although Law helped to spearhead the resistance that led eventually to Joseph's death, his account has the ring of truth. It is reasonable to believe that Emma struggled with plurality and that it brought her to a line she feared to cross.[10]

Both Brigham Young and Orson Pratt talked about the arguments between Joseph and Emma and what plurality implied for her. When Hyrum first showed her a dictated revelation on the subject in mid-1843, her instinct was to destroy it, as if ruining the draft would run the doctrine out of her life. Fortunately, Young stated, "Joseph had wisdom enough to take care of it, and he handed the revelation to Bishop [Newel K.] Whitney, and he wrote [i.e., copied] it all off. After Joseph had been to Bishop Whitney's he went home, and Emma began teasing for the revelation. She said–'Joseph, you promised me that revelation, and if you are a man of your word you will give it to me.' Joseph took it from his pocket and said–'Take it.' She went to the fire-place and put it in, and put a candle under it and burnt it, and she thought that was the end of it."[11]

The fissures that plurality caused in Joseph's household were impossible to bridge completely. Questions about dealing fairly with those whom he cared most deeply about were complicated by the overlay of jealousy, competition, differences in age and temperament that already colored Joseph and Emma's relationship. The result was a situation at least one of them found impossible to endure.

Emma's role in building Zion was related to Joseph's role as prophet.

9. See William Law's affidavit, in Charles A. Shook, *True Origin of Mormon Polygamy*, 132. See also W. Wyl's interview with Law in Thomas Gregg, *Prophet of Palmyra*, 508.

10. William Law, Affidavit, in Shook, *True Origin of Mormon Polygamy*, 132.

11. Brigham Young, Aug. 9, 1874, JD 17:159. Orson Pratt's version is more critical of Emma: "But what became of the original? An apostate destroyed it; you have heard her name. … That same woman has brought up her children to believe that no such thing as plurality of wives existed in the days of Joseph, and has instilled the bitterest principles of apostasy into their minds …" Pratt, Oct. 7, 1869, JD 13:194.

Her identity became, at least in part, a function of his, and the demands of his work and personality required her patience and forgiveness. Joseph knew that he tested Emma's goodness, especially when he married women from among their own circle of friends. He depended on Emma's integrity of spirit. He worked around Emma, sometimes keeping her in the dark, and other times calming her until her tears ceased. It mattered greatly that Emma support him in his life-altering demands. She had significant potential for stirring up trouble for Joseph with Nauvoo's women. Still, the one thing Joseph knew for sure was that his first wife was a good woman, dedicated to hm as prophet, to their marriage, and to the Church.

The 1843 Plural Wives

Joseph's first plural union of 1843 may have been to thirty-three-year-old Ruth Vose Sayers, perhaps sealed to him in February 1843.[12] Sometime during the same spring (date not known), he was also apparently sealed to sixteen-year-old Flora Ann Woodworth. Her mother, Phebe, had joined the Relief Society on May 13, 1842,[13] and her father, Lucien, worked on the Nauvoo House as both designer and construction manager. Flora attended the common school of William Woodbury.[14] Although the primary motivation for this marriage may have been dynastic, it is also true that physical attraction played a role. William Clayton noted at least two carriage rides in which Joseph and Flora were alone, on May 2 and June 1. There may have been other encounters as well. This teenager's youth must have been a telling affront to Emma, almost thirty-nine, worn by ten pregnancies and the tension required to maintain normalcy in the midst of doctrinal evolution. How could she not feel discarded, betrayed?

Despite Joseph's attention, Flora did not refuse the company of nineteen-year-old Orange Wight, one of Apostle Lyman Wight's sons. Once, as they strolled along a Nauvoo street in the spring of 1843, Joseph pulled up alongside them in his carriage and invited them to join him for a ride through the countryside. They spent a pleasant afternoon, passing by the temple lot and eventually stopping in front of the Woodworth house. After all three had entered, Flora's mother took Orange into a private room to confide, as

12. See Ruth Vose Sayers, Affidavit, Joseph F. Smith Affidavits, May 1, 1869. See also Andrew Jenson, Papers, ca.1871-1942, Ms 17956, box 49, fld. 16, fifth document, LDS Church History Library.

13. Relief Society, Minutes, May 13, 1842.

14. Lyman D. Platt, ed., "Nauvoo School Records," *Nauvoo Journal* 1 (1989): 16.

Orange recalled, the unthinkable–Flora was already one of Joseph's wives.[15] "I was aware or believed that Eliza R. Snow and the two Partridge Girls were his wives," Orange reported years later, "but was not informed about Flora. But now Sister Woodworth gave me all the information necessary, so I knew Joseph Believed and practiced Polygamy." Orange delivered a "mild lecture" to Flora, then "left her and looked for a companion in other places and where I could be more sure."[16] The layering of such encounters must have confused those outside the secret, but others, like Orange, suspected long before they received confirmation of the sacred but secret practice.

William Clayton records that Emma went to the Woodworth home with Joseph on August 23, 1843, but when they returned, she threw an angry fit over a gold watch that Joseph had given to the young woman. Two days earlier, Emma had asked Clayton about two letters Eliza R. Snow had written to Joseph. According to Clayton, "President Joseph found them in his pocket. E[mma] seemed vexed and angry." Joseph, Hyrum, and Clayton then rode to Flora's house where Joseph and Flora talked with her mother.[17] Two days later, Joseph "met Ms Wdth [Miss Woodworth]" at Clayton's house.[18]

Following Joseph's marriage to Flora came two of the best-known and most perplexing of his plural marriages, complicated by Emma's reluctant involvement after the fact.

Eliza and Emily Partridge

The story of Joseph's marriages to the Partridge sisters reveals the cost of both the complexity and duplicity of plurality. "The first intimation I had from Brother Joseph that there was a pure and holy order of plural marriage," Emily later wrote, "was in the spring of 1842," but they were not married until 1843.[19] Thus, Joseph waited almost a year, after the sisters had been living in his home for two years, before taking the next step. Emily turned nineteen on February 28, 1843, Eliza twenty-three on April 20.

Decades later, Emily wrote a reminiscence about the strange courtship, which she kept secret both from her sister and her father. In one version of her first encounter with the prophet, Emily reported "shut[ting] him up so

15. "Recollections of Orange L. Wight."

16. Ibid.

17. William Clayton, Journal, Aug. 26, 1843, in George D. Smith, ed., *An Intimate Chronicle*, 118-19.

18. William Clayton, Journal, Aug. 28, 1843 (Smith, *An Intimate Chronicle*, 119).

19. Emily Dow Partridge Smith Young, Autobiography, at http://www.boap.org/LDS/Early-Saints/EmPart.html.

quick that he said no more to me untill the 28th of Feb. 1843, (my nineteenth birth day)."[20] In a second version, she said he introduced the topic by saying, "'Emily, if you will not betray me, I will tell you something for your benefit.' Of course I would keep his secret, but no opportunity offered for some time to say anything to me . ... he asked me if I would burn it if he would write me a letter."[21] Joseph may have intended a missive similar to the one he had composed a year earlier to Nancy Rigdon.

As a properly raised girl, Emily was startled at the request and "I was about as miserable as I ever would wish to be for a short time," she recalled in 1884. "I went to my room and knelt down and asked my father in heaven to direct me in the matter." Although she does not say she felt inspired to act as she did, she "received no comfort till I went back and [said] I could not take a private letter from him." She wanted the discussion to end, but continued to feel miserable.

Not long afterwards, Joseph's plural wife Elizabeth Durfee invited Emily and Eliza to come to her home. Emily remembered that Durfee wanted to mediate a meeting between Joseph and the two sisters: "Joseph would like an opportunity to talk with me. I asked if she knew what he wanted. She said she thought he wanted me for a wife." In 1893, Emily reflected, "I think I was thoroughly prepared for anything."[22]

A week later, Durfee told Emily again that Joseph wanted to talk to her. This time Emily consented to meet Joseph at Heber and Vilate Kimball's house in the evening. When she arrived, only young Helen Mar and her younger brother were present, but Joseph and Heber soon arrived. Heber sent the children to a neighbor's house and, acting as if it was a usual social occasion, told her, "Vilate is not at home, and you had better call another time." Emily hurried off "as fast as I could so as to get beyond being called back, for I still dreaded the interview." She was not fast enough, however, and Kimball called her back.[23]

The setting for what happened next is not clear–whether Joseph and Emily met outside, whether Kimball sent away the family members who were there, or whether Kimball, Joseph, and Emily found a neutral corner. But Emily seems to remember the results clearly: Joseph "said the Lord had

20. Emily Dow Partridge Smith Young, "Incidents of the Early Life of a Mormon Girl," holograph, 185, LDS Church History Library.

21. Emily Dow Partridge Smith Young, Reminiscences, 1.

22. Ibid.

23. Ibid.

commanded [me] to enter into plural marriage and had given me to him and although I had got badly frightened he knew I would yet have him." By this time, Emily's resistance was apparently over: "My mind was now prepared and would receive the principles. … that was the only way that [it could] be done then. Well I was married there and then," presumably with Kimball performing the ceremony. Then "Joseph went home and I [went] my way alone. A strange way of getting married wasn't it?"[24] Of course, "home" for both of them was the same location–Emma's home. Without specifying a date, Emily later testified that she "roomed" with Joseph that night and that the couple had "carnal intercourse."[25]

Emily was reportedly sealed to Joseph on March 4, sister Eliza four days later–Kimball officiating at both.[26] Because Eliza did not write as extensively about her marriage, there is little to flesh out the series of events that transpired. Joseph taught her about celestial marriage the same time as Emily. Emily recorded of Eliza's and her life with the Smiths in her autobiography: "I continued to live in his [Joseph's] family for a length of time after this but did not reside there when he was martyred. … A woman living in polygamy dare not let it be known, and nothing but a firm desire to keep the commandments of the Lord could have induced a girl to marry in that way."[27]

Emma reluctantly acceded to Joseph's repeated requests and selected the Partridge sisters as acceptable plural wives not knowing that they had already secretly been married to her husband. So, according to Emily, "To save family trouble Brother Joseph thought it best to have another ceremony performed. … [Emma] had her feelings, and so we thought there was no use in saying anything about it so long as she had chosen us herself." She also remembered that Emma "helped explain the principles to us."[28]

On May 11, the secret ceremonies were performed a second time, with Emma as a witness and James G. Adams, a judge and Mormon priesthood

24. Ibid.

25. Emily Dow Partridge Smith Young, Deposition Testimony, 364, Part 3, pp. 371, 384, questions 480-84, 747-62; questions, 756, 762: "Question: Did you ever have carnal intercourse with Joseph Smith? Answer: Yes sir … Question: Did you make the declaration that you never slept with him but one night? Answer: Yes sir. Question: And that was the only time and place that you ever were in bed with him? Answer: No sir." Perhaps she meant that they had had sexual relations on more than one occasion, but had only slept together once.

26. See H. Michael Marquardt, "Emily Down Partridge Smith Young on the Witness Stand," 120, 130; George D. Smith, *Nauvoo Polygamy*, 177.

27. Eliza Marie Partridge Smith Lyman, at http://www.boap.org/LDS/Early-Saints/EMPSLyman.html.

28. Emily Dow Partridge Smith Young, Autobiography, at http://www.boap.org/LDS/Early-Saints/EMPart.html.

holder from Springfield, officiating.[29] "She [Emma] gave her free and full consent. She had always up to this time, been very kind to me and my sister Eliza, who was also married to the Prophet Joseph Smith with Emma's consent," remembered Emily.[30] However, Emma soon grasped that the marriages would need to be consummated, changed her mind, and began actively to resent the girls' presence in her home.

Emma's change of heart was painful for the girls, and one can only imagine Emma's own distress as well. Perhaps most bitterly, the girls–and not Joseph–became the target of Emma's wrath. "But ever after she was our enemy," continued Emily. "She used every means in her power to injure us in the eyes of her husband, and before strangers."[31] Emily saw Emma's desperation but was nevertheless "indignant towards Joseph for submitting to Emma," even though she felt a pang of pity for him. "His countenance was the perfect picture of despair." She wrote, "[Emma] insisted that we should promise to break our [marriage] covenants that we had made before God. Joseph asked her if we made her the promise she required, if she would cease to trouble us, and not persist in our marrying someone else. She made the promise. Joseph came to us and shook hands with us and the understanding was that all was ended between us. I for one meant to keep this promise I was forced to make."

After this conversation, Joseph followed Emily downstairs. "You know my hands are tied," she remembered him telling her. He seemed to want to "sink into the earth." Her heart quickly "melted" and she was no longer angry. However, then Emma entered the room. "Emily, what did Joseph say to you?" "He asked me how I felt." "You might as well tell me. … I am determined that a stop shall be put to these things …" "I shall not tell you," Emily replied. "He can say what he pleases to me, and I shall not report it to you, there has been mischief enough made by doing that. I am as sick of these things as you can be." Tensions escalated, and "Emma could not rest till she had us out of the house and then she was not satisfied, but wanted us to leave the city. She offered to give us money to pay our expenses if we would go. We consulted Joseph, he said we might make a visit to some of our relatives, who were living up the river two or three hundred miles. So we agreed to go, and she gave us ten dollars. Joseph said it was insufficient and for us not to go so

29. Ibid.
30. Ibid.
31. Ibid.

we gave it up and returned the money to Emma." Joseph found the sisters a place with a "respectable family."[32]

William Clayton tells his own version of Emma's capitulation and repudiation. On August 16, 1843, Clayton recorded that Joseph told him that Emma resisted vehemently the "Principle in toto" after she had returned from St. Louis to purchase goods for the store and supplies for the hotel wing of her home accompanied by Lorin Walker, Lucy Walker's brother who helped out at the store. Attempting to calm her, Joseph offered to "relinquish all for her sake." But Emma retreated, changing her position, and "said she would give him Eliza and Emily Partridge." Doubting her sincerity, Joseph told Clayton that "he knew if he took them she would … obtain a divorce and leave him. He however, told me he should not relinquish anything."[33]

Emily watched Emma struggle. "I have nothing in my heart towards her but pity. I know it was hard for Emma, and any woman to enter plural marriage in those days, and I do not know as anybody would have done any better than Emma did under the circumstances. I think Emma always regretted having any hand in getting us into such trying circumstances. But she need not have blamed herself for that, in the least, for it would have been the same with or without her consent … It has been to me like an anchor cast within the well."[34] Yet even as the sisters may have appreciated Emma's kindness and acknowledged her sacrifice, they also competed with her for her husband's attention.

Almera Woodward Johnson

Joseph married the Partridge sisters in March. The next month, William Clayton sealed Joseph to Almera Woodward Johnson, the thirty-year-old sister of Benjamin Johnson.[35] Her widowed older sister, Delcena Johnson Sherman, age thirty-eight or thirty-nine, had been sealed to Joseph in July 1842.[36] (See chap. 12.)

Joseph traveled the twenty miles east to Ramus/Macedonia, where he preached on May 16, 1843. He took Eliza Partridge, her younger sister

---

32. Ibid.

33. William Clayton, Journal, Aug. 16, 1843, in George D. Smith, *An Intimate Chronicle*, 117.

34. Emily Dow Partridge Smith Young, "Testimony That Cannot Be Refuted," *Woman's Exponent* 12 (Apr. 1, 1884): 164.

35. Almera W. Johnson Smith Barton, Affidavit, Jan. 28, 1903, in Joseph Fielding Smith, *Blood Atonement and the Origins of Plural Marriage*, 71.

36. Benjamin F. Johnson, Letter to George Gibbs, in Dean R. Zimmerman, ed., *I Knew the Prophets*, 45.

Lydia, George Miller, and Clayton, staying in Benjamin's home.[37] According to Benjamin's later reminiscence, Joseph "had come to Ramus to teach Me Plural Marriage," and then slept with Almera on at least two occasions.[38] Six weeks earlier on April 2, Benjamin later recalled, Joseph had slept in the same bedroom with the "Daughter of the Late Bishop Partridge."[39]

Clayton's contemporary version fleshes out the picture:

> Before we retired the prest. [Joseph Smith] gave bro [Benjamin F.] Johnson & wife some instructions on the priesthood. He put his hand on my [Clayton's] knee and says "'your life is hid with Christ in God,' and so is many others." Addressing Benjamin, he says "nothing but the unpardonable sin can prevent him (me) [Clayton] from inheriting eternal glory for he is sealed up by the power of the priesthood unto eternal life having taken the step which is necessary for that purpose." He said that ["]except a man and his wife enter into an everlasting covenant and be married for eternity while in this probation by the power and authority of the Holy priesthood they will cease to increase when they died (ie. they will not have any children in the resurrection), but those who are married by the power & authority of the priesthood in this life and continue without committing the sin against the Holy Ghost will continue to increase and have children in the celestial glory. The unpardonable sin is to shed innocent blood or be accessary thereto. All other sins will be visited with judgement in the day of the Lord Jesus." … Prest. J[oseph] said that the way he knew in who to confide, God told him in whom he might place confidence. He also said that in the celestial glory there was three heavens or degrees, and in order to obtain the highest a man must enter into this order of the priesthood and if he dont he cant obtain it.

Joseph's "step which is necessary"–as applied to Clayton–clearly referred to plural marriage.[40]

The next day Joseph's party dined at Almon Babbit's. Again, the topic was plurality. Joseph said that when Joseph Bates Noble "was first taught this doctrine [plural marriage] [he] set his heart on one [potential plural

37. *History of the Church*, 5:391 (May 16, 1843).

38. Benjamin F. Johnson, Letter to George Gibbs, in Zimmerman, *I Knew the Prophets*, 44; Benjamin F. Johnson, *My Life's Review*, 85; Almera W. Johnson Smith Barton, Affidavit, Aug. 1, 1883, in Joseph F. Smith Affidavit Books.

39. Benjamin F. Johnson, Letter to George Gibbs, in Zimmerman, *I Knew the Prophets*, 40, 44. Johnson's original 1903 letter, in the LDS Church History Library, dates the marriage incorrectly at May 15.

40. William Clayton, Journal, May 16, 1843, in George D. Smith, *An Intimate Chronicle*, 102.

wife] & pressed J[oseph Smith]. to seal the contract but he never could get opportunity. It seemed that the Lord was unwilling. Finally another [potential plural wife] came along & he then engaged that one and is a happy man. I learned from this anecdote never to press the prophet but wait with patiences & God will bring all things right. I feel to pray that God will let me live so that I may come to the full knowledge of truth and salvation & be prepared for the enjoyment of a fulness of the third heavens."[41]

It is easy to detect in the records of the Saints how enthusiastically they welcomed Joseph to their homes, sharing meals as he expounded on religious topics. It was a simple matter for Joseph to visit his plural wives without creating a scandal. This was true for Louisa Beaman, with whom Joseph sometimes dined at the homes of friends, or with Delcena Johnson Sherman. Benjamin Johnson noted that in June 1842 he visited Delcena who had moved in with Louisa. It was clear to him "that they ware in his [Joseph Smith's] Care and that he provided for there [their] Comfort."[42] When Almera married Joseph in April 1843, Louisa reportedly witnessed the ceremony, which occurred in Delcena's house.

Lucy Walker

Lucy Walker's account of her sealing on May 1, 1843, portrays the level of deception required for the courtship process. A hired girl in the Smith household, Lucy had to interact daily with Emma. She also later asserted that Emma knew of Joseph's marriages to the Partridge sisters. When he proposed a plural marriage to Lucy, first in 1842, Joseph advised her to pray for "light and understanding in relation thereto, and promised me if I would do so sincerely, she should receive a testimony of the correctness of the principle."[43] By 1843, Lucy recalled, Joseph's proposals had "aroused every drop of Scotch in my veins. For a few moments I stood fearless before him, and looked him in the eye. I felt at this moment that I was called to place myself

41. Ibid., May 17, 1842, 103. Recall that Noble performed Joseph's Nauvoo plural marriage to Noble's sister-in-law Louisa Beaman. According to Noble family history, Joseph performed Noble's plural marriage to Sarah B. Alley on April 5, 1843 (Joseph Noble, "Individual Record," www.familysearch.org; Jenson, "Plural Marriage," 6:221). The next month, on May 11, Joseph rebaptized Louisa and probably Eliza R. Snow (Joseph Smith, Diary, May 11, 1843, in Scott H. Faulring, ed., *An American Prophet's Record*, 377). Later that same day, Joseph re-wed the Partridge sisters, in Emma's presence.

42. In Zimmerman, *I Knew the Prophets*, 40.

43. Lucy Walker Kimball, "Brief Biographical Sketch of the Life and Labors of Lucy Walker Smith," 15, 12. See also Rodney Wilson Walker and Noel Stephenson, comps., *The Second Edition of Ancestry and Descendants of John Walker*, 33.

upon the altar a living sacrifice–perhaps to brook the world in disgrace and incur the displeasure and contempt of my youthful companions."[44]

According to her later reminiscence, Lucy told him, "Although you are a Prophet of God, you could not induce me to take a step of so great importance, unless I knew that God approved my course. I would rather die." At that, Joseph moved to stand directly in front of her. She thought the emotion that swept over his face was a "most beautiful expression of countenance," as he reportedly assured her: "God Almighty bless you. You shall have a manifestation of the will of God concerning you; a testimony that you can never deny. I will tell you what it shall be. It shall be that joy and peace that you never knew."

"Oh how earnestly I prayed for these words to be fulfilled," she wrote. Near dawn after yet another sleepless night, "my room was lighted up by a heavenly influence. To me it was in comparison like the brilliant sun bursting through the darkest cloud. My soul was filled with a calm, sweet peace that I never knew. Supreme happiness took possession of me, and I received a powerful and irresistible testimony of the truth of the marriage covenant called 'Celestial or plural marriage.'"[45]

Lucy married Joseph on May 1, 1843–neither her father, John, nor Emma was there. Lucy said that Joseph introduced her to Heber Kimball and Brigham Young as his wife but that the marriage was otherwise not public. Like all of Joseph's wives, Lucy kept her maiden name. William Clayton performed the marriage.[46] "Weddings were not performed publicly in those days," Lucy later explained, "Emma Smith was not present, and she did not consent to the marriage; she did not know anything about it at all." Lucy declined to say if she cohabited with Joseph that night or any other night during their marriage.[47]

Sarah and Maria Lawrence

In the summer of 1841, Joseph became guardian of the minor children of Edward and Margaret Lawrence.[48] Their mother, Margaret, was still alive, but

44. Lucy Walker Smith Kimball, qtd. in Lyman Omer Littlefield, *Reminiscences of Latter-day Saints*, 47.

45. Ibid.

46. Lucy Walker Kimball, Testimony, Temple Lot Case, Complainants Abstract, 374.

47. Ibid., 373, 374.

48. Although this guardianship is not fully understood, Gordon Madsen's research describes some of the legal complexities of the arrangement, concluding that Joseph fulfilled his fiduciary responsibilities. Gordon Madsen, "Joseph Smith as Guardian."

their father had left town, and the children were legally considered "orphans." Margaret married a widower, Josiah Butterfield, a member of the Quorum of Seventy, by 1842; but Joseph, continued to transact their business. The relationship between Joseph and Butterfield was unsteady at best.[49] Joseph's diary traces the disintegration that occurred over time. On April 4, 1842, Joseph notes: "Transacted business at his house with Josiah Butterfield concerning the Lawrence estate."[50] Not quite a year later, on March 28, 1843, Joseph recorded: "Josiah Butterfield came to my house and insulted me so outrageously that I kicked him out of the house, across the yard, and into the street."[51]

As part of Joseph's détente with Emma, she apparently agreed that he could take new wives as long as she chose them. The Partridge sisters had been the first. Emma next selected the Lawrence sisters, who were sealed to Joseph the same month (May), although the exact dates are not known. Sarah was seventeen, Maria nineteen.[52] Unlike Emily Partridge, neither Maria nor Sarah left an account detailing her marriage to Joseph. After their marriages, they continued their lives with the Smith family. Emily Partridge said Emma knew about the marriages,[53] but did not say if they preceded or followed her and Emily's second sealings to Joseph. Lucy Walker testified that the Lawrences told her of the marriage, "and the prophet told me so himself."[54]

Because he was a friend to the Lawrence family, William Law knew about Joseph's marriages to Maria and Sarah. Law wanted to force Joseph to abandon the practice and to punish him for enacting it with the town's women. After he had been excommunicated on April 16, 1844, Law filed suit on May 23 in Hancock County's circuit court accusing Joseph of living in an open state of "adultery" since October 12, 1843.[55]

Three days later on May 26, 1844, Joseph denied Law's accusation, scoffing to an audience of Saints, "What a thing it is for a man to be accused of committing adultery, and having seven wives, when I can only find one."[56] Denying these well-known marriages would eventually hurt Joseph–he was

49. The spring 1842 Nauvoo ward census lists "Maria Laurence" as living with Josiah and Margaret Butterfield in the Nauvoo Third Ward.

50. Joseph Smith, Diary, Apr. 4, 1842, in Dean C. Jessee, *The Papers of Joseph Smith*, 2:374.

51. *History of the Church*, 5:316 (Mar. 28, 1843).

52. Jenson, "Plural Marriage," 6:223.

53. Emily Dow Partridge Smith Young, "Incidents of the Early Life of a Mormon Girl," 186.

54. Lucy Walker, Testimony in Temple Lot Case, 373.

55. *History of the Church*, 6:403 (May 23, 1844). See also John Dinger, "Joseph Smith's Indictment for Adultery and Fornication," August 16, 2015, at www.rationalfaiths.com/joseph-smiths-indictment-for-adultery-and-fornication (Aug. 21, 2015).

56. *History of the Church*, 6:411 (May 26, 1844).

less than a month away from assassination–but he clearly believed that his only option was to deny plurality's existence. Then, conscious of public perception, he and his counselors filed a countersuit accusing Law of slandering Maria Lawrence.[57]

Helen Mar Kimball

A year after Newel K. and Elizabeth Ann Whitney had agreed to give their daughter Sarah Ann to Joseph in mid-1842, Heber C. Kimball offered his fourteen-year-old daughter, Helen Mar, to the prophet in mid-1843. Almost forty years later, Helen recalled that her father taught her about celestial marriage during the spring-summer of 1843.[58] She reported her father asking her if "I would believe him if he told me that it was right for married men to take other wives." Raised to believe this was immoral, she was outraged. "My sensibilities were painfully touched," she wrote. "I felt such a sense of personal injury and displeasure; for him to mention such a thing to me I thought altogether unworthy of my father, and as quick as he spoke, I replied to him, short and emphatically, *No I wouldn't!*" He stood his ground and proceeded to teach his daughter about the principle and its relationship to their life on the earth.[59]

For Helen, the news was a "small earthquake," but when she acquiesced, her father suggested a marriage to Joseph. "Having a great desire to be connected with the Prophet," she said in 1881, her father "offered me to him."[60] When she hesitated,

> [he] left me to reflect upon it for the next twenty-four hours … I was skeptical–one minute believed, then doubted. I thought of the love and tenderness that he felt for his only daughter, and I knew that he would not cast her off, and this was the only convincing proof that I had of its being right. I knew that he loved me too well to teach me anything that was not strictly pure, virtuous and exalting in its tendencies; and no one else could

57. See Joseph Smith, Diary, June 4, 1843, in Faulring, *An American Prophet's Record*, 487.

58. Helen Mar Kimball, "Scenes and Life Incidents in Nauvoo," *Woman's Exponent* 11 (Aug. 1, 1882): 39.

59. Ibid.

60. "Helen Mar Kimball Whitney's Retrospection About her Introduction to the Doctrine and Practices of Plural Marriage in Nauvoo at age 15." Also titled "Helen Mar Kimball Smith Whitney to her Children, March 30, 1881. Similar statements to be opened at Centennial," LDS Church History Library. In Jeni Brobert Holzapfel and Richard Neitzel Holzapfel, eds., *A Woman's View*, 482; http:rsc.byu.edu/archived/womans-view-helen-mar-kimball-whitneys-reminiscences-early-church-history/11-appendix-one; June 16, 2013.

> have influenced me at that time or brought me to accept of a doctrine so utterly repugnant and so contrary to all of our former ideas and traditions.[61]

If Helen's memory his correct, she had only a day to consider the radical new idea. When Joseph, in company with Helen's parents, broached the topic the next morning, "I heard him [Joseph] teach & explain the principle of Celestial marriage–after which he said to me, 'If you will take this step, it will ensure your eternal salvation & exaltation and that … of your fathers household & all of your kindred.'" Helen agreed, recalling, "None but God & angels could see my mother's bleeding heart."[62] When Joseph asked Vilate Kimball if she agreed, she answered simply: "If Helen is willing I have nothing more to say." Helen wrote, "She had witnessed the sufferings of others, who were older & who better understood the step they were taking, & to see her child, who had scarcely seen her fifteenth summer, following in the same thorny path, in her mind she saw the misery which was so sure to come as the sun was to rise and set; but it was all hidden from me."[63]

A poem written by an elderly Helen captures her memory of what she both gained and lost.

> They saw my youthful friends grow shy and cold.
> And poisonous darts from sland'rous tongues were hurled,
> Untutor'd heart in thy gen'rous sacrafise,
> Thou dids't not weigh the cost nor know the bitter price;
> Thy happy dreams all o'er thou'st doom'd alas to be
> Bar'd out from social scenes by this thy destiny,
> And o'er thy sad'nd mem'ries of sweet departed joys
> Thy sicken'd heart will brood and imagin future woes,
> And like a fetter'd bird with wild and longing heart,
> Thou'lt dayly pine for freedom and murmur at thy lot.[64]

Helen, like many of the young wives of Nauvoo, did not understand the parameters of plurality. There is no reason why she would have. Unburdening her heart to a friend who later became a critic of the Church, Helen reportedly said, "I would never have been sealed to Joseph had I known it was

61. Helen Mar Kimball, "Scenes and Incidents in Nauvoo," *Woman's Exponent* 11, no. 3 (Aug. 1, 1882): 39.

62. Holzapfel and Holzapfel, *A Woman's View*, 482, 486.

63. Ibid., 486.

64. "Helen Mar Kimball Whitney's 1881 Autobiography," in Holzapfel and Holzapfel, *A Woman's View*, 486.

anything more than ceremony. I was young, and they deceived me, by saying the salvation of our whole family depended on it."[65]

Instructing William Clayton

William Clayton first learned about plurality from Joseph as they walked together on a brisk February morning in 1843 about the time of the growing tension between Emma Smith and Eliza Partridge. Clayton later affirmed that the meeting changed his life from that point forward. "During our walk, he [Joseph] said he had learned that there was a sister back in England, to whom I was very much attached. I replied there was, but nothing further than an attachment such as brother and sister in the Church might rightfully entertain for each other."

To Clayton's surprise, Joseph bluntly asked, "Why don't you send for her?"

Clayton replied, "In the first place, I have no authority to send for her, and if I had, I have not the means to pay the expenses."

Joseph brushed the objections aside: "'I give you authority to send for her, and I will furnish you with means,' which he did. This was the first time the Prophet Joseph talked with me on the subject of plural marriage."[66] Clayton became a polygamist because he believed Joseph's prophet-narrative. On April 27, 1843, Joseph sealed Clayton to his first plural wife, Margaret Moon.[67] Three days earlier, Clayton had noted in his journal his impression of Moon: "She is a lovely woman and desires to do right in all things and will submit to council with all her heart."[68] It was not, initially, a happy marriage. Margaret had been engaged to another convert, Aaron Farr, and was obviously depressed by becoming a second wife.[69] When Lorin Walker, Lucy Walker's brother, subsequently told Clayton that he thought Clayton had "done wrong" to break up Margaret and Farr and that Emma

---

65. Qtd. in Catherine Lewis, *Narrative of Some of the Proceedings of the Mormons* (Lynn, Massachusetts: n.p., 1848), 19. (Lewis's "narrative" is hostile to Joseph and the Mormons.)

66. "Sworn statement of William Clayton, February 16, 1874," reproduced in Jenson, "Plural Marriage," 6:225. On July 12, 1843, Clayton recorded the revelation on plural marriage at Joseph's dictation (now LDS D&C 132).

67. Joseph Smith, Diary, Apr. 27, 1843, in Faulring, *An American Prophet's Record*, 396: "W[illia]m Clayton and Margaret Moon by J[oseph] S[mith] at H[eber] C. K[imball]'s."

68. Smith, *An Intimate Chronicle*, 99.

69. Clayton cherished Joseph's expressions of trust. On June 23, Joseph told him that Emma "wanted to lay a snare for me. He told me last night of this and said he had felt troubled. He said [Emma] had treated him coldly and badly since I came. ... He cautioned me very kindly for which I felt thankful." William Clayton, Journal, June 23, 1843, in George D. Smith, *An Intimate Chronicle*, 108.

"was considerably displeased" about it, Clayton asked Joseph "if I had done wrong in what I had done he answered no you have a right to get all [plural wives] you can."[70]

Clayton clung to such reassurances as he eventually married plural wives and later proudly testified: "From him [Joseph Smith] I learned that the doctrine of plural and celestial marriage is the most holy and important doctrine ever revealed to man on the earth, and that without obedience to that principle no man can ever attain to the fullness of exaltation in celestial glory."[71] Joseph wove through his restorationist narrative comparisons with Old Testament prophets whom God had also commanded to practice polygamy. Joseph's teachings positioned plurality in an ancient order and justified his marriages as part of a prophet's role. By linking plurality to salvation, Joseph made it an indispensable doctrine.

Eliza R. Snow: Discovery

Emma had invited Eliza R. Snow to join the Smith household on August 13, 1842, perhaps six months before she realized that Eliza was one of her husband's plural wives. Neither Emma nor Eliza (nor Joseph, for that matter) ever left an account of what actually happened during their months under the same roof.[72] Six months later on February 11, 1843, Eliza abruptly moved out, recording only: "Took board and had my lodging removed to the residence of br. [Jonathan] Holmes."[73] (Elivra Holmes, Relief Society treasurer, was Eliza's friend.) It requires little stretch of the imagination to attribute the sudden move to Emma's discovery of the marriage between her children's teacher and her husband.

Eliza did not write in her journal for another five weeks. Perhaps she was angry with both Joseph and Emma. Her poem, "Who Needs Consolation," written in May 1843, seems to suggest as much:

I feel thy woes–my bosom shares
Thy spirit's agony–
How can I love a heart that dares
Suspect thy purity?

70. Ibid., Aug. 11, 1843, 115.

71. Clayton, Affidavit, in Jenson, "Plural Marriage," 6:226. See also Orson Pratt, Oct. 7, 1874, JD 17:225-26; B. Carmon Hardy, *Solemn Covenant*, 14-19, 84-113.

72. Maureen Ursenbach Beecher, Linda King Newell, and Valeen Tippetts Avery, "Emma, Eliza, and the Stairs," 87-96.

73. Eliza R. Snow, Journal, Feb. 11, 1843, in Beecher, *The Personal Writings of Eliza Roxcy Snow*, 64.

I'll smile on all that smile on thee
As angels do above–
All who in pure sincerity
Will love thee, I will love.
Believe me, thou hast noble friends
Who feel and share thy grief;
And many a fervent pray-r ascends
To heav-n, for thy relief.[74]

Eliza's diary both conceals and reveals the truth of her life as a plural wife of Joseph Smith. She erased Emma from her life's narrative by never again referring to Emma by name in her journal. She created emotional distance between her and her husband's civil wife by terms like "Prest. Smith and Mrs. Smith," effectively rendering Emma an appendage to her husband.[75]

Multiple versions of Eliza's and Emma's presumed confrontation have survived, none contemporary or completely reliable, and each embedded in the lore that later grew up around the sometimes gossip-riddled story of Nauvoo plurality. It is virtually impossible to detect which parts of the story are based on fact and which have been embellished over time.

Wilhelm Wyl's exposé, published in 1886, gave the earliest printed variant of the story without articulating a source. Instead, he presented the narrative as if everyone already knew the story: "There is scarcely a Mormon unacquainted with the fact that Sister Emma … soon found out the little compromise arranged between Joseph and Eliza. Feeling outraged as a wife and betrayed as a friend, Emma is currently reported as having had recourse to a vulgar broomstick as an instrument of revenge; and the harsh treatment received at Emma's hands is said to have destroyed Eliza's hopes of becoming the mother of a prophet's son."[76] Without reliable independent corroboration, Wyl's lurid story is strictly folklore. In fact, Wyl's account illustrates the problems of such sensational ex post facto stories as a whole: They may make for compelling storytelling, but they are not reliable history.

It is also unclear in Wyl's story if the woman involved is Eliza Snow or Eliza Partridge, and to complicate further the analysis of this episode, Clayton on May 23, 1843, recorded: "President [Smith] stated to me that he had had a little trouble with sis. E[mma]. He was asking E[liza] Partridge

74. Ibid., May 1843, 77.
75. Ibid., 64.
76. Wilhelm Wyl [pseud. Wilhelm Ritter von Wymetal], *Mormon Portraits*, 58.

concerning [Joseph] Jackson conduct during Prest. absence & E[mma] came up stairs. he shut to the door not knowing who it was and held it. She came to the door & called Eliza 4 times & tried to force open the door. Prest. opened it & told her the cause etc. She seemed much irritated."[77]

Although the details of the two stories vary, it is possible that the mythic telling of the Eliza and Emma confrontation was rooted in such casual notations. According to the work of Maureen Ursenbach Beecher, Linda Newell, and Valeen Avery, Clayton's journal was a principal source used to compile the *History of the Church,* and is the "only know contemporary version of any such event involving Emma and an Eliza."[78]

Eliza Snow's brother, Lorenzo, indicated that when she married Joseph, Eliza was thirty-eight and later "lived in an unmarried state until she was beyond the condition of raising a family."[79] In 1885, Eliza remembered how central the doctrine was to her identity. "I was sealed to the Prophet, Joseph Smith, for time and eternity, in accordance with the *Celestial Law* of Marriage which God has revealed–the ceremony being performed by a servant of the Most High–authorized to officiate in sacred ordinances. This, one of the most important circumstances of my life, I never have had cause to regret."[80] After four decades of justifying her life in plurality, Eliza focused on the authoritative, sacred nature of the marriage, the fact that it had God's sanction, and that it was at the core of who she was as a Latter-day Saint woman.

There was not always conflict between the two women; in fact, they were similar in many ways–smart and attractive–leaders among women, and looked to by others. Eliza did record in her journal a visit from a distraught Emma on July 20, 1843:

> Sister [blank in original] called to see me. Her appearance very plainly manifested the perturbation of her mind. How strangely is the human countenance changed when the powers of darkness reign over the empire of the heart! Scarcely, if ever, in my life had I come in contact with such forbidding and angry looks; yet I felt as calm as the summer eve, and received her as smilingly as the playful infant; and my heart as sweetly reposed upon the bosom of conscious innocence, as infancy reposes in the arms of paternal tenderness & love. It is better to suffer than to do wrong, and it is sometimes better to submit to injustice rather than contend; it is

77. Clayton, Journal, May 23, 1843, in George D. Smith, *An Intimate Chronicle*, 105.
78. Beecher, Newell, and Avery, "Emma and Eliza and the Stairs," 89.
79. Ibid., 91.
80. Eliza R. Snow, "Life Sketch," in Beecher, *The Personal Writings of Eliza Roxcy Snow*, 17.

certainly better to wait the retribution of Jehovah than to contend where effort will be unavailable.[81]

Eliza pondered the significance of this encounter the next evening. She termed it a "season for contemplation," and reflected on the angry encounter: "The likeness and unlikeness of disposition & character with which we come in contact, is a fruitful theme of thought; and the very few, who have strength of mind, reason & stability; to act from principle; is truly astonishing, and yet only such are persons worthy of trust."[82] Clearly, Eliza counted herself among the latter, while scorning Emma's lack of loyalty to Joseph. It was a nuanced perception; the only proof Emma could have given of her wifely devotion was to accept another wife.

The Emma and Eliza story became embedded in Joseph's story from that point forward, regardless of its accuracy. Despite Emma's efforts to avoid a collision with the reality of Joseph's increasingly complex familial situation, such a jarring discovery was inevitable. The tension between the two women kept them separate thereafter. Eliza's identity would always be wrapped around Joseph's as prophet, as was also true for Emma. Even after Joseph's death, their marriages represented the defining event of their lives.

Joseph was also still spending an exhausting amount of energy publicly denying rumors of polygamy. On February 21, 1843, ten days after Eliza Snow had moved from his house, Joseph said: "If the stories about Joe Smith are true, then the stories of John C. Bennett are true about the ladies of Nauvoo; and he says that the Ladies' Relief Society are all organized of those who are to be the wives of Joe Smith. Ladies, you know whether this is true or not. It is no use living among hogs without a snout. This biting and devouring each other I cannot endure. Away with it. For God's sake, stop it."[83] Less than five months later, he insisted: "I have constantly said no man shall have but one wife at a time, unless the Lord directs otherwise."[84]

After Lorenzo Snow returned from England on April 12, 1843, Joseph explained plurality to him while walking along the banks of the river. Snow would later tell the story of this life-changing session: "[H]e said that the Lord had revealed it unto him, and commanded him to have women sealed to him as wives; that he foresaw the trouble that would follow, and sought to turn away from the Commandment; that an angel from Heaven appeared

81. Eliza R. Snow, Journal, July 20, 1843, ibid., 80.

82. Ibid., July 21, 1843, 81.

83. *History of the Church*, 5:286 (Feb. 21, 1843).

84. Ibid., 501.

before him with a drawn Sword, threatening him with destruction unless he went forward and obeyed the Commandment." All this was by way of preface: "He further said that my sister Eliza R. Snow had been sealed to him as his wife for time and eternity. He told me that the Lord would open the way, and I should have women sealed to me as wives."[85] The motifs in this hour-plus exchange captured Joseph's rhetorical positioning of plurality. An angel with a drawn sword enhanced the imperativeness of obedience–the threat of destruction that gave Joseph, and those who followed him, little choice but to obey.

Emma's Continued Resistance

After the explosion over Eliza Snow in February 1843, Emma continued to trouble Joseph about plurality.[86] Between then and July, Clayton notes conflict between Joseph and Emma five times.[87] In contrast, Joseph thought that, as president of Nauvoo's Relief Society, Emma should lead out in plurality, demonstrating how other women might accept the difficult doctrine through her own faithfulness. Emma's example of loyalty, faithfulness, and deference was key. How could he ask the wives of the apostles to acquiesce if his own wife was unwilling? But unlike the wives of apostles like Heber Kimball and Brigham Young, Emma refused to capitulate to her husband's wishes. The stories that developed around Joseph's enmeshment in plurality made Emma's struggle emblematic of the more generalized struggle to understand the teachings of a prophet of God.

May 1843 seems to have been a brief pause in Emma's resistance. On the 6th, Joseph, his military staff, their wives, and friends rode out on a prairie east of his farm. Despite the cool weather and a high wind, they enjoyed the outing. Emma must have valued the time with Joseph when she did not have to wonder where he was. In the afternoon, Emma led a group of horsewomen to the parade ground accompanying Joseph and his staff. There they reviewed new Nauvoo Legion uniforms, while the brass band played. Joseph candidly addressed the legionnaires: When the Mormons petitioned the government for help, "they have always told us they had no power to help

85. Lorenzo Snow, Affidavit, Aug. 28, 1869, in Joseph F. Smith, Affidavit Books, 2:20; for another discussion of this conversation, see also Eliza R. Snow, *Biography and Family Record of Lorenzo Snow*, 68-69.

86. Newell and Avery, *Mormon Enigma*, 157-60.

87. Clayton, Journal, in George D. Smith, *An Intimate Chronicle*: May 23, 1843, 105; May 29, 1843, 106; June 23, 1843, 108; July 12, 1843, 110; July 13, 1843, 110.

us. Damn such power! When they give me power to protect the innocent /I will never say I can do nothing/. I will ex[er]cise that power /for/ their good. So help me God."[88] The *Nauvoo Neighbor* reported: "We felt proud to be associated with a body of men which in point of discipline, uniform, appearance, and a knowledge of military tactics, are the pride of Illinois, one of its strongest defenses, and a great bulwark of the western country."[89] In addition to a fine sorrel and a new carriage that Joseph gave Emma, she was finally sealed to him for time and eternity a few days later on May 28 in recognition of her sanctioning his marriages to the Partridges and the Lawrences. That same day, Emma also went to St. Louis on a shopping spree for the Mansion House. Emma's role in building Zion was both supportive of and oppositional to Joseph's role as prophet.

On May 18, Joseph H. Jackson, who grandiloquently portrayed himself as a student of human nature, arrived in Nauvoo to worm his way into Joseph's confidence "that I might discover and disclose to the world his real designs and the nature of his operations," he wrote in an exposé published before the end of 1844.[90] Bragging that his unorthodox means were justified by the ends, he reportedly told Joseph he "had committed the darkest crimes"[91] and asked Joseph's protection. Joseph's diary notes that Jackson posed as a "Catholic priest,"[92] a detail Jackson did not mention. Jackson wove a tale that placed him in the confidence of the Mormon prophet, alleging that Joseph "admitted me into all of his secret councils, and was confided in so far, that he disclosed to me every act of his life."[93] He may have been speaking a partial truth of the too-trusting Joseph. On May 20, Clayton recorded Joseph saying that "Jackson appears a fine and noble fellow but is reduced in circumstances. The prest. [Joseph] feels disposed to employ him & give him a chance in the world. Jackson says he shall be baptized ere long."[94] Three days later, however, Joseph had decided that "Jackson is rotten," summarized Clayton, who then attached his own

88. Joseph Smith, Diary, May 6, 1843, in Faulring, *An American Prophet's Record*, 376. In his editing of Joseph's diary, Faulring used angled slashes to indicate written material inserted above the line in the original document.

89. "Military," *Nauvoo Neighbor* 1 (May 10, 1843): 2.

90. Joseph H. Jackson, *A Narrative of the Adventures and Experience of Joseph H. Jackson in Nauvoo*, 3. Thomas Gregg, *Prophet of Palmyra*, 328, described Jackson's exposé as on par with John C. Bennett's.

91. Jackson, *A Narrative*, 9.

92. Joseph Smith, Diary, May 18, 1843, in Faulring, *An American Prophet's Record*, 378.

93. Jackson, *A Narrative*, 19.

94. Clayton, Journal, May 20, 1843, in George D. Smith, *An Intimate Chronicle*, 105.

prayer: "May the Lord preserve me [Clayton] from committing a fault to cause me to lose the confidence of my friends for I desire to do right thou Lord knowest."[95]

Some ten months later, Jackson with William and Wilson Law, Robert Foster, and Chauncey Higbee "held a caucus designing to destroy all the Smith family." In response to the men's efforts between March and May 25, 1844, Joseph "instructed the officers to have him [Jackson] arrested for threatening life."[96] Lucy Mack Smith, in her 1844-45 memoir, said that Jackson had attempted to woo Hyrum Smith's sixteen-year-old daughter, Lovina. When Hyrum refused permission for the marriage, Jackson, according to Lucy, came out against the Smith family and played a role in Joseph's and Hyrum's murders.[97] Lovina eventually married Lorin Walker, Lucy Walker's brother.

Not surprisingly, Jackson tells a different story. According to Jackson, Joseph tried to get "Mrs. William Law for a spiritual wife," and also announced a spurious revelation "that Law was to be sealed up to Emma, and that Law's wife was to be his; in other words there was to be a spiritual swop." He added that Joseph "had never before suffered his passion for any woman to carry him so far as to be willing to sacrifice Emma for its gratification."[98] In 1887, William Law contradicted Jackson's account: "Joseph Smith never proposed anything of the kind to me or to my wife; both he and Emma knew our sentiments in relation to polygamy in any and every form." While Law said that Joseph had not offered him Emma, he had heard rumors "that Joseph offered to furnish his wife, Emma, with a substitute for him, by way of compensation for his neglect of her, on condition that she would stop her opposition to polygamy and permit him to enjoy his young wives in peace and keep some of them in the house."[99] It is impossible to know which story is true because of the conflict that poisoned memories of the events and because neither Joseph nor Emma left an account.[100]

95. Clayton, Journal, May 23, 1843, in George D. Smith, *An Intimate Chronicle*, 106.

96. Joseph Smith, Diary, Mar. 23 and May 25, 1844, in Faulring, *An American Prophet's Record*, 460, 483.

97. Lavina Fielding Anderson, ed., *Lucy's Book*, 736-37.

98. Jackson, *A Narrative*, 21.

99. William Law, Letter to Dr. W. Why, Jan. 7, 1887, in the Salt Lake City *Daily Tribune*, Jan. 1887. D&C 132:51-52 ambiguously suggests what might be this arrangement: "A commandment I give unto my handmaid, Emma Smith, your wife, whom I have given unto you, that she stay herself and partake not of that which I commanded you to offer unto her; for I did it, saith the Lord, to prove you all, as I did Abraham."

100. Doctrine and Covenants 132:54–"I command mine handmaid, Emma Smith, to abide

Clayton recorded a month later, on June 23, 1843, that Emma had another argument with Joseph, and reportedly threatened, "If he would indulge himself," she "might too."[101] Clearly, the story had traction. A year later, Alexander Neibaur recounted another version, based on hearsay, at best, of the story on May 24, 1844. He said that William Law asked Joseph to seal him to his wife, Jane, in May 1843 for eternity but Joseph refused. Neibaur recorded: "Some days after Mr. Smith [was] going toward his office, Mrs. Law stood in the door [and] beakoned to him ... as no one but herself [was] in the hous, she drawing her Arms around him [said] if you won't seal me to my husband Seal myself unto you, he Said stand away and pussing her Gently aside giving her a denial and going out, when Mr. Law came home to Inquire who had been [there] in his Absense, she said no one but Br. Joseph, he then demanded what had passed. Mrs. L[aw] then [said] Joseph wanted her to be married to him."[102]

A third account comes from Joseph Lee Robinson's journal, reporting a second-hand account from his sister-in-law Angeline Robinson, brother Ebenezer's wife. (The Robinsons lived across the street from the Laws.) Angeline "had some time before this watched Brother Joseph the Prophet, had seen him go into some house that she had reported to sister Emma." When Emma learned about these visits, she "was determined he should not get another [wife]. If he did she was determined to leave and when she heard [of Joseph visiting another woman] she became very angry and said she would leave and was making preparations to go to her people in the State of New York. It came close to breaking up his family." Robinson said "he succeeded in saving her at that time but the Prophet felt dreadful bad over it" and intervened. Joseph asked Ebenezer to stop his wife from talking to Emma, but he would not. Joseph then sent the couple to Philadelphia to work for Sidney Rigdon's printer. Joseph Robinson reflected: "[T]here was something wrong or Joseph would not have sent him away that way and with that man, but Ebenezer thought sure his character stood clear in the eyes of the Prophet."[103] This same day, April 18, 1844, William and Jane Law were excommunicated for "unchristianlike conduct."[104]

---

and cleave unto my servant Joseph, and to none else"–may be read as suggesting that Joseph would probably not have considered giving Emma to another man.

101. Clayton, Journal, June 23, 1843, in George D. Smith, *An Intimate Chronicle*, 108.

102. Alexander Neibaur, Journal, May 24, 1844.

103. Joseph Lee Robinson, Journal excerpts, 1811-92, typescript, 81.

104. *History of the Church*, 6:341 (Apr. 18, 1844).

Hyrum's Conversion

By mid-May 1843, Hyrum Smith had come to sense more than he dared to guess about his younger brother's teachings. Apparently, sometime between May 23 and May 26, he confronted Brigham Young. Young at first feigned ignorance, then relented: "I told Hyrum the whole story, and he bowed to it and wept like a child, and said, 'God be praised.'"[105] With his older brother now having embraced plurality, at least in principle, Joseph on May 26 began re-performing endowment ceremonies for men he had the previous year inducted into the Quorum of the Anointed.[106] Hyrum would soon become one of his brother's stauchest supporters. Less than two months later, Joseph dictated for the first time a revelation on plural marriage (now LDS Doctrine and Covenants 132), in part, to convert Emma.

On July 12, Hyrum told Joseph to write a revelation down and he would take it to Emma, challenge her to pray, and ask if it was true.[107] But when he read the revelation to Emma, she turned "very bitter and full of resentment and anger," as Joseph had evidently predicted.[108] Reportedly, Emma may have burned the original, but a copy had been made, thus helping to assure the survival of Joseph's teaching.[109]

On July 13, Joseph sent for Clayton. When he arrived, he was informed that the Smiths had "mutually entered into" a special "arrangement." Joseph and Emma "both stated their feelings on many subjects and wept considerable. O may the Lord soften her heart," Clayton shortly afterwards recorded, "that she may be willing to keep and abide by his Holy Law."[110] Evidently, Joseph and Emma had talked incessantly about the revelation and its implications. But try as she might, Emma could not submit.[111]

Joseph's revelation was six pages in length and included sixty-six

105. Brigham Young, Address, Oct. 8, 1866, qtd. in Ehat, "Introduction of Temple Ordinances and the 1844 Succession Question," 57-59.

106. Joseph Smith, Diary, May 26, 1843, in Faulring, *An American Prophet's Record*, 381.

107. William Clayton, Affidavit, Feb. 16, 1874, in Jenson, "Plural Marriage," 6:223-26.

108. Ibid., 226.

109. Joseph Kingsbury, Affidavit, May 22, 1886, in Jenson, "Plural Marriage," 6:226; Joseph Kingsbury, Affidavit, Mar. 7, 1870, in Joseph F. Smith, Affidavit Books, 2:16.

110. Clayton, Journal, July 13, 1843, in George D. Smith, *An Intimate Chronicle*, 110.

111. See William Law's affidavit, in Shook, *True Origin of Mormon Polygamy*, 132. See also William Law, Interviewed by Wyl, in Gregg, *Prophet of Palmyra*, 508; and Bathsheba Smith, Affidavit, Nov. 19, 1903, in Joseph F. Smith, Affidavit Books, 2:51. A shorthand entry in Joseph's diary for July 17, 1843, uses the term "purgatory" to describe the Smiths' previous four days, presumably because of Emma's negative response to Joseph's revelation. See Andrew H. Hedges, Alex D. Smith, and Brent M. Rogers, eds., *The Joseph Smith Papers: Journals, Volume 3: May 1843-June 1844* (Salt Lake City: Church Historian's Press, 2015), 62.

verses separated into two–possibly three–parts. Each section begins with a question, and creates a discourse in answer to Joseph's query about Old Testament prophets who had "many wives and concubines." Passages about adultery refer to the conflict between Emma and Joseph over plurality. The document takes Emma to task, instructing her "to receive all those [wives] that have been given unto my servant Joseph, and who are virtuous and pure before me" (D&C 132:52).

More important, the revelation links celestial marriage to exaltation and eternal progression. Stressing that exaltation is only possible through the "new and everlasting covenant" (v. 4), it locates priesthood authority and the keys to perform binding unions in Joseph and promises nothing less than a reunion with God: "they shall pass by the angels, and the gods, which are set there, to their exaltation and glory in all things, … which glory shall be a fullness and a continuation of the seeds forever and ever" (v. 19). Joseph is told that "this promise is yours also, because ye are of Abraham, and … by this law is the continuation of the works of my Father, wherein he glorifieth himself" (v. 30). Finally, the revelation reassures readers–specifically Emma–that Joseph is indeed a prophet:

> And again, verily I say unto you, my servant Joseph, that whatsoever you give on earth, and to whomsoever you give any one on earth, by my word and according to my law, it shall be visited with blessings and not cursings, and with my power, saith the Lord, and shall be without condemnation on earth and in heaven (v. 48).

For his many sacrifices, Joseph is promised "a throne for you in the kingdom of my Father, with Abraham your father" (v. 49).

Heber Kimball, then on a mission in the Eastern states, explained from Pittsburgh his own evolving understanding of the complicated doctrine in a letter on July 15, 1843, to his wife, Vilate. Conscious of the danger he was putting her in with this secret knowledge, he cautioned:

> … be carful. [W]ho you read these letrs to, you may hurt feelings. Not that I calculate to write one word that would cast one reflection upon anny person or upon you, fore you are wright in what you said to me, do not read these letrs to anny ones Excpt you think best. and our own family then not all. read your self. … now remember me to Sister Sariah Noon [Kimball's plural wife] if you think it is best to read this leter to hur, be wise. so as not hurt feelings. I shall wright to her soon, you will hear from me again when I get to the City of Philadelphia tell me how the

> Children get along. and all things. direct your leters to Phidaldelphia. … Elder [Parley P.] Pratt said he had agreeded he and his wife, if Either of them should die while he was gon, that the one that Should live should see that the Covent betwen them should be ratlefide [ratified] fore Eternity. so you see they have got some under standing. he asks me menny qustions that I dare not answer.[112]

This letter is poignant on several levels. Kimball was struggling to understand what plurality required of him, the accommodations Vilate and he needed to make for it to work, and their efforts to welcome others into the circle they had created with their marriage. It was new, and surely bewildering, but he was determined to make it work. What is more, it imposed heavy demands on Vilate who had been raised, like him, in a monogamous family, had married her husband in a monogamous union, and had addressed her life with one set of assumptions. Now everything had been turned upside down.

On June 27, Vilate wrote back, revealing how much plurality had expanded in his absence and confiding her own fears by telling him about the struggles of others.

> I have had a viset from brother Parley [P. Pratt] and his wife [Mary Ann Frost]. They are truly converted [to plural marriage]. It appears that J[ose] p[h] has taught him some principles and told him his privilege and even appointed one for him [i.e., Elizabeth Brotherton]. I Dare not tell you what it is [as] you would be astonished and I guess some tried. She has be[e]n to me for counsel. I told her I did not wish to advise in such matters. Sister Pratt has be[e]n rageing against these things. She told me her self that the devel had ben in her until within a few days past. She said the Lord has shown her it was all right. She wants Parley to go ahead, says she will do all in her power to help him. They are so ingagued I fear they will run to[o] fast. They asked me many questions on principle. I told them I did not know much and I rather they would go to those that had authority to teach.

Vilate's letter hints at the complicated reactions to the new doctrine and its scope, including anger, astonishment, and despair.[113]

---

112. Heber C. Kimball, Letter to Vilate Kimball, July 15, 1843; also see Helen Mar Kimball, "Scenes and Incidents in Nauvoo," *Woman's Exponent* 10, no. 10 (Oct. 15, 1881): 74.

113. Vilate Kimball, Letter to Heber C. Kimball, June 27, 1843; also quoted in Holzapfel and Holzapfel, *A Woman's View*, 211-12.

Hyrum's conversion to plurality was evidently wholehearted. His first wife, Jerusha Barden, had died on October 14, 1837. He married Mary Fielding two months later on December 24. Then, not quite six years later, in August 1843, he took two plural wives: Catherine Phillips and Mercy Fielding. Hyrum also performed at least nine plural marriage sealings himself, while expounding the principle to others.[114] For example, in July 1843, he taught plural marriage to Howard and Martha Coray. Howard was Joseph's clerk and later assisted his wife in polishing Lucy Mack Smith's dictated memoirs in 1844-45. Previous to their meeting with Hyrum, Martha had had a confusing dream, and Howard and she sought out Hyrum to interpret it:

> ... he commenced rehearsing the revelation on celestial marriage and carefully went through with the whole of it, then reviewed it, explaining such portions of it as he deemed necessary. This was on the 22nd of July 1843. The dream was in harmony with the revelation and was calculated to prepare her mind for its reception. She never doubted the divinity of it, nor rebelled against it. ... Brother Hyrum asked my wife if she was willing to be sealed to me. After a moment's thought, she answered yes. He then asked me if I wished to be sealed. I replied in the affirmative and after telling us that he knew by the spirit of the Lord that it was His will for us to be sealed, he performed the ceremony, then and there.[115]

Other Plural Wives

Between June and November 1843, Joseph reportedly added another seven wives with known sealing dates or seasons. On June 1, William Clayton sealed Joseph to twenty-nine-year-old Elvira Annie Cowles; Heber Kimball performed the ceremony, and Eliza Partridge was witness. Elvira had been married to Jonathan Holmes six months earlier and was the treasurer of the Relief Society. When she was later re-sealed after to Joseph after his death, with Jonathan as proxy, Elvira continued to live with Jonathan after her plural marriage.[116] Before her marriage, Elvira had lived with the Smith family between 1840 and 1842, and became a friend to Emma, the Partridge girls, and Eliza Snow, fellow Relief Society sisters and relatives of Church leaders.

114. Bergera, "Identifying the Earliest Mormon Polygamists," Appendix, 52-74.

115. Howard Coray, "Autobiography."

116. Elvira A. Cowles Holmes, Affidavit, Aug. 28, 1869, in Joseph F. Smith, Affidavit Books, 1:78; Jenson, "Plural Marriage," lists "Elvira A. Cowles, afterwards the wife of Jonathan H. Holmes," as one of Joseph's wives.

On June 12, Joseph married Rhoda Richards, Willard Richards's fifty-eight-year-old unmarried sister. Willard performed the ceremony.[117] At an unspecified date that summer, Joseph married Hannah S. Ells, a single woman in her late twenties, a British convert, and a seamstress.[118] Hannah knew Emma through the Relief Society. Charlotte Haven, who met Hannah in May 1843, described her as "very, very tall."[119] Also at some point that summer, Joseph married twenty-seven-year-old Olive Grey Frost (previously never married) and Desdemona Wadsworth Fullmer, who resided at William Clayton's house at the time. (Brigham Young performed the last marriage, and Heber Kimball was witness.)[120]

On June 29, five of Joseph's plural wives–Eliza Snow, Elvira Cowles, Eliza Partridge, Elizabeth Ann Whitney, and Elizabeth Durfee–took a carriage ride to Melissa Lott's parents' house, perhaps to counsel her about her marriage to Joseph that would occur in late September.[121] Each woman shared a knowledge of Joseph's secret teachings that united them in a special way. They understood what was going to happen Melissa,[122] then nineteen. Joseph probably noticed her when she had worked the previous year in his and Emma's home. Her father, Cornelius, helped to manage the Smiths' farm. Joseph Smith III described Melissa as "a tall, fine-looking woman with dark complexion, dark hair and eyes. She was a good singer, quite celebrated in a local way, I have heard her sing at parties and receptions in private home, on the stage where theatrical performances were given, and on the political rostrum when William Henry Harrison was running for president."[123] Melissa's plural marriage is recorded in her family Bible.[124] In 1893, she testified that she was Joseph's wife "in all that word implies," confirmation that this

---

117. Rhoda Richards Smith, Affidavit, May 1, 1869, in Joseph F. Smith, Affidavit Books, 1:17. Joseph Smith, Diary, June 12, 1843, in Faulring, *An American Prophet's Record*, "[Joseph Smith] married to Rhoda Richards and Willard Richrds married to Susan[nah Lee] Liptrot."

118. Jenson included Ells in his list of Joseph's wives, supporting it with an affidavit by John Benbow. John Benbow, Affidavit, Aug. 28, 1869, in Jenson, "Plural Marriage," 6:222-23.

119. Charlotte Haven, "A Girl's Letters from Nauvoo," *Overland Monthly*, 2d series, 96 (Dec. 1890): 629.

120. Joseph Smith, Diary, June 12, 1843, in Faulring, *An American Prophet's Record*, 387; Desdemona Fullmer Smith, Affidavit, June 17, 1869, in Joseph F. Smith, Affidavit Books.

121. See Temple Lot, Complainants Abstract, 314, for date of September 27, and Jenson, "Plural Marriage," 234, for September 20.

122. Eliza R. Snow, Journal, June 29, 1843, in Beecher, *The Personal Writings of Eliza Roxcy Snow*, 78.

123. Mary Audentia Smith Anderson and Bertha A. Anderson Hulmes, *Joseph Smith III and the Restoration*, 35.

124. Lott Family Bible.

marriage, and probably others with younger wives, was consummated.[125] She acknowledged, "I did not go to church [with him] ... was never seen on the streets or in public places with him as his wife."[126] The layering of knowledge defined personal relationships, creating insiders and outsiders among the Church membership and a hierarchy of persons most trusted by Joseph. Melissa married Joseph and her parents were sealed for eternity on the same day. Later that fall, her parents joined the Anointed Quorum.

Historian Todd Compton believes that Joseph's sealing to Nancy Maria Winchester most likely occurred before the end of 1843 when she was fourteen or fifteen years old.[127] Joseph's final known sealing that year was to Fanny Young Carr Murray, a fifty-six-year-old widow, and Brigham Young's sister, reportedly on November 2, 1843 (see chap. 21). Joseph turned thirty-eight the next month.[128]

In an important understatement, Joseph said on May 1, 1843: "Excitement has become almost the essence of my life. When that dies away I feel almost lost. When a man is reined up continually by excitement, he becomes strong and gains power and knowledge."[129] Speaking perhaps intuitively of creative genius as religious ecstasy, Joseph was seemingly filled to bursting with a sense of purpose and meaning, linked to the understandings which flooded his mind and which he believed came from God.

If ritual is a regressive act and if plurality was a ritual sweeping Joseph into a liminal state, it is easy to understand the moral fluidity that prevailed after Hyrum Smith on August 12, 1843, read his brother's revelation on plurality to the Nauvoo High Council. Ritual's fundamental motivation, according to Victor Turner, is to break free of social structure, temporarily transcending the alienation, distance, and inequality inherent in status and role differentiation.[130] The dialectic between ritual and social structure repeated itself in various forms in Nauvoo, as the Saints struggled endlessly to transcend the limitations of the secular world. Through this process, ritual changed the rules, making "not merely acceptable but glowing the hardships

---

125. Melissa Lott, in *Reorganized Church vs. Church of Christ*, Deposition Testimony, 17, 237-38, 255.

126. Melissa Lott, Testimony, Temple Lot Suit, Complainant's Abstract, 314; Melissa Lott, Affidavit, Aug. 4, 1893, Stanley Ivins Papers, Utah State Historical Society, Salt Lake City.

127. Compton, *In Sacred Loneliness*, 606. Nancy Winchester is included in Andrew Jenson's list of Joseph's wives, Jenson, "Plural Marriage," 6.

128. Jenson, "Plural Marriage," 6:234: "Fanny Young, a sister of Prs. Brigham Young, married Joseph 2 Nov. 1843. Brigham Young officiating."

129. *History of the Church*, 5:389 (May 1, 1843).

130. Victor Turner, *Dramas, Fields, and Metaphors*, 272.

and unforeseen disasters of long journeys across several national frontiers."[131] Most important, for the story of Joseph's plurality, ritual presented the possibility of experiencing temporary freedom from many–but probably not all–prevailing behavioral norms, cognitive rules, and structural constraints.[132]

Turner once described ritual's liminal stage as "a time and place lodged between all times and spaces defined and governed ... by the rules of law, politics, and religion, and by economic necessity. Here the cognitive schemata that give sense to everyday life no longer apply, but are, as it were suspended."[133] Plurality, the endowment, and the other rituals enacted in the Quorum of the Anointed and other groups in the Church suspended the Saints from earthly concerns, made them believe that anything was possible. Ritual carried them away to heaven.

131. Victor Turner, *The Drums of Affliction*, 7, 15.
132. Turner, *Dramas, Fields, and Metaphors,* 273.
133. Victor Turner, *From Ritual to Theatre*, 84.

CHAPTER 20

At Work and at Play

If I live, I will yet take these brethren through the United States and through the world, and we will make just as big a wake as God Almighty will let me.
–Joseph Smith, History of the Church, *5:256 (Jan. 20, 1843)*

The men around Joseph hung on his every word, believing them to be precious, treasured, internalized. Men like Wilford Woodruff, Willard Richards, and William Clayton recorded his utterances in both public and private meetings with equal attentiveness. A curious interaction played out between Joseph and his scribes. He was at once observer and observed, sometimes dictating the daily activities of an extraordinary life, while also interpreting that significance with scribes to add layer upon layer of observation, especially when the scribes also kept their own diaries.

Meetings reserved for only the most faithful, or for the performance of only the most special rituals, such as meetings of the Quorum of the Anointed, were of particular importance. Regardless of how often these meetings were held or how routine the rituals became, they were perhaps the most noteworthy times prophet and disciples spent together each week. They were times that transformed the ordinary world. In them, men and women believed they could become gods and build their own eternal kingdoms. They saw themselves as preparing for the fulfillment of latter-day prophecy and the glorious rewards promised to the faithful.

Joseph expanded on his dream of the kingdom in 1843. According to LDS historian Klaus Hansen, "the desire to build a Zion in the wilderness had become a peculiarly American expression of this dream."[1] Dependent on missionary work and the gathering of new members, Joseph needed

1. Klaus Hansen, *Quest for Empire*, 8.

a continued influx of new Saints for his vision of Zion to materialize. "I prophesy [that] as soon as we get the Temple built," Joseph asserted on January 20 at a council meeting of the Twelve Apostles held in Brigham Young's house, "… we will have means to gather the Saints by thousands and tens of thousands." He promised an elite group of trusted leaders, "[W]e will take ship for England and so on to all countries where we shall have a mind to go. … We must send kings and governors to Nauvoo, and we will do it."[2]

Even as he wove a narrative space that stretched beyond the territory of the two sides of the Mississippi River, Joseph agonized over the difficulties of managing both the socialization of new Saints and a financially steady path to the future. Three weeks after the January 1843 meeting of the Twelve, Joseph spent the evening at Orson Hyde's house. In the company of friends, he let his frustration show: those "brethren who came here having money, and purchased without the Church and without counsel, must be cut off."[3] It had proven impossible to convince converts to turn the money they had brought with them over to Joseph and the Church. Despite Joseph's effort to frame this instruction with his prophetic narrative, a type of ambiguity challenged the promise of American individualism and resurrected a historic tension between community and individual. Besides the infusion of religious fervor and talent that each boatload of Saints brought, only money itself in the specie-poor Mormon town promised welcome relief from the complicated debts Joseph managed. Understandably, when he could not shape his future according to his designs, he sometimes unloaded his frustrations on friends.

When Joseph spoke again to his apostles on April 19, he evoked a prophetic voice. He talked about himself in the third person at times and laced reminders that he spoke from God's revelations to him. Seven of the Twelve were there–Young, Parley P. Pratt, William Smith, John Taylor, Wilford Woodruff, George A. Smith, and Willard Richards. "I hereby command the hands to go to work on the house," Joseph pronounced.[4] God told him, Joseph attested, to tell Lucien Woodworth, leader of the temple building committee and father of his plural wife Flora, to continue to dedicate himself to the building of the Nauvoo House and to be patient until workers could be found to help him.[5]

2. *History of the Church*, 5:256 (Jan. 20, 1843).
3. Ibid., 272-73 (Feb, 13, 1843).
4. Ibid., 366 (Apr. 19, 1843).
5. Joseph Smith, Diary, Apr. 19, 1843, in Scott H. Faulring, ed., *An American Prophet's*

Joseph exhorted the Twelve to stay united, promising that they would accomplish more through their efforts together than alone.[6] Sympathizing with the difficulties they encountered, he said, "it is difficult for a man to have strength of lungs and health, to be instant in season and out of season." Rather than send the Twelve back to England, he wanted some to travel through the United States. Ominously, he added, "The Twelve must travel to save their lives." "I will not designate," Joseph said, where each of the Twelve should serve but did mention that Lorenzo Snow could stay home and rest and that Willard Richards should work on Joseph's history which was appearing serially in the *Times and Seasons.*[7] But regardless of other important Church business, he urged them all to remember that building the Nauvoo House was their mission. Joseph requested that the Twelve write to Oliver Cowdrey, one of the Three Witnesses to the Book of Mormon who had been excommunicated for apostasy in 1838, asking if he was ready to rejoin the Church. Joseph left the meeting at 4:30 p.m. that day.[8]

When nine of the Twelve had launched missionary work in the British Isles in 1840-41, they changed the nature of the Church. British converts flooded into Nauvoo, brought expertise and skills, and became consumers of real estate and other fledgling industries. According to Mormon historians James B. Allen, Ronald K. Esplin, and David J. Whittaker, "No other single assignment has had such a profound and far-reaching effect upon the Church. The apostles and their co-workers baptized thousands of people and created a missionary system that made an extraordinary contribution to continuing Church growth."[9] As important as the expansion and diversification of Church membership that resulted, the Twelve also expanded the armature of Church leadership beyond Joseph that, when they returned, became critical to the business of the Church. Events in 1843 show the maturation of that role and a shift in the emphasis on British missions to U.S. missions.

For more than a decade, the Church had moved in and out of crisis as if it were a normal state of being, and leaders had lived lives shadowed by millennial expectations. But in a little more than a year, the Twelve would move decisively to fill in the void created by Joseph's unexpected death.

Record, 370; *History of the Church*, 5:366 (Apr. 19, 1843).

6. Quorum of the Twelve Apostles, Minutes, Apr. 19, 1843.

7. Joseph Smith, Diary, Apr. 19, 1843, in Faulring, *An American Prophet's Record*, 371.

8. Joseph Smith, Diary, Apr. 19, 1843, in ibid., 372. See also Scott G. Kenney, ed., *Wilford Woodruff's Journal, 1833-1898*, 2:228 (Apr. 19, 1843); hereafter Woodruff, *Journal.*

9. James B. Allen, Ronald K. Esplin, and David J. Whittaker, *Men with a Mission*, xvi.

Although they did not know it at the time, the work they did in 1843 strengthened their experience and ability to lead in Joseph's absence–some managing publications or real estate, others new missions or preaching at home. Each had, by Joseph's death, been introduced to plurality. The parameters of their family lives were shifting radically. It was not easy; but as a group, they were persuaded that Joseph was a prophet and that Mormonism was the restoration of an ancient religion. They were men mostly in their thirties or early forties. Some had known Joseph for ten years; each measured his life by his beliefs.

Joseph called Brigham Young to the Quorum of Twelve Apostles in February 1835. Charged with bringing the restored gospel "to all the nations, kindreds, tongues, and people," the apostles worked for the Church at home and abroad.[10] In Kirtland, Ohio, Young spent summers as a missionary in the East. He moved with the Church to Missouri, then helped to organize the exodus to Illinois. In Great Britain, as president of the Twelve, he developed the organizational skills that made him a colonizer in the Great Basin Kingdom. Helping to direct missionary work included the production of hymnals, launching the *Millennial Star,* and organizing the immigration of nearly 1,000 converts to Nauvoo. Once back in Nauvoo, Young helped to supervise missionary efforts, to negotiate land purchases for the new immigrants, and absorbed Joseph's new teachings.

William Clayton was converted to the Mormon message in Preston, England, in 1837 at age twenty-three. Described by biographer George D. Smith as "never swerving in his belief in the church and its leaders,"[11] Clayton was a meticulous scribe to the prophet of a growing church. He was serious and dependable, the "soul of punctuality." His daughter remembered his "love for order, which he believed was the first law of heaven. … [H]e would not carry a watch that was not accurate."[12] Though never an apostle, Clayton nonetheless witnessed some of the most critical moments in the evolution of Church doctrine. He heard Joseph speak to a variety of audiences, and through his own journal and notes he took for Joseph, he interpreted the history of the Church for future generations.

Unlike the individualism that swept Jacksonian America during the time of the Mormon sojourn in Nauvoo, Joseph's vision for the good society included an all-encompassing religion that seeped into every aspect

10. Ibid., 1603.
11. George D. Smith, ed., *An Intimate Chronicle*, xvii.
12. Qtd. in ibid., xvi.

of life. His followers willingly threw their whole selves into their work, weaving mundane chores into the same cultural milieu as proselytizing or preaching. The good of the community reigned supreme over the good of the individual, and the lines between the sacred and the profane blurred. Society had always had an interest in marriage and familial relations; but in the Latter-day Saint world, family became the sacred landscape of the plural marriage ritual and ascent toward godhood. "At the deepest level," Lawrence Foster has said, plural marriage "was a fundamental protest against the careless individualism of romantic love, which seemed to threaten the very roots of family life and social solidarity."[13]

One can only imagine the way adherents leaned in to hear Joseph speak or reached out for his handshake upon welcome or departure. He drew them in with a brightness and optimism so potent as to be tangible. Separated from the outside world by the boundaries that their distinctive beliefs created, they became unquestioning in their loyalty to Joseph, clamoring for his attention, his interpretation of scripture or of any natural event. This fascination was centered in his charisma to be sure, but only to a certain degree. For them, Joseph was first of all a prophet, and his role as prophet positioned him, in their minds, as one who spoke with God. His prophet-narrative, a frame more powerful than wealth or political influence, rendered everything he said significant, even critical.[14] Prophethood functioned as a lens through which followers examined the world and Joseph's role in it. It framed the rituals of plurality, the endowment, and the restoration message with new meaning. Importantly, it initiated followers "into a largely unknown new condition of being. In effect, Smith was attempting to demolish an old way of life and build a new social order from the ground up."[15]

Revelations that Joseph received between 1841 and 1843 created a platform for the temple endowment and plurality. At their core was a connection between the living and the dead and the ways ritual bridged the gap, made operational by priesthood authority. Baptism for the dead, marriage sealings, and endowments gave the Saints new understandings about their part in the salvation of human beings–living and dead. The temple became the threshold between the spiritual and material worlds. In the same way, Joseph rendered God and godhood knowable. This made the

13. Lawrence Foster, *Religion and Sexuality*, 139.
14. See ibid., 143.
15. Ibid.

temple ceremonies turning points. Everyday men and women became *de facto* priests and priestesses, gods and goddesses. Like them, God became a being with whom Joseph conversed.

As chaos built gradually around him toward a crescendo, Joseph turned inward, making decisions in an increasingly private, inward way. In fact, according to Foster, it was in the "context of this rapidly increasing tension that Smith chose to represent in Nauvoo doctrines that had long been germinating in his mind. Apparently foreseeing the possibility of his eventual martyrdom, Smith became obsessed with teaching even his most controversial ideas to his close associates, lest those ideas die with him."[16]

The liminality that sprang from Joseph's developing religious theology and ritual colored the "now" and bestowed sacred significance and power on even routine moments. The intensity of his followers' friendship–their shared *communitas*–produced the sense that each brought something powerful and valued to the grand unfolding drama. The feeling was exhilarating. They were building the kingdom of God; their lives were special, distinct, sacred.[17]

It is difficult to imagine the force it took to sweep some of Joseph's followers–men like William Law–away from the light his leadership cast. But during the next year, a steady stream of such men turned away. Foster captures this ripping asunder: "Joseph Smith's passionate sincerity and direct emotional engagement with his followers was a key element of his appeal and charisma. But such emotional power was a two-edged sword; it could lead to passionate love or, equally, to passionate hatred. There often seemed to be no middle ground. Either one was for the prophet, or one was against him."[18]

Challenges to Joseph's Prophethood

In some ways, Joseph was a ready target for charlatans or critics determined to disprove his claims to revelation or powers of translation. It was inevitable that, as his life played out as a prophet, his activities would collide with the less-than-scrupulous agenda of others. The Kinderhook Plates episode was one such event. A layered history, it was understood one way by contemporaries and insiders, another way by critics hoping to discredit the Church, and still a third way by contemporary historians.

16. Ibid., 142.
17. See ibid., 168.
18. Ibid., 169.

The story began in 1843 Kinderhook, Pike County, Illinois, seventy-two miles from Nauvoo. Three men buried a set of six bell-shaped brass plates measuring about 2 ⅞ inches by 2 ¼ inches. The men placed them in an ancient burial mound, then pretended to uncover them near the body of an unidentified man. They went public with their "discovery," displaying the plates in the nearby town of Quincy. Motivation for such a ruse must have included the promise of financial reward; but framing it in Illinois was the Book of Mormon and Joseph's prophet-narrative–his claims to translate ancient texts. Much of what we know about this episode comes from local papers. A few Saints also noted the discovery in their personal journals, thus helping to create the Mormon vantage point.

According to the *Quincy Whig:*

> There were but few bones found in the mound; and it is believed, that it was but the burial place of a small number, perhaps of a person, or family of distinction, in ages long gone by. … The plates above alluded to, were exhibited in this city [Quincy] last week, and are now, we understand, in Nauvoo, subject to the inspection of the Mormon Prophet. The public curiosity is greatly excited, and if Smith can decipher the hieroglyphics on the plates, he will do more towards throwing light on the early history of this continent, than any man now living.[19]

The *Times and Seasons* announced the find on May 1, 1843, speculating, "Circumstances are daily transpiring which give additional testimony to the authenticity of the Book of Mormon." As much the reflection of gossip as of fact, the discovery seemed significant to those who had banked their lives on the translation of ancient scripture. The *Times and Seasons* continued:

> Mr. Smith has had those [Kinderhook] plates, what his opinion concerning them is, we have not yet ascertained. The gentleman that owns them has taken them away, or we should have given a fac smilie of the plates and characters in this number. We are informed however, that he purposes returning with them for translation; if so, we may be able yet to furnish our readers with it.[20]

19. "Singular Discovery–Material for Another Mormon Book," *Quincy Whig* 6, no. 2 (May 3, 1843).

20. "Ancient Records," *Times and Seasons* 4, no. 12 (May 1, 1843): 186. The *Times and Seasons* was published bi-monthly, and released with less than predictable regularity. In this example, the May 3 story published in the *Quincy Whig* was published in the *Times and Seasons* dated May 1, 1843.

From the later confession of the hoaxsters, here are the facts: Bridge Whitton, Robert Wiley, and Wilbur Fugate concocted a plan to see if Joseph could tell the difference between an authentic document and a forgery. Whitton cut six copper sheets in bell shapes, Wiley and Fugate etched marks intended to look like writing on them, then applied acid to age the plates artificially. Bound together with pieces of rusted hoop iron and then buried with Native American bones in an old mound in the area, the plates lay beneath the earth waiting to be "discovered." Cautious about possible hoaxes and perhaps because the *New York Herald* had recently reported that the Egyptian language had been fully deciphered and that a grammar had been published in England,[21] Joseph never published even a partial translation (which may also explain why his Book of Abraham translation apparently stalled).

On May 1, William Clayton recorded that Joseph had "translated a portion" and "says they contain the history of the person with whom they were found and he was a descendant of Ham through the loins of Pharaoh king of Egypt, and that he received his kingdom from the ruler of heaven and earth." Clayton reported that he had seen the "6 brass plates" himself. The mound was nine feet high and the skeleton on whose breast they were found was "about 6 feet from the surface of the earth." Clayton sketched one plate in his journal. "This diagram shows the size of the plates being drawn on the edge of one of them," he noted. "They are covered with ancient characters of language containing from 30 to 40 on each side of the plates."[22] The *History of the Church* placed Clayton's diary entry in Joseph's voice: "I insert fac-similes of the six brass plates found near Kinderhook, in Pike County, Illinois, on April 23, by Mr. Robert Wiley and others, while excavating a large mound. They found a skeleton about six feet from the surface of the earth, which must have stood nine feet high. The plates were found on the breast of the skeleton and were covered on both sides with ancient characters."[23]

A second contemporary source is a letter written by non-Mormon

21. "Egyptian Antiquities," *New York Herald*, Dec. 28, 1842, 2.

22. Allen, *Nor Toil Nor Labor Fear*, 393.

23. *History of the Church*, 5:372 (May 1, 1843). Stanley W. Kimball, "Kinderhook Plates," 2:789, acknowledges that extensive tests on one of the original Kinderhook plates "proved conclusively that the plate was one of the Kinderhook six; that it had been engraved, not etched; and that it was of nineteenth-century manufacture. There thus appears no reason to accept the Kinderhook plates as anything but a frontier hoax." This conclusion leaves unanswered what his scribe, William Clayton, meant when he said Joseph "translated" the plates or, more fundamentally, what he understood by the word "translation."

Charlotte Haven, who wrote to "My dear home friends," on May 2, 1843. Joshua Moore, who exhibited the plates to Joseph, alleged that Joseph said "the figures or writing on them were similar to that in which the Book of Mormon was written, and if Mr. Moore could leave them, he thought that by the help of revelation he would be able to translate them."[24]

Like Clayton, Brigham Young sketched the plates in his diary, with the comment, "I took this at Joseph Smiths house found near Quincy."[25] Parley P. Pratt described the discovery in a letter dated May 7: "Six plates having the appearance of Brass have lately been dug out of a mound … They are small and filled with engravings in Egyptian language and contain the genealogy of one of the ancient Jaredites back to Ham the son of Noah."[26] The similarities in these accounts suggest how the story spread through Nauvoo. In ways, it mirrored Joseph's story about the Book of Mormon plates, but the differences in the narrative were critical. It was not precipitated by a prayerful request, framed by a heavenly messenger as sacred text, or brought into the company of the other ancient scripture.

Joseph was allowed to keep the plates at his home for a short period of time. Reuben Hedlock, who earlier had made woodcuts of three facsimiles from the Book of Abraham Egyptian papyri, also made woodcuts of the Kinderhook Plates–a total of twelve, two for each plate. A broadside with the images was published on June 24, 1843, and sold for a dollar a dozen.[27] A decade after Joseph had died, W. P. Harris, in a letter to W. C. Flagg on April 25, 1855, reported a second-hand version of the hoax. "Bridge Whitton said to me that he cut and prepared the plates and he (B. Whitton) and R. Wiley engraved them themselves, and that there was nitric acid put upon them the night before that they were found to rust the iron ring and band. And that they were carried to the mound, rubbed in the dirt and carefully dropped into the pit where they were found."[28]

Twenty-four years later, in 1879, Wilbur Fugate admitted his deceit in a letter. He claimed they manufactured the items complete with "hieroglyphics by making impressions on beeswax and filling them with acid."[29]

24. Charlotte Haven, Letter to "My dear home friends," May 2, 1843, in *Overland Monthly* 16 (Dec. 1890): 630.

25. Brigham Young, Journal, May 3, 1843, LDS Church History Library.

26. Parley P. Pratt, May 7, 1843, qtd. in Stanley B. Kimball, "Kinderhook Plates Brought to Joseph Smith Appear to Be a Nineteenth-Century Hoax," 73.

27. "Discovery of the Brass Plates," broadside, June 24, 1843.

28. W. P. Harris, Letter to W. C. Flagg, Apr. 25, 1855, in "A Hoax: Reminiscences of an Old Kinderhook Mystery," 272.

29. Wilbur Fugate, Mound Station, Illinois, Letter to James T. Cobb, June 30, 1879, qtd. in

He described the alleged excavation as "a HUMBUG, gotten up by Robert Wiley, Bridge Whitton and myself." They were reacting to the claims of Mormon missionaries: "We read [Parley P.] Pratt's prophecy that 'Truth is yet to spring out of the earth.' We concluded to prove the prophecy by way of a joke."[30]

In 1980, Mormon historian Stanley B. Kimball, with the cooperation of both the LDS Church and the Chicago Historical Society, where the plates resided, conducted a series of tests on one of the plates. Kimball's conclusion was that the plate was a brass alloy dating from the mid-nineteenth century.[31] According to Kimball, "[S]peculation about the plates and their possible content was apparently quite unrestrained in Nauvoo when the plates first appeared. … Whether or not [Clayton] was present when Joseph Smith saw the plates is unknown."[32] Because Clayton was Joseph's secretary, it is likely he had access to the plates in Joseph's possession. Kimball asserts that much of what men like Clayton, Pratt, and others who commented on the discovery said about the Kinderhook Plates and their significance in relation to Mormon scripture was based on "hearsay stories circulating in Nauvoo."[33] It is clear the plates caused a reaction; the broadside is concrete evidence, and so are the mentions in the diaries and letters of Church leaders. But no translation from Joseph survives in written form.

Business of the Kingdom

On Sunday, May 21, 1843, Joseph preached on 2 Peter 1. That afternoon the sacrament of bread and water was administered in the temple for the first time.[34] Two days later, he met in his office with some of the Twelve including Brigham Young, Heber Kimball, Parley Pratt, Orson Pratt, Orson Hyde, Wilford Woodruff, John Taylor, George A. Smith, Willard Richards, and other leaders to bless and set them apart for their new missions.[35] The following Saturday, Young, Kimball, Hyde, Woodruff, Taylor, George A. Smith, and Richards met as a council with Joseph and

Wilhelm Wyl [pseud. Wilhelm Ritter von Wymental], *Mormon Portraits*, 207-208. Also reproduced in W. A. Linn, *The Story of the Mormons*, 87.

30. Fugate to Cobb, in Wyl, *Mormon Portraits*, 207-208.

31. Kimball, "Kinderhook Plates Brought to Joseph Smith Appear to be a Nineteenth-Century Hoax," 69.

32. Ibid., 67, 71.

33. Ibid., 73.

34. Clayton, Journal, May 21, 1843, in Smith, *An Intimate Chronicle*, 105.

35. *History of the Church*, 5:404 (May 23, 1843).

Hyrum. Their main business centered on mission assignments, and Hyde read a copy of a letter of recommendation and identification that the missionaries would carry.

Before adjoining, the men also took up the case of Benjamin Winchester in Philadelphia "for improper conduct, for slandering the Saints in Philadelphia," and specifically to investigate a letter from Sybella Armstrong.[36] Claiming that he was not prepared to respond to the allegations, Winchester rebutted by summarizing at length the gossip he had heard about Armstrong.[37] Winchester was thirty-six years old and the president of the Church's Philadelphia branch. A zealous missionary, he claimed to have baptized thousands of converts and was an original member of the Quorum of the Seventy. He could also be mercurial, self-centered, and imperious. Unpersuaded, Joseph "rebuked Elder Winchester in the sharpest manner. Said he had a lying spirit & had lied about him & told him of many of his errors" and that Joseph himself had been "under the ire of his tongue." Joseph and Hyrum disagreed about the way to proceed: "Hyrum pleaded for mercy, Joseph for justice."[38] Young thought Winchester should relinquish his license and cease preaching altogether.

According to Woodruff, Young was defiant and

> said his mind was made up & the remarks of Brother Hyrum or of Br Joseph had not altered it. As for himself he would not sit upon the case another day. He considered it an insult upon his office & calling as an apostle of Jesus Christ & he would not bear it. As for the rest of the Twelve [they] might do as they pleased. As for himself he would not do it. Benjamin Winchester has despised & rejected the council of the presidency & the Twelve had said they had no Jurisdiction over him in Philadelphia & to say whare he should go &c. But he & others will find their is power in the Twelve. ... Benjemin Winchester has never for the first time received our council but has gone contrary to it. No one is safe in his hands. He calls Hiram an old granny & slanders evrybody. He says their is a contradiction between Hiram & the Twelve. Their is no contradiction between us & Hiram is there Br Hiram? (Hiram answers no.)

When Young sat down, Joseph responded, telling the men he would offer some instruction, if they would accept it. He had changed his mind

36. Ibid., 403 (May 22, 1843). See also Woodruff, *Journal*, 2:234 (May 27, 1843).
37. "History of Joseph Smith," *Millennial Star* 21 (1859): 171.
38. Ibid.

under Young's rhetoric, and now thought it was proper to "take [Winchester's] lisence & have him come to Nauvoo & if he would not do that let him go out of the Church. It was then Mooved & seconded that Elder Winchester be silenced & give up his lisence & come with his family to Nauvoo which was carried unanimously."[39] Joseph "instructed the Twelve [Apostles] to call up[on] the whole Philadelphia Church while in the council."[40]

At the Twelve's next meeting, three more missionaries were assigned, and the whole Philadelphia branch was "counselled … to come to Nauvoo," with notice being posted in the *Times and Seasons*.[41] This reactionary, punitive directive would impact the 200 members of the branch.

Noah Rogers, Addison Pratt, Benjamin F. Grouard, and Knowlton Hanks left for missions to the Sandwich Islands on June 1 on board the "steamer *Sarah Ann*."[42] Reuben Hedlock was sent to "preside over the churches" in England, and to manage immigration and Church business more generally.[43] Also on June 1, the Twelve met "[t]o make some arrangements to start on their missions" to the East Coast and other locations in the United States to "collect funds for the Nauvoo House & temple."[44] "We each one of us bound ourselves under bonds of two thousands Dollars," wrote Wilford Woodruff, "for the faithful performance of our duty in making strict returns of all property put into our hands to the trustee in trust." Joseph gave each man a letter identifying him to the Saints and affirming that he was authorized to collect donations. Woodruff copied this letter, peppered with purple prose, into his journal:

> Dear Brethren & friends I Joseph Smith a servant of the Lord and Trustee in trust for the Church of Jesus Christ of Latter Day Saints do hereby certify that the bearer hereof Wilford Woodruff an Elder and one of the Twelve Apostles of the Church of Jesus Christ of Latter Day Saints has deposited with me his bond and security to my full satisfaction according to the resolution of the conference held in this city on the 6th day of April last. He therefore is recommended to all Saints & honorable people as a legal agent to collect funds for the purpose of Building the Nauvoo house and Temple of the Lord Confident that he will honor this high trust as

39. Woodruff, *Journal*, 2:235-36 (May 27, 1843).
40. Joseph Smith, Diary, May 27, 1843, in Faulring, *An American Prophet's Record*, 381.
41. Ibid., May 29, 1843 (Faulring, 382); Quorum of the Twelve Apostles, Minutes, May 29, 1843.
42. *History of the Church*, 5:417 (June 1, 1843).
43. Ibid., 405.
44. Woodruff, *Journal*, 2:237 (June 1, 1843).

> well as ardently fulfill his Commission as a messenger of peace and Salvation as one of the Lords noble men I can fervently say may the Lord clear his way before him, and bless him and bless those that obey his teachings wherever there are ears to hear & hearts to feel. … Laus Deus. Praise God.

Finally, Joseph reminded the Saints that he was "one that greatly desires the salvation of man" and urged them "to strive with a godly zeal for virtue, holiness, and the commandments of the Lord. Be good. Be wise; be just, be liberal; and above all be charitable always abounding in all good works. And may health peace and the love of God our Father and the grace of Jesus Christ our Lord be and abide with you all is the Sincere Prayer of your devoted brother & friend …"[45] Although signed by Joseph, the letter was doubtless drafted by W. W. Phelps, whose penchant for rhetorical excess was well known.[46]

By 1843, the role of the twelve apostles had "significantly expanded."[47] Brigham Young and the rest of the Twelve called and appointed missionaries and helped the newly baptized settle in Nauvoo. On July 30, Woodruff noted that six apostles met in Temperance Hall in Pittsburgh and were "addressed by Elder H. C. Kimball who gave some of his experience & bore testimony to the work of the Lord much to our edifycation. He was followed by Elder B Young who also bore testimony to the work of the Lord."[48] Their remarks conjured up their prophet, whom they carried with them on their mission to strangers and Saints. "Joseph Smith is the Prophet of God as an instrument in the hands of God is the Author of it. He is the greatest man on earth. No other man of this age has power to assemble such a great people from all the Nations of the earth with all their varied dispositions as assimulate them & cement them together so that they will be subject to rule & order."[49] This conviction more than justified anything Joseph ever asked of them.

Intimate Glimpses

Joseph may have been a prophet, but he was also a man with an appetite for action and stimulation. His temporal roles as father, friend, civic

45. Ibid., 238. See also Brigham Young's letter in *History of the Church* 5:416-17 (June 1, 1843).
46. Samuel Brown, "The Translator and the Ghostwriter," 26, 31, 47.
47. Allen, Whittaker, and Esplin, *Men with a Mission*, 315.
48. Woodruff, *Journal*, 2:267 (July 30, 1843).
49. Ibid., 268, lists the apostles called to this eastern mission.

leader allowed him to act one way, while his role as prophet another. In a typical layering of temporal and spiritual matters, on February 8, 1843, Joseph bundled up to exercise "by sliding on the ice" with his seven-year-old son Frederick.[50] The next day, he received a revelation that later would be canonized as Doctrine and Covenants 129: "there are two kinds of beings in heaven"–resurrected angels, who have bodies of flesh and bones, and "the spirits of just men."[51] Moving between the sacred and profane spheres required agility, and Joseph was usually adept at the requisite shifts. For him–though not always for others–life was an integrated whole. He visited the various chautauquas[52] that came through town, brushing up against the curious and intellectual. His interests ranged from phrenology to astronomy to German to political intrigue. His mind was curious and absorbent, pulling in the new and exotic and positioning them within the framework of ancient doctrines.

As mayor, Joseph held city court on March 10, 1843, deciding a medical malpractice suit. At the end of the day, he and friends stood outside to watch rays of light streak across the sky in the shape of a sword. The next day, he prophesied that the "sword seen last evening is the sure sign thereof," presumably meaning a sign of coming battle.[53] He then traveled with Brigham Young from Nauvoo to Ramus, where he challenged the strongest man in town to a stick-pulling contest, exerting himself so much that the next day, as he blessed nineteen children, he suddenly turned pale and lost strength.[54] He attributed the weakness to Satan, who would "exert his influence to destroy the children" whom he was blessing.[55] Exhausted from hours of study and contemplation, Joseph collapsed in sleep on a pile of law books in his office on March 18. Reinvigorated by his nap, he later played ball with young boys in the street.[56] He was a physically vigorous man, who loved a good challenge and moved easily between mind and body.

Coming upon two boys, muddy and sweaty from wrestling in the middle of the street one day, Joseph pulled them apart, scolded them, and

---

50. *History of the Church*, 5:265 (Feb. 8, 1843).

51. Ibid., 267 (Feb. 9, 1843).

52. Chautauquas were a kind of nineteenth-century/early-twentieth-century adult education program. Traveling lecturers and performers visited rural American towns and presented a wide range of topics. They brought culture to the backwoods village or mid-sized town.

53. Woodruff, *Journal*, 2:219 (Mar. 10, 1843); see also *History of the Church*, 5:301 (Mar. 10, 1843).

54. *History of the Church*, 5:302 (Mar. 11, 13, 1843).

55. Ibid., 303 (Mar. 12, 1843).

56. Ibid., 307 (Mar. 18, 1843).

reprimanded onlookers for failing to intervene. He then "returned to the court, and told them that nobody was allowed to fight in Nauvoo but myself," he joked.[57]

It is important to retain sight of the prophet's earthy warmth. Joseph wanted the world he inhabited to be fair and good. Despite the elaborate theological vision he narrated, Joseph loved most people, particularly children, and embraced common humor upon occasion. He loved to jolly up those who took themselves too seriously. A range of concerts given by local musicians out-of-doors never failed to entertain him. Lectures on phrenology, natural disasters, or the latest medical contraption–no topic was too sophisticated or commonplace for his attention. Dances and dinners were frequent events at the Nauvoo House; both Emma and he loved to entertain. For him, heaven consisted of the same kinds of joys and pleasures he found so appealing on earth.

57. Ibid., 282-83 (Feb. 20, 1843).

CHAPTER 21

Secrets

Iniquity of any kind cannot be sustained in the Church, and it will not fare well where I am; for I am determined while I do lead the Church, to lead it right.
–Joseph Smith, History of the Church, *5:411 (May 27, 1843)*

Joseph could not wait for the completion of the Nauvoo temple. The secular space of the upper level of his red brick store or the various other locations where the endowment ceremony was performed were rendered sacred through the language, clothing, and imagined spaces of the rituals themselves. Participants received new names and donned special clothing, including special garments bearing Masonic-like marks to be worn from that time forward. They moved from space to space where they noticed a curtain hanging from one side to the other. Passing solemnly from "chamber" to "chamber," they received "instructions … signs, tokens, penalties with the Key words."[1] At the core of the endowment was new knowledge about the plan of salvation and finding one's way back into God's presence. Hope and fear both coexisted in the narrative. Joseph and the others who led the ritual showed them ways their faithfulness could be tested. Then participants gathered in a circle near the conclusion of the ceremony in the "true order of prayer." The special rite empowered them to "ask questions of God with confidence that their prayers would be answered."[2]

Only the most faithful Saints were to be initiated in the mysteries of the endowment. The rhetoric of the ritual promised members they could become "kings and priests" and "queens and priestesses,"[3] and offered them nothing

1. L. John Nuttall, Diary, Feb. 7, 1877.
2. Devery S. Anderson and Gary James Bergera, eds., *Joseph Smith's Quorum of the Anointed,* xxii.
3. See George Miller, Autobiography, in "De Tal Palo Tal Astilla," qtd. in Anderson and

less than the fullness of blessings prepared for the Church of the First Born.[4] Instruction framed by ritual tied what was possible to a set of understandings by which Joseph would help members of his Quorum of the Anointed know what God required. The endowment ordinance became perhaps the most powerful way the men and women remembered their collective identity as forming a sort of *communitas*. It focused their attention on Joseph's leading them back into heaven.

The prayer circle was part of the ritual first introduced on May 4, 1842. Historian D. Michael Quinn points to the "binding" quality of the circle, the way it connected "religious participants as a group distinct from the unenlightened, the unconverted, and the uninitiated."[5] As a ritual, it symbolically depicted the coming together of persons in a holy community. Participants would clasp the hands of those next to them, a gesture that evoked the uniting goal of building the kingdom of God. Like other ordinances they would later perform in the temple, there was a precedent for prayer circles among the Masons and other groups. "Lodges were opened at sunrise, the Master taking his station in the East and the brethren forming a half circle around him."[6] David Bernard describes the circle and accompanying use of symbols in Masonic ritual: "The brethren assemble around the altar, and form a circle and stand in such a position as to touch each other, leaving a space for the Most Excellent Master; [who] … then kneels, [and] joins hands with the others, which closes the circle."[7]

The men and women in the Anointed Quorum were the elite in the Church. Between 1842 and 1844, they met in four primary locations: (1) September to November 1843, in a second-floor room in the Mansion House facing the street; (2) November to December 1843, in the southeast room of the Homestead; (3) December 1843 to June 1844, in the upper chambers of the red brick store; and (4) a few times in Brigham Young's house between January and February 1844.[8] Joseph used these meetings to teach new doctrines, notably plurality, and to spell out strategies to help his followers detect those who held sincere beliefs and those who camouflaged more complicated, suspicious motivations.

Bergera, *Joseph Smith's Quorum of the Anointed*, 7, 9; Joseph Smith, Diary, Sept. 28, 1843, in Scott H. Faulring, ed., *An American Prophet's Record*, 416.

4. *History of the Church*, 5:2 (May 4, 1842).
5. D. Michael Quinn, "Latter-day Saint Prayer Circles," 1.
6. Albert G. Mackey, *An Encyclopedia of Freemasonry*, 2:595.
7. David Bernard, *Light on Masonry*, 116-17.
8. Quinn, "Latter-day Saint Prayer Circles," 86.

When the Anointed Quorum met on May 26, 1843, members received instructions "on the priesthood, and the new and everlasting covenant" of celestial marriage.[9] The next day, the same men and a few others met again in Joseph's store, where Joseph taught them how to judge conflicts: "in all our counsels, especially while on trial of any one we should see and observe all things appertaining to the subject, and discern the spirit by which either party was governed. … We should keep order and not let the council be imposed upon by unruly conduct. … Iniquity of any kind cannot be sustained in the Church, and it will not fare well where I am; for I am determined while I do lead the Church, to lead it right."[10] Thus, Joseph extended his influence through a small, tightly knit force of devoted disciples.

May 28 was an unseasonably cold, rainy day, but one with sacred significance for Emma. For that day she was finally sealed "for eternity" to her husband of sixteen years.[11] It was a bold, if calculated, effort on Joseph's part to assure Emma of her unchanged place in his affections and of her eternal place by his side. It also seems to have been intended to compensate for the nine women to whom he had already been eternally sealed that year, perhaps as many as sixteen in total, including the Partridge sisters. In the same meeting, James Adams was sealed to his wife, Harriett.

The prayers voiced in that meeting expressed the concerns that challenged the Saints' security. Members hoped "that James Adams might be delivered from his enemies, that O[rrin] P. Rockwell [be released from prison in Missouri for the attempted assassination of ex-Governor Lilburn Boggs], and [that] the Twelve be prospered in collecting means to build the Nauvoo House."[12] The next day, Hyrum was sealed to Jerusha Barden, his deceased first wife, with his second wife, Mary Fielding, acting as her proxy. Then Hyrum and Mary were sealed. Willard and Jennetta Richards were also sealed in the same meeting.[13] A network of familial and spiritual relationships resulted, a web of connections that rent the veil between their temporal and spiritual lives.

Women had been excluded from the Anointed for the first year. Then,

---

9. Joseph Smith, Diary, May 26, 1843, qtd. in Anderson and Bergera, *Joseph Smith's Quorum of the Anointed*, 17.

10. *History of the Church*, 5:411 (May 27, 1843).

11. Joseph Smith, Diary, May 28, 1843, in Faulring, *An American Prophet's Record*, 381. See also Anderson and Bergera, *Joseph Smith's Quorum of the Anointed*, 19n6.

12. Joseph Smith, Diary, May 28, 1843, qtd. in Anderson and Bergera, *Joseph Smith's Quorum of the Anointed*, 19.

13. "Minutes of the Anointed Quorum," May 29, 1843, qtd. in Anderson and Bergera, *Joseph Smith's Quorum of the Anointed*, 21n8.

on September 28, 1843, Emma was allowed to join, followed by the wives of men who were already members. By the time Joseph died, sixty-six persons had been endowed.[14] According to Devery S. Anderson and Gary James Bergera, "an important aspect of the quorum … was family relatedness."[15] Lucy Mack Smith (Joseph's mother), Agnes M. Coolbrith Smith (Don Carlos Smith's widow and a plural wife of Joseph), Fanny Young Murray (the widowed sister of Brigham Young and a plural wife of Joseph), Mercy R. Fielding Thompson (the widowed sister-in-law and plural wife of Hyrum), and "Sister Durfee" (Joseph's plural wife, Elizabeth Durfee) expanded family definitions in new ways.[16]

The locale of that significant September 28 meeting was the upper front room of the Mansion House, with William Law and William Marks also in attendance. Joseph led the group in prayer "that his [Joseph's] days might be prolonged until his mission on the earth is accomplished, have dominion over his enemies, all their households be blessed, and all the Church and the world."[17] According to his diary, Joseph and Emma then received what has come to be known as the second anointing.[18] Also sometimes called the "fullness of the priesthood," the second anointing ordinance functioned to fulfill the latent promises of the first anointing.[19]

This meeting foretold the expansion of Joseph's power beyond the spiritual into a domain with no apparent boundaries.[20] It is impossible to miss the strategic importance of this rhetorical move for men and women who had experienced the poverty and privation of Missouri. In the tenuous security of Nauvoo, they were seizing power, moving beyond the uncertainty of the present into a grand future of limitless possibility. For Church leaders, the inclusion of their wives in this honored and powerful state strengthened their loyalty by committing their spouses to support the heavenly kingdom.[21]

14. Anderson and Bergera, *Joseph Smith's Quorum of the Anointed*, xxxiii.

15. Ibid., xxx.

16. Ibid., xxxiv-xxxv.

17. *History of the Church*, 6:39 (Sept. 28, 1843).

18. Joseph Smith, Diary, Sept. 28, 1843, in Faulring, *An American Prophet's Record*, 416.

19. See David John Buerger, "'The Fulness of the Priesthood,'" 10-44; see also David John Buerger, *The Mysteries of Godliness*, 62-63. The first anointing promised recipients they could become priests and priestesses, gods and goddesses. The second anointing confirmed these titles on them.

20. D. Michael Quinn, *The Mormon Hierarchy: Origins of Power*, 124, 643. See also D. Michael Quinn, "The Council of Fifty and Its Members, 1844-1945," 164-66, 185-86; Andrew F. Ehat, "'It Seems Like Heaven Began on Earth,'" 254-57, 264, 267, 268; and Hyrum L. Andrus, *Doctrines of the Kingdom*, 550-60.

21. Joseph's initiation of the endowment did not mean that he saw the temple as less

Yet however grandiose and exaggerated the hope that the language of second anointing portrayed for the faithful, it generated rumors that swirled around the state from that point forward, alarming Joseph's enemies who were already concerned about the Mormons' undemocratic tendencies. Stories about kings and presidents in the Latter-day Saint secret world helped to create the conditions that led to Joseph's and Hyrum's deaths in June 1844.

On November 2, 1843, Fanny Young Carr Murray, Brigham Young's fifty-six-year-old widowed sister, overheard Young and Joseph talking about the link between celestial marriage and exaltation. "When I get into the celestial kingdom," she reportedly said, "if I ever do get there, I shall request the privilege of being a ministering angel ... I don't want any companion in that world ..."[22] Joseph told her not to talk so "foolishly," adding, "you do not know what you will want." He then instructed Young to seal her to him on the spot, an ordinance Fanny accepted meekly.[23] It was Joseph's last known plural marriage.

Like many of Joseph's marriages, this sealing linked the two men as kin for time and eternity. The marriage was a demonstration of Fanny's faith and her deference to male authority. Although it would have been difficult for her to resist this proposal from the prophet, it was nevertheless proof of her devotion to his leadership. For her faithfulness, Fanny was further honored the next month, on December 23, when she received her endowment along with several other members of the Relief Society.

Twenty-one-year-old Bathsheba Bigler Smith, wife of Joseph's cousin, George A. Smith, years later described the ritual of her endowment, also on December 23: Mary Fielding Smith, Hyrum's wife, "anointed me in Emma's bedroom blessed me; she said I was a good girl ... poured oil on my head, and blessed me that was all that was done, and all that was said. ... I had different clothing on from what I wore when I went to the house first. This anointing was for the purpose of initiating me in the secret society and order of endowments." The women then proceeded into the "hall where these endowments were given, there was no curtain separating the ladies from the gentlemen; we did not have any curtain at all. I did not take any oath or make any promises in Sister Emma's bedroom" where the initial washing

important; rather, he pushed its construction vigorously as a sacred setting for these special ordinances. See *History of the Church*, 5:423, 424 (June 11, 1842).

22. Brigham Young, Aug. 31, 1873, JD 16:167.

23. Fanny is mentioned as Joseph's plural wife in several affidavits included in Andrew Jenson, "Plural Marriage," 6:233; see also Benjamin F. Johnson, in Dean R. Zimmerman, ed., *I Knew the Prophets*, 38.

and anointing was done. "Afterwards we promised not to reveal our endowments, or tell what it was."[24]

At the same time that the Anointed Quorum enhanced the layers of loyalty, secrecy, and ritual required of those most committed to Joseph's prophetic vision, the subterranean practice of plurality expanded. Although Ebenezer Robinson later left the Church, he apparently was privy to some of these private introductions during the summer of 1843. He later claimed that the subject of the plurality of wives was "so closely pressed that I felt that the time was at hand when I must determine whether to accept or reject it." The idea caused him "much turmoil and prayer," but he finally decided he could not accept it. Plurality made it impossible for him to stay in the fellowship of the Saints. According to Robinson, Nauvoo Stake President William Marks also opposed the practice.[25]

By Robinson's recollection, the members of Nauvoo's stake high council did not know how to react on August 12, 1843, when Hyrum read Joseph's revelation (LDS D&C 132) to them.[26] The council members who were present were James Allred, Austin A. Cowles, Samuel Bent, David Fullmer, Thomas Grover, George W. Harris, William Huntington, Levi Jackman, Aaron Johnson, William Marks, Phineas Richards, Leonard Soby, and Dunbar Wilson. Some had already heard rumors about the secret doctrine and were anxious to understand what it meant, but none had yet been approached about entering plurality.[27] Hyrum read the revelation and testified to its truth; then, according to Grover, Hyrum announced: "Now you that believe this revelation and go forth and obey the same shall be saved, and you that reject it shall be damned."[28]

Marks, Cowles (Joseph's father-in-law in plurality), and Soby refused to support the radical new doctrine. Cowles resigned his position, and "after that … was looked upon as a seceder, and no longer held a prominent place in the Church, although morally and religiously speaking he was one of the

24. Bathsheba Smith, Temple Lot Case, Complainant's Abstract, 361.

25. Ebenezer Robinson, "Items of Personal History of the Editor," *The Return* 2, no. 10 (Oct. 1890): 347; 3 (Feb. 1891): 29; http://www.boap.org/LDS/Early-Saints/ERobinson.html (June 13, 2013).

26. Thomas Grover, Letter to Amos M. Musser, Jan. 10, 1885, qtd. in Jenson, "Plural Marriage," 6:227.

27. Thomas Grover, "Something Related to Celestial Marriage," *Deseret News*, June 13, 1883, 12.

28. Thomas Grover, Letter to Amos M. Musser, Jan. 10, 1885, qtd. in Jenson, "Plural Marriage," 6:227.

best men in the place."[29] Cowles subsequently published an affidavit in the dissident *Nauvoo Expositor* describing the episode: "In the latter part of the summer, 1843, the Patriarch, Hyrum Smith, did in the High Council, of which I was a member, introduce what he said was a revelation given through the Prophet … contain[ing] the following doctrines; … 2nd, the doctrine of a plurality of wives, or marrying virgins; that 'David and Solomon had many wives, yet in this they sinned not save in the matter of Uriah.'"[30] An affidavit by William and Jane Law appeared in the same issue of the *Expositor* confirming the existence of the revelation.[31] Cowles left Nauvoo in June 1844 when William Law and Robert Foster also fled from the city after the destruction of the *Expositor.*

Joseph's creation of the Quorum of the Anointed generated circles of insiders within the insiders, a development of new in- and inner-groups that occurred in quick succession during 1843. His criteria for selecting those whom he invited to become one of the Anointed remain mysterious. But some patterns in membership suggest that a strong influence was both kinship and affective networks. Those whom he most trusted and loved surrounded him in this sacred exchange of ritual. Strong familial relationships connected thirty-nine of quorum members (44 percent) to Joseph. These individuals spread out from Joseph in concentric circles of relatives, disciples, and friends. They protected Joseph's person, doctrine, and practice, ensuring that the concepts and rituals he shared in quorum meetings would endure regardless of what happened to him.[32]

At least sixteen of the thirty-seven men in the Quorum of the Anointed and twenty-two of the twenty-nine women were polygamists–already proven to keep secrets. Nineteen men and seventeen women received the second anointing before Joseph died. Of the nineteen men who received the second anointing, eleven were polygamists and eight monogamists.[33] These included Joseph's immediate relatives and their spouses or plural partners, the relatives of his plural wives and their partners, and, forming a slightly more removed circle, close associates like Brigham Young or Willard Richards and their wives and relatives.

29. Robinson, "Items of Personal History of the Editor," 3 (Feb. 1891): 29-30; http://www.boap.org/LDS/Early-Saints/ERobinson.html (June 13, 2013).

30. Austin Cowles, Affidavit, May 4, 1844, *Nauvoo Expositor*, June 7, 1844, 2.

31. William and Jane Law, Affidavits, in *Nauvoo Expositor*, June 7, 1844, 2.

32. Anderson and Bergera, *Joseph Smith's Quorum of the Anointed*, xxx.

33. Ibid., xxxiii.

Second Attack from Missouri

Joseph's life was never about just one thing. Simultaneous with his entry into the rituals of the endowment and the second anointing, he dealt with political pressures that threatened to destroy both him and his religious experiment. Once again the specter of Missouri overshadowed the summer of 1843. In the layering typical of Joseph's years in Nauvoo, the layers created by temple ritual, plurality, and family and kingdom building were obscured by political conflict that spun out of Missouri and linked Joseph's destiny again with that of ex-Governor Lilburn Boggs. A prophet's secrets threatened to destroy Joseph as well as the people who sustained his role in the LDS world. More than anything else, "during these troubled times," as legal historians Edwin Firmage and Richard Mangrum write, "the value of the writ of habeas corpus in saving Smith and others from legal harassment seemed to escalate."[34]

While it is impossible to say for certain that Joseph was complicit in the attempted murder of Boggs on May 6, 1842, he unquestionably had reasons to wish for Boggs's death. It was inevitable that the crime would be blamed on Joseph. Boggs's infamous order authorizing the "extermination" of the Mormons in 1838 was central to the persecution motif drawn by the Saints after Missouri and was well known through the region. Anticipating accusations of culpability, Joseph publicly denied his involvement;[35] but John C. Bennett responded sensationally that Joseph had not only predicted Boggs's death "by violent hands within a year," he had "offered a reward of five hundred dollars to any man that would secretly assassinate Governor Boggs."[36]

In the aftermath of the first attempt to extradite Joseph to Missouri in the summer of 1842 (see chap. 15), Bennett tried to keep the story of the Mormon prophet in front of the press and encouraged Missouri officials to arrest Joseph during the spring of 1843.[37] Bennett was a potent enemy. Deviating from his moderate course during Joseph's January 1843 trial in Springfield, Illinois, Governor Thomas Ford joined Missouri's Governor Thomas Reynolds to issue a new warrant for Joseph's arrest on June 17, 1843.[38] The charge was treason.

34. Edwin Brown Firmage and Richard Collin Mangrum, *Zion in the Courts*, 101.

35. "Letters," *Warsaw Signal*, July 23, 1842, www.sidneyrigdon.com/dbroadhu/IL/sign1842.htm#0709 (Dec. 26, 2008).

36. John C. Bennett, *The History of the Saints*, 281.

37. Morris Thurston, "The Boggs Shooting and Attempted Extradition: Joseph Smith's Most Famous Case," *BYU Studies Quarterly* 48, no. 1 (2009): 10-11.

38. George R. Gayler, "Attempts by the State of Missouri to Extradite Joseph Smith, 1841-1843," 32.

Four days earlier, Joseph and Emma had taken the children and traveled in their new carriage to visit Emma's sister, Elizabeth Hale Wasson, 170 miles to the north in Dixon. The next day, June 18, Hyrum received word by Judge James Adams's messenger that Ford had dispatched two law officials after them, Joseph H. Reynolds, sheriff of Jackson County (no relation to Governor Reynolds), and Harmon T. Wilson, constable of Carthage, Illinois. Hyrum immediately sent William Clayton and Stephen Markham to warn Joseph.[39] The two galloped out of Nauvoo toward Dixon at 12:30 a.m.

The next day and a half inched by, hours heavy with dread. Joseph had planned to speak to the Saints in Dixon, but instead "kept myself quiet all day," telling "the people there was a writ out for" his arrest.[40] On the morning of June 23, Joseph sent Clayton into Dixon to see if he could find out what had happened. Joseph waited at the Wassons' farm about eight miles outside of town. Ironically, Clayton met the two sheriffs disguised as Mormon elders.[41] They rode out to the farm, knocked on the door of the farmhouse, got no response, then spotted Joseph out back in the yard.

Reynolds and Wilson sneaked up to Joseph, surprised him, and "presented cocked pistols to my breast." Joseph remembered that Reynolds shouted, "God damn you, if you stir I'll shoot." Although he must have been frightened, Joseph's narrative presents him as unmoved. "I am not afraid to die," he allegedly replied. Contributing to the drama, he thrust his breast forward and taunted: "I have endured so much oppression, I am weary of life; and kill me, if you please. I am a strong man, however, and with my own natural weapons could soon level both of you; but if you have any legal process to serve, I am at all times subject to law, and shall not offer resistance." Hearing the commotion, Markham rushed to Joseph's side. In a scene that rivaled the stereotypical western display of male bravado, the two sheriffs pointed their pistols first at Joseph and then swung around to threaten Markham.[42] At gunpoint, the two forced Joseph into a wagon and drove toward Dixon, periodically punching him with the butts of their pistols to establish their control.

En route, Joseph demanded to know their authority and also insisted on a writ of habeas corpus. They retorted, "God damn you, you shant have [it]."[43] When they arrived in Dixon, they locked him in a room on the

39. *History of the Church*, 5:433, 435, 439 (June 18, 1843).
40. Ibid., 439.
41. Ibid., 440 (June 23, 1843).
42. Ibid.
43. Ibid., 441 (June 23, 1843); see also Andrew F. Ehat and Lyndon W. Cook, eds., *The*

second story of a tavern.[44] Markham jumped on his own horse and rode the distance as quickly as he could into town. Joseph threw open the window and shouted out to a man walking by: "I am falsely imprisoned here, and I want a lawyer." Unpopular strangers in this Illinois town, Reynolds and Wilson tried unsuccessfully to drive away the crowd that had gathered outside; but rather improbably, according to official accounts, they did nothing to silence Joseph.[45]

One of the Dixon residents, Lucian P. Sanger, reportedly challenged Reynolds: "[If] that was their mode of doing business in Missouri, they had another way of doing it in Dixon. They were a law-abiding people ... that he should not take me away without giving me the opportunity of a fair trial."[46]

Reynolds and Wilson guarded Joseph through the night. Two different lawyers, Shepard G. Patrick and Edward Southwick, visited him briefly. He told them he had been seized "without process," that he had been "insulted and abused," and again that he wanted "a writ of habeas corpus."[47]

Meanwhile, in Nauvoo, the Fifth Legion, second cohort, of the Nauvoo Legion, mustered under the direction of Hosea Stout as colonel, Theodore Turley lieutenant-colonel, and Jesse D. Hunter major. Prepared to do whatever was necessary, they waited for further orders.[48] Joseph, by unspecified means, sent an urgent message to Cyrus Walker, local head of the Whig Party who was campaigning nearby for a seat in the U.S. House of Representatives. Joseph knew Walker was "considered the greatest criminal lawyer in that part of Illinois." Originally from Virginia, Walker was living in McDonough County, Illinois. Joseph also sent a message six miles from Dixon to where a Mr. Chamberlain, the master-in-chancery, lived, requesting a writ of habeas corpus.[49]

The next morning, Saturday, June 24, Emma and her children left for Nauvoo with nephew Lorenzo Wasson. Clayton and Markham had traveled the 170 miles between Dixon and Nauvoo, riding hard for sixty-six hours. It would have taken Emma and the children longer.[50] They were no doubt

---

Words of Joseph Smith, 219. Unless otherwise noted, the details of Joseph's imprisonment and the legal contest that ensued are taken from *History of the Church*, 5:441-59 (June 23-30, 1843).

44. *History of the Church*, 5:442 (June 23, 1843).
45. Ibid., 442.
46. Ibid.
47. Ibid., 441.
48. Ibid., 443.
49. Ibid., 443.
50. Ibid., 445 (June 24, 1843).

frantic with fear, all of the nightmares of Missouri awakening in them again. As they jolted southward, at 8:00 a.m. the master-in-chancery arrived in Dixon to issue a first writ of habeas corpus returnable before John D. Caton, judge of the Ninth Judicial Circuit in Ottawa, and served on Reynolds and Wilson for threatening Markham's life.[51]

Meanwhile, rumors ran rampant: John C. Bennett was going to invade Nauvoo with a mob. Ford's willingness to honor Reynolds's extradition order meant that he was seeking an occasion to betray Joseph. The citizens at Carthage were in an uproar against Joseph. The Nauvoo City Council established what amounted to martial law on June 24 as soon as word of the arrest reached the city. Troops organized and waited for instructions. Strangers entering the city were required to give name, address, and occupation. Local police enforced a 9:00 p.m. curfew. Tensions mounted steadily. Emma and the children reached Nauvoo that evening, safe despite the fact that part of their carriage had caught fire and burned.

Because Judge Caton was in New York, Markham and a small group of men traveling with him went back to Dixon and secured a second writ of habeas corpus from the master-in-chancery. The first writ was effectively canceled; the new writ was made returnable "before the nearest tribunal in the Fifth Judicial District authorized to hear and determine writs of habeas corpus." Presumably, that tribunal would be Stephen Douglas's, since he was the Supreme Court judge assigned to Quincy.[52]

Cyrus Walker also reached Dixon on Saturday morning and met with Joseph in the tavern. According to the *History of the Church,* he told Joseph he could not make time to represent him because he was busy campaigning unless Joseph "could promise him [his] vote."[53] Desperate, Joseph agreed. At 10:00, the Circuit Court of Lee County issued a second writ–this one against Reynolds and Wilson for false imprisonment.[54] It claimed $10,000 damages on the grounds that Ford's writ was "void writ in law." In an almost comical turn of affairs, an unidentified Lee County sheriff put them in custody on $10,000 bail.

Understandably, Reynolds and Wilson chafed under the reversal of accusations and arrests. They secured another writ of habeas corpus from the Circuit Court of Lee County–the third in the case–also to be discharged

51. Ibid., 443-44.
52. Ibid., 447 (June 25, 1843).
53. Ibid., 444 (June 24, 1843).
54. Ibid.

before Caton. Caton, however, was still in New York. Making haste, the two again secured Joseph and began traveling north parallel to the river toward Ottawa, by way of Pawpaw Grove, thirty-two miles from Dixon. Angered by Joseph's resistance and legal maneuverings, they again roughed him up. Joseph seems more amused than frightened at this point. According to the *History of the Church,* a large group of bystanders gathered to see the Mormon prophet in the "largest room in the hotel," "anxious to hear" him preach, and "requested [him] to address them."[55] He "addressed the assembly for an hour-and-a-half on the subject of marriage. My freedom commenced from that hour."[56]

Wilson and Reynolds planned to travel to Quincy by boat, bypassing Nauvoo. Instead, the entire party proceeded by land. As a result, Nauvoo was identified as having the court in the Fifth Judicial District which would hear and determine writs of habeas corpus.

Meanwhile, in Nauvoo, Hyrum called a meeting of Saints near the Masonic Hall. According to Wilford Woodruff, "The whole city flocked together."[57] The men, Woodruff continued, "formed a hollow square on the green, where Hyrum told them that Joseph had been arrested, that he had been roughed up, and that the sheriffs were planning to take the prophet to Missouri." Hyrum called for volunteers; immediately "two or three hundred" cried out their willingness to help.[58] Brigham Young, acting in concert with Hyrum, raised $700 to support an expedition.

"When Joseph was kidnapped in Dixon, his brother Hyrum called for volunteers, and I volunteered to go to rescue Joseph," William Fawcett remembered. "I felt willing to lay down my life for him. I loved him, and have ever believed that that offering of mine was acceptable to the Lord."[59] Between 100-300 men rode out of Nauvoo on June 25; Wilson Law and Charles C. Rich led 100 men that very night. Another seventy-five left on the *Maid of Iowa* under the command of Dan Jones the next morning.[60] Rumors criss-crossed the air like angry hornets, so threatening that Ford sent an agent to Nauvoo to investigate the Mormon response.[61]

---

55. Ibid., 444-45.

56. Ibid.

57. Scott G. Kenney, ed., *Wilford Woodruff's Journal, 1833-1898*, 2:245-46 (June 25, 1843); hereafter Woodruff, *Journal.*

58. Ibid., 246.

59. William Fawcett, "Recollections of the Prophet Joseph Smith," 66.

60. Woodruff, *Journal*, 2:246 (June 25, 1843).

61. Gayler, "Attempts by the State of Missouri to Extradite Joseph Smith," 35, quoting

On June 25, Joseph, still in Dixon, sent a letter to Wilson Law, general in the Nauvoo Legion, asking him to come to Monmouth "with sufficient force to prevent my being kidnapped into Missouri," where he worried he would be killed.[62] He feared a trial "without any shadow of law or justice, although they well knew that I had not committed any crime worthy of death or bonds." The nightmare shadow of Missouri had fallen over Joseph, and he was flailing toward safety through emotional ups and downs during June's last week.[63]

On Tuesday, June 27, Joseph "with the company" crossed the Fox River (between Dixon and Monmouth) and saw not very far away two galloping horsemen–Mormons Peter Conover and William Cutler. As soon as he recognized them, he exclaimed with relief: "I am not going to Missouri this time. These are my boys!" These two were forerunners of the large company that joined them that day, bringing with them Joe Duncan, Joseph's favorite horse.[64]

Near Monmouth on Thursday, June 28, James Campbell, sheriff of Lee County, arrested Reynolds and Wilson for breaking the law by threatening citizens of the state and committing false imprisonment.[65] The entire group–the two sheriffs, Wilson, Joseph, Markham, Walker, and others–was en route to Quincy where they planned to appear at Stephen Douglas's court. On the 29th, they traveled as far as the Henderson River where they met Generals Wilson and William Law and sixty of the Nauvoo cavalry. At Honey Creek, their company, which by then included 100 or more men, slaughtered turkeys and chickens to feed the group. Walker peeled off from the group and hurried to Nauvoo to be sure his client's writ of habeas corpus could be heard promptly and also, by changing the venue from Quincy, sidestepping political maneuvers.

Before the group reached Nauvoo on Friday, June 30, a messenger brought the welcome news that the prophet would soon arrive. Willard Richards, Wilford Woodruff, and Brigham Young prepared the courtroom for an expeditious hearing.[66] Joseph's party left Honey Creek at 8:00 a.m., June 30, as Emma, Hyrum, and the Nauvoo Brass Band prepared to meet

Evarts Bottell Green and Charles Manfred Thompson, eds., "Governors' Letterbooks, 1840-1853," *Collections of the Illinois State Historical Society* (Springfield, 1911), 94-95.

62. *History of the Church*, 5:448 (June 25, 1843).

63. Ibid.

64. Ibid., 449-50 (June 27, 1843).

65. Ibid., 452 (June 28, 1843).

66. Ibid., 458 (June 30, 1843); Woodruff, *Journal*, 2:246 (June 30, 1843).

them on the road into town with a "train of carriages" carrying some of Nauvoo's most prestigious citizens. The meeting, Woodruff wrote, "was a seen of Great Joy."[67] They met at 11:45 a.m. a mile and a half east of the temple, near Hyrum's farm. Joseph was in the first carriage, Reynolds, Wilson, Walker, Patrick, and Southwick in a stagecoach that followed behind.[68] Cannon boomed in the distance announcing his arrival. Emma, dressed in her finest riding habit, and Hyrum were waiting about a mile and a half outside the city. They wept with relief as they embraced Joseph. The brass band played in the background. Joseph mounted another of his favorite horses, Old Charley, and, flanked by Emma and Hyrum, rode through crowds of people and a parade of the Nauvoo Legion welcome. Whatever the continued legal peril, Joseph threw himself joyfully into the moment.

At that point, the law had been stretched and twisted in a display of impressive elasticity. Sheriff Campbell turned over his two law-officer prisoners and their prisoner, Joseph, to Colonel Stephen Markham of the Nauvoo Legion.[69] In Woodruff's view, Reynolds and Wilson "looked as though they had had the ague [i.e., malaria]," for they had "treated Joseph Smith shamfully deprived him of the wright of Hebeas Corpus & of speaking to any friend & intended to run him into Missouri as soon as possible."[70] Brigham Young's history underscores the message for the subdued Reynolds and Wilson: "[O]n this occasion the officers who arrested him, who were still with him, witnessed the devotion and good feeling in the hearts of the Saints towards their Prophet."[71]

At the Mansion House, Joseph dismounted Charley, jumped onto his yard fence, and proclaimed, "I am out of the hands of the Missourians again, thank God." He promised that he would speak "at the Grove near the Temple, at four o'clock this afternoon." Many in the crowd wept.[72] Emma mobilized friends to cook a celebratory dinner for fifty at midday, among whom were, at Joseph's invitation, Reynolds and Wilson.[73] Joseph's generosity was noted by his friends, who thought he was "treating them well" by "setting them to the head of his table & giving them the best he had served unto them by his own wife."[74]

67. Woodruff, *Journal*, 2:246 (June 30, 1843).
68. *History of the Church*, 5:458 (June 30, 1843).
69. Firmage and Mangrum, *Zion in the Courts*, 102.
70. Woodruff, *Journal*, 2:246 (June 30, 1843).
71. Elden J. Watson, ed., *Manuscript History of Brigham Young*, 132.
72. *History of the Church*, 5:459 (June 30, 1843).
73. Ibid., 460.
74. Woodruff, *Journal*, 2:247 (June 30, 1843).

With evident satisfaction, Joseph Fielding described the scene in his diary, stressing Joseph's seeming invulnerability:

> A little before they [i.e., Joseph and party] reached here they were met by our band and hundreds of others in haste to congratulate our beloved head and leader on his escape from the hands of the wicked. I suppose so great tokens of respect and honor had never before been manifested towards him, and although it was attended with considerable expense, yet it was a day of great rejoicing with us, to see our beloved Prophet instead of being taken a prisoner into the hands of those that thirsted for his blood, riding on his horse, his brother on one side and his wife on the other, and hundreds or thousands of his friends and a band of music in full play, as though he had been a mighty monarch returning from some glorious victory, and all this in the sight of his enemies.[75]

That same afternoon, as soon as his scribes could put pen to paper, Joseph submitted a petition to the Nauvoo municipal court outlining what he had suffered during and after the arrest and asking for a writ of habeas corpus to render the Missouri writ void. After dinner, the group went to the courtroom, where the municipal court issued a new writ ordering Reynolds to deliver Joseph to the court, which he did, then heard the testimony about the arrest, the writ, and the questions about the legality of the extradition order itself.[76]

Joseph, demonstrating the liberation he felt, told the court that he "had an appointment to preach to the people, and requested the privilege from the court, which they granted, and adjourned until eight o'clock tomorrow morning."[77] Joseph's petition argued that the writ identified him improperly as Joseph Smith Jr., while he was actually Joseph Smith Sr. Since his father had died in 1840, this point was technically correct. He also claimed that he had not fled from justice, had not committed treason against Missouri, and that, most important, he had already been tried for these alleged offenses in Warren County and acquitted.[78] Perhaps the larger legal issue was whether the Nauvoo court could overturn a writ that lay within the jurisdiction of the state court. Walker gave a three-hour address before the court, arguing that the court could quash the arrest order, based on unique provisions in the city charter. In part a technical plea, his speech was undoubtedly also public

75. Andrew F. Ehat, "'They Might Have Known That He Was Not a Fallen Prophet,'" 144.
76. *History of the Church*, 5:461-65.
77. Ibid., 465 (June 30, 1843).
78. Ibid., 461-63.

electioneering. Later when Ford wrote about the case, he dismissed Walker's argument: "Thus the Mormons were deluded and deceived by men who ought to have known and did know better."[79]

Walker was not the first opportunist to use Joseph's difficulties as a springboard to bolster his own interests. Nor would he be the last. But in any case, the court welcomed an argument so attuned to their own preferences. Clamoring for attention, both Walker and his Democratic rival, Joseph P. Hoge of Galena, defended Joseph in his extradition hearing.[80] Not surprising, on Saturday, July 1, the court dismissed Joseph "for want of substance in the warrant upon which he was arrested."[81]

Joseph stood at the stand that Friday afternoon on June 30 at 5:00 p.m., an hour later than promised, to reassure his people. One imagines the emotion running though the gathering, estimated at 8,000, as they listened to Joseph's narrative of triumph over persecution. Walker, his attorney, remained at his side. Joseph was simultaneously grateful, angry, defiant: "I wish you to know and publish that we have all power; and if any man from this time forth says anything to the contrary; cast it into his teeth."[82] He predicted, "If our enemies are determined to oppress us and deprive us of our constitutional rights and privileges as they have done," and "if the authorities ... will not sustain us in our rights, ... I swear"–he mounted toward a rhetorical climax–"I will not deal so mildly with them again, for the time has come when forbearance is no longer a virtue; and if you or I are again taken unlawfully, you are at liberty to give loose to blood and thunder." "But be cool, be deliberate, be wise," he said, but "act with almighty power."[83]

When it came to Reynolds and Wilson, the prophet's language seesawed between violence and pacification: He had treated his arrestors kindly when he brought them to Nauvoo, despite their having "deprive[d] me of my rights, and would have run me to Missouri to have been murdered if Providence had not interposed." He "pledged my honor and my life that a hair of their heads shall not be hurt." However, if Missouri would not stop its persecution, "[I will] lead you to the battle; and if you are not

79. Thomas Ford, *History of Illinois*, 2:148.

80. "Municipal Court of the City of Nauvoo," *Times and Seasons*, 4, no. 16 (July 1, 1843): 246-56; see also *History of the Church*, 5:461-63 (June 30, 1843); Gayler, "The Mormons and Politics in Western Illinois, 1839-1844," 56.

81. *History of the Church*, 5:474 (July 21, 1843).

82. Ibid., 466 (June 30, 1843).

83. Ibid., 467.

afraid to die, and feel disposed to spill your blood in your own defense, you will not offend me."[84]

Joseph wove this latest episode into his larger tapestry of persecution: "[W]e have been deprived of our rights and privileges of citizenship, driven from town to town, place to place, and state to state, with the sacrifice of our homes and lands, our blood has been shed, many having been murdered, and all this because of our religion …" He thundered: "Shall we longer bear these cruelties which have been heaped upon us for the last ten years in the face of heaven, and in open violation of the constitution and laws of these United States and of this state?" "God forbid," he answered. "I will not bear. If they take away any rights, I will fight, for my rights manfully and righteously until I am used up. … I swear, in the name of Almighty God, and with uplifted hands to heaven, I will spill my heart's blood in its [Nauvoo's] defense. … If they don't let me alone, I will turn up the world–I will make war."[85]

Joseph had, once again, won the battle, but control of the war was slipping from his grasp. He saw the writ of habeas corpus as a fully legal protection; his opponents saw it as a barely legal circumvention of the law. Reynolds and Wilson left the city that evening (it is unclear whether they stayed for Joseph's screed) but vowed to return with a militia.[86]

The next day, Sunday, July 2, the *Maid of Iowa* docked at about 6:00 p.m. Joseph was on hand to welcome the scores of men who had embarked in his defense. He blessed them for their loyalty and efforts.[87] Hugging them and slapping them on the back, he walked with them to his store where he again shook hands with each before blessing them. Then, taking off his hat, he told the gathering the story of his arrest and triumphant return to Nauvoo. At dusk, they dispersed to their homes.[88]

The next day, Joseph addressed yet another group of would-be rescuers who, under the direction of Charles C. Rich, had ridden to Dixon. Again he thanked them for their support.[89] In each of these encounters, Joseph interpreted his arrest as part of the prophet-narrative. He repeated the story for a general audience at the temple stand on the morning of Tuesday, July 4.[90]

84. Ibid., 468.

85. Ibid., 471.

86. Ibid., 473.

87. Ibid., 481 (July 2, 1843).

88. Manuscript *History of the Church*, July 2, 1843, qtd. in Ehat and Cook, *Words of Joseph Smith*, 225-26.

89. *History of the Church*, 5:486 (July 3, 1843).

90. Joseph Smith, Diary, July 4, 1843, in Faulring, *An American Prophet's Record*, 393.

Enmeshed in an increasingly complicated set of loyalties, deals, and counter-deals, Joseph turned to politics:

> ... I never tell any man how to vote or whom to vote for. But I will show you how we are situated by bringing a comparison. Should there be a Methodist Society here and two candidates running for office, one says, "if you will vote for me and put me in governor, I will exterminate the Methodists, take away their charters," etc. The other candidate says, "If I am governor, I will give all an equal privilege." Which would the Methodists vote for? Of course they would vote en masse for the candidate that would give them their rights. ... Thus it has been with us. Joseph Duncan [Whig gubernatorial candidate] said if the people would elect him he would exterminate the Mormons, and take away their charters. As to Mr. [Thomas] Ford, he made no threats, but manifested a spirit in his speeches to give every man his rights; hence the members of the Church universally voted for Mr. Ford and he was elected governor. But he has issued writs against me the first time the Missourians made a demand for me, and this is the second one he has issued against me, which has caused me much trouble and expense.[91]

Three steamboats arrived that afternoon: one from St. Louis, another from Quincy, and the third from Burlington. Each brought curiosity seekers. Stories about the Mormon prophet's arrest had circulated widely. It was estimated that as many as 900 visitors came that day. The Nauvoo Brass Band played as they proceeded with escorts to the stand where they were entertained with cannon fire and patriotic speeches. Swelled by celebrating Saints, the crowd reached an estimated 15,000. Again, Joseph talked about the arrest and triumph. By then, the story was familiar and proof of Mormon righteousness. The persecution narrative demonized Missouri, which provided a useable foil to the Saints' identity as Zion.

After word of the Nauvoo court's decision reached Missouri, Governor Reynolds, incensed, immediately issued another writ on July 5 and asked Ford to send a military force to accompany his sheriffs to Nauvoo. Foreseeing political confusion, Ford declined.[92] Still, the Mormon question increasingly demanded Ford's attention. Among newspapers picking up the story was the *Niles' National Register*, published in Baltimore that, in the

91. *History of the Church*, 5:490 (July 4, 1843).

92. Gayler, "Attempts by the State of Missouri to Extradite Joseph Smith," 34, quoting Green and Manfred, "Governors' Letterbooks," 97-101; see also *History of the Church*, 4:492 (which misdates the letter as July 6, 1843).

early nineteenth century, was known nationally for its coverage of current events. On September 30, the paper claimed that Ford's refusal "has awakened a spirit which we fear may end in bloodshed."[93] The paper also reported that Hancock County citizens had rallied at Carthage on September 6 "to call in the citizens of the surrounding counties and states, to assist them in delivering up Joe Smith, if the governor of Illinois refused to comply with the requisition of the Governor of Missouri."[94]

George R. Gayler, a historian of Illinois politics, correlates the rise in Mormon political power with the rise in anti-Mormon activity in Illinois and Iowa.[95] Ford wrote later, revealing his own contempt for Joseph's rule, "His followers were divided into the leaders and the led."[96] Ford believed that since Joseph had been tried and acquitted in Illinois, it was not within his power to send him to Missouri. What is more, Ford said he would resist efforts to capture Joseph in the future. Jacob B. Backenstos, a non-Mormon, brought independent assurances from Ford to Joseph that Ford would not consent to extradition "so long as the Mormons continued to vote the Democratic ticket." According to Gayler, Ford "later admitted that such a pledge had been given by a prominent Democrat (whom he did not name), but without his (Ford's) knowledge."[97] Joseph had reason to distrust Ford, but after this, no further attempts to extradite Joseph to Missouri were made.

What might have been, in another circumstance, an ordinary procedure became the fulfillment of religious myth. Joseph kept his promise to Walker that the Whig candidate could count on his vote in the election of November 1843 (see chap. 16), but publicly announced Hyrum's "revelation" that the Mormons should vote for Joseph Hoge, Walker's rival and gave unqualified support to Hyrum's accuracy as a revelator.[98] Hoge won, and with what many interpreted as a bait-and-switch maneuver, the Saints threw fuel on the fire of anti-Mormon sentiment that was growing throughout the region.

Later that summer, a reporter from the *Pittsburg Gazette* visited Nauvoo. He framed his report with a description of how Joseph performed his

93. "Mormons," *Niles' National Register*, Sept. 30, 1843.

94. Ibid.

95. George R. Gayler, "The Mormons and Politics in Illinois: 1839-1844," 49. The *Warsaw Signal* articulated this view in its May 19, 1841, issue: "whenever they, as a people, step beyond the proper sphere of a religious denomination; and become a political body, as many of our citizens are beginning to apprehend will be the case, then this press stands pledged to take a stand against them." www.sidneyrigdon.com/dbroadhu/IL/sign1841 (Dec. 26, 2008).

96. Ford, *History of Illinois*, 2:214.

97. Gayler, "The Mormons and Politics in Western Illinois," 55-56.

98. See *History of the Church*, 5:526; and Ford, *History of Illinois*, 2:152.

multiple roles as prophet, politician, and social leader. "After ten we walked out past the house of the prophet, who has a very good garden containing about an acre, with a very fine fence around it, painted white, as is also his house, a moderate sized and humble looking frame dwelling." He painted a vivid picture of the scene. "Near the prophet's house, on the bank of the river, is the site of the 'Nauvoo House' ... The basement is finished. It is built of a good, hard, white stone. The front on the river is about 140 feet and is entirely above ground of cut stone. It has a wing running back about 100 feet. All this work is of the best and most substantial character. When this building is finished, it will be equal to any hotel in the western country. By special revelation, the prophet and his heirs are to have a suite of rooms in this house forever."[99]

The reporter had earlier constructed a skewed picture of the Mormon prophet from third-hand sources, but much of what he now saw challenged that image:

> The next morning, after breakfast, we paid a visit to the prophet. We were received in a common sitting room, very plainly furnished, where the prophet and the older members of the family had just been breakfasting, and his numerous children and dependents were then sitting at the table. He received us in quite a good humored, friendly manner, asked us to sit down, and said he hoped for a better acquaintance. Once the gentleman who accompanied me asked him how he prospered, he replied, "None can get ahead of me, and few can keep behind me." He seemed to think he had said something very witty, for he laughed very heartily. We spent about an hour conversing on various subjects, the prophet himself, with amazing volubility, occupying the most of the time, and his whole theme was himself. ... He said he had never asked the Lord anything about politics; if he had done so, the Lord would have told him what to do.[100]

Joseph contextualized this last statement with a jocular intimacy with the Almighty. The Lord had "promised to give us wisdom, and when I lack wisdom I ask the Lord, and he tells me, and if he didn't tell me, I would say he was a liar ..." "But I never asked him anything about politics," Joseph maintained. "I am a Whig, and I am a Clay man. I am made of Clay, and I

---

99. "The Prairies, Nauvoo, Joe Smith, the Temple, the Mormons, &c.," *Pittsburgh Weekly Gazette*, Sept. 15, 1843, 3, qtd. in John E. Hallwas and Roger D. Launius, eds., *Cultures in Conflict*, 41.

100. Ibid.

am tending to Clay, and I am going to vote for Henry Clay, that's the way I feel." Laughing, Joseph continued, "But I won't interfere with my people, religiously, to affect their votes, though I might to elect Clay, for he ought to be president. ... I am a democrat myself. I am a [George] Washington democrat, a Jefferson democrat, a Jackson democrat, and I voted for [William Henry] Harrison, and I am going to vote for Clay."[101] Comical at the moment, this pragmatic voting was indeed how Joseph managed his people's politics, and his insouciance was dangerous.

When the reporter asked for his views on race, Joseph gave a surprisingly liberal denial of alleged racial inferiority. "Change their situations with the whites, and [African-Americans] would be like them," he affirmed. However, he opposed intermarriage and integration. "Had I anything to do with the negro," he announced, "I would confine them by strict law to their own species, and put them on a national equalization."[102]

Joseph and Race

As is the case with much of the story of Joseph's years in Nauvoo, Missouri set the stage for his views on race. In the 1830s, Missouri was a hotbed of conflict over slave ownership. Seeking a new home for the Church in the area, the Mormons unintentionally interjected themselves into the argument.[103] Joseph tended not to articulate clearly his position on race, and we are left to tease meaning from the way he engaged in dialogue over the issues of slavery and abolitionism. In this, his views were very much of his age and cultural milieu.

Not long after the movement of the Saints into different parts of Missouri in the mid-1830s, Joseph received a revelation regarding slavery, saying "it is not right that any man should be in bondage to another."[104] For Joseph, the question was: Is it morally right to have a hierarchy of human beings? Two years later, he argued the point differently, focusing on the legality of the relationship between an owner and his "property." Joseph decided that it is "unlawful and unjust, and dangerous to the peace" for an

101. Ibid.

102. Ibid.

103. "Mormon antipathy for slavery, initially evident in the Book of Mormon, rained in eclipse throughout the 1830s," writes historian Newell Bringhurst. "However, by the 1840s, Mormonism's antislavery impulse would reemerge and become the dominant Mormon response to the slavery issue for the remainder of Joseph Smith's lifetime" (Newell Bringhurst, *Saints, Slaves and Blacks*, 46).

104. *History of the Church*, 1:463 (Dec. 16, 1833).

individual or church "to interfere with bond-servants, neither preach the gospel to, nor baptize them contrary to the will and wish of their masters …"[105] What resulted was a relativistic measurement that dictated the way LDS missionaries interacted with potential converts. In September 1835, Joseph clarified that the Church was to preach "the doctrine of repentance in all the world," but that missionaries were to ask for an owner's permission before teaching his slaves.[106]

For Joseph, abolitionism was "calculated to … set loose, upon the world a community of people who might peradventure, overrun our country and violate the most sacred principles of human society,–chastity and virtue."[107] Locating his argument in scripture, he said that blacks, who he believed were the children of Canaan (or Ham), remained cursed through a "decree of Jehovah."[108] By 1836, he had reversed his position on proselytizing among slaves, saying, "It would be much better and more prudent, not to preach at all to the slaves, until after their masters are convened."[109] However, six years later, he published an article in the *Times and Seasons* entitled "UNIVERSAL LIBERTY," praising John C. Bennett and Charles V. Dyer, a Chicago physician and abolitionist, for their opposition to slavery. With the horrors of the Mormon war in Missouri still fresh, Joseph now aligned the anti-slavery effort with the fight against persecution: "The cause of humanity cries aloud for help, while suffering Justice, is bleeding at every pore."[110] "Though none of these arguments were truly unique to this period or even to the nineteenth century," researchers Lester Bush and Armand Mauss observe, "their prominence in national debate was greatest during the years from 1830 to 1860."[111] They suggest that by 1842, the situation of the Church had changed significantly: "The slavery issue was no longer threatening to the Mormons."[112]

Joseph also participated in the expression of attitudes about race in his work on the Egyptian papyri, published in 1842 as the Book of Abraham. Though Joseph's text seems to argue that the descendants of one of Noah's sons were "forbidden to hold the priesthood" because of a marriage link to a

105. Ibid., 2:249 (Jan. 14, 1836).
106. Ibid.
107. "For the Messenger and Advocate," *Messenger and Advocate* 2, no. 19 (Apr. 1836): 289.
108. Ibid., 290.
109. Ibid., 291.
110. "UNIVERSAL LIBERTY," *Times and Seasons* 3, no. 19 (Mar. 15, 1842): 723.
111. Lester E. Bush and Armand L. Mauss, *Neither White Nor Black*, 59.
112. Ibid., 62.

woman of "Canaanite descent,"[113] there is no reliable evidence that he "ever used the Book of Abraham to justify priesthood denial (nor apparently did any other Church leader, until the Utah period)."[114] Indeed, the "first known documentation" of the policy of denying priesthood ordination and temple admission to blacks came some five years after Joseph's death. Even if Joseph "contemplated denying blacks the priesthood at the time that the earliest book of Abraham texts were in preparation," he "never publicly espoused this potential application of his scripture."[115]

The difference between Joseph's positions on slavery in the mid-1830s and in the 1840s is clear in his *Views on the Government and Policy of the United States* (1844), a treatise that accompanied his audacious bid for the U.S. presidency. Joseph addressed the issue of slavery with sympathy for the plight of blacks. "Some two or three millions of people are held as slaves," he wrote, "because the spirit in them is covered with a darker skin than ours." He asked for nothing less than the "break down [of] slavery" and taking "the shackles from the poor black man."[116] Stopping short of calling for the end to all race-based discrimination, he stated, "[W]ere I the president of the United States, by the voice of the virtuous people … when the people petitioned to abolish slavery in the slave states, I would use all honorable means to have their prayers granted … that the whole nation might be free indeed!"[117] Joseph may have "shared the common belief that Negroes were descendants of Ham," but his views eventually "reflected a rejection of the notion that this connection justified Negro slavery."[118]

Joseph's opposition to slavery in the 1840s dramatized how much had changed for the Church after Missouri. Despite the Saints' difficulties, Joseph felt confident enough to take a stand that hinted of a millennial

113. Bringhurst, *Saints, Slaves and Blacks*, 16; D&C 134:58-59.

114. Lester E. Bush, "A Commentary on Stephen G. Taggart's Mormonism's Nego Policy: Social and Historical Origins," *Dialogue: A Journal of Mormon Thought* 4 (Winter 1969): 86-103; reprinted in Bush and Mauss, *Neither White Nor Black*, 31-52.

115. Lester E. Bush, "Whence the Negro Doctrine?," in Bush and Mauss, *Neither White nor Black*, 207, 205. For speculations regarding the LDS Church's race-based prohibitions (lifted in 1978), see ibid., 208; Dean L. May, "Mormons"; Klaus Hansen, *Mormonism and the American Experience*, 190-98); and Rex Cooper, *Promises Made to the Fathers*, 77, also 116-18. For the LDS Church's repudiation of racism, see "Race and the Priesthood," at https://www.lds.org/topics/race-and-the-priesthood?lang=eng (Aug. 26, 2015).

116. Joseph Smith, *Views on the Government and Policies of the United States*, 3; written with the aid of W. W. Phelps.

117. Ibid.

118. Bush and Mauss, *Neither White Nor Black*, 65.

world view.[119] His attitudes toward race may be best situated in his sense of the imminence of Christ's coming. The lens of Mormon millennialism provides yet another way of interpreting Joseph's attitudes toward slavery. He seems to have believed genuinely that God wanted to "ameliorate the condition of every man."[120]

---

119. Bringhurst, *Saints, Slaves and Blacks*, 56.

120. Wilford Woodruff, qtd., in Bringhurst, *Saints, Slaves and Blacks*, 59. In linking themselves to adoptive membership in the tribes of ancient Israel, "the Mormons were able simultaneously to carve out for themselves a special niche and a special connection to the whole redemptive history and destiny of God's chosen people" (Armand L. Mauss, *All Abraham's Children*, 7, 9). For a recent consideration of Joseph's views on race, see W. Paul Reeve, *Religion of a Different Color: Race and the Mormon Struggle for Whiteness* (New York: Oxford University Press, 2015), references throughout.

CHAPTER 22

A Gathering Storm

> *... Jesus Christ, who was, and is, and is to come, has borne me safely over every snare and plan laid in secret or openly ... to destroy me.*
> *–Joseph Smith,* History of the Church, *6:74 (Nov. 13, 1843)*

Visitors to Joseph's Nauvoo often commented on the location's beauty. "The site of Nauvoo is one of the most beautiful on the Mississippi River," wrote David N. White, editor of the *Pittsburgh Weekly Gazette* in mid-September 1843. He continued with a rich description of the city of the Saints:

> The river at this place makes a large bend, forming a semi-circle, within which lies the lower part of the city, running back to the bluff. This semi-circular piece of ground is perfectly level, and lies above the high water mark ...and is about a mile and a half in length along the bluff. The bluff rises gradually, and is not very high, and presents most beautiful building sites. On the bluff ... a mile from the river, stands the temple. The site is beautifully chosen, as it is in a central and elevated position and can be seen from the river, all around the bend, and from every part of town.[1]

Despite the surface beauty and calm, Nauvoo was a city on the verge of disaster. Wary of Mormon ambitions to build the literal kingdom of God on the earth, outsiders watched the growing strength of the Mormon city with alarm. Nauvoo's trajectory appeared to be fulfilling John C. Bennett's

1. David N. White, "The Prairies, Nauvoo, Joe Smith, the Temple, the Mormons, &c.," *Pittsburgh Weekly Gazette*, Sept. 15, 1843, 3, qtd. in John E. Hallwas and Roger D. Launius, eds., *Cultures in Conflict*, 42. At the same time, White added:

> ... no part of the town is compactly built. The whole space is a conglomeration of houses, fences, gardens, corn fields, stables, huts, etc. One looks in vain for anything like a compactly built street. The object seems to have been to scatter as widely as at all convenient, and to cover as much ground as possible. ... Everybody seems engaged in putting up houses, taking care of gardens, and getting in hay from the prairies. (Ibid., 42.)

allegations the previous year that the Mormons had "a vast and deep laid scheme … for conquering the states of Ohio, Indiana, Illinois, Iowa, and Missouri, and erecting upon the ruin of their present governments a despotic military and religious empire, the head of which, as emperor and pope [would be] Joseph Smith …"[2]

Far from the gathering storm, on September 9, 1843, eight of the twelve apostles met in conference with local converts in Boston. The Church's Boston branch included 182 members, all "strong in the faith of gathering," Wilford Woodruff reported.[3] Representatives from sixteen branches, including Lowell, New Bedford, and Salem, were also present (a total of 878 members).[4] Although potential converts and curious townspeople were present as well, the apostles' message was directed to the baptized: Gather to Zion. "We know & all the Saints aught to know that God has pointed out a place & time of gathering," Parley P. Pratt propounded,

> and has raised up a Prophet to bring it about of which we are witnesses. We have not got to go along round about. The time & place is pointed out the foundations of the city & Temple laid and a people already gatherd & we know [we] have to go & to reject the revelations of God that have pointed out these things to us ownly brings Condemnations & if this is not the Case then our faith is vain & our works & hopes are vain also. We have already got the opinions of men enough concerning the coming of Jesus Christ. But we need the voice of a Prophet in such a Case & we have it & I am willing to risk my all upon it.[5]

Brigham Young reinforced the centrality of Joseph's message: "Had we lived in the days of Jesus Christ we would say we would receive his work. But Judge ye if the people are better now than then. They are not. … And now the full set time is come for the Lord God Almighty to set his hand to redeem Israel." He continued:

> We are not bound to make the people believe but to preach the gospel & then our garments are Clear. The Lord does not require evry soul to leave his home as soon as he believes but he requirs him to harken to council & follow that course that the lord points out. The spirit of the Lord & this work is on the elert , and those that keep up with the work

2. *History of the Church*, 5:80n (July 22, 1842).

3. Scott G. Kenney, ed., *Wilford Woodruff's Journal, 1833–1898*, 2:286 (Sept. 9, 1843); hereafter Woodruff, *Journal*.

4. *History of the Church*, 6:10 (Sept. 9, 1843).

5. Parley P. Pratt, qtd. in Woodruff, *Journal*, 2:287–88.

> must be on the alert also. When the Lord says gather yourselves together why do you ask the Lord what for? … if he commands us to come out & gather together He will not save us by staying at home.[6]

The idea of living in the company of like-minded men and women was seductive indeed. Young then connected the gathering to the temple:

> … the Lord requires us to build a house unto his name that the ordinances & blessings of his kingdom may be revealed & that the Elders may be endowed & go forth & gather together the Blood of Ephraim the people of God from the ends of the earth. Can you get an endowment in Boston? No & ownly in that place that God has pointed out. … Now will you help us to build the Nauvoo House & Temple? If so you will be blessed. If not we will build it alone. And if you dont harken you will not have the spirit of the Lord for the spirit of the Lord is on the moove.[7]

While the Mormon message originated with Joseph's revelations and interpretations, the elaboration on doctrine by the Twelve represents an evolutionary process. It is more than just the differences between what each man heard Joseph say and what he thought the prophet meant. Rather, these doctrinal expositions positioned Joseph's teachings in practical examples or metaphors easy for listeners to cling to. Like Joseph, these missionaries were weaving the story of the kingdom of God, the gathering of Zion, and why the lives of ordinary men and women would be transformed by entering the waters of baptism. When Young, Pratt, Kimball, or Woodruff joined Joseph's narration, they subtly transformed the core narrative. Mormonism became theirs perhaps as much as Joseph's. Joseph taught as much by the way he was as by what he said.

Preparing for every exigency, including spiritual and physical war fare, on September 11, 1843, Joseph assigned W. W. Phelps, Henry Miller, and Hosea Stout to obtain permission from Governor Ford to purchase firearms for the Nauvoo Legion that would be owned by the city rather than the Church.[8] That evening, "Joseph, Hyrum, W[illia]m Law, N[ewel] K. Whitney and Willard [Richards] had a season of prayer in Joseph's east room New House for Laws little daughter who was sick and Emma who was some better."[9]

6. Brigham Young, qtd. in ibid., 288-89.

7. Ibid., 290.

8. *History of the Church*, 6:31 (Sept. 11, 1843).

9. Joseph Smith, Diary, Sept. 11, 1843, in Scott H. Faulring, ed., *An American Prophet's Record*, 413.

Always trying to engineer ways to support his family financially and to deal with the hordes of visitors who clamored for his attention, on September 15, Joseph reached another goal. "I put up a sign" announcing the opening of the "Nauvoo Mansion" (also Nauvoo House), a hotel operated in the interests of both town and Church.[10] The public notice situated the hotel in the context of an especially complicated life:

> In consequence of my house being constantly crowded with strangers and other persons wishing to see me, or who had business in the city, I found myself unable to support so much company free of charge, which I have done from the foundation of the Church. My house has been a home and resting place for thousands, and my family many times obliged to do without food, after having fed all they had to visitors; and I could have continued the same liberal course, had it not been for the cruel and untiring persecution of my relentless enemies. I have been reduced to the necessity of opening "The Mansion" as a hotel. I have provided the best table accommodations in the city; and the Mansion, being larger and convenient, renders travelers more comfortable than any other place on the upper Mississippi. I have erected a large and commodious brick stable, and it is capable of accommodating seventy-five horses at one time, and storing the requisite amount of forage, and is unsurpassed by any similar establishment in the State.[11]

The next day, Joseph reviewed a parade of the Nauvoo Legion on Water Street in front of the new hotel.[12]

As always, Joseph was ready for a vigorous intellectual duel and the next evening debated a Mr. Blodgett, a visiting Unitarian minister who was curious about the Mormon prophet. Joseph later commented: "I was gratified with his sermon in general, but differed in opinion on some points, on which I freely expressed myself to his great satisfaction, on persecution making the work spread, like rooting up a flower-garden or kicking back the sun!"[13] Beneath the genial, confident exterior, however, worry gnawed, prompted by rumors about a mob of anti-Mormons organizing in Carthage.[14] Joseph expressed his concerns in a letter to Governor Ford. In reply, Ford considered it his obligation to "prevent the invasion of this State … for any hostile

10. *History of the Church*, 6:33 (Sept. 15, 1843).
11. Ibid.
12. Ibid., 34 (Sept. 16, 1843).
13. Ibid. (Sept. 17, 1843).
14. Ibid. (Sept. 19, 1843).

purposes whatever." While he believed there was little chance of hostilities at that time, he worried that "some other mode of annoyance [might] be adopted," but declined to speculate how he might respond. Ford also asked Joseph to send him a copy of "the resolutions passed at the meeting of the mob at Carthage."[15] Back in Nauvoo on the same day, Joseph expelled a hotel guest because he insulted one of the hired girls.[16]

Joseph's secret life formed a powerful current under the glamorous public facade. The fall of 1843–the last of Joseph's life–was one of spiritual feasting. Prayer meetings held several nights each week brought those consumed by the desire to understand Joseph's message to the room over the red brick store. The spiritually earnest listened, rapt, as he taught, inspired, and welded them together with bonds solid enough to carry them through the troubles ahead and keep them focused on building the kingdom.

He had not abandoned his commitment to plurality. On September 23, Hyrum sealed his prophet-brother to nineteen-year-old Melissa Lott, with her parents, Cornelius and Parmelia Lott (who were also that day sealed for eternity), who witnessed the marriage.[17] That same day, Austin Cowles, unable to sustain plurality, resigned as a counselor to Nauvoo Stake president William Marks. Plurality would pull men and women like the Lotts into kinship with Joseph, but repel others who found in it evidence that their prophet had fallen away from God's truth.

An undated sealing apparently occurred late in 1843 to Nancy Maria Winchester, who was fourteen or fifteen years old.[18] Nancy had been a member of the Relief Society since May 27, 1842. Hyrum had explained polygamy to her brother, Benjamin Winchester, who immediately rejected the principle out of hand. According to historian David Whittaker, Winchester "refused to believe that the practice was anything more than satanic."[19] Neither Benjamin nor Nancy explained why he rejected and she accepted the teaching. Like Emily and Eliza Partridge or Lucy Walker, Nancy placed her faith in Joseph alone. Such a test of faith placed the new relationship beyond any possibility

15. Ibid., 35 (Sept. 13, 1843).

16. William H. Walker, "Righteous Indignation," in McConkie, *Remembering Joseph*, 99-100.

17. Andrew Jenson, "Plural Marriage," 6:234; Lott Family Bible, inscription on title page, LDS Church History Library; Malissa Lott, Affidavit, May 20, 1869, in Joseph F. Smith, Affidavits Books, 1:23. Lott provided a second date in her testimony at the Temple Lot Case in 1892 (Respondents' Testimony, Part 3, 63-64): September 27.

18. Todd Compton, *In Sacred Loneliness*, 6; Jenson, "Plural Marriage," 6:234. Nancy was later sealed to Heber Kimball.

19. Benjamin Winchester, "Primitive Mormonism," *Salt Lake Tribune*, Sept. 22, 1889, 2; David J. Whittaker, "East of Nauvoo," 64.

of equality. Seven weeks later, Joseph had Brigham Young seal him to his sister Fanny Young Carr Murray, a widow for the second time at fifty-six.[20]

A meeting of the Anointed Quorum on September 28 marked the first time women were admitted. Quorum meetings continued several times each week at irregular intervals. Attendees Wilford Woodruff, William Clayton, and Joseph Smith kept journals. Although the entries are terse and guarded, a sense emerges about the critical role these meetings played in the formation of Mormon identity and the deepening of their dedication to Joseph. While William and Wilson Law, Chauncey and Francis Higbee, and Robert Foster were moving away from Joseph, alarmed by his doctrinal expansions, other men and women drew even closer to him and became more strongly convinced that his words were God's words.

Despite the embarrassing departure of John C. Bennett, the Masonic lodges in Nauvoo had continued to grow. On June 24, 1843, the "free and accepted ancient York Masons" gathered for ritual at the lodge room, formed a procession and walked to Main Street, where they gathered for a cornerstone ceremony led by Hyrum, as Worshipful Master, for a Masonic temple. The men sang two Masonic hymns, and then retired to the grove by the temple where John Taylor delivered a rousing oration.[21] Four months later, in October, the Grand Lodge of Illinois issued a statement that it found irregularities in the four Mormon Masonic lodges and was suspending their charters. Complaints included "gathering members without regard to character," advancing members too quickly, and failing to present their records before the "Committee on Returns and Work of Lodges" as requested.[22] The Nauvoo lodges ignored the suspension.[23]

At the Quorum of the Anointed meeting on October 1, 1843, Jane Law, Rosannah Marks, Elizabeth Durphy, and Mary Fielding Smith were initiated, while "Joseph &c. reanointed. [William] Law &c."[24] Redoing the ritual embedded its meaning more deeply and fused powerful bonds of secrecy. Until October 1, Emma had been the only woman initiated into the Quorum. Jane, Rosannah, and Mary were the wives of Mormon leaders, but Elizabeth Durfee (also Durphy) was not, at least, not publicly. Her husband, Jabez Durfee, was a mainstream member in many ways–faithful,

20. Brigham Young, Aug. 31, 1873, JD 16:167. Also Jenson, "Plural Marriage," 6:234.

21. *History of the Church*, 5:446 (June 24, 1843).

22. *Proceedings of the Grand Lodge of Illinois, from its Organization in 1840–1850 Inclusive*, 78; Michael W. Homer, "'Similarity of Masonry in Mormonism,'" 31.

23. Homer, "'Similarity of Masonry in Mormonism,'" 31.

24. Joseph Smith, Diary, Oct. 1, 1843, in Faulring, *An American Prophet's Record*, 417.

loyal, devoted, but nevertheless outside this special circle. The most plausible explanation for Elizabeth's inclusion is that she was one of Joseph's plural wives. An energetic, generous member of Relief Society, she had remained loyal to Joseph when gossip and dissension had estranged others. Perhaps by coincidence, her next-door neighbor in Nauvoo was another polyandrous wife, Zina Huntington Jacobs.[25]

On October 3, Joseph turned from the sacred to the mundane. Emma and he hosted a dinner at the newly opened Nauvoo Mansion, inviting their close friends and associates. It was simultaneously a housewarming and a launching the new enterprise.[26] Framing the evening with his own interpretation of the past few months, Joseph emotionally "tendered his thanks to the company for the encomiums and honors conferred on him." Returning to the "many woes through which he had passed," he expressed gratitude for "the pleasing prospects that surrounded him to the great Giver of all good." He compared himself to Job, whom "the Lord had remembered" and blessed.[27] The merry association mirrored the celestial relationships for which all present hoped. Such socials formed a layer of civic contentment that veiled the subterranean level of ritual where some of Joseph's most creative expressions emerged. The *Nauvoo Neighbor* reported on the event, and a "Thank You" drafted by Robert Foster read, "General Joseph Smith, whether we view him as a Prophet at the head of the Church, a General at the head of the Legion, a Mayor at the head of the City Council, or as a landlord at the head of his table, ... if he has equals, he has no superiors."[28]

Also in October, Joseph again turned on Sidney Rigdon, his former ally. The latest controversy had been brewing for months. Orson Hyde had told Joseph during the summer that Rigdon had passed on information about Joseph's whereabouts to the Missouri sheriff and Carthage constable who had arrested him the previous June.[29] Although the report was false, Joseph exploded in a series of public denunciations from which Rigdon defended himself. The Church on August 13 had voted to disfellowship Rigdon.[30] (See chap. 18.)

25. Nauvoo Ward Census, "A Record of the Names ... in Spring of 1842," LDS Church History Library.

26. *History of the Church*, 6:42 (Oct. 3, 1843).

27. Ibid., 43 (Oct. 3, 1843).

28. Ibid.

29. Apparently a lie, the story contributed to the erosion of their relationship. Richard S. VanWagoner, *Sidney Rigdon*, 320.

30. Van Wagoner, *Sidney Rigdon*, 320; Faulring, *An American Prophet's Record*, 406; see also

Significantly, the account of October 1843's general conference printed in the *Times and Seasons* differs from later published versions, with the effect of creating, according to Rigdon's biographer, "an erroneous image of Rigdon that prevails in Mormon tradition to this day and warrants rectification."[31] When conference opened on Saturday, October 7, Joseph began with the "case and standing" of Rigdon. He recited a laundry list of increasingly scandalous complaints.[32] One of Joseph's few specifics was that Rigdon had deliberately delayed documents sent by Justin Butterfield that were necessary for Joseph's defense in the January 1843 hearing at Springfield.

Rigdon pleaded with Joseph and the audience for a fair hearing. He defended himself against the charge of negligence by saying that the Butterfield documents had been delivered to him when he was "sick, and unable to examine it" in a timely fashion. He tried to explain away Joseph's other complaints. The meeting closed before the matter was concluded.

Sunday morning, Rigdon picked up where he had left off. But this time instead of meeting each of Joseph's accusations, he took a different tack. Recounting their shared narrative, he offered "a moving appeal to President Joseph Smith concerning their former friendship, associations and sufferings, and expressed his willingness to resign his place, though with sorrowful and indescribable feelings." His remarks impacted the audience, and "the sympathies of the congregation were highly excited," according to the *Times and Seasons.*

Although still unsure of Rigdon's "integrity and steadfastness," Joseph "expressed entire willingness to have elder Sidney Rigdon retain his station, provided he would magnify his office, and walk and conduct himself in all honesty, righteousness, and integrity."[33] Hyrum, following Joseph, urged forgiveness for Rigdon, with "appropriate and expressive remarks on the attribute of mercy … especially towards their aged companion and fellow servant in the cause of truth and righteousness."[34]

It seems extraordinary that Joseph would so publicly reveal his insecurities. Airing his dirty linen was not only histrionic but embarrassing to those whom he accused. Inevitably, it created enmity that would come back to haunt him. Furthermore, it must have heightened anxiety among

History of the Church, 5:531-32 (Aug. 13, 1843); "Book of the Law of the Lord," qtd. in Van Wagoner, *Sidney Rigdon*, 327n32.

31. Van Wagoner, *Sidney Rigdon*, 321.

32. "Minutes of a Special Conference," *Times and Seasons* 4, no. 21 (Sept. 15, 1843): 330.

33. Ibid.

34. Ibid.

those who had reservations about Joseph, even if they had, so far, kept those doubts to themselves.

When conference reconvened at 2:00 p.m. on October 8, Joseph, in a more expansive mood, began to discourse about our "true relation to God." "The organization of the spiritual and heavenly worlds, and of spiritual and heavenly beings, was agreeably to the most perfect order and harmony ... their limits and bounds were fixed irrevocably, and voluntarily subscribed to by themselves ... hence the importance of embracing and subscribing to principles of eternal truth." He continued by describing "distinction between the spirits of the just, and angels."[35] The *Times and Seasons* reported: "Such is a faint outline of the discourse of Joseph Smith, which was delivered with his usual feeling and pathos; and was listened to with the most profound and eager attention by the multitude, who hung upon his instructions, anxious to learn and pursue the path of eternal life."[36] What must Joseph have felt when he read such words? Relief? Swept up with his own sense of rightness? A satisfying connection between his followers and his effort to teach them what they needed to know?

During the multi-day public conference, the Quorum of the Anointed continued to meet. On October 8, the women in attendance included "Sis[ters Harriet] Adams, [Elizabeth Ann] Whitney, Uncle John's wife [Clarissa], [and] Mother [Lucy Mack] Smith. Hiram [Smith] and his wife [Mary Fielding Smith] were blessed, ord[ained], and anointed."[37] The image of Hyrum and Mary surrounded in such a sacred setting by a band of the most faithful Saints must have left a potent mark. Each must have yearned for the same blessings, for such holiness, for such a confirmation of divine standing.

Joseph must have found it immensely gratifying to see thousands of men and women leave their homes within minutes of each other to proceed to the stand to receive his instructions. On Sunday morning, October 15, Joseph moved effortlessly among topics: the U.S. Constitution, the Bible, and the economy of Nauvoo. His paranoia flared briefly as he urged greater production of "wool and raw materials ... Set our women to work and stop this ... talking about spiritual wives."[38] His conclusion returned to the temple: "Some say It is better, say some to give [to] the poor than build the

35. Ibid., 331-32.

36. Ibid., 332.

37. Joseph Smith, Diary, Oct. 8, 1843, in Faulring, *An American Prophet's Record*, 418; also in Devery S. Anderson and Gary James Bergera, eds., *Joseph Smith's Quorum of the Anointed*, 29.

38. Joseph Smith, Diary, Oct. 15, 1843, in Faulring, *An American Prophet's Record*, 421.

temple.–the building of the temple has kept the poor who were driven from Missouri from starving. as has been the best means for this object which could be devised." He continued, "[A]ll ye rich men of the Latter Day Saints.–from abroad I would invite to bring up some of their money and give to the temple."[39]

Joseph and William Clayton left Nauvoo on October 19 for Macedonia, returning on the 22nd in time for an afternoon prayer meeting in Joseph's house, where William and Rosannah Marks were installed as members of the Quorum of the Anointed and received their second anointings in the presence of twenty-four members.[40]

Afternoon meetings must have been sometimes inconvenient, as members would be required to suspend their usual daily activities. But attendees' willingness to put the meetings first indicates how rewarding they found the important gatherings to be. Whether the ritual was for themselves or others, it created a sacred space they shared–one they believed was real, important, meaningful, in which God's living prophet spoke.

Two days later, twenty-nine were present at the evening meeting of the Anointed Quorum. "(Sister[s] Fielding, Richards, Taylor, Young, Kimball" were anointed.[41] In much the same way that a mantra instills quietude during meditation, participation in these rituals created a sort of tonal rhythm in which men and women moved in synchronization with Joseph, believing they were traveling with him to a better place. On November 2, Joseph met with Church leaders John Taylor, Hyrum Smith, Brigham Young, Heber C. Kimball, Willard Richards, William Clayton, and William Law. With their help, he drafted letters to the five leading U.S. presidential candidates–Henry Clay, John C. Calhoun, Richard M. Johnson, Martin Van Buren, and Lewis Cass–in the 1844 election. The purpose was to ask them what "their course of action would be in relation to the cruelty and oppression that we have suffered."[42] Two days later, Joseph met with Richards and Taylor to read over the letters.[43]

According to Joseph's diary, on November 5 the Anointed Quorum convened. However, neither Joseph nor Emma dressed in the special ceremonial

39. Ibid., 421-22.

40. Joseph Smith, Diary, Oct. 22, 1843, in Faulring, *An American Prophet's Record*, 423; also in Anderson and Bergera, *Joseph Smith's Quorum of the Anointed*, 30.

41. Joseph Smith, Diary, Nov. 1, 1843, in Faulring, *An American Prophet's Record*, 425.

42. *History of the Church*, 6:63 (Nov. 2, 1843).

43. Ibid., 64-65 (Nov. 2, 1843).

robes.[44] Three days later, the quorum met again, this time without Joseph.[45] Though no participant left an account of the meeting, Joseph's absence must have cast a kind of pall over the proceedings.

On November 7, Joseph met in his office with Brigham Young, Parley Pratt, Orson Pratt, Wilford Woodruff, John Taylor, George Smith, and Willard Richards to discuss raising $500 to reprint the Doctrine and Covenants, a compilation of Joseph's revelations, first published in 1833 as the Book of Commandments.[46] He also asked Joseph C. Cole to help move tables to the room above the red brick store so Willard Richards and W. W. Phelps could work on Joseph's history.[47]

The following Sunday, Joseph joined the Anointed Quorum in the southeast room of the Homestead where Reynolds and Thirza Cahoon received the second anointing.[48] The next evening, Joseph wrote to James Arlington Bennet in New York City, offering a proof of the factual truthfulness of his calling as prophet.[49]

> … truth is a matter of fact; and the fact is, that by the power of God I translated the Book of Mormon from hieroglyphics, the knowledge of which was lost to the world, in which wonderful event I stood alone, an unlearned youth, to combat the worldly wisdom and multiplied ignorance of eighteen centuries, with a new revelation, which (if they would receive the everlasting Gospel,) would open the eyes of more than eight hundred millions of people, and make "plain the old paths," wherein if a man walk in all the ordinances of God blameless, he shall inherit eternal life; and Jesus Christ, who was, and is, and is to come, has borne me safely over every snare and plan laid in secret or openly, through priestly hypocrisy, sectarian prejudice, popular philosophy, executive power, or law-defying mobocracy, to destroy me.
>
> If, then, the hand of God in all these things that I have accomplished towards the salvation of a priest-ridden generation, in the short space of twelve years, through the boldness of the plan of preaching the Gospel, and the boldness of the means of declaring repentance and baptism for

44. Joseph Smith, Diary, Nov. 5, 1843, in Faulring, *An American Prophet's Record*, 426; also in Anderson and Bergera, *Joseph Smith's Quorum of the Anointed*, 34.

45. Joseph Smith, Diary, Nov. 8, 1843, in Faulring, *An American Prophet's Record*, 426; also in Anderson and Bergera, *Joseph Smith's Quorum of the Anointed*, 34.

46. *History of the Church*, 6:66 (Nov. 7, 1843).

47. Ibid., 66.

48. Joseph Smith, Diary, Nov. 12, 1843, in Faulring, *An American Prophet's Record*, 426; also in Anderson and Bergera, *Joseph Smith's Quorum of the Anointed*, 35.

49. *History of the Church*, 6:73-78 (Nov. 13, 1843).

> the remission of sins, and reception of the Holy Ghost by laying on of the hands, agreeably to the authority of the Priesthood, and the still more bold measures of receiving direct revelation from God, through the Comforter, as promised, and by which means all holy men from ancient times till now have spoken and revealed the will of God to men, with the consequent "success" of the gathering of the Saints, throws any "charm" around my being, and "points me out as the most extraordinary man of the age," it demonstrates the fact that truth is mighty and must prevail, and that one man empowered from Jehovah has more influence with the children of the kingdom than eight hundred millions led by the precepts of men. God exalts the humble, and debases the haughty.[50]

Joseph's letter may have subsequently provoked grand dreams, for on November 15, he spoke to the Anointed Quorum of a "Proclamation to the kings. Letter to Bennet and Petition to Congress &c."[51] The proclamation would articulate his religious beliefs and doctrine.

On November 21, Joseph distributed assignments. Phelps was to write an appeal to the citizens of Vermont and, with Willard Richards, John Taylor, and Orson Hyde, "a proclamation to the Kings /&c./ of the Earth."[52] The next night, at a Quorum of the Anointed meeting, "B Young [was] (anointed and wife) &c."[53] At this point in the late fall of 1843, the Anointed Quorum was meeting approximately every three days.

Two years earlier, John C. Bennett had proposed building a dam north of Main Street to harness the power of the Mississippi as it dipped through the Des Moines Rapids. Joseph returned to the idea on November 23, 1843, and "[s]uggested the idea of petitioning congress for a grant to make a canal over the falls, or a dam to turn the water to the city, so that we might erect mills and other machinery."[54] Two weeks later, the city council supported a plan for improvements with an ordinance that gave Joseph "and his successor for the term of perpetual succession" authority to build dams and use them to propel "mills and machinery." The ordinance also specified the right to use the catch basin as a harbor where riverboats could dock and tolls could be collected for the road leading to the top of the dam. All fees and

50. Ibid., 74.

51. Joseph Smith, Diary, Nov. 15, 1843, in Faulring, *An American Prophet's Record*, 427.

52. Joseph Smith, Diary, Nov. 21, 1843, in Faulring, *An American Prophet's Record*, 428.

53. Ibid., Nov. 22, 1843; also in Anderson and Bergera, *Joseph Smith's Quorum of the Anointed*, 37.

54. Ibid.

compensation would be monitored by the council itself.[55] Interest in the plan ran high but stalled with the political difficulties of 1844.

Problems with plurality also erupted that fall. By November, Joseph had been sealed to at least thirty-three wives, and twenty-four other men had also enlarged their "privileges" in this way.[56] Between the loyal outer circle of members, who presumably believed the public denials, and the inner circle, who knew otherwise, came a midrange of those who knew that the practice existed but not its purpose or rules. Confused, faulty, and partial understandings were a consequence of the doctrine's subterranean nature. As mayor and Church leader, Joseph was responsible for prosecuting moral law-breakers, regardless of the apparent hypocrisy.

One of these cases came before the Nauvoo High Council on November 25, at which Joseph accused thirty-eight-year-old Harrison Sagers with "trying to seduce a young girl, living at his house by the name of Phebe Madison" (Sagers's sister-in-law), and "for using my name in a blasphemous manner, by saying that I tolerated such things in which thing he is guilty of lying." Sagers had joined the Church in New York state in 1833, had served missions to New Orleans and Jamaica, was part of Zion's Camp, and had served on the Adam-ondi-Ahman High Council. According to Joseph's account:

> I ... told them that the Church had not received any permission from me to commit fornication, adultery, or any corrupt action; but my every word and action has been to the contrary. If a man commit adultery, he cannot receive the celestial kingdom of God. Even if he is saved by any kingdom, it cannot be the celestial kingdom. I did think that the many examples that have been made manifest, such as John C. Bennett's and others, were sufficient to show the fallacy of such a course of conduct. I condemned such actions in toto, and warned the people present against committing such evils ...[57]

Sagers pled not guilty, and the high council simply ruled that "he had taught false doctrine which was corrected by President Joseph Smith."[58]

On November 26, Joseph and some of the apostles again consulted with Colonel John Frieson, a Quincy supporter of John C. Calhoun, about the draft "memorial" for Congress (the third), detailing Missouri's persecutions

55. Ibid., Dec. 8, 1843, in Faulring, *An American Prophet's Record*, 431.
56. George D. Smith, *Nauvoo Polygamy*, 575-639.
57. *History of the Church*, 6:81 (Nov. 25, 1843).
58. Nauvoo High Council, Minutes, Nov. 25, 1843.

and other grievances.[59] Frieson had heard from Calhoun's friend, R. B. Rhett, a representative from South Carolina, that Rhett would be willing to present the petition.[60] The memorial emphasized the importance of granting the mayor power "to call to his aid a sufficient number of United States troops, in connection with the Nauvoo Legion, to repel the invasion of mobs, keep the public peace, and protect the innocent from the unhallowed ravages of lawless banditti that escape justice on the western frontier."[61] The idea of establishing a Mormon "territory" was ingenious. It would have bypassed the Illinois legislature and also have provided federal funds to maintain the Nauvoo Legion. In short, it would have guaranteed on-going independence.

The story of Missouri so engrossed Joseph that he wrapped his sense of his and the Church's future and past around it. Driven by anger, humiliation, and a desire for retribution, he brandished the Mormon story before the federal government yet again. More than failed judgment, culpable human nature, or pride, Joseph's preoccupation with Missouri doomed him to failure and eventually to death. Critical to understanding Joseph's sense of his prophet-role was the unsteady relationship between Joseph and Missouri that so shaped his years in Illinois. Joseph still believed that the City of Zion would be located in Missouri and that Satan-inspired persecution had twice thwarted his divinely directed efforts, once in 1833 and again in 1838. His failure to achieve a temple in Independence had compromised his mission, resulting in an adaptation and even abdication of his original vision. Perhaps he felt compelled to settle the score, not just because of the property and lives lost, the injustice of the prosecutions and imprisonment, or even his personal sufferings and continued fears of extradition. Rather, the loss of Zion forced him to resurrect the issue of retribution over and over again. Throughout the Nauvoo period, Missouri haunted him, and he struck back with three formal memorials. Reminded by the most recent petition of his anger toward Missouri, Joseph returned to the subject on six recorded occasions during the next two weeks.

Later in the day, Joseph lectured to a small group and then had Phelps read his draft "Appeal to the Green Mountain Boys" soliciting help from residents in Joseph's birth state of Vermont.[62] The "appeal" announced that

59. *History of the Church*, 6:84-97 (Nov. 29, 1843).

60. Ibid., 83 (Nov. 28, 1843).

61. Ibid., 131 (Nov. 29, 1843).

62. Manuscript *History of the Church*, Nov. 9, 1843: also in Ehat and Cook, *The Words of Joseph Smith*, 258. The Green Mountain Boys, commanded by Ethan Allen, had organized in Vermont in 1770 to protect their lands against claims by New York property owners.

Joseph had used his influence to prevent Mormons from fighting the Missouri mobs, which he now regretted. But the letter's main point was his hope that the "Green Mountain Boys" would

> help bring Missouri to the bar of justice. If there is one whisper from the spirit of an Ethan Allen; … let it mingle with our sense of honor, and fire our bosoms for the cause of suffering innocence,–for the reputation of our disgraced country, and for the glory of God; … if Missouri, blood-stained Missouri;–escapes the due demerit of her crimes, the vengeance she so justly deserves, that Vermont is a hypocrite–a coward–and this nation the hot bed of political demagogues! …[63]

According to one writer, "Vermonters were unimpressed," so much so that some Green Mountain Boys penned their own sarcastic response two months later.[64]

Joseph's dwelling on the wrongs of Missouri must have intensified his own insecurities. On December 8, he presided over the Nauvoo City Council at 4:00 p.m., which passed an extraordinary law that anyone who brought an arrest warrant against Joseph on the Missouri charges would be subject to life imprisonment.[65] At the same meeting, Joseph also "suggested to the Council the idea of petitioning Congress … to acknowledge the Nauvoo Legion as U.S. troops, and to assist in fortifications and other purposes."[66] This petition–which would have given Joseph the power to mobilize U.S. troops–reflected still more poor judgment, since it was sure to be rejected and its originator branded as audacious. Joseph seems to have recognized its mediocre chances; but instead of charting a more realistic course, he issued a "prophecy" when he signed it on December 16: "if Congress will not hear our petition and grant us protection, they shall be broken up as a government."[67]

On December 9, six days after the first reading of the appeal to the Green Mountain Boys and the Congressional petition, Joseph gave a rousing speech on the street to a "very large meeting of citizens." He asserted that the "Legion was a part of the militia of Illinois, and that his commission declared that he [Joseph Smith] was the Lieutenant-General of the Nauvoo

63. Joseph Smith, "An Appeal to the Freemen of the State of Vermont, the 'Brave Green Mountain Boys,' and Honest Men," in *The Essential Joseph Smith*, 209. Phelps included snippets from seventeen foreign languages in a bravura display of–largely mock–erudition, including Chaldean, Egyptian, Greek, Syrian, Samaritan, Hebrew, and Latin.

64. Samuel Brown, "The Translator and the Ghostwriter," 47.

65. *History of the Church*, 6:105 (Dec. 8, 1843).

66. Ibid., 99. After "all had spoken upon it," the "Appeal" was "dedicated by prayer."

67. Ibid., 116 (Dec. 16, 1843).

Legion & of the militia of the State of Illinois."[68]Increasing the pitch of his arguments and the violence of his rhetoric, Joseph used every opportunity in early December to hammer home the persecution narrative. He was positioning his people to see themselves primarily–if not only–as a despised minority who would have to fight for their rights. The frequency and intensity of these meetings toward the end of 1843 all but predicted some dramatic outcome. Besides regular meetings of the city council, high council, the Twelve, and the Quorum of the Anointed, Joseph addressed six citizens' meetings in December alone. Such intensity must have taken a toll on him; but perhaps intuiting how important it was for him to arouse the spiritual and emotional ecstasy his followers had come to expect, Joseph continued to dazzle them with on-going ritual and a grander view of the heavenly glory that awaited the faithful.

Another reason Joseph felt justified in putting the city on alert was news that reached him on December 10 that Daniel Avery, a Mormon carpenter, had been arrested with his son, Philander, at Bear Creek near Warsaw, and that both men were being held in Missouri.[69] Quickly, Joseph drafted a letter and affidavit to Governor Thomas Ford on December 11.[70] Ford responded a day later, claiming that he had no way of interfering in another state's legal proceedings,[71] and explained that Joseph could only "appeal to the laws of Missouri."[72] Joseph probably received Ford's letter on December 13, which may help to explain his violent illness on December 15. "I was never prostrated so low, in so short a time, before," he marveled. But thanks to "herbs and mild drink," by evening he was "considerably revived."[73] On the 20th, Clayton, perhaps sensing that money issues may have also contributed to Joseph's distress, issued a public letter urging immigrants to buy land from the Church:

> ... there is in the hands of the Trustee in Trust, a large quantity of lands, both in the city and adjoining Townships in this county, which is for sale,

68. Ibid., 107 (Dec. 9, 1843).
69. Ibid., 108 (Dec. 10, 1843).
70. Ibid., 109-10 (Dec. 11, 1843).
71. Ibid., 114 (Dec. 12, 1843).
72. Thomas Ford, Letter to Joseph Smith, Dec. 12, 1843, qtd. in *History of the Church*, 6:114. Ford also reminded Joseph that, the previous August, he had been "furnished by your friends with a very large amount of affidavits and evidence, said to be intended to show cause why no further writs should be issued against you. I have not read them and probably never will, unless a new demand should be made in which case they will receive a careful perusal and you may rest assured, that no Steps will be taken by me but such as the Constitution and laws may require."
73. *History of the Church*, 6:115-16 (Dec. 15, 1843).

> some of which belongs to the church and is designed for the benefit of the poor, and also to liquidate debts owing to the church, for which the Trustee in Trust is responsible. … Let all the brethren, therefore, when they move into Nauvoo, consult President Joseph Smith, the trustee in trust, and purchase their lands of him; and I am bold to say that God will bless them.[74]

Joseph, Hyrum, and Brigham Young continued to deal in land privately, giving some lots to the poor or as compensation for land lost in Missouri.[75] During this period of intense land exchange, Nauvoo had no formal institution for lending money. Instead, land served as a means of exchange, a sort of floating capital one could borrow from or lend against with some security.

On December 17, the Anointed Quorum met in the red brick store, anointing Joseph's younger brother, Samuel Harrison Smith. Joseph was still jumpy, preoccupied by Missouri: "[H]e lifted up his hands towards heaven & declaired that if Missouri Came against us any more he would fight them & defend his rights."[76] The next week, another couple, Isaac and Lucy Morley, and Orson Pratt were anointed along with six women, two of them Joseph's plural wives: "Sister Lot, Fanny Murray, Sister Woodruff, Geo[rge] A. Smith's wife, Sister O[rson] Spencer, [and] Sister Phelp[s]."[77] According to Wilford Woodruff, on Christmas Eve "I again met with the quorum in Company with Mrs Woodruff. We recieved some instruction concerning the Priesthood."[78]

By December 1843, women were fully involved in the Quorum of the Anointed. They were not explicitly promised priesthood or the power embedded in men in the Latter-day Saint view of heaven, but as priestesses, they occupied a position beside their husbands as partners in their family kingdoms.

On Christmas morning, a small group of women serenaded Joseph and his family. That night, Emma and he hosted a dinner party for fifty couples in their home, which turned into an impromptu celebration of Porter Rockwell's return from Missouri. Rockwell, after spending the winter of 1842-43 in Philadelphia, tried unsuccessfully to become employed in Indiana or

74. William Clayton, "To Emigrants and Latter-Day Saints Generally," *Nauvoo Neighbor*, Dec. 20, 1843, 2.

75. Robert B. Flanders, *Nauvoo*, 126.

76. Woodruff, *Journal*, 2:332 (Dec. 18, 1843).

77. Joseph Smith, Diary, Dec. 23, 1843, in Faulring, *An American Prophet's Record*, 435; also Anderson and Bergera, *Joseph Smith's Quorum of the Anointed*, 44.

78. Woodruff, *Journal*, 2:333 (Dec. 24, 1843).

Ohio.[79] He decided to return to Nauvoo; but when he docked across the river from Nauvoo on March 5, 1843, a Missouri sheriff seized and jailed him in Independence. A full five months later in August, a grand jury failed to indict Rockwell.[80] Rockwell escaped from jail once, was captured, and jailed again. A second grand jury indicted him for breaking out of jail. Tried on this charge, he was found guilty but served only "Five minutes confinement in the County Jail."[81] After nine months, Rockwell was released on December 14, 1843.

When Rockwell walked back into Nauvoo, his hair was long, stringy, and filthy. His clothes hung loosely on an underfed body. Trusting in Joseph's sense of humor, he pushed his way past the guards, exaggerating his staggering stride to give the impression he was drunk. Alarmed that the stranger might be from Missouri, Joseph at first recoiled, then saw Rockwell's face and embraced him, pounding his back affectionately. The women stopped screaming and joined in the laughter.[82]

On the afternoon of December 27, Joseph shared with W. W. Phelps letters drafted to presidential candidates Lewis Cass and John Calhoun, expounding Joseph's own political views and asking their positions on the treatment the Church had received.[83] The episode illustrates a striking difference in the scale of the nineteenth-century world. Joseph drafted letters that would have been read personally by Calhoun or Cass. Nauvoo and the Church sent petitions and memorials to Congress in a line more direct than that circumscribed by today's administrative staff, committees, and layers of bureaucracy. On December 28, Joseph mused with John Bernhisel, a physician and political economist, and Joseph H. Jackson, still in Joseph's good graces, about his life as a prophet.[84]

Also on the 28th, Joseph confided to a group of Nauvoo policemen his anxieties about his personal security: "I am exposed to far greater danger from traitors among ourselves than from enemies without. … I can live as Caesar might have lived, were it not for a right-hand Brutus." He then added ominously, "Judas was one of the Twelve."[85] "My life is in more danger from

79. Harold Schindler, *Orrin Porter Rockwell*, 86.

80. Ibid., 101.

81. Ibid., 106.

82. *History of the Church*, 6:134 (Dec. 25, 1843).

83. Joseph Smith, Diary, Dec. 29, 1843, in Faulring, *An American Prophet's Record*, 436.

84. Ibid., Dec. 28, 1843, 436; *History of the Church*, 6:152 (Dec. 29, 1843); Joseph H. Jackson, *A Narrative of the Adventures and Experience of Joseph H. Jackson in Nauvoo*, 19, 7.

85. *History of the Church*, 6:152 (Dec. 29, 1843).

some little dough-head of a fool in this city than from all my numerous and inveterate enemies abroad," he stated.[86] Despite evidence of Nauvoo's success all around them, Joseph's spreading influence, and the Church's swelling ranks, trouble criss-crossed the Mormon world. Some who had long been Joseph's trusted allies questioned his leadership because of plurality or other doctrines that were equally difficult to accept.

On December 30, Joseph preached to the Quorum of the Anointed on "the principles of integrity," its lack leading "to apostasy."[87] William and Jane Law did not come to this final meeting of 1843. Though endowed, they either had not been invited or had absented themselves intentionally, foreshadowing the bruising dissension that would mark the next six months and lead ultimately to Joseph's death at Carthage Jail.

Joseph celebrated New Year's Eve in a meeting of the Anointed lasting from "early candle light till ten o'clock."[88] Fifty carolers and musicians sang to Joseph and Emma beneath their bedroom window with W. W. Phelps's "New Year's hymn."[89] But any sense of celebration and well-being would be short-lived.

86. Ibid.; "dough head": blockhead; stupid.

87. Joseph Smith, qtd. in Elden J. Watson, ed., *Manuscript History of Brigham Young*, 157. Also in Anderson and Bergera, *Joseph Smith's Quorum of the Anointed*, 49.

88. Joseph Smith, Diary, Dec. 31, 1843, in Faulring, *An American Prophet's Record*, 437.

89. *History of the Church*, 6:153 (Dec. 31, 1843).

CHAPTER 23

Dissension

I should be like a fish out of water, if I were out of persecutions.
–Joseph Smith, History of the Church, *6:408 (May 26, 1844)*

It is difficult to say if the hostility of outsiders or the dissension of insiders was more dangerous to Joseph's role as prophet. Both made 1844 a year of mounting tensions for the Mormon leader–and ultimately led to the prophet's death. Non-Mormon enemies in Illinois perceived Joseph as representing an even greater threat than in Missouri. The growing empire on the banks of the Mississippi created unease, mistrust, and animosity. Joseph's increasingly expansive view of his destiny as a religious and political ruler and their relationship to plurality alienated previously loyal men like William Law and William Marks, especially as Joseph crossed line after line.

Despite the winter storm, New Year's Eve ushering in 1844 featured "a large party … at my house and continued music and dancing till morning," Joseph recorded, adding, oddly for a host, "I was in my private room with my family and John Taylor &c."[1] By January 2, it had snowed an inch, the first storm "of consequence," Joseph observed.[2]

Joseph also responded on New Year's day to Governor Thomas Ford's letter of December 12, 1843, about the arrest of Philander and Daniel Avery in Missouri, released on Christmas day, after a writ of habeas corpus had been issued.[3] Joseph could not have been pleased with Ford's lecture on jurisdiction, but he tried to be conciliatory. He found Ford's analysis "consistent with the spirit and genius of the [Nauvoo] charter and the common law of the land, as well as the intention of our constitution." As mayor, he had a "devout calculation to magnify the law and safely confide in it" and would be

1. Joseph Smith, Diary, Jan. 1, 1844, in Scott H. Faulring, ed., *An American Prophet's Record*, 37.
2. Ibid., Jan. 2, 1844 (Faulring, 437).
3. See *History of the Church*, 6:108, 147-48 (Dec. 25, 1843).

sure that his people would act only in "self defence." However, Joseph then launched into his engrained persecution narrative, focusing on the sufferings of Orrin Porter Rockwell who had spent nine months in a Missouri jail.[4]

After two years overseeing construction on the Nauvoo House, Joseph gave up its management within four months of moving in. Although he continued to live in the building, he complained of debt, distractions, and complex ecclesiastical and civic responsibilities, and on January 23 decided to lease the Mansion House to Ebenezer Robinson for $1,000 per year.[5] The agreement included setting aside a suite of three rooms for the Smith family and room in the barn for Joseph's horses. Attempting to create order in other business operations that blended the personal and public, Joseph also unloaded the *Times and Seasons* "printing office and lot," "printing apparatus," bindery, and foundry for $2,832, a price suggested by W. W. Phelps, Willard Richards, and Newel K. Whitney.[6] Although Joseph respected their judgment, he thought the valuation was "low" and expressed himself as "disappointed."[7] He had bought the paper for twice the price. These two transactions reveal the lack of realism that pulled the economic rug out from Joseph's over-optimistic feet. When Joseph died, his estate was smothered with debt.

Besides the financial, Joseph's troubles included dissension at home. Emma's resistance to, and Joseph's embrace of, plurality was poisoning their marriage. John Taylor remembered Emma working actively against celestial marriage. "Emma Smith, at first professed having faith in the revelation on celestial marriage," Taylor later commented, "but afterwards forsook it, and used her influence against it to my wife and others." Leonora Taylor had been initiated into the Quorum of the Anointed on November 1, 1843,[8] and had agreed to John's taking his first plural wife the next month on December 12.[9] Almost four decades later, Taylor recounted a conversation with Joseph about Emma's resistence: "Brother Joseph, do you know that sister Emma has been talking thus and so to my wife, and telling her such and such things, and said that you have denied the revelation yourself?" Joseph

4. Joseph Smith, Letter to Thomas Ford, Jan. 1, 1844, in Dean C. Jessee, ed., *Personal Writings of Joseph Smith*, 489.

5. Robert B. Flanders, *Nauvoo*, 177.

6. *History of the Church*, 6:185 (Jan. 22, 1843).

7. Ibid. (Jan. 24, 1844).

8. Devery S. Anderson and Gary James Bergera, eds., *Joseph Smith's Quorum of the Anointed*, 32.

9. George D. Smith, *Nauvoo Polygamy*, 627.

allegedly answered: "Brother Taylor, Sister Emma would dethrone Jehovah himself, if she could, for the accomplishment of her purposes."[10]

Eudocia Baldwin Marsh, a teenage visitor from Carthage, also remembered Emma's resistance. She did not include the date of her visit, but it was after September 1843. Eudocia's sister was in "the hotel [i.e., Mansion House] parlor" where "ten or twelve young women were assembled, laughing and talking. Mrs. Emma Smith presently joined them, and recognizing my sister, whom she had met before, entered into conversation with her. My sister asked, 'Mrs. Smith, where does your church get this doctrine of spiritual wives?' [H]er face flushed scarlet, and her eyes blazed as she replied, 'Straight from hell, madam.'"[11]

Emma must have been outraged at having to field such questions. Anger, humiliation, and desperation must have accompanied many such encounters. Some of the young women present were only amused by Emma's distress; others, like John Taylor, were angry at her intransigence. The emotion and tension that marked this period of time emerge in the bizarre accusation by Joseph that Emma tried to poison him on November 5, 1843. The illness and vomiting that accompanied it were, no doubt, the result of simple food poisoning.[12] Emma may have felt profoundly betrayed by Joseph's practice of plurality, but it stretches credibility to think that she would try to murder him.

Throughout the winter of 1843-44, Emma attended meetings of the Anointed Quorum, performing washings and anointings for the women in her own bedroom. Heber Kimball recorded on January 17, 1844: "My wife Vilate and menny feemales was received into the Holy order and was washed and inointed by Emma."[13] Emma may have viewed these meetings as opportunities to voice her apprehensions regarding plural marriage.

Rather than acknowledge how these new doctrines frayed the loyalty of some of his most trusted friends, Joseph continued to link his identity to persecution: "I, like Paul," he announced on May 26, 1844, a month before his death, "have been in perils, and oftener than anyone in this generation. … I should be like a fish out of water, if I were out of persecutions."[14] Persecution

10. John Taylor, qtd. in, "Minutes of a General Meeting Held in the Fourteenth Ward Assembly Hall," July 18, 1880, *Woman's Exponent* 9 (Sept. 1, 1880): 50.

11. Eudocia Baldwin Marsh, "Mormons in Hancock County: A Reminiscence," Apr. 1, 1916, 375, qtd. in Linda King Newell and Valeen Tippets Avery, *Mormon Enigma*, 172.

12. See Newell and Avery, *Mormon Enigma*, 164.

13. Heber C. Kimball, Journal, Jan. 20, 1844, in Stanley B. Kimball, ed., *On the Potter's Wheel*, 56.

14. *History of the Church*, 6:408 (May 26, 1844).

was a badge of membership, dividing God's chosen people from outsiders. The Church's collective memory was forged in part by this story of God's truth persecuted endlessly by evil.

Joseph swore in forty city policemen at the city council meeting on December 29, instructing them to obey the city ordinances and his own orders as mayor.[15] "If the bloodthirsty hell-hounds of Missouri continue their persecution, we will be forbearing, until we are compelled to strike; then do it decently and in good order, and break the yoke effectually, so that it cannot be mended." He added, "We will be in peace with all men, so long as they will mind their own business and let us alone."[16] He continued to lament Porter Rockwell's suffering, but then returned to his own situation: "I am exposed to far greater danger from traitors among ourselves than from enemies without ... I can live as Caesar might have lived, were it not for a right-hand Brutus. I have had pretended friends betray me." Joseph may have had John C. Bennett in mind, but his next statements hinted at new traitors: "All the enemies upon the face of the earth may roar and exert all their power to bring about my death, but they can accomplish nothing, unless some who are among us and enjoy our society, have been with us in our councils, participated in our confidence, taken us by the hand, called us brother, saluted us with a kiss, join with our enemies, turn our virtues into faults, and, by falsehood and deceit, stir up their wrath and indignation against us, and bring their united vengeance upon our heads."[17]

Joseph's allusions to "Brutus" and "Judas" had the effect of putting him in the positions of noble Caesar and blameless Christ. Rumors bloomed that he meant William Law, his second counselor in the First Presidency, which Joseph shrewdly confirmed by refusing to deny that he meant Law. Feeling betrayed and condemned, Law subsequently testified under oath to the Nauvoo City Council that he had been "informed that some of the policemen had another oath administered besides the one administered to them publicly: that one of them said there was a Judas in General Smith's cabinet,–one who stood next to him; and he must be taken care of, and that he must not be allowed to go into the world, but must be taken care of; and he was not only a ... a traitor like Judas, but an assassin like Brutus: that the idea had been advanced that the scriptures support such a doctrine." According to the official account, Law's source was officer Daniel Carn. Joseph countered by querying

15. Ibid., 149 (Dec. 29, 1843).
16. Ibid., 150.
17. Ibid., 152.

all of the policemen, including Carn, directly: "On conditions I have had no private conversation with any of you, rise up and change the breech of your gun upwards."[18] All of the officers stood up and swung their weapons into position. Joseph continued: "The reason why I made the remarks I did was on account of the reports … that my enemies were determined to get me into their power and take my life."[19] Joseph defiantly made his accusation even more bold. "[T]hey feared that 'Mormonism' would destroy their present religious creeds, organizations, and orthodox systems." Then, distinguishing the particular threat they present, "They did not design to try me, but hang me, or take my life anyhow: that they had a man in our midst who would fix me out, if they could not get me into their power without."[20]

Law's version of events after the council meeting display the distance that had grown between the two men and how differently they interpreted the same set of events. Law, his brother Wilson, and Hyrum Smith sought out Joseph to question him personally about the rumors swirling in the air. Joseph "became very angry," according to Law's journal, "that any should have any fears or suspect that he would encourage such a thing, and said that he had a good mind to put them (the police) on us any how." Law described the "indignation" it caused him, to find "the mayor of the City, threaten two innocent men, with forty armed poliece, because they complained to him of threats having been made by them, against their lives; some hard words passed between us."[21]

Joseph Fielding described another meeting during this tense time, showing Joseph testing the loyalty of those surrounding him. On March 7, he wrote, "[A] meeting was called and several addresses delivered by the Prophet and others on some Evils in the City, Several received a severe Exposure in the Church and out." Charles Foster asked if Hyrum had "alluded to him … but did not get a direct Answer." Then, Foster confronted Joseph. Joseph asked why he thought so. Foster repeated the question, insisting, "If you will not hear me you soon shall hear from me. Did you allude to me?" Joseph answered, "You say it," and instructed the police to fine Foster "5 or 10 Dol[lars]." "Thus it ended for the time," Fielding remembered, "but the reproof and exposure which he and several others had received stirred up feelings that could not be suppressed."[22] Such public humiliations were, at a minimum, injudicious.

18. Nauvoo City Council, Minutes, *History of the Church*, 6:163 (Jan. 3, 1844).
19. Ibid., 164.
20. Ibid.
21. William Law, Diary, January 4, 1844, in Lyndon W. Cook, ed., *William Law*, 42.
22. Andrew F. Ehat, ed., "'They Might Have Known that He Was Not a Fallen Prophet,'"

"A few weeks after this," Joseph took the stand again, according to Fielding, this time claiming "that a conspiracy was formed by the two Fosters, the Laws, C[hauncey]. Higby, and J[oseph] H. Jackson and others against himself and all the Smiths by some of them it was declared that there should not be one of the Smith Family alive in a few Weeks. ... They had formed a Caucus and had invited others to join it but much of this was found to be the false statement of the said Joseph H. Jackson, [who] proved to as corrupt and guilty as a man could well be." Jackson left Nauvoo after the meeting with the Law brothers, William and Wilson, which Fielding interpreted as a blatant advertisement of their affiliation.[23]

Some, men like the Laws, who once had been close to Joseph, had become troubled by the developing discrepancies between his prophetic persona and his all-too-human grandiosity and over-reactions. Still for the ordinary members of Nauvoo, Joseph's charisma was dazzling. "I saw him on parade one fourth of July riding his black horse named Joe Duncan," wrote admiring disciple Mary Dunn Ensign seventy years later: "I thought I had never seen a more beautiful sight. I have also witnessed him on the ball grounds many times. None could excel him in the games."[24] "His appearance was that of a fine, portly gentleman, six feet high, weighing about two hundred pounds," Fawcett also recalled. "He was pleasant and kind. His character was unimpeachable among the Saints. They loved him and he loved them." Joseph obviously relied on this foundation of adoration that enabled him to minimize resistance, perplexity, and challenges to his authority. Fawcett's faith in Joseph's prophethood dominated all competing interpretations: "My testimony of Joseph Smith is that he was a Prophet of the living God, and held the keys of the Holy Melchizedek Priesthood, and of the everlasting gospel to this generation; and that he saw God and His Son Jesus Christ, and talked with them, and also holy angels who ordained him to this priesthood, and talked with and called him to establish God's Church upon the earth again in our day."[25]

The story of the division between William Law and Joseph takes the

---

145-46. The exchange between Joseph Smith and Charles Foster is also recorded in the conference minutes, *History of the Church*, 6:240 (March 7, 1844).

23. Andrew F. Ehat, ed., "'They Might Have Known that He was Not a Fallen Prophet,'" 145-46.

24. Ivy H. B. Hill, ed., *Autobiography of Mary Dunn Ensign, daughter of Simeon Adams Dunn and Adaline Rawson Dunn*, 193.

25. Fawcett, "Recollections of the Prophet Joseph Smith," http://www.boap.org/LDS/Early-Saints/REC-JS.html (June 30, 2013).

form of myriad affronts–the split over the doctrine of plurality (see chap. 19) and disagreements over business deals with serious financial ramifications. In this environment, it was almost impossible to respond calmly to public accusations about what Joseph had (or had not) said or meant (or not meant). Joseph's relationships with William Law, Robert Foster, and Chauncey and Francis Higbee eroded especially during the early months of 1844. By June, there was no mutual trust or respect left.

Joseph's alienation from William Law was particularly troublesome. Law looked like the perfect Saint. He had been a loyal supporter, steady and true both to the Church and its leadership. With his wife, Jane, and their children, he had arrived in Nauvoo in 1839. Already wealthy, his investments included construction industries, mills, and small manufacture. In Nauvoo, he and brother Wilson bought real estate, started a steam mill, and was known as a "man of means."[26] Joseph named Law second counselor in the First Presidency in 1841.[27]

But Law developed qualms about how real estate was handled in Nauvoo and grew increasingly uneasy about the prophet's monopoly of land sales and potential profits. Furthermore, he questioned Joseph's investment in the publication of a revised version of the Bible.[28] Biographer Lyndon W. Cook describes Law as justifying his dissent in five ways. First, he deemed Joseph "totally ungovernable and defiant" and was alarmed that Joseph seemed "determined to obey or disobey the law of the land at his own convenience." He found unacceptable Joseph's way of erasing the distinction between church and state. Second, his manipulation of the Mormon vote and encouragement of influence-peddling to politicians seeking the Church's support was repugnant to Law. Third, judicial order under Joseph's rule, was, according to Law, "trampled under foot." Fourth, the Mormon prophet also used his ecclesiastical role to control his people's finances. Finally, Law repudiated the plurality of wives and of gods as false doctrine.[29]

Wilson Law was a convert who, like his brother, had been in Joseph's favor as a member of the Nauvoo City Council after 1841. Also in 1841, he was appointed brigadier general in the Nauvoo Legion with a further elevation in rank in 1842 to major general. Loyally, he had helped to secure Joseph's

---

26. Lyndon W. Cook, "William Law, Nauvoo Dissenter," 53.

27. "Traveling Agents," *Times and Seasons* 2 no. 7 (Feb. 1, 1841): 310: "William Law has recently, by revelation, been appointed one of the first Presidency in the place of Hyrum Smith."

28. *History of the Church*, 6:164-65 (Jan. 3, 1844).

29. Cook, "William Law," 56.

return to Nauvoo after the prophet's arrest at Dixon. When he and William finally broke with Joseph, Wilson became his brother's counselor in the presidency of the dissenting True Church of Jesus Christ of Latter Day Saints.[30]

The Law brothers were united in their opposition to plural marriage, a position they shared with William Marks, Austin Cowles, and Leonard Soby. Marks, born in Rutland, Vermont, had joined Mormonism in New York in 1835. A devoted follower, he was a Church leader–president of the Kirtland and Nauvoo stakes–and a civic leader, serving as an alderman in Nauvoo. Joseph trusted him enough to make him a member of the Council of Fifty.[31] Marks's counselor was fifty-six-year-old Austin Cowles, a Methodist Episcopal minister who converted and moved to Kirtland. In Nauvoo, he was on the high council, as was Leonard Soby.[32]

Besides the Laws, Marks, Cowles, and Soby, the two Higbee brothers, Chauncey and Francis, aligned themselves against Joseph. Several of these men had conflicted relations with Joseph over real estate and business affairs. When he was twenty-two years old, Francis had associated with Bennett during the controversy over Joseph's overtures to Nancy Rigdon. In 1844, he would be excommunicated for apostasy; brother Chauncey had been expelled from the Church on May 24, 1842, for his collusion with Bennett.[33] Yet another on the side of dissenters, Hiram Kimball, a wealthy entrepreneur and merchant and later convert to Mormonism, had been welcoming as the Saints built up the town, partly because his wife, Sarah Melissa Granger Kimball, had joined the Church in 1833.[34] But in 1842, Joseph had proposed plural marriage to Sarah. Sarah refused, and Hiram developed serious doubts about the prophet. The record suggests tension between Joseph and Hiram that was most likely rooted in plurality but which also included conflict over business. Hiram owned land along the steamboat wharves and planned to collect wharfage as a profit. Joseph claimed that the city should get the money instead. Kimball bristled at this violation of the simplest principle of capitalism.[35]

During the winter of 1843-44, William Law and Robert Foster became so strongly opposed to Joseph's Church-centric economy that they initiated

30. Jessee, *Personal Writings of Joseph Smith*, 680.

31. Ibid., 682.

32. Glen Leonard, *Nauvoo*, 446.

33. *History of the Church*, 5:18 (May 24, 1842).

34. Mary Stovall Richards, "Sarah Granger Kimball," 2:784; see also Jill C. Mulvay, "The Liberal Shall Be Blessed: Sarah M. Kimball," 205-21; Sarah M. Kimball, "Auto-Biography," 51.

35. *History of the Church*, 5:12 (May 19, 1842).

independent business ventures. Buying lumber that came down the Mississippi from the Church's operations in Wisconsin, they launched significant construction projects, hiring men for hard currency and better wages than the tithing script paid to workers on the temple or Mansion House.[36] These signs of entrepreneurship challenged Joseph's view of Zion and his economic monopoly. They divided loyalties and created a market economy mentality, both of which were anathema to the unity that Joseph felt could be achieved only by hierarchical order.

Once Joseph lost William Law's loyalty, Law found fault with much of what Joseph did. He criticized Joseph's emphasis on donations for the temple and the Nauvoo House as unwise, given the poverty-stricken Saints' need to establish homes and invest in their own farms and businesses. In 1842 and 1843, he saw Joseph use money collected from the Saints for the hotel and temple to buy more land. Law condemned the diversion.[37] Joseph insisted that the Nauvoo House "must be built. Our salvation depends upon it." He also played the authority card: "I will say to those who have labored on the Nauvoo House, and cannot get their pay–Be patient; and if any man takes the means which are set apart for the building of that house, and applies it to his own use, let him, for he will destroy himself. If any man is hungry, let him come to me, and I will feed him at my table. … I will divide with them to the last morsel; and then if the man is not satisfied, I will kick his backside!"[38] It was a mixed message for even the most faithful men who labored without assurance of wages and who came home to a starving family.

The circles of increasingly privileged insiders surrounding Joseph made it easy to disregard questioners and dissenters. At the same time, the same complexity of insidership and the politics of critics that afflicted Joseph is revealed as a subtle undercurrent in Joseph's diary during the first six months of 1844. Dispassionate in some ways, the brief descriptions of hearings, court appearances, and other complications that he endured almost daily suggest a growing chaos that Joseph struggled to resist but could not escape.

Joseph spent much of a cold, cloudy January 3 at home except for a noon meeting of the city council.[39] There, William Law argued with the prophet. "If you see a man stealing," Joseph stressed, "and you have told him three times to stand, and warned him that he is a dead man if he does not stand,

36. Flanders, *Nauvoo*, 188.

37. Cook, "William Law," 62.

38. *History of the Church*, 5:286 (Feb. 21, 1843).

39. Ibid., 6:162 (Jan. 3, 1844).

and he runs[,] shoot off his legs. The design of the office of the police is to stop thieving; but an enemy should not be harmed until he draws weapons upon you."[40] Though he spoke in metaphors and veiled references, Joseph's message to Law was clear.

Law, however, was not intimidated. He threatened sometime before January 8 that unless Joseph repented of his sins and confessed, Law would make Joseph's promiscuity public. According to Law, Joseph retorted that he would rather be "damned." Law made good on his threat, publishing the details of his allegations in the first and only issue of the *Nauvoo Expositor* on June 7, 1844. According to Law, Joseph told him: If I admitted to the charges, it would "prove the overthrow of the Church!" "Is not that inevitable already?" When Law questioned his former friend, Joseph tried to turn it into a joke: Then "we would all go to Hell together and convert it into a heaven by casting the Devil out!" "Hell is by no means the place this world of fools suppose it to be," Joseph continued, perhaps taken by his own whimsy, "but on the contrary, it is quite an agreeable place." Law could not be cajoled and left, announcing, "You can enjoy it then, but as for me, I will serve the Lord our God!"[41]

Joseph spent the morning of Friday, January 5, at home, then, at William Marks's request, attended another city council meeting, at 11:00 a.m., which again erupted into discord. Francis Higbee testified that some opposed Joseph's interpretation of doctrine. The minutes report his testimony as: "Have received the impression from rumor that Mr. [William] Law, Mr. [William] Marks, and probably one or two others, could not subscribe to all things in the church, and there were some private matters that might make trouble." Such threats had become relatively frequent, but Joseph's response was impatient and *ad hominem:* "Francis Higbee had better stay at home and hold his tongue, lest rumor turn upon him and disclose some private matters, which he would prefer kept hid; did not believe there was any rumor of the kind afloat, or he could have told some of the names of his informants." Characterizing Higbee as a troublemaker, Joseph made no effort to temper his wrath: "Thought the young men of the city had better withdraw from his [Higbee's] society, and let him stand on his own merits; I by no means consider him the standard of the city. There has been a system of corruption and debauchery which these rumors have grown out of, and the individuals who are the authors of them are those who do not want a police, they want

40. Nauvoo City Council, Minutes, Jan. 3, 1844, in ibid., 163.
41. William Law, "Preamble," *Nauvoo Expositor*, June 7, 1844, 2.

to prowl in the streets at pleasure without interruption."[42] The pressure to maintain the secret ritual of plurality was immense. Many of the men in the room had uneven knowledge of the doctrine at best, others had plural wives.

Earlier in the same meeting, Joseph had pointed to examples of his patience with his critics: "My long forbearance to my enemies [e.g., John C. Bennett] ought to be sufficient testimony of my peaceful disposition toward all men." And his dictated diary entry is again dismissive, almost too impatient to record the details: "Another tempest in a tea-pot, or big fuss about nothing at all," he said, rejecting the possibility the conflict might escalate. Because the night was bitterly cold, some citizens built a bonfire to ward off the chill across from William Marks's house. Marks, according to Joseph's account, "then became afraid, and concluded he must either be the Brutus or the dough-head, and lay awake all night, thinking the police had built the fire to kill him by!" The next morning, Marks, alarmed, described the scene of the night before. "[A]nother session of inquiry was held by the city council at his request, and the police sworn and questioned."[43]

Joseph's scoffing at Law's and Marks's concerns show more wishful thinking and denial than a realistic appraisal of the situation. The *History of the Church* continues with Joseph lashing out: "What can be the matter with these men? Is it that the wicked flee when no man pursueth, that hit pigeons always flutter, that drowning men catch at straws, or that Presidents Law and Marks are absolutely traitors to the Church, that my remarks should produce such an excitement in their minds. Can it be possible that the traitor whom Porter Rockwell reports to me as being in correspondence with my Missouri enemies, is one of my quorum?"[44]

In this case, Law left his own account: "Joseph [Smith] said he would not think such a thing of Bro. Law or Bro Marks for they were lovely men both of them. I made some remarks, said Joseph had nothing to fear from me, I was not his enemy (I did not say I was his friend). I said that if he and I had any difficulties or should have any hereafter I thought we could settle them between ourselves without calling on the Poliece ." Law's version of Joseph's attack on Higbee is equally judicious. First, he summarized Joseph's threat: "F. M. Higbee had better be careful or a train of facts would be

42. *History of the Church*, 6:168, 169 (Jan. 5, 1844).

43. Ibid., 166 (Jan. 5, 1844); Faulring, *An American Prophet's Record*, 437.

44. *History of the Church*, 6:170 (Jan. 5, 1844). This angry speculation does not appear in Joseph's journal. See Joseph Smith, Diary, Jan. 5, 1844, in Faulring, *An American Prophet's Record*, 438.

disclosed concerning him that he would not like." According to Law, Joseph "gave us to understand that he [Higbee] was conniving with Missouri &c.," and that he "would not allow him to associate with his females &c; that he [Smith] had been called on to lay hands on him [Higbee] when he stank from a cause that he did not like to name (or such a saying). I did not believe the story at all, and cannot see why he [Smith] should tell it." The "cause" Joseph did not name was a venereal disease.[45]

The whiplash-sharp changes in subjects throughout these few days–from the apostasy of his former friends to his possible U.S. presidential campaign–were profound. Despite Joseph's anger and denial, he would have suffered at their defection and feared what they could disclose. Although listening to his letter to John C. Calhoun might have been a welcome respite, sober reflection on the splintering of the Church required uninterrupted time for deliberations with his most trusted advisors. Unfortunately, the record kept by his scribes provides no glimpse of any such pause. Rather it shows him too swiftly enveloping new proselytes in a kaleidoscope of unrelenting demands and too swiftly discarding men of substance with proven loyalty to Mormonism's core principles.

On February 7, the *Warsaw Message* published the anonymous "Buckeye's Lamentation for Want of More Wives," a lengthy, satirical poem.[46] Joseph, no doubt annoyed, characterized the work as "doggerel" of a "very foul and malicious spirit."[47] Yet despite its hyperbole, "Lamentation" showed considerable insider knowledge, reading, in part:

> I once thought I had knowledge great,
> But now I find 'tis small.
> I once thought I'd religion too,
> But now I find I've none at all–
> For I have but ONE LONE WIFE,
> And can obtain no more;
> And the doctrine is I can't be saved,
> Unless I've HALF A SCORE.

45. William Law, Journal, Jan. 5, 1844, in Lyndon W. Cook, ed., *William Law*, 45-46. That Joseph meant venereal disease is clear in the original minutes of Francis Higbee's trial, May 8, 1844. The published account which appeared in "Municipal Court, City of Nauvoo, Illinois," *Times and Seasons* 5, no. (May 15, 1844): 537-41, is based on Thomas Bullock's notes, Nauvoo City Records Collection, LDS Church History Library.

46. "Buckeye's Lamentation for Want of More Wives," *Warsaw Message*, Feb. 7, 1844, 3.

47. *History of the Church*, 6:210 (Feb. 7, 1844). See also Gary James Bergera, "Buckeye's Laments: Two Early Insider Exposés of Mormon Polygamy and Their Authorship," *Journal of the Illinois State Historical Society* 96 (Winter 2003): 350-90.

A TENFOLD glory–that's the prize!
Without it you're undone!
But with it you will shine as bright
As the bright shining sun.
There you may shine like mighty Gods.
Creating worlds so fair
At least a WORLD for every WIFE
That you take with you there.[48]

On Saturday, January 6, Joseph took Emma, two months pregnant, out for a sleigh ride.[49] The sweeping prairie and snow-blanketed earth offered a welcome break from the previous week's conflict. Prayer meetings of the Anointed Quorum were also a place of refuge, where he could act fully in an unchallenged prophetic role, sustained and supported by believers. On Sunday afternoon, Joseph traveled to his farm three miles outside Nauvoo with Reynolds Cahoon, stopping to "preach" at Cornelius P. Lott's.[50] Lott managed Joseph's farm, and his daughter, Melissa, had been one of Joseph's wives since September 1843. Joseph returned to Nauvoo in time for a meeting of the prayer circle at 6:00 p.m. Significantly, he recorded: "Law absent. Marks not present."[51] Wilford and Phebe Woodruff also attended the meeting, and Wilford recorded "an interesting time of instruction. I spoke during the day upon the relationship that we sustained towards our Progenitures & posterity in the resurrection of the dead."[52] Excluded from the fellowship that took place in these gatherings of the most elite, William and Jane Law and the Markses were increasingly outsiders, both literally and figuratively. Robert Foster and Wilson Law had their fallings-out with Joseph before achieving that final step across the most intimate threshold into the Quorum of the Anointed.

On the 8th, William Law noted another affront from Joseph: "I was passing along the street near my house, when call'd to by Joseph Smith, he said

48. "Buckeye's Lamentation," 3. "Buckeye" had no doubt once cherished his status as someone who "had knowledge great" of Mormonism's teachings, only to discover that Joseph had not confided every new doctrine to him, and that, as a result, he found himself excluded from Joseph's most trusted circle of friends. Alarmed that salvation was tied to plurality, he adopted the premise (for rhetorical effect) that his doom was predestined and struck back by denying the validity of the vision that had previously framed his life.

49. Joseph Smith, Diary, Jan. 6, 1844, in Faulring, *An American Prophet's Record*, 438.

50. *History of the Church*, 6:171 (Jan. 7, 1844).

51. Joseph Smith, Diary, Jan. 7, 1844, in Faulring, *An American Prophet's Record*, 438.

52. Scott G. Kenney, ed., *Wilford Woodruff's Journal, 1833-1898*, 2:339 (Jan. 7, 1844); hereafter Woodruff, *Journal*.

I was injuring him by telling evil of him."[53] Joseph remarked on the encounter in his diary, saying he met with Law in the street in front of "Bro[ther] Phelps."[54] The public display of animosity drove the two men farther apart. An otherwise mundane chance encounter became a showdown that strained civility and made apparent the chasm separating the two. It would be Law's last known conversation with Joseph.

On January 10, Joseph ordained his uncle John Smith a patriarch, continuing with the routine business of running the Church despite the growing storm around him.[55] Construction on the temple likewise continued, bolstering morale and anticipation, but simultaneously draining the Church's resources with its continual demands for greater sacrifice. Joseph's own needs sometimes imposed on the goodwill of the Saints. On January 11, "The Twelve issued notices to the Saints at Nauvoo to cut and draw 75 or 100 cords of wood for the Prophet on the 15th and 16th January."[56]

Much about the five months before Joseph's death either foreshadowed his martyrdom or revealed his anxiety about his increasing vulnerability. Reportedly, he explored the issue of succession if he were to die. The most important of these possible successors was eleven-year-old Joseph Smith III. According to a second-hand account, in early 1844 George J. Adams, a high priest who had served several missions after his 1840 conversion, left an intimate meeting of the Church leaders to look for Emma.[57] He told her, as if she knew the importance of their conversation, that the matter is "now settled." We "now kn[o]w who Joseph's successor [will] be: it is little Joseph, [for] I have just seen him ordained by his father."[58] Lyman Wight also later remembered that Joseph blessed his namesake during a special leaders' meeting in the red brick store's second-floor chamber.[59]

53. William Law, Journal, Jan. 8, 1844, in Cook, *William Law*, 46.

54. Joseph Smith, Diary, Jan. 8, 1844, in Faulring, *An American Prophet's Record*, 439.

55. Ibid., Jan. 10, 1844, 439.

56. Ibid., Jan. 11, 1844, 440.

57. Roger D. Launius, *Joseph Smith III*, 15: "Among those present, according to some accounts, were Joseph and Hyrum Smith, John Taylor, Willard Richards, Newel K. Whitney, Reynolds Cahoon, Alpheus Cutler, Ebenezer Robinson, George J. Adams, W.W. Phelps, and John M. Bernhisel, all important individuals in the church's complex hierarchy." See also Newell and Avery, *Mormon Enigma*, 169-70.

58. Adams did not leave a personal account of this experience; but on May 14, 1865, William W. Blair recorded Emma's memory of Adams's statement. *Saints Herald* 8 (Oct. 1, 1885). Since Emma would doubtless have reported Joseph's words, rather than Adams's, had she heard about the episode from her husband, it is likely that Joseph never told her about it. See also Newell and Avery, *Mormon Enigma*, 169.

59. Lyman Wight, Letter to *Northern Islander*, July 1855, qtd. in Joseph Smith III and Heman C. Smith, eds., *The History of the [Reorganized] Church of Jesus Christ of Latter Day Saints*, 2:789.

Almost forty years after the fact, Joseph's financial clerk, James Whitehead, reported overhearing a conversation that occurred in Joseph's office about Joseph III's ordination as Joseph's successor. He said there were about twenty-five individuals at the meeting, which he recalled as being held on January 17, 1844. "Just before Joseph's death, Young Jos was ord[ained] in a Council by his father, John Taylor[,] Willaird Richards[,] Alph[eus] Cutler, W W Phelps. Dr. Bernhisel & Bishop Whitney were present. Bishop W. held the horn of oil & pou[red it on the boy's head]. ... Young Joseph was ordained by Joseph & Hyrum, in the council room in the Brick Store; and that Hyrum was appointed his guardian till he should become of age."[60] When Joseph spoke the next Sunday about "sealing the hearts of the fathers to the children and the heart of the children to the fathers," Whitehead thought he was reflecting on the blessing he made to his son. Historian and biographer of Joseph Smith III Roger D. Launius speculates that Joseph might have wondered whether he would live much longer "and needed to bless his son to carry on after him." Over young Joseph's lifetime, "this blessing became increasingly important to Joseph Smith III as he matured and took the leadership of the Reorganized Church."[61]

Joseph had administered the second anointing or "fullness of the priesthood" to Brigham Young on November 22, 1843.[62] By the end of January 1844, nine of the Twelve had received the second anointing and believed they had the authority–or, the "keys to the kingdom"–to administer all Church ordinances and affairs if anything happened to Joseph. Even so, as historians Linda King Newell and Valeen Tippets Avery have pointed out, Joseph had apparently given the blessing of presidential succession, not to the Twelve, but to Joseph III.[63]

The Holy Order met for prayer on the afternoon of January 14, again in the chamber over the store. The weather was "warm, rainy towards night and evening," according to Joseph.[64] The Twelve "preached at private houses in

60. William W. Blair, Diary, May 14, 17, 1865; Alexander H. Smith, Diary, entry after May 14, 1864. See also *True Latter Day Saints Herald* 8 (Oct. 1, 1865): 101: W. Grant McMurray, "'True Son of True Father,'" 141. Whitehead's later testimony is in *Autumn Leaves* 1 (May 1888): 202; Whitehead, Testimony, Temple Lot Case, 28, 32, 36.

61. Roger D. Launius, *Joseph Smith III*, 15-16. See also Joseph Smith III, Letter to A. V. Gibbons, June 1, 1893, qtd. in Newell and Avery, *Mormon Enigma*, 170.

62. Anderson and Bergera, *Joseph Smith's Quorum of the Anointed*, 37.

63. Newell and Avery, *Mormon Enigma*, 172.

64. *History of the Church*, 6:176 (Jan. 14, 1844); Anderson and Bergera, *Joseph Smith's Quorum of the Anointed*, 53.

various parts of the city."[65] This seemingly commonplace entry gives a picture of only illusory peace. The next day, at 10:00 a.m. Orson Pratt made an affidavit against Francis Higbee "for absenting himself from City Council without leave … and for slanderous and abusive language towards" Joseph Smith.[66] Shortly afterwards, Higbee appeared first before the municipal court, then the city council and, improbably, "a reconciliation took place with Francis M. Higbee, who had written a slanderous letter concerning me [Joseph Smith], and said many hard things, which he acknowledged, and I forgave him. I went before the council, and stated that all difficulties between me, and F. M. Higbee were eternally buried, and I was to be his friend for ever; to which F. M. Higbee replied, 'I will be his friend for ever, and his right hand man.'"[67]

The over-emotional language reveals both the desire of both men to draw back from the brink of the cliff but also the disconnect between the Higbees and Laws and the men who had stepped into the ranks of Joseph's supporters. The alienation ran deeper than barbed remarks hurled in a public arena, nor could reconciliation be achieved by scuffing them into a corner with florid protestations of eternal friendship. These divisions were based on fundamentally varied interpretations of prophetic authority and doctrine. These men were believers, believed God spoke through prophets, but also believed Joseph was flawed and that his communication with God was blocked.

Outside Nauvoo, mistrust and unease narrowed the window for calmer actions. On January 17, firebrand journalist Thomas Gregg luridly condemned Joseph in the *Warsaw Signal:*

> that hoary monster who rules at Nauvoo; whose black heart would exult in carnage and bloodshed, rather than yield one iota of what power he has obtained by his hellish knavery. … We would not compromise with Joe Smith, one inch in the acknowledgement of his right to plunder, and to destroy, and tyrannize, and dupe, as he is doing. … We see no use in attempting to disguise the fact that many in our midst contemplate a total extermination of that people; that the thousands of defenceless women and children, aged and infirm, who are congregated at Nauvoo, must be driven out–aye, DRIVEN–SCATTERED–like the leaves before the Autumn blast![68]

---

65. *History of the Church*, 6:176 (Jan. 14, 1844).
66. Joseph Smith, Diary, Jan. 15, 1844, in Faulring, *An American Prophet's Record*, 440.
67. Ibid., Jan. 16, 1844 (Faulring, 440-41).
68. Thomas Gregg, "Remarks on the Above," *Warsaw Signal*, Jan. 17, 1844, 2.

Gregg's fiery rhetoric suggests a revulsion that Joseph would have been wise to address. Instead, 1844 churned relentlessly forward like a wave of churning lava.

The following Friday, January 19, Joseph preached on the U.S. Constitution and the likely presidential candidates. The disequilibrium his experiment with playing Whigs against Democrats the previous August had not subsided, but he had not learned caution from it.[69] Instead, he was developing his dangerous political philosophy before only friendly audiences.

Two days later, a crowd of several thousand braved inclement weather to fill the street in front of Robert D. Foster's Mammoth Hotel from which Joseph preached about the coming of Elijah and of "sealing the hearts of the fathers to the children and the hearts of the children to the fathers."[70] He wanted his audience to understand the interconnectedness of ritual and doctrine with Mormonism's concept about the thin line between the living and the dead. "Somewhat out of health" and complaining of "weak lungs," he asked for "the prayers and faith of my brethren that God may strengthen me and pour out His special blessing upon me."[71] He promised them that they would become saviors by "building their temples erecting their Baptismal fonts & going forth & receiving all the ordinances, Baptisms, Confirmations, washings anointings ordinations & sealing powers upon our heads in behalf of all our Progenitors who are dead." The work would make it possible for them, too, to come "forth at the resurrection and be exalted to thrones of glory" binding "the hearts of the fathers to the Children," so as to fulfil the mission of Elijah.[72] Everyone who seeks the "highest mansion," Joseph explained, must abide the "Celestial law."[73]

Joseph probably had a cold Sunday night and was still under the weather on Monday, but he joined the Quorum of the Anointed for a prayer meeting at which Parley P. Pratt received his second anointing.[74] The importance of such meetings, particularly in the midst of conflict, was great. Here the few chosen Saints were suspended in a liminal space where they stood as kings and queens.

Although some patterns emerged over time for these meetings, they did

69. Joseph Smith, Diary, Jan. 19, 1844, in Faulring, *An American Prophet's Record*, 441.

70. Ibid., Jan. 21, 1844 (Faulring, 442).

71. *History of the Church*, 6:183 (Jan. 21, 1844).

72. Joseph Smith, "When I Consider the Surrounding Circumstances," in *The Essential Joseph Smith*, 211-12; see also Woodruff, *Journal*, 2:341-43.

73. Woodruff, *Journal*, 2:341-43 (Jan. 21, 1844).

74. Joseph Smith, Diary, Jan. 21, 1844, in Faulring, *An American Prophet's Record*, 442.

not have a regular schedule. In November 1843, the group met eight times, eleven times in December, thirteen in January 1844. Clearly, frequency was related to, among other factors, tensions in the city. The meetings acted as a sort of safety value, reassuring elite members that everything was still right in Zion, that their prophet was safe, and that the doors to heaven remained open. For Joseph, the rituals provided relief from the strain of dissension and assured him of the devotion of those most in touch with the pulse of Mormonism.

Joseph was anxious that all the apostles receive their second anointings. On January 26, "Elder O. Pratt Received his 2d Anointing."[75] The next day, Willard and Jennetta Richards, who had been kept away "for a number of days" by illness, "Received their 2d Anointing and sealing."[76] On the 28th, Woodruff was "anointed to the fullness of the priesthood," according to Joseph. Woodruff's version was more descriptive: "a benefit by Prayers and laying on of hands. The Subject of Elijah's coming to seal the hearts of the fathers to the Children &c was spoken of. Seal the hearts of the children to the fathers Malachi IVth Ch. 6 vers."[77]

During the last week of January, the Anointed Quorum met four nights out of seven. No detailed record has survived, but it is not difficult to imagine the emotional and spiritual pitch of the gatherings. The gaps between meetings shortened, until at some point they seemingly blended into a single religious ecstasy–the drive for solidarity, union, and sacrament, pulling members together again and again. But regardless of their efforts, or of their faith, they could not ward off the danger bearing down on their Church.

75. Woodruff, *Journal*, 2:343 (Jan. 26, 1844).

76. Ibid. (Jan. 27, 1844); Joseph Smith, Diary, Jan. 27, 1844, in Faulring, *An American Prophet's Record*, 443.

77. Joseph Smith, Diary, Jan. 28, 1844, in Faulring, *An American Prophet's Record*, 443; Woodruff, *Journal*, 2:344 (Jan. 28, 1844).

CHAPTER 24

Political Ambitions

> *[Y]e are a chosen generation, a royal priesthood, an holy nation, a peculiar people ...*
>
> *–1 Peter 2:9*

The opening months of 1844 had been marred by festering conflicts between Joseph and formerly close associates who could not accept, among other doctrines, plurality. They would first resist, then dissent, and finally be termed apostates. Keeping his conflicts in the public eye was intentional–a way of lining up the Saints behind him. Joseph announced on March 24, 1844, at the stand near the temple:

> I have been informed by two gentleman that a conspiracy is got up in this place for the purpose of taking the life of President Joseph Smith, his family, and all the Smith family, and the heads of the Church. One of the gentleman will give his name unto the public, and the other wishes it to be hid for the present; they will both testify to it on oath, and make an affidavit upon it. The name of the persons revealed at the head of the conspiracy are as follows:–Chancey L. Higbee, Dr. Robert D. Foster, Mr. Joseph H. Jackson, William and Wilson Law. ... I won't swear out a warrant against them, for I don't fear any of them; they would not scare off an old setting hen.[1]

Joseph's direct confrontation both angered and humiliated critics since they could not reciprocate in kind. It almost certainly distanced them from the rest of the Saints. As a strategy, Joseph gambled that naming names would isolate his enemies and leave them powerless, but it did not. As a positive effect, it communicated Joseph's confidence; but it also had the negative effect of revealing his desperation and frustration. He was constructing

1. *History of the Church*, 6:272 (Mar. 24, 1844).

elaborate stories that some in his audience knew to be untrue. Engaging in bullying would not produce compliance or self-exile. And it was not halting the conspiracy he had all but guaranteed by making these trusted friends the next chapter in his narrative of persecution.

In March and April, evidently not satisfied with the Quorum of the Anointed as a medium for political action, Joseph established another inner circle of confidants–the all-male, ultra-secret Council of Fifty. Meanwhile, Emma used the spring meetings of the Relief Society to call the women of Nauvoo back to a standard of virtue. And outside Nauvoo, hostility and suspicion about the Mormon kingdom's political aspirations continued to churn.

During Nauvoo's pleasant spring that year, Joseph gave the Twelve Apostles new responsibilities, carving out another layer of activity and allegiance. To insider Wilford Woodruff, recalling in 1869 the events of 1844,

> Joseph Smith was what he professed to be, a prophet of God, a seer and revelator. He laid the foundation of this Church and kingdom, and lived long enough to deliver the keys of the kingdom to the Elders of Israel, unto the Twelve Apostles. He spent the last winter of his life, some three or four months, with the Quorum of the Twelve, teaching them. It was not merely a few hours ministering to them the ordinances of the Gospel; but he spent day after day, week after week and month after month, teaching them and a few others the things of the kingdom of God. Said he, during that period, "I now rejoice. I have lived until I have seen this burden, which has rested on my shoulders, rolled on to the shoulders of other men; now the keys of the kingdom are planted on the earth to be taken away no more for ever."[2]

Benjamin F. Johnson, another member of the Council of Fifty, also remembered of Joseph's unburdening himself of God's kingdom:

> With great Feeling & Animation he [Joseph Smith] graphically Reviewed his Life of Persicution, Labor and Sacrafise for the church & the Kingdom of God–Both of which he diclared now organized upon the earth. The burden of which had become too great for him longer to carry. That he was weary & Tired with the weight he [had] So long born, and he then Said, with great Vehimence: "And in the name of the Lord, I now Shake from my shoulders the Responsability of bearing off the Kingdom of God to all the world–and here & now I place that Responsability, with all the Keys, Powers & Privilege pertaining there too, upon the shoulders

2. Wilford Woodruff, Dec. 12, 1869, JD 13:164.

of you the Twelve Apostles, in connection with this council: and shall open your way, and if you do it not you will be damned."[3]

The past decade and a half, laced with persecution and the introduction of new doctrine that tested the loyalty of his followers, had been unbelievably difficult for the young prophet. It is easy to imagine why, after fourteen years, he would have been tempted to pass the burden to someone else. "He told us," Woodruff recollected, "that he was going away to leave us, going away to rest." Exhausted by the seemingly endless search for meaning in the narrative of his life, he instructed them, in effect: "Round up your shoulders to bear up the kingdom. No matter what becomes of me. I have desired to see that Temple built, but I shall not live to see it. You will; you are called upon to bear off this kingdom." For Woodruff, the words would make more sense after Joseph's death, but he was bewildered in 1844: "He [Joseph] said this time after time to the Twelve and to the Female Relief Societies and in his public discourses; but none of us seemed to understand that he was going to seal his testimony with his blood ..."[4]

Resilient through challenges that threatened to destroy him and the Church, Joseph faced at the beginning of 1844 no easy end to his troubles. Joseph's sense of fate closing in was strong during these months, and his hints acquired new meaning when loving friends went back over the evidence. "I remember what Joseph said, a short time before he was slain in one of the last sermons I ever heard him preach," recalled Woodruff in 1856 in the Salt Lake tabernacle. "Said he, 'Men are here to-day who are seeking my blood, and they are those who have held the Priesthood and have received their washings and anointings; men who have received their endowments.' I saw the faces of those men at that time," averred Woodruff, "and they had a hand in slaying the Prophet."[5]

On March 10, 1844, Joseph received two letters from Lyman Wight and George Miller, dated the previous February 15, proposing that the pineries missionaries move to Texas.[6] Native American agents had been interfering with their attempts to acquire tribal forests for the Church's use. But more important, Wight and Miller felt that, in Texas, they could create a new gathering place–outside the United States and therefore free from

3. Benjamin F. Johnson, Letter to George Gibbs, in Dean Zimmerman, ed., *I Knew the Prophets*, 10.

4. Woodruff, Dec. 12, 1869, JD 13:164.

5. Wilford Woodruff, Dec. 21, 1856, JD 4:149.

6. *History of the Church*, 6:255-56 (Feb. 15, 1844).

government harassment. They estimated that they would have cut between "8 to 12 hundred thousand" feet by July–"sufficient to finish the two houses [the temple and Nauvoo House], which will accomplish the Mission on which we started this country."[7]

They had consulted with members of the pineries committee, who also saw many benefits.[8] The Church would be present "in all the South and Southwestern States, as also Texas, Mexico, Brazil, etc., together with the West Indian Islands." In such a location, the Mormons could "employ our time and talents in gathering together means to build according to the commandments of our God, and spread the gospel to all nations." They asked, "[A]re there not thousands of the rich planters who would embrace the Gospel, and, … if rightly taught, for building up the Kingdom; … Yes, we believe they would."[9]

Joseph added to the confusion in Nauvoo by preaching hard-hitting sermons about building Zion on the Mississippi and by simultaneously preparing for a range of eventualities. The specter of the Missouri shadowed the present, conditioning the Latter-day Saint future with a perpetual need to accommodate worst-case scenarios. Knowing that they might be driven out of Illinois by the Church's enemies, the Twelve discussed moving the Church again and what that would mean for their future.

The proposal of a new settlement in the West supported Joseph's grand ambitions. Without commentary, the *History of the Church* describes simply how on the evening of March 10 the "brethren went into council on the subject matter of the letters …" Joseph's diary recorded greater detail. After reading the letters from Miller, Wight, and the others, Joseph asked the Twelve, "[C]an this council keep what I say, not make it public[?]" All the men raised their hands in agreement.[10] At that point, the prophet began to organize the Council of Fifty, yet another secretive layer of loyal men around him, with the intent that it would function as the government of

7. Ibid., 258.

8. Ibid.

9. Ibid; see also Robert B. Flanders, *Nauvoo*, 296.

10. *History of the Church*, 6:260 (Mar. 10, 1844); Joseph Smith, Diary, Mar. 10, 1844, in Scott H. Faulring, ed., *An American Prophet's Record*, 458. "For the time being, this was to remain *a perfect secret* until God should reveal to the contrary," wrote George T. M. Davis. Joseph "swore them all to present secrecy, *under penalty of death!" (An Authentic Account of the Massacre of Joseph Smith, the Mormon Prophet, and Hyrum Smith, His Brother* …, 7; Davis mistakenly identifies the year as 1842 instead of 1844). Clerk William Clayton recorded that they "covenanted before God with uplifted hands to maintain all things inviolate agreeable tot he order of the Council" (Clayton, Journal, Mar. 1, 1845, in George D. Smith, ed., *An Intimate Chronicle*, 158).

the kingdom of God on the earth. Responsible for the safety of the Church, it would direct the resettlement of the Church. The next day, the council met to "take into consideration the … [Miller-Wight] letters, and also the best policy for this people to adopt to obtain their rights from the nation and insure protection for themselves and children: and to secure a resting place in the mountains, or some uninhabited region."[11] Its members were "as princes in the Kingdom of God,"[12] ruling in what one described as the "highest court on earth."[13]

Contemplating such a move must have entailed a recognition, on some level, that Joseph was leading his people down the road of irreconcilable conflict. It had always been true that he surveyed possible alternatives even as his people settled into a new place. Inadvertently predicting the Church's future, two years earlier, in 1842, Joseph had reportedly stated that "the Saints would continue to suffer much affliction and would be driven to the Rocky Mountains, many would apostatize, others would be put to death by our persecutors or lose their lives in consequence of exposure or disease," but that as a whole, they would thrive in cities of Zion and "become a mighty people in the midst of the Rocky Mountains."[14] On a personal level, the West–untamed, wild, and exotic–was a perfect test of Joseph's creative energies. The Council of Fifty became his instrument toward materializing that expansion.

Joseph imposed secrecy on this new council. In fact, of all the secret circles formed in Nauvoo, the Council of Fifty may have been the most secretive, largely invisible to most of the Church's membership. In fact, only during the second decade of the twenty-first century did the LDS Church begin to release its records and minutes.[15] Prior to this era of openness, enough of the group's history was contained in the journals and reminiscences of some of its members, including William Clayton, Joseph Fielding, and George Miller, to enable a reconstruction. The original membership in the Council of Fifty included fifty Latter-day Saint men and three non-members: thirty-two-year-old Marenus G. Eaton, thirty-six-year-old Edward Bonney, and fifty-nine-year-old Uriah Brown, a longtime friend and intimate of Joseph's. Latter-day Saints included: George Adams, Almon W. Babbitt,

11. *History of the Church*, 6:261 (Mar. 11, 1844).

12. George Miller, *Correspondence of Bishop George Miller …*, 20.

13. Dale Morgan, ed., "The Reminiscences of James Holt," 107.

14. *History of the Church*, 5:85 (Aug. 6, 1842).

15. See, for example, "Council of Fifty Summary," at http://josephsmithpapers.org/topic?name=Council+of+Fifty; and "Plenary Session Focuses on Council of Fifty Minutes," June 19, 2014, at http://josephsmithpapers.org/news/2014 (both Sept. 1, 2015).

Alexander Badlam, Samuel Bent, John Bernhisel, Edward Bonney, Reynolds Cahoon, William Clayton, Joseph W. Coolidge, Alpheus Cutler, James Emmett, Amos Fielding, Joseph Fielding, Jedediah M. Grant, John P. Greene, Abram Hatch, Peter Haws, David S. Hollister, Orson Hyde, Samuel James, Benjamin F. Johnson, Heber C. Kimball, John D. Lee, Cornelius P. Lott, Amasa M. Lyman, William Marks, John D. Parker, John Phelps, William W. Phelps, Orson Pratt, Parley P. Pratt, Charles C. Rich, Willard Richards, Sidney Rigdon, Orrin Porter Rockwell, Elias Smith, George Smith, Hyrum Smith, John Smith, Joseph Smith Jr., William Smith, Erastus Snow, Orson Spencer, John Taylor, Lorenzo D. Wasson, Newel K. Whitney, Lyman Wight, Wilford Woodruff, David D. Yearsley, and Brigham Young.[16] More than half were members of the Anointed Quorum and were familiar with Joseph's more esoteric doctrines.[17] Most were also Masons, a fact that D. Michael Quinn believes rendered "membership in Smith's theocratic council ... more completely an extension of Freemasonry than any other dimension of Nauvoo society."[18]

Though revealed in principle as early as 1842 (see chap. 13),[19] the Council of Fifty was organized beginning on March 10 at 4:30 p.m. in the "lodge rooms" at Henry Miller's house.[20] John D. Lee described the secrecy that veiled their activities from easy view: "the members of this order were placed under the most sacred obligations that language could invent. They were sworn to stand by and sustain each other; *sustain, protect, defend,* and *obey* the leaders of the church under any and all circumstances unto death."[21] It is likely that Joseph spoke with participants, perhaps individually, before the formal meeting, stressing the group's role in the kingdom of God. For the first three days, Willard Richards served as interim chair until March 13 when Joseph became chair, with Richards as recorder and William Clayton as clerk.[22]

---

16. D. Michael Quinn, "The Council of Fifty and Its Members 1844 to 1945."

17. D. Michael Quinn, *The Mormon Hierarchy: Origins of Power*, 129.

18. Ibid., 130.

19. Council of Fifty, Minutes, Apr. 10, 1880, identify April 7, 1842, as the day "it was organized by the Lord." It is not known why Joseph waited two years before formally organizing the council except for the pressures of other activities and events.

20. Scott G. Kenney, ed., *Wilford Woodruff's Journal, 1833-1898*, 2:366 (Mar. 10, 1844); hereafter Woodruff, *Journal*. Franklin D. Richards, Journal, Apr. 10, 1880. Joseph's March 10, 1844, diary entry comments that, at the organization meeting, "Copy the constitution of the U.S. ... [placed in the] hands of a select committee [as a guide in drafting a constitution for the council]. No law can be enacted but what every man can be protected [from]." In Faulring, *An American Prophet's Record*, 458. William Clayton and Joseph Fielding recorded March 11, 1844, as the first day Joseph admitted members.

21. John D. Lee, qtd. in M. W. Montgomery, *The Mormon Delusion*, 44.

22. Joseph Smith, Diary, Mar. 10, 11, 1844, in Faulring, *An American Prophet's Record*, 458-59. See also William Clayton, Journal, Mar. 13, 1844, in Smith, *An Intimate Chronicle*, 127.

Though evidently christened in 1842 as "the Kingdom of God and His Laws with the Keys and Power[s] thereof and judgment in the hands of his servants," the council in 1844 quickly acquired briefer, more cryptic names: "Grand Council," "Council of God (or the Gods)," "Grand Council of Heaven,"[23] "special council," "general council,"[24] "Council of the Kingdom," "Living Constitution,"[25] and "Kingdom of God."[26]

The council had barely begun to function as a kind of shadow government before Joseph died. Conceptually it plotted politics and economics, facilitated business, and formulated policies for dealing with enemies. The potential was immense, although what actually transpired before June was more modest. To historian D. Michael Quinn, the council was "an important symbol of the unattained ideal of a democratically functioning Kingdom of God."[27] It created plans for a future world, organizing temporal power as the Quorum of the Anointed organized sacred power, modeling the hierarchy, loyalties, and behaviors required to make the kingdom materialize. Importantly, the Council of Fifty and Quorum of the Anointed differentiated functions and domains–the sacred and profane–with varied agendas, justifications, and membership. Even a member of both would have been conscious of when he was acting as an agent of Joseph's theological government and when he was engaging in sacred ritual. The line would have been clear, distinct, and meaningful.

Brigham Young later remembered that Joseph organized the council to take into consideration the necessary steps to obtain redress "for the wrongs which had been inflicted upon us by our persecutors, and also the best manner to settle our people in some distant and unoccupied territory; where we could enjoy our civil and religious rights, without being subject to constant oppression and mobocracy, under the protection of our laws, subject to the constitution."[28] Related in every way to the narrative of

---

23. Joseph Fielding, Journal, entry after Apr. 6, 1884, in Andrew F. Ehat, "'They Might Have Known that He Was Not a Fallen Prophet,'" 148; Lyman Wight, *An Address by Way of an Abridged Account and Journal of My Life …*, 9, 11, 13, 14. See also Hansen, *Quest for Empire*, 61; Quinn, "The Council of Fifty," 3-4.

24. *History of the Church*, 6:274, 286, 331, 341, 343, 351, 356, 369. See also Quinn, "Council of Fifty," 4; Hansen, *Quest for Empire*, 61.

25. Lee, *Mormonism Unveiled*, 173; see also William Clayton, Journal, Jan., 1845, in Smith, *An Intimate Chronicle*, 153 (Clayton uses the singular of powers). Franklin D. Richards, Journal, Mar. 16, 1880.

26. Heber C. Kimball, Journal, Feb. 4, 1845, qtd. in Quinn, "Council of Fifty," 28n12.

27. Quinn, "Council of Fifty," 11; see also Jedediah S. Rogers, ed., *The Council of Fifty: A Documentary History* (Salt Lake City: Signature Books, 2014).

28. "History of Brigham Young," *Millennial Star* 26 (May 21, 1864): 328; Arrington, *Brigham Young*, 109.

persecution–past and especially future–the council was one way to impose order on ambiguity.

The term "in council" came to represent special gatherings as well as specific meetings and differentiated the gatherings of insiders from rituals such as the endowment. "In council" was coded language for meetings of those whom Joseph most trusted and that occurred beyond public view. "In council," they shared special rituals, learned new doctrines, and envisioned a new world order. And, finally, "in council" they occupied a treasured liminal space where the relationships between men and women were redefined and where the line between heaven and earth became permeable. On March 10, Clayton "attended Council with the First Presidency and the Twelve on important business." The next day, "In Council again all day, as last night many great and glorious ideas were advanced."[29] "In council 9 to 12 a.m.," Joseph's diary reads for March 13. Then, after several blank lines: "Joseph and Hiram Smith gave Amos Fielding a letter of Attorney to transact business in England. In council on the 'The Kingdom of God.'"[30] "I met in Council with the brethren for the first time during the week," recorded Woodruff the same day.[31] Clayton's record was more detailed: "At 11 the Council [of Fifty] was called together. ... p.m. in council [of Fifty] again, also in the evening O. Hyde, W. Woodruff, and James Emmett were admitted members. The President appointed W. Richards Recorder, and me the Clerk of the Kingdom."[32]

Benjamin Johnson described the Council of Fifty as "a select circle of the prophet's most trusted friends." It included all of the Twelve but not all of the other Church leaders.[33] The idea for the council evolved over time, according to George Miller:

> Joseph said to me ... we will call together some of our wise men and proceed to set up the kingdom of God by organizing some of its officers. And from day to day he called some of the brethren about him, organizing them as princes in the kingdom of God, to preside over the chief cities of the Nation, until the number of fifty-three were called. In this council we ordained Joseph Smith as King on earth.[34]

29. William Clayton, Journal, March 10, 1844, in Smith, *An Intimate Chronicle*, 126.
30. Joseph Smith, Diary, Mar. 13, 1844, in Faulring, *An American Prophet's Record*, 459.
31. Woodruff, *Journal*, 2:366 (Mar. 13, 1844).
32. Smith, *An Intimate Chronicle*, 127 (Mar. 13, 1844).
33. Benjamin F. Johnson, Letter to George Gibbs, 9.
34. George Miller, qtd. in Donna Hill, *Joseph Smith*, 368.

The Church president was president of the council. As John D. Lee understood it, the nature of the Council of Fifty was political in the context of the political kingdom of God: "This council aluded to is the Municipal department of the Kingdom of God set up on the Earth, from which all law eminates, for the rule, government & controle of all Nations Kingdoms & toungs and People under the whole Heavens but not to controle the Priesthood but to council, deliberate & plan for the general good & upbuilding of the Kingdom of God on the earth."[35] William Marks remembered: "I was witness … of the introduction (secretly) of a kingly form of government, in which Joseph suffered himself to be ordained a king, to reign over the House of Israel forever." Marks added: "I could not conceive [the kingly government] to be in accordance with the laws of the Church, but I did not oppose this move, thinking it to be none of my business."[36] Thus, rather than a president who was elected by the people, the Fifty received Joseph as their king. This "coronation" created a different sort of power–absolute rather than sovereignty distributed by the rule of law.

Despite Marks's tactful language implying that Joseph reluctantly allowed this new calling, it was Joseph himself who initiated the act. But use of "king" and the implication that God approved of kings in America were incendiary in the American political landscape. The concept that the laws of the political kingdom of God would be different from those of the American political system was equally unnerving. It was unclear how these conflicting systems would co-exist. Perhaps the laws of God would be put in place by the Church in conference, while the political laws would be determined by the Council of Fifty. Yet in every practical way, such contradictions between the spiritual and the temporal were danger signals for the city's stability. Like the Nauvoo City Charter and use of habeas corpus, the dichotomy manufactured essential political power to protect such special Church practices as plurality.

Benjamin Johnson recorded in his autobiography details about the council meetings: "Its settings were always strictly private, and its rules [directives] were carefully and promptly observed. … I was present at every session, and being about the youngest member of that Council"–he turned twenty-six in 1844–"I was deeply impressed with all that transpired, or was taught by the Prophet." The men, he said, began "in a degree to understand

35. Robert Glass Cleland and Juanita Brooks, eds., *A Mormon Chronicle*, 1:80.

36. William Marks, Letter to "Beloved Brethren," June 15, 1853, in *Zion's Harbinger and Baneemy's Organ* 3 (July 1853): 53. See also Andrew H. Hedges, Alex D. Smith, and Brent M. Rogers, eds., *The Joseph Smith Papers: Journals, Volume 3: May 1843-June 1844* (Salt Lake City: Church Historian's Press, 2015, 227n1021.

the meaning of what he [Joseph] had so often publicly said, that should he teach and practice the principles that the Lord had revealed to him, and now requested of him, that those then nearest to him in the stand would become his enemies and the first to seek his life."[37]

John D. Lee remembered Joseph's explanation of sacred responsibility: "Members of this council should be men of [such] firmness and integrity, that when they leave this council Room that the things that belong to this council should be as safe as though it was locked up on the silent vaults of Eternity but such things must be overcome or the men who indulge in them will be dropped from this council."[38] When Lee recorded details about meetings in his journal, he employed an unsubtle cipher: YTFIF ("Fifty" backwards). It was assumed that eventually the council's activities would become public, but not until the world was ready to accept them. To the men involved, the council was the key to political power they had never before tasted.[39]

For the two weeks after the Council of Fifty was organized, it met almost daily in sessions that could stretch for hours. Exploring various avenues for expanding and strengthening the Kingdom of God, the council considered options for settling new regions. It brought in new members and decided to found a colony in Texas, looking for land that might make the Mormon state a buffer between Texas and Mexico.[40] On March 14, the council went into session at 9:00 a.m., broke from 1:00 to 4:00 p.m., then had another three-hour session, and authorized sending Lucien Woodworth to Texas "to negotiate a treaty in behalf of the Council of Fifty."[41]

Orson Hyde said Joseph was "somewhat depressed in Spirit" at a March 17 meeting, but was willing to "open his heart ... concerning his presentiments [about the future]." Stressing the importance of finishing the temple, Hyde said that Joseph announced, "It may be that my enemies will kill me, and in case they should, and the Keys and power which rest on me not be imparted to you, they will be lost from the Earth; but if I can only succeed in placing them on your heads, then let me fall a victim to murderous hands if God will suffer it." He could rest easily if "the foundation laid on which the kingdom of God is to be reared in this dispensation of the fullness of times" was secure. He placed great faith in the Twelve, and his sadness for what

37. Benjamin F. Johnson, qtd. in James R. Clark, "The Kingdom of God, the Council of Fifty, and the State of Deseret," 141; Benjamin F. Johnson, Letter to George Gibbs, 32.

38. Cleland and Brooks, *A Mormon Chronicle*, 1:104; see also Hansen, *Quest for Empire*, 65.

39. Ibid., 80.

40. Miller, *Correspondence*, 20.

41. Joseph Smith, Diary, Mar. 13, 1844, in Faulring, *An American Prophet's Record*, 459.

that meant for them was immense. "You will know what it is to be bound with chains and with fetters for this cause sake. God knows I pity you and feel for you; but if you are called to lay down your lives, die like men, and pass immediately beyond the reach of your enemies." Joseph paced anxiously back and forth. "Should you have to walk right into danger and the jaws of death, fear no evil; Jesus Christ has died before you." Satisfied that he had given every "key and every power that he ever held himself," he felt a certain sort of relief.[42]

The Council of Fifty absorbed much but not all of Joseph's attention. On Monday, March 18, for example, he spent the day at home, and despite the considerable cold, he met with Alexander Neibaur, who tutored him in German. On the 21st, the Fifty held another meeting with a future-focused agenda. Despite the decision about Texas only a week earlier, Joseph assigned Willard Richards to draft a memorial (the fourth) to "Congress for the privilege of raising troops"–a breathtaking 100,000 men–for possible U.S. expansion into either Oregon or Texas.[43] Unlike the Missouri memorials that focused on persecution in the past, this memorial held the hope of the future, a vision for the settlement of a new place, in the West. The final version of the document, which communicates the expansionist vision of the Council of Fifty and the Church, begins with an affirmation of Joseph's patriotism. The preamble is phrased in grand language intended to impress:

> Whereas, many of the citizens of these United States have been and are migrating to Texas, Oregon, and other lands contiguous to this nation; and whereas Texas had declared herself a free and independent nation, without the necessary power to protect her rights and liberties, and whereas Oregon is without any organized government [or] protection … and whereas the United States desire to see the principles of her free institutions extended to all men, especially where it can be done without loss of blood and treasure to the nation, and whereas there is almost boundless extent of territory on the west and south of these United States, where exists little or no organization of protective government, and whereas the lands thus unknown, unowned, or unoccupied, are among some of the richest and most fertile on the continent, and whereas many … would gladly embrace the opportunity of extending their researches and acquirements so soon as they can receive protection [from] the red man, the robber, and the desperado … and whereas Joseph Smith … does

42. Qtd. in Anderson and Bergera, *Joseph Smith's Quorum of the Anointed*, 72-73.
43. *History of the Church*, 6:270 (Mar. 21, 1844); Klaus J. Hansen, *Quest for Empire*, 87.

> hereby offer to prevent … bloodshed on our frontiers, to extend the arm of deliverance to Texas, to protect … Oregon from foreign aggression and domestic western and southern borders … to open the vast regions … to our enterprising yeomanry … and thus strengthen the government and enlarge her borders. …

The document reveals the allure Joseph found at the possibility of moving yet again into a region more distant than before, a land promising refuge, security, and hope. The document also threatened fines and imprisonment for anyone who hindered Joseph, who would be acting as an officer of the U.S. army "in raising said volunteers, and marching and transporting them to the borders of the United States and Territories."

The document bound Joseph and his forces not to "disturb the peace of any nation or government acknowledged as such, break the faith of treaties between the United States and any other nation, or violate any known law of nations, thereby endangering the peace of the United States." Joseph promised that his action would "save the national revenue" required to fund an army; instead, the Mormon force could explore the western regions, "search out antiquities," and "break down tyranny and oppression."[44]

The Fifty approved the grandiose memorial on March 26 and instructed Orson Pratt and Orson Hyde to present it to Congress, with a second one for the "President, in case the other should fail."[45] Hyde left on April 4 for Washington, D.C., with the second assignment of exploring the possibility of securing land in other parts of the trans-Mississippi West, while Lucien Woodworth simultaneously explored settlement in Texas.[46]

In Washington, Hyde and Pratt met with Illinois Senator James Semple on April 24, then with other senators who seemed "deeply interested in the Oregon question." Hyde announced his intention to consult about Oregon's suitability for settlement.[47] Hyde's first progress report to Joseph on the 25th was optimistic about the government's willingness to offer protection, but that "we believe that the generosity of our government towards us will be equal to our enterprise and patriotism; and that they will allow us a grant or territory of land, which will be both honorable to them and satisfactory to us." Semple had told the two apostles that he did not think Congress would act on the Oregon question in this session and that Illinois's delegates

44. *History of the Church*, 6:275-77 (Mar. 26, 1844).
45. Ibid.
46. Ibid., 286 (Apr. 14, 1844).
47. Ibid., 369 (Apr. 25, 1844).

believed the Mormons had an "undoubted right to go to Oregon with all the emigrants" they could raise. "They say the existing laws protect you as much as law can protect you," Hyde wrote, "and should Congress pass an additional law, it would not prevent wicked men from shooting you down as they did in Missouri." Hyde was less hopeful about Missouri's response to the Mormons' relocation plans, and concurred that Congress would not act on either Texas or Oregon during its current session.[48]

Hyde wrote again the next day, more enthusiastic about Oregon: "There is no government established there, and it is so near California that when a government shall be established there, it may readily embrace that country likewise." Stephen A. Douglas gave Hyde a map of Oregon and John C. Fremont's description of the Kansas and "Great" Platte River-South Pass route. In important ways, the issue came down to simple political expedience. "I have learned this much," Hyde wrote, "that if we want Congress to do anything for us … we must not ask what is right in the matter, but we must ask what kind of a thing will Congress pass? Will it suit the politics of the majority? Will it be popular or unpopular?"[49]

Chicago's John Wentworth introduced the Mormons' memorial to the House of Representatives; unsurprisingly, it was declined. Throughout this episode, the Church agents acted as if the political kingdom of God were an actuality, and they were diplomats from a real state, rather than a church. It was clear that boundaries were blurred in their minds.

Campaign for the U.S. Presidency

Joseph's quixotic decision to run for the U.S. presidency makes best sense when seen against both his psychological propensity for excitement and the increasingly hostile political climate in Illinois. Thus, he could announce off-handedly to Charles Francis Adams and his cousin Josiah Quincy, two Bostonians who visited Nauvoo on April 25, that "he [Joseph] might one day so hold the balance between the parties as to render his election [as U.S. president] … by no means unlikely."[50]

The increased distance Mormonism saw between the promises of American constitutionalism and the reality of the persecution that they had suffered alienated Joseph and his leadership from both political parties

48. Orson Hyde, Letter to Joseph Smith, ibid., 371.

49. Orson Hyde, Letter to Joseph Smith, *History of the Church*, 6:375 (Apr. 26, 1844).

50. Josiah Quincy, excerpted in William Mulder and A. R. Mortensen, eds., *Among the Mormons*, 142.

and many politicians who had campaigned for the support and favor of the Mormons. Only presidential aspirants Henry Clay and John Calhoun had responded to Joseph's November 1843 letters.[51] Both saw the separation of powers between federal and state governments as placing the Mormon conflict as the state's responsibility.[52]

Although Joseph expected Clay to enter the presidential race, Clay replied discouragingly: "I can enter into no engagements, make no promises, give no pledge to any particular portion of the people of the United States. If I ever enter into that high office I must go into it free and unfettered." He sympathized with the "sufferings under injustice" of the Mormon people, and thought that "in common with other religious communities, they ought to enjoy the security and protection of the Constitution and laws."[53]

Such responses were predictable, but Joseph reacted indignantly. He dictated replies that expanded on his views on government, shaped by the persecution experience of the Mormons and the government's lack of response to pleas for redress. Joseph questioned the view that "the powers of the Federal Government are so specific and limited that it has no jurisdiction of the case,"[54] and said that he pondered "what can be done to protect the lives, property, and rights of a virtuous people, when [President and Congress] are unbought by bribes, uncorrupted by patronage … unawed by fear, and uncontaminated [by] tangling alliances."[55] The prophet's reaction was injudicious, but the weight of his frustrations was sincere.

On October 1, 1843, the *Times and Seasons* asked: "Who shall be our next President?," framing the question in the rhetoric of persecution:

> The Latter Day Saints have had their property destroyed and their houses made desolate by the hands of the Missourians; murders have been committed with impunity, and many in consequence of oppression, barbarism and cruelty, have slept the sleep of death. They have been obliged to flee from their possessions into a distant land, in the chilling frost of December … and have had to wander as exiles in a strange land, without as yet, being able to obtain any redress for their grievances. We have hitherto adopted

51. *History of the Church*, 6:65 (Nov. 4, 1843); see also Arnold K. Garr, "Joseph Smith: Candidate for President of the United States," 151-67.

52. John C. Calhoun, qtd. in *History of the Church*, 6:156 (Jan. 2, 1844).

53. *History of the Church*, 6:376 (Nov. 15, 1843).

54. Ibid., 157 (Jan. 2, 1844).

55. Ibid., 160 (Jan. 2, 1844). "Vexed by remembrance of the cruelty and injustice endured by the Saints in Missouri and the general indifference to their suffering among public men, the letter was written in a caustic and, at times, vehement vein."

> every legal measure. First, we petitioned to the state of Missouri, but in vain. We have memorialized Congress, but they have turned a deaf ear to our supplication and referred us again to the state and *justice* of Missouri.[56]

The implication was clear: in the absence of ethical government, individuals had both the right and the responsibility to intervene:

> As American citizens we claim the privilege of being heard in the councils of our nation. ... We may fix upon the man who will be the most likely to render us assistance in obtaining redress for our grievances–and not only give our own votes, but use our influence to obtain others, and if the vote of suffering innocence will not sufficiently arouse the rulers of our nation to investigate our case, perhaps a vote of from fifty to one hundred thousand may rouse them from their lethargy.[57]

The same issue of the *Times and Seasons* announced George J. Adams's departure on a diplomatic mission to Russia, hinting that it involved "some of the most important things concerning the advancement and building up of the kingdom of God in the last days, which cannot be explained at this time."[58] Mormon missionaries were proselytizing in various locations throughout the world; but this mysterious reference makes it clear that Adams's mission was different. He took with him a document signed by Joseph and Hyrum but not by Sidney Rigdon or William Law, neither of whom would be members of the Council of Fifty.[59]

Joseph's penchant for seeing persecution instead of taking responsibility for his own actions showed up in a letter he wrote on January 2, 1844, to Calhoun, who had solicited Joseph's views on national affairs two months earlier: "If the Latter-day Saints are not restored to all their rights and paid for all their losses [in Missouri]," blustered Joseph, "... God will come out of His hiding place, and vex this nation with a sore vexation: yea the consuming wrath of an offended God shall smoke through the nation."[60] In some ways the letter was a recapitulation of the Missouri persecution narrative's key themes, but Joseph personalized it this time against Calhoun:

> O ye people who groan under the oppression of tyrants! ... pay in your money to the treasury to strengthen the army and the navy; worship

56. *History of the Church*, 6:39-40 (Oct. 1, 1843).
57. Ibid., 40-41.
58. *Times and Seasons*, qtd. in ibid., 41.
59. *History of the Church*, 6:41 (Oct. 1, 1843).
60. Joseph Smith, Letter to John C. Calhoun, *History of the Church*, 6:158 (Jan. 2, 1844).

> God according to the dictates of your own consciences; pay in your taxes to support the great heads of a glorious nation; but remember a *"sovereign State"* is so much more powerful than the United States, the parent Government, that it can exile you at pleasure, mob you with impunity, confiscate your lands and property, have the Legislature sanction it,–yea, even murder you as an edict of an emperor, *and it does no wrong;* for the noble Senator of South Carolina says the power of the federal Government is *so limited and specific, that it has no jurisdiction of the case!*[61]

Joseph's disdain for government would have made it virtually impossible for Calhoun to work with the Saints on any level. But by this time, Joseph was clearly reaching for a broader national stage.

On January 29, Joseph lectured to unnamed visitors from Warsaw on politics, religion, and other topics. They were tourists, to be sure, but they symbolized the encroachment of the outer world. Nor were the topics merely of passing interest. Perhaps a result of these musings on heaven and earth, the Twelve met at the mayor's office at 10:00 a.m. and voted by acclamation to declare Joseph's candidacy for the U.S. presidency, pledging the Church to use "all honorable means to secure his election."[62] Even though it was an extremely cold day, Joseph warmly instructed the Twelve to send every Mormon "who could speak throughout the land to electioneere, [to give] stump speech/es/–advocate the Mormon religion, purity of elections, and call upon the people to stand by the law and put down mobocracy."[63] Laying out a plan for the next few months, he said:

> Tell the people we have had Whig and Democratic Presidents long enough: we want a President of the United States. If I ever get in the presidential chair, I will protect the people in their rights and liberties. I will not electioneer for myself. Hyrum, Brigham, Parley, and [John] Taylor must go. [William] Clayton must go, or he will apostatize.[64]

The self-absorption in this announcement maps Joseph's distance from political reality. He had launched himself into a public game, daring his enemies to thwart him. At that moment, only Martin Van Buren and Henry Clay

61. Ibid., 157; emphasis his.

62. Joseph Smith, Diary, Jan. 29, 1844, in Faulring, *An American Prophet's Record*, 443. The previous evening, a Captain White from Warsaw had toasted: "May all your enemies be skinned, and their skins be made into drum heads for your friends to beat upon." Also "May Nauvoo become the empire seat of government" (at http://josephsmithpapers.org/paperSummary/history-1838-1856-volume-e-1-1-july1843-30-april-1844?p=242&highlight=drum).

63. *History of the Church*, 6:188 (Jan. 29, 1844).

64. Ibid.

had declared their candidacies. Van Buren was repugnant, since the Saints believed he had "criminally neglected his duties as chief magistrate." Joseph's insulting, sarcastic letter to Clay had burned a possible bridge there, even if Clay's position had been more welcoming.

In 1902, B. H. Roberts, a Mormon general authority with political ambitions of his own, saw Joseph's optimism as excessive: "Of course there could be no hope seriously entertained that ... [Joseph] would be elected; but, ... if the Saints could not succeed in electing their candidate, they would have the satisfaction of knowing that they had acted conscientiously; they had used their best judgment, under the circumstances, and if they had to throw away their votes, it was better to do so upon a worthy than upon an unworthy individual who might use the weapon they put into his hands to destroy them."[65]

It is perhaps ironic that Joseph's candidacy represented such a biting critique of American government. Often during the preceding five years, he had spoken glowingly of his love for the United States, affirming that the Constitution had been divinely inspired to protect the religious lives of its people, and that its establishment was part of a heavenly design leading to the restoration of ancient things.

At the same time, the narrative of persecution played out against the backdrop of American individualism and the separation of church and state. In a confusing dichotomous relationship with the state, Joseph and his proposed theocratic state seemed simultaneously to love Americanism and to loathe it. Self-identified as both a persecuted people and a government-loving people, Mormonism presented Joseph's candidacy as a sort of rejection of Americanism and as a bold assertion of something else. Joseph revealed specifically what that "something else" was over a series of weeks, first in private, and then in public. The Mormons had always generated opposition and controversy. What was different here were the strength of their numbers, their legal manipulations in Joseph's defense, and the lack of reasonable alternatives.

At some point in the 1830s, before the Church moved to Nauvoo, Joseph had begun to think of the kingdom of God as temporal, transferring his vision of a heavenly state to life on the earth. Organizing a government to rule the Mormon sovereign state was part of a natural evolution of his theology about space and power. These developments made his understanding of

65. B. H. Roberts, "Joseph Smith's Candidacy for the Presidency," *History of the Church*, 6:xxxiv.

the kingdom of God more complete, metaphorically dictating what needed to be done next. For him, this central theme joined the Church's past and present, and anticipated the future. Moreover, it unified a range of Church doctrines, including plurality and temple endowments.

The moment of Mormon ascendancy had arrived. Almost four years earlier in May 1840, Parley P. Pratt had announced the changes that were afoot in a letter to Queen Victoria. This letter, published in the *Millennial Star,* undoubtedly impacted conversions in England. "All the political, and all the religious organizations that may previously exist, will be swallowed up into one entire union, one universal empire, having no laws but God's laws, and Saints to administer them."[66] In 1840, Pratt's remarks were, at best, hopeful; but by 1844, Joseph had created–or believed he had created–the mechanism to implement God's laws–a complete temporal subterranean government.

The task of the political government of God was nothing short of the transformation of the world. Apostles, missionaries, and other emissaries sent from Nauvoo were the equivalent of diplomats and ambassadors, extending the Church's power throughout the United States and abroad. The kingdom of God would coexist with worldly political institutions until the Mormons had sufficient financial and cultural stability to take control. It was the high point of Mormon millennialism.

Like the Shakers and the Oneida Perfectionists, the Mormons believed literally that they were building a landscape for Jesus' second coming, which would usher in the Millennium. This belief explained the evil that led to their expulsion from Missouri and the persecution they had felt through the 1830s. This millennial lens colored everything they did and endowed it with heightened significance. Prudently, Joseph avoided predicting the literal date of Jesus' advent but felt certain enough on March 10, 1844, to challenge William Miller's forecast that the Second Coming would occur later that year on October 22. Joseph said, "I prophesy, in the name of the Lord, that Christ will not come in forty years."[67]

Substantiating the Mormon belief that the end was near, and that they were, in fact, the Saints of the Last Days, Church newspapers recorded portentous "signs of the times" with care: natural calamities and political disasters. War, persecution, and conflict framed the kingdom, confirming the

66. "The Millennium," *Millennial Star* 1 (1840): 8.
67. *History of the Church,* 6:254 (Mar. 10, 1844).

approaching advent. At the same time, the Millennium would not result from a series of miracles but from hard work by human beings to create the potentialities of heaven and a spiritual domain.

Joseph's vision for government grew out of the persecution narrative. Majority rule to Mormons had meant persecution and a denial of civil liberties. Priesthood, universally available to worthy Mormon men, gave Church leaders the right–in fact, the obligation–to rule. Such attitudes, present in the Council of Fifty, alarmed observers because they directly challenged traditional American values: the separation of church and state, individual rights, and states rights.

Joseph dictated to W. W. Phelps a political treatise that became the core of a pamphlet designed for distribution during the campaign: *General Smith's Views of the Powers and Policy of the Government of the United States.*[68] Historian Bruce Van Orden finds that "Joseph Smith relied heavily upon" Phelps in the drafting of the document which is laced with the literary flourishes typical of Phelps's own writing, but it is clear that Joseph had long thought deeply on these issues.[69] However, Joseph did not record the extent of Phelps's contribution, merely noting briefly on February 7, "met the Twelve [Apostles] and Hyrum at my office /at their request/ to devise means to promote the interest of the gen[eral] Government."[70] The *History of the Church* adds to the narrative, "I completed and signed my 'Views.'"[71]

Despite the February 7 date, Joseph's political manifesto was not published in the *Times and Seasons* until May 15, about six weeks before Joseph's death. "Born in a land of liberty, and breathing an air uncorrupted with the sirocco of barbarous climes, I ever feel a double anxiety for the happiness of all men, both in time and eternity," he began. Joseph argued that the Constitution provided equality of rights and that government existed to protect those rights. "As long as our government ... secures to us the rights of person and property, liberty of conscience, and of the press, it will be worth defending." However, "calamity and confusion will sooner or later, destroy

68. *History of the Church*, 6:189 (Jan. 29, 1844); also in *Times and Seasons* 5, no. 10 (May 15, 1844): 528-33; as "Views of the Powers and Policy of the Government of the U.S." in *The Voice of Truth* (Nauvoo: Printed by John Taylor, 1844), 26-38, with William W. Phelps; and reprinted in *The Essential Joseph Smith*, 213-25; *History of the Church*, 6:197-209.

69. Bruce Van Orden, "William W. Phelps's Service in Nauvoo as Joseph Smith's Political Clerk," 24n.

70. Joseph Smith, Diary, Feb. 7, 1844, in Faurling, *An American Prophet's Record*, 444. "/at their request/" was added above the line in the original diary.

71. *History of the Church*, 6:197 (Feb. 7, 1844).

the peace of the people." He then spelled out a list of radical reforms. The first was "pardon[ing] every convict ... and saying to them in the name of the Lord, *go thy way and sin no more.*" He argued for setting 1850 as the year for abolishing slavery–to "save the abolitionist from reproach or ruin, infamy and shame." Congress should compensate for the slaves out of land revenues or by deducting the sum from Congressmen's salaries. He preached civil morality: "Make HONOR the standard with all men: be sure that good is rendered for evil in all cases: and the whole nation, like a kingdom of kings and priests, will rise up in righteousness ..."[72]

Although what distinguished Joseph's candidacy was his role as prophet, he made no other mention of either religion or any distinctive Mormon doctrines. Instead, *Views* detailed political issues that, as a whole, impacted individual civil rights. Historian Arnold Garr calls Joseph's interpretation of presidential powers his key plank.[73]

Phelps read *Views* at an evening meeting on February 8. Joseph, Orson Hyde, and John Taylor detailed the document's contents. "I feel it to be my right and privilege to obtain what influence and power I can, lawfully, in the United States, for protection of injured innocence; and if I lose my life in a good cause I am willing to be sacrificed on the altar of virtue," Joseph said.[74] Two weeks later, Joseph's electioneers had printed 1,500 copies and mailed them to U.S. President John Tyler, the members of his cabinet, the Supreme Court justices, members of Congress, the press and other important private citizens they had identified.[75] Until Joseph died, both the *Times and Seasons* and the *Nauvoo Neighbor* carried banners in their mastheads reading "For President–General Joseph Smith."

When Joseph told the people what he would do, he sounded like an Old Testament prophet: "I would lend the influence of a chief magistrate to ... extend the mighty efforts and enterprise of a free people from the east to the west sea; and make the wilderness blossom as the rose. And when a neighboring realm petitioned to join the union of the sons of liberty, my voice would be, *come:* yea come Texas; come Mexico; come Canada; and come all the world, let us be brethren; let us be one great family; and let there be universal peace." Let "reason and friendship reign over the ruins of ignorance and barbarity," he said, "I would, as the universal friend of man, open the

72. Ibid., 205.
73. Arnold K. Garr, "Joseph Smith: Candidate for President of the United States," 155.
74. *History of the Church*, 6:210-11 (Feb. 8, 1844).
75. Ibid., 224-25.

prisons; open the eyes; open the ears and open the hearts of all people, to behold and enjoy freedom, unadulterated freedom; and God."[76]

Joseph blended government with God. "The world is governed too much, and as there is not a nation or a dynasty now occupying the earth which acknowledges Almighty God as their lawgiver, and as 'crowns won by blood, by blood must be maintained,' I go emphatically, virtuously, and humanely, for a Theodemocracy, where God and the people hold the power to conduct the affairs of men in righteousness."[77] He dismissed the two-party system as corrupt. Hyrum clarified Joseph's commitment to a single-party government: "We want a President of the United States, not a party President, but a President of the whole people; for a party President disfranchises the opposite party. … Damn the system of splitting up the nation into opposite belligerent parties."[78]

The latter-day prophet's opponents found his campaign a ludicrous, possibly dangerous, grasp at power. Thomas Gregg was outraged: "Do you think that, of all the men, women and children you have so foull[y] wronged, that no one will be so bold as to avenge their own wrongs? … we tell you that your career of infamy cannot continue but a little longer! Your days are numbered! The handwriting is on the wall!"[79] Long after Joseph's death, Josiah Quincy responded more judiciously: "Born in the lowest ranks of poverty, without book-learning and with the homeliest of all human names, he had made himself at the age of thirty-nine a power upon earth. … His influence whether for good or for evil, is potent to-day and the end is not yet."[80]

Despite the commencement of the political campaign–perhaps in part because of it–the prayer circle met on the successive nights of February 10 and 11. The minutes do not reveal a preoccupation with Joseph's candidacy,[81] clearly indicating the diverging roles of the Fifty and the Anointed.

The choice of a presidential candidate was a matter "of the most

76. Ibid., 208.

77. Joseph Smith, "The Globe," *Nauvoo Neighbor*, Apr. 17, 1844.

78. *History of the Church*, 6:323 (Apr. 9, 1844). Joseph's disdain for Congress reflected the Church's experience. "Reduce Congress at least two thirds. Two Senators from a State and two members to a million of population will do more business than the army that now occupy the halls of the national Legislature. Pay them two dollars and their board per diem (except Sundays). That is more than the farmer gets, and he lives honestly" (ibid., 204-205).

79. Thomas Gregg, "A Word of Parting to Brother Joe," *Warsaw Signal*, Feb. 7, 1844, www.sidneyrigdon.com/dbroadhu/IL/sign1844.htm#0207 (Feb. 13, 2009).

80. Josiah Quincy, *Figures of the Past from the Leaves of Old Journals* (Boston: Roberts Brothers, 1883), 377-400, qtd. in John E. Hallwas and Roger D. Launius, eds., *Cultures in Conflict*, 51.

81. Joseph Smith, Diary, Feb. 10, 1844, Faulring, *An American Prophet's Record*, 445.

paramount importance and requires our most serious , calm, and dispassionate reflection," wrote John Taylor, editor of the *Nauvoo Neighbor,* in issues dated February 7 and February 14. If the president is a "man of an enlightened mind, and a specious soul–if he is a virtuous, a statesman, a patriot, and a man of unflinching integrity; ... and wishes to promote the universal good of the whole republic, he may indeed be made a blessing to community."[82]

Connecting Joseph's campaign to his failed appeal to Martin Van Buren in 1840, Taylor referenced the narrative of the Saints' efforts at compensation. "It is a fact well understood, that we have suffered great injustice from the State of Missouri, ... and have obtained the heartless reply that 'congress has no power to redress your grievances." In the face of such unreasonable justice, Taylor stressed that the only candidate worthy of the Saints' support was none other than "General Joseph Smith. A man of sterling worth and integrity, and of enlarged views; a man who has raised himself from the humblest walks of life." Rather than become the targets "for the filthy demagogues of the country to shoot their loathsome arrows at," Taylor closed, "we withdraw."[83]

Missionary work and political campaigning proceeded in tandem. In fact, according to Arnold Garr, ten of the twelve members of the Twelve–Brigham Young, Heber C. Kimball, Orson Hyde, Parley P. Pratt, William Smith, Orson Pratt, John E. Page, Wilford Woodruff, George A. Smith, and Lyman Wight–"served as electioneer missionaries."[84] Willard Richards predicted in early March: "If God goes with [the campaigners], who can withstand their influence?"[85] Certainly, Joseph threw the Church's best human resources into this campaign. His vigor reflects his belief that, regardless of the sacrifices the effort required from the Saints, he was fulfilling prophecy.

On March 7, he told the Saints: "When I get hold of the Eastern papers, and see how popular I am, I am afraid myself that I shall be elected."[86] A few days later, he half-joked: "The Lord once told me that what I asked for I should have. I have been afraid to ask God to kill my enemies, lest some of them should, peradventure, repent."[87] It was, perhaps, an ill-advised statement considering that the Lilburn Boggs attempted assassination affair was

82. John Taylor, "For President–General Joseph Smith," *Nauvoo Neighbor*, Feb. 7, 14, 1844.
83. Ibid.
84. Arnold K. Garr, "Joseph Smith: Campaign for President of the United States," *Ensign*, Feb. 2009.
85. *History of the Church*, 6:232 (Mar. 4, 1844).
86. Ibid., 243 (Mar. 7, 1844).
87. Ibid., 253 (Mar. 10, 1844).

less than two years behind him; worse, the statement would lose all vestige of good humor as violence overwhelmed the Mormons–and their prophet–within four months.

Although the Church was one organization and the campaign another, no one was surprised that the pulpit at April's general conference doubled as a politicking stump. Spiritual and political themes wove through sermons on April 9. Brigham Young and Heber Kimball proclaimed their intention to go into the field to "preach the gospel and electioneer."[88] Catching the enthusiasm Joseph projected from the stand, when Young called for volunteers, a surge of 244 individuals showed their willingness to serve by moving to the "right of the stand."[89] By April 15, the number of campaigner-missionaries had reached almost 340. Their plans included visiting each of the twenty-six states and Wisconsin territory, holding a total of forty-seven national conferences, the last in Washington, D.C., on September 15, a few weeks before the election. The largest number of missionaries–forty-seven–would travel to New York State. The Quorum of the Twelve scheduled the first such conference for Quincy, Illinois, on May 4.[90] Men representing each state and ten of Illinois's 102 counties nominated Joseph for the president.[91] Although Joseph had asked James Arlington Bennet to run as vice-president, Bennet had declined because he had been born in Ireland.[92] The convention nominated Sidney Rigdon, evidence that the two men's relationship had improved from the previous year. Besides rousing political speeches, those in attendance proposed a national convention for Baltimore on May 17 and named a "correspondence" (public relations) committee for the campaign.[93]

Wilford Woodruff, who had set out on May 9 toward the East, described a missionary experience presumably typical of the proselytizing-electioneering. In two months, he preached the gospel ten times and delivered speeches at six "political meetings."[94] He would introduce Joseph's political platform and frame his candidacy with a narrative of persecution. On May 20, he "spoke of

88. Ibid., 322 (Apr. 9, 1844).

89. Ibid., 325. See also Garr, "Joseph Smith: Campaign for President."

90. *History of the Church*, 6:334-40 (Apr. 9, 1844).

91. Arnold K. Garr, "Joseph Smith: Candidate for President of the United States," 160. Garr's research establishes that many of these representatives were representing their home states but were now living in Nauvoo.

92. Joseph Smith, Diary, Mar. 4, 1844, in Faulring, *An American Prophet's Record*, 451.

93. Willard Richards, John M. Bernhisel, William W. Phelps, and Lucian R. Foster were appointed a central correspondence committee. *History of the Church*, 6:386-90 (May 17, 1844).

94. Garr, "Joseph Smith: Campaign for President."

our persecutors, & the danger the whole people of the United States were in of being destroyed by misrule & mob law if they permitted that principle to triumph."[95] Usually, the campaign meeting came first, followed by a meeting with a more spiritual emphasis.[96] However, the degree to which such a procedure was representative of other preacher-campaigners is not clear.

Joseph knew for certain he would have the vote of the 12,000 Mormons in Nauvoo, another 4,000 in towns nearby. But who else would support his candidacy? Either for public relations purposes or from wishful thinking, he exaggerated the numbers of converts swarming into Illinois, putting the number of Mormons at a staggering 200,000.[97]

During these final months of his life, Joseph moved between anxiety and expansiveness. He fed off excitement in the same way some people experience extreme highs or lows, the extremity itself providing evidence that the individual is alive.[98] Although Joseph had expressed relief at rolling off responsibility for the kingdom onto the shoulders of the Twelve, he was spending less time in meditation, prayer, or working on his translation of the Bible. Instead, he hovered over the Council of Fifty, making himself the center of it. He spent hours instructing members and had himself named king on April 11, 1844. He was not walking away from the turbulent, secretive system he had created but enmeshing himself more inextricably into it.

A New Refuge?

Joseph's vision of his people expanding into the West was almost innocent in its Americanness. In 1844, talk about the annexation of Texas and Oregon swirled in the air over local and national politics, coloring discussions about slavery, diplomatic relations with both England and Mexico, and the deal-making that forged loyalties and party politics on the national scene. Coupled with this near-brutal *realpolitik,* however, was the promise of life returning to the garden, of a utopian world where justice and truth prevailed. For Joseph, the template for the kingdom of God perfectly fit a western landscape, seeming to promise propitious conditions for the establishment of a government which would protect the Church and its people, and allow them to worship unimpeded by persecution.

---

95. Woodruff, *Journal*, 2:399 (May 20, 1844).

96. Ibid., 394-424 (May 7-July 18, 1844). See also Timothy L. Wood, "The Prophet and the Presidency"; Ehat, "It Seems Like Heaven Began on Earth."'

97. "Correspondence between Gen. Joseph Smith and the Hon. Henry Clay," 547.

98. *History of the Church*, 5:389 (May 14, 1843).

Oregon

During an era of Manifest Destiny, the West was seen as a safety valve for the Latter-day Saints along with contemporaries searching for the landscape of the American dream. As Joseph looked to resolve the Missouri conflict in 1839, Henry Clay recommended that the Saints relocate to Oregon.[99] Fur traders of the Hudson Bay Company had been traversing Oregon for decades before migration into the area began in earnest in 1836. Boosted by eastern entrepreneurs as a desirable location for settlement, the combination of the lure of Manifest Destiny and a missionary instinct pulled Methodists, Presbyterians, and Congregationalists to the Willamette Valley. The image of the Willamette Valley that reached the Midwest was of a new Garden of Eden, a place to start fresh in a pastoral landscape. Three years after Clay recommended the Mormons try this new place, the *Quincy Whig*, on September 24, 1842, picked up the same theme, recommending that Joseph "locate his new Jerusalem, away to the far West, in the Oregon country and there … govern the Saints in his own way," with an altruistic allusion to the common good: "it greatly needs settlers in that region; and doubtless, Government would do something right handsome for Joseph, in the grant of a gift of lands, etc., if he would guarantee the emigration of any number of settlers."[100]

Long before Oregon became an appealing alternative, another of Joseph's advisors, James Arlington Bennet, also saw the West as a solution to the "Mormon problem." The Latter-day Saint notion of Zion was compatible with the Western concept of the garden, a physical place where anything was possible, not unlike the liminal space in a temple. In an 1841 letter to *New York Herald* editor James Gordon Bennett, he said that Missouri and Illinois might finally leave the Mormons alone if they had an independent government in the West. "Indeed, I would recommend to the Prophet to pull up stakes and take possession of the Oregon territory in his own right, and establish an independent empire. In one hundred years from this time, no nation on earth could conquer such a people." Then Joseph could "make his own laws by the voice of revelation, and have them executed like the act of one man."[101] Joseph had the letter reprinted in the *Wasp* with a series of articles promoting emigration to Oregon. Orson Hyde's overtures in that direction, however, did not find a welcome in Washington, D.C.; and Joseph focused instead on Texas.

99. Ibid., 393 (May 18, 1843).

100. Rpt. as "Cold Comfort," *Times and Seasons* 3, no. 23 (Oct. 15, 1842): 953.

101. *History of the Church*, 5:171 (Oct. 16, 1841).

Texas

Joseph's support of Texas annexation had begun even before the organization of the Council of Fifty. On March 7, 1844, he preached on liberating the slaves in "two or three states, indemnifying their owners, and send[ing] the Negroes to Texas, and from Texas to Mexico, where all colors are alike. And if that was not sufficient, I would call upon Canada, and annex it. … We should grasp all the territory we can."[102]

Before the winter of 1843-44, Joseph had not acted on this belief, except to send Jonathan Dunham to the "western country" in July and August of 1843 to explore possible routes between the Mississippi and Missouri Rivers.[103] Dunham's mission was kept quiet, but it clearly anticipated the Church's move. Published in the *History of the Church*, Dunham's account of his travels concluded with the simple note, "I have seen much delightful country, but the prospect for bee hunting is not as good as I could wish."[104]

After the failure of the December 1843 memorial to Congress, discussion became more public about a western move.[105] On February 21, 1844, according to Brigham Young, "Brother Joseph directed the Twelve to select an exploring company to go to California to select a location for the settlement of the Saints: Jonathan Dunham, David Ful[l]mer, Phinehas H. Young and David D. Yearsley volunteered to go, and Alphonzo Young, James Emmett, George D. Watt and Daniel Spencer were selected to go."[106] Young understood the organization of the Council of Fifty as part of a strategy to find "the best manner to settle our people in some distant and unoccupied territory, [free from] constant oppression and mobocracy, under the protection of our own laws, subject to the constitution."[107] The establishment of the Council of Fifty the next month coalesced with this purpose.

On March 14, Joseph sent Lucien Woodworth, who had designed the Nauvoo House, to Austin, Texas, to negotiate with its government.[108] Woodworth made a glowing report on May 3 to the Council of Fifty. George Miller recalled: "It was altogether as we could wish it. On the part of the church there were commissioners appointed to meet the Texan Congress to sanction or ratify the said treaty, partly entered into by our minister

102. Ibid., 6:244 (Mar. 7, 1844).
103. Ibid., 5:541ff.
104. Ibid., 549 (Aug. 26, 1843).
105. Ibid., 6:125 (Dec. 21, 1843).
106. Elden J. Watson, ed., *Brigham Young, Manuscript History*, 160.
107. "History of Brigham Young," *Millennial Star* 26 (May 21, 1864): 328.
108. *History of the Church*, 6:264 (Mar. 14, 1844).

and the Texan cabinet. A. W. Brown, Lucien Woodworth and myself were the commissioners appointed to meet the Texan Congress." Wight's assignment included beginning to organize the move of the colony to the "newly acquired territory" over the summer, then to "report to the Council of the kingdom."[109]

Meanwhile, Woodworth's instructions were to acquire "all that country north of a west line from the falls of the Colorado River [the Texas Colorado, not the great river of the Far West] to the Nueces, thence down the same to the Gulf of Mexico, and along the same to the Rio Grande, and up the same to the United States territory." This extraordinary request would have included about three-fifths of the eventual boundaries of the State of Texas, the eastern half of New Mexico, the Oklahoma panhandle, part of Kansas, a third of Colorado, and even a section of south-central Wyoming. In exchange, Texas would recognize the Mormon nation, which stood "as a go-between between the belligerent powers"–Texas and Mexico. Upon Woodworth's return, Wight and Miller would lead the first pioneers to Texas to take possession of the territory.[110]

Nationally, the political climate was incendiary at best, annexation being an issue with international dimensions, complicated by the slavery debate, constitutional restraints, and fear of war. President Van Buren had firmly opposed annexation; but his successor, John Tyler, saw annexation as the best way to prevent Texas from becoming controlled by Great Britain.

Spreading the word beyond Illinois, Young wrote on May 3, the same day as Woodworth's report, to Reuben Hedlock, who was in England on a mission: "If any of the brethren wish to go to Texas [instead of Nauvoo], we have no particular objection. ... In eighteen months ... you may send a hundred thousand there."[111] But before momentum could build further, Joseph was killed; and Young cancelled the Texas move. Wight resented it and, believing that his commission from Joseph outweighed Young's dictum, established a colony on the Pedernales, and was eventually excommunicated. The issue became moot in any case on February 28, 1845, when Congress passed a resolution annexing Texas.[112]

The Council of Fifty emerged from a strongly democratic political

109. Joseph Smith III and Heman C. Smith, *History of the Reorganized Church of Jesus Christ of Latter Day Saints*, 2:794.

110. Miller, *Correspondence*, 201.

111. *History of the Church*, 6:354 (May 3, 1844).

112. Joel H. Silbey, *Storm over Texas*; David M. Pletcher, *The Diplomacy of Annexation*; Eugene C. Barker, "The Annexation of Texas"; George Pierce Garrison, ed., *Diplomatic Correspondence*

tradition. Its members understood and accepted power and sovereignty based in part on goodness, or correctness. Moreover, when mixed with biblical traditions of kings and authority from God, the transformation from president to king was an easy one. Still, Joseph's theocratic kingdom ushered the Saints into a new form of government in which the line between church and state disappeared. Expansively, Joseph preached on May 11, 1844: "I calculate to be one of the instruments of setting up the kingdom of Daniel by the word of the Lord, and I intend to lay a foundation that will revolutionize the whole world. ... It will not be by sword or gun that this kingdom will roll on, the power of truth is such that all nations will be under the necessity of obeying the Gospel."[113]

Resistance in the Relief Society

The unfathomable nature of plurality confused sexual relations and mores in Nauvoo in profound ways. The layering of knowledge and boundaries between insiders and outsiders became ambiguous and confused. In late February 1844, Hyrum was the subject of innuendo that reflected a fractured version of the truth. Orsimus F. Bostwick, according to a complaint filed by Hyrum, had uttered "slanderous language concerning [Hyrum] and certain females of Nauvoo."[114] Bringing what amounted to gossip to the court, Hyrum's display of self-righteousness exhibited a disconnect between the truth and what looked like the truth. In boastful and gendered humor, Hyrum, according to Bostwick, had said "he could take a half bushel of meal and get what accommodation he wanted with almost any woman in the city."[115] Attempting to control the conversation over the sacred practice of plurality, Joseph moved through a web of secrets, incomplete knowledge, and loyalties to preserve the ritual of a plurality of wives. In response to Bostwick's story and to manage the conflict in his own home, Joseph had W. W. Phelps draft an essay defending the reputations of the women of the Relief Society.[116]

The Relief Society's first meeting of 1844 convened on March 9. By then, more than a thousand women had found power in the gatherings they shared. By then, they had articulated a sense of contribution and meaning to

of the Republic of Texas; Joseph William Schmitz, *Texan Statecraft, 1836-1845*; Justin Harvey Smith, *The Annexation of Texas*.

113. *History of the Church*, 6:365 (May 11, 1844).

114. Ibid., 225 (Feb. 26, 1844).

115. Orsimus F. Bostwick, qtd. in Linda King Newell and Valeen Tippetts Avery, *Mormon Enigma*, 173.

116. Joseph Smith, Diary, Feb. 28, 1844, in Faulring, *An American Prophet's Record*, 449.

their work. Perhaps best understanding the influence the women held with their husbands, their president, Emma Smith, presented Phelps's document, the "Voice of Innocence," and asked them to support it. She read the text to the women at four overflow meetings, two each on March 9 and 16. These repetitions indicate Emma's intent to give as many as possible the chance to hear it in person and to create solidarity around its discourse. Thomas Bullock transcribed one copy of the document, and Willard Richards wrote a preface that framed it with his own interpretation of its significance.[117]

The language of the "Voice of Innocence" is rich with hidden meaning and innuendo, extravagant and gaudy in its extreme point of view, but direct in its intent: to put rumors to rest, defend the women's character, and denounce promiscuity:

> The corruption of wickedness which manifested itself in such horrible deformity on the trial of Orsemus F. Bookwich [Bostwick] last week, for slandering President Hyrum Smith and the widows of the City of Nauvoo has awakened all the kindly feelings of female benevolence, compassion and pity, for the softer side to spread forth the mantle of charity to shield the character of the virtuous mothers, wives and daughters of Nauvoo, from the *blasting breath* and *poisonous touch* of debauchers, vagabonds, and rakes, who have jammed themselves into our city to offer *strange fire* at the divines of infamy, disgrace and degradation; as they and their kindred spirits have done in all the great cities throughout the world; corrupting their way on the earth and bringing women, poor defenseless women to wretchedness and ruin.[118]

In a way, it was another version of the persecution narrative, but this time the victims were pure women. "Curse the man that preys upon female virtue!" Emma read aloud. "Curse the man that slanders a woman." Seething with righteous anger, she continued, "My God! My God! Is there not female virtue and valor enough in this city to let such mean men die of the rot[?]" The women then unanimously voted to support proposed specific resolutions, including:

> Resolved … that we view with unqualified disapprobation and scorn the conduct of any man or woman, whether in word or deed, that reflects dishonor, upon the poor persecuted mothers, widows, wives and

117. Relief Society, Minutes, Mar. 9, 16, 1844.

118. "The Voice of Innocence from Nauvoo, March 9, 1844"; emphasis in original; not paginated.

daughters of the Saints in Nauvoo; they have borne aspersions, slander and hardships enough: for forebearance has ceased to be a virtue …

Resolved unanimously that while we render credence to the doctrines of Paul, that *neither the man is without the woman; neither is the woman without the man in the Lord,* yet we raise our voices and hands against John C. Bennett's "Spiritual Wife System," as a scheme of profligates to seduce women; and they that harp upon it, wish to make it popular for the convenience of their own cupidity; wherefore, while the marriage bed, undefiled is honorable, let polygamy, bigamy, fornication, adultery, and prostitution, be forced out of the hearts of honest men to drop in the gulf of fallen nature, "where the worm dieth not; and the fire is not quenched!"[119]

After the sisters' unanimous vote, Emma convened the second meeting, "exhorting all to take heed to their ways; and follow the teachings of Brother Joseph."[120] She was constructing a sort of word trap for the women. "When he Preaches against vice take heed of it," for "he meant what he said."[121] Emma knowingly moved into dangerous territory, using language that revealed what she really meant behind words that suggested something different.

At the outset of the March 16 meeting, Emma told the women "the time had come when we Must thro throw the Mantle of Charity round to Shield those who will repent."[122] While some still taught Bennett's doctrine, if they wanted to know Joseph's doctrine, they should look in the Book of Mormon and the Doctrine and Covenants.[123]

Tension must have cracked in the air as she deployed her strategy against plurality. She told them not to vote in support unless "they where willing to maintain their integrity through time & Et[e]rnity." Again she warned them to follow her husband's teachings "from the Stand," saying there "could not be stronger language used than that just read."[124] It was her last address as president of the society.

Only seven days separated the Relief Society's first and last meetings of 1844. The society never met again in Nauvoo; whatever power struggle must have resulted in its suspension was never recorded and has never been fully explained. Perhaps it was intended only as a temporary suspension that became permanent when overtaken by the calamities of the next few

119. Ibid.; emphasis in original.
120. Relief Society, Minutes, Mar. 9, 1844.
121. Ibid.
122. Ibid., Mar. 16, 1844.
123. Ibid.
124. Ibid. "The Voice of Innocence" was published in the *Nauvoo Neighbor* on March 20.

weeks. But, clearly, Emma had challenged the gap between Joseph's private teachings about plurality and traditional Christian standards. The society's suspension would later be blamed on the "disharmony with larger priesthood structure of the church,"[125] but John Taylor insisted almost four decades later that "Emma Smith the Pres. taught the Sisters that the principle of Celestial Marriage as taught and practiced by Joseph Smith was not of God."[126] The language suggests that, in addition to the defense of sexual virtue that could have been made from any national pulpit, Emma, pregnant with a child conceived after her endowment and sealing in celestial marriage, may have begun to launch private teachings against plurality. If so, such a woman-to-woman approach mirrors her husband's own manner of inviting women and men to enter plurality.

The minutes of the society help to sort out the way Emma's simultaneous defense and critique of Joseph's plurality. Although she never spoke specifically about the practice, she argued against it in principle, giving women language to use when their husbands came to them with similar propositions or, worse, propositions from Joseph himself.

Parallel to the reading of the "Voice of Innocence" in the Relief Society, Hyrum published a stern letter on March 15, denying again the existence of plurality:

> Whereas brother Richard Hewitt has called on me to-day, to know my views concerning some doctrines that are preached in your place [China Creek, Illinois], and states to me that some of your elders say, that a man having a certain priesthood, may have as many wives as he pleases, and that doctrine is taught here [in Nauvoo]; I say unto you that that man teaches false doctrine, for there is no such doctrine taught here; neither is there any such thing practised here. And any man that is found teaching privately or publicly any such doctrine, is culpable, and will stand a chance to be brought before the High Council, and lose his license and membership also; therefore he had better beware what he is about.[127]

Hyrum had accepted plurality a year earlier and was at this point married to two, and possibly five, plural wives.[128] Paradoxically, Hyrum was known

125. Jill Mulvay Derr, "Strength in Our Union," in Lavina Fielding Anderson and Maureen Ursenbach Beecher, eds., *Sisters in Spirit*, 162.

126. John Taylor, Statement, June 29, 1881.

127. Hyrum Smith, "Our City, and the Present State of Affairs," *Times and Seasons* 5, no. 6 (Mar. 15, 1844): 474.

128. George D. Smith, *Nauvoo Polygamy*, 620-21.

for his integrity. Lying for the Lord and for his brother must have exacted a high price. Perhaps he did not see it as a lie but as a sort of layering to remove the sacred doctrine from profane view. In that case, it is possible to place his lying in the context of ritual. The behavior required to practice plurality was, in part, about such layering, whether with words or with acts. For plurality to move forward, it could only exist beyond public view.

The political kingdom of God had developed in fits and starts during the past decade, only to be repeatedly thwarted. The gathering impacted the relative success of Zion that was a place, a process, a set of relationships. In Nauvoo, Joseph found all three. By 1844, as spring inched toward summer, Joseph's political ambitions, the creation of another secret organization, continuing tensions over plurality, and the growing resistance to his leadership formed strands weaving into a stronger and stronger net, one that would, within a few months, bring him down.

CHAPTER 25

The *Nauvoo Expositor* Affair

> *... it may be that the Saints will have to beat their ploughs into swords, for it will not do for men to sit down patiently and see their children destroyed.*
>
> –*Joseph Smith,* History of the Church, *6:364–65 (May 12, 1844)*

The ultimate flaw in the design of a religious community based on ritual secrecy is that it requires absolute loyalty from fallible human beings. Ideal behavior rarely plays out consistently in the real world, and it proved impossible in the religious world Joseph built. Too many people had heard about plurality from Joseph or been exposed to its practice. Despite a remarkable level of acceptance, some were repelled and turned away, causing schisms in the Church that led to Joseph's and Hyrum's deaths.

Embraced when they first arrived in Illinois, the Saints had worn out that welcome by 1844. Governor Thomas Ford, in retrospect, saw Joseph as "a man who, though ignorant and coarse, had some great natural parts, which fitted him for temporary success, but which were so obscured and counteracted by the inherent corruption and vices of his nature, that he never could succeed in establishing a system of policy which looked to permanent success in the future."[1]

It was Joseph's charisma that rendered his followers most vulnerable in Ford's opinion:

> He could, as occasion required, be exceedingly meek in his deportment; and then again rough and boisterous as a highway robber; being always able to satisfy his followers of the propriety of his conduct. He always quailed before power, and was arrogant to weakness. At times he could put on the air of a penitent, as if feeling the deepest humiliation for his

1. Thomas Ford, *History of Illinois ...*, 2:213.

> sins, and suffering unutterable anguish, and indulging in the most gloomy forebodings of eternal woe. At such times he would call for the prayers of the brethren in his behalf, with a wild and fearful energy and earnestness.[2]

Ford's comments capture the drama of the prophet's mood swings. Joseph was many things to different people, slipping in and out of personas easily. Unlike Ford, believers were touched differently by this prophet who changed their lives so completely. Jacob Gibson arrived at Nauvoo from New Jersey with his wife and child on April 13, 1844. After a couple of days' rest, the Gibson family "were introduced to the Prophet, who spoke very pleasantly *and turned and looked a look in my face,* giving me an earnest look, and said, 'Brethren stick to me or by me, and you shall always have light.' Which saying I have often proved true." Gibson attributed Joseph's presidential candidacy to "the other candidates' non-attention to the church to redress their wrongs, the wrath of the surrounding country became so enraged that, mob us out they must, so we had to take up arms to defend or retreat and organize."[3]

The apostles were poised to depart on their electioneering missions on April 1; but before they left, Joseph tutored them on key doctrines. After Joseph's death, Orson Hyde remembered Joseph explaining and conferring upon them "every ordinance of the holy priesthood." Joseph exclaimed at the end of this instruction: "you have got all the keys, and all the ordinances and you can confer them upon others, and the hosts of Satan will not be able to tear down the kingdom as fast as you will be able to build it up."[4] In point of fact, however, succession was nowhere near that clear leading up to Joseph's death. (See chap. 23.)

In other activities, the Masons in Nauvoo completed the Masonic Hall, begun with the cornerstone ceremony on June 24, 1843, and dedicated less than a year later on April 5, 1844.[5] Hyrum Smith, as Worshipful Master, conducted both. The tallest building in town, it served flexibly as the backdrop to funerals, and many Church meetings.[6] The Nauvoo Legion was headquartered there, and the police force used it as an office.[7] Masons

---

2. Ibid., 214.

3. "The Book of the Generations of Jacob Gibson 1849-1881," 6-7.

4. Orson Hyde, qtd. in "Conference Minutes," *Times and Seasons* 5, no. 17 (Sept. 15, 1844): 651.

5. Nauvoo Masonic Lodge Minute Book, June 24, 1841; "Record of Na[u]voo Lodge under Dispensation," 1841-1846.

6. Richard Neitzel Holzapfel and T. Jeffrey Cottle, *Old Mormon Nauvoo and Southeastern Iowa*, 108-109; Michael W. Homer, "'Similarity of Masonry in Mormonism,'" 32.

7. Larry C. Porter and Susan Easton Black, eds., *The Prophet Joseph*, 254-55.

met on the third floor that was sometimes also used for dances or dinners. The ground floor was a good venue for plays and other social events. Both Hyrum and Joseph spoke at the dedication and Apostle Erastus Snow gave a special Masonic speech to an audience of more than 550 Masons.[8]

April's general conference convened on a crisp, clear Saturday morning in the temple grove at 10:00 a.m. on the 6th. It would be Joseph's last general conference, his forum to inspire *communitas* among his people, spin a narrative about prophets, heaven, and earth, and place his followers in a meaningful world where anything seemed possible. A warm breeze blew up from the south.

Joseph and Hyrum did not arrive until a quarter past ten, when Brigham Young called the meeting to order. Joseph welcomed the large congregation. William Law had asked to address the conference, but Joseph said no: "It had been expected by some that the little petty difficulties which have existed, would be brought up, but it will not be the case; these things are of too trivial a nature to occupy the attention of so large a body." Rather, Joseph intended to instruct them about eternal principles of truth: "The great Jehovah has ever been with me, and the wisdom of God will direct me in the seventh hour; I feel in closer communion, and better standing with God than ever I felt before in my life."[9] It was a bold, confident stance.

W. W. Phelps offered the opening prayer, followed by a hymn. Sidney Rigdon, the first speaker, detailed the history of the Church and asserted firmly, "We *know* this is the Church of God." Four Native Americans joined them on the stand, then Rigdon continued, denouncing apostates in the audience who "know how far they could go and not get punished by the law."[10]

On the next day, at 3:00 p.m., Joseph delivered what has become known as the King Follett sermon,[11] perhaps his most important theological exposition. Fittingly, Nauvoo's largest audience ever assembled heard him–reportedly, upwards of ten thousand or more individuals.[12] Although he

---

8. *History of the Church*, 6:287 (Apr. 5, 1844); Scott G. Kenney, ed., *Wilford Woodruff's Journal, 1833-1898*, 2:373 (Apr. 5, 1844); hereafter Woodruff, *Journal.*

9. "Conference Minutes: April 6, 1844, Saturday Morning, In Grove," *Times and Seasons* 5, no. 9 (May 1, 1844): 522.

10. Joseph Smith, Diary, Apr. 6, 1844, in Scott H. Faulring, ed., *An American Prophet's Record*, 463.

11. King Follett (1788-1844), who joined the Church in 1831, had been digging a well when a bucket of rocks fell on him, crushing him. Stan Larson, ed., "The King Follett Discourse," 198.

12. Woodruff, *Journal*, 2:379 (Apr. 7, 1844); also in Andrew F. Ehat and Lyndon W. Cook, eds., *The Words of Joseph Smith*, 343. Thomas Bullock, one of the scribes for this address, estimated attendance at between 15,000 and 20,000 and, despite the tensions in the city, the "good order that

chose not to couch his remarks in the language of "thus saith the Lord," the weight of its content was immense.[13] He spoke about the nature of God, the potential humans had for becoming Gods, and about the relation between earthly life and the life hereafter. His discourse ranged over the "glory of knowledge, the multiplicity of gods, the eternal progression of the human soul," yet his comments were shadowed by an acknowledgment of how precarious his position had become. He concluded with a statement of intense vulnerability: "You don't know me; you never knew my heart," he said plaintively. "No man knows my history. I cannot tell it: I shall never undertake it. I don't blame anyone for not believing my history. If I had not experienced what I have, I would not have believed it myself."[14]

The discourse fits into the larger prophet-narrative that Joseph constructed of his life. The animating impulse behind autobiography is always the individual's desire for meaning, wholeness, unity, and understanding. Our stories attempt to make sense of the raw material of our lives. Joseph's narrative of his life as a prophet interpreted his history, gave meaning, promoted his liberation, and actively directed the next chapter in that story. "This moment," "this day," "this year," or even "this life" on the earth had for him an expanse that he sensed and understood but feared that others could not. "Soon as we begin to understand the character of Gods he begins to unfold the heavens to us," he said. "All mind & spirit God ever sent into the world are susceptible of enlargement."[15] Although nothing Joseph said that day may have been entirely new, he delivered his message with such eloquence and emotion that it deeply moved his audience and convinced many that indeed he did speak with God.[16]

Joseph focused on the necessity of understanding God's nature: "few understand the character of God. they do not understand their relationship to God. the world know[s] no more than the brute beast, & they know no

---

was preserved, when we consider the immense number that were present, speaks much in favour of the morality of our city." Bullock, qtd. in Ehat and Cook, *Words of Joseph Smith*, 400n123.

13. According to Donald Q. Cannon, "The King Follett Discourse," 179. Joseph touched on twenty-seven subjects in this two-hour-plus discourse, including "the character of God, the origin and destiny of man, the unpardonable sin, the resurrection of children and the Prophet's love for all men."

14. *History of the Church*, 6:317 (Apr. 7, 1844).

15. Joseph Smith, Diary, Apr. 7, 1844, in Faulring, *An American Prophet's Record*, 466.

16. For Joseph Fielding, "Joseph's discourse on the origin of man, the nature of God and the resurrection were the most interesting matters of this time and any one that could not see in him the spirit of inspiration of God must be dark." In Andrew F. Ehat, "'They Might Have Known That He Was Not a Fallen Prophet,'" 148.

more than to eat drink and sleep & this is all man knows about God or his existence, except what is given by the inspiration of the Almighty." He asked the congregation, "[W]hat kind of a being is God?" The scriptures tell us, he said, that "eternal life [is] to know" God and his son Jesus Christ. He then elaborated: "I will tell you & hear it O Earth! God who sits in yonder heavens is a man like yourselves That GOD if you were to see him to day that holds the worlds you would see him like a man in form, like yourselves. Adam was made in his image and talked with him & walkd with him." Humans too "may converse with him," Joseph said, because he was once a man.

What was more, "man exhisted in spirit & mind coequal with God himself" before God created bodies for us, as Joseph taught. "I am dwelling on the immutibility of the spirit of man," meaning that the spirit has neither beginning nor end. "God has power to institute laws to instruct the weaker intelligences that thay may be exhalted with himself this is good … it tastes good, I can taste the principles of eternal life, so can you," he promised. "They are given to me by the revelations of Jesus Christ and I know you believe it. All things that God sees fit to reveal to us in relation to us, reveals his commandments to our spirits, and in saving our spirits we save the body."[17] The truly unpardonable sin, Joseph explained, was to know God and then sin against him. This is what the apostates had done, he continued, connecting his argument to his complicated interpersonal relationships.[18] Joseph insisted that he had never harmed "any man since I have been born in the world[.] my voice is always for peace[.] I cannot lie down until my work is finished[.] I never think evil nor think any thing to the harm of my fellow man–& when I am called at the trump & weighed in the balance you will know me then."[19]

On April 8, the day after the King Follett address, Joseph told the audience that his "lungs" had given out.[20] But he needed to explain a crucial fact about Zion to the elders, who were asked to stay after the meeting was dismissed. Questions about the role of Jackson County, Missouri, had persisted despite the settlement of Nauvoo. "I will make a proclamation that will cover a broader ground," he said. "The whole of America is Zion itself from north south, and is described by the Prophets, who declare that it is the

17. Woodruff, *Journal*, 2:383-86 (Apr. 7, 1844).

18. Ibid., 387.

19. Bullock, report, Apr. 7, 1844, http://www.boap.org/LDS/Parallel/1844/7Apr44.html (May 31, 2013).

20. William Clayton, report, Apr. 8, 1844, in Ehat and Cook, *Words of Joseph Smith*, 362.

Zion where the mountains of the Lord should be, and that it should be in the center of the land." Nauvoo now stands as the center place, "the particular spot for the salvation of our dead." Joseph emphasized that expansion would not detract from temple building efforts. "[T]he greatest responsibility resting upon us is to look after our dead. They without us cannot be made perfect."[21] Linked to the expansion of Zion and to the "dominion of the Kingdom," Joseph's candidacy for the U.S. presidency made sense in a millennial frame. Although the idea had been formulated before the Council of Fifty's organization, it became the specific assignment of that group to nurture the kingdom of God. For many, the rationale explained why the group existed at all.

The Council of Fifty met in both the morning and the afternoon on April 11 in the Masonic Hall. Woodruff noted they talked about the "principle of toleration";[22] Clayton portrayed it as "a glorious interview." He noted "President Joseph was voted our P[rophet] P[riest] and K[ing]."[23] "Had a very interesting time. The Spirit of the Lord was with us, and we closed the council with loud shouts of Hosanna!"[24] The Quorum of the Twelve met the next day.[25] But the harmony felt at both meetings glossed over the tension that ran just beneath the surface of Nauvoo.

With the acceleration of Joseph's political campaign, formation of the Council of Fifty, and expansion of plural marriage, Joseph's personal, political, and economic relationships with a growing group of dissenters preoccupied him and played out in the public and private arenas of Nauvoo.

On April 13 at 1:00 p.m., Nauvoo's Municipal Court met. Robert Foster had been claiming that he had paid for Joseph's journey to Washington, D.C. Joseph demanded: "Have I ever misused you any way?" Foster replied, "I do not feel at liberty to answer this question under existing circumstances." Joseph repeated his question, and Foster repeated his answer, twice. Then Joseph said, "Tell me where I have done wrong and I will ask your forgiveness. I want to prove to this company by your own testimony that … I have treated you honorably." Foster refused to answer any additional questions.[26]

Hurt and angry, Joseph accused Foster of "unchristian like conduct in general for abusing my character privately, for throwing out slanderous

21. Joseph Smith, Diary, Apr. 8, 1844, in Faulring, *An American Prophet's Record*, 468.
22. Woodruff, *Journal*, 2:391 (Apr. 11, 1844).
23. William Clayton, Journal, Apr. 11, 1844, in Smith, *An Intimate Chronicle*, 129.
24. *History of the Church*, 6:331 (Apr. 11, 1844).
25. Ibid. (Apr. 12, 1844).
26. Joseph Smith, Diary, Apr. 13, 1844, in Faulring, *An American Prophet's Record*, 470.

insinuation against me, for conspiring against my peace and Safety, for conspiring against my life, for conspiring against the peace of my family" and "for lying."[27] Obviously, he worked himself into a rage the longer he talked, culminating in this accusation of conspiracy to murder. But by 5:00 p.m., the *Maid of Iowa* docked at the Nauvoo House wharf, bringing 210 converts from Liverpool, ready to start their lives in Nauvoo, an event that may have altered Joseph's bad mood. "Nearly all arrived in good health and spirits," the *History of the Church* reported cheerfully.[28]

The evening of April 18, a group of thirty-two men–the Twelve, the Nauvoo High Council, and the presidents of the Seventies–met for an excommunication trial, with Brigham Young presiding. Neither Joseph nor Hyrum was present. The business was what to do with the Laws, the Fosters, and other apostates who were directly challenging Joseph's authority.[29] Law, who knew the rules of Church courts, had previously pointed out that "B. Young has no right to preside in this Stake only over his own Quorum."[30] He had also challenged the court's jurisdiction over him as a member of the First Presidency. (Joseph had dismissed him in January 1844, but the action had not yet been ratified by conference action.) The correct presiding officer, according to Law, was William Marks, president of the Nauvoo Stake. Law also knew that he had a right to "know how our accuser was, what accused of, who the witnesses were, what they proved."[31] Ignoring Law's objections, the men voted unanimously that he be cut off from the Church. Before the meeting ended, William, Wilson, and Jane Law, and Robert Foster–none of them present–were all excommunicated for "unchristian like conduct."[32] Law heard about the proceedings from Marks on April 19, recording: "they said we were opposed to Joseph Smith and that was enough, some charges had been preferred against Foster, but they cut him off before the day of trial, ... But we consider this cutting off as illegal."[33]

Law believed in much of what Joseph had taught but had come to the conclusion that, primarily because of plurality, he was a fallen prophet. The excommunication roused Law's ire: "The fact is," he continued his diary

27. Ibid., 471 (Apr. 13, 1844). See also *History of the Church*, 6:333 (Apr. 13, 1844).

28. *History of the Church*, 6:333 (Apr. 13, 1844).

29. Ibid., 341 (Apr. 18, 1844).

30. William Law, Diary, Apr. 19, 1844, in Lyndon W. Cook, *William Law*, 50-51.

31. Ibid., 51 (Apr. 21, 1844).

32. *History of the Church*, 6:341 (Apr. 18, 1844). See also Joseph Smith, Diary, Apr. 18, 1844, Faulring, *An American Prophet's Record*, 472.

33. William Law, Diary, Apr. 19, 1844, in Lyndon W. Cook, *William Law*, 50-51.

entry, "they are afraid to bring us to trial, knowing that they cannot prove anything against us, and they know we could prove them guilty of base & damning crimes, they fear that we might bring charges against them, and therefore they want to cut us off lest we should expose their wicked acts."[34] Law then began to draft a letter to Marks, asking who had accused them, what they were accused of, and who had given testimony against them.[35] When he asked Willard Richards for a copy of the trial minutes, according to Law's account, Richards lied and told him that no one took minutes.[36] Being cut off from the Church did not, however, eliminate them as thorns in the Church's side. What it did was remove the last vestige of Church control over them and harden their conviction that Joseph was no longer acting in accordance with God's will.

Whether for business or to clear the air, Emma boarded a steamboat on April 20 for St. Louis, her ostensible purpose: to buy more "states" goods for the store.[37] Joseph rode with sons Frederick and Alexander into the prairie to find respite in the pastoral landscape.[38] Critics quickly spread the word that Joseph and Emma had separated. On April 23, the *St. Louis Republican* proclaimed that "the Mormon prophet Joe Smith, has turned his wife out of doors for being in conversation with a gentleman of the sect which she hesitated or refused to disclose." The *Boston Post* reprinted the tittle-tattle but added the correction: "Jo Smith's wife did not leave him for good; she only went to St. Louis on business and has returned to Mahomet."[39] Almira Covey, Lucy Mack Smith's niece, corrected misinformation in a letter to her sister reporting that Emma, then two months pregnant, "is not very well," and categorically denying problems in the marriage: "The report … about her being turned out of doors is false … Never could a man use a wife better than he has her."[40]

On April 24, Emma returned from St. Louis on the same boat as the brother of a *St. Louis Gazette* writer. After disembarking, the visitor asked Joseph "by what principle" he had acquired so much power. "I told him I obtained power on the principles of truth and virtue which would last when

34. Law, Diary, Apr. 19, 1844, in Cook, *William Law*, 51.

35. Ibid., Apr. 21, 1844, 51.

36. Ibid., 52.

37. *History of the Church*, 6:342 (Apr. 20, 1844).

38. Ibid.

39. *St. Louis Republican*, Apr. 23, 1844, reprinted in the *Boston Post* 24 (May 6, 1844), 108, qtd. in Linda King Newell and Valeen Tippetts Avery, *Mormon Enigma*, 178.

40. Ibid.

I was dead and gone &c."[41] Joseph spent most of the day with the Council of Fifty planning a state nominating convention at Nauvoo on May 17. He also passed a brief but significant portion of the day in intense conference with Emma.

When she entered the Mansion House, Emma was surprised to find a saloon bar–including liquor–on the main room, and sent eleven-year-old Joseph III to get his father. She chastised Joseph, "How does it look for the spiritual head of a religious body to be keeping a hotel in which a room is fitted out as a liquor-selling establishment?" When Joseph responded that all hotels have bars and serve liquor, she announced flatly: "As for me, I will take my children and go across to the old house and stay there, for I will not have them raised up under such conditions as this arrangement imposes upon us, nor have them mingle with the kind of men who frequent such a place. You are at liberty to make your choice; either that bar goes out of the house, or we will!"[42] Joseph agreed to have it removed.[43] Within a month, construction began on a modest building, away from the prophet's home, to house the bar.

Joseph had fewer than a hundred days left to live, and his activities were spinning faster, threads criss-crossing. He had apparently married his last plural wife in November 1843 and was devoting efforts at publicly denying the practice. His political ambitions drew off much of his energy, and the mounting opposition from former devotees frightened him. He reacted violently, and frequently overreacted. The chronology of his days shows the layers of activities, meanings, and new interpretations as he tried to impose order on chaos.

On April 26, Nauvoo's marshal, John P. Greene, climbed the hill to Augustine Spencer's house, arrest warrant in hand. Augustine's brother, Orson, had accused him of assaulting him in his own house. Robert Foster, Charles Foster, and Chauncey Higbee agreed with Augustus that the arrest was unjust, an attempt to punish Augustus for his association with the outcasts. They marched down to Joseph's office and demanded that he meet with them on the street.[44] According to Joseph's account, "Charles Foster drew a pistol towards me on the steps of my office. I ordered him to be arrested and the pistol taken from him. A struggle ensued." The three men resisted,

41. Qtd. in *History of the Church*, 6:343 (Apr. 25, 1844).

42. Mary Audentia Smith Anderson and Bertha A. Anderson Hulmes, eds., *Joseph Smith III and the Restoration*, 75.

43. Newell and Avery, *Mormon Enigma*, 179.

44. Joseph Smith, Diary, Apr. 26, 1844, in Faulring, *An American Prophet's Record*, 473.

and Joseph also ordered their arrests. The marshal fined Augustus $100 for resisting arrest and ordered him to "keep the peace" for "6 months."[45] They immediately appealed to the municipal court. Whether the accounts contain elements of exaggeration, it is clear that tensions were mounting quickly and that the line between the two camps was hardening. Conflict violence seemed inevitable if not imminent.

After their excommunication, William and Jane Law remained in Nauvoo, determined to present an alternative to Joseph's mistaken course. On April 28, the Law brothers, Austin Cowles, John Scott, Francis Higbee, Robert Foster, and Robert Pierce organized a rival church. Law, named president, chose Cowles and Wilson Law as counselors.[46] Law clearly longed for some way to remain faithful to Joseph's original vision while rejecting what he saw as wrong. The method he took was reform, which led to founding the *Nauvoo Expositor.*

Higbee filed a formal charge against Joseph for slander on May 4. Intending to avoid a hearing in Nauvoo, Higbee had Joseph served by John D. Parker, circuit court clerk in Carthage, on the 6th. What is less clear is why Higbee wanted to revisit the slander charge he had made four months earlier on January 10.[47] Higbee's animosity toward Joseph was long-standing, fueled by the Nancy Rigdon affair and the aftermath of mudslinging. Joseph, Hyrum, and the Church's other general authorities had used the pulpit to criticize their enemies and had in private maligned the Higbees, Laws, and Fosters.[48]

On Tuesday morning, May 7, Joseph rode out on the prairie with a group of men to show them some land they were interesting in buying. "A tremendous thunder storm in the afternoon," Joseph's diary noted, "with a strong wind and rain, which abated about sunset." Although he reported the weather, he did not mention a detail that, in retrospect, was portentous: The printing press for the dissidents' *Nauvoo Expositor* had arrived in town the week before.[49] The impending storm was almost too pat as a symbol of the apostasy that was rapidly changing the landscape of enemies and supporters.

On Wednesday, May 8, Joseph responded to Higbee's complaint by asking for a writ of habeas corpus and asking Higbee to explain why he should continue to be restricted by the arrest.

45. *History of the Church*, 6:344 (Apr. 26, 1844).
46. Ibid., 346-47 (Apr. 28, 1844).
47. Ibid., 174 (Jan. 10, 1844).
48. Ibid., 356 (May 7, 1844).
49. Ibid., 357.

> Your petitioner further states that he is not guilty of the charge preferred against him …
>
> Your petitioner further states, that he verily believes that another object the said F. M. Higbee had in instituting the proceeding, was, and is, to throw your petitioner into the hands of his enemies …
>
> Your petitioner further states that the suit which has been instituted through malice, private pique, and corruption.
>
> Your petitioner would therefore most respectfully ask your honorable body, to grant him the benefit of the write of habeas corpus …

The published testimony portrays a nasty, personal battle between the men. At one point, the transcript is annotated as being "too indelicate for the public eye or ear" and portrays Higbee's behavior as "revolting, corrupt, and disgusting."[50] Joseph's charges were designed to deflect Higbee's damage. "He was determined to prosecute me, because I slandered him, although I tell nothing but the truth." Despite Hyrum's claim that the accusations were "a mistake," others testified they were not. The result was Joseph's exoneration, and a ruling that "Francis M. Higbee's character having been so fully shown, as infamous, the court is convinced that this suit was instituted through malice, private pique and corruption; and ought not be countenanced."[51] Higbee chose not to be present.[52]

Compounding the insults, William Law, on May 9, was court-martialed by the Nauvoo Legion for ungentlemanly conduct.[53] The next day, another marker of social disapproval was chalked up against Robert D. Foster when he was court-martialed and dismissed as surgeon-general of the legion for "unbecoming and unofficer-like conduct."[54] On the same day, the prospectus of the *Nauvoo Expositor* appeared, promising "the [w]hole tale and by

50. In the unredacted account, Joseph asserted: "I went and found him [i.e., Higbee] on the floor, he stunk very bad. I took Dr. [John C.] Bennett out of doors and asked him what was the matter with Francis, when he told me he was nearly dead with the Pox–he said he had caught it on the 4th of July [1842] , or it might be a day or two after, it was before Dr. Bennett left, a French lady [i.e., a prostitute] come up from Warsaw, a very pretty lady. Francis M. Higbee got in company with this woman and so got this disease. I afterwards talked with him, when he acknowledged that he had got the Pox–he got better, but shortly after was down again, Dr. Bennett said he could not keep him away from the women until he could get him well, and if he would not keep away from them, he would die of it" (from Smith v. Higbee, May 8, 1844, MS 16800, Bx. 5, fd. 26, LDS Church History Library).

51. *History of the Church*, 6:361. Higbee was ordered to pay the costs of the hearing, slightly more than $32.00.

52. See the testimony in "Municipal Court," *Nauvoo Neighbor*, May 15, 1844, in *Times and Seasons* 5, no. 10 (May 15, 1844): 536-39.

53. *History of the Church*, 6:363 (May 9, 1844).

54. Ibid. (May 10, 1844).

all honorable means to bring to light and justice," "a general diffusion of useful knowledge," and to "advocate the pure principles of morality, the pure principles of truth; designed not to destroy, but strengthen the mainspring of God's moral government." The new publication's supporters identified as focal points the Mormons' misuse of political and spiritual power, unfair involvement in real estate dealings, Joseph's political ambitions and doctrinal innovations, violations of democratic procedures, the plurality of gods doctrine, and what they deemed "gross moral imperfections … found, either in the Plebian, Patrician, or self-constituted MONARCH."[55]

In a belated, but nonetheless meaningful, victory, the same day a jury in Lee County, Illinois, awarded Joseph forty dollars in damages for having suffered "unlawful imprisonment and abuse" from Joseph H. Reynolds and Harmon T. Wilson, the two sheriffs who had arrested him the previous June.[56] As one legal battle concluded, another began.

On Sunday, May 12, Joseph preached a message that Thomas Bullock, and no doubt others, found comforting. The prophet assured listeners that the "Savior has the words of Eternal life–nothing else can profit us–there is no salvation in believing an evil report against our neighbor." Joseph advised his listeners to "go on to perfection and search deeper and deeper into the mysteries of Godliness–a man can do nothing for himself unless God direct him in the right way, and the Priesthood is reserved for that purpose." "When those tribulations should take place," Joseph related, "it should be committed to a man, who should be a witness over the whole world[.] … it has always been my province to dig up hidden mysteries, new things, for my hearers–just at the time when some men think that I have no right to the keys of the Priesthood just at that time, I have the greatest right."[57]

Besieged, Joseph fought back, launching his message like cannon fire: "My enemies say that I *have* been a true prophet. Why, I had rather be a fallen true prophet than a false prophet. … False prophets"–probably John C. Bennett and William Law–"always arise to oppose the true prophets and they will prophesy so very near the truth but they will deceive almost the very chosen ones. … It will not be by sword or gun that this kingdom will roll on. … [I]t may be that the Saints will have to beat their ploughs

55. "Prospectus" for the *Nauvoo Expositor*, May 10, 1844.

56. *History of the Church*, 6:362 (May 10, 1844).

57. Joseph Smith, "The Savior Has the Words of Eternal Life," May 12, 1844, in *The Essential Joseph Smith*, 246.

into swords, for it will not do for men to sit down patiently and see their children destroyed."[58]

Later in the sermon, Joseph reminded listeners that he was ordained to "this very office in that grand Council" in heaven before the world began, and that "the Ancient Prophets declared in the last days the God of Heaven shall set up a Kingdom which should never be destroyed, nor, left to other people; and the very time that was calculated on." Then, in a sudden descent to the personal, Joseph announced, "I never carry a weapon with me. God will always protect me until my mission is fulfilled." Joseph counseled his listeners to judge whether he was a good man or a bad one by the measure of what he taught them, emphasizing the validity of his message. "I never told you I was perfect–but there is no error in the revelations which I have taught–must I then be thrown away as a thing of nought?"[59] According to Joseph's account: "A full room prayed for deliverance from our enemies and exaltation to such officers as will enable the Servants of God to execute Righteousness in the Earth."

Also on May 12, Joseph attended a prayer meeting,[60] in which all present petitioned heaven for deliverance from their enemies, for the ability to fulfill God's commandments, and to spread righteousness throughout the earth.[61]

Three days after the publication of the *Nauvoo Expositor*'s prospectus, William Law recorded: "We feel determined to oppose iniquity and vindicate truth, and although our numbers are few yet we trust in God and [are] not afraid; our enemies rage violently and speak evil of us but it matters not so long as God is for us."[62] The parallels between this statement and the persecution rhetoric at the heart of Joseph's narrative are striking. Sidney Rigdon brought Law a message of conciliation from Joseph on May 13. According to Law, "He said it was that if we would let all difficulties drop that we ([Wilson Law], my wife Jane Law, R. D. Foster and myself[)] should be restored to our standing in the Church ... We told him that we had not been cut off from the Church legally, and there fore did not ask to be restored."

58. *History of the Church*, 6:364-65 (May 12, 1844).

59. Ibid., 364-66. Touched by the prophet's message, Joseph Fielding "never felt more delighted with his discourse than at this time." In an allusion that, all things considered, might have been unfortunate, Fielding continued: "It put me in Mind of Herod when they said at his Oration. It is the voice of a God and not of a Man." Joseph Fielding, Journal, May 12, 1844, http://www.boap.orgLDS/Parallel/1844/12May44.html (May 31, 2013).

60. *History of the Church*, 6:367 (May 12, 1844).

61. Joseph Smith, Diary, May 12, 1844, in Faulring, *An American Prophet's Record*, 478.

62. William Law, Diary, May 13, 1844, in Cook, *William Law*, 52.

Rigdon admitted that the excommunications had been handled incorrectly but insisted that "they wanted peace." Law countered that if Joseph admitted that "he had taught and practiced the doctrine of the plurality of wives," acknowledged the doctrine was "from Hell," agreed that "the persecution against me and my friends was unjust," then Law "would agree to cease hostilities, otherwise we would publish all to the world." Rigdon knew he did not have authority to make such a commitment but repeated that they would restore the Laws to their former status in the Church.[63] It was too late for such measures.

The meetings of the Anointed Quorum and the Council of Fifty throughout April, May, and June brought Joseph's most devoted disciples together, determined to resist pressures from outsiders and complications from apostates within. The meetings were important for simultaneously creating and maintaining boundaries that unified members in their resolve, forged bonds of shared conviction, and allowed them to perpetuate the myth that certain secret doctrines were still inviolate.

The list of issues they addressed speaks of lofty concerns. Sometimes, they dealt with the particular challenges of the Saints who became ill or struggled financially. On other days, they dreamed more largely of kingdoms and powers. They dashed off correspondence to Washington, D.C., explored escape routes from a Nauvoo envisioned in flames, and called on the Lord to fight enemies who became more real the more they prayed. The repeated performance of ritual brought an increased number of men and women into the sacred circle. The intensity and spiritual fervor of such gatherings stimulated prayers soliciting God's help.

On May 14, at the awkward hour of 4:00 p.m. in the middle of spring planting, a "few" of the Anointed Quorum met for "Prayer Meeting." Lyman Wight was initiated into the group, which prayed for "Bro[ther] Woodworth's daughter who was sick."[64] This daughter was probably eighteen-year-old Flora, whom Joseph had married the previous spring.

On May 16, the day before the presidential nominating convention, the *Nauvoo Neighbor* published an informal poll of *Osprey* passengers: "General Joseph Smith, 26 gentlemen, 3 ladies. Henry Clay, 6 gentlemen, 2 ladies. Van Buren, 2 gentlemen. 0 ladies. The ladies are altogether forsaking Van Buren, and the gentlemen as a matter of course are following after. There is a

---

63. Ibid., 52-53.

64. Joseph Smith, Diary, May 14, 1844, in Faulring, *An American Prophet's Record*, 479.

wonderful shrinkage in Henry Clay, but the General is going it with a rush. *Hurrah for the General!*"[65]

Joseph's presidential candidacy was launched in grand style with a state convention on Friday, May 17. Thanks to Mormonism's broad net sweeping in converts, it could muster representatives from virtually every state in the union. The convention opened with a reading of several letters of support, solicited from friends of the Church. They applauded Joseph for the "principles of … Jefferson democracy, free trade, and sailor's rights, and the protection of person and property," one read.[66]

Nine resolutions were adopted, articulating Joseph's platform and the Church's views on government, each generating a rousing response, but the fifth received particular acclamation: "Resolved, … we will support General Joseph Smith, of Illinois, for the President of the United States"[67] and to support Sidney Rigdon as vice president.

Joseph heard the flattering comments in the morning meeting but missed the evening caucus because he was with Emma, who was ill.[68] The ailment is unspecified, but she was, at the time, forty years old, and three months pregnant with her eleventh full-term pregnancy. Nor had the previous year been stress free.

That night, a group gathered on the street outside the Mansion House and burned a barrel of tar. The scent may have reminded Joseph of being mobbed in Hiram, Ohio, dragged from his house on a frosty night, tarred and feathered, and perhaps threatened with poison and emasculation. Now it signaled a celebration. The group toasted him, "carried me on their shoulders twice round the fire and escorted me to my Mansion by a band of music," he reported, enjoying the support.[69] The next day at 5:00 p.m, "cannons were fired in front of my old home and [the] regiment dismissed."[70] Rallying around Joseph, the show of camaraderie must have assuaged his suffering at the betrayal of former friends.

Emma was still "very sick" on May 20. Again, Joseph spent an anxious day with her. He must have been exasperated to receive a summons to appear in court on another complaint of one of the Higbee brothers. The

65. "Steamboat Election," *Nauvoo Neighbor*, May 16, 1844, in *History of the Church*, 6:384-85.
66. *History of the Church*, 6:386 (May 17, 1844).
67. Ibid., 391.
68. Joseph Smith, Diary, May 17, 1844, in Faulring, *An American Prophet's Record*, 480.
69. *History of the Church*, 6:397 (May 17, 1844).
70. Ibid., 398 (May 18, 1844).

lawyers agreed to an "abatement," and a change of venue to McDonough County was ordered.[71]

On Tuesday, May 21, Brigham Young, Heber Kimball, and forty other men sailed downriver to St. Louis on the *Osprey.* Their ultimate destination was the eastern United States. Joseph was there to bid them farewell at 7:00 in the morning. An hour later, Dan Jones's and Levi Moffatt's *Maid of Iowa* arrived with sixty-two Saints from the Eastern states.[72] All were reportedly "in good health and spirits." Avoiding yet another sheriff hoping to subpoena him, Joseph and Orrin Porter Rockwell rode out to the prairie for some relief. Joseph came back in the evening, relieved that "Emma … is somewhat better." He rolled up his shirt sleeves and shoveled dirt on the ditch bank near their house, while Lorenzo D. Wasson stood watch at the corner of the fence. The alertness of Emma's cousin explains why the officer of the court who came searching for Joseph could not find him. Constantly vigilant, the men around Joseph were attentive to his safety. Later that evening Joseph rode out to the countryside to see a sick child with William Clayton.[73] By May 23, Emma was much improved.[74]

On May 22, Joseph invited a group of Sac and Fox natives, who had earlier inhabited the site of Nauvoo, into his kitchen and listened as they pronounced: "You preach a great deal so say great Spirit, you be as great and good as our fathers that will do. Our worship is different, but we are good as other men. … We wish friendship with all men. Our chiefs done wrong in selling our country." They told Joseph that Black Hawk's brother, whose full name was Maquisto Fox Nation, had worshipped on the ground where Nauvoo now stood. Overall, it was a friendly visit, in Joseph's mind.[75] Joseph told them he believed that they "had been wronged," but deflected what might have been an attempt to claim Nauvoo's site. From his perspective, the Saints had bought the land, paid for it, and had fair title to it. In the future, he advised them to not sell "any more land. Cultivate peace with all men with the different tribes." He said the Book of Mormon "told me about your fathers.

71. Joseph Smith, Diary, May 20, 1844, in Faulring, *An American Prophet's Record*, 480; *History of the Church*, 6:398-99 (May 20, 1844).

72. Ronald K. Esplin, "Life in Nauvoo, June 1844: Vilate Kimball's Martyrdom Letters," *BYU Studies* 19, no. 2(Fall 1978): 231.

73. *History of the Church*, 6:399 (May 21, 1844).

74. Joseph Smith, Diary, May 23, 1844, in Faulring, *An American Prophet's Record*, 481.

75. Ibid., May 22, 1844, 481. Faulring uses right slanting lines to frame words added above the line in the original text.

... You must send to all the tribes you can and tell them to live in peace and when any of our people come to see you treat them as we treat you."[76]

Long accustomed to being the object of curiosity, Joseph loved entertaining dignitaries, and welcomed the visit to Nauvoo of Josiah Quincy, Boston brahmin, and his friend Charles Francis Adams on May 14. Quincy was so impressed by this encounter that he wrote about it almost forty years later in *Figures of the Past* (1883). He described the Mormon prophet as a "phenomenon" difficult to interpret. "If the reader does not know just what to make of Joseph Smith, I cannot help him out of the difficulty. I myself stand helpless before the puzzle."[77]

Quincy and Adams woke up on the morning of the 15th to torrential rain outside the old mill, which had been converted into an Irish shanty. The next day, Joseph sent his own carriage to bring them the two miles over muddy roads to the Mansion House. In the doorway stood their host, "a man of commanding appearance, clad in the costume of a journeyman carpenter when about his work." Quincy described him as a "hearty, athletic fellow, with blue eyes standing prominently out upon his light complexion, a long nose, and retreating forehead. He wore striped pantaloons, a linen jacket, which had not lately seen the washtub, and a beard of some three days' growth." Their companion, Dr. Goforth, a fellow passenger, introduced them to the prophet, who said loudly, "God bless you, to begin with!" As he spoke, he placed his hands in a familiar way on Adams's shoulders. Quincy assessed the gesture as "official familiarity, such as a crowned head might adopt on receiving the heir presumptive of a friendly court. The greeting to me was cordial with that sort of cordiality with which the president of a college might welcome a deserving janitor and a blessing formed no part of it." Joseph then said, "And now come, both of you, into the house!"[78]

Quincy considered that Joseph was a "remarkable individual who had fashioned the mold which was to shape the feelings of so many thousands of his fellow-mortals. But Smith was more than this, and one could not resist the impression that capacity and resource were natural to his stalwart person." Joseph drove the men around the city after pausing briefly to preach informally in the yard outside his house and engage in debate with a Methodist minister who happened to be present. After surveying the prairie

---

76. Ibid., 482.

77. Josiah Quincy, *Figures of the Past*, in John E. Hallwas and Roger D. Launius, eds., *Cultures in Conflict*, 51.

78. Ibid., 46-50.

land near the temple, they stopped at the grove "where there were seats and a platform for speaking." Joseph explained that this was where they held worship services when the weather was good, but once the temple was completed they would move them indoors.

For some, Joseph's use of "thus saith the Lord" for a wide range of revelations, both formal or informal inspirations, was a stretch of legitimacy and a quesitonable use of power. Quincy prodded Joseph on this point. Joseph responded, "In your hands or that of any other person," he said, "so much power would, no doubt, be dangerous. I am the only man in the world whom it would be safe to trust with it. Remember, I am a prophet!" The last five words were spoken, Quincy remarked, "in a rich, comical aside, as if in hearty recognition of the ridiculous sound they might have in the ears of a Gentile." They talked briefly about Joseph's position on slavery. He recognized the "curse and iniquity" of slavery, though he opposed the methods of the abolitionists. The nation should pay for the slaves from the sale of the public lands.

Joseph then denounced the Missouri Compromise "as an unjustifiable concession for the benefit of slavery." Positioning it as part of Henry Clay's bid for the presidency, he dismissed it as a political ploy. Joseph's ideas about governmental reform ranged from reducing the number of members of the House of Representative to increasing the powers of the president. Obviously shaped by Missouri, he advocated that the president be given the "authority to put down rebellion in a state, without waiting for the request of any governor; for it might happen that the governor himself would be the leader of the rebels." Quincy found some value in what Joseph proposed but said "the man mingled Utopian fallacies with his shrewd suggestions. He talked as from a strong mind utterly unenlightened by the teachings of history."

Journalist James Gordon Bennett, of the *New York Herald,* followed Joseph's campaign with interest. On May 23, Bennett editorialized: "They claim possession of from two hundred thousand to five hundred thousand votes in Nauvoo and throughout the Union ... Well, if so, they may be worth looking after. ... It seems by this movement that Joe Smith does not expect to be elected President but he still wants to have a finger in the pie, and see whether something can't be made out of it."[79] That night, Joseph went for a walk with Willard Richards; the two men encountered "several police." Hyrum also cautioned his younger brother "about speaking so freely about my enemies and in such a manner they could make it actionable. I told him 6

79. "Mormon Movements," *New York Herald,* May 23, 1844, 2.

months would not roll over his head before they would swear 12 as palpable lies about him as they had about me."[80]

Although Joseph spent the 24th at home, politics created a vortex, drawing energy as it grew in size. Joseph Jackson, William Law, and Robert Foster continued to spread stories about plurality and Joseph's absolute power. Joseph counseled with Willard Richards and W. W. Phelps at his home at 6:00 p.m., ordering an emergency council meeting for the next day. Richards came to the Smith home with news of a grand jury convened in Carthage to issue two writs against Joseph for adultery, one based on the testimony of William Law that Joseph had married Maria Lawrence as a plural wife, the other based on the testimonies of Joseph H. Jackson and Robert D. Foster.[81]

Also on the 24th, Orrin Porter Rockwell and Aaron Johnson, who had been in Carthage attempting unsuccessfully to deflect legal attention to Foster, had more bad news. The grand jury of which Richards warned had heard testimony from Jackson, now a bitter enemy.[82] At 2:00 p.m. the next day, Jackson arrived in town and Joseph ordered "the officers to have him arrested for threatening life &c." By the next day, some of the grand jurors were in Nauvoo, confirming that two indictments had been issued: "one for false swearing by R[obert] D. Foster and Joseph Jackson and one for polygamy or something else by the Laws." Francis Higbee swore "so hard," among other charges, that Joseph had stolen state property that the judge ordered him removed from the courtroom. The jury rejected Higbee's testimony.[83] Joseph sought refuge by meeting with the Council of Fifty.

The agony Joseph suffered from dissension was personal, surfacing in his sermons over the next few weeks, as he struggled to understand what to do next. On Sunday morning, May 26, Joseph's remarks were fueled by both anger and disgust. He denounced Jackson and the other "mobocrats" and challenged critics: "I am the only man that has ever been able to keep a whole church together since the days of Adam." He compared himself to "Paul, John, Peter [and] Jesus. ... I boast that no man ever did a work as I ..." Particularly bitter over William Law's treason, he derided Law as "this new holy prophet" who had "gone to Carthage and swore that I had told him that I was guilty of adultery. This spiritual wifeism! Why, a man dares not speak

80. *History of the Church*, 6:403 (May 23, 1844).
81. Ibid., 405 (May 25, 1844).
82. Joseph Smith, Diary, May 24, 1844, in Faulring, *An American Prophet's Record*, 483.
83. Ibid., May 25, 1844 (Faulring, 483).

or wink, for fear of being accused of this."[84] The former confidant had sworn "under oath that he was satisfied that he was ready to lay down his life for me, and [now] he swears that I have committed adultery."[85] He blamed his troubles in part on the "Voice of Innocence," rather inconsistently–and unfairly.[86] Joseph continued to play a dangerous word game: publicly denying what he was privately promoting.

Far from being crushed, he boasted: "I glory in persecution. I am not nearly so humble as if I were not persecuted. If oppression will make a wise man mad, much more a fool. If they want a beardless boy to whip all the world, I will get on the top of a mountain and crow like a rooster: I shall always beat them. When facts are proved, truth and innocence will prevail at last. My enemies are no philosophers: they think that when they have my spoke under, they will keep me down; but for the fools, I will hold on and fly over them."[87]

Joseph ran down the list of accusers, condemning each for hypocrisy. In retrospect, what Joseph needed most was a period of calm to focus his energies on his political campaign and the move west. Instead, he jumped into battle, his rhetorical extravagance betraying how much in thrall he was to his narrative of persecution. Toward the conclusion of his address, his anger turned to pathos: "As I grow older, my heart grows tenderer for you," he confessed. "I am at all times willing to give up everything that is wrong, for I wish this people to have a virtuous leader ... When I shrink not from your defense will you throw me away for a new man who slanders you? I love you for your reception of me."[88]

The next day, May 27, Joseph first rode on horseback with a few friends to Carthage, leaving at 8:00 a.m., "to meet my enemies before the Court and have my Indictments investigated." He did not record why he had so quickly changed his mind. As he rode past the temple, other horsemen joined the group until it was a party of about twenty-four.[89] One of the riders was Robert Foster's brother, Charles A. Foster, secretary of the recently organized Nauvoo Library and Literary Institute. They reached the Hamilton Hotel in Carthage about noon. Joseph Jackson, Francis Higbee, and Chauncey Higbee were already there. Charles Foster took Joseph aside and confided

84. *History of the Church*, 6:409-10 (May 26, 1844).
85. Ibid., 411.
86. Ibid.
87. Ibid., 408.
88. Ibid., 412.
89. Joseph Smith, Diary, May 27, 1844, in Faulring, *An American Prophet's Record*, 484.

that there "was a conspiracy against" his life.[90] Even his own brother, Robert, "told some of the brethren there was evil determined against me ... and that there were those who were determined I should not go out of the village alive &c. Jackson was seen loading his pistol and swore he would have satisfaction of me and Hiram." Joseph does not say how seriously he took this information. Joseph's attorneys tried to have the indictments heard the next day, but the prosecution moved for a postponement, and the trial was deferred to the next term.[91]

Disappointed, they left the next afternoon, even though Chauncey Higbee tried to detain Joseph about another case. Joseph made particular note that "Jackson stood on the green with one or 2 men some distance off."[92] Because it was raining, Joseph switched from horseback to a carriage that tipped over at Temple Hill. No one was hurt, so Joseph mounted Joe Duncan, a favorite horse, and reached Nauvoo at 9:00 p.m. Emma was once more ill in bed.[93]

It rained most of the week, trapping Joseph and the Saints indoors. On Wednesday, June 5, more than a week later, Joseph ventured out to the prairie to show some land to a potential buyer. It was 8:00 or 9:00 p.m. before he returned, lingering outdoors "to watch the lightning in the North. It was most beautiful and sublime, a little thunder. ... I told my clerk Dr. Richards it would be fair weather tomorrow."[94] This moment of simple pleasure is poignant in retrospect. Concerned about the legal machinations, angry at the apostasy of former friends, entertaining grandiose ambitions, and basking in the adulation of members, Joseph was handling more intense emotions than were probably healthy. His own reserves of good judgment were wearing away.

Joseph's plural marriages had evidently stopped after November 1843, and it is unclear whether he meant to continue or to halt the practice. Brigham Young, in an address delivered on October 8, 1866, admitted that "Joseph was worn out with it," but issued a less-than-categorical denunciation of the denial story: "As to his denying any such thing I never knew that he denied the doctrine of polygamy. Some have said that he did, but I do not believe he ever did."[95]

90. Ibid.
91. Ibid., 485.
92. Ibid.
93. Ibid.
94. Ibid., June 5, 1844 (Faulring, 487).
95. Brigham Young, Address, Oct. 8, 1866, Brigham Young Papers, LDS Church History Library.

Joseph cared deeply about the welfare of the Saints, of the beloved men among the Twelve, of their wives, and particularly of Emma. But he believed God wanted him to introduce plurality and use his powers of persuasion and discretion to ensure that it would work in the context of the lives of his followers. When it failed and instead caused heartache, he would have grieved; and it seems likely that he would have assumed, on some level, that it was because of something he lacked or a mistake he had made. Prone to plunge into fits of depression, he sometimes took action based on his vacillating feelings rather than on sober reflection. Joseph knew that the misery he saw in the faces of the women and men he loved was, in part, his own doing. Empathizing with their plight but understanding the importance of what they were trying to do, he was powerless to help them through the darkest trials of their lives. Yet regardless of Joseph's own cessation, plural marriages continued: on Wednesday, May 8, 1844, Brigham Young married fifteen-year-old Clarissa Decker as his third plural wife.[96]

A small group of the faithful gathered in the Mansion House on June 6 at 9:00 a.m. to hear Joseph reread his most recent, third letter to Henry Clay. Joseph described the letter as an argument to "show the subject [the presidential election] in its true light and showed [Clay] that no man could honestly vote for a man like Clay who had violated his oath and not acted on constitutional principles." At noon, Dimick B. Huntington came with a message from Robert D. Foster. Foster "felt bad and he thought there was a chance for him to return if he could be reinstated in his office in the Legion &c. that he had all the anties [anti-Mormons] affidavits &c. at his control." Joseph brightened at the prospect of reconciliation and offered: "I told him if he would return, withdraw all his suits &c. and do right he should be restored."[97]

However, it was too late. On the very next day, the dissidents published the first and sole issue of the *Nauvoo Expositor.* Those loyal to Joseph saw the paper as an unmitgated frontal assault. The publishers did not. William Law, Wilson Law, Charles Ivins, Francis M. Higbee, Chauncey L. Higbee, Robert D. Foster, and Charles A. Foster signed an editorial laying out the paper's objectives: "We all verily believe, and many of us know of a surety, that the religion of the Latter-day Saints, as originally taught by Joseph Smith, which is contained in the Old and New Testaments, Book of Covenants, and Book of Mormon, is verily true." But "we have many items of doctrine, as now taught,

96. Brigham Young genealogical records, at www.familysearch.org (Jan. 8, 2007).

97. Joseph Smith, Diary, June 6, 1844, in Faulring, *An American Prophet's Record*, 488; *History of the Church*, 6:428 (June 6, 1844).

some of which, however, are taught secretly and denied openly … [which] considerate men will treat with contempt."[98] It announced that the Mormons practiced plurality and confined itself to a description that may have been motivated by respect for the women who had been pulled into a practice they felt powerless to resist. The editorial gave equal time to Joseph's political activities and identified several points of reform to restore democracy.

For William Law, Joseph was still the Church's prophet but had fallen from grace through sin. According to his biographer, Law's change represented a "psychological reorientation that had begun early in 1843, even before William first suspected the prophet was involved in polygamy."[99] Law was still reeling from Joseph's accusation made the previous December that there was a "Judas" in the Church's midst.[100] Assuming rightly that he was one of the probable suspects, Law denounced Joseph's accusations and the implied threat of retribution. Making public what had been private, Law chastised Joseph for excommunicating him, Wilson, and Jane three weeks earlier "without their knowledge" and for refusing to let Law address the Saints at April's general conference.[101]

The *Expositor* also published separate affidavits signed by William Law, Jane Law, and Austin Cowles describing the revelation on plurality each had read (now LDS D&C 132), which guaranteed men the privilege of marriage to ten virgins and forgave them of all sin except the "shedding of innocent blood."[102] Questioning Joseph's efforts to combine the Church with civil government, the editors of the paper said, "We do not believe that God ever raised up a Prophet to christianize a world by political schemes and intrigue. It is not the way God captivates the heart of the unbeliever; but on the contrary, by preaching truth in its own native simplicity." The group continued their challenge to Joseph's kingdom-building: "We will not acknowledge any man as king or lawgiver to the church: for Christ is our only king and law-giver."[103] Through the paper, dissenters questioned Joseph's flawed judgment, his desire for power and influence, and his distance from his original prophetic role. They questioned his management of the Church's finances, manipulation of the city charter, "moral imperfections," and disobedience to God's laws.

98. "Preamble," *Nauvoo Expositor*, June 7, 1844, 1.
99. Lyndon Cook, "William Law, Dissenter," 70.
100. *History of the Church*, 6:152 (Dec. 29, 1843).
101. "Preamble," *Nauvoo Expositor*, June 7, 1844, 2.
102. Ibid.
103. "Affidavits," *Nauvoo Expositor*, June 7, 1844, 2.

Even from the perspective of hindsight, it is impossible to reconstruct the thinking by which Joseph justified continuing to deny plurality in public, a policy that left him powerless to combat the threat posed by the *Expositor*. Ironically, the truth might have been his best weapon. Enough people knew first hand about plurality that Joseph no doubt would have had the backing of the most loyal members. But instead, secrecy seemed to be the higher value. It seems that, in Joseph's mind, secrecy was an integral, sacred part of the ritual itself.

Each of Joseph's friends who had traveled with him through the difficult terrain that led to Nauvoo but who could not accept plurality had to measure the personal cost on both public and private levels. Their opposition was an agonizing judgment. The revelations in the *Expositor* were not, in themselves, the moment of crisis; but they aroused Joseph's anger to its highest pitch and took him across a line from which he could not step back. The real crisis was the number of men who failed to follow him and ultimately denied his prophethood. Their desertion and the image of himself that he saw in their eyes–an image counter to the one he held of himself–brought him to the desperation of his final days.

In his rage and despair, Joseph burst into yet another liminal state in which he again rejected civil law as a limitation. In the grip of his passions, he decided to utterly destroy the *Expositor*. Even though he masked his action behind that of the city council and even though the destruction itself was carried out by the city marshal, the decision was Joseph's and represented the prophet at his most injudicious. Joseph's defense of plurality and his placement of it as the centerpiece of the Mormon vision of heaven fell flat in the face of his own flawed humanity. And in the end, it was not his enemies' actions but his own anger, frustration, and impatience that rendered him powerless.

The city council met to talk about the *Expositor* on Saturday, June 8, with the first session running from 10:00 a.m. to 1:00 p.m. and the second from 3:00 to 6:30 p.m. As the group began to focus on the nature of the dissenting group's behavior–what Edwin Brown Firmage and Richard Collin Mangrum term the "character and conduct of the paper's editors"[104]–an avalanche of ills burst forth. Hyrum Smith demanded to know "what good [Robert] Foster and his brother and the Higbees and Laws had ever done." A series of testimonies then paraded offenses that had been ignored earlier

104. Firmage and Mangrum, *Zion in the Courts*, 107.

and held up slights that had been forgiven. Joseph Jackson emerged as a particular scoundrel. Hyrum told the story of Jackson's plan to kidnap and marry Hyrum's sixteen-year-old daughter Lovina, as the most recent crime in a history of villainy. Jackson, Joseph's most recent favorite, was a good target as he was the man least known by the Saints.[105]

While witnesses raised the specter of crimes and scandalous behavior, Joseph repeatedly steered the conversation back to the *Expositor.* Resolving to destroy the press, but conscious of the need for legal justification, he encouraged the council to pass an ordinance preventing "misrepresentations and libelous publications." "The conduct of such men and such papers are calculated to destroy the peace of the city," Joseph insisted, "and it is not safe that such things should exist, on account of the mob spirit which they tend to produce." A thorn in his side since it was first aired publicly, Joseph referred to Emma's document, "Voice of Innocence," and claimed that the Laws had "said if God ever spake by any man, it will not be five years before this city is in ashes and we in our graves."[106]

Backing up his brother with a lie, Hyrum vowed that the revelation he had read to the high council on July 12, 1843, "was in reference to former days, and not the present time as related by [Austin] Cowles." Joseph went farther, claiming that he "had never preached the revelation in private, as he had in public–had not taught it to the anointed in the church in private." Desperately, Joseph launched on an explanation of marriages on earth and marriages in heaven. "Man in this life must marry in view of eternity, otherwise they must remain as angels, or be single in heaven."[107]

Exhausted, his "health not very good. Lungs wearied," Joseph stayed home on Sunday, June 9; Hyrum preached at the stand in his place.[108] The city council reconvened on Monday, June 10, with Joseph again presiding as mayor. The sessions remained lengthy: from 10:00 a.m. to 1:30 p.m., and from 2:20 to 5:30 p.m. By now, the council had adopted a view of the sinister efforts of the Laws, Higbees, Fosters, and their cronies, how they had "formed a conspiracy for the purpose of destroying [Joseph's] life, and scattering the Saints or driving them from the state."[109]

Joseph scorned the council's slowness to act: "If he had a City Council

105. See Driscoll, *Hyrum Smith*, 333.

106. *History of the Church*, 6:438 (June 8, 1844).

107. "A Brief Synopsis of the Proceedings of the Municipality of the City of Nauvoo," June 8, 1844, *Nauvoo Neighbor*, June 19, 1844, [2-3].

108. Joseph Smith, Diary, June 9, 1844, in Faulring, *An American Prophet's Record*, 489.

109. *History of the Church*, 6:432 (June 10, 1844).

who felt as he did, the establishment (referring to the *Nauvoo Expositor*) would be declared a nuisance before night." Reading the editorial from the *Expositor*, he demanded to know who had ever said a word against the Laws or Jackson "until they came out against the city?" He, for one, was willing "to subscribe his name to declare the *Expositor* and whole establishment a nuisance."[110] It was clear that the prophet was encouraging the council to take an action that ostensibly solved his problem without also considering what the consequences of that action could be.

Willard Richards, Joseph's clerk, took sketchy minutes that under-represented the mounting crisis; but as the hours passed, the city council gradually took on the role of a court. Unlike a court of law, no lawyers presented the defense, no witnesses testified for the accused. Besides Joseph, those present were Hyrum, John Taylor, Lorenzo Wasson, Lucien Woodworth, Daniel Carn, Cyrus Hills (described simply as "a stranger"), Orrin Porter Rockwell, Andrew L. Lamoreaux, Peter Haws, Aaron Johnson, Benjamin Warrington, Elias Smith, Orson Spencer, Levi Richards, Phineas Richards, W. W. Phelps, John Birney, Stephen Markham, Warren Smith, and George W. Harris.[111] Blurring the roles of judge and jury, and backing up Joseph's accusations, the council determined that "traitors in the Church" had "pollut[ed], degrad[ed] and convert[ed] the blessings and utility of the press to the sin-smoking and blood-stained ruin of innocent communities–by publishing lies, false statements, coloring the truth, slandering me [Joseph], women, children, societies, and countries–by polishing the characters of blacklegs, highwaymen, and murders as virtuous."[112] Joseph claimed that Joseph Jackson had been "proved a murderer" as well.[113]

At the close of that Monday afternoon, the council voted to order Joseph, as head of the council and mayor, to "abate the said nuisance." To make it legal, they passed an ordinance to define the *Expositor* as a public nuisance. Significantly, the ordinance framed this latest confrontation in the rhetoric of the Missouri persecution narrative:

> ... the Church of Jesus Christ of Latter day Saints, from the moment that its first truth sprang out of the earth till now, has been persecuted with death, destruction, and extermination; and, ... men to fulfill the Scriptures

110. Ibid., 441-42.

111. Ibid., 434-48. See also the entry in John S. Dinger, ed., *The Nauvoo City and High Council Minutes.*

112. *History of the Church*, 6:433 (June 10, 1844).

113. Ibid., 441.

> that a man's enemies are they of his own household, have turned traitors in the Church, and combined and leagued with the most corrupt scoundrels and villains that disgrace the earth unhung ...[114]

They claimed they were forced to take action by a "body of degraded men that have got up a press in Nauvoo to destroy the charter of the city–to destroy Mormonism, men, women, and children as Missouri did; by force of arms–by fostering laws that emanate from corruption and betray with a kiss." In addition to invoking the Judas image, the council pitched its reaction in the rhetoric of good citizenship, doing so "to honor the State of Illinois, and those patriots who gave the charter, and for the benefit, convenience, health, and happiness of said city."[115] As a thunderstorm swept over Nauvoo in the late afternoon, the city council ordered Jonathan Dunham "to assist the [City] Marshall with the [Nauvoo] Legion if called upon so to do."[116]

Immediately, Joseph "ordered the marshal to destroy [the paper] without delay"[117]–office, equipment, press, type, and published copies. The council read the resolution, then all signed it with the exception of Benjamin Warrington, a non-Mormon.[118] At about 8:00 p.m., Marshal John P. Greene "reported that he had removed the press, type, and printed papers and fixtures into the street and fired them."[119] It is not clear exactly how many men were involved, but Joseph described a "possey consisting of some hundred" who accompanied Greene back to the Mansion House.[120] Joseph praised the posse, blessing them "in the name of the Lord" and promising that they would be "protected from harm."[121]

The Law brothers and Robert Foster had been in Carthage on Monday where they were speaking on "Nauvoo legislation, usurpation &c." Ironically, William Law noted that he "urged the policy and necessity of being patient, and allowing the law to have its course in all cases."[122] He told listeners that he had been warned the press would be destroyed, "but I did not believe it." To his astonishment, when they returned to Nauvoo that night, he heard that Greene had "the office door broken open by sledges, the press & type

114. Ibid., 433.
115. Ibid., 434.
116. Ibid., 432.
117. Ibid.
118. Ibid.
119. Ibid.
120. Joseph Smith, Diary, June 10, 1844, in Faulring, *An American Prophet's Record*, 489.
121. Ibid.; *History of the Church*, 6:433.
122. William Law, Diary, June 10, 1844, in Cook, *William Law*, 55.

carried out into the street and broken up, then piled the tables, desks, paper &c on top of the press and burned them with fire." The marshal said that if anyone resisted, he was "to burn the houses of the proprietors if they offered any resistance." Law noted, "Our absence on that occasion was perhaps for the best as it may have saved the shedding of blood."[123]

The publishers and their families "thought it wisdom to retire from the midst of a den of robbers, and murderers." Their lives in Nauvoo were ended. "It is truly mortifying to be under the necessity of leaving good comfortable homes, with but a few hours to prepare, yet it is the only course left, and so we commenced packing our goods &c,"[124] Law wrote on Tuesday, June 11.

On Wednesday, the 12th, William and Jane Law, Wilson Law, Robert Foster, and the other families boarded a steamboat for Burlington, Iowa. Their belongings, piled on the deck, were drenched by the rain that fell steadily during the journey upriver. Two days later, Jane went into labor early in the morning. Within the hour, Foster delivered her of a premature but "fine boy." "She had suffered great fatigue and anxiety from our leaving home so suddenly, and our lives being threatened," William noted, "but the Lord was very kind to her." Still, "to find ourselves driven from a comfortable home (unjustly)," he wrote, "lodged at a strange tavern under such circumstances was most bitter and wounding to our feelings."[125]

One could speculate endlessly about the different decisions Joseph might have made. Perhaps his fatal flaw was anger, but equally serious was the illusion he seems sometimes to have cherished about his own invulnerability. He could not have more thoroughly prepared the stage for his enemies. He had given those who hated him cause for both prosecution and pursuit. He provided the dissidents with evidence of how far he had traveled from reason, democracy, and respect for law. Even to fair-minded outsiders, Joseph had become a prophet gone wrong, deluded by his own visions of himself.

Joseph's reaction was an emotional response colored by memories of Missouri. Firmage and Mangrum argue that suppression was, at least, technically, a legal response. They assert, "In common law, conduct that injured the public health, morals, safety, or general welfare was a public nuisance. If less drastic measures could not effectively remove the danger, public officials

123. Ibid., 56.
124. Ibid., June 11, 1844, 56.
125. Ibid., June 14, 1844, 57.

could 'abate' the nuisance, that is, remove or destroy it."[126] But this view was not commonly held at the time to apply to newspapers. As Governor Thomas Ford wrote to Joseph on June 22, the suppression of the *Expositor* not only violated the Constitution but also was a "very gross outrage upon the laws and liberties of the people."[127]

Joseph counseled with supporters at his home on Tuesday, June 11, in the aftermath of the destruction.[128] Present were Hyrum, Willard Richards, and George Adams, and others such as W. W. Phelps, who, on Joseph's instructions, drafted a proclamation to the Saints of Nauvoo.[129] At 2:00 p.m., hearing that a crowd had gathered at the municipal court, which was meeting at his house, Joseph strode out to meet them and again gave his version of events, telling them, "I was ready to fight, if the mob compelled me to."[130] He asked listeners "if they would stand by Me and they cried yes from all quarters."[131] Joseph spent the afternoon at home with Willard and Hyrum. Adams, who had been a lay Methodist preacher and actor before joining the Saints, preached at Joseph's house that night. Afterwards, a man told them that Francis M. Higbee had said that if "they lay their hand upon it or break it, (speaking of the *Expositor* press) They may date their downfall from that very hour."[132] Threats and counter threats, magnified by rumors, hung in the air like a disorienting fog. Joseph noted that "runners have gone in different directions to get up a mob &c. Mobites selling their homes."[133]

Within days, groups of anti-Mormon men gathered in Warsaw and Carthage, reportedly plotting the death of Joseph and the destruction of his power base in Nauvoo. Latter-day Saints living in the outskirts of both towns and areas in-between feared for their safety, not knowing what would happen next, images of Missouri suddenly fresh in their minds.

One of the first to react was Thomas Sharp in Warsaw, drawing on his

126. Edwin Brown Firmage and Richard Collin Mangrum, *Zion in the Courts*, 112, 109.

127. *History of the Church*, 6:534 (June 22, 1844).

128. Joseph Smith, Diary, June 11, 1844, in Faulring, *An American Prophet's Record*, 489.

129. Joseph Smith, Diary, June 11, 1844, in Faurling, *An American Prophet's Record*, 490.

130. *History of the Church*, 6:449-50 (June 11, 1844).

131. Ibid. See also, Joseph Smith, Diary, June 11, 1844, in Faulring, *An American Prophet's Record*, 490.

132. Ibid.

133. Ibid. "Nauvoo was the scene of excitement last night," Vilate Kimball wrote to her husband, Heber, then campaigning for Joseph in the East. "Some hundreds of the brethren turned out and burned the printing press of the opposite party. This was done by order of the City Council. They had published one paper *[Expositor]* which is considered a public nuisance. They have sworn vengeance, and no doubt they will have it" (Vilate Kimball, Letter to Heber C. Kimball, June 11, 1844).

love of uppercase type in fueling ire against Joseph's kingdom on Wednesday, June 12: "War and extermination is inevitable! CITIZENS ARISE, ONE AND ALL!!! Can you stand by and suffer such INFERNAL DEVILS! TO ROB MEN of their property and Rights, without avenging them? We have no time for comments; every man will make his own. LET IT BE MADE WITH powder and ball!!!"[134]

In a prompt legal backlash, Francis Higbee preferred charges against Joseph and seventeen others: Samuel Bennett, John Taylor, William W. Phelps, Hyrum Smith, John P. Greene, Stephen Perry, Dimick B. Huntington, Jonathan Dunham, Stephen Markham, William Edwards, Jonathan Holmes, Jesse P. Harmon, John Lytle, Joseph W. Coolidge, Harvey D. Redfield, Orrin Porter Rockwell, and Levi Richards.[135] The accusation was that, on June 10, these men, "with force and violence broke into the office of the Nauvoo Expositor" and "unlawfully and with force burned and destroyed the printing press, type and fixtures of the same ..."[136] Constable David Bettisworth, from Carthage, arrested Joseph that day at 1:15 p.m., and within the hour Joseph petitioned for a writ of habeas corpus.[137]

Bettisworth arrested the eighteen Mormons on a writ to be heard by Hancock County justice of the peace, Thomas Morrison, "or some other justice of the peace." Seizing its remaining power to control the explosive episode, the Nauvoo Municipal Court, headed by Daniel H. Wells, a friendly non-Mormon and later counselor to Brigham Young, went into session at 5:00 p.m.[138] After hearing twenty-one witnesses, Wells ruled that "Joseph Smith had acted under proper authority in destroying the establishment of the *Nauvoo Expositor* ..." Wells's court countered with an accusation of its own–that the charge was "a malicious prosecution" on Higbee's part who was required to "pay the costs of suit," while Joseph and the other seventeen men were "honorably discharged."[139]

The next day, Joseph presided over the municipal court in the Seventies Hall. Associate justices William Marks, Newel K. Whitney, George W. Harris, Gustavus Hills, and Elias Smith heard Higbee's complaint against the remaining seventeen defendants. Like Joseph, they all obtained writs and

134. Thomas Sharp, Editorial, *Warsaw Signal*, June 12, 1844, 1.
135. *History of the Church*, 6:453 (June 12, 1844).
136. Ibid., 453 (June 12, 1844).
137. Ibid., 453-54 (June 12, 1844).
138. Ibid., 456-58.
139. Ibid.

were "set free by Municipal Court."[140] Instead, the court decided "that said Higbee pay the costs; whereupon execution was issued for the amount."[141]

That night, two men arrived from Carthage with the news that about 300 "mobbers" were determined to seize the Mormon prophet.[142] On Friday, Joseph wrote to Governor Ford to justify the city council's action.[143] He stressed the council's conclusion "that the proprietors were a set of unprincipled, lawless debauchers, counterfeiters, bogus-makers, gamblers, peace-disturbers, and that the grand object of said proprietors was to destroy our constitutional rights and chartered privileges."[144] Even as he rehearsed this story of justification, Joseph was convincing himself that he had acted correctly and that any truly unbiased observer would surely see things his way.[145] Joseph denied rumors that two men had been killed in the process or that a mob had carried out the action. The mayor and city council only performed their civic duty "by removing the paper, press, and fixtures into the street, and burning the same, all which was done without riot, noise, tumult, or confusion."[146]

The next day, Saturday, Joseph received another report from Carthage, this time that a much reduced number of men–forty–were training for confrontation. Another report was that "several boxes of arms" had arrived at Warsaw and that "there was some excitement." Joseph sent back the conflicting and not very consoling counsel that nearby Saints should "give up their arms," and "give up their lives as dear as possible."[147] He then retreated to the consolations of theology. To the small group of men in his office, he lectured on the "key word to which the heavens is opened ... The g[rand] key word was the first word Adam spoke and is a word of supplication."[148]

Joseph preached at the stand the next morning, ignoring the rain that dampened the shoulders of the thousands who had gathered. He told them to "make no disturbance" but to organize and to "send delegates to all the

---

140. Joseph Smith, Diary, June 13, 1844, in Faulring, *An American Prophet's Record*, 491; *History of the Church*, 6:487 (June 17, 1844).

141. *History of the Church*, 6:461 (June 13, 1844).

142. Ibid., 462.

143. Ibid., 466-67 (June 14, 1844).

144. Ibid., 466.

145. Joseph Smith, Letter to Thomas Ford, June 14, 1844, in Dean C. Jessee, ed., *The Personal Writings of Joseph Smith*, 604.

146. Ibid., 605.

147. Joseph Smith, Diary, June 15, 1844, in Faulring, *An American Prophet's Record*, 491.

148. William Clayton, Journal, June 15, 1844, in George D. Smith, ed., *An Intimate Chronicle*, 134.

surrounding towns and villages and explain the cause of the disturbance and show them all was peace at Nauvoo and no cause for Mobs."[149] He also reviewed the themes of the plurality of gods, the organization of heaven, and God's making human beings in his own image.[150] William McIntire, a convert from Pennsylvania, noted in his "Minute Book" that Joseph read Revelation 3:6: "And hath made us Kings & priests unto God & his father &c He then preceded to show the plurality of Gods ..."[151] Joseph reminded them that Jesus had said, "I said Ye are Gods." Joseph wanted his listeners to remember that "God always sent a new dispensa[tio]n into the world–when men come out & build upon o[the]r men's foundat[io]n.–did I build on anot[he]r mans found[a]t[io]n but my own–I have got all the truth & an indepen[den]t rev[elation]n in the bargain–God will bear me off triumphant."[152]

Also on Sunday, Jesse B. Thomas, justice of the Illinois Supreme Court and the circuit judge of both Adams and Hancock Counties, went into Nauvoo to talk with Joseph. He had jurisdiction for the writ that the Nauvoo Municipal Court had dismissed. He concluded that Joseph must appear before another court–one not composed of Mormons. Such action would, he believed, "allay all excitement, answer the law, and cut off all legal pretext for a mob."[153] Joseph told him he would follow his instructions on Monday.

Other developments that day were more militaristic. Isaac Morley wrote from Lima that a hostile citizens' committee had given Morley and the Mormons there three choices: arm themselves and accompany the mob to Nauvoo to arrest Joseph, leave, or stay put and remain quiet.[154] Clearly Joseph's encouragement to "give up their arms" had had little impact. Men like Morley, some distance from Nauvoo, worried about false messengers, and panicked.

Such alarm motivated Joseph to launch letters, missives, and lectures to anyone who he thought would listen. It must have been confusing to those who depended on his lead. Joseph dashed off another alarmed letter to Ford on Sunday to apprise him of these most recent developments. They had heard, he wrote, "that an energetic attempt is being made by some of

149. Joseph Smith, Diary, June 16, 1844, in Faulring, *An American Prophet's Record*, 492.

150. Thomas Bullock, Report, June 16, 1844, http://www.boap.org/LDS/Parallel/1844/16June1844.html (May 30, 2013).

151. William Patterson McIntire, Minute Book, qtd. in Ehat and Cook, *Words of Joseph Smith*, 383.

152. Bullock, "K[ings] & P[riests] unto God & His Fa[the]r," 255.

153. *History of the Church*, 6:479.

154. Ibid., 481-82.

the citizens of this and the surrounding counties to drive and exterminate 'the Saints' by force of arms, … I ask at your hands immediate counsel and protection."[155] He urged "your Excellency to come down in person with your Staff, and … cause peace to be restored to the Country …"[156]

The next day, Joseph had Hyrum draft anxious letters to the apostles:

> There has been for several days a great excitement among the inhabitants in the adjoining counties. Mass meetings are held upon mass meetings drawing up resolutions to utterly exterminate the Saints. The excitement has been gotten up by the Laws, Fosters and the Higbees, and they themselves have left the city and are engaged in the mob. They have sent their runners into the State of Missouri to excite them to murder and bloodshed, and the report is that a great many hundreds of them will come over to take an active part in murdering the Saints.[157]

The Twelve should return immediately to Nauvoo, but "do it without noise. You know we are not frightened, but think it best to be prepared and be ready for the onset; and if it is extermination, extermination it is …" He encouraged them to pack "a little powder, lead and a good rifle," but without "creating any suspicion."[158] He had sent word to both the governor and the president, and was preparing for attack.[159]

Monday morning, June 17, Joseph and the others were arrested on a writ issued by Daniel H. Wells, "on complaint of W. G. Ware, for a riot on the 10th inst. in destroying the *Nauvoo Expositor.*" The party appeared before Wells at his house at 2:00 p.m. After a "long and close examination," they were discharged.[160]

Also on the 17th, Joseph had sent Anson Call and David Evans to take an affidavit from an unidentified individual about the *Expositor*'s destruction and political aftermath. The two men carried a communication from Joseph to Jesse B. Thomas, judge of the circuit court and Illinois Supreme Court, whose office was eighty miles away. At this critical moment, Joseph trusted that Thomas's judgment would be sound and asked that he clarify Joseph's legal rights and options.[161]

---

155. Ibid., 480.
156. Joseph Smith, Letter to Ford, June 16, 1844, *History of the Church*, 6:480.
157. *History of the Church*, 6:486-87 (June 17, 1844).
158. Ibid., 487.
159. Ibid.
160. Ibid.; Joseph Smith, Diary, June 17, 1844, in Faulring, *An American Prophet's Record*, 493.
161. "The Life and Record of Anson Call, Commenced in 1839," 11-12.

Since Nauvoo's men first organized in the ranks of the Nauvoo Legion, demonstrations on the militia field had helped citizens rally and create a united front. In the face of an increasingly uncertain future, the legion contributed to Joseph's grasping for composure. On Tuesday, June 18, legionnaires arrived on the parade ground at 9:00 a.m. to face Joseph. They waited in the humid heat until 11:00 a.m., when their prophet arrived. Within a few hours, their numbers had swelled to as many as 4,000, and they moved to a position near the Mansion House. Joseph declared martial law.[162] In the atmosphere charged with outrage, W. W. Phelps read aloud the preamble and resolutions "of the mob in which they threaten extermination to the whole Church in Nauvoo." Everyone present believed history was repeating itself, and a sense of doom spread out before them like a black swamp. For much of their lives as Saints, their prophet had interpreted their past and present as a religious drama laced with sacred significance. He did the same for them now, addressing them for an hour and a half.[163] He branded, not just his, but his people's opponents as a mob who "waged a war of extermination upon us because of our religion." Joseph called "upon the Citizens to defend the lives of their wives and children, fathers and mothers, brothers and sisters from being murdered by the mob." If we die, he told them, "we die like men of God and secure a glorious resurrection."[164] At the high point of his speech, Joseph thrust his sword toward heaven, exclaiming:

> I call God and angels to witness that I have unsheathed my sword with a firm and unalterable determination that this people shall have their legal rights, and be protected from mob violence, or my blood shall be split upon the ground like water, and my body consigned to the silent tomb. ... I do not regard my own life. I am ready to be offered a sacrifice for this people; for what can our enemies do? Only kill the body, and their power is then at an end. Stand firm, my friends; never flinch. Do no seek to save our lives, for he that is afraid to die for the truth, will lose eternal life.[165]

More than an hour later, at 3:15 p.m., the legion moved up Main Street, marking time with Joseph and his staff.[166] Women, children, and

162. *History of the Church*, 6:497 (June 18, 1844); see also William Clayton, Journal, June 18, 1844, in George D. Smith, *An Intimate Chronicle*, 134.

163. Joseph Smith, Diary, June 18, 1844, in Faulring, *An American Prophet's Record*, 494.

164. *History of the Church*, 6:499 (June 18, 1844); see also Clayton, Journal, June 18, 1844, in George D. Smith, *An Intimate Chronicle*, 134-35.

165. *History of the Church*, 6:499 (June 18, 1844); Joseph Smith, Diary, June 18, 1844, in Faulring, *An American Prophet's Record*, 494.

166. Joseph Smith, Diary, June 18, 1844, in Faulring, *An American Prophet's Record*, 494.

men too old to be in the legion crowded the sides of the street, watching the force march forward. The scene must have inspired them to believe–if only for a moment–that everything would work out, that Joseph and the Saints would be safe.

That evening, at about 9:00 p.m., messengers galloped in from Carthage, repeating the warning about mobs but also news of Governor Ford's instructions to trust him to resolve the conflict legally. But the men in the mob "damned the Gov[ernor] as being as bad as Joe Smith. [They] Did not care for him [and would] be as willing [to act even if] he would not help."[167] Joseph's terse notes that night record only the skeleton of what had happened, but carried a sliver of hope that Ford would side with the Saints. A bitterly cold wind blew in from the east.[168]

On Wednesday, the 19th, additional Nauvoo Legion troops swarmed into town, were addressed by Joseph, and escorted to join the rest of the encamped troops. More legionnaires arrived that afternoon.[169] Joseph called for guards to be posted throughout the city, on the roads leading out of town, and along the river banks.[170]

For the next four days, June 20-23, Thursday through Sunday, Joseph stayed most of the time in the Mansion House, with Alpheus Cutler and Reynolds Cahoon guarding the door. Periodically, he went out to encourage the legionnaires. The suspense made him restless. He wrote letters to the President of the United States, John Tyler; Willard Richards drafted letters to James Arlington Bennet and to the apostles.[171]

Joseph strategized with Richards, John Taylor, and John Bernhisel, among others. The prophet's sense of urgency was immense. On the 20th, he wrote new letters instructing the Twelve to return. Anticipating his eventual arrest, he gathered affidavits about the raid on the *Expositor* press and arms. The affidavits from Isaac Morley, Gardner Snow, John Edmiston, Edmund Durfee, Solomon Hancock, Allen T. Waite, James Guyman, Obadiah Bowen, Alvah Tippetts, Hiram B. Mount, and John Cunnington[172] affirmed the claims Joseph had made in his letters to Ford and others. Joseph also instructed Theodore Turley to begin manufacturing artillery while,

167. Ibid.
168. *History of the Church*, 6:433 (June 18, 1844).
169. Joseph Smith, Diary, June 18, 1844, in Faulring, *An American Prophet's Record*, 494.
170. *History of the Church*, 6:505 (June 18, 1844).
171. Joseph Smith, Diary, June 18, 1844, in Faulring, *An American Prophet's Record*, 495.
172. *History of the Church*, 6:519 (June 20, 1844).

contradictorily, assuring him "that there would not be a gun fired on our part during this fuss."[173]

Despite his defiance, Joseph had to consider the possibility of his own death. At one point, he told Hyrum to take his family and leave on the next steamboat to Cincinnati. "Joseph, I can't leave you," his brother replied. Joseph did not argue but said to others standing nearby, "I wish I could get Hyrum out of the way, so that he may live to avenge my blood, and I will stay with you and see it out."[174]

Governor Ford, not wishing to overact to Joseph's urgent letter of June 16, arrived in Carthage on Friday, June 21, to investigate. He interviewed the Laws, the Fosters, and the Higbees.[175] Ford wanted to hear both the accusations and the defense before taking action and asked Joseph to send "one or more well-informed and discreet persons, who will be capable of laying before me your version of the matter …"[176]

Long after Joseph's death, Ford reflected:

> [A] cause of mobs is that men engaged in unpopular projects expect more protection from the laws than the laws are able to furnish in the face of popular excitement. … In such a case, it may happen that the whole people may be on one side, and merely the public officers on the other. … If the government cannot suppress an unpopular band of horse thieves … how is it to suppress a popular combination which has the people on its side? I am willing enough to acknowledge that all this is wrong, but how is it to be avoided?[177]

From the time Ford had entered the race for governor in 1842, he had advocated the repeal of the Nauvoo Charter, foreseeing the role it would play in fomenting discontent and suspicion.

After Ford's interview with the dissidents, Joseph met with the city council, who chose twenty-four testimonials and assigned John M. Bernhisel, John Taylor, and Willard Richards to take them to Ford. Taylor and Bernhisel left immediately; Richards stayed longer to prepare some additional documents.[178] Ford reviewed the documents and wrote to Joseph on Saturday, the 22nd. Not surprisingly, he found significant contradictions

173. Theodore Turley, qtd. in *History of the Church*, 6:520 (June 20, 1844).
174. Ibid., 520 (June 21, 1844).
175. Ibid., 521 (June 21, 1844).
176. Ibid.
177. Thomas Ford, *History of Illinois*, 2:41.
178. *History of the Church*, 6:522 (June 21, 1844).

between the two versions of events. His own position, however, was clear: "Your conduct in the destruction of the press was a very gross outrage upon the laws and the liberties of the people. It may have been full of libels, but this did not authorize you to destroy it." Joseph and the city council had, Ford wrote, violated freedom of the press, freedom from unreasonable searches and seizures, unified legislative and judicial powers in the council's resolution, and had "assumed to yourselves more power than you are entitled to in relation to writs of *habeas* under your [city] charter."[179]

In the same letter, Ford responded for the first time to Joseph's request to call out the militia: "I can call no portion of the militia for your defense until you submit to the law." He warned: "If you, by refusing to submit, shall make it necessary to call out the militia, I have great fears that your city will be destroyed … [S]uch is the excitement of the country that I fear the militia, when assembled, would be beyond legal control." If the Saints did not submit, Ford warned, "I will be obliged to call out the militia; and if a few thousand will not be sufficient, many thousands will be."[180]

Joseph responded the same day, arguing that he had already been tried and released. He again begged Ford to come to Nauvoo to hear "the whole matter … in its true colors."[181] Again, he appealed to the persecution narrative that defined his reality: "Our troubles are invariably brought upon us by falsehood & misrepresentations by designing men …" Throttling back considerably on the name-calling, he claimed that he had ordered the press destroyed because the men "had already set themselves at defiance of the laws, … and had threatened the lives of some of its principle officers."[182] John Taylor, accompanied by Lucien Woodworth, James Woods (Joseph's non-Mormon attorney), and John Bernhisel, carried this latest missive to Ford that evening.

When he read Ford's letter to Hyrum, Willard Richards, W.W. Phelps, William Marks, and others, Joseph concluded: "There is no mercy–no mercy here." Hyrum agreed: "Just as sure as we fall into their hands, we are dead men."[183] They discussed the possibility of taking their grievances again to Washington but concluded it would most likely be futile. "If Hyrum and I are ever taken again," Joseph mused to Stephen Markham, "we shall be

179. Ibid., 535.

180. Ford, Letter to Smith, in *History of the Church*, 6:536 (June 22, 1844).

181. Smith, Letter to Ford, June 22, 1844, in Jessee, *The Personal Writings of Joseph Smith*, 613.

182. Ibid., 613-14.

183. Ibid., 545 (June 22, 1844).

massacred, or I am not a prophet of God."[184] Obviously, the anger that had fueled his attack on the *Expositor* and the optimism with which he had addressed the troops were fading.

Joseph then apparently realized that if the authorities only wanted Hyrum and him, perhaps a new way to escape their difficulties was open. "[T]ell everybody to go about their business," he remarked to the small group of supporters, "and not to collect in groups, but to scatter about. There is no doubt they will come here and search for us. Let them search; they will not harm you in person or property, and not even a hair of your head. We will cross the river tonight, and go away to the West."[185]

Joseph walked to the door. Outside in the late afternoon air, he told two men to bring the *Maid of Iowa* to the upper landing, to take Emma, Mary Fielding Smith, and the children in both families on board, then to go down river to Portsmouth, Illinois, where they would later be contacted.[186] Relief must have settled on Joseph as he contemplated his next move.

184. Ibid., 546.
185. Ibid., 545-46.
186. Ibid.

CHAPTER 26

Last Days

> *The power of religion depends, in the last resort, upon the credibility of the banners it puts in the hands of men as they stand before death, or more accurately, as they walk, inevitably, toward it.*
>
> –*Peter Berger,* The Sacred Canopy, *51*

Clearly, Joseph set events in motion that careened beyond his control. The non-Mormon response to the destruction of the *Nauvoo Expositor* was swift. Within days, rallies of critics of Mormonism converged in Carthage and Warsaw. Illinois state troops flooded into the county seat from the surrounding countryside. To maintain order, Governor Ford was forced to act, which triggered more reactions.

As Nauvoo mayor, Joseph issued a proclamation on Tuesday, June 11, the day after the destruction of the *Nauvoo Expositor*, calling for peace while justifying the city council's action. In a notably lengthy sentence, he argued:

> As attempts have already been made to excite the jealousy and prejudice of the people of the surrounding country, by libels, and slanderous articles upon the citizens and City Council, for the purpose of destroying the "Charter" of said city, and for the purpose of raising suspicion, wrath, and indignation among a certain class of the less honorable portion of mankind, to commit acts of violence upon the innocent and unsuspecting, in a certain newspaper called the "Nauvoo Expositor," recently established for such purposes in said city, and which has been destroyed as a nuisance according to the provisions of the Charter, I further call upon every Officer, authority and citizen to be vigilant in preventing by wisdom, the promulgation of false statements, libels, slanders, of any other malicious or evil designed concern that may be put in operation to excite and foment the passions of men to rebel against the rights and privileges of the city, citizens or laws of the land, to be ready to suppress the gathering of

> mobs; to repel by gentle means and noble exertion, every foul scheme of unprincipled men, to disgrace and dishonor the city, or State, or any of their legally constituted authorities; and finally to keep the peace, by being cool, considerate, virtuous, unoffending, manly and patriotic as the free sons of liberty ever have been and honorably maintain the precious boon our illustrious fathers won.[1]

Equating the "public peace" with a lack of dissension among followers, Joseph positioned his life as a prophet in a world that was both public and private yet also sacralized by the Church's restoration mission. Any activity that challenged Joseph's view of what he believed God wanted him to do should be stopped. His enemies were unqualifiedly evil–fomenting a host of sins inside and outside the Church. He portrayed the opposition, not as attacking him personally, but as assaulting the "rights and privileges of the city, citizens or laws of the land." Preying on the stories of Missouri's horrors, he warned them to be ready for mobs and the "foul scheme[s] of unprincipled men." Although his own forces had destroyed the press, he called on supporters to be "cool, considerate, virtuous, unoffending, manly and patriotic as the free sons of liberty."

Whatever the strict legality of his action, Joseph's choices turned Illinois against the Saints and, of equal importance, threatened to erode the Church's solidarity. According to Linda King Newell and Valeen Tippetts Avery, "Joseph and the Nauvoo city council had unleased a tornado which threatened to suck them into its vortex."[2] Prepared in some ways for a possible exodus into the west, the Church was poised on the brink, ready to act or react. Lawrence Moore suggests: "Although one may confidently state that Smith did not plan his death, he knowingly courted it and did not forget to prepare his followers for it."[3]

The number of ways for trying to understand Joseph's last days may be endless. Was he so disconnected from the effects of his acts on others? Was he encased in a sense of invulnerability that rendered him oblivious to danger? Was he carried away by hubris, boasting of his powers and taunting his enemies with invocations of dominion? Was he acting out a divine script of martyrdom, spelled out in the pages of the Bible and culminating in the

---

1. Joseph Smith, "Proclamation," June 11, 1844, in Dean C. Jessee, ed., *The Personal Writings of Joseph Smith*, 603.
2. Linda King Newell and Valeen Tippetts Avery, *Mormon Enigma*, 182.
3. R. Laurence Moore, *Religious Outsiders and the Making of Americans*, 37.

redemptive sacrifice of Jesus himself? His religious belief certainly provided an understanding that positioned him in a larger religious drama.

Sociologist Peter Berger suggests that such empowerment is the natural outcome of the effective creation of a religious world "capable of maintaining itself in the ever-present face of chaos." It makes possible for prophets and their followers to do outrageous or unthinkable things. It imposes order on a world that spins out of control. In fact, Berger argues, this need for order is, in part, why religion exists and why humans shape their lives according to its parameters: "The precariousness of every such world is revealed each time men forget or doubt the reality-defining affirmations, each time they dream reality-denying dreams of 'madness,' and most importantly, each time they consciously encounter death. Every human society is, in the last resort, men banded together in the face of death."[4] Thus, Joseph positioned himself to observe and participate in the fulfillment of scripture and belief, a fulfillment that explained his suffering, his people's persecution, and even his own death.

Joseph's decision to destroy the *Expositor* was, at the minimum, ill advised and began a process that reached its climax in Carthage Jail. Perhaps the most judicious analysis of the legality of Joseph's actions was made by attorney-historian Dallin H. Oaks, who argued that suppression may have been within the law but not its destruction:

> The common law authorities ... were emphatic in declaring that [nuisance] abatement must be limited by the necessities of the case, and that no wanton or unnecessary destruction of property could be permitted. ... *there was no legal justification in 1844 for the destruction of the* Expositor *press as a nuisance.* Its libelous, provocative, and perhaps obscene output may well have been a public and a private nuisance, but the evil article was not the press itself but the way in which it was being used.[5]

Appreciating the finer points of the controversy was no doubt lost in the climate of fear that followed the Nauvoo City Council's actions.

When, on Saturday, June 22, Joseph stepped outside his home, his mind fixed on escape to the West, it was Nauvoo that drew him back. Accompanied by Porter Rockwell, he began walking, no doubt trying to diffuse some of his tension. As twilight fell, Hyrum exited the Mansion House and approached Reynolds Cahoon. He confided, his words making it more real:

4. Berger, *The Sacred Canopy*, 51.

5. Dallin H. Oaks, "The Suppression of the *Nauvoo Expositor*," 890-91; emphasis added, paragraphs combined.

"A company of men are seeking to kill my brother Joseph, and the Lord has warned him to flee to the Rocky Mountains to save his life. Good-by, Brother Cahoon, we shall see you again."[6] Joseph came up to Cahoon as well. He wiped at the tears on his checks, but did not attempt to speak through his sadness.

A quick river storm blew up; and between 9:00 and 10:00 p.m., Joseph, Hyrum, and Willard Richards waited in the rain for Aaron Johnson's rowboat to transport them across the river. When W. W. Phelps arrived, Joseph instructed: "Go to our wives, and tell them what we have concluded to do, and learn their feelings on the subject; and tell Emma you will be ready to start by the second steamboat, and she has sufficient money wherewith to pay the expenses. If you ascertain by tomorrow morning that there is anything wrong, come over the river to Montrose, to the house of Captain John Killien, and there you will learn where we are." He intended to send new petitions to the President and to Congress to "see if they would grant the Church liberty and equal rights."[7] On some level, he must have known that it was a futile tactic.

Not until 2:00 a.m., June 23, did the four men start to cross the river. Rockwell began rowing vigorously as Joseph, Hyrum, and Richards bailed with their boots. The boat was leaky, the water rough, and the Mississippi overflowing after weeks of storms. Many remembered it as the worst flooding in a decade.[8] They did not reach the other side until daybreak later that Sunday morning.[9]

In Iowa, Joseph remained a wanted man, since the governor had never lifted the extradition order received on September 15, 1840, from Missouri.[10] But it was still a temporary haven.

After arriving, Joseph penned a terse note to Emma, listing three men who owed him money. She could collect the sums and use them for expenses. He also authorized her to sell property in his name "for your support and children & Mother." "Do not despair," he wrote. "If God ever opens a door that is possible for me I will see you again. I do not know where I

6. *History of the Church*, 6:547 (June 22, 1844).

7. Ibid., 548.

8. Ibid.

9. Ibid., 548 (June 23, 1844).

10. Ibid., 4:198 (Sept. 15, 1840). Firmage and Mangrum, *Zion in the Courts*, 93, point to another factor in the ambiguous legal situation that Joseph experienced: "In their petition to Congress for redress in early 1840, the Mormons had cited the failure of Missouri authorities to seek extradition as evidence that the charges against Smith were vexatious and intended to merely drive the Mormons from Missouri." See also *History of the Church*, 4:35-36 (Nov. 28, 1840).

shall go, or what I shall do, but shall if possible endeavor to get to the city of Washington"–implying that he planned to make an in-person appeal to elected officials. "May God almighty bless you & the children–& mother & all my friends. My heart bleeds." He ended with: "No more at present. If you conclude to go to Kirtland, Cincinnati, or any other place, I wish you would contrive to inform me, this evening."[11] Without resting, Rockwell rowed back across the river and delivered the note to Emma at about 8:00 a.m.

After they arrived, at sunrise, Joseph with Hyrum and Willard went first to the home of Captain John Killien. Failing to find him, and both drenched and tired, they walked next to Brother William Jordan's.[12]

At about 1:00 p.m., Emma sent Reynolds Cahoon, Hiram Kimball, and Lorenzo Wasson back across the river with Rockwell, his third crossing in less than twelve hours.[13] Cahoon carried her letter entreating Joseph to confront those who accused them and arguing that, unless he gave himself up, the city would certainly be destroyed.[14] She also begged that Cahoon encourage "Joseph to come back and give himself up,"[15] which Cahoon agreed to do since everything they had worked for hinged on Joseph's return. Cahoon also told Joseph that Ford guaranteed Joseph's safety and a fair, speedy trial. Joseph's friends suffered with him, aware how difficult he found it to discern the right path.[16]

Joseph resisted, still intent on flight. Cahoon, Wasson, and Kimball reminded him that "he had always said that if the church would stay by him he would stay with them." Cahoon and Kimball raised the specter of "cowardice for wishing to leave the people," and noted that "their property would be destroyed, and that they left without house or home." Cahoon worried that Joseph was leaving "the sheep to be devoured." Joseph reportedly signed, "If my life is of no value to my friends, it is of none to myself."[17]

Joseph had been wavering for days. Now, fatigued and rootless, he also may have felt ashamed. The judgement of cowardice, or at least selfishness, was an intolerable situation in a culture of honor. He asked Rockwell, "What shall I do?" Rockwell said simply: "You are oldest and ought to know best;

11. Joseph Smith, Letter to Emma Smith, June 23, 1844, in Jessee, *Personal Writings of Joseph Smith*, 616.
12. *History of the Church*, 6:548 (June 23, 1844).
13. Ibid., 549.
14. William Clayton, qtd. in Newell and Avery, *Mormon Enigma*, 189.
15. *History of the Church*, 6:549 (June 23, 1844).
16. Ibid.
17. Ibid.

and as you make your bed, I will lie with you." Joseph also consulted Hyrum, who proposed giving up. Hyrum's oldest daughter, Lovina, was going to be married that very evening and he hoped to be there. "If you go back," Joseph conceded, "I will go with you, but we shall be butchered."[18]

Feeling defeated–or reconciled–Joseph drafted a note to Ford, agreeing to meet his posse at the Mound, six miles east of Nauvoo at 2:00 p.m. Monday afternoon when he and the other seventeen defendants would surrender. "I now offer to come to you at Carthage on the morrow ... provided we can have a fair trail, not be abused nor have my witnesses abused, and have all things done in due form of law, without partiality, and you may depend on my honor without the show of a great armed force to produce excitement in the minds of the timid."[19] He asked Cahoon to tell Captain Daniel E. Davis to "have his boat ready at half-past five to cross the river." It is unclear who delivered the letter to Ford.[20]

At 4:00 p.m., Rockwell made his fourth and final trip across the river rowing his beloved prophet, Hyrum, Cahoon, Wasson, and Kimball. Joseph became reflective as the boat neared the shore. He wished he could "get the people once more together," but added: "It is of no use to hurry, for we are going back to be slaughtered." Rockwell suggested: "We can send out word, and have them hear you by starlight."[21] Joseph's recent talks had been defiant. Surrounded by loyal followers, he no doubt would have found his conviction of invulnerability rising to the fore once more–and armed resistance by Nauvoo would have almost certainly triggered the bloodbath that he was trying to avoid. Ultimately, it is just as well that the idea of a starlight sermon never materialized.

Remembering how painful the night had been, her anxiety perhaps as intense as she had ever experienced, Emma later said, "When he came back I felt the worst I ever did in my life, and from that time I looked for him to be killed."[22] Vilate Kimball wrote a more optimistic, but less realistic, view of the situation to Heber: "Joseph went over the river out of the United States, and composed his mind, and got the will of the Lord concerning him, and that was, that he should return and give himself up for trial. ... My heart

18. Ibid., 549-50.

19. Joseph Smith, Letter to Thomas Ford, June 23, 1844, in Jessee, *Personal Writings of Joseph Smith*, 618; also *History of the Church*, 6:550 (June 23, 1844).

20. *History of the Church*, 6:550.

21. Ibid., 551.

22. Emma Smith Bidamon, qtd. in Edmund C. Briggs, "Visit to Nauvoo in 1856," 453-54.

said Lord bless those Dear men, and presurve them from those that thirst for their blood."[23]

As Joseph walked up the slight rise to the Mansion House, his family crowded around him. Rather than preach to the Saints, he relished what remaining time he had with Emma and children.[24] The oldest of the children, Julia, was not even a woman yet at thirteen, and Emma was four months pregnant with David Hyrum. Joseph III, twelve years old at the time, remembered that their father called the family into the parlor, savoring what time he had left. Reportedly, he again blessed his namesake son: "If anything should happen to me, you will know who is to be my successor. This, my son, has been blessed and set apart, and will in time succeed me."[25]

Emma asked for her own blessing. Overwhelmed, he told her to "write out the best blessing she could hope for and that he would sign the same on his return." It was probably late at night when she allegedly poured out "the desires of my heart. … First of all that I would crave as the richest of heaven's blessings would be wisdom from my Heavenly Father bestowed daily, so that whatever I might do or say, I could not look back at the close of the day with regret, nor neglect the performance of any act that would bring a blessing. I desire the Spirit of God to know and understand myself, that I desire a fruitful, active mind, that I may be able to comprehend the designs of God, when revealed through his servants without doubting."

"I desire a spirit of discernment," she continued, according to a surviving transcript,

> I desire a spirit of discernment, which is one of the promised blessings of the Holy Ghost. I particularly desire wisdom to bring up the children that are, or may be committed to my charge, in such a manner that they will be useful ornaments in the Kingdom of God, and in a coming day arise up and call me blessed. I desire prudence that I may not through ambition abuse my body and cause it to become prematurely old and care-worn, but that I may wear a cheerful countenance, live to perform all the work that I covenanted to perform in the spirit-world and be a blessing to all who may in any wise need aught at my hands. I desire with all my heart to honor and respect my husband as my head, ever to live in his confidence and by acting in unison with him retain the place which God has given

23. Vilate Kimball, Letter to Heber C. Kimball, June 24, 1844.

24. *History of the Church*, 6:551-52.

25. Joseph Smith [III], Letter to J. M. Stubbart, May 19, 1896, Joseph III Letterbook, 6:458, qtd. in Newell and Avery, *Mormon Enigma*, 189 and n23.

> me by his side, and I ask my Heavenly Father that through humility, I may be enabled to overcome that curse which was pronounced upon the daughters of Eve. I desire to see that I may rejoice with them in the blessings which God has in store for all who are willing to be obedient to his requirements. Finally, I desire that whatever may be my lot through life I may be enabled to acknowledge the hand of God in all things.[26]

Meanwhile, the local militia, known as the Carthage Greys, "bitterly resentful of Joseph Smith's military pretensions," pitched their tents on the public square at Carthage.[27] While Joseph recrossed the river on Sunday, a regiment marched into town from neighboring McDonough County. Within a couple of days, a battalion from Schuyler County joined them. In Carthage, more than 1,400 men gathered in anticipation of a confrontation.[28]

On Monday, June 24, the respite ended. Before they left for Carthage, Joseph, Hyrum, and John Taylor apparently removed their endowment undergarments, perhaps choosing to keep private what the outside world could misunderstand. Sarah Richards offered an explanation in a letter to Zina Huntington: "[T]he order came that in every habitation where any of the endowment clothes were found, [it] would [mean] death to the inmates …"[29] In another account, Oliver Huntington, then a twenty-one-year-old, wrote in 1909: "Joseph said before taking [the garments] off, that he was going to be killed… and he did not want his garments to be exposed to the sneers and jeers of his enemies."[30] Huntington does not say how he knows this.[31] In a third account, Julia Bowen Dalton, a hired girl who boarded at the Smiths, reported that Joseph said: "It was to be that he should lay down his life as a martyr to the testimony he bore but that his enemies could not take his life while he was wearing his garments. He took them off before leaving for Carthage."[32]

According to Joseph Fielding, Hyrum and Joseph met with trusted counselors most of the night, although it is not clear what business they transacted

26. Emma Smith, Letter to Joseph Smith, n.d. but probably June 24, 1844, typescript, Utah State Historical Society. Only a typescript of the letter and blessing exists.

27. Dallin H. Oaks and Marvin S. Hill, *Carthage Conspiracy*, 18.

28. Williams, Samuel Otho, "Such an Excitement I Never Witnessed in My Life," in Hallwas and Launius, *Cultures in Conflict*, 223.

29. Sarah Richards, Letter to Zina D. Huntington, Sept. 20, 1890, LDS Church History Library.

30. "History of the Life of Oliver B. Huntington," 406.

31. Avery and Newell, *Mormon Enigma*, 189-90.

32. Qtd. in Sarah Louise Dalton Elder, Statement, ca. Oct. 10, 1931, 9:85.

or, indeed, if Joseph was able to make coherent plans. It had been at least forty-eight hours since he had slept more than a couple of hours at a time.[33]

Joseph started for Carthage at about 6:30 a.m. with Hyrum, Willard Richards, Dan Jones, Henry G. Sherwood, Alfred Randall, James Davis, Cyrus H. Wheelock, Abram C. Hodge, and "several other brethren." James W. Woods accompanied them as legal counsel.[34] As he gazed upon Nauvoo's landscape–his Kingdom of God, Joseph said, "This is the loveliest place and the best people under the heavens; little do they know the trials that await them." The men stopped at Daniel Wells's home. Wells "was unwell," and Joseph told him, "I wish you to cherish my memory, and not think me the worst man in the world either."[35]

The thousand-plus Mormon troops camped near the temple had been joined by additional men from other towns in the area. When his twelve-year-old cousin, John Lyman Smith, the son of John and Clarissa, saw Joseph, he ran to him and threw his arms around his legs. The boy's feet were bleeding. Seeing a shoemaker in the doorway of his shop, Joseph called out, "Let these men have some shoes." When the shoemaker said, "I have none," Joseph ordered, "Let them have boots then!" Speaking gently to his young cousin, Joseph said, "Have no fears, for you shall yet see Israel triumph and in peace."[36] Perhaps at about this same time, if not earlier, Joseph sent Abram Hodge to Carthage to assess the situation.[37]

The last of the three times Joseph said goodbye to Emma and their children that day, Edwin Rushton reportedly overheard the couple's exchange. Joseph asked Emma to train his children to follow in his footsteps. Emma replied, "Oh, Joseph, you're coming back!" As her eyes teared up, she staunchly insisted, "[Y]ou are coming back."[38] Leonora Cannon Taylor, John Taylor's wife, said that Joseph asked Emma to come with him. But she would not leave their children and said she had "chills and fever."[39] Joseph opened the garden gate and walked out to join the waiting men.

At 6:00 p.m. or a little later, the company rode by the Masonic Hall on their way out of town. Joseph shouted to men standing along the road,

---

33. Joseph Fielding, Journal, June 22, 1844, http://www.boap.org/LDS/Early-Saints/JFielding.html (June 10, 2013).

34. *History of the Church*, 6:554 (June 24, 1844).

35. Ibid., 554.

36. John Lyman Smith, "Journals of John Lyman Smith, Born November 17, 1832, Son of John Smith, a Cousin to the Prophet Joseph Smith."

37. *History of the Church*, 6:557 (June 24, 1844).

38. Edwin Rushton, "Bridge Builder and Faithful Pioneer," 3.

39. Leonora C. Taylor, Statement, n.d., qtd. in Newell and Avery, *Mormon Enigma*, 190.

"Boys, if I don't come back, take care of yourselves." When they got as far as Joseph's farm on the outskirts of town, he looked at the fields with their sprouting crops and commented, "If some of you had got such a farm and knew you would not see it any more, you would want to take a good look at it for the last time."

At that point, Hodge rode to Joseph to report what he had seen in Carthage. He told Hyrum to stay in Nauvoo: "they say they will kill you, if you go to Carthage."[40] Hyrum's resolve to stay with his brother remained unshaken.

By 9:00 p.m. Joseph and Hyrum and a group of men riding ahead of the main company reached Albert Fellows's house, four miles west of Carthage. They stopped for a half hour's rest.[41] A Captain Dunn and his mounted militia caught up with them. Escorted by Dunn's group, the party reached Carthage just after midnight and made their way to the Hamilton House, a hotel-tavern where Governor Ford was staying. As they rode past the public square, the local militia jeered: "Where is the damned prophet?" "[L]et us shoot the damned Mormons." "God damn you, old Joe, we've got you now." "Clear the way and let us have a view of Joe Smith, the prophet of God. He has seen the last of Nauvoo."[42]

In the center of town, scores of restless men created chaos that threatened to erupt in violence. The Carthage Greys brandished bayonets as if they were Bowie knives, throwing them into the air in arcs, then picking them up and whooping, cursing, and yelling.[43] Almost certainly they had been drinking, and now their target was finally in view. Working themselves into a frenzy, the men lost their individual moral judgment. Although any one of them might not have plotted the murders of the Latter-day Saint men in custody, as a group they experienced less inhibitions. This process of deindividuation explains how normal constraints on behavior become loosened in groups, which is what happened in Carthage.[44]

Disturbed by the troops, Ford stuck his head out a second-floor window and asked them to quiet down. "I know your great anxiety to see Mr. Smith, which is natural enough," he said, "but it is quite too late tonight for you to have the opportunity; but I assure you, gentlemen, you shall have that privilege tomorrow morning, as I will cause him to pass before the troops upon

40. *History of the Church*, 6:558 (June 24, 1844).

41. Ibid., 559.

42. Ibid., 559; hyphens replaced with letters.

43. Ibid., 559-60.

44. See Richard A. Berk, *Collective Behavior;* Bill Buford, *Among the Thugs;* Elias Canetti, *Crowds and Power;* and Clark McPhail, *The Myth of the Madding Crowd.*

the square, and I now wish you, with this assurance, quietly and peaceably to return to your quarters." Not long afterward the men settled down.[45] Also staying at the Hamilton were the Law brothers, the Higbee brothers, the Foster brothers, Augustine Spencer, Henry O. Norton, John A. Hicks, and others of their friends.

Early the next morning, Tuesday, June 25, the prisoners "voluntarily surrendered themselves to the constable, Mr. David Bettisworth, who held the writ against them." Ford pledged that the "Smiths and other persons should be protected from personal violence, and should have a fair and impartial trial," a point he repeatedly made to Joseph's attorneys, James W. Woods and Hugh T. Reid. While Joseph met with William G. Flood of Quincy, the U.S. Receiver of Public Moneys, at 8:00 a.m., Bettisworth formally arrested Joseph for "treason against the state of Illinois"–the treason being his declaration of martial law, which was exclusively the governor's prerogative. This second charge was a capital offense, and a similar writ had been issued against Hyrum.[46]

A half hour later, at 8:30 a.m., Ford ordered the troops to form a square, lining up in four rows, in the center of which his men placed an old table. He climbed up on the unsteady dias to address the troops for twenty or thirty minutes. According to the *History of the Church,* he roused them to "feelings of indignation against General Joseph and Hyrum Smith, which were already burning in their breast ..." He opined that Joseph and Hyrum were "guilty of all that they might have alleged against them, still they were in the hands of the law, which must have its course." He asked the troops to line up in two rows, then had Joseph and Hyrum walk in front of them, affording the good view he had promised.[47]

At about 9:15 a.m., Ford went back to the hotel. There, Joseph had his first consultation with Ford, during which Ford again reassured him that "he and his friends should be protected from violence."[48] Afterward, Ford escorted Joseph, Hyrum, and Willard Richards to the hotel room of Brigadier-General Miner R. Deming of the state militia, and then paraded the men outside in front of the Carthage Greys. Joseph was flanked by Deming on the right and Hyrum on his left. Richards, John Taylor, and W. W. Phelps followed behind. Giving the Smith brothers their full military titles

45. *History of the Church*, 6:560.
46. Ibid., 561-62 (June 25, 1844).
47. Ibid., 563.
48. Ibid.

("Generals of the Nauvoo Legion"), Ford introduced them to the troops about "twenty times along the line."[49] Ford walked a tightrope between exerting his authority and placating the group of armed men. However, from the record, he consistently insisted on procedures as fair as they could be under the unique circumstances.

Back in the hotel about 10:00 a.m., Joseph must have felt under siege. Rumors swirled into the hotel, first, that the Carthage Greys had "revolted," then that they had quieted, that the Laws, Fosters, Higbees, and their group were going to "plunder" Nauvoo. He asked Ford to send troops to guard the city. Although the rumor seemed improbable, Ford ordered a company of county militia to work with the Nauvoo police in keeping the peace. It is less certain why he also pledged to call out the Nauvoo Legion if necessary.[50] The second pledge was empty. Some of the Mormon guns and munitions had been deposited in the Masonic Hall and the rest taken away by Dunn's men. The Saints were essentially unarmed, unable to protect the city in any meaningful way.

That same day, Tuesday, June 25, Joseph found time to pen Emma a message: "Myself and Hyrum have been again arrested for treason because we called out the Nauvoo Legion, but when the truth comes out we have nothing to fear. We all feel calm and composed."[51] Considering the feelings of Ford, the Carthage Greys, and the troops who held Joseph in custody, this comment must have been a deliberate exaggeration to set a tone of masculine calm. "I think the Governor has and will succeed in enforcing the laws," he reassured Emma.[52] Joseph said that Ford planned to send troops to "Nauvoo to protect the citizens." He encouraged her to treat them with kindness, was generally optimistic about the results, and erroneously promised that "the prisoners, all that can, will be admitted to bail."[53] Joseph further described Ford as introducing him and Hyrum to the troops in "a very appropriate manner."[54] He immediately sent it by messenger; Emma received it later that night.

Ford, later criticized for selecting the Greys to guard the jail, justified his decision: "It has been said that this company had already been guilty of mutiny

49. Ibid., 564.

50. Ibid., 565.

51. Joseph Smith, Letter to Emma Smith, June 25, 1844, in *History of the Church*, 6:565 (June 25, 1844).

52. Ibid.

53. Joseph Smith, Letter to Emma Smith, June 25, 1844, in Jessee, *Personal Writings of Joseph Smith*, 620-21.

54. Joseph Smith, Letter to Emma Smith, June 25, 1844, in *History of the Church*, 6:565; see also Jessee, *Personal Writings of Joseph Smith*, 620.

and had been ordered to be arrested whilst in the encampment at Carthage; and that they and their officers were the deadly enemies of the prisoners." But in his mind, "it would have been difficult to find friends of the prisoners under my command unless I had called in the Mormons as a guard."[55] He had a point, but ten years earlier, when he had been the state attorney, he had already found the Greys difficult to govern and prone to violence.

The previous afternoon, the Carthage justice of the peace, Robert Smith, had heard the riot charge against Joseph, Hyrum, and thirteen others and ordered them all bound over for trial Tuesday. Smith was "Captain" Smith, head of the Carthage Greys and an avowed anti-Mormon.[56] Another of Joseph's enemies, Chauncey Higbee, made a motion to adjourn the proceedings, which would free the defendants but require that they "acknowledge their guilt." On their attorneys' advice, the Smiths "waived the examination of witnesses against them and entered into recognizances in the sum of five hundred dollars each" so that the case could be heard at the Circuit Court for Hancock County instead of before Justice Smith.[57] While all of the men could have gone free at this point, the Smith brothers could not. As Oaks and Hill point out, the second writ against the Smith brothers for treason for having declared martial law was still outstanding."[58]

At 5:00 p.m., Justice Smith adjourned the hearing and left the courthouse, returning more than an hour later without addressing the issue of bail on the treason writ, and before Joseph and Hyrum were placed under arrest for treason.[59] Bail for capital offenses could be established only by a circuit court judge. The nearest judge with jurisdiction over the case "was a day's ride away."[60] Instead, the defendants were ordered to jail until they could be released, or until June 29, when a hearing would be held on the treason writ.[61] The defendants returned to the Hamilton Hotel.

Joseph, feeling that Hyrum and he were detained illegally, was granted a meeting with Ford at 7:30 p.m. They talked briefly, then went to dinner without resolving the matter. At 8:00 p.m., Bettisworth appeared at the hotel with the order requiring them to be housed in the jail and a false

55. Ford, *History of Illinois . . .*, 2:195.

56. Oaks and Hill, *Carthage Conspiracy*, 18.

57. George T. M. Davis, *An Authentic Account of the Massacre of Joseph Smith*, 15; see also *History of the Church*, 6:567-68 (June 24-25, 1844).

58. Oaks and Hill, *Carthage Conspiracy*, 18.

59. *History of the Church*, 6:568.

60. Oaks and Hill, *Carthage Conspiracy*, 18.

61. *History of the Church*, 6:590-91 (June 26, 1844). See also Oaks and Hill, *Carthage Conspiracy*, 18-19; Oaks, "The Suppression of the *Nauvoo Expositor*," 866-67.

mittimus, issued the day before, on the treason charge, which required him to put them in jail until a hearing with material witnesses could be held.[62] Joseph protested "against such bare-faced, illegal and tyrannical proceedings," but Bettisworth insisted and Ford refused to interfere.[63]

A crowd gathered outside, as Dunn and twenty men escorted the prisoners to the jail, a block northwest of the public square. A sturdy, two-story stone building facing Walnut Street, it was setback eighteen feet from the street and measured thirty-four feet long by twenty-eight feet wide. The south facing facade featured two windows to the right of the door and three windows on the upper level, but a single window on each level to the sides. The door led to a small entranceway, big enough for a staircase to the second floor and a doorway to the room to the right on the main floor. The jailer, George W. Stigall, and his wife lived on the ground floor where they prepared food for the prisoners in their kitchen. Their sitting room on the southeast end of the second story was sometimes used for prisoners as well, described in the *History of the Church* as a place "where prisoners and their friends had amusing conversations on various interesting subjects which engaged them till late."[64] The prisoners would spend some of their time in the second-story jail cell, a room that had mattresses stuffed with straw, iron bolts on the walls for prisoners that needed to be restrained with chains. Stigall could also move them to the spartan ground-floor cell for security.[65]

Although only Joseph and Hyrum were charged with treason, the other eight men accompanied their leaders: Willard Richards, John Taylor, John P. Greene, Stephen Markham, Dan Jones, John S. Fullmer, Dr. Southwick, and Lorenzo D. Wasson to the jail. Jones and Markham flanked Joseph, both holding canes that were probably intended for defense.[66] Stigall initially put them in the criminals' cell but then moved them to the debtors' apartment on the second floor.

Once again, in the evening, the prisoners and their friends talked for hours. Except for Joseph and Hyrum, the rest could have returned to Nauvoo–Wasson, Southwick, Greene, and Fullmer eventually did, while Richards and Taylor stayed. The men prayed together, "which made Carthage prison into the gate of heaven for a while," as Joseph's narrative put it, then slept

62. *History of the Church*, 6:569-70.
63. Ibid., 570.
64. Ibid., 574 (June 25, 1844).
65. Samuel W. Richards, Journal, June 25, 1844.
66. *History of the Church*, 6:574 (June 25, 1844).

together on the floor that night. Exhausted, they slept from 11:30 p.m. until 6:00 a.m. Wednesday morning, June 26.[67]

The jailer served breakfast to the men at 7:00 a.m., then they returned to the debtors' chamber. Joseph chatted with Stigall who reportedly told them that, the week before, a mob had plotted an "attack on Nauvoo, and they expected about 9,000 persons, but only about 200 came." At 8:00 a.m., Joseph penned a note to Ford to request a meeting, and although Ford had not intervened on Tuesday, Joseph made another appeal: "We desire the time may be hastened when all things shall be made right, and we relieved from this imprisonment."[68] Within a half-hour, Ford himself replied that he "was taken by surprise last evening, and was very sorry." He told them he "was afraid we would think he had forfeited his word about having an interview, that the wrath of his people was about to turn on the head of … the mob."[69] Ford arrived at the jail about an hour later.[70]

The two leaders faced off over issues that seemed unbridgeable–varied interpretations of the destruction of the *Expositor*, Ford's responsibility to protect Joseph and the other prisoners, and Ford's legal ability to intervene in the crisis at all. One last time, Joseph framed his plight in the larger prophet-narrative of persecution. His intentions were "pacific," Joseph stressed, despite the fact that his people had endured "every conceivable indignity and lawless outrage … since [their] settlement" in Illinois. At the same time, he positioned the destruction of the press in his understanding of the "principles of equal rights that have been instilled into our bosoms from our cradles, as American citizens." It was this, he said, that "forbid[s] us submitting to every foul indignity, and succumbing and pandering to wretches so infamous as these. But, independent of this, the course that we pursued we considered to be strictly legal …"[71]

Obviously dissatisfied because Ford did not see the situation from his perspective, Joseph dictated to Willard Richards a brief letter for Jesse B. Thomas, the judge who had originally heard the complaints on Sunday, June 16. He begged Thomas, who was based in Springfield, to go at once to Nauvoo, take up residence in Joseph's home, and prepare the papers necessary "to bring us on Hab[e]us. Our witnesses are all at Nauvoo–there you can easily

67. Ibid., 574.

68. Joseph Smith, Letter to Thomas Ford, June 26, 1844, in Jessee, *Personal Writings of Joseph Smith*, 625.

69. *History of the Church*, 6:576 (June 26, 1844); Davis, *An Authentic Account*, 15.

70. Ibid., 575-76.

71. Ibid., 580-81.

investigate the whole matter."[72] Joseph sent the letter by messenger. There is no record that Thomas responded.

Coincidentally, a forty-man unit of the McDonough County militia arrived in Nauvoo that same Wednesday morning. Commander James Singleton announced: "I see no cause of having a military force stationed here unless it is for the apprehension of your fears that a mob will come against you. … I was somewhat excited when I left home but am not now, for I see harmony and peace is with you, and I don't think the mob will make an attack upon you."[73] He also stated that within a few hours Ford himself would arrive. Emma made and served both breakfast and dinner to the McDonough militia.

The editor of the *Alton Telegraph,* George T. M. Davis, stayed in Carthage, knowing that he was witness to a great story. "No one could close his ears against the murmurs that ran throughout the entire community. Little squads could be seen at the taverns, at the tents of the soldiers, and in every part of town … expressions falling from the lips of numbers, there assembled, could leave no other impression upon any sane mind, than that they were determined the Smiths should not escape summary punishment."[74]

During the day, Joseph and the men prayed, talked, and even sang.[75] At 4:00 p.m., the constable and a group of Carthage Greys "compelled the jailor, against his will and conviction of duty, to deliver Joseph and Hyrum to the Constable" who escorted them to the court room for a hearing on the treason charge. Joseph put his hat on before leaving, then "locked arms" with Hyrum and Willard Richards for security. They were followed not far behind by John Taylor, Dan Jones, Stephen Markham, and John Fullmer. After Robert Smith called the court to order, attorneys Reid and Woods asked for subpoenas for witnesses for their clients and proposed that the examination begin as soon as the witnesses arrived. Forty-five minutes later, Woods suggested that the court adjourn until noon the next day. At 5:30 p.m., the men returned to jail.[76] That night, Joseph's uncle John Smith visited. Joseph later read a letter from William Clayton reporting on conditions in Nauvoo: "many threats keep coming that the mob are determined to attack the city

72. Joseph Smith, Letter to Jesse B. Thomas, June 26, 1844, in Jessee, *Personal Writings of Joseph Smith*, 628.

73. Samuel W. Richards, Journal, June 26, 1844; verb tenses changed for greater readability.

74. Davis, *An Authentic Account*, 17.

75. *History of the Church*, 6:593 (June 26, 1844).

76. Ibid., 595-97.

in your absence, but we have no fears."[77] About 6:20 p.m., Joseph began to dictate a letter to Emma but left it unfinished as the slow darkness of late June descended.[78]

By this time, only Richards, Markham, Fullmer, and Jones remained with Joseph and Hyrum. The others had left to deliver messages for Joseph or to return to their families in Nauvoo. The men talked by candlelight in the front room after 9:15 p.m. Hyrum read and interpreted passages from the Book of Mormon, lingering on scriptures that seemed to address their situation. Seizing what might be one of his last opportunities to preach, Joseph bore witness of the "authenticity of the Book of Mormon, the restoration of the Gospel, the administration of angels, and that the kingdom of God was again established upon the earth." He interpreted his incarceration as persecution rather than as a criminal violation.[79]

As they had the night before, the two brothers lay down on the "sole" bedstead in the room; the other men made do with blankets spread out on the floor. Richards continued to write until the candle flickered out. When a gunshot later rang, startling Joseph awake, he joined the men on the floor, lying between Jones and Fullmer. Fullmer, also awake, and Joseph whispered. Reportedly, Joseph admitted that he had "presentiments that he had to die," but also that he "would like to see [his] family again." After Fullmer had slipped back to sleep and Richards had carefully joined the men on the floor, Welsh convert and ship captain Jones looked at Joseph, who whispered, "Are you afraid to die?" Jones responded, "Has that time come, think you? Engaged in such a cause I do not think that death would have many terrors." "You will yet see Wales," Joseph promised, and "fulfill the mission appointed you before you died."[80] The next morning, Joseph instructed Fullmer to return to Nauvoo.[81]

In addition to the gunshot, the troops had racketed about during the night. The next morning, June 27, Joseph sent Jones to Ford at 5:30 a.m. for information about the shot. En route, Jones overheard a man announce to a group: "Our troops will be discharged this morning in obedience to the orders, and for a sham we will leave the town; but when the Governor and the McDonough troops have left for Nauvoo this afternoon, we will return and

77. Ibid., 599.
78. Jessee, *Personal Writings of Joseph Smith*, 629.
79. *History of the Church*, 6:600.
80. Ibid., 601.
81. Clara Fullmer Bullock, *The John Solomon Fullmer Story*, 28.

kill those men, if we have to tear the jail down."[82] Alarmed, Jones reported this exchange to Ford; but Ford dismissed his concern: "[T]he people are not that cruel."

When Jones returned to the jail, a guard prevented him from entering. Instead, he walked back to the Hamilton Hotel. Ford was in the front yard, talking with the McDonough troops who would accompany him to Nauvoo. Jones asked him for passes permitting Joseph's friends to move safely "in and out of the prison." Ford refused to give them all passes but asked his secretary to issue one for Willard Richards, Joseph's scribe. Chauncey Higbee came up to the men and reportedly "threatened" Jones: "We are determined to kill Joe and Hyrum, and you had better go away to save yourself."[83]

The jailer's wife served breakfast at about 7:00 a.m.[84] A little more than an hour later, Joseph returned to his letter to Emma. Dictating to Richards, Joseph said that Ford would not be coming to Nauvoo with troops. She should tell the people to stay at home. He urged calm both among the people and the members of the Nauvoo Legion, though he simultaneously affirmed their duty to protect their lives and those of their families if necessary. "I am very much resigned to my lot, knowing I am justified and have done the best that could be done give my love to the children and all my Friends ... who inquire after me as for treason I know that I have not committed any and they cannot prove one apearance of any thing of the kind. So you need not have any fears that any harm can happen to us on that score. may God bless you all. Amen." A little later, he added the postscript that Ford had disbanded his troops but established a guard to protect the prisoners and keep the peace. Ford was once again planning to go to Nauvoo. "This is right as I suppose." He noted the time of this postscript: "20 mi[nutes] to 10."[85] Ford indeed disbanded the Carthage Greys "with the exception of three companies, two of which were retained as a guard to the jail." Dunn accompanied Ford along with sixty mounted soldiers to Nauvoo.[86] The Greys on duty at the jail were commanded by Robert Smith. Ford was confident the Greys would demonstrate "loyalty and integrity."[87] Some members of a group of 200 soldiers in a regiment from

82. *History of the Church*, 6:602-603.

83. Ibid., 604.

84. Ibid.

85. Joseph Smith, Letter to Emma Smith, June 27, 1844, in Jessee, *Personal Writings of Joseph Smith*, 630.

86. *History of the Church*, 7:17; John W. Williams, testimony, in "Minutes of Trial of Members of Mob Who Helped Kill Joseph Smith, the Prophet," 82, qtd. in Oaks and Hill, *Carthage Conspiracy*, 19.

87. *History of the Church*, 7:17-20.

Warsaw refused to turn back and continued toward Carthage.[88] It was a warning about Ford's overconfidence in the militia's "honor."

Thirty-one-year-old Latter-day Saint Cyrus H. Wheelock, who was supposed to accompany Ford to Nauvoo, warned him: "sir, I am about to leave for Nauvoo, and I fear for those men; they are safe as regards the law, but they are not safe from the hands of traitors, and midnight assassins who thirst for their blood and have determined to spill it; and under these circumstances I leave with a heavy heart." Ford responded: "I was never in such a dilemma in my life; but your friends shall be protected, and have a fair trial by the law; in this *pledge* I am not alone; I have obtained the *pledge* of the whole of the army to sustain me."[89]

Before they left, Wheelock entered the jail sometime between 9:20 a.m. and 10:00 a.m., wearing an overcoat against the rain. Concealed in its pocket was an Allen's Patent Pepperbox pistol with six cartridges.[90] He gave the revolver to Joseph who slipped it into his pocket. John S. Fullmer had also smuggled in a single-barrel pistol that he gave to Hyrum. Hyrum said that he hated "to use such things or to see them used." Joseph agreed but said that they might have "to defend ourselves." The men deluged Wheelock with verbal and written messages to take to Nauvoo. Joseph told him to keep their friends and families "calm and quiet"[91] and gave him a list of witnesses to call for the trial that was planned for Saturday, June 29.[92] Joseph asked his lawyer, James Woods, to represent him and to help usher his people through this impossible time: "They have determined to murder me, and I never expect to see you again. I have no doubt you have done the best you could for me."[93]

The remaining Greys pitched their tents in the southwest corner of the square in front of the hotel and "took up their quarters in the court house." The jail where Joseph, Hyrum, Taylor, and Richards were imprisoned was 500 yards to the west.[94] Detachments of six to eight men from the Greys guarded the jail, with each detachment being relieved every several hours. En route to Nauvoo, Ford was told the jail could be stormed, which he

88. Ibid., 6:606 (June 27, 1844); Oaks and Hill, *Carthage Conspiracy*, 19.

89. *History of the Church*, 6:607.

90. Wicks and Foister, *Junius and Joseph*, 169.

91. *History of the Church*, 6:608.

92. Ibid., 609.

93. James W. Woods, Memoirs, qtd. in Edward H. Stiles, *Recollections and Sketches of Notable Lawyers and Public Men of Early Iowa*, 269-70.

94. Ibid., 269. See also Samuel Otho Williams, Letter to John Prickett, July 10, 1844: "A guard of six men was placed at the jail with a sergeant to command it which was relieved about every three hours."

knew would expose "my life and the life of my companions to the sudden vengeance of the Mormons …"[95] Regardless, and hoping to avoid "mere possibilities," Ford sent Robert Smith a "special order" to do his duty "to guard the jail strictly, and at the peril of his life, until my return."[96]

Some of the soldiers from Warsaw had chosen to stay, and many anticipated a violent confrontation. Two captains, Davis and Grover, each chose ten soldiers for a select unit who "were marched a short distance to one side."[97] Their leaders told them only as much as they needed to know. Ford sent orders to Colonel Levi Williams to disband his troops who were camped southeast of Warsaw at Golden's Point.[98] Williams read the order aloud. Now they were once again part of the public citizenry, and no longer under military command.[99]

While some of the troops returned to Warsaw, others were hungry for violence. A number of militia men wanted to give up on Ford and return to Carthage, saying that they "must either take the matter into [their] hands, and avenge [their] wrongs, or [their] most implacable enemies [the Smiths] would escape."[100] Davis, Grover, and another officer called for volunteers to return to Carthage. Eighty-four responded affirmatively.[101]

When Ford and his party reached Nauvoo, Emma welcomed them. She provided Ford a room in the Mansion House where he could clean up. Orrin Porter Rockwell hovered close to the governor and his entourage. Twelve years later, Rockwell alleged that he overheard Ford's aide say, "The deed is done before this time."[102] Ford claimed that he did not know about a specific plot to kill the prophet, that he had disbanded the militia in an effort to keep the peace, and that he had gone to Nauvoo with his military unit because he had agreed to do so.[103]

Although Nauvoo's militia had previously been ordered to turn over its state-issued arms, Ford wanted to prevent violence and bring some measure

95. Ford, qtd. in *History of the Church*, 7:22.

96. Ibid., 23.

97. William M. Daniels and Lyman O. Littlefield, *Correct Account of the Murder of the Generals Joseph and Hyrum Smith …*, 9; see also Davis, *An Authentic Account*, 28.

98. *History of the Church*, 7:163 (July 4, 1844).

99. William M. Daniels, Affidavit, July 4, 1844, in *History of the Church*, 7:163. According to Illinois law, the men could not be arrested as they traveled to their homes; Wicks and Foister, *Junius and Joseph*, 171.

100. Davis, *An Authentic Account*, 28.

101. Daniels, *A Correct Account*, 8; Benjamin Brackenberry, Oct. 1844, Grand Jury Testimony, Community of Christ Library-Archives.

102. Harold Schindler, *Orrin Porter Rockwell*, 134-35.

103. "Salt Lake City, April 1856," *Millennial Star* 24 (1862): 409.

of control over the Latter-day Saints. While his men collected the arms, Ford called the Mormons to assemble at the same platform where Joseph had, nine days earlier, brandished his sword at the sky. As many as 5,000 citizens heard Ford speak.[104] The governor began by summarizing the accusations against Joseph and the other defendants. He reminded them that there was considerable "hatred and prejudice" towards them, and that "if any vengeance should be attempted openly or secretly against the persons or property of the citizens who had taken part against their leaders, that … thousands would assemble for the total destruction of their city and the extermination of their people." Ford was stern: "You ought to be praying Saints, not military Saints. Depend upon it, a little more misbehavior on the part of the citizens, and the torch which is now already lighted, will be applied; the city may be reduced to ashes, and extermination would inevitably follow." Ford declined Emma's invitation to stay overnight and rode away at 6:30 p.m., his escorts "giving all the passes, guards, cuts and thrusts, taking up the entire width of the street, and making as imposing a show as they could," perhaps to "intimidate the people."[105]

Back in Carthage, Stephen Markham lingered with Joseph, sitting next to him on the bed. "I wish you would tell me how this fuss is going to come out as you have at other times before hand," Markham asked. Joseph responded, "Brother Markham, the Lord placed me to govern this kingdom on the earth but the people has taken away from me the [reins] of government." Joseph talked about the long night he had spent across the river, allegedly admitting that he had given in to those who had criticized him for leaving Nauvoo. "[T]he whisperings of the spirit left me," he reportedly stated, in despair, "& I am now no more [than] a common man."[106]

When Willard Richards began to feel nauseous, Joseph asked Markham to leave the jail and find Richards something to "settle his stomach."[107] Markham borrowed a pipe from Sheriff Jacob Backenstos, then walked across the street to purchase tobacco. A man spotted him and "threw out considerable threats against the Mormons" coupled with personal insults to Markham.[108] Glancing out the front window of the Hamilton Hotel, Artois Hamilton rushed to help. He pulled Markham aside and warned him to get

104. *History of the Church*, 7:23.
105. Ibid., 6:623-24 (June 27, 1844).
106. Stephen Markham, Letter to Wilford Woodruff, June 20, 1856.
107. *History of the Church*, 6:614 (June 27, 1844).
108. Markham, Letter to Woodruff, June 20, 1856.

out of town. "You will only get killed if you remain," he insisted. He offered to bring Markham his horse. Markham refused. Then some of the Greys surrounded him, forcing him on a horse and running him out of town "at the point of a bayonet."[109] Markham reached Nauvoo during Ford's speech. He reported on the tension in Carthage and on his own treatment. "That is nothing to what you have done here," Ford reportedly said.[110]

With the departure of Ford's party, Joseph, Hyrum, and their companions settled down to another muggy day. As the minutes dragged, the brothers bore testimony to the work of the Church, the Book of Mormon, and the missionary work that had brought the gospel to Saints from across the world. Joseph found parallels between his own experience and that of Jesus. According to Cyrus Wheelock's later account, Joseph said:

> Our lives have already become jeopardized by revealing the wicked and bloodthirsty purposes of our enemies; and for the future we must cease to do so. All we have said about them is truth, but it is not always wise to relate all the truth. Even Jesus, the Son of God had to refrain from doing so, and had to restrain His feelings many times for the safety of Himself and His followers, and had to conceal the righteous purposes of His heart in relation to many things pertaining to His Father's kingdom. ... So it is with the Church of Jesus Christ of Latter-day Saints; we have the revelation of Jesus, and the knowledge within us is sufficient to organize a righteous government upon the earth, and to give universal peace to all mankind, if they would receive it, but we lack the physical strength, as did our Savior when a child, to defend our principles, and we have of necessity to be afflicted, persecuted and smitten, and to bear it patiently until Jacob is of age, then he will take care of himself.[111]

This passage reveals Joseph's conviction that he was a prophet, the possessor of privileged knowledge and truth. His words are more a dialogue between his self-knowledge, his understanding of the role of Jesus and God, and the Saints' identity as chosen people. As players in Joseph's prophet-narrative, the other men in the room accompanied Joseph to this climatic moment, and helped to explain what it meant.

At noon, Joseph wrote Orville H. Browning of Quincy, asking him to serve as his attorney at Saturday's hearing. It was a last-ditch effort to seek

109. *History of the Church*, 6:614.

110. Markham, Letter to Woodruff, June 20, 1856.

111. Cyrus Wheelock, London, England, Letter to George A. Smith, Salt Lake City, Dec. 29, 1854, LDS Church History Library.

justice with the help of a friend and it again reveals Joseph's view of reality as shaped by persecution.[112] Dan Jones left on horseback with the letter, while the other men ate lunch.[113]

Throughout the day, a storm sputtered outside, a natural backdrop for the tempest brewing in Carthage. Taylor sang in his resonant tenor voice "A Poor Wayfaring Man of Grief," which he had learned on his mission to England in 1840. At Joseph's request, he sang it again while Joseph, Hyrum, and Richards listened closely:

> A poor wayfaring man of grief
> Had often cross'd me on my way,
> Who sued so humbly for relief,
> That I could never answer "Nay."
> I had not power to ask his name,
> Whither he went, or whence he came,
> Yet there was something in his eye
> That won my love, I knew not why. ...[114]

At 4:00 p.m., the guard changed to a squad of eight, seven soldiers and their sergeant. The remainder of the Greys were still camped about a quarter of a mile away in the town square. An hour later, Stigall urged the men to move into the cell rather than the room upstairs for greater security. Joseph said they would after supper, then asked Willard Richards, "If we go into the cell, will you go with us?" He answered, "Brother Joseph you did not ask me to cross the river with you–you did not ask me to come to Carthage–you did not ask me to come to jail with you–and do you think I would forsake you now? But I will tell you what I will do; if you are condemned to be hung for treason, I will be hung in your stead, and you shall go free." Joseph responded, "You cannot." Richards insisted simply, "I will."[115]

At 5:00 p.m., a teenage son of Artois Hamilton, posted at the top of the Carthage courthouse as an outlook, spotted a group of men marching in from the west. He reported to Captain Smith, who told him to keep the news to himself and to let him know if they proceeded toward the jail. The

112. Joseph Smith, Letter to Orville H. Browning, June 27, 1844, in Jessee, *Personal Writings of Joseph Smith*, 635.

113. *History of the Church*, 6:614 (June 27, 1844).

114. Ibid., 614-15. Originally titled "The Stranger and His Friend," the seven-stanza work was written by James Montgomery in 1826 as a poem.

115. *History of the Church*, 6:615-16.

instructions to tell no one were useless.[116] The group of 150-200 men soon arrived at the jail.[117] Many of the men had darkened their faces to disguise their identities.[118]

Captain Smith issued orders to the men posted at the square to line up and prepare their arms. Some bystanders ran toward the jail, but the Greys marched slowly in response to Smith's command. Trained in parades on their town green, they followed their flag forward, holding their guns diagonally across their bodies. The eight-man squad of Greys at the jail "elevated their firelocks, and boisterously threatening the mob discharged their firearms over their heads" into the air.[119] Upstairs, Richards looked through the curtains and saw some 200 men gathered in the yard below. Shoving the guards aside, the Warsaw militiamen stormed up the stairs and fired into the door.

Joseph and Hyrum drew their pistols and struggled to hold the door, which had no lock or latch. Some fired through the door. One of the first bullets hit Hyrum on the left side of his nose, throwing him to the floor. Another bullet caught him in the throat under his chin. Opening the door just wide enough to fire, Joseph emptied his pistol into the men. A bullet fired from outside caught Taylor in the thigh. A third bullet hit his hip just as he rolled under the bed. Lying in a pool of blood, he lost consciousness. The mob forced the door open, pushing Richards behind it. As Joseph moved toward the window, bullets riveted his body. Reportedly shouting, "O Lord my God!," the first four words of a Masonic cry of distress, and raising his arms in a gesture similar to a Masonic distress signal, he tottered on the wide window sill, then fell to the ground.[120] A member of the mob propped Joseph's body against the base of the well. In a final act of degradation, mobbers fired repeatedly into Joseph's lifeless body.[121] Then someone yelled, "The Mormons are coming!" The mob quickly dispersed. According to researchers Joseph Lyon and David Lyon, Joseph was "shot through the right upper thigh, right lower abdomen, right breast, right shoulder near the neck, and under his heart–with a likely exit wound behind the right clavicle. The wound in his right hip and shoulder may have been exit wounds."[122]

116. Oakes and Hill, *Carthage Conspiracy*, 20.

117. *History of the Church*, 6:629 (June 29, 1844).

118. Ibid.

119. Ibid., 617 (June 27, 1844).

120. Ibid., 620.

121. John D. Lee, *Mormonism Unveiled*, 153; D. Michael Quinn, *The Mormon Hierarchy: Origins of Power*, 646; and Glen M. Leonard, *Nauvoo*, 397, all interpret Joseph's last remarks as a "Masonic signal of distress."

122. Joseph L. Lyon and David W. Lyon, "Physical Evidence at Carthage Jail and What It

Richards, who had received only a minor cut to his earlobe, dragged Taylor into the cell next door and covered him with straw. "If your wounds are not fatal," he told Taylor, "I want you to live to tell the story."[123] Samuel Smith, Joseph's younger brother, and Richards carried Hyrum's and Joseph's bodies to the Hamilton Hotel, then came back for Taylor.[124]

As events played out in the jail, Ford left a small group of men to maintain an official presence in Nauvoo and headed for Carthage at about 6:30 p.m. About two miles out of Nauvoo, they met two Mormons who gave them the news that the Smiths "had been assassinated in jail, about five or six o'clock that day. The intelligence seemed to strike every one with a kind of dumbness." According to Ford, "As to myself it was perfectly astounding, and I anticipated the very worst consequences from it."[125] Ford took the two men with his party back to Carthage, thus delaying news of the murders from reaching Nauvoo. He arrived at midnight and immediately sent men to Warsaw, carrying word to the citizens there about the murders and warning them of possible retribution.[126]

In Nauvoo, Emma managed the production of another meal for a large guest list at the Mansion House. Her children needed to be feed as did the guests staying in the hotel. More difficult to host were the soldiers Ford had left to watch the Mormons.

Orrin Porter Rockwell decided he could wait no longer, saddled a horse, and rode toward Carthage. There he met Lorenzo Wasson and George D. Grant. Wasson told Rockwell that Joseph was dead. Rockwell galloped back to Nauvoo, screaming into the night streets a dreadful lament, "Joseph is killed–they have killed him! Goddam them! They have killed him!"[127]

Agnes Coolbrith Smith had put her two young daughters to sleep, then gone to bed herself. Lucy Walker had shared Agnes's home for a couple of years by that time. Tense and anxious, they prayed for Joseph's safety. But not long after Agnes had dozed off, a neighbor knocked at their door, crying, "Joseph and Hyrum have been murdered." Shocked, the two widows "returned to our chamber and on our bended Knees poured out the

Reveals about the Assassination of Joseph and Hyrum Smith," 41.

123. *History of the Church*, 6:621 (June 27, 1844).

124. Ibid., 624-25.

125. Ibid., 7:24-25.

126. Ibid.

127. Porter Rockwell, qtd. in Anson Call, "Life and Record," 27, Utah State Historical Society Library, Salt Lake City; Wandle Mace, "The Journal of Wandle Mace," typescript, LDS Church History Library; www.boap.org/LDS/Early-Saints/Wmace.html (Dec. 8, 2008).

Anguish of our Souls to that God who holds the destinies of his children in his own hands."[128]

Sweeping across town like a thunderstorm, grief engulfed the Saints, biting especially hard at the hearts of Joseph's wives. The private sorrow they shared meant that they could only lament him as a prophet, not as a husband. According to an account written after her own death, Eliza R. Snow

> was prostrated with grief, and besought the Lord with all the fervency of her soul to permit her to follow the Prophet at once, and not leave her in so dark and wicked a world. … she did not and could not cease that prayer of her heart until the Prophet came to her [in spirit] and told her that she must not continue to supplicate the Lord in that way … Joseph told her that his work upon earth was completed as far as the mortal tabernacle was concerned, but hers was not; the Lord desired her, and so did her husband, to live many years, and … turn her thoughts away from her own loneliness, and seek to console her people in their bereavement and sorrow.[129]

Willard Richards wrote a hasty announcement to the people of Nauvoo from the Hamilton Hotel that both John Taylor and he signed: "CARTHAGE JAIL, 8:05 o'clock, P.M., June 27th, 1844 Joseph and Hyrum are dead. Taylor wounded, not very badly. I am well. Our guard was forced, as we believe, by a band of Missourians from 100 to 200. The job was done in an instant, and the party fled towards Nauvoo instantly. This is as I believe it. The citizens here are afraid of the Mormons attacking them. I promise them no!"[130] The statement was given to two men described as "mobocrats" in the *History of the Church,* who feared that the Mormons would "kill them" and instead took it to Arza Adams, "who was sick with the ague and fever," lying prostrate at a farm two-and-a-half miles north of Carthage. He struggled out of bed after midnight and arrived at Nauvoo at sunrise. The news had already arrived, but Ford attributed the "good conduct of the Mormons" to "the influence of this letter."[131]

In Carthage, Ford asked Richards to instruct the Mormons to stay in Nauvoo. Richards also penned a letter to Emma and Major-General Jonathan Dunham, telling them that the citizens should "stay at home, and be prepared for an attack from Missouri mobbers." With a touch of irony, he

---

128. Lucy Walker Kimball, "A Brief Biographical Sketch," 22.
129. "Eliza R. Snow," in Andrew Jenson, *LDS Biographical Encyclopedia,* 1:695.
130. *History of the Church,* 6:621-22 (June 27, 1844).
131. Ibid., 7:28.

added, the "people of the county … fear the Mormons will come out and take vengeance." He had given his word that they would not.[132] The letter reached Emma Friday morning long after daybreak. She asked the Saints to "remain quiet and peaceable."[133]

Nauvoo seethed with anxiety. Some wanted to attack Carthage; others took the more moderate position of maintaining a defensive perimeter around Nauvoo. Many others, terrified, wanted to flee. Adding to the confusion was uncertainty about who was authorized to act as authority now seemed to be distributed somewhat among the city council, the Quorum of the Twelve, and Nauvoo High Council.[134]

Artois Hamilton, with the aid of his sons, quickly constructed simple pine caskets. The two funeral wagons carrying the caskets and shaded with green boughs left Carthage at 8:00 a.m. on Friday, the 28th. Traveling through the countryside, they reached Nauvoo about noon. The Nauvoo Brass Band led a somber cortege, while an honor guard of twelve men marked time next to the wagons. Bystanders wept; some struggled with rage. Jacob Gibson remembered: "[t]he procession marched in solemn file to the mansion [house] where, oh terrible to relate, the families met them, but I can not describe the scene, no, no, no."[135] Helen Mar Kimball watched from the door of her parents' house. Thirty-seven-years later, she bitterly recalled having heard Ford pledge "his honor and faith of the State that *they should be protected.*" In her mind, "it was the popularity of Joseph as candidate for the Presidency, and the power and influence that the 'Mormon' people were gaining, that created a feeling of fear among the apostates and corrupt politicians, and a deeper hatred took possession of their hearts, similar to that which was felt by the Jews towards Jesus Christ, and like them they were

132. John Taylor and Willard Richards, Letter to the Saints, June 27, 1844, in ibid., 6:624-25.

133. *History of the Church*, 6:624-25. *Western Sun and General Advertiser* (Vincennes, Indiana), July 13, 1844, reports the proclamation, qtd. in Newell and Avery, *Mormon Enigma*, 196.

134. Jacob Gibson remembered the poignant scene once word reached Nauvoo that Joseph and Hyrum were dead:

> After breakfast [on Friday, June 28] I met with some thousand others on the public stand in the Temple Block, to hear the awful news read, by W. W. Phelps and confirmed. The first murmurs, were revenge from almost every quarter, but in a moment the line was turned and the speaker said, "Be still and know that God reigneth, be composed and return to your homes," which was done amidst many a heavy heart, at the thoughts of being thus betrayed, having the servants of God murdered or crucified, while we felt sufficient strength to protect our selves and them. But all was quiet, all was deep mourning, lamentation and sorrow ("The Book of the Generations of Jacob Gibson 1849-1881," 8).

135. Ibid.

determined by the Jews towards Jesus Christ, and like them they were determined to put an end to his earthly career."[136]

Allen Joseph Stout recalled, "I there and then resolved in my mind that I would never let an opportunity slip unimproved of avenging their blood. … I knew not how to contain myself, and when I see one of the men who persuaded them to give up to be tried, I feel like cutting their throats yet."[137] The caskets were carried into the Mansion House and "the doors were closed immediately."[138]

William Marks and the brothers of Joseph's plural sister-wives Zina Jacobs and Presendia Buell, Dimick and William Huntington, washed the bodies, then dressed them "with fine plain drawers and shirt, white neckerchiefs, white cotton stockings and white shrouds." When the bodies were thought to be sufficiently presentable, the women and children came in. Still, the condition of the corpses must have been terrible. Emma, who was pregnant, nearly fainted. Dimick supported her. She threw herself on Joseph, kissing him and begging him to speak to her again.[139] For those who loved Joseph, the pain was inexpressible. Weeping filled the air. "Joseph, Joseph," one observer recalled Emma's disbelieving words, "are you dead? Have the assassins shot you?" "[G]rief that words cannot embody seemed to overwhelm the whole group."[140]

Joseph III remembered his mother's broken heart: "Oh, Joseph, Joseph! My husband, my husband! Have they taken you from me at last!"[141] Lucy Mack Smith had prepared herself for the ordeal but cried out at the sight of the bodies, asking why God had so forsaken her family.

The next day, Saturday, Joseph's and Hyrum's bodies were placed in finished coffins lined with soft white cambric, black velvet, and held together with brass nails.[142] Squares of glass set in the lids allowed the Saints to see what remained of the murdered brothers' faces. Beginning at 8:00 a.m., a train of Saints entered the mansion through the west entrance, filed through the dining room where the bodies lay in state, and exited to the north. Joseph Fielding's reaction to the sight of the bodies was unmitigated horror. "I had

136. Helen Mar Whitney, "Scenes and Incidents in Nauvoo," *Woman's Exponent* 11, no. 15 (Jan. 1, 1883): 114.

137. Wayne Stout, ed., "Journal Allen Joseph Stout, 1818-1848," 19, typescript, Lee Library; Wayne Stout, "Allen Joseph Stout: A Great Champion of Mormonism," not paginated.

138. *History of the Church*, 6:626 (June 28, 1844).

139. Ibid., 627.

140. B. W. Richmond, "The Prophet's Death!" *Deseret News*, Nov. 27, 1875.

141. Joseph Smith III, qtd. in Roger D. Launius, *Joseph Smith III*, 21.

142. *History of the Church*, 6:627 (June 29, 1844).

often read of the martyrs of old, but now here I saw two of the greatest of men who sealed the truth which they had held and taught with their blood. Is this an earnest of what has to take place in this Last Dispensation? Is the blood of the sheep again to be shed like that of the shepherd as in former days?"[143]

Although many of Joseph's wives had already left Nauvoo for other households, the events in Nauvoo that night had implications for their futures. Not all of them recorded how they felt. But Eliza R. Snow recalled, "To look upon the noble, lifeless forms … was a sight that might well appal the heart of a true American citizen; but what it was for loving wives and children, the loyal heart may feel."[144] Thus, she implicitly included herself in the group of most intimate mourners. Oblivious to the reaction of many women who filed past the bodies, Joseph III later wrote, "It is a source of gratification to me now to remember that no other women bowed beside the bodies of these brothers … as wives to mourn and exhibit their grief … save my mother at my father's side and Aunt Mary at the side of my Uncle Hyrum. The scene was sacred to their grief and theirs alone."[145]

Struggling to come to terms with the brutal crisis, many Saints marked the dark day with letters to loved ones, passages in their diaries, or mournful poetry or prose. Nathan Calhoun Cheney's letter to Charles Beebe, his wife Eliza Ann Beebe's father, written from Nauvoo on the 28th, predicted that, by the time his relatives received his letter, "you will [also] hear that our enemies are trying to take our lives." It seemed impossible to view the prophet's death without seeing themselves as the next victims of persecution. "This gang of murderers," he wrote, "sought to destroy the Church of Latter-day Saints in every way they could. They sought to have our charter taken away from us, they bought a printing press and commenced to print. They printed all the lies the devil could think of and some that he could not think of." On Saturday morning, he completed his letter: "To-day Joseph and Hyrum are put in the tomb. When this excitement will end I know not. The mob are threatening to destroy us daily …"[146]

143. Joseph Fielding, Diary, June 27, 1844.

144. Eliza R. Snow, "Sketch of My Life," in Maureen Ursenbach Beecher, ed., *The Personal Writings of Eliza Roxcy Snow*, 17.

145. Mary Audentia Smith Anderson and Bertha A. Anderson Hulmes, eds., *Joseph Smith III and the Restoration*, 85. Emma evidently stayed upstairs much of the day but sometimes came down to greet visitors. "I saw Emma walking back and forth in [another part] … of the Mansion," one woman wrote, "she spoke to me, and I answered her, and then continued on my way" (Sarah Griffin Richards, Letter to Zina D. Young, July 17, 1889).

146. Nathan Cheney, Letter to Charles Beebe, Sandusky, Cattauraugus County, New York, June 28-29, 1844; spelling and punctuation modernized.

More than 10,000 Saints walked through the Smith home that Friday until 5:00 p.m. when the doors to the Mansion House shut. Finally, his wife of two decades, Emma, and his sister-in-law Mary said goodbye to the husbands they had loved. With their children gathered around, comforting them even as they sought their own consolation, they stood together unaware of what they would face next. Fearing a mob might attempt to steal the bodies, men placed the corpses in the inner caskets and hid them in a small northeast bedroom, while the finished coffins were filled with sand. William Huntington drove the wagon carrying the sand-filled caskets to the meeting ground for a public funeral on Saturday.

Like so much of Joseph's life of religious ritual, his funeral began with an illusion–a hearse carrying coffins filled only with sand. The weeping Saints gathered to hear W. W. Phelps deliver the sermon he had written the day before. Longtime friend and scribe to the prophet, Phelps was a poet, an editor, and Joseph's ghostwriter. Historians Richard Van Wagoner and Steven C. Walker see significance in the way Phelps's address dramatized "the ambivalence of feelings in Nauvoo toward avenging the Martyrdom" and found Phelps "surprisingly incendiary."[147]

Phelps began by quoting Revelation 14:13: "And I heard a voice from heaven saying unto me, Write, Blessed are the dead which die in the Lord from henceforth: Yea, saith the Spirit, that they may rest from their labours; and their works do follow them." He framed Joseph's and Hyrum's lives as events of primarily religious, not civic or political, significance: "Two of the greatest and best men," he said, "who have lived on the earth, since the Jews crucified the Savior, have fallen victims to the popular will of mobocracy in this boasted 'Asylum of the oppressed'–the only far famed realms of liberty–or freedom, on the globe." Persecution had plagued them in life and brought them down in death. Phelps, completing the prophet-narrative, positioned Joseph among God's ancient seers. "Joseph Smith was the first apostle and seer that held the priesthood of God, and promulgated the fullness of the everlasting gospel, since this church was driven into the wilderness, after the old apostles fell a sleep."[148]

Governments had failed Joseph, who had come out of "gentile furnaces without the smell of fire from his garments." Joseph's life ended unjustly, yet

147. Richard Van Wagoner and Steven C. Walker, "The Joseph/Hyrum Smith Funeral Sermon," 4.

148. Ibid., 5.

he now had "gone to his royal kindred in paradise … and remember, beloved friends," Phelps pointed out, "that while he lived here upon the earth, he conferred all the keys and blessings of the priesthood, and Endowments, upon the apostles and others, that are needed for the gathering of Israel." Twining Mormon doctrine about heaven and earth into a single thread, he placed Joseph's life in the context of an everlasting priesthood. "The bodies of our brethren are marred, by physical force; because the flesh was weak, … but the priesthood remains unharmed–that is eternal without beginning of days or end of years; and the 'Twelve,' (mostly now absent) are clothed with it."[149]

"He was a man of God," Phelps proclaimed. "Like the sun in his meridian splendor, Joseph Smith shown a full man, at home, among his friends, in the fields, on the bench, or before the world; a pattern parent; a worthy friend; a model general; a righteous judge, and the wisest man of the age, sustained by truth, and 'God was his right hand man.' Surely, as one of the holy ones commissioned by God the Father among the royal seventy, when the council of heaven set them apart to come down and 'multiply and replenish this earth,' he was the 'last,' and who knows but the 'greatest,' for he declared–we–*knew not who he was!*"[150]

Phelps had stumbled onto the central question of Joseph's identity: to speak with God, to speak for God, and to weave a prophet-narrative from his life.

At Saturday-Sunday midnight, June 29-30, Dimick and William Huntington, Edward Hunter, William Marks, Jonathan H. Holmes, Gilbert Goodsmith, Alpheus Cutler, Lorenzo D. Wasson, and Philip B. Lewis carried the bodies to the dirt basement of the unfinished Nauvoo House and buried them in the pine caskets, carefully smoothing out all traces of what they had done. A rainstorm that night helped to complete the obliteration.[151]

The Sunday after the funeral was dreadful. "Every heart is filled with sorrow, and the very streets of Nauvoo seem to mourn," Vilate Kimball wrote to Heber in Boston on June 30. "Where it will end the Lord only knows. We are kept awake night after night by the alarm of mobs. These apostates say, 'Their damnation is sealed, their die is cast, their doom is fixed.'" Were the mobs the most immediate threat to the city? Would Mormons in other locales become targets? Vilate longed to have her husband home and safe.

149. Ibid., 6; emphasis in original.
150. Ibid., 8.
151. *History of the Church*, 6:628 (June 29, 1844).

"My constant prayer now," she ended, "is for the Lord to preserve us all to meet again. I have no doubt but your life will be sought, but may the Lord give you wisdom to escape their hands."[152] As Joseph's narrative ended, the question became: What would his people do now that the man they loved and for whom they had sacrificed everything was gone?

152. Vilate Kimball, Letter to Heber C. Kimball, June 30, 1844.

Epilogue

Whose mills does this stream activate? Who is utilizing its power? Who dammed it? These are the questions which historical materialism asks and it changes the picture of the landscape by naming the forces which have been operative in it.

–Walter Benjamin, qtd. in Ulf Strohmayer, Space and Social Theory, *162*

How is a prophet's life different from that of an ordinary human being? What does an encounter with what one believes to be the sublime do? How does the belief that God lives and talks with humanity cast shadows over such a person, over his life?

It would be impossible for a historian to wade through the voluminous source material that surrounds Joseph Smith's prophet-narrative without ending up with as many, if not more, questions as she had at the beginning. For example, how does one reconcile the tension between prophethood and mortality? The diaries kept largely by secretaries generate still more questions. In them, Joseph's life is interpreted, framed by the scribes' understandings of the importance of their belief in his prophethood. The rarer passages that Joseph wrote himself obscure his personality behind grammatical clumsiness. Despite excellent historical interpretation and more than a century and a half of analysis, Joseph remains elusive, in death as in life.

Another question concerns plurality or, framed more largely, how Joseph related to the women in his life. Although the scribes who told Joseph's story are partly complicit in distancing them, the women became shadows in the background of the central drama. Even Emma is present primarily as an actor in a play. These complicate the storyline and become pawns in political power plays between Joseph and men such as John C. Bennett. Their reputations, their need to be protected or led, enhanced the masculinity of priesthood leadership, of the construction of ideas about kingdom, family, and the veil between heaven and earth. As was true for all men who believed the framework that plurality created for the Latter-day Saint interpretation of heaven, Joseph's right to celestial kingdoms–to eternal kingship and godhood–was tied to women. The fact that they were present rendered plurality possible. Although women met in private prayer meetings, delivered each other's babies, made homes, and tended to the sick, they stood outside the governing councils. In the exercise of actual power–the power of God through priesthood–and the metaphoric exercise of power through ritual, Joseph prescribed their involvement in ways grounded by assumptions about gender in both public and private life. Although women are not absent from Joseph's story–indeed, it is largely because of them that we know today about Joseph's plurality–their experience is different from that of men; and in the narratives that emerge from Joseph's series of scribes and other contemporary sources, the picture closely matches the larger social context in which women's lives were largely domestic and private while men's were public. Joseph's story is a gendered narrative that has a meaning particular to the Mormon understanding of heaven, marriage, and family. It is gendered in its interpretation of the possibility of godhood for every righteous man who participated in temple ordinances and who engaged in the sacred ritual of celestial marriage. Associated with male godhood in this way, women accompanied men into heaven, but were not endowed in the same way with the power of priesthood, godhood, and the potentialities of heaven. They are supporting actors–"privileges," in the language of plurality–in Joseph's drama.

While Joseph's notions about the plurality of gods and wives may have been radical in the context of the times, his notions about women and their roles were not. Women did not join the Council of Fifty despite their association in the Female Relief Society. They did not decide the fate of dissenters who threatened to overturn the Church or call for the destruction of the *Nauvoo Expositor* press, but they rallied with the Saints at the stand in worship services as supportive members of community, contributed to the creation of *communitas,* and engaged in sacred ritual in gendered ways appropriate to Joseph's view of the world. When they, like Sarah Pratt or Nancy Rigdon, resisted the prophet-narrative in public ways, they risked ruination.

As soon as Joseph died, his life took on new meaning. Indeed, the martyrdom of the Mormon prophet became the sacred defining myth, unifying the Saints so strongly that they could leave Nauvoo, make a new Zion in the Rocky Mountains, and continue to draw thousands of converts across seas and continents, braiding them into the warp and weft of that narrative. It would be impossible to overestimate the power of the story Joseph created with and from his life, in countless sermons delivered in the sunshine in fields near the temple, or in correspondence to presidents and senators, to strangers and friends alike. Brigham Young and the other powerful men who mourned Joseph's death from their standing within the elite circles he created took from Joseph's narrative the salient points, episodes, and themes, interpreting them repeatedly in sermons of their own.

Whether one believes Joseph was a prophet, those who followed him were filled with the potent, reality-reorienting sense of what that meant. It meant that he had communed with God, that his mind and heart–his whole being–had been filled with what he interpreted as answers to prayers. And with those understandings came a sometimes overwhelming responsibility to teach those around him what he believed to be true and what they must do with their lives regardless of how outrageous or revolutionary his instructions to them would seem at times.

The church that he founded continued to use its first prophet's narrative to inspire faith and devotion, a willingness to follow his description of the true path to heaven. The Prophet Joseph is where Latter-day Saint identity begins. His life is the central design motif of the dominant imperative: that God speaks to human beings and obligates them to live in particular ways. But at the same time and apart from the kind of history that enhances faith, parallel streams run through his story, confusing or even alienating the historian. Imperfect knowledge and incomplete understandings of his rituals provide some with absolute answers but stimulate more questions for others.

Joseph was an earthy man, who loved women and children, opened his heart in friendship to many men, not all of whom deserved it, who marveled at a bizarre news account, or responded to a sentimental story. Yet he was also sometimes petty or even greedy for both power and possessions. It makes him more human and therefore more interesting to consider the many ways in which he struggled to understand himself. Perhaps that struggle is what makes his narrative so arresting for Mormon audiences. For what Joseph's life demonstrates, even in the midst of his flawed, conflicted humanity, is that he was like us: yes, a compelling genius, gifted in creating organizations and community, a holy man in embodying aspirations for the sacred in ritual–but also deeply flawed. Capable of failure along with success, hopeful of a better world but grappling with one that was not, the story of Joseph's struggle with prophethood shows us what may be possible in our own lives. Joseph's narrative demonstrates that it is impossible to be perfect even if one communicates with God and gives himself to the Lord's work. And as depressed as Joseph became in the midst of his own confusion, he nonetheless believed that God was and that he could become godly himself.

Perhaps no episode in Joseph's life demonstrates this belief as convincingly as his destruction of the *Nauvoo Expositor.* Unquestionably one of the most ill-conceived moves of his life, it demonstrates an unattractive sense of entitlement anchored both in priesthood and political power. It shows him motivated by anger, vengeance, and a reckless insistence that his view of reality was the only correct view. The fact that he was able to bend the city council to his will after eight hours of persuasion and only after creating a flimsy shield of legal technicalities makes it clear that other views struggled to compete but went down before the power of his will. And in the aftermath, Joseph's predictable response was a campaign to justify what he could see only as righteous action. His letters to the governor, to local newspapers, to his critics and supporters defended his actions with righteous indignation and the belief that God could not have allowed him to err, that once again he was being persecuted by the forces of evil.

More questions surface at this point. What was his mental state? He swung between exultation, defiance, and blood-spattered rhetoric at one extreme and despondency, despair, and passivity at the other. It is difficult to imagine the intensity of emotion and pressure that brought him to such a point. Did he see himself as an Old Testament prophet, calling down floods or plagues? Did his claim that "God is my right-hand man" manifest faith, arrogance, or both?

What is clear is that, when Mayor Joseph Smith ordered the destruction of the *Expositor,* he launched an attack that ended in his own death sixteen days later. There is a tragic inevitability about the narrative from the moment his defiant eyes met those of his obedient city marshal across the city council chamber. It becomes clear–not only what would happen next–but what must happen. The prophet-narrative had a beginning, a middle, and an end. It forms a perfect myth, one that shapes the identities of believers and reaches out in song, tale, and testimony to draw other believers into its powerful and empowering world.

The story my father told us children as we traveled the miles between

Michigan and Salt Lake City was his own version of this myth. Critical to our own identity as Mormons, he helped us know who we were and why we lived the way we lived. But Joseph's life had more layers than the dramatic moments suggested by the bullet holes in Carthage Jail. The complexity of relationships between Latter-day Saint men and women belied the normalcy suggested by the brick walls of Nauvoo houses lining the streets of the Mormon town. A series of veils, literal in temple ritual and metaphoric in the subterfuge required to keep ritual private, created hierarchies of actors in a sacred religious drama around the person of a latter-day prophet.

There will be an endless debate over whether Joseph actually saw God, but I assert my belief that Joseph genuinely believed his was the prophet's role and that he spent his entire life trying to understand what that meant. The responsibilities this belief brought colored every move he made and shadowed the principal events and relationships of his life–his marriage to Emma and his association with his closest friends and Church leaders. He required a startling intensity of commitment and engagement from those around him. They had to learn to accept his word as a prophet and to adapt their lives to his instruction about how they should live. Those who could not either withdrew, drifting away from myth, or were driven to the margins or cast out in terms that left them stranded outside heaven. The line was drawn around Joseph by his prophet's role, and it was sharp and defined, impossible to contest unless one chose to challenge God himself.

Other powerful charismatic figures of the mid-nineteenth century sketched millennial world views and devised communal social experiments, but Joseph's is the one that thrives today. His prophet-narrative is one reason. It evokes a shared history, interprets the meaning of heaven and earth, and gives Joseph's followers a course of action–an eye turned to heaven, a desire for godhood, and the tools to build a holy city and a sanctified community on earth. Their belief and the work it inspires is evidence that it is indeed possible for a human being to escape the confines of ordinariness and capture the potential of heaven.

Where does identity originate? The question is deceptively simple, because it presupposes an identity that comes with birth, with a lifetime spent in a family or a group. But for Joseph, his identity as a prophet began when he believed God first spoke to him as if from heaven. Joseph's understanding of the vision he believed he experienced in his youth expanded over time. In 1832, he emphasized the personal nature of the vision and the promise of the forgiveness of sins; six years later, he stressed the instructions to join no church and his role as prophet, seer, and revelator.

Like a monument, an individual with the mythic dimensions of Joseph encourages memory to consider the formation of identity. His figure encourages us to remember some things and to forget others. The process of creating a prophet's narrative shapes public memory and collective identity.

When memory is located in a place, as might be true with a person, place-making suggests Walter Benjamin's notion of "digging," in which the body brings past and present into the same place. Benjamin was a German-Jewish Marxist literary critic, who observed the way individuals make meaning out of their lives in particular places:

> He who wishes to approach his own buried past must act like a man who digs. ... Facts of the matter are only deposits, layers which deliver only to the most meticulous examination what constitutes the true assets hidden within the inner earth: the images which, torn from all former contexts, stand–like ruins or torsos in the collector's gallery–as the treasures in the sober chambers of our belated insights. And, in order to dig successfully, a plan is certainly required. Yet just as indispensable is the spade's careful, probing penetration of the dark earthen realm; and he who only keeps the inventory of his finds, but not also this dark bliss of the finding itself, cheats himself of the best part. The unsuccessful search belongs to it just as fully as the fortunate search. This is why memory must not proceed by way of narrative, much less by way of reports, but must, rather assay its spade, epically and rhapsodically in the most rigorous sense, in ever new places and, in the old ones, to delve into ever deeper layers.[1]

Joseph's life was a layered existence. As we delve into deeper layers, we experience a broader range of emotions. Confusion and anger come long before clarity, for it takes effort to interpret the meaning of the rituals that coursed through everything Joseph did. What looks like subterfuge, intended to obscure one's vision, may have been embedded in ritual. We must struggle to understand it as he did. Joseph adopted Freemasonry because he sensed the power of its hiddenness, but it was not enough. He went on to hide plurality, sacred temple endowments, prayer circles, and the political kingdom of God in ever-deepening layers of secrecy because he believed they were necessary to fulfil God's will. Over time, a complex web of relationships and intrigues encased Joseph and his ritualized world of belief

1. Walter Benjamin, "A Berlin Chronicle," 611.

like a cocoon, impossible to unravel and understand as a single strand. We cannot say with consistency "this is how Joseph acted, this is what Joseph believed," for each layer looks different. There is an intentionality about what Joseph let people see or understand. Their movement through layers of knowledge or experience resulted in a hierarchy of persons most in line for God's blessings. Perhaps this same sensed movement is true for all of us; but for a human being who had experiences both of the earth and of heaven, who experienced the liminality and anomie that accompanies ritual, Joseph whirled through a kaleidoscope life promising infinite, divine potentialities. Those who saw what he saw were true disciples who believed in his vision of Zion. They already lived and loved in the kingdom of God and the life that awaited them upon death.

In some ways, Joseph's life was a palimpsest–a set of overlapping stories that positioned him as a prophet, a human being with access to the authority and power of God, and the gatekeeper to heaven. The Mormon people he called into being used the content of his narrative to frame contemporary claims to truth and a particular set of understandings about the meaning of the present. This type of memory work contributed to social identity. Nauvoo became a material setting, central to the narrative structure of the story, a scene that localized time, mood, and affect. It became a symbol of key turning points or relations among the characters around him and came to signify the social relations that would take place in an as-yet-unrevealed future.

A multitude of unfolding plots ran parallel to his–most notably the story of Emma Hale Smith, his wife, his disciple, his beloved, his opponent. Prominent among Nauvoo narratives were those of Sidney Rigdon, William Law, and brother Hyrum. Nauvoo came to connote the complex social and emotional interactions of love, jealousy, and anger among the main players. Nauvoo was eyewitness to past events and social interactions, a central character in the story itself that imprinted the fears, hopes, and desires of the Mormons in Nauvoo, of Joseph himself, becoming both a memory and a symbol that has not lost its power for modern Mormonism.

Benjamin suggests, "As consciousness translates into self-consciousness, as we embark upon knowledge about ourselves, something new emerges. Taming this new has become the task we set ourselves."[2] We can frame this process with the image of layerings, but the effect is the same. "The point of departure" becomes a circle; "inside the circle, someone speaks, writes and

2. Qtd. in Strohmayer, *Space and Social Theory*, 164.

listens." Joseph engaged in this process, this compulsively driven search for self-understanding. He was compelled by a passion for knowing why God chose him, why his life, why this people.

Joseph's desire pulled him toward God, shaped his life as a prophet, and made it impossible for him to turn from the life that his particular knowledge obligated him to live. Desire for life with God, desire to walk always with God became Joseph's master-passion, a hungry constancy that colored all he did. Desire may be tied to identity, suggesting that what we are stems from what we most ardently yearn for: "Desire becomes … a permanent mediator between individual and society; identify your desire and the means are yours to transcend it. Speak. Think. And see what happens to your I."[3] Joseph's life as a prophet was not an object–a reality "out there"–but an interior reality inaccessible to others and that one believed or not. Joseph's desire to understand what God wanted of him as a prophet, his passion to live the life of a prophet–to explain to others what that meant–was the central occupation of his life. As much as desire was a part of Joseph's narrative, so was fear–fear of the alternative.

Italian journalist and novelist Italo Calvino imagines conversations in *Invisible Cities* between Marco Polo and Kublai Khan about places they both might have visited or seen. When the Khan asks Polo to name one of the cities he describes, Polo responds:

> It has neither name nor place. I shall repeat the reason why I was describing it to you: from the number of imaginable cities we must exclude those whose elements are assembled without a connecting thread, an inner rule, a perspective, a discourse. With cities, it is as with dreams: everything imaginable can be dreamed, but even the most unexpected dream is a rebus that conceals a desire or, its reverse, a fear. Cities, like dreams, are made of desires and fears, even if the thread of their discourse is secret, their rules are absurd, their perspectives deceitful, and everything conceals something else.[4]

Zion, for members of the Church of Jesus Christ of Latter-day Saints, was at once a place and an idea that concealed both a desire for heaven and a fear of the alternative. Memory, identity, and narrative wove through the lines etched in the plat of the City of Zion, the Mormon blueprint for the good society. Religious people build and inhabit spaces that are narratives

3. Ibid., 166.
4. Italo Calvino, *Invisible Cities*, 43-44.

of the values and beliefs they hold dear. Those spaces shape their decisions about family and politics, work and play, holiness and sin. They reveal patterns of social relationships that are expressed in a spatial language.

Historian B. Carmon Hardy reminds us of the caution given by William James at the turn of the twentieth century: "Not only are supposedly objective methods of analysis the products of time and place," as James says, "but the 'enchantment' of religious transport 'is not rationally or logically deducible from anything else.' It is a category of experience having unique qualities of its own. While historians are always obliged to challenge collective memory, they must also respect it as an additional lens for exploring the past. We cannot, if we are to comprehend the Mormon polygamous phenomenon, disregard the fact that when formally dictating his only explicit statement on plural marriage that was not also a denial, Smith commenced with the imprimatur 'Verily, thus saith the Lord unto you my servant Joseph.'"[5]

In Joseph's narrative, God himself is a character with emotion, dimension, presence. He is companion and mentor to Joseph the student-prophet; his life mirrors what is possible for Joseph in his own. The lusciousness of God's vision of Earth and Heaven promises a future that Joseph tastes as he lives and feeds his own desire for the same. We struggle to understand how deeply personal God was for the Mormon prophet. It is impossible to know for sure if Joseph would or could have opted out of his life as a prophet or whether he was simply swept forward in a course carved out by undeniable inevitabilities. But the God in it rendered it certain, for Joseph craved the presence of God, desired the presence of God, yearned for a home with God. As compelling as the most powerful addiction, the knowledge of life's meaning that God shared with Joseph rendered his life meaningful, special, significant in ways that lie beyond common human comprehension. That unique way of seeing and being obligated Joseph to explain God with his own life to disciples who sensed and desired that same uniqueness but who glimpsed its glory only in furtive, blinding glances.

The source of power, the activator of the earth's forces, Joseph's God became meaningful in the context of the story of the Latter-day Saints and was made manifest through the life they constructed on the banks of the Mississippi River. The temple, the Nauvoo House, and the Masonic Hall would have been only buildings without the life practices of the Mormons.

5. B. Carmon Hardy, *Doing the Works of Abraham*, 32; the James quotation is from *Varieties of Religious Experience*.

But inhabited by the Saints, the buildings became ritualized spaces in but not of the profane world. Rituals made everything the Saints did sacred, dedicated to God. Joseph spent his life trying to understand what being a prophet meant. For Joseph's followers, his life-ritual was a narrative that, despite his many human failings, God made complete with revelations of the sublime.

Bibliography

Abbreviations

Community of Christ	Library-Archives, Community of Christ, Independence, Missouri.
D&C	[Joseph Smith Jr. et al.]. *Doctrine and Covenants of the Church of Jesus Christ of Latter-day Saints: Containing Revelations Given to Joseph Smith the Prophet, with Some Additions by His Successors in the Presidency of the Church.* Salt Lake City: Deseret Book, for the Church, 1981.
History of the Church	Joseph Smith Jr. et al., *History of the Church of Jesus Christ of Latter-day Saints,* edited by B. H. Roberts, 2d ed. rev. (6 vols. 1902-12, Vol. 7 1932. Rpt., Salt Lake City: Deseret Book, 1977 printing).
JD	*Journal of Discourses.* 26 vols. Liverpool and London: Latter-day Saints Book Depot, 1853-86.
Journal History	Journal History of the Church of Jesus Christ of Latter-day Saints. Chronological scrapbook of typed entries and newspaper clippings, 1830-present. LDS Church History Library.
LDS Church History Library	Archives-Library, Church History Department, Church of Jesus Christ of Latter-day Saints, Salt Lake City.
Lee Library	L. Tom Perry Special Collections, Harold B. Lee Library, Brigham Young University, Provo, Utah.
Marriott Library	Special Collections, J. Willard Marriott Library, University of Utah, Salt Lake City.
USHS	Utah State Historical Society Archives, Salt Lake City, Utah.

Frequently Cited Works

Abzug, Robert H. *Cosmos Crumbling: American Reform and Religious Imagination.* New York: Oxford University Press, 1994.

Achorn, Erik. "Mary Cragin, Perfectionist Saint." *New England Quarterly* 28 (Dec. 1955): 490-518.

Adams, Charles Francis. "Charles Francis Adams Visits the Mormons in 1844." Edited by Henry Adams. *Proceedings of the Massachusetts Historical Society* 68 (1944-47): 267-300.

Affidavits and Certificates, Disproving the Statements and Affidavits Contained in John C. Bennett's Letters. Broadside. Nauvoo, Illinois, Aug. 31, 1842.

Affidavits on Celestial Marriage, 1869-1915. See Smith, Joseph F., comp.

Alexander, Bobby C. "Correcting Misinterpretations of Turner's Theory: An African American Pentecostal Illustration," *Journal for the Scientific Study of Religion* 30, no. 1 (Mar. 1991): 26-44.

_____. *Victor Turner Revisited: Ritual as Social Change.* Atlanta, Georgia: Scholars Press, 1991.

Alexander, Thomas G. "Joseph Smith." In *Research Guide to American Historical Biography.* Edited by Robert Muccigrosso and Suzanne Niemeyer. Washington, D.C.: Beacham Publishers, 1988, 1404-11.

_____. "The Place of Joseph Smith in the Development of American Religion: A Historiographical Inquiry." *Journal of Mormon History* 5 (1978): 3-17; reprinted in Bryan Waterman, ed., *The Prophet Puzzle,* 1-24.

_____. "The Reconstruction of Mormon Doctrine." In Gary James Bergera, ed., *Line upon Line,* 53-66.

_____. *Things in Heaven and Earth: The Life and Times of Wilford Woodruff, a Mormon Prophet.* Salt Lake City: Signature Books, 1991.

Allen, James B. "Emergence of a Fundamental: The Expanding Role of Joseph Smith's First Vision in Mormon Religious Thought." *Journal of Mormon History* 7 (1980): 43-61.

_____. "The Historian's Corner." *BYU Studies* 18, no. 3 (Spring 1978): 475-80.

_____. "Nauvoo's Masonic Hall." *John Whitmer Historical Association Journal* 10 (1990): 39-49.

_____. "One Man's Nauvoo: William Clayton's Experience in Mormon Illinois." *Journal of Mormon History* 6 (1979): 37-59.

_____. "The Significance of Joseph Smith's 'First Vision' in Mormon Thought." *Dialogue: A Journal of Mormon Thought* 1, no. 1 (Autumn 1966): 29-45.

_____. *Trials of Discipleship: The Story of William Clayton, a Mormon.* Urbana: University of Illinois Press, 1987.

_____. "Was Joseph Smith a Serious Candidate for the Presidency of the United States?" *Ensign,* Sept. 1973, 21-22.

_____. "'We Were Willing Because We Were Obliged to': The Mormons, Their Religion, and Why They Left Nauvoo." In *The Iowa Mormon Trail.* Edited by Susan Easton Black and William G. Hartley. Orem, Utah: Helix Publishing, 1997, 3-20.

_____. "Why Did People Act that Way?" *Ensign,* Dec. 1978, 21-24.

_____. "William Clayton." In *Utah History Encyclopedia.* Edited by Allan Kent Powell. Salt Lake City: University of Utah Press, 1994, 99.

_____, and Thomas B. Alexander, eds. *Manchester Mormons: The Journal of William Clayton 1840-1842.* Santa Barbara, California: Peregrine Smith, 1974.

_____, Ronald K. Esplin, and David J. Whittaker. *Men with a Mission: The Quorum of the Twelve Apostles in the British Isles, 1837-1841.* Salt Lake City: Deseret Book, 1992.

_____, and Glen M. Leonard. *The Story of the Latter-day Saints.* 2d ed. rev. Salt Lake City: Deseret Book, 1992.

_____, and Marvin S. Hill, eds. *Mormonism and American Culture.* Interpretations of American History Series. New York: Harper & Row, 1972.

American Almanac and Repository of Useful Knowledge for the Year 1842. Boston: David H. Williams, 1842.

"Ancient Records." *Times and Seasons* 4 (May 1, 1843): 185-87.

Anderson, Devery S. "The Anointed Quorum in Nauvoo, 1842-45." *Journal of Mormon History* 29, no. 2 (2003): 137-57.

_____, and Gary James Bergera, eds. *Joseph Smith's Quorum of the Anointed, 1842-1845: A Documentary History.* Salt Lake City: Signature Books/Smith-Pettit Foundation, 2005.

Anderson, Lavina Fielding, ed. *Lucy's Book: A Critical Edition of Lucy Mack Smith's Family Memoir.* Salt Lake City: Signature Books, 2001.

_____. "139-Year-Old Portraits of Joseph and Emma Smith." *Ensign,* Mar. 1981, 62-64.

Anderson, Mary Audentia [Smith]. *Ancestry and Posterity of Joseph Smith and Emma Hale.* 1929; 2d ed., Independence, Missouri: Herald House, 1952.

_____, and Bertha A. Anderson Hulmes, eds. *Joseph Smith III and the Restoration.* Independence, Missouri: Herald House, 1952. [Joseph Smith III memoirs].

Anderson, Richard Lloyd. "The Reliability of the Early History of Lucy and Joseph Smith." *Dialogue: A Journal of Mormon Thought* 4 (Summer 1969): 13-28.

Anderson, Robert D. *Inside the Mind of Joseph Smith: Psychobiography and the Book of Mormon.* Salt Lake City: Signature Books, 1999.

Andrew, David S., and Laurel B. Blank. "The Four Mormon Temples in Utah." *Journal of the Society of Architectural Historians* 30, no. 1 (Mar. 1971): 51-65.

Andrew, Laurel B. *The Early Temples of the Mormons: The Architecture of the Millennial Kingdom in the American West.* Albany: State University of New York Press, 1978.

Andrus, Hyrum L. *Doctrines of the Kingdom.* Vol. 3 in *Foundations of the Millennial Kingdom of Christ.* Salt Lake City: Bookcraft, 1973.

_____. *Joseph Smith, Man and Seer.* Salt Lake City: Deseret Book, 1960.

_____. "Joseph Smith, Social Philosopher, Theorist, and Prophet." Ph.D. diss., Syracuse University, 1955.

_____, and Helen Mae Andrus, eds. *They Knew the Prophet.* Salt Lake City: Bookcraft, 1974.

"Another Abortive Attempt to Arrest Joe Smith." *Sangamo Journal,* Sept. 16, 1842, 3.

Arrington, Joseph Earl. "Destruction of the Mormon Temple at Nauvoo." *Journal of the Illinois State Historical Society* 40 (1947): 414-25.

_____. "William Weeks, Architect of the Nauvoo Temple." *BYU Studies* 19, no. 3 (1979): 337-59. www.byustudies.byu.edu/shop/pdfSRC/19.3Arrington.pdf (Jan. 20, 2009).

Arrington, Leonard J. "Brigham Young." *Encyclopedia of Mormonism.* 4 vols. New York: Macmillan Publishing, 1992, 4:1601-1609.

_____. *Brigham Young: American Moses.* New York: Alfred A. Knopf, 1985.

_____. "Centrifugal Tendencies in Mormon History." In *To the Glory of God.* Edited by Truman G. Madsen and Charles D. Tate Jr. Salt Lake City: Deseret Book, 1972, 165-80.

_____. "Church Leaders in Liberty Jail." *BYU Studies* 13, no. 1 (1972): 20-26.

_____. "Early Mormon Communitarianism: The Law of Consecration and Stewardship." *Western Humanities Review* 7 (1953): 341-69.

_____. *Great Basin Kingdom: An Economic History of the Latter-day Saints, 1830-1900.* Cambridge, Massachusetts: Harvard University Press, 1958.

_____. "The Human Qualities of Joseph Smith, the Prophet." *Ensign,* Jan. 1975, 35-38.

_____. "Joseph Smith." In *The Presidents of the Church.* Edited by Leonard J. Arrington. Salt Lake City: Deseret Book, 1986, 3-42.

_____. "Joseph Smith and the Lighter View." *New Era,* Aug. 1976, 8-13.

_____. "Joseph Smith, Builder of Ideal Communities." In *The Prophet Joseph.* Edited by Larry C. Porter and Susan E. Black. Salt Lake City: Deseret Book, 1988, 115-37.

_____, and Davis Bitton. *The Mormon Experience.* New York: Alfred A. Knopf, 1979.

_____, Dean L. May, and Feramorz Y. Fox. *Building the City of God: Community and Cooperation among the Mormons.* 2d ed. Salt Lake City: Deseret Book, 1976.

Ashment, Edward H. "The Facsimiles of the Book of Abraham: A Reappraisal." *Sunstone* 4 nos. 5-6 (1979): 33-48.

Ashurst-McGee, Mark. "Joseph Smith, the Kinderhook Plates, and the Question of Revelation." Paper at the Mormon History Association annual meeting, 1996.

_____. "A Pathway to Prophethood: Joseph Smith Junior as Rodsman, Village Seer, and Judeo-Christian Prophet." M.A. thesis, Utah State University, 2000.

"Assassination of Ex-Governor Boggs of Missouri." *Wasp,* May 28, 1842, 4.

"Assassination of Ex-Governor of Missouri, Lilburn Boggs." *Quincy Whig,* May 21, 1842, 1, www.sidneyrigdon.broadhu/IL/whit1842.html@0521 (Nov. 7, 2007).

Autobiography of Andrew Dickson White. 2 vols. New York: Century Co., 1957.

Avery, Valeen Tippetts. *From Mission to Madness: Last Son of the Mormon Prophet.* Urbana: University of Illinois Press, 1998.

Bachman, Danel. "New Light on an Old Hypothesis: The Ohio Origins of the Revelation on Eternal Marriage." *Journal of Mormon History* 5 (1978): 19-32.

_____. "A Study of the Mormon Practice of Plural Marriage before the Death of Joseph Smith." M.A. thesis, Purdue University, 1975.

Backenstos, J. B. Affidavit, July 28, 1842. In *Affidavits and Certificates, Disproving the Statements and Affidavits Contained in John C. Bennett's Letters.*

Backman, Milton V., Jr., and Richard O. Cowan. *Joseph Smith and the Doctrine and Covenants.* Salt Lake City: Deseret Book, 1992.

Bailey, Raymond T. "Emma Hale: Wife of the Prophet Joseph Smith." M.A. thesis, Brigham Young University, 1952.

Barker, Eugene C. "The Annexation of Texas." *Southwestern Historical Quarterly* 50 (July 1946): 357-79.

Barnes, Lorenzo. "Letter." *Times and Seasons* 1, no. 5 (Mar. 1840): 78-79.

Barnett, Steven G., ed. "Wilson Law: A Sidelight on the *Expositor* Incident." *BYU Studies* 19, no. 2 (1979): 244-46.

Barrett, Ivan J. *Joseph Smith and the Restoration.* Provo, Utah: Brigham Young University Press, 1973.

Bates, Irene M. "William Smith, 1811-93: Problematic Patriarch." *Dialogue: A Journal of Mormon Thought* 16, no. 2 (Summer 1983): 11-23.

_____, and E. Gary Smith. *Lost Legacy: The Mormon Office of Presiding Patriarch.* Urbana: University of Illinois Press, 1996.

Baugh, Alexander L. "'For This Ordinance Belongeth to My House': The Practice of Baptism for the Dead Outside the Nauvoo Temple." *Mormon Historical Studies* 3 (Spring 2002): 47-58.

_____. "'We took Our Change of Venue to the State of Illinois': The Gallatin Hearing and the Escape of Joseph Smith and the Mormon Prisoners from Missouri, April 1839." *Mormon Historical Studies* 2, no. 1 (Spring 2001): 59-82.

Beadle, John H. *Polygamy, or the Mysteries and Crimes of Mormonism.* Philadelphia: National Publishing Co., 1882.

Bean, Nellie Stary. "Reminiscences of the Granddaughter of Hyrum Smith." *Relief Society Magazine* 9 (Jan. 1922): 8-10.

Beardsley, Harry M. *Joseph Smith and His Mormon Empire.* Boston: Houghton Mifflin, 1931.

Beck, James. Notebook, 1859-65. LDS Church History Library.

Bederman, Gail. *Manliness and Civiliation.* Chicago: University of Chicago Press, 1995.

Beecher, Maureen Ursenbach, ed. "'All Things Move in Order in the City': The Nauvoo Diary of Zina Diantha Huntington Jacobs." *BYU Studies* 19, no. 3 (Spring 1979): 285-320.

_____. *Eliza and Her Sisters.* Salt Lake City: Aspen Books, 1991.

_____. "Eliza R. Snow's Nauvoo Journal." *BYU Studies* 15 (Summer 1975): 391-416.

_____. *The Personal Writings of Eliza Roxcy Snow.* Salt Lake City: University of Utah Press, 1995.

_____, and Lavina Fielding Anderson, eds. *Sisters in Spirit: Mormon Women in Historical and Cultural Perspective.* Urbana: University of Illinois Press, 1987.

_____, Linda King Newell, and Valeen Tippetts Avery. "Emma, Eliza, and the Stairs." *BYU Studies* 22, no. 1 (Winter 1982): 87-96.

Bell, F. A., comp. *Order of the Eastern Star: An Instructive Manual on the Organization and Government of Chapters of the Order with Ceremonies and Ritual.* Chicago: Ezra A. Cook Publications, 1948.

Benamou, Michel, and Charles Caramello, eds. *Performance in Postmodern Culture.* Madison: Center for Twentieth-Century Studies, University of Wisconsin-Milwaukee, 1977.

Benjamin, Walter. "A Berlin Chronicle." In *Selected Writings, Volume 2, 1927-1934.* Eds. Michael W. Jennings, Howard Eiland, and Gary Smith. Cambridge, Massachusetts: Belknap Press of Harvard University, 1999, 594-637.

Bennet, James Arlington. "From the Mormon Country." *New York Herald,* Jan. 19, 1842, 1.

_____. "The Mormons: A Leaf from Joe Smith." *New York Herald,* Apr. 3, 1842, 2.

Bennett, Archibald F. "The Ancestry of Joseph Smith the Prophet." *Utah Genealogical and Historical Magazine,* Pt. 1, 20 (Jan. 1929): 1-34; Pt. 2, 20 (Apr. 1929): 49-74.

Bennett, John C. Letter. July 2, 1842. *Sangamo Journal,* (July 15, 1842). www.sidneyrigdon.com/dbroadhu/Il/sang1842.html#0702 (July 21, 2008).

_____. "Bennett's Second and Third Letters." *Sangamo Journal,* July 15, 1842. www.sidneyrigdon.com/dbroadhu/Il/sang1842.html#0715 (July 21, 2008).

_____. "For the Sangamo Journal." *Sangamo Journal,* July 8, 1842, 2.

_____. "From the Louisville Journal." *Sangamo Journal,* Sept. 2, 1842, 2.

_____. *The History of the Saints: or, An Exposé of Joe Smith and Mormonism.* 3rd ed. 1842; rpt., Urbana: University of Illinois Press, 2000.

_____. Letter to James Strang, June 2, 1846. Strang Manuscripts, Beinecke Library, Yale University, New Haven, Connecticut.

_____. "Now for the Records." *Sangamo Journal,* July 22, 1842, 2.

_____. "To the Editor of the Journal." *Sangamo Journal,* Aug. 19, 1842.

"Bennett's Letters." *Wasp,* Aug. 27, 1842, 2.

Bentley, Joseph I. "In the Wake of the Steamboat *Nauvoo:* Prelude to Joseph Smith's Financial Disasters." *Journal of Mormon History* 25, no. 1 (Winter 2009): 23-49.

Berger, Peter. *The Sacred Canopy: Elements of a Sociological Theory of Religion.* New York: Doubleday, 1967.

Bergera, Gary James. "Buckeye's Laments: Two Early Insider Exposés of Mormon Polygamy and Their Authorship." *Journal of the Illinois State Historical Society* (Winter 2002/2003), 350-90. http://findarticles.com/p/articles/mi_qa3945/is_200301/ai_n9170043/print (Dec. 20, 2008).

_____. *Conflict in the Quorum: Orson Pratt, Brigham Young, Joseph Smith.* Salt Lake City: Signature Books, 2002.

_____. "The Earliest Eternal Sealings for Civilly Married Couples Living and Dead." *Dialogue: A Journal of Mormon Thought* 35, no. 3 (2002): 41-66.

_____. "Identifying the Earliest Mormon Polygamists, 1841-44." *Dialogue: A Journal of Mormon Thought* 38 (Fall 2005): 1-74.

_____. "'Illicit Intercourse,' Plural Marriage, and the Nauvoo Stake High Council." *John Whitmer Historical Association Journal* 23 (Winter 2003): 59-90.

_____. "John C. Bennett, Joseph Smith, and the Beginnings of Plural Marriage in Nauvoo." *John Whitmer Historical Association Journal* 25 (2005): 52-92.

_____. "Joseph Smith and the Hazards of Charismatic Leadership." *John Whitmer Historical Association Journal* 6 (1986): 33-42; reprinted in Bryan Waterman, ed., *The Prophet Puzzle,* 239-58.

_____, ed. *Line upon Line: Essays on Mormon Doctrine.* Salt Lake City: Signature Books, 1989.

_____, ed., "The Personal Cost of the 1838 Mormon War in Missouri: One Mormon's Plea for Forgiveness." *Mormon Historical Studies* 4 (Spring 2003): 139-44.

Berk, Richard A. *Collective Behavior.* Dubuque, Iowa: Wm. C. Brown, 1974.

Bernard, David. *Light on Masonry: A Collection of All the Most Important Documents on the Subject of Speculative Free Masonry.* Utica, New York: William Williams, 1829.

Bestor, Arthur. *Backwoods Utopias: The Sectarian and Owenite Phases of Communitarian Socialism in America, 1663-1829.* Philadelphia: University of Pennsylvania Press, 1950.

Bigler, Henry W. Autobiography, 1815-1846. Holograph, Lee Library. Also wwwboap.org/LDS/Early-Saints/HBigler.html (Dec. 8, 2008).

Billington, Ray Allen. "The Frontier in Illinois History." *Journal of the Illinois State Historical Society* 43 (Spring 1950): 28-45.

Biographical Review of Hancock County, Illinois. Chicago: Hobart Publishing Co., 1907.

"Biographical Sketch of the Life of Peter Wilson Conover." 1807-82. Typescript. LDS Church History Library.

"Biography of Mary Dunn Ensign, daughter of Simeon Adams Dunn and Adaline Rawson Dunn." In Mark L. McConkie, ed., *Remembering Joseph.*

Bishop, M. Guy. "'What Has Become of Our Fathers?': Baptism for the Dead at Nauvoo." *Dialogue: A Journal of Mormon Thought* 23, no. 2 (Summer 1990): 85-97.

Bitton, Davis. *A Guide to Mormon Diaries and Autobiographies.* Provo, Utah: Brigham Young University Press, 1977.

_____. *Images of the Prophet Joseph Smith.* Salt Lake City: Aspen Books, 1996.

Black, Susan Easton. "Isaac Galland: Both Sides of the River." *Nauvoo Journal* 8, no. 2 (1996): 3-9.

_____. "Membership of the Church of Jesus Christ of Latter-day Saints, 1830-1848." 48 vols. Provo, Utah: Religious Studies Center, Brigham Young University, 1987. On Infobase, CD-ROM, Collector's Library. Orem, Utah: Infobase, 1997.

_____, and Richard E. Bennett, eds. *A City of Refuge: Quincy, Illinois.* Salt Lake City: Millennial Press, 2000.

_____, and Charles D. Tate Jr., eds. *Joseph Smith: The Prophet, the Man.* Provo, Utah: Brigham Young University Religious Studies Center, 1993.

Blair, Karen J. *The Clubwoman as Feminist: True Womanhood Redefined, 1868-1914.* New York: Holmes & Meier, 1980.

Blair, William W. "Dear Herald." *Saints Herald* 8 (Oct. 1, 1885): 101.

_____. "Divine Authority of Joseph Smith the Martyr." *Saints Herald* 8 (Oct. 1, 1865): 101.

_____. Journal/Diary. Typescript. Community of Christ Archives. Entries May 14 and 17, 1865, and June 17, 1875, in *Saints Herald* 8 (Oct. 1, 1865): 101.

Bloom, Harold. *The American Religion: The Emergence of the Post-Christian Nation.* New York: Simon & Schuster, 1992.

_____. *Genius: A Mosaic of One Hundred Exemplary Creative Minds.* New York: Warner Books, 2002.

Blum, John M., Edmund S. Morgan, Willie Lee Rose, Arthur M. Schlesinger Jr., Kenneth M. Stampp, and C. Vann Woodward. *The National Experience: A History of the United States.* New York: Harcourt Brace Jovanovich, 1981.

Boggs, William M. "A Short Biographical Sketch of Lilburn W. Boggs, by His Son." *Missouri Historical Review* 4 (Jan. 1910): 106-10.

"The Book of the Generations of Jacob Gibson 1849-1881." LDS Church History Library.

"A Book of Proxy." Nauvoo Temple Proxy Sealings, Jan. 7-Feb. 5, 1846. Photocopy. Marriott Library.

Boorstin, Daniel J. *The Americans: The National Experience.* New York: Random House, 1965.

Bowen, Walter Dean. "The Versatile W. W. Phelps: Mormon Writer, Educator, and Pioneer." M.A. thesis, Brigham Young University, 1958.

Bowes, John. *Mormonism Exposed, in Its Swindling and Licentious Abominations, Refuted in Its Principles, and in the Claims of Its Head, the Modern Mohammed, Joseph Smith, Who Is Proved to Have Been a Deceiver, and No Prophet of God.* London: E. Ward, 1849.

Brackenberry, Benjamin. Grand Jury Testimony, Oct. 1844. Community of Christ Library-Archives.

Bradley, Martha Sonntag. "Polygamy." In *Historical Atlas of Mormonism.* Edited by Kent Brown et al. New York: Simon and Schuster, 1994, 116-17.

_____. "'Seizing Sacred Space': Women's Engagement in Early Mormonism." *Dialogue: A Journal of Mormon Thought* 27 (Summer 1994): 57-70.

_____, and Mary Brown Firmage Woodward. *Four Zinas: A Story of Mothers and Daughters on the Mormon Frontier.* Salt Lake City: Signature Books, 2000.

_____, and Mary Brown Firmage Woodward. "Plurality, Patriarchy and the Priestess: Zina D. H. Young's Nauvoo Marriages." *Journal of Mormon History* 20 (Spring 1994): 84-118.

"A Brief Synopsis of the Proceedings of the Municipality of the City of Nauvoo." June 8, 1844, *Nauvoo Neighbor,* June 19, 1844, [2-3].

Briggs, Edmund C. "Visit to Nauvoo in 1856." *Journal of History* 9 (Oct. 1916): 446-62.

Bringhurst, Newell G. *Brigham Young and the Expanding American Frontier.* Boston: Little, Brown and Co., 1986.

_____. *Saints, Slaves and Blacks: The Changing Place of Black People Within Mormonism.* Westport, Connecticut: Greenwood Press, 1981.

_____, and Darron T. Smith, eds. *Black and Mormon.* Urbana: University of Illinois Press, 2004.

Brodie, Fawn M. *No Man Knows My History: The Life of Joseph Smith.* 1946; 2d ed. rev. New York: Alfred A. Knopf, 1971; New York: Vintage Books, 1995.

Brooke, John L. *The Refiner's Fire: The Making of Mormon Cosmology, 1644–1844.* New York: Cambridge University Press, 1994.

Brooks, Juanita. *John Doyle Lee: Zealot–Pioneer Builder–Scapegoat.* Glendale, California: Arthur H. Clark, 1962.

_____, ed. *On the Mormon Frontier: The Diary of Hosea Stout.* 2 vols. Salt Lake City: University of Utah Press, 1964.

Brown, Lisle G, comp. *Nauvoo Sealings, Adoptions, and Anointings: A Comprehensive Register of Persons Receiving LDS Temple Ordinances, 1841-1846.* Salt Lake City: Smith-Pettit Foundation, 2006.

Brown, Samuel. "The Translator and the Ghostwriter: Joseph Smith and W. W. Phelps." *Journal of Mormon History* 34, no. 1 (Winter 2008): 26-62.

"Buckeye's Lamentation for Want of More Wives." *Warsaw Messenger,* Feb. 7, 1844, 3.

Buerger, David John. "'The Fulness of the Priesthood': The Second Anointing in Latter-day Saint Theology and Practice." *Dialogue: A Journal of Mormon Thought* 16, no. 1 (Spring 1983): 10-44.

_____. *The Mysteries of Godliness: A History of Mormon Temple Worship.* San Francisco: Smith Research Associates, 1994.

_____. "Salvation in the Theology of Joseph Smith." In Gary James Bergera, ed., *Line upon Line,* 159-69.

Buford, Bill. *Among the Thugs: The Experience, and the Seduction, of Crowd Violence.* New York: W. W. Norton & Co., 1992.

Buley, Raymond Carlyle. *The Old Northwest: A Pioneer Period, 1815-1840.* 2 vols. Indianapolis: Indiana Historical Society, 1950.

Bullock, Clara Fullmer. "The John Solomon Fullmer Story." 1968. Unpublished typescript. Marriott Library. Also available www.geocities.com/richardwinmill/john_s_fullmer.html (Jan. 12, 2009).

Bullock, Thomas. Diary, 1844-50. Holograph. LDS Church History Library.

_____. "K[ings] & P[riests] unto God & His Fa[the]r." www.boap.org/LDS/Parallel/1849/16 June 1844.html (Feb. 13, 2010).

Burgess, Margarette McIntire. "Recollections of the Prophet Joseph Smith." *Juvenile Instructor* 27 (1892): 66-67.

Burnett, Peter H. *Recollections and Opinions of an Old Pioneer.* New York: Appleton, 1880. Rpt. as *An Old California Pioneer.* Oakland, California: Biobooks, 1946.

Burton, Alma P., comp. *Discourses of the Prophet Joseph Smith.* 3d ed. Salt Lake City: Deseret Book, 1956.

Burton, Richard F. *The City of the Saints and across the Rocky Mountains to California.* New York: Harper & Brothers, 1862.

Bush, Lester E., and Armand L. Mauss, eds., *Neither White Nor Black: Mormon Scholars Confront the Race Issue in a Universal Church.* Midvale, Utah: Signature Books, 1984.

Bushman, Richard Lyman. "The Character of Joseph Smith." *BYU Studies* 42, no. 2 (2003): 23-34.

_____. "The Character of Joseph Smith: Insights from His Holographs." *Ensign*, Apr. 1977, 10-13.

_____. "How Did the Prophet Joseph Smith Respond to Skepticism in His Time?" *Ensign*, Feb. 1990, 61-63.

_____. *Joseph Smith and the Beginnings of Mormonism.* Urbana: University of Illinois Press, 1984.

_____. *Joseph Smith: Rough Stone Rolling.* New York City: Alfred A. Knopf, 2005.

_____. "Joseph Smith as Translator." In *Believing History: Latter-day Saints Essays.* Edited by Reid L. Neilson and Jed Woodworth. New York: Columbia University Press, 2004, 233-47.

_____. *Making Space for the Mormons: Ideas of Sacred Geography in Joseph Smith's America.* Leonard J. Arrington Mormon History Lecture Series, No. 2. Logan: Utah State University Press, 1997.

_____. "Mormon Persecutions in Missouri, 1833." *BYU Studies* 3 (Autumn 1960): 11-20.

_____, and Dean C. Jessee. "Smith, Joseph: The Prophet." *Encyclopedia of Mormonism.* 4 vols. New York: Macmillan, 1992, 3:1331-39.

Butler, John. Autobiography. Typescript. Lee Library.

Cahoon, William. Qtd. in "Recollections of the Prophet Joseph Smith." *Juvenile Instructor* 27 (Aug. 15, 1892): 492-93.

Calvino, Italo. *Invisible Cities.* New York: Harcourt, 1974.

Campbell, Eugene, and Bruce Campbell. "Divorce among Mormon Polygamists: Extent and Explanations." *Utah Historical Quarterly* 46 (Winter 1978): 4-23.

Canetti, Elias. *Crowds and Power.* New York: Viking Press, 1962.

Cannon, Angus M. "Joseph Smith, the Prophet." *Young Woman's Journal* 17, no. 12 (Dec. 1906): 546-47.

_____. Statement of Interview with Joseph Smith III, 1905. Typescript. LDS Church History Library.

Cannon, Brian Q. "John C. Calhoun, Jr., Meets the Prophet Joseph Smith Shortly Before the Departure for Carthage." *BYU Studies* 33, no. 4 (1993): 773-80.

Cannon, Donald Q. "King Follett Discourse: Joseph Smith's Greatest Sermon in Historical Perspective." *BYU Studies* 18, no. 2 (Winter 1978): 179-225.

Cannon, George Q. *The Life of Joseph Smith.* Salt Lake City: Juvenile Instructor Office, 1888.

Cannon, Janath R., and Jill Mulvay Derr. "Relief Society." *Encyclopedia of Mormonism.* 4 vols. New York: Macmillan Publishing Co., 1992, 3:1200.

Cannon, M. Hamlin, ed. "Documents: Bankruptcy Proceedings Against Joseph Smith in Illinois." *Pacific Historical Review* 14, no. 4 (1945): 425-33.

_____. "A Further Note on the Bankruptcy of Joseph Smith in Illinois." *Pacific Historical Review* 15 (June 1946): 214-15.

_____. "Migration of English Mormons to America." *American Historical Review* 52 (1947): 436-55.

Cannon, Oa J. "Henry Bailey Jacobs." Ca. 1980. Typescript. Oa Cannon Collection, LDS Church History Library.

_____. Untitled narrative about Zina Diantha Huntington [Jacobs Smith Young]. N.d. Typescript. Oa J. Cannon Collection, LDS Church History Library.

Capers, Gerald M. *Stephen A. Douglas: Defender of the Union.* Boston: Little, Brown, 1959.

Carden, Maren L. *Oneida: Utopian Community to Modern Corporation.* Baltimore: Johns Hopkins Press, 1969.

Carlson, Theodore Leonard. *Illinois Military Tract.* Urbana: University of Illinois Press, 1951.

Carnes, Mark C. *Secret Ritual and Manhood in Victorian America.* New Haven, Connecticut: Yale University Press, 1989.

Carter, Gideon. Affidavit. Feb. 27, 1894. Holograph. LDS Church History Library.

Carter, Jared. Autobiography. Holograph. LDS Church History Library. Also typescript, n.d., LDS Church History Library.

Carter, Kate B., ed. *Heber C. Kimball, His Wives and Family.* Salt Lake City: Daughters of Utah Pioneers, 1967.

Caswall, Henry. *The Prophet of the Nineteenth Century; Or, the Rise, Progress, and Present State of the Mormons, or Latter-day Saints.* London: J.G.F. and J. Rivington, 1843.

"Celebration of the Anniversary of the Church–Military Parade–Prest. Rigdon's Address–Laying the Corner Stones of the Temple." *Times and Seasons* 2 (Apr. 15, 1841): 375-77.

"Certificate of Sidney Rigdon," "Certificate of George W. Robinson," and "Certificate of Colonel Henry Marks." *Sangamo Journal,* Sept. 23, 1842, 2.

Chase, Daryl. "Sidney Rigdon: Early Mormon." M.A. thesis, University of Chicago, 1931.

Cheney, Elam Sr. "Joseph Smith, the Prophet." *Young Woman's Journal* 17, no. 12 (Dec. 1906): 539-40.

Cheney, Nathan. Letter to Charles Beebe, Sandusky, Cattauraugus Co., New York, June 28-29, 1844. LDS Church History Library. Spelling, punctuation modernized.

"Chief Corner Stone." *Times and Seasons* 2, no. 12 (Apr. 15, 1841): 382-87.

"Church History." *Times and Seasons* 3, no. 10 (Mar. 15, 1842): 705.

"Citizens of Illinois–Read and Consider." *Sangamo Journal,* Jan. 21, 1842, 3.

"City of Nauvoo." *Times and Seasons* 2, no. 19 (Aug. 2, 1841): 495-97.

"City of Nauvoo." *Times and Seasons* 3, no. 2 (Nov. 15, 1841): 599.

"City of Nauvoo." *Times and Seasons* 3, no. 6 (Jan. 15, 1842): 663.

"City of Nauvoo." *Times and Seasons* 3, no. 17 (July 1, 1842): 839-41.

"City of Nauvoo." *Times and Seasons* 3, no. 12 (Apr. 15, 1842): 765.

"City of Nauvoo." *Times and Seasons* 3, no. 13 (May 2, 1842): 775-76.

"City of Nauvoo." *Times and Seasons* 4, no. 22 (Oct. 1, 1843): 343-44.

Clark, James R. "The Kingdom of God, the Council of Fifty and the State of Deseret." *Utah Historical Quarterly* 26, no. 2 (1958): 131-48.

Clarke, S. J. *History of McDonough County, Illinois.* Springfield, Illinois: D. W. Lusk, State Printer and Binder, 1878.

Clawson, Margaret Gay Judd. "Mothers of Our Leaders: Rambling Reminiscences of Margaret Gay Judd Clawson." *Relief Society Magazine* 6 (June 1919): 257-62; 317-27.

Clayton, William. Affidavit. Feb. 16, 1874. LDS Church History Library.

_____. Affidavit, Feb. 16, 1874. in Andrew Jenson, ed., *Historical Record* 6 (May 1887): 224-25.

_____. "Historian's Corner: To the Saints in England: The Impressions of a Mormon Immigrant (The 10 December 1840 William Clayton Letter from Nauvoo to Manchester)." *BYU Studies* 18, no. 3 (Spring 1978): 477.

_____. "History of the Nauvoo Temple History Journal." Microfilm. LDS Church History Library.

_____. Letter to "Beloved Brothers and Sisters." Dec. 10, 1840. LDS Church History Library.

_____. Letter to Madison M. Scott, Nov. 11, 1871. William Clayton Letterbooks, Marriott Library.

_____. "Testimony." Feb. 16, 1874. In Andrew Jenson, ed., *Historical Record* 6 (May 1887): 224-26.

_____. *William Clayton's Journal: A Daily Record of the Journey of the Original Co. of Mormon Pioneers from Nauvoo, Illinois, to the Valley of the Great Salt Lake.* Salt Lake City: Clayton Family Association, 1921.

Cleland, Robert Glass, and Juanita Brooks, eds. *A Mormon Chronicle: The Diaries of John D. Lee, 1848-1876.* 2 vols. Salt Lake City: University of Utah Press, 1984.

Cleveland, Sarah [M. Kingsley]. "To the Presidency, and Ladies of the Female Relief Society of Nauvoo." *Times and Seasons* 4 (May 1, 1843): 187.

Clift, Mary. Affidavit. Aug. 29, 1842; Sept. 4, 1842. LDS Church History Library.

Coil, Henry Wilson. *Coil's Masonic Encyclopedia.* New York: Macoy Publishing & Masonic Supply Co., 1961.

"Cold Comfort." *Times and Seasons* 3, no. 23 (Oct. 15, 1842): 953-54.

Collier, Fred, ed. *The Nauvoo High Council Minutes Books.* Hannah, Utah: Collier Publishing Co., 2005.

"A Communication from Another Seceding Mormon." *Sangamo Journal,* Oct. 7, 1842. www.sidneyrigdon.com/dbroadhu/IL/sang1842.html#1007 (Nov. 20, 2008).

"Communications." *Times and Seasons* 1, no. 6 (Apr. 1840): 82-86.

Compton, Todd. "Fawn Brodie on Joseph Smith's Plural Wives and Polygamy: A Critical View." In *Reconsidering No Man Knows My History: Fawn M. Brodie and Joseph Smith in Retrospect.* Edited by Newell G. Bringhurst. Logan: Utah State University Press, 1996, 164-73.

_____. *In Sacred Loneliness: The Plural Wives of Joseph Smith.* Salt Lake City: Signature Books, 1997.

_____. "A Trajectory of Plurality: An Overview of Joseph Smith's Thirty-three Plural Wives." *Dialogue: A Journal of Mormon Thought* 29, no. 2 (Summer 1996): 1-38.

"Conference Minutes." *Times and Seasons* 5, no. 17 (Sept. 15, 1844): 646-47.

"Conference Minutes: April 6, 1844, Saturday Morning, In Grove." *Times and Seasons* 5, no. 9 (May 1, 1844): 522-24.

Conkling, J. Christopher. *A Joseph Smith Chronology.* Salt Lake City: Deseret Book, 1979.

Cook, Lyndon W. "'Brother Joseph Is Truly a Wonderful Man, He Is All We Could Wish a Prophet to Be': Pre-1844 Letters of William Law." *BYU Studies* 20, no. 2 (1980): 207-18.

_____. "Isaac Galland–Mormon Benefactor." *BYU Studies* 19 (Spring 1979): 261-84.

_____. "James Arlington Bennet and the Mormons." *BYU Studies* 19 (Winter 1979): 247-49; www.byustudies.byu.edu/shop/pdfsrc/19.2Cookpdf (Dec. 20, 2008).

_____. *Nauvoo Marriages, Proxy Sealings: 1843-1846.* Provo, Utah: Grandin Books, 2004.

_____. *William Law: Biographical Essay, Nauvoo Diary, Correspondence, Interview.* Orem, Utah: Grandin Book, 1994.

_____. "William Law, Nauvoo Dissenter." *BYU Studies* 22 (Winter 1982): 47-72.

_____, ed. *The Revelations of the Prophet Joseph Smith: A Historical and Biographical Commentary of the Doctrine and Covenants.* Provo, Utah: Seventy's Mission Bookstore, 1981.

Cooper, Rex Eugene. *Promises Made to the Fathers: Mormon Covenant Organization.* Salt Lake City: University of Utah Press, 1990.

Coray, Howard. Affidavit. June 12, 1882. LDS Church History Library.

_____. "Autobiography, 1817-1883." Microfilm. LDS Church History Library.

_____. Journal, 1867-68. Holograph. Lee Library.

_____. Letter to Martha Jane [Coray] Lewis, Aug. 2, 1889. LDS Church History Library.

Corbett, Pearson H. *Hyrum Smith, Patriarch.* Salt Lake City: Deseret Book, 1963.

"Correspondence between Gen. Joseph Smith and the Hon. Henry Clay." *Times and Seasons* 5, no. 11 (June 1, 1844): 544-49.

Cottam, Thomas. "Recollections of the Prophet Joseph Smith." *Juvenile Instructor* 27, no. 2 (Jan. 15, 1892): 65.

Council of Fifty. Minutes. Photocopy, H. Michael Marquardt Collection, Marriott Library.

Cowley, Matthias. Autobiography, 1829-53. Typescript. LDS Church History Library.

_____. Reminiscences, 1856. Typescript. LDS Church History Library.

_____. *Wilford Woodruff: History of His Life and Labors as Recorded in His Daily Journals.* Salt Lake City: Deseret News, 1909.

Cox, Elias. "Joseph Smith, the Prophet." *Young Woman's Journal* 17, no. 12 (Dec. 1906): 544.

Cox, Henrietta. "Recollections of the Prophet Joseph Smith." *Juvenile Instructor* 27, no. 7 (Apr. 1, 1892): 203.

Crang, Mike, and Nigel Thrift, eds. *Thinking Space.* London: Routledge, 2000.

Crawley, Peter. *A Descriptive Bibliography of the Mormon Church, Volume One, 1830-1847.* Provo, Utah: BYU Religious Studies Center, Brigham Young University, 1998.

Crites, Steven. *In the Twilight of Christendom: Hegel vs. Kierkegaard on Faith and History.* Chambersberg, Pennsylvania: American Academy of Religion, 1972.

_____. "Narrative Quality of Experience." *Journal of the American Academy of Religion* 239 (Sept. 1971): 291-311.

Crocheron, Augusta. *Representative Women of Deseret: A Book of Biographical Sketches to Accompany the Pictures of the Same Title.* Salt Lake City: J. C. Graham, 1884.

Crockwell, James. *Pictures and Biographies of Brigham Young and His Wives.* Salt Lake City: James Crockwell, n.d. [1887].

Crookston, Robert. "Autobiography of Robert Crookston Senior." 1865. Microfilm. LDS Church History Library.

Cross, Whitney R. *The Burned-Over District: The Social and Intellectual History of Enthusiastic Religion in Western New York: 1800-1850.* Ithaca: Cornell University Press, 1950.

Crowther, Duane S. *The Life of Joseph Smith: An Atlas, Chronological Outline, and Documentation Harmony.* Springville, Utah: Horizon Publishers, 1989.

Cummings, B[enjamin] F[ranklin]. "The Prophet's Last Letters." *Improvement Era* 18 (Feb. 1915): 388-93.

Cummings, Horace. "Joseph Smith and Polygamy." *Contributor* 5 (Apr. 1884): 205-24.

Dana, Charles Root. Journal, 1847. Microfilm. LDS Church History Library.

Daniels, William M., with Lyman Littlefield. *Correct Account of the Murder of the Generals Joseph and Hyrum Smith at Carthage on the 27th Day of June, 1844.* Nauvoo, Illinois: John Taylor, 1845, http://lincoln.lib.niu.edu/cgi-bin/hilogic/getobject.p1?c.967:2.lincoln (Feb. 14, 2009).

Davis, David Brion. "Some Themes of Counter-Subversion: An Analysis of Anti-Masonic, Anti-Catholic, and Anti-Mormon Literature." *Mississippi Valley Historical Review* 47 (Sept. 1960): 205-24.

Davis, George T. M. *An Authentic Account of the Massacre of Joseph Smith, the Mormon Prophet, and Hyrum Smith, His Brother, Together with a Brief History of the Rise and Progress of Mormonism and All the Circumstances Which Led to Their Death.* St. Louis: Chambers & Knapp, 1844.

Daynes, Kathryn M. *More Wives Than One: Transformation of the Mormon Marriage System, 1840-1910.* Urbana: University of Illinois Press, 2001.

de Leon, Edwin. *Thirty Years of My Life on Three Continents.* London: Ward and Downey, 1890.

De Toqueville, Alexis. *Democracy in America.* Trans. Henry Reeve. 2 vols. 1840; rpt., New York: Shocken, 1961.

deCerteau, Michel. *The Practice of Everyday Life.* Berkeley: University of California Press, 1988.

"Democratic Platform of 1840." http://edsitement.neh.gov/view_lesson_plan.asp?id=554. 11/20/2007 (Feb. 2008).

de Pillis, Mario S. "The Quest for Religious Authority and the Rise of Mormonism." *Dialogue: A Journal of Mormon Thought* 1, no. 1 (1966): 68-88.

Derr, Jill Mulvay. "'Strength in Our Union': The Making of Mormon Sisterhood." In Maureen Ursenbach Beecher and Lavina Fielding Anderson, eds., *Sisters in Spirit,* 153-207.

_____, Janath Russell Cannon, and Maureen Ursenbach Beecher. *Women of Covenant: The Story of the Relief Society.* Salt Lake City: Deseret Book, 1992.

"The Difficulties at Nauvoo–The Other Side of the Story–John C. Bennett–'Spiritual Wives,' &c, &c." *Quincy Whig,* July 16, 1842, 1.

Dinger, John S. *The Nauvoo City and High Council Minutes.* Salt Lake City: Signature Books, 2011.

"Disclosures–The Attempted MURDER OF BOGGS! To the Editors of the St. Louis Bulletin." *Sangamo Journal,* July 16, 1842, 2.

"Discovery of the Brass Plates." Broadside published at Nauvoo, Illinois, June 24, 1843.

Ditzion, Sidney. *Marriage Morals and Sex in America: A History of Ideas.* New York: Bookman Associates, 1953.

Dixon, William Hepworth. *Spiritual Wifery.* 2 vols. London: Hurst and Blackett, 1868.

Document Containing the Correspondence, Orders &c. in Relation to the Disturbances with the Mormons; And the Evidence Given Before the Hon. Austin A. King, Judge of the Fifth Judicial Circuit of the State of Missouri, at the Court-House in Richmond, in a Criminal Court of Inquiry, Begun November 12, 1838, on the Trial of Joseph Smith, Jr., and Others, for High Treason and Other Crimes Against the State. Fayette, Missouri:

Published By Order of the General Assembly. Printed at the office of the Boon's Lick Democrat, 1841). www.farwesthistory.com/docc01.html.

Dumenil, Lynn. *Freemasonry and American Culture, 1880-1939.* Princeton, New Jersey: Princeton University Press, 1984.

Durkheim, Emile. *Suicide: A Study in Sociology.* Ed. George Simpson. Trans. John A. Spaulding and George Simpson. New York: Free Press, 1966.

"Effects of Apostasy." *Times and Seasons* 4, no. 6 (Feb. 1, 1843): 89-90.

"Egyptian Antiquities." *New York Herald,* Dec. 28, 1842, 2.

"Egyptian Antiquities." *North American Review* 29 (Oct. 1829): 361-89.

Ehat, Andrew F. "'It Seems Like Heaven Began on Earth': Joseph Smith and the Constitution of the Kingdom of God." *BYU Studies* 20, no. 3 (Spring 1980): 253-79.

_____. "Joseph Smith's Introduction of Temple Ordinances and the 1844 Mormon Succession Question." M.A. thesis, Brigham Young University, 1982.

_____. "'Who Shall Ascend into the Hill of the Lord?': Sesquicentennial Reflections of a Sacred Day, 4 May 1842." In *Temples of the Ancient World: Ritual and Symbolism.* Edited by Donald W. Parry. Salt Lake City: Deseret Book/Provo, Utah: FARMS, 1994, 48-62.

_____, ed. "'They Might Have Known That He Was Not a Fallen Prophet': The Nauvoo Journal of Joseph Fielding." *BYU Studies* 19, no. 2 (Winter 1979): 133-66. Also at www.byustudies.byu.edu/shop/pdfSRS/19.2Ehatpdf (Jan. 12, 2008).

_____, and Lyndon W. Cook, eds. *The Words of Joseph Smith: The Contemporary Accounts of the Nauvoo Discourses of the Prophet Joseph.* Vol. 6 in the Religious Studies Monograph Series. Provo, Utah: Brigham Young University Religious Studies Center, 1980.

"Elder Rigdon, &c." *Times and Seasons* 3, no. 22 (Sept. 15, 1842): 922-23.

Elder, Sarah Louise Dalton. Statement. Ca. Oct. 10, 1931. Church Manuscripts Collection, 9:85. Compiled by Alan H. Gerber. Microfilm. Lee Library.

Eldredge, Horace. Diary, 1816-60. *Tullidge's Quarterly Magazine* 1 (1880-81): 406-14.

Eliade, Mircea. *The Sacred and the Profane: The Nature of Religion.* New York: Harcourt Brace Jovanovich, 1959.

Ellis, John B. *Free Love and Its Votaries, Etc.* New York: United States Publishing Co., 1870.

Ellsworth, Paul. D. "Mobocracy and the Rule of Law: American Press Reaction to the Murder of Joseph Smith." *BYU Studies* 20, no. 1 (1979): 71-82.

Ellsworth, S. George. "A History of Mormon Missions in the United States and Canada, 1830-1860." Ph.D. diss., University of California, 1951.

Enders, Donald L. "A Dam for Nauvoo: An Attempt to Industrialize the City." *BYU Studies* 18, no. 2 (1978): 246-54.

_____. "Platting the City Beautiful: A Historical and Archaeological Glimpse of Nauvoo Streets." *BYU Studies* 19, no. 3 (1979): 408-15.

England, Breck. *Life and Thought of Orson Pratt.* Salt Lake City: University of Utah Press, 1985.

England, Eugene, ed. "George Laub's Nauvoo Journal." *BYU Studies* 18, no. 2 (1978): 151-78.

"An Epistle of the Twelve." *Times and Seasons* 3, no. 2 (Nov. 15 1841): 600-602.

Epperson, Steven. "'The Grand, Fundamental Principle': Joseph Smith and the Virtue of Friendship." *Journal of Mormon History* 23, no. 2 (1997): 77-105.

Erickson, Dan. *"As a Thief in the Night": The Mormon Quest for Millennial Deliverance.* Salt Lake City: Signature Books, 1998.

Esplin, Ronald K. "Hyrum Smith: The Mildness of a Lamb, the Integrity of Job." *Ensign,* Feb. 2000, 30-36.

_____. "Joseph Smith's Mission and Timetable: 'God Will Protect Me Until My Work is Done.'" In Larry C. Porter and Susan Easton Blacks, eds., *The Prophet Joseph,* 280-319.

_____. "Sickness and Faith: Nauvoo Letters." *BYU Studies* 15, no. 4 (1975): 425-34.

_____. "The Significance of Nauvoo for Latter-day Saints." *Journal of Mormon History* 16 (1990): 71-86.

_____, ed. "Life in Nauvoo, June 1844: Vilate Kimball's Martyrdom Letters." *BYU Studies* 19, no. 2 (1979): 231-40.

The Essential Joseph Smith. Salt Lake City: Signature Books, 1995.

Evans, John Henry. *Joseph Smith: An American Prophet.* New York: MacMillan Co., 1943.

"Evidence of John Taylor." *Saints Herald* 52 (July 11, 1905): 28.

Faulring, Scott H., ed. *An American Prophet's Record: The Diaries and Journals of Joseph Smith.* Salt Lake City: Signature Books/Smith Research Associates, 1989.

Fawcett, William. "Recollections of the Prophet Joseph Smith." *Juvenile Instructor* 27, no. 2 (Jan. 15, 1892): 66.

Fielding, Joseph. Diary, 1797-1863. www.boap.org/LDS/Early-Saints/JFielding.html (Dec. 20, 2008).

Firmage, Edwin Brown, and Richard Collin Mangrum. *Zion in the Courts: A Legal History of the Church of Jesus Christ of Latter-day Saints, 1830-1900.* Urbana: University of Illinois Press, 1988.

Fisher, Josephine Lyon. Statement, Feb. 24, 1915. Holograph. LDS Church History Library.

Flake, Chad J., and Larry W. Draper, eds. *A Mormon Bibliography, 1830-1930: Books, Pamphlets, Periodicals, and Broadsides Relating to the First Century of Mormonism.* 2 vols. 2nd ed., rev. and enl. Provo, Utah: BYU Religious Studies Center, 2004.

Flanders, Robert B. "The Kingdom of God in Illinois: Politics in Utopia." *Dialogue: A Journal of Mormon Thought* 5 (Spring 1970): 26-36. Rpt. in *Kingdom on the Mississippi Revisited: Nauvoo in Mormon History,* edited by Roger D. Launius and John E. Hallwas. Urbana: University of Illinois Press, 1996, 147-59.

_____. *Nauvoo: Kingdom on the Mississippi.* Urbana: University of Illinois, 1965.

_____. "To Transform History: Early Mormon Culture and the Concept of Time and Space." *Church History* 40 (1971): 108-17.

Fogarty, Robert S., ed. *Dictionary of American Communal and Utopian History.* Westport, Connecticut: Greenwood Press, 1980.

"For the Neighbor." *Nauvoo Neighbor,* Aug. 2, 1843, 2.

"For the Sangamo Journal." *Sangamo Journal,* July 1, 1842.

Ford, Thomas. *History of Illinois from its Commencement as a State in 1818 to 1847: Containing a Full Account of the Black Hawk War, the Rise, Progress, and Fall of Mormonism, the Alton & Lovejoy Riots, and Other Important and Interesting Events.* 2 vols. 1854. Rpt., Chicago: Lakeside, 1946.

_____. "Message of the Governor of Illinois in Relation to the Disturbances in Hancock County, December 21, 1844." *Reports Made to the Senate and House of Representatives of the State of Illinois, 1844.* Springfield, Illinois: Walters & Weber, Public Printer, 1845.

Foster, Lawrence. "A Little-Known Defense of Polygamy from the Mormon Press in 1842." *Dialogue: A Journal of Mormon Thought* 9 (Winter 1974): 21-34.

_____. "The Psychology of Prophetic Charisma: New Approaches to Understanding Joseph Smith and the Development of Charismatic Leadership." *Journal of Mormon History* 36 (Winter 2003): 1-14.

_____. "The Psychology of Religious Genius: Joseph Smith and the Origin of New Religious Movements." In Bryan Waterman, ed., *The Prophet Puzzle,* 183-208.

_____. *Religion and Sexuality: The Shakers, the Mormons and the Oneida Community.* Urbana: University of Illinois Press, 1984.

_____. *Religion and Sexuality: Three American Communal Experiments of the Nineteenth Century.* New York: Oxford University Press, 1981.

_____. *Women, Family, and Utopia: Communal Experiments of the Shakers, the Oneida Community, and the Mormons.* Syracuse, New York: Syracuse University Press, 1991.

Francaviglia, Richard V. *The Mormon Landscape: Existence, Creation, and Perception of a Unique Image in the American West.* New York: AMS Press, 1978.

Francis, Simeon. "The Mormons." *Sangamo Journal,* July 1, 1842.

Franco, Barbara. "The Ritualization of Male Friendship and Virtue in Nineteenth-Century Fraternal Organizations." In *The Material Culture of Gender, the Gender of Material Culture.* Edited by Katherine A. Martinez and Kenneth L. Ames. Winterthur, Delaware: University Press of New England, 1997, 281-98.

Freemasonry Letters. Nauvoo, 1842. LDS Church History Library.

Freemasons. Grand Lodge of the District of Columbia. Reprint of the *Proceedings of the Grand Lodge of Illinois from Its Organization in 1840 to 1850, Inclusive.* Washington, D.C.: John F. Shieiry, Printer, 1903.

Fullmer, John S. Letter to Wilford Woodruff, Oct. 18, 1844. LDS Church History Library.

Fulwider, A. L. *History of Stephenson County, Illinois.* Chicago: S. J. Clarke Publishing, 1910.

Galland, Isaac. Letter to Joseph Smith, Dec. 11, 1841. LDS Church History Library.

Ganzevoort, R. Ruard. "Religious Coping Reconsidered: An Integrated Approach." *Journal of Psychology and Theology* 26 , no. 3 (1998): 260-75.

Gardner, Hamilton. "The Nauvoo Legion, 1840-1845: A Unique Military Organization." *Journal of the Illinois Historical Society* 54, no. 2 (1961): 181-97.

Garr, Arnold K. "Joseph Smith: Campaign for President of the United States," *Ensign,* Feb. 2009.

_____. "Joseph Smith: Candidate for President of the United States." *Regional Studies in Latter-day Saint Church History: Illinois.* Edited by H. Dean Garrett. Provo, Utah: BYU Department of Church History and Doctrine, 1995, 151-68.

Garrett, H. Dean. "The Coming Forth of the Doctrine of Covenants." In *Regional Stuides in Latter-day Saint Church History: Ohio.* Edited by Milton V. Backman. Provo, Utah: BYU Department of Church History and Doctrine, 1990, 89-103.

_____. "Disease and Sickness in Nauvoo." In *Regional Studies in Latter-day Saint Church History: Illinois.* Edited by H. Dean Garrett. Provo, Utah: BYU Department of Church History and Doctrine, 1995, 169-82.

Garrison, George Pierce, ed. *Diplomatic Correspondence of the Republic of Texas.* 3 Parts. Washington, D.C.: Government Printing Office, 1908-11.

Gates, Susa Young. *History of the Young Ladies' Mutual Improvement Association.* Salt Lake City: General Board of the YLMIA, 1911.

_____. Introduction to "Olivia Pratt Driggs." *Relief Society Magazine* 11, no. 8 (Aug. 1924): 385-39.

Gaustad, Edwin Scott, and Philip L. Barlow. *New Historical Atlas of Religion in America.* New York: Oxford University Press, 2001.

Gayler, George R. "Attempts by the State of Missouri to Extradite Joseph Smith, 1841-1843." *Journal of the Illinois State Historical Society* 58 (Oct. 1963): 21-36.

_____. "The 'Expositor' Affair: Prelude to the Downfall of Joseph Smith." *Northwest Missouri State College Studies* 25 (Feb. 1961): 3-15.

_____. "Governor Ford and the Death of Joseph and Hyrum Smith." *Journal of the Illinois State Historical Society* 50 (Winter 1957): 391-411.

_____. "The Mormons and Politics in Illinois 1839-1844." *Journal of the Illinois State Historical Society* 49 (Spring 1956): 48-66.

_____. "A Social, Economic, and Political Study of the Mormons in Western Illinois, 1839-1846: A Re-Evaluation." Ph.D. diss., University of Chicago, 1938.

Geddes, Joseph A. *The United Order among the Mormons: (Missouri Phase).* New York City: Columbia University, 1922.

Gergen, Kenneth J., and Mary M. Gergen. "Narrative Form and the Construction of Psychological Science." In *Narrative Psychology: The Storied Nature of Human Conduct.* Edited by Theodore R. Sarbin. New York: Praeger Publishers, 1986, 22-44.

Glaser, John Frederick. "The Disaffection of William Law." *Restoration Studies* 3(1986): 163-75.

Goddard, Stephen H. Statement, July 23, 1842. In *Affidavits and Certificates, Disproving the Statements and Affidavits Contained in John C. Bennett's Letters.*

Goddard, Zeruiah N. Affidavit. In *Affidavits and Certificates, Disproving the Statements and Affidavits Contained in John C. Bennett's Letters.*

Godfrey, Kenneth W. "Causes of Mormon/Non-Mormon Conflict in Hancock County, Illinois, 1839-1846." Ph.D. diss. Brigham Young University, 1967.

_____. "Joseph Smith and the Masons." *Journal of the Illinois State History Society* 64, no. 1 (Spring 1971): 79-96.

_____. "A New Look at an Alleged Little Known Discourse by Joseph Smith." *BYU Studies* 9 (Autumn 1968): 49-53.

_____. "Non-Mormon Views of the Martyrdom: A Look at Some Early Published Accounts." *John Whitmer Historical Association Journal* 7 (1987): 12-20.

_____. "The Road to Carthage Led West." *BYU Studies* 7 (Winter 1968): 204-15.

_____, Audrey M. Godfrey, and Jill Mulvay Derr. *Women's Voices: An Untold History of the Latter-day Saints, 1830-1900.* Salt Lake City: Deseret Book, 1982.

Goodwin, Samuel H. *Mormonism and Masonry.* Washington, D.C.: The Masonic Service Association of the United States, 1924.

Gordon, Sarah Barringer. *The Mormon Question: Polygamy and Constitutional Conflict in Nineteenth-Century America.* Chapel Hill: University of North Carolina Press, 2002.

"The Government of God." *Times and Seasons* 3, no. 11 (July 15, 1842): 855-58.

"Governor Ford's Inaugural Address." *Sangamo Journal,* Dec. 15, 1842. www.sidneyrigdom.com/dbroadhu/IL/sang1842.html#1215 (Dec. 20, 2008).

Gowans, Alan. "Freemasonry and the Neoclassic Style in America." *Antiques* vol. 77, no. 2 (1960): 171-75.

Grant, Bryan J. "The Church in the British Isles." *Encyclopedia of Mormonism.* 4 vols. New York: Macmillan Publishing, 1992, 1:226-32.

Green, Arnold H. "Jews in LDS Thought." *BYU Studies* 34, no. 4 (1994-95): 137-64.

Green, Doyle L. "Are These Portraits of the Prophet Joseph Smith?" *Improvement Era* 69 (Dec. 1966): 1074-77.

Gregg, Thomas. *History of Hancock County, Illinois, Together with an Outline History of the State and a Digest of State Laws.* Chicago: C. C. Chapman, 1880.

_____. *Portrait and Biographical Record of Hancock, McDonough, and Henderson Counties, Illinois, Containing Biographical Sketches of Prominent and Representative Citizens of the County.* Chicago: Lake City Publishing, 1894.

_____. *Prophet of Palymyra; Mormonism Reviewed and Examined in the Life, Character, and Career of Its Founder, from "Cumorah Hill" to Carthage Jail and the Desert. Together with a complete history of the Mormon Era in Illinois, and an Exhaustive Investigation of the "Spalding Manuscript" Theory of the Origin of the Book of Mormon.* New York: J. B. Alden, 1890.

Griggs, Thomas. "Remarks on the Above." *Warsaw Signal,* Jan. 17, 1844, 2.

_____. "A Word of Parting to Brother Joe." *Warsaw Message,* Feb. 24, 1844.

Grover, Thomas. "Something Related to Celestial Marriage." *Deseret News,* June 13, 1883, 12.

Gue, Benjamin F. *History of Iowa,* 2 vols. New York: Century History Co., 1903.

Halbwachs, Maurice. *The Collective Memory.* New York: Harper and Row, 1950.

Hale, Aroet Lucius. Autobiography. Typescript. Lee Library.

_____. Journal, 1828-80s. Holograph. LDS Church History Library.

Hale, Van. "The Doctrinal Impact of the King Follett Discourse." *BYU Studies* 18, no. 2 (1978): 209-25.

_____. "The King Follett Discourse: Textual History and Criticism." *Sunstone* 8, no. 5 (1983): 4-12.

Hales, Brian C. "The Joseph Smith-Sylvia Sessions Plural Sealing: Polyandry or Polygyny?" *Mormon Historical Studies* 9, no. 1 (2008): 41-57.

_____. *Joseph Smith's Polygamy,* 3 vols. Salt Lake City: Greg Kofford Books, 2013.

Hall, William. *The Abominations of Mormonism Exposed.* Cincinnati: I. Hart, 1852.

Hallwas, John E. "Mormon Nauvoo from a Non-Mormon Perspective." *Journal of Mormon History* 16 (1990): 53-66.

_____, and Roger D. Launius, eds. *Cultures in Conflict: A Documentary History of the Mormon War in Illinois.* Logan: Utah State University Press, 1995.

Hamilton, C. Mark. *Nineteenth Century Mormon Architecture and City Planning.* New York: Oxford University Press, 1995.

Hampshire, Annette. "Nauvoo Politics." *Encyclopedia of Mormonism.* 4 vols. New York City: Macmillan Publishing, 1992, 3:999-1000.

_____. "Thomas Sharp and Anti-Mormon Sentiment in Illinois, 1842-1845." *Journal of the Illinois State Historical Society* 72, no. 2 (1979): 82-100.

Hancock, Mosiah. "The Prophet Joseph–Some of His Sayings." *Deseret News,* Feb. 21, 1884.

Hanks, Maxine, ed. *Women and Authority: Re-emerging Mormon Feminism.* Salt Lake City: Signature Books, 1992.

Hansen, Klaus J. "The Making of King Strang: A Re-Examination." *Michigan History* 44 (Sept. 1962): 201-19.

_____. *Quest for Empire: The Political Kingdom of God and the Council of Fifty in Mormon History.* East Lansing: Michigan State University Press, 1967.

Hardy, B. Carmon. *Doing the Works of Abraham: Mormon Polygamy: Its Origin, Practice, and Demise.* Vol. 9 of Kingdom in the West: The Mormons and the American Frontier, Norman, Oklahoma: Arthur H. Clark Co., 2007.

_____. *Solemn Covenant: The Mormon Polygamous Passage.* Urbana: University of Illinois Press, 1992.

Harrington, Virginia C., and J. C. Harrington. *Rediscovery of the Nauvoo Temple.* Salt Lake City: Nauvoo Restoration, 1971.

Hartley, William G. "Close Friends as Witnesses: Joseph Smith and the Joseph Knight Families." In Susan Easton Black and Charles D. Tate Jr., eds., *Joseph Smith,* 271-83.

_____. "Nauvoo Stake, Priesthood Quorums, and the Church's First Wards." *BYU Studies* 32, nos. 1-2 (1992): 57-80.

_____. *Stand by My Servant Joseph: The Story of the Joseph Knight Family and the Restoration.* Provo, Utah: Joseph Fielding Smith Institute for LDS History; Salt Lake City: Deseret Book, 2003.

Hatch, Ephraim. "What Did Joseph Smith Look Like?" *Ensign,* Mar. 1981, 65-73.

Hatch, Nathan O. *The Democratization of American Christianity.* New Haven, Connecticut: Yale University Press, 1989.

Haven, Charlotte. "A Girl's Letters from Nauvoo." [variously titled]. *Overland Monthly* 16, 2nd ser.: Dec. 16, 1890, 618-38. http://olivercowdery.com/smithhome/1880s-1890s/havn1890.html (Jan. 29, 2009).

Hayden, Dolores. *The Power of Place: Urban Landscapes as Public History.* Cambridge, Massachusetts: MIT Press, 1995.

Heidegger, Martin. "Language." In *Poetry, Language, Thought.* Edited by Albert Hofstader. New York: Perennial Classics, 1971, 185-208.

Hendricks, Drusilla Dorris. "Historical Sketch." Typescript. LDS Church History Library.

Hickman, Jared Winston. "'The Whole of America Is Zion': Joseph Smith, the New World Baroque, and Comparative American Literary Studies." Honor's thesis, Bowdoin College, 2001.

Hicks, Michael. "Joseph Smith, W. W. Phelps, and the Poetic Paraphrase of 'The Vision.'" *Journal of Mormon History* 20 (Fall 1994): 63-84.

Higbee, Chauncey L. Affidavit. May 17, 1842. Statements Collection. LDS Church History Library.

Higham, John. *From Boundlessness to Consolidation: The Transformation of American Culture, 1848-1860.* Ann Arbor, Michigan: William L. Clements Library, 1969. Rpt. in Bobbs-Merrill Reprint Series in American History. Indianapolis: Bobbs-Merrill Co., n.d.

"The Higher Ordinances." *Deseret News Semi-Weekly,* Feb. 15, 1884, 2.

Hill, Donna. *Joseph Smith: The First Mormon.* Garden City, New York: Doubleday, 1977.

Hill, Ivy H. B. ed. *Autobiography of Mary Dunn Ensign, daughter of Simeon Adams Dunn and Adaline Rawson Dunn, 1914.* Logan, Utah: J. P. Smith and Son, 1962.

Hill, Marvin S. "Brodie Revisited: A Reappraisal." *Dialogue: A Journal of Mormon Thought* 7 (Winter 1972): 72-85.

_____. "Counter-Revolution: The Mormon Reaction to the Coming of American Democracy." *Sunstone* 13, no. 3 (1989): 24-33.

_____. "Foreword." *The Essential Joseph Smith.*

_____. "Joseph Smith the Man: Some Reflections on a Subject of Controversy." *BYU Studies* 21 (Spring 1981): 175-86.

_____. "Quest for Refuge: An Hypothesis as to the Social Origins and Nature of the Mormon Political Kingdom." *Journal of Mormon History* 2 (1975): 3-20.

_____. *Quest for Refuge: The Mormon Flight from American Pluralism.* Salt Lake City: Signature Books, 1989.

_____. "The Role of Christian Primitivism in the Origin and Development of the Mormon Kingdom, 1830-1844." Ph.D. diss., University of Chicago, 1968.

_____. "Secular or Sectarian History? A Critique of *No Man Knows My History.*" *Church History* 43 (Mar. 1974): 78-96.

_____, and James B. Allen, eds. *Mormonism and American Culture.* New York: Harper and Row, Publishers, 1972.

Hills, Gustavus. *Map of the City of Nauvoo, 1842.* Facsimile. Nauvoo Restoration, 1972.

Hinchman, Lewis P., and Sandra K. Hinchman, eds. *Memory, Identity, Community: The Idea of Narrative in the Human Sciences.* Albany, New York: SUNY Press, 1997.

Historian's Office Journal. LDS Church History Library.

Historical Encyclopedia of Illinois and History of McDonough County. Chicago: Munsell Publishing, Bateman, Newton, and Paul Selby, Alonzo St. Clair Wilderman, and Augusta A. Wilderman, 1907.

Historical Record. For Andrew Jenson's affidavits/article on plural marriage in Nauvoo, see Jenson, Andrew, "Plural Marriage."

"History and Life of William Greenhalgh, son of Robert and Ellen Greenhalgh, Born July 29, 1811, in Bregmat (Brightmat) (Near Belton, Lanceshire, England)." In Mark L. McConkie, ed., *Remembering Joseph,* 397-99.

"History of Brigham Young." *Millennial Star* 26 (May 21, 1864): 328.

"History of Emma Maria Zundel (1836-1926)." Excerpted from "A Record of the Ancestry and Descendants of John Jacob Zundel, Known as Jacob Zundel." In Mark L. McConkie, ed., *Remembering Joseph.* CD.

"History of Joseph Smith." *Times and Seasons* 3, no. 10 (Mar. 15, 1842): 727-28, 748-49, 753.

History of Lee County, Iowa, Containing a History of the County, Its Cities, Towns, etc. Chicago: Western Historical Co., 1979.

History of Sangamon County, Illinois. Chicago: Interstate Publishing Co., 1881.

"History of Women's Freemasonry." www.womenfreemasonsusa.com/history.html (Nov. 13, 2007).

"A Hoax: Reminiscences of an Old Kinderhook Mystery." *Journal of the Illinois State Historical Society* 5 (July 1912): 272.

Hogan, Mervin B. *The Confrontation of Grand Master Abraham Jonas and John C. Bennett in Nauvoo.* Privately printed, 1976.

_____. "Erection and Dedication of the Nauvoo Masonic Temple." Salt Lake City: N.p., Dec. 27, 1976. In Marvin B. Hogan Papers, Marriott Library.

_____. *Freemasonry and Mormon Ritual.* Salt Lake City: Author, 1991.

_____. "The Involvement of John Cook Bennett with Mormonism and Freemasonry at Nauvoo." N.d. Marriott Library.

_____. "Mormonism and Freemasonry: The Illinois Episode." *The Little Masonic Library* 2 (1977): 311. Rpt., Salt Lake City: Macoy Publishing and Masonic Supply, Campus Graphics, ca. 1977, 1980.

_____. *The Official Minutes of Nauvoo Lodge U.D.* Des Moines, Iowa: Research Lodge, No. 2 [1971].

_____, ed. *Founding Minutes of the Nauvoo Lodge, U.D.* Des Moines, Iowa: Research Lodge No. 2, 1971.

Holt, James. "The Reminiscences of James Holt: A Narrative of the Emmett Co." Edited by Dale Morgan. *Utah Historical Quarterly* 23 (Apr. 1955): 1-33.

Holzapfel, Jeni Brobert, and Richard Neitzel Holzapfel, eds. *A Woman's View: Helen Mar Whitney's Reminiscences of Early Church History.* Provo, Utah: BYU Religious Studies Center, 1997.

Holzapfel, Richard Neitzel, and T. Jeffrey Cottle. *Old Mormon Nauvoo and Southeastern Iowa.* Provo, Utah: Grandin Book, 1990.

_____, and Jeni Broberg Holzapfel. *Women of Nauvoo.* Salt Lake City, Utah: Bookcraft, 1992.

Homer, Michael W. "'Similarity of Priesthood in Masonry': The Relationship between Freemasonry and Mormonism." *Dialogue: A Journal of Mormon Thought* 27, no. 3 (Fall 1994): 1-116.

Horne, Robert. "Reminiscences of the Church in Nauvoo." *Millennial Star* 55 (Sept. 4, 1893): 585.

Hovey, Joseph G. "Autobiography (1812-47)." July 1868. Typescript. LDS Church History Library.

Howard, Richard P., ed. *The Memoirs of President Joseph Smith III (1832-1914).* Photo rpt., from *Saints Herald,* Nov. 6, 1934-July 31, 1937.

_____. *Restoration Scriptures: A Study of Their Textual Development.* Independence, Missouri: Herald House, 1969.

_____. "A Tentative Approach to the Book of Abraham." *Dialogue: A Journal of Mormon Thought* 3, no. 2 (1968): 88-92.

_____. "What Sort of Priesthood for Women at Nauvoo?" *John Whitmer Historical Association Journal* 13 (1993): 18-30.

Howe, Eber D. *History of Mormonism: Or, A Faithful Account of That Singular Imposition and Delusion.* Painesville, Ohio: Author, 1840.

_____. *Mormonism Unvailed: or, A Faithful Account of That Singular Imposition and Delusion, from Its Rise to the Present Time.* Painesville, Ohio, 1834.

Huntington, Oliver B. "History of the Life of Oliver B. Huntington: Also His Travels and Troubles Written by Himself, 1878-1900." Typescript, Utah State Historical Society. Carbon copy of typescript, LDS Church History Library. Copy also at Marriott Library.

_____. Journals, 1835-1900. Typescript, Utah State Historical Society.

Huntington, William. Autobiography, 1784-1846. Typescript. Zina D. H. Young Collection. LDS Church History Library.

_____. Diaries and Autobiography, 1784-1846. Lee Library.

Huntington, Zina Diantha. Autobiographies (not differentiated by title or date). Zina D. H. Young Collection. LDS Church History Library.

_____. "Nauvoo Journal." June 5, 1844-Sept. 21, 1845. Holograph. In Zina Card Brown Collection, LDS Church History Library.

Huntress, Keith. "Governor Thomas Ford and the Murders of Joseph Smith." *Dialogue: A Journal of Mormon Thought* 4, no. 2 (1969): 41-52.

Hyde, John. *Mormonism: Its Leaders and Designs.* New York: W.P. Fetridge, 1857.

Hyde, Mary Ann Price. "Autobiography." Aug. 20, 1888. Holograph, Bancroft Library. Microfilm, Utah State Historical Society and LDS Church History.

Hyde, Myrtle Stevens. *Orson Hyde: The Olive Branch fo Israel.* Salt Lake City: Agreka Books, 2000.

Hyde, Orson. *Speech of Elder Orson Hyde, Delivered Before the High Priests' Quorum, in Nauvoo, April 27th, 1845, upon the Course and Conduct of Mr. Sydney [sic] Rigdon, and upon the Merits of His Claims to the Presidency of the Church of Jesus Christ of Latter-day Saints.* Liverpool, England: James and Woodburn, 1845.

Irving, Gordon. "The Law of Adoption: One Phase of the Development of the Mormon Concept of Salvation, 1830-1890." *BYU Studies* 14, no. 3 (1974): 291-314.

Jackson, Joseph H. Affidavit. June 21, 1844. LDS Church History Library.

_____. *A Narrative of the Adventures and Experience of Joseph H. Jackson in Nauvoo: Disclosing the Depths of Mormon Villainy Practiced in Nauvoo.* Warsaw, Illinois: n.p., 1844.

Jackson, Richard H. "The Mormon Village: Genesis and Antecedents of the City of Zion Plan." *BYU Studies* 17, no. 2 (1977): 223-40.

Jacob, Udney Hay. *An Extract, From a Manuscript Entitled The Peace Maker, or the Doctrines of the Millennium: Being a Treatise on Religion and Jurisprudence, Or a New System of Religion and Politicks.* Nauvoo, Illinois: Joseph Smith, 1842.

Jacobs, Zebulon. Diary, 1867-78. Typescript. Zina D. H. Young Collection. LDS Church History Library.

James, William. *Varieties of Religious Experience: A Study in Human Nature.* New York: New American Library, 1958.

Jamison, Kay Redfield. *Touched with Fire: Manic Depressive Illness and the Artistic Temperament.* New York: Free Press, 1993.

Jennings, Warren A. "Two Iowa Postmasters View Nauvoo: Anti-Mormon Letter to the Governor of Missouri." *BYU Studies* 11 (Spring 1971): 275-92.

Jensen, Richard L. "Transplanted to Zion: The Impact of British Latter-day Saint Immigration upon Nauvoo." *BYU Studies* 31, no. 1 (Winter 1991): 77-89.

Jenson, Andrew. "Joseph Smith the Prophet." *Historical Record* 7 (Jan. 1888): 353-576. Jenson published nine volumes of this periodical in Salt Lake City, between 1882 and 1890.

_____. *Latter-day Saint Biographical Encyclopedia: A Compendium of Biographical Sketches of Prominent Men and Women in the Church of Jesus Christ of Latter-day Saints.* 4 vols. Salt Lake City: Andrew Jenson History Co., 1901-30.

_____. "Plural Marriage." *Historical Record* 6 (May 1887): 219-40.

Jessee, Dean C. "The Early Accounts of Joseph Smith's First Vision." *BYU Studies* 9, no. 3 (Spring 1969): 275-94.

_____. "Joseph Smith's 19 July 1840 Discourse." *BYU Studies* 19, no. 3 (Spring 1979): 390-94. Martha Jane Knowlton Coray's notes.

_____. "Howard Coray's Recollections of Joseph Smith." *BYU Studies* 17, no. 3 (Spring 1977): 341-47.

_____, ed. *The Papers of Joseph Smith.* 2 vols. Salt Lake City: Deseret Book. *Volume 1: Autobiographical and Historical Writings* (1989). *Volume 2: Journal, 1832-1842* (1992).

_____. "The Reliability of Joseph Smith's History." *Journal of Mormon History* 3 (1976): 23-46.
_____. "The Writing of Joseph Smith's History." *BYU Studies* 11 (Spring 1971): 439-73.
_____, ed. "The John Taylor Nauvoo Journal, January 1845-September 1845." *BYU Studies* 23, no. 3 (1983): 1-105.
_____, ed. *The Personal Writings of Joseph Smith.* Salt Lake City: Deseret Book, 1984.
_____. "Priceless Words and Fallible Memories: Joseph Smith as Seen in the Effort to Preserve His Discourses." *BYU Studies* 31 (Spring 1991): 19-40.
_____, and John W. Welch. "Revelations in Context: Joseph Smith's Letter from Liberty Jail, March 20, 1839." *BYU Studies* 39, no. 3 (2000): 125-45.
"John C. Bennett." *Times and Seasons* 3, no. 19 (July 22, 1842): 868-76.
"John C. Bennett, Affidavit." *Sangamo Journal,* July 5, 1842, 2.
Johnson, Benjamin F. "Biographical Sketch of Zina D. Young, 1896." Typescript. Zina D. H. Young Collection. LDS Church History Library.
_____. Letter to George Gibbs, 1903. See Zimmerman, Dean.
_____. *My Life's Review.* 1947; rpt. Provo, Utah: Grandin Book Co., 1997.
Johnson, Clark V., ed. *Mormon Redress Petitions: Documents of the 1833-1838 Missouri Conflict.* Provo, Utah: BYU Religious Studies Center, 1992.
Johnson, Melvin C. *Polygamy on the Pedernales: Lyman Wight's Mormon Villages in Antebellum Texas, 1845-1858.* Logan: Utah State University Press, 2006.
Jonas, Abraham. Letter to George Miller, May 4, 1842, LDS Church History Library.
Jones, A. J., and R. M. Anservitze. "Saint-Simone and Saint-Simonism: A Weberian View." *American Journal of Sociology* 80, no. 5 (Mar. 1975): 1095-23.
Joseph F. Smith Affidavit Books. See Smith, Joseph F. Affidavit Books.
"Joseph Smith and Celestial Marriage." *Deseret News,* May 20, 1866. Rpt. in *Woman's Exponent* 15 (June 15, 1886): 10.
Josephson, Marba C. "What Did the Prophet Joseph Smith Look Like?" *Improvement Era* 56 (May 1953): 311-15, 371-75.
Journal History of the Church of Jesus Christ of Latter-day Saints. Chronological multi-volume scrapbook, 1830-present. LDS Church History Library.
Katich, Samuel. "A Tale of Two Marriage Systems: Perspectives on Polyandry and Joseph Smith." Foundation for Apologetic Information and Research, 2004 .www.fairlds.org/pubs/polygandry.pdf. (Feb. 2007).
Kenney, Scott G., ed. See Woodruff, Wilford. *Wilford Woodruff's Journal, 1833-1898.*
Kephart, William M. "Experimental Family Organization: An Historico-Cultural Report on the Oneida Community." *Marriage and Family Living* 25 (Aug. 1963): 261-71.
Kern, Louis J. *An Ordered Love: Sex Roles and Sexuality in Victorian Utopias–The Shakers, the Mormons, and the Oneida Community.* Chapel Hill: University of North Carolina Press, 1981.
Kessler, Frederick. Diary. Sporadic entries 1860-98. Holograph. Marriott Library.
Kilbourne, David W. *Strictures on Dr. I. Galland's Pamphlet, entitled, "Villainy Exposed," with Some Account of His Transactions in Lands in the Sac and Fox Reservations, etc., in Lee County, Iowa.* Fort Madison, Iowa: n.p., 1850.
Kimball, Heber C. *Journal of Heber C. Kimball.* Salt Lake City: Juvenile Instructor's Office, 1882.

_____. Letter to Helen Mar Kimball, June 9, 1844. Holograph. LDS Church History Library.

_____. Letter to Parley P. Pratt and Mary Ann Pratt, June 17, 1842. Parley P. Pratt Papers, LDS Church History Library.

_____. Letters to Vilate Kimball, Oct. 25, 1842, June 15, 1843. LDS Church History Library.

Kimball, Helen Mar. Autobiography, Mar. 30, 1881. Microfilm. LDS Church History Library.

_____. "Helen Mar Kimball's Retrospection about Her Introduction to the Doctrine and Practice of Plural Marriage in Nauvoo at Age 15." LDS Church History Library.

Kimball, James L. "The Nauvoo Charter: A Reinterpretation." In Roger D. Launius and John E. Hallwas, eds., *Kingdom on the Mississippi Reconsidered,* 39-47.

Kimball, Lucy Walker Smith. Affidavit. Dec. 17, 1902. LDS Church History Library.

_____. "A Brief Biographical Sketch, in the Life and Labors of Lucy Walker Smith." Typescript. Lucy Walker Smith Kimball Papers, LDS Church History Library.

_____. "Brief Biographical Sketch of the Life and Labors of Lucy Walker Smith." Typescript. LDS Church History Library.

_____. "A Brief But Intensely Interesting Sketch of Her Experience Written by Herself." Copied for the Federal Writers Project by Elvera Manful, Ogden, Utah, 1940. Typescript, Utah State Historical Society, Salt Lake City.

_____. Testimony. In Andrew Jenson, "Plural Marriage," 6:29-30.

Kimball, Presendia Lathrop Huntington Smith. Autobiographical Sketch. Apr. 1, 1881. Typescript. Zina D. H. Young Collection, LDS Church History Library.

Kimball, Sarah M. Granger. "Auto-biography." *Woman's Exponent* 12 (Sept. 1, 1883): 51.

Kimball, Stanley B. *Heber C. Kimball: Mormon Patriarch and Pioneer.* Urbana: University of Illinois Press, 1981.

_____. "Heber C. Kimball and Family: The Nauvoo Years." *BYU Studies* 15 (Summer 1975): 447-79.

_____. "Kinderhook Plates." *Encyclopedia of Mormonism.* 4 vols. New York: Macmillan Publishing, 1992, 2:789.

_____. "Kinderhook Plates Brought to Joseph Smith Appear to be a Nineteenth-Century Hoax." *Ensign,* Aug. 1981, 66-74.

_____, ed. *On the Potter's Wheel: The Diaries of Heber C. Kimball.* Salt Lake City: Signature Books/Smith Research Associates, 1987.

Kimball, Vilate. Letters to Heber C. Kimball, June 27, 1842, June 29, 1843, June 11, 24, and 30, 1844. LDS Church History Library.

Kimmel, Michael S. "Introduction: The Power of Gender and the Gender of Power." In *The Material Culture of Gender.* Edited by Katherine A. Martinez and Kenneth L. Ames. Lebanon, New Hampshire: University Press of New England, 1997.

King, Arthur Henry. *The Abundance of the Heart.* Salt Lake City: Bookcraft, 1986.

Kingsbury, Joseph C. Affidavit. May 22, 1886. LDS Church History Library.

_____. Autobiography. Holograph. Marriott Library. University of Utah. Salt Lake City.

_____. "The History of Joseph C. Kingsbury." Typescript, n.d. Marriott Library.

Knight, Newel. "Sketch." Microfilm, LDS Church History Library.

Larson, Andrew, and Katherine Miles Larson, eds. *Diary of Charles Lowell Walker.* 2 vols. Logan: Utah State University Press, 1980.

Larson, Stan, ed. "The King Follett Discourse: A Newly Amalgamated Text." *BYU Studies* 18, no. 2 (1978): 193-208.

"The Late Proceedings." *Times and Seasons* 2 no. 16 (June 15, 1841): 447-49.

Launius, Roger D. "Anti-Mormonism in Illinois: Thomas C. Sharp's Unfinished History of the Mormon War, 1845." *Journal of Mormon History* 15 (1989): 27-45.

_____. "The Awesome Responsibility: Joseph Smith III and the Nauvoo Experience." *Western Illinois Regional Studies* 11 (Fall 1988): 55-68. Rpt., in Roger D. Launius and John E. Hallway, eds., *Kingdom on the Mississippi Revisited,* 231-50.

_____. "Don Carlos Smith: Brother of the Prophet." *Restoration Witness,* Aug. 1980, 4-10.

_____. *Joseph Smith III: Pragmatic Prophet.* Urbana: University of Illinois Press, 1988.

_____. "Methods and Motives: Joseph Smith III's Opposition to Polygamy, 1860-1890." *Dialogue: A Journal of Mormon Thought* 20 (Winter 1987): 105-20.

_____. "The Murders in Carthage: Non-Mormon Reports of the Assassination of the Smith Brothers." *John Whitmer Historical Association Journal* 15 (1995): 17-34.

_____, and F. Mark McKiernen. *Joseph Smith, Jr.'s Red Brick Store.* Macomb: Western Illinois University, 1985.

_____, and John E. Hallwas, eds. *Kingdom on the Mississippi Revisited.* Urbana: University of Illinois Press, 1996.

Law, William. "Preamble." *Nauvoo Expositor,* June 7, 1844, 5, www.utlm.org/onlineresources/nauvooexpositor.html (Jan. 8, 2008).

Lazar, Aryeh, Shlomo Kravetz, and Peri Frederich-Kedem. "The Multidimensionality of Motivation for Jewish Religious Behavior: Content, Structure, and Relationship to Religious Identity." *Journal for the Scientific Study of Religion* 41, no. 3 (2002): 509-19.

LeBaron, E. Dale. *Benjamin Franklin Johnson: Friend to the Prophets.* Provo, Utah: Benjamin F. Johnson Family Organization, 1997.

Lee, John D. *Mormonism Unveiled: The Life and Confessions of the Late Mormon Bishop.* Edited by W. W. Bishop. St. Louis: Bryan, Brand & Co., 1877.

Lefebvre, Henri. *The Production of Space.* Translated by Donald Nicholson-Smith. Oxford, England: Blackwell, 1991.

Leonard, Glen M. *Nauvoo: A Place of Peace, A People of Promise.* Salt Lake City: Deseret Book/Provo, Utah: Brigham Young University Press, 2002.

_____. "Picturing the Nauvoo Legion." *BYU Studies* 35, no. 2 (1995): 95-135.

Lester, Andrew. *Hope in Pastoral Care and Counseling.* Louisville: Westminster John Knox Press, 1995.

LeSueur, Stephen C. *The 1838 Mormon War in Missouri.* Columbia: University of Missouri Press, 1987.

"Letter to Orson Pratt." *Wasp,* July 27, 1842. www.sidneyrigdon.com/dbroadbu/LDS/waspl.html#072742 (Dec. 20, 2008).

"Letters." *Warsaw Signal,* July 23, 1842. www.sidneyrigdon.com/dbroadhu/IL/sign1842.html#0709 (Dec. 26, 2008).

"Letters from General Bennett, Joe Smith's Letter to Miss. Rigdon." *Sangamo Journal,* Aug. 19, 1842, 2.

"Life and Record of Anson Call, Commenced in 1839." Typescript, Utah State Historical Society.

"Life and Testimony of Mary E. Lightner." *Utah Genealogical and Historical Magazine,* July 1926, 1-44.

Liggett, Helen. "City Sights/Sites of Memories and Dreams." In *Spatial Practices: Critical Explorations in Social/Spatial Theory.* Edited by Helen Liggett and David C. Perry. London: Sage, 1995, 243-73.

Lightner, Mary Elizabeth Rollins. "Autobiography." N.d. Typescript. Utah State Historical Society, Salt Lake City.

_____. Journal, 1818-ca. 1860s. Typescript. Lee Library.

_____. Letter to John R. Young, Jan. 25, 1892. Holograph. George A. Smith Family Collection, Marriott Library.

_____. *The Life and Testimony of Mary Lightner.* Dugway, Utah: Pioneer Press, 1969.

_____. "Remarks at Brigham Young University. She is 87 Years of Age, Apr. 14, 1905." LDS Church History Library.

_____. "Statement." Feb. 8, 1902. Typescript. Lee Library.

"Lilburn W. Boggs." *Times and Seasons* 2, no. 5 (Jan. 1, 1841): 264-65.

Limerick, Patricia Nelson. "Believing in the American West." In her *Something in the Soil: Legacies and Reckonings in the New West.* 2d ed. New York: W. W. Norton, 2001.

Linn, W. A. *The Story of the Mormons.* New York: Macmillan, 1902.

Littlefield, Lyman Omer. "Autobiography (1819-1848)." In *Reminiscences of Latter-day Saints: Giving an Account of Much Individual Suffering Endured for Religious Conscience.* Logan: Utah Journal Co., 1888.

_____. Letter to Joseph Smith, Feb. 10, 1844. Joseph Smith Collection, LDS Church History Library.

_____. *Reminiscences of Latter-day Saints: Giving an Account of Much Individual Suffering Endured for Religious Conscience.* Logan: Utah Journal Co. Printers, 1888.

Lott Family Bible. LDS Church History Library.

Lucas, James W., and Warner P. Woodworth. *Working toward Zion: Principles of the United Order for the Modern World.* Salt Lake City: Aspen Books, 1996.

Luce, W. Ray. "Building the Kingdom of God: Mormon Architecture before 1847." *BYU Studies* 30, no. 2 (1990): 33-45.

Lyman, Amy Brown. Statement on Relief Society history. Oct. 20, 1872 Typescript. LDS Church History Library.

Lyman, Eliza Maria Partridge. Affidavit. July 1, 1869. LDS Church History Library.

_____. "Life and Journal of Eliza Maria Partridge Lyman." Holograph. Marriott Library.

Lynch, Kevin. *The Image of the City.* Cambridge, Massachusetts: MIT Press, 1960.

Lyon, Joseph L., and David W. Lyon. "Physical Evidence at Carthage Jail and What It Reveals about the Assassination of Joseph and Hyrum Smith." *BYU Studies* 47, no. 4 (2008): 5-50.

Lyon, T. Edgar. "Free Masonry at Nauvoo." *Dialogue: A Journal of Mormon Thought* 6, no. 1 (1971): 76-78.

_____. "Orson Pratt: Early Mormon Leader." M.A. thesis, University of Chicago Divinity School, 1932.

Lyotard, Jean-Francois. *The Postmodern Condition: A Report on Knowledge.* Translated by Geoff Bennington and Brian Massumi. Manchester, England: Manchester University Press, 1984.

Mace, Wandle. Autobiography. www.boap.org/LDS/EarlySaints/WMace.html (Feb. 13, 2010).

_____. "Excerpts from the Life Story of Wandle Mace, 1809-1890." Typescript. LDS Church History Library.

_____. "The Journal of Wandle Mace." Holograph, LDS Church History Library; typescript, n.d. Lee Library. www.boap.org/LDS/EarlySaints/Wmace.html (Dec. 8, 2008).

Mackey, Albert G. *An Encyclopedia of Freemasonry.* 2 vols., rev. ed. New York: Masonic History Co., 1920.

_____. *A Lexicon of Freemasonry.* 2nd ed., enl. Charleston: Walker & James, 1852.

Madsen, Carol Cornwall, ed. *In Their Own Words: Women and the Story of Nauvoo.* Salt Lake City: Deseret Book, 1994.

_____. "Mormon Women and the Temple: Toward a New Understanding." In Maureen Ursenbach Beecher and Lavina Fielding Anderson, eds., *Sisters in Spirit,* 80-110.

Madsen, Gordon A. "Joseph Smith as Guardian: The Lawrence Estate." Paper given at Mormon History Association, May 18, 1996. Also in *Journal of Mormon History* 36, no. 3 (Summer 2010): 172-211.

Madsen, Truman G., ed. *The Concordance of the Doctrinal Statements of Joseph Smith.* Salt Lake City: I.E.S. Publishing, 1985.

_____. *Joseph Smith among the Prophets.* Salt Lake City: Deseret Book, 1965.

_____. "Joseph Smith and the Problem of Ethics." In *Seminar on the Prophet Joseph Smith, 1961.* Compiled by Truman G. Madsen. Provo, Utah: BYU Adult Education Center, Office of Special Courses and Conferences, 1962, 23-58. Rpt. in *Perspectives in Mormon Ethics: Personal, Social, Legal, and Medical.* Edited by Donald G. Hill Jr. Salt Lake City: Publishers Press, 1983, 29-48.

_____. *Joseph Smith the Prophet.* Salt Lake City: Bookcraft, 1989.

_____. *The Radiant Life.* Salt Lake City: Bookcraft, 1994.

Mahoney, Timothy R. "Urban History in a Regional Context: River Towns on the Upper Mississippi, 1840-1860." *Journal of American History* 72, no. 2 (1985): 318-39.

Markham, Stephen. "Affidavit." *Wasp,* July 27, 1842. www.sidneyrigdon.com/dbroadhu/LDS/wasp1.html@072742 (July 21, 2008).

_____. Letter to Wilford Woodruff, June 20, 1856. LDS Church History Library.

Marks, William. "Letter to Beloved Brethren." *Zion's Harbinger and Baneemy's Organ* 3 (July 1853): 22-26.

_____. Letter to Hiram Falk and Josiah Butterfield, Oct. 1, 1865. Paul M. Hansen Papers, Community of Christ Library-Archives.

_____. "Opposition to Polygamy." *True Latter Day Saints Herald* 1 (Jan. 1860): 22-26.

Marquardt, H. Michael. "Early Texts of Joseph Smith's Revelations, 1828-1833." *Restoration* 1 (July 1982): 8-11.

_____. "Emily Dow Partridge Smith Young on the Witness Stand: Recollection of a Plural Wife." *Journal of Mormon History* 35, no. 3 (Summer 2008): 110-41.

_____. *The Joseph Smith Revelations: Text and Commentary.* Salt Lake City: Signature Books, 1999.

_____. *The Strange Marriages of Sarah Ann Whitney to Joseph Smith the Mormon Prophet, Joseph C. Kingsbury, and Heber C. Kimball.* Salt Lake City: Modern Microfilm, 1973.

_____, and Wesley P. Walters. *Inventing Mormonism: Tradition and the Historical Record.* San Francisco: Smith Research Associates, 1994.

Marsden, George M. *Religion and American Culture.* Fort Worth, Texas: Harcourt Brace College Publishers, 1990.

Marsh, Eudocia Baldwin. "Mormons in Hancock County." *The Bellman*, Apr. 1, 8, 1916. Photocopy in Linda King Newell Collection, Marriott Library.

Martin, David, ed. "Mormon Miscellaneous." *New Nauvoo Neighbor Press* 2 (Mar. 1977): 4.

Matthews, Robert J. *A Bible! A Bible!* Salt Lake City: Bookcraft, 1990.

_____. *A Plainer Translation: Joseph Smith's Translation of the Bible.* Provo, Utah: Brigham Young University Press, 1975.

Mauss, Armand L. *All Abraham's Children: Changing Mormon Conceptions of Race and Lineage.* Urbana: University of Illinois Press, 2003.

_____. "Culture, Charisma and Change: Reflections on Mormon Temple Worship." *Dialogue: A Journal of Mormon Thought* 20 (Winter 1987): 77-83.

May, Dean L. "Mormons." In *Harvard Encyclopedia of American Ethnic Groups,* ed. Stephen Thernstrom. Cambridge, Massachusetts: Harvard University Press, 1980, p. 730.

McBrien, Dean Depew. "The Influence of the Frontier on Joseph Smith." Ph.D. diss., George Washington University, 1929.

McCarl, William B. "The Visual Image of Joseph Smith." M.A. thesis, Brigham Young University, 1962.

McConkie, Bruce R. *Mormon Doctrine.* Salt Lake City: Bookcraft, 1958. 2nd ed., 1966.

McConkie, Mark L. *The Father of the Prophet: Stories and Insights from the Life of Joseph Smith, Sr.* Salt Lake City: Bookcraft, 1993.

_____, ed. *Remembering Joseph: Personal Recollections of Those Who Knew the Prophet Joseph Smith.* Salt Lake City: Deseret Book, 2003. Also on CD.

McGavin, Elmer Cecil. *Nauvoo, the Beautiful.* Salt Lake City: Stevens and Wallis, 1946.

McKiernan, F. Mark. *The Voice of One Crying in the Wilderness: Sidney Rigdon, Religious Reformer 1793-1876.* Lawrence, Kansas: Coronado Press, 1971.

McLaws, Monte B. "The Attempted Assassination of Missouri's Ex-Governor, Lilburn W. Boggs." *Missouri Historical Review* 60, no. 1 (Oct. 1965): 50-62.

McMurray, W. Grant. "'True Son of True Father': Joseph Smith III and the Succession Question." *Restoration Studies 1.* Independence, Missouri: Herald House Publishing House, 1980.

McPhail, Clark. *The Myth of the Madding Crowd.* New York: Aldine de Gruyter, 1991.

Melder, Keith. *Beginnings of Sisterhood: The American Woman's Rights Movement.* New York: Schoken Books, 1977.

"Memoirs of President Joseph Smith." *Saints Herald,* Jan. 1, 1935; Dec. 18, 1934,

Michalko, Michael. *Cracking Creativity: The Secrets of Creative Genius.* Berkeley: Ten Speed Press, 2001.

Miles, Carrie A. "Polygamy and the Economics of Salvation." *Sunstone* 21 (Aug. 1998): 34-45.

"Military." *Nauvoo Neighbor* 1 (May 10, 1843): 2.

"The Millennium." *Millennial Star* 1 (1840): 5.

Miller, David E., and Della S. Miller. *Nauvoo: The City of Joseph.* 3rd ed. 1966. Rpt. Layton, Utah: Peregrine Smith, 1974.

Miller, George. *Correspondence of Bishop George Miller with the Northern Islander from His First Acquaintance with Mormonism Up to Near the Close of His Life, 1855.* Pamphlet. Burlington, Wisconsin: Wingfield Watson, 1916.

_____. Letter to Joseph Smith. *Times and Seasons* 3 (July 1, 1842): 839-42.

Minutes of the Quorum of the Twelve Apostles. Jan. 20, 1843; Apr. 18, 1844. Holograph. Brigham Young Papers, LDS Church History Library.
"Minutes of a Special Conference." *Times and Seasons* 4, no. 21 (Sept. 15, 1843): 329-32.
Montgomery, W. W. *The Mormon Delusion: Its History, Doctrines, and the Outlook in Utah.* Boston: Congregational Sunday-School & Publishing Society, 1890.
Moore, R. Laurence. *Religious Outsiders and the Making of Americans.* New York: Oxford University Press, 1986.
"More Disclosures." *Sangamo Journal,* July 8, 1842, 2.
Morgan, Dale. *The Bancroft Research Guide: A Guide to the Manuscript Collection of the Bancroft Library.* Berkeley: University of California Press, 1963.
_____, ed. "The Reminiscences of James Holt: A Narrative of the Emmett Co." *Utah Historical Quarterly* 2 (1955): 1-33.
"Mormon Movements." *New York Herald,* May 23, 1844, 2.
"The Mormon Prophet and the Mormon General at Daggers' Points." *Illinois State Register,* July 15, 1842. www.sidneyrigdon.com/dbroadhu/Il/miscill2.html#071542 (July 20, 2008).
"Mormonism." *Times and Seasons* 4 (May 15, 1843): 200.
"The Mormons." *New York Herald,* Oct. 21, 1842. www.sidneyrigdon.com/dbroadhu/NewYork/New Yorkherld0.html@102142 (July 21, 2008).
"The Mormons in Western Illinois." *Niles National Register,* Feb. 1, 1840, 6.
"Mother Poulterer Dead." *Deseret Evening News,* Aug. 20, 1879, 3.
"Mr. Editor." *Wasp,* May 28, 1842, 2.
Mulder, William. *Homeward to Zion: The Mormon Migration from Scandinavia.* 1957. Rpt., Provo, Utah: Brigham Young University Press, 1985.
_____. "Mormonism's 'Gathering': An American Doctrine with a Difference." *Church History* 23, no. 3 (1954): 248-64.
_____. "Nauvoo Observed." *BYU Studies* 32, nos. 1-2 (1992): 95-118.
_____, and A. R. Mortensen, eds. *Among the Mormons: Historic Accounts by Contemporary Observers.* New York: Alfred A. Knopf, 1958.
Mulvay, Jill C. "The Liberal Shall Be Blessed: Sarah M. Kimball." *Utah Historical Quarterly* 44 (Summer 1976): 205-21.
"Municipal Court of the City of Nauvoo." *Times and Seasons* 4 (July 1, 1843): 243-56.
Murdock, Miriam. "'Stepping Stones' of Understanding: Patterns of Priesthood in Universalism, Freemasonry, and Mormonism." *Archive of Restoration Culture: Summer Fellows Papers, 1997-1999.* Provo, Utah: Joseph Fielding Smith Institute for Latter-day Saint History, 2000, 51-57.
"My Dear Sir." *Joliet Courier,* June 22, 1841, 1.
Myres, Sandra L. *Westering Women and the Frontier Experience, 1800-1915.* Albuquerque: University of New Mexico Press, 1982.
"Nauvoo." *Sangamo Journal,* Feb. 9, 1841, 2.
"Nauvoo." *Times and Seasons* 3, no. 23 (Oct. 1, 1842): 936-37.
"Nauvoo." *Warsaw Signal,* July 9, 1843. www.sidneyrigdon.com/dbroadhu/IL/sign1842.html#0709 (Dec. 8, 2008).
Nauvoo City Council. Minutes, 1841-45. LDS Church History Library.
Nauvoo High Council, Minutes. 1840-45. LDS Church History Library.
"Nauvoo, Ill.: Sept., 1840." *Times and Seasons* 1, no. 11 (Sept. 1840): 169-70.
Nauvoo Legion. Records, 1841-44. LDS Church History Library.

Nauvoo Masonic Lodge. Minutes, 1841-46. LDS Church History Library.

Nauvoo Municipal Court. Docket, 1841-74. LDS Church History Library.

Nauvoo Sealings and Adoptions, 1846-57. Photocopy of holograph. Marriot Library.

Nauvoo Ward Census. "A Record of the Names of the Members of the Church of Jesus Christ of Latter-day Saints: Begun in Spring of 1842." Microfilm. Family History Library, Church of Jesus Christ of Latter-day Saints, Salt Lake City.

Navone, John. *Toward a Theology of Story.* Slough, England: St. Paul Publications, 1977.

Needham, John. "Letter from Nauvoo." *Millennial Star* 4 (Oct. 1843): 87-88.

Neibaur, Alexander. Journal. Feb. 1841-April 1862. Microfilm of holograph. LDS Church History Library.

_____. Journal. Typescript, 1841-62. Lee Library.

Nelson, Lowry. *The Mormon Village: A Pattern and Technique of Land Settlement.* Salt Lake City: University of Utah Press, 1952.

Neusner, Jacob. "Conversations in Nauvoo about the Corporeality of God." *BYU Studies* 36, no. 1 (1996-97): 7-30.

Newell, Linda King. "Cousins in Conflict: Joseph Smith III and Joseph F. Smith." *John Whitmer Historical Association Journal* 9 (1989): 3-16.

_____. "Emma Hale Smith and the Polygamy Question." *John Whitmer Historical Association Journal* 4 (1984): 3-15.

_____. "Gifts of the Spirit." In Maureen Ursenbach Beecher and Lavina Fielding Anderson, eds., *Sisters in Spirit,* 111-50.

_____. "The Historical Relationship of Mormon Women and Priesthood." *Dialogue: A Journal of Mormon Thought* 18 (Fall 1985): 21-32.

_____. "In Search of Emma Smith: Techniques Used in Recovering Her Personal History." In *World Conference on Records: Preserving Our Heritage, Aug. 12-15, 1980.* No. 4, series 347, 1-9. Salt Lake City: Church of Jesus Christ of Latter-day Saints, 1980, 1-9.

_____, and Valeen Tippets Avery. *Mormon Enigma: Emma Hale Smith, Prophet's Wife, "Elect Lady," Polygamy's Foe.* Garden City, New York: Doubleday & Co., 1984.

_____, and Valeen Tippets Avery. "New Light on the Sun: Emma Smith and the *New York Sun* Letter." *Journal of Mormon History* 6 (1979): 23-35.

Nibley, Preston. *Joseph Smith the Prophet.* Salt Lake City: Deseret News Press, 1944.

Noall, Claire. *Intimate Disciple: A Portrait of Willard Richards.* Salt Lake City: University of Utah Press, 1957.

Noble, Joseph Bates. Affidavit, June 26, 1869. Smith, Joseph F., Affidavit Books.

_____. Journal, 1810-34. Typescript. Lee Library.

_____. Testimony in Temple Lot Case. *Reorganized Church of Jesus Christ of Latter Day Saints, Complainant, vs. the Church of Christ at Independence, Missouri: Richard Hill, trustee; Richard Hill, Mrs. E. Hill, C.A. Hall [et al.] as members of and doing business under the name of the Church of Christ, at Independence, Missouri, respondents. In equity: Complainant's abstract of pleading and evidence.* Lamoni, Iowa: Herald Publishing House, 1893, 364-71.

Norberg-Schultz, Christian. *Genius Loci: Toward a Phenomenology of Architecture.* 1979; rpt., New York: Rizzoli, 1991.

Norman, Mary Bailey Smith. Letter to Ina Coolbrith, ca. Jan.-Mar. 1908. Community of Christ Library-Archives.

"Notice." *Times and Seasons* 3, no. 16 (June 15, 1842): 830.

"Notice." *Times and Seasons* 3, no. 19 (Aug. 1, 1842): 872.
"Notice." *Times and Seasons* 4, no. 2 (Dec. 1, 1842): 32.
Nuttall, L. John. Diary, 1879-92. Lee Library.
Oakes, Len. *Prophetic Charisma: The Psychology of Revolutionary Religious Personalities.* Syracuse, New York: Syracuse University Press, 1997.
Oaks, Dallin H. "Habeas Corpus in the State, 1776-1865." *University of Chicago Law Review* 32, no. 2 (1965): 243-88.
_____. "The Suppression of the *Nauvoo Expositor.*" *Utah Law Review* 9 (Winter 1965): 862-903.
_____, and Joseph I. Bentley. "Joseph Smith and Legal Process: In the Wake of the Steamboat *Nauvoo.*" *Brigham Young University Law Review* 2 (1976): 735-782.
_____, and Marvin S. Hill. *Carthage Conspiracy: The Trial of the Accused Assassins of Joseph Smith.* Urbana: University of Illinois Press, 1975.
"Officers." *Times and Seasons* 3 (Jan. 1, 1842): 646.
"Olivia Pratt Driggs." *Relief Society Magazine* 11, no. 8 (Aug. 1924): 385-90. Introduction by Susa Young Gates.
Olney, Oliver. *The Absurdities of Mormonism Portrayed.* Hancock County, Illinois: n.p., 1843.
Olsen, Steven L. "Joseph Smith and the Structure of Mormon Identity." *Dialogue: A Journal of Mormon Thought* 14 (Autumn 1981): 89-99.
_____. "Joseph Smith's Concept of the City of Zion." In Susan Easton Black and Charles D. Tate Jr., eds., *Joseph Smith,* 203-11.
_____. "The Mormon Ideology of Place: Cosmic Symbolism of the City of Zion, 1830-1846." Ph.D. diss., University of Chicago, 1985; Rpt., Provo, Utah: Joseph Fielding Smith Institute for Latter-day Saint History/*BYU Studies,* 2002.
"On Marriage." *Times and Seasons* 3 (Oct. 1, 1842): 939-40.
Order of the Eastern Star. *An Instructive Manual on the Organization and Government of Chapters of the Order with Ceremonies and Ritual.* Arranged by F. A. Bell. Chicago: Ezra A. Cook Publications, 1948.
"An Ordinance Regulating the Fees, and Compensation of the Several Offices, and Persons Therein Mentioned." *Wasp,* Jan. 28, 1843, 4.
Owens, Lance S. "Joseph Smith: America's Hermetic Prophet." In Bryan Waterman, ed., *The Prophet Puzzle,* 155-72.
Palmer, James. Reminiscences, n.d. LDS Church History Library.
Palmer, Spencer, ed. "Eliza R. Snow's 'Sketch of My Life': Reminiscences of One of Joseph Smith's Plural Wives." *BYU Studies* 12 (Autumn 1971): 125-30.
Pargament, K. I, and C. L. Park. "Merely a Defense? The Variety of Religious Means and Ends." *Journal of Social Issues* 51, no. 2 (1995): 13-32.
Parker, Robert A. *A Yankee Saint: John Humphrey Noyes and the Oneida Community.* New York: G. P. Putnam's Sons, 1935.
Paulsen, David C. "The Doctrine of Divine Embodiment Restoration: Judeo-Christian and Philosophical Perspectives." *BYU Studies* 35, no. 4 (1995-96): 6-94.
Penrose, Charles W. "Joseph Smith and Celestial Marriage." *Deseret Evening News,* May 20, 1886.
_____. "What Is the True Character of Joseph Smith?" *Millennial Star* 20, no. 15 (Apr. 10, 1858): 225-27.
Pepper, Stephen. *World Hypotheses.* Berkeley: University of California Press, 1942.

Perego, Ugo A., Natalie M. Myres and Scott R. Woodward. "Reconstructing the Y-Chromosome of Joseph Smith: Genealogical Applications." *Journal of Mormon History* 31 (Summer 2005): 70-88. Corrected version printed in 31 (Fall 2005): 42-60.

Phelps, William W. Letter to Brigham Young. Aug. 12, 1861. LDS Church History Library.

Pitzer, Donald E., ed. *America's Communal Utopias.* Chapel Hill: University of North Carolina Press, 1997.

Platt, Lyman D., ed. "Nauvoo School Records." *Nauvoo Journal* 1 (1989): 13-17.

Pletcher, David M. *The Diplomacy of Annexation: Texas, Oregon, and the Mexican War.* Columbia: University of Missouri Press, 1973.

"Pluto" (pseud.). "Mr. Editor." *Wasp,* Apr. 16, 1842, 3.

Poll, Richard D. "Joseph Smith and the Presidency, 1844." *Dialogue: A Journal of Mormon Thought* 3, no. 3 (Aug. 1968): 17-21.

Pooley, William Vipard. *Settlement of Illinois: From 1830-1850.* Madison, Wisconsin: N.p., 1908.

Porter, Larry C., Milton V. Backman, and Susan Easton Black, eds. *Regional Studies in Latter-day Saint Church History: New York.* Provo, Utah: BYU Department of Church History and Doctrine, 1992.

Porter, Larry C., and Susan Easton Black, eds. *The Prophet Joseph: Essays on the Life and Mission of Joseph Smith.* Salt Lake City: Deseret Book, 1998.

Poulsen, Richard C. "Fate and the Persecutors of Joseph Smith: Transmutations of an American Myth." *Dialogue: A Journal of Mormon Thought* 11 (Winter 1978): 63-70.

"The Prairies, Nauvoo, Joe Smith, the Temple, the Mormons, &c." *Pittsburgh Weekly Gazette,* Sept. 15, 1843, 3.

Pratt, Orson. *Interesting Account of Several Remarkable Visions, and the Late Discovery of Ancient American Records.* Edinburgh, Scotland: Ballantyne and Hughes, 1840.

_____. "Mr. Editor." *Wasp,* Sept. 2, 1842, 3.

Pratt, Parley Parker. *Autobiography of Parley Parker Pratt: One of the Twelve Apostles of the Church of Jesus Christ of Latter-day Saints, Embracing His Life, Ministry, and Travels, with Extracts in Prose and Verse, from his Miscellaneous Writings.* Ed. Parley P. Pratt Jr. 1874. Salt Lake City: Deseret Book, 1968 and 1985 printings.

_____. "Government and Institutions of Nauvoo." *Millennial Star* 4, no. 3 (Aug. 1842): 69.

_____. *A Voice of Warning and Instruction to All People, Containing a Declaration of the Faith and Doctrine of the Church of the Latter Day Saints, Commonly called Mormons.* New York: W. Sandford, 1837; rpt., Independence, Missouri: Herald Publishing House, 1950.

Prince, Gregory A. *Power from On High: The Development of Mormon Priesthood.* Salt Lake City: Signature Books, 1995.

Prior, Samuel A. "A Visit to Nauvoo." *Times and Seasons* 4 (May 15, 1843): 197-99.

Proceedings of the Grand Lodge of Illinois, at a Grand Annual Community in the Town of Jacksonville, commencing October Third A.L. 5842. Jacksonville, Illinois: A. V. Putnam Book and Job Printers, 1842.

Proceedings of the Grand Lodge of Illinois, from its Organization in 1840-1850 Inclusive. 1892; rpt., Freeport, Illinois: Journal Reprint, 1895.

"A Proclamation, to the Saints Scattered Abroad." *Times and Seasons* 2, no. 6 (Jan. 15, 1841): 273-77.

"Prospectus." *Nauvoo Expositor*, June 7, 1844. www.utlm.org/onlineresources/nauvooexpositor.html (Jan. 8, 2008).

Public Statues at Large of the United States of America, 1789-1845. Boston, n.p., 1848.

"Quincy Branch Manuscript History and Historical Report." LDS Church History Library.

Quincy, Josiah. *Figures of the Past: From the Leaves of Old Journals.* Boston: Roberts Brothers, 1883.

Quinn, D. Michael. "The Council of Fifty and Its Members, 1844-1945." *BYU Studies* 20 (Winter 1980): 163-97.

_____. *Early Mormonism and the Magic World View.* Salt Lake City: Signature Books, 1987.

_____. "The Evolution of the Presiding Quorums of the LDS Church." *Journal of Mormon History* 1 (1974): 21-38.

_____. "Joseph Smith III's 1844 Blessing and the Mormons of Utah." *John Whitmer Historical Association Journal* 1 (1981): 12-27.

_____. "Latter-day Saint Prayer Circles." *BYU Studies* 19, no. 1 (Fall 1978): 79-105.

_____. *The Mormon Hierarchy: Extensions of Power.* Salt Lake City: Signature Books/Smith Research Associates, 1996.

_____. *The Mormon Hierarchy: Origins of Power.* Salt Lake City: Signature Books/Smith Research Associates, 1994.

_____. "The Mormon Succession Crisis of 1844." *BYU Studies* 16 (Winter 1976): 187-233.

_____. "Organizational Development and Social Origins of the Mormon Hierarchy, 1832-1934: A Prosopographical Study." M.A. thesis, University of Utah, 1973.

_____. "The Practice of Rebaptism at Nauvoo." *BYU Studies* 18, no. 2 (1978): 226-32.

_____, ed. *The New Mormon History: Revisionist Essays on the Past.* Salt Lake City: Signature Books, 1992.

Quorum of the Twelve. Minutes, 1841-46. Brigham Young Papers. LDS Church History Library.

"Recollections of the Prophet Joseph Smith." *Juvenile Instructor* 27 (1892): 174. www.boap.org/LDS/Early-Saints/REC-JS.html (Dec. 20, 2008).

"Record of Na[u]voo Lodge under Dispensation," 1841-1846. LDS Church History Library.

Relief Society. Minutes of the Female Relief Society of Nauvoo, Mar. 17, 1842-Mar. 16, 1844. Holograph and typescript in LDS Church History Library.

"Remarks by Sister Mary E. Lightner Who Was Sealed to Joseph Smith in 1842. She is 87 Years of Age," at Brigham Young University, Apr. 14, 1905. Typescript. LDS Church History Library.

"Remarks on Chartered Rights." *Times and Seasons* 4 no. 3 (Dec. 15, 1842): 41-47.

Remini, Robert V. *The Revolutionary Age of Andrew Jackson.* New York: Harper Torchbooks, 1987.

Reorganized Church of Jesus Christ of Latter Day Saints v. Church of Christ of Independence, Missouri, et al. 60 F. 937 (W.D. Missouri, 1894). Deposition testimony.

Reps, John W. *The Making of Urban America: A History of City Planning in the United States.* Princeton, New Jersey: Princeton University Press, 1965.

Reynolds, John C. *History of the M. W. Grand Lodge of Illinois …* Springfield, Illinois: H. G. Reynolds Jr., 1869.
Richards, Franklin D. Journal, Jan. 1869, loose sheet in Franklin D. Richards Papers. LDS Church History Library.
_____. Journals. Franklin D. Richards Papers. LDS Church History Library.
_____. Letter to John Taylor, Dec. 26, 1883. Holograph. LDS Church History Library.
Richards, Jane S. "Joseph Smith, the Prophet." *Young Woman's Journal* 16, no. 12 (Dec. 1905): 550.
Richards, Levi. Diaries, 1840-53. Holograph. LDS Church History Library.
Richards, Mary Stovall. "Sarah Granger Kimball." *Encyclopedia of Mormonism.* 4 vols. New York City: Macmillan Publishing, 1992, 2:784-85.
Richards, Samuel W. Journals, 1839-1909. Microfilm of holograph. LDS Church History Library.
Richards, Sarah Griffin. Letter to Zina D. Young. July 17, 1889. Holograph. LDS Church History Library.
Richards, Willard. Journals, 1836-52. Holograph. LDS Church History Library.
Richmond, B. W. "The Prophet's Death!" *Deseret News,* Nov. 27, 1875.
Ricoeur, Paul. *Figuring the Sacred: Religion, Narrative, and Imagination.* Trans. David Pellauer. Minneapolis, Minnesota: Augsburg Fortress, 1995.
"Rigdon &c." *Times and Seasons* 3 (Sept. 15, 1842): 922-93.
Rigdon, John Wickliffe. Affidavit, June 18, 1882. In Joseph Fielding Smith, *Blood Atonement and the Origin of Plural Marriage,* 81-84.
_____. "The Life Story of Sidney Rigdon." Typescript. LDS Church History Library.
_____. Statement, July 28, 1905. Holograph, Sidney Rigdon Collection. LDS Church History Library.
Rigdon, Sidney. "Editor of the Wasp." Rpt., *Sangamo Journal,* Sept. 23, 1842, 2.
_____. "Editor of the Wasp." *Wasp.* Extra edition. July 27, 1842, 2.
_____. "[Letter to the] Editor of the Wasp, Nauvoo, Aug. 27, 1842." *Wasp,* Sept. 3, 1842, 2.
_____. "The Government of God." *Times and Seasons* 3 (July 15, 1842): 855-58.
_____. Letter to Joseph Smith, July 1, 1842. Joseph Smith Letterbooks, LDS Church History Library.
_____. Letter to Joseph Smith, July 11, 1842. LDS Church History Library.
_____. "To the Sisters of the Church of Jesus Christ of Latter Day Saints." *Latter Day Saint's Messenger and Advocate* (Pittsburgh) 1, no. 10 (Mar. 15, 1845): 154-58.
Riley, I. Woodbridge. *The Founder of Mormonism: A Psychological Study of Joseph Smith, Jr.* New York: Dodd, Mead & Co., 1907.
Roberts, B. H. *A Comprehensive History of the Church of Jesus Christ of Latter-day Saints, Century I.* 6 vols. 1930; rpt. Provo, Utah: BYU Press, 1965.
_____. *Joseph Smith: The Prophet-Teacher.* 1908. Rpt., Princeton, New Jersey: Deseret Club of Princeton University, 1967.
_____. *The Life of John Taylor; Third President of the Church of Jesus Christ of Latter-day Saints.* Salt Lake City: George Q. Cannon and Sons, 1892; rpt., Salt Lake City: Bookcraft, 1963, 2002.
_____. *Succession in the Presidency of the Church.* Salt Lake City: George Q. Cannon & Sons Publishing, 1900.

Roberts, Nelson C., and Samuel W. Moorehead. *Story of Lee County.* Chicago: S.J. Clarke Publishing Co., 1914.

Robertson, Margaret C. "The Campaign and the Kingdom: The Activities of the Electioneers in Joseph Smith's Presidential Campaign." *BYU Studies* 39, no. 3 (2000): 147-80.

Robinson, Ebenezer. "Discourse by Joseph Smith." *The Return* 2 (Sept. 1890): 321-25.

_____. "Horticulture." *Times and Seasons* 3 (Feb. 1, 1842): 678.

_____. "Items of Personal History of the Editor." *The Return.* www.sidneyrigdon.com/RigWrit/m&a/Return1.html (Dec. 20, 2008).
2, no. 4 (Apr. 1890): 253-54.
2, no. 5 (May 1890): 257-62.
2, no. 6 (June 1890): 284-87.
2, no. 9 (Sept. 1890): 321-45.
2, no. 10 (Oct. 1890): 346.
2, no. 11 (Nov. 1890): 287.
3, no. 1 (Jan. 1891): 12-13.
3, no. 2 (Feb. 1891): 29-30.

Robinson, George W. Letter to James Arlington Bennett, July 27, 1842. In John C. Bennett, *History of the Saints,* 245-47.

Robinson, Joseph Lee. Autobiography and Journals, 1883-92. Holograph and typescript. LDS Church History Library.

Robison, Charles and Jerusha. Family Group Record, LDS Family History Library, Salt Lake City. Ancestral Index (Nov. 12, 2006).

Rogers, David W. Statement. Feb. 1, 1839. Microfilm. LDS Church History Library.

Romig, Ronald E. "David Whitmer: Faithful Dissenter, Witness Apart." In *Differing Visions: Dissenters in Mormon History.* Edited by Roger D. Launius and Linda Thatcher. Urbana: University of Illinois Press, 1994, 23-44.

_____. "The Temple Lot Suit after 100 Years." *John Whitmer Historical Association Journal* 12 (1992): 3-15.

Rowley, Dennis. "The Mormon Experience in the Wisconsin Pineries, 1841-1845." *BYU Studies* 32, nos. 1-2 (1992): 119-48.

_____. "Nauvoo: A River Town." *BYU Studies* 18, no. 2 (1978): 255-72.

Rowley, William. Diary, 1798-1870. Photocopy of holograph. Marriott Library.

Roukema-Konig, B. "Religious Coping Reconsidered." *Journal of Psychology and Theology* 26, no. 3 (1998): 260-75. www.ruardganzevoort.no/a98rclc2.html (May 18, 2007).

Rushton, Edwin. "Bridge Builder and Faithful Pioneer." N.d. *Pioneer Journals.* Lee Library.

Ryan, Mary. "The Power of Female Networks: A Case Study of Female Moral Reform in Antebellum America." *Feminist Studies* 5 (Spring 1979): 66-86.

"Salt Lake City, April 1856." *Millennial Star* 24 (1862): 409.

Salt Lake City School of the Prophets. Minutes. Typescript in Leonard J. Arrington Papers, Special Collections, Merrill-Cazier Library, Utah State University, Logan.

Sandeen, Ernest R. "John Humphrey Noyes as the New Adam." *Church History* 40 (Mar. 1971): 82-90.

Sarbin, Theodore R. "The Narrative as a Root Metaphor for Psychology." In *Narrative Psychology: The Storied Nature of Human Conduct.* Edited by Theodore R. Sarbin. New York: Praeger Publishers, 1986, 3-21.

"Saturday, Apr. 23, 1842." *Wasp*, Apr. 23, 1842, 2.
Schindler, Harold. *Orrin Porter Rockwell: Man of God, Son of Thunder.* 1966; rpt., Salt Lake City: University of Utah Press, 1983.
Schmitz, Joseph William. *Texan Statecraft, 1836-1845.* San Antonio: Naylor, 1941.
Schweitzer, A. *The Age of Charisma.* Chicago: Nelson-Hall, 1984.
"Sealing and Adoption Book A, Nauvoo Temple." Photocopy. Marriott Library.
Searle, Howard C. "Authorship of the History of Joseph Smith: A Review Essay." *BYU Studies* 21 (Winter 1981): 101-22.
_____. "Willard Richards as Historian." *BYU Studies* 31 (Spring 1991): 41-62.
Secord, Jessie Rigdon. Letter to Arlene Hess, May 19, 1967. Hess Collection, Lee Library.
Sessions, Patty Bartlett, Journal, 1846-80. Holograph. LDS Church History Library.
Shann, Ben. *The Shape of Content.* New York: Vintage, 1957.
Sharp, Thomas. Editorial note. *Warsaw Signal,* June 12, 1844, 1.
_____. "Our Position Again." Editorial. *Warsaw Signal,* June 16, 1841, 2.
_____. "Unparalleled Outrage at Nauvoo." *Warsaw Signal,* June 12, 1844, 1.
Shipps, Jan. "A Little Known Account of the Murders of Joseph and Hyrum Smith." *BYU Studies* 14, no. 3 (1974): 389-92.
_____. *Mormonism: The Story of a New Religious Tradition.* Urbana: University of Illinois Press, 1985.
_____. "The Prophet Puzzle: Suggestions Leading toward a More Comprehensive Interpretation of Joseph Smith." *Journal of Mormon History* 1 (1974): 3-20.
_____. *Sojourner in the Promised Land: Forty Years among the Mormons.* Urbana: University of Illinois Press, 2000.
_____, and John W. Welch, eds. *The Journals of William E. McLellin, 1831-1836.* Urbana: University of Illinois Press/Provo, Utah: BYU Studies, 1994.
Shirts, Kathryn H. "Joseph Smith: The Prophet Voice." In *Women and Christ: Living the Abundant Life.* Edited by Dawn H. Anderson, Susette F. Green, and Marie Cornwall. Salt Lake City: Deseret Books, 1993, 57-66.
Shook, Charles A. *True Origin of Mormon Polygamy.* Cincinatti: Standard Publishing Co., 1914.
Short, Dennis, ed. *For Women Only.* Salt Lake City: Author, 1977.
Silbey, Joel H. *Storm over Texas: The Annexation Controversy and the Road to Civil War.* New York: Oxford University Press, 2005.
Silverstein, Sanford. "The Early Development of the Mormon Church: A Study of the Routinization of Charisma." M.A. thesis, University of Illinois, Urbana, 1953.
"Singular Discovery–Material for Another Mormon Book." *Quincy Whig,* 6, no. 2 (May 3, 1843). www.sidneyrigdon.com/dbroadhu/IL/whig1843.html#0503 (Dec. 8, 2008).
"A Sketch of the Life of Eunice Billings Snow." *Woman's Exponent* 39, no. 2 (Aug. 1910): 14.
Skinner, Andrew C. "John C. Bennett: For Prophet or Profit?" In *Regional Studies in Latter-day Saint History: Illinois.* Edited by H. Dean Garrett. Provo, Utah: BYU Department of Church History and Doctrine, 1995, 249-85.
Smart, Donna Toland, ed. *Mormon Midwife: The 1846-1888 Diaries of Patty Barlett Sessions.* Logan: Utah State University Press, 1997.

Smith, Alexander H. Journal, Mar. 25, 1862; Aug. 6, 1863-May 16, 1864, with gaps. Holograph. Community of Christ Archives.

Smith, Andrew F. Introduction to John C. Bennett. *The History of the Saints: or, An Exposé of Joe Smith and Mormonism.* 3rd ed. Urbana: University of Illinois Press, 2000, vi-xi.

_____. *The Saintly Scoundrel: The Life and Times of Dr. John Cook Bennett.* Urbana: University of Illinois Press, 1997.

Smith, Bathsheba W. Affidavit. Nov. 19, 1903, LDS Church History Library.

_____. "Autobiography," 1822-ca. 1906. Microfilm of holograph. LDS Church History Library.

_____. "Recollections of the Prophet Joseph Smith." *Juvenile Instructor* 27 (June 1, 1892): 344-45.

Smith, Emma. Letter to Joseph Smith, Mar.7, 1839. Holograph. LDS Church History Library.

_____. Letter to Joseph Smith, Dec. 6, 1839. Holograph, Joseph Smith Letterbooks, LDS Church History Library.

_____. Letter to Joseph Smith, n.d. but probably June 24, 1844. Typescript. Utah State Historical Society.

_____. Letter to Thomas Carlin, Aug. 27, 1842. Photocopy of holograph, Linda King Newell Collection, Special Collections, Marriott Library.

Smith, George A. Letter to Joseph Smith III. Oct. 9, 1869. Holograph in Community of Christ Archives. Retained copy in George A. Smith Collection, Letterbook No. 6, item 891, LDS Church History Library.

Smith, George D. "How Joseph Smith Cultivated Thirty to Forty Young Women for Plural Marriage in Nauvoo, Illinois." Paper presented at the Mormon History Association annual conference, May 2002, Tucson, Arizona.

_____, ed. *An Intimate Chronicle: The Journals of William Clayton.* Salt Lake City: Signature Books/Smith Research Associates, 1991.

_____. *Nauvoo Polygamy: "... But We Called It Celestial Marriage"* Salt Lake City: Signature Books, 2008.

_____. "Nauvoo Roots of Mormon Polygamy, 1841-46: A Preliminary Demographic Report." *Dialogue: A Journal of Mormon Thought* 16, no. 1 (Spring 1994): 1-72.

Smith, Hyrum. "Affidavit." *Times and Seasons* 3 (Aug. 1, 1842): 870-71.

_____. Diary, 1839-40. LDS Church History Library.

_____. Diary and Accounts, 1831-44. Photocopy of holograph. LDS Church History Library.

_____. Discourse, Apr. 8, 1844. Miscellaneous Minutes Collection, LDS Church History Library.

_____. "Municipal Court of the City of Nauvoo, Illinois." *Times and Seasons* 4, no. 16 (July 1, 1843): 243-56.

_____. "Nauvoo, March 15, 1844." Rpt., in "Our City, and the Present Aspect of Affairs." *Times and Seasons* 5, no. 6 (Jan. 1, 1845): 474.

_____. "Our City, and the Present State of Affairs." *Times and Seasons* 5, no. 6 (Mar. 15, 1844): 471-72.

_____. Qtd. in "Words of the Prophets, Sprictural [sic]." N.d. Holograph. LDS Church History Library.

Smith, John. Journal. LDS Church History Library.

_____. "Sermon delivered in Lee County, Iowa on August 9, 1840." http://www.boap.org/LDS/Parallel/1840/9Aug40.html (July 26, 2013).

Smith, John Lyman. "Journals of John Lyman Smith, Born November 17, 1832, Son of John Smith, a Cousin to the Prophet Joseph Smith." Microfilm of holograph. LDS Church History Library.

_____. "Recollections of the Prophet Joseph Smith." *Juvenile Instructor* 27, no. 6 (Mar. 15, 1892): 172.

Smith, Joseph. "The Globe." *Nauvoo Neighbor,* Apr. 17, 1844; www.sidneyrigdon.com/dbroadhu/LLDS/wasp2.html#041744 (Dec. 20, 2008).

_____. Letter to "Dear, and Beloved, Brother and Sister Whitney, and &c.," Aug. 18, 1842. Photocopy. LDS Church History Library.

_____. Letter to James Sloan, May 17, 1842. Joseph Smith Collection, LDS Church History Library.

_____. Letter to Oliver Granger, May 4, 1841. *Journal of the Illinois State Historical Society* 40 (1947): 85-86.

_____. *The Prophet Joseph Smith's Views on the Powers and Policy of the Government of the United States.* Salt Lake City: Joseph Hyrum Parry, 1886.

_____. Revelation to Newel K. Whitney. July 27, 1842. LDS Church History Library.

_____. "State Gubernatorial Convention." *Times and Seasons* 3, no. 5 (Jan. 1, 1842): 651.

_____. "Wentworth Letter." Reprint. *BYU Studies* 9, no. 3 (Spring 1969): 295-96.

_____. *Views on the Government and Policies of the United States.* Nauvoo, Illinois, 1844.

Smith, Joseph, III. Letter to Mrs. D. C. Chase, May 5, 1893. Community of Christ.

_____. Memoirs. See Anderson, Mary Audentia Smith, and Bertha A. Anderson Hulmes, eds. *Joseph Smith III and the Restoration.* Independence, Missouri: Herald House, 1952.

_____. "Memoirs of President Joseph Smith." *Saints Herald,* Jan. 22, 1935, 110.

_____. "Pleasant Chat." *True Latter Day Saints' Herald* 14 (Oct. 1868): 105.

_____, and Heman C. Smith, eds. 4 vols. *The History of the [Reorganized] Church of Jesus Christ of Latter Day Saints.* Lamoni, Iowa: Herald House, 1897-1903. Rpt., 1967-73.

Smith, Joseph F., comp. Affidavit Books. 1869. 4 vols. (two bound vols. with two holograph copies). LDS Church History Library. Some affidavits are holograph; others are fill-in-the-blank printed forms. Some deponents made more than one affidavit, and many but not all of the affidavits are duplicated between vols. 1 and 2.

Smith, Joseph Fielding. *Blood Atonement and the Origin of Plural Marriage: A Discussion.* 1905; rpt., Salt Lake City: Deseret News Press, 1950. Also Joseph F. Smith Jr. [Joseph Fielding Smith] and Richard C. Evans, eds. *Blood Atonement and the Origin of Plural Marriage.* Rpt., Whitefish, Montana: Kessinger Publishing, n.d.

_____, comp. and ed. *Teachings of the Prophet Joseph Smith.* 1938; Salt Lake City: Deseret News Press, 1954 printing.

Smith, Justin Harvey. *The Annexation of Texas.* 4th ed. New York: AMS Press, 1971.

Smith, Lucy Mack. *Biographical Sketches of Joseph Smith the Prophet and His Progenitors for Many Generations.* Liverpool, England: Published for Orson Pratt by S. W. Richards, 1853.

_____. *History of Joseph Smith by His Mother, as Revised by George A. Smith and Elias Smith.* Salt Lake City: Bookcraft, 1958 ed.

Smith, Lucy Meserve. "Statement." May 18, 1892. George A. Smith Papers, Marriott Library.

Smith, Mary Fielding. Collection, ca. 1832-48. LDS Church History Library.

Smith, Paul Thomas. "John Taylor." *Encyclopedia of Mormonism.* 4 vols. New York: Macmillan, 1992, 4:1438-41.

Smith, Prescindia L. Kimball. Letter to her eldest granddaughter living in 1930. Apr. 1, 1881. LDS Church History Library.

Smith, William. "Introduction." *Wasp,* Apr. 6, 1842, 2.

Smith-Rosenberg, Carroll. *Disorderly Conduct: Visions of Gender in Victorian America.* New York: Alfred A. Knopf, 1985.

_____. "The Female World of Love and Ritual: Relations Between Women in Nineteenth-Century America." *Signs* 1, no. 1 (Autumn 1975): 1-29.

Snider, Cecil A. "Development of Attitudes in Sectarian Conflict: A Study of Mormonism in Illinois in Contemporary Newspaper Sources." M.A. thesis, University of Iowa, 1933.

Snow, Eliza R. *Biography and Family Record of Lorenzo Snow.* Salt Lake City: Deseret News, 1884.

_____. Letter to Joseph F. Smith, n.d. Holograph. Joseph F. Smith Collection, LDS Church History Library.

_____. "Poetry." *Wasp,* Aug. 20, 1842, 3.

_____. "To Who Needs Consolation." *Wasp,* Sept. 10, 1842, 1.

Snow, Erastus. Affidavit. Oct. 17, 1879. In Andrew Jenson, comp., "Plural Marriage," *Historical Record* 6 (May 1887): 232-33.

_____. Journal, June 1841-Feb. 1847, opposite p. 50.

_____. Qtd. in "A Sinopsas [sic] of Remarks made by Apostle E[rastus] Snow July 22 [1883] at Nephi [Utah] Sunday evening." Reported by Thomas Crawley, clerk of the Juab Utah Stake Conference, LDS Church History Library.

Snow, Lorenzo. Affidavit. Aug. 28, 1869. LDS Church History Library.

_____. "Discourse." *Millennial Star* 61 (Aug. 31, 1899): 545-49.

Speech of Elder Orson Hyde, Delivered before the High Priest's Quorum in Nauvoo Apr. 27th, 1845, upon the course and Conduct of Mr. Sidney Rigdon. Nauvoo, Illinois: John Taylor, 1845.

Spieres, John. Autobiography and Diary, 1822-77. Unpaginated holograph. LDS Church History Library.

Staker, Susan. "'The Lord Said, Thy Wife Is a Very Fair Woman to Look Upon': The Book of Abraham, Secrets, and Lying for the Lord." In Bryan Waterman, ed., *The Prophet Puzzle,* 289-318.

_____. "Secret Things, Hidden Things: The Seer Story in the Imaginative Economy of Joseph Smith." In *American Apocrypha: Essays on the Book of Mormon.* Edited by Dan Vogel and Brent Lee Metcalfe. Salt Lake City, Utah: Signature Books, 2002, 235-74.

"State Gubernatorial Convention." *Times and Seasons* 3 (Jan. 1, 1842): 651.

"State of Illinois, Hancock County." *Times and Seasons* 5, no. 6 (May 15, 1844): 537-41.

"The State Register and the Mormons." *Alton Telegraph,* June 4, 1842. www.sidneyrigdon.com/dbroadh/IL/aHn1838.html#060442 (Nov. 20, 2007).

"Statement of L[ucy] W[alker]. [Smith] Kimball," n.d. Typescript. Lucy Walker Kimball Papers. LDS Church History Library.

Stenhouse, Fanny. *Exposé of Polygamy in Utah: A Lady's Life among the Mormons.* New York: American News Co., 1872.

_____. *"Tell It All": The Story of a Life Experience in Mormonism.* Hartford, Connecticut: A. D. Worthington & Co., 1874.

Stenhouse, T. B. H. *The Rocky Mountain Saints.* New York: D. Appleton and Co., 1873.

Stevens, Frank E. *History of Lee County, Illinois.* Chicago: S. J. Clarke Co., 1914.

_____. "Life of Stephen Arnold Douglas." *Journal of the Illinois State Historical Society* 16 (1923-24): 247-673.

Stiles, Edward H. *Recollections and Sketches of Notable Lawyers and Public Men of Early Iowa.* Des Moines: Homestead Publishing, Co., 1916.

Stocks, Hugh Grant. "The Book of Mormon, 1830-1879: A Publishing History." M.L.S. degree, U.C.L.A., 1979.

"Story of the Organization of the Relief Society." *Relief Society Magazine* 6 (Mar. 1919): 127-42.

Stout, Allen Joseph. Journal, 1818-48. Typescript. Lee Library.

Stout, Wayne. "Allen Joseph Stout: A Great Champion of Mormonism." N.d. Typescript. LDS Church History Library.

Strohmayer, Ulf. *Space and Social Theory: Interpreting Modernity and Postmodernity.* Hoboken, New Jersey: Wiley-Blackwell, 1997.

Stroup, George. *Promise of Narrative Theology: Recovering the Gospel in the Church.* Atlanta: John Knox Press, 1981.

Stuy, Brian H. ed. *Collected Discourses.* 5 vols. Burbank, California/Woodland Hills, Utah: B.H.S. Publishing, 1987-92.

Talmage, James E. *House of the Lord: A Study of Holy Sanctuaries, Ancient and Modern.* Salt Lake City: Deseret Book, 1912.

Taylor, J. Lewis. "Joseph the Prophet: A Self-Portrait." *Ensign,* June 1973, 40-44.

Taylor, John. "Editorial." *Nauvoo Neighbor,* May 29, 1844, 3.

_____. "The History of Joseph Smith." *Millennial Star* 23 (Mar. 30, 1881): 215.

_____. "For President–General Joseph Smith." *Nauvoo Neighbor,* Feb. 7, 14, 1844.

_____. "Relief Society Reports." *Woman's Exponent* 9 (Sept. 1, 1880): 53.

_____. Statement, June 29, 1881. LDS Church History Library.

_____. Qtd. in Minutes of Meeting, Oct. 14, 1882, L. John Nuttall Papers, Lee Library.

Taylor, Leonora C. Statement, n.d. Holograph. LDS Church History Library.

Taylor, Nellie T. "John Taylor, His Ancestors and Descendants." *Utah Genealogical and Historical Magazine* 21 (July 1930): 105-106.

"The Temple." *Times and Seasons* 2, no. 13 (May 2, 1842): 776.

Temple Lot Case. U.S. Court of Appeals (8th Circuit) 1892. Transcript. LDS Church History Library. A condensed, expurgated published version is *Complainant's Abstract of Pleading and Evidence, In the Circuit Court of the United States, Western District of Missouri, Western Division, at Kansas City. The Reorganized Church of Jesus Christ of Latter-Day Saints. Complainant vs. The Church of Christ at Independence, Missouri …* Lamoni, Iowa: Herald Publishing House, 1893.

"Temple Ordinance Chronology." *Deseret News 1975 Church Almanac.* Salt Lake City: Deseret News, 1975, F5-F6.

"The Terrible Trouble in the Mormon Country–More Disclosures Relative to the Alleged Seduction and Adulteries of Joe Smith and Others–Crimination and

Re-crimination." *New York Herald*, July 24, 1842. www.sidneyrigdon.com/dbroadhu/NewYork/NewYorkherld0.html#072442 (July 20, 2008).
Thompson, Mercy Rachel Fielding Smith. "An Important Testimony." *Deseret News*, Feb. 17, 1886, 79.
_____. Letter to Joseph Smith III, Sept. 5, 1883. LDS Church History Library.
_____. "Recollections of the Prophet Joseph Smith." *Juvenile Instructor* 27, no. 13 (July 1, 1892): 398-400.
Tinney, Thomas Milton. "The Royal Family of the Prophet Joseph Smith Junior: First President of the Church of Jesus Christ of Latter-day Saints." Typescript; various states. Salt Lake City: Thomas Milton Tinney, 1973. LDS Church History Library.
"To the Church of Jesus Christ of Latter Day Saints, and to All the Honorable Part of Community." *Wasp* 1 (June 25, 1842), 2.
"Tour East." *Messenger and Advocate of the Church of Christ* 2 (Dec. 1845): 401.
Tracy, Nancy Naomi Alexander. "Autobiography." Typescript. Lee Library.
_____. "Autobiography." *Woman's Exponent* 28 (1909-10): 15-18, 26, 39-40, 48, 55-56, 63-64.
"Traveling Agents." *Times and Seasons* 2 no. 7 (Feb. 1, 1841): 310.
"Try the Spirits." *Times and Seasons* 3, no. 11 (Apr. 1, 1842): 743-48.
Tuan, Yi-Fu. *Space and Place: The Perspective of Experience.* Minneapolis: University of Minnesota Press, 1977.
Tullidge, Edward W. *Life of Joseph the Prophet.* 1878; 2d ed., New York: Tullidge and Crandall, 1880. The first edition concludes in 1844 with Joseph Smith's death; the second edition includes the history of the RLDS Church.
_____. *The Women of Mormondom.* New York: Tullidge & Crandall, 1877.
Turner, Victor. *Dramas, Fields, and Metaphors: Symbolic Action in Human Society.* Ithaca, New York: Cornell University Press, 1974.
_____. *The Drums of Affliction: A Study of Religious Processes among the Ndembu of Zambia.* Oxford, England: Clarendon Press, 1968.
_____. *The Forest of Symbols: Aspects of Ndembu Ritual.* Ithaca, New York: Cornell University Press, 1967.
_____. "Frame, Flow and Reflection: Ritual and Drama as Public Liminality." In *Performance in Postmodern Culture.* Edited by Michel Benamou and Charles Caramello. Madison: Center for Twentieth Century Studies, University of Wisconsin-Milwaukee, 1977, 465-99.
_____. *From Ritual to Theater: The Seriousness of Human Play.* New York: Performance Art Journal Publications, 1982.
_____. *The Ritual Process: Structure and Anti-Structure.* Chicago: Aldine Publishing, 1969.
_____. "Variations on a Theme of Liminality." In *Secular Ritual.* Edited by Sally F. Moore and Barbara G. Meyerhoff. Assen, Netherlands: Van Gorcum & Comp., 1977, 36-52.
_____, and Edward M. Bruner. *The Anthropology of Experience.* Urbana: University of Illinois Press, 1986.
_____, and Edith L. B. Turner. *Image and Pilgrimage in Christian Culture: Anthropological Perspectives.* New York: Columbia University Press, 1978.
Underwood, Grant. *The Millenarian World of Early Mormonism.* Urbana: University of Chicago Press, 1993.

"An Unpublished Letter of the Prophet Joseph Smith." *Improvement Era,* Dec. 1905, 168-69.

"Valdictory." *Times and Seasons,* 4, no. 1 (Nov. 15, 1842): 8.

Van Der Zee, Jacob. "The Half-Breed Tract." *Iowa Journal of History and Politics* 13 (Apr. 1915): 151-64.

Van Deusen, Glyndon G. *The Jacksonian Era, 1828-1848.* New York: Harper Torchbooks, 1959.

Van Dusen, Increase McGee. *The Mormon Endowment; Secret Drama, or Conspiracy, in the Nauvoo Temple, in 1846; to Which Is Added a Sketch of the Life of Joseph Smith …* Syracuse, New York: N. M. D. Lathrop, 1847.

_____. *The Sublime and Ridiculous Blended.* New York: Author, 1848.

Van Orden, Bruce A. "Sidney Rigdon." *Encyclopedia of Mormonism.* 4 vols. New York: Macmillan Publishing, 1992, 3:1233-35.

_____. "Stephen A. Douglas and the Mormons." In *Regional Studies in Latter-day Saint Church History: Illinois.* Edited by H. Dean Garrett. Provo, Utah: BYU Department of Church History and Doctrine, Brigham Young University, 1995, 359-79.

_____. "William W. Phelps's Service in Nauvoo as Joseph Smith's Political Clerk." *BYU Studies* 32 (Winter/Spring 1991): 81-94.

Van Wagenen, Michael Scott. *The Texas Republic and the Mormon Kingdom of God.* College Station: Texas A&M University Press, 2002.

Van Wagoner, Richard S. "The Making of a Mormon Myth: The 1844 Transfiguration of Brigham Young." *Dialogue: A Journal of Mormon Thought* 28, no. 4 (1995): 1-24.

_____. *Mormon Polygamy: A History,* 2d ed. Salt Lake City: Signature Books, 1992.

_____. "Sarah M. Pratt: The Shaping of an Apostate." *Dialogue: A Journal of Mormon Thought* 19 (Summer 1986): 69-99.

_____. *Sidney Rigdon: A Portrait of Religious Excess.* Salt Lake City: Signature Books, 1994.

_____, and Steven C. Walker. "The Joseph/Hyrum Smith Funeral Sermon." *BYU Studies* 23, no. 1 (1983): 3-18, www.byustudies.byu.edu/Products/MoreInfoPage/MoreInfo.axps?Type=7&ProdID=643 (January 12, 2008).

Vogel, Dan. *Early Mormon Documents.* 5 vols. Salt Lake City: Signature Books, 1996-2004.

_____. *Joseph Smith: The Making of a Prophet.* Salt Lake City: Signature Books, 2004.

"The Voice of Innocence from Nauvoo, 1844, March 9." Published in the *Nauvoo Neighbor,* Mar. 20, 1844.

von Wymetal, Wilhelm Ritter. See Wyl, Wilhelm.

W. "Communication Mr. Editor." *Warsaw Signal,* June 11, 1845, 2.

Waite, Catherine V. *The Mormon Prophet and His Harem.* Cambridge, Massachusetts: Riverside Press, 1866.

Waite, Frederick C. "The First Medical Diploma Mill in the United States." *Bulletin of the History of Medicine* 20 (Nov. 1946): 495-504.

Walgren, Kent L. "James Adams, Early Springfield Mormon and Freemason." *Journal of the Illinois State Historical Society* 75, no. 2 (Summer 1982): 126-36.

Walker, Charles Lowell. *Diary of Charles Lowell Walker.* 2 vols. Edited by A. Karl Larson and Katharine Miles Larson. Logan: Utah State University Press, 1980.

_____. "Ode to the Ague." In his "Book of Verse." N.p., n.d., LDS Church History Library.

Walker, Rodney Wilson, and Noel Stevenson, comps. *The Second Edition of Ancestry and Descendants of John Walker.* Salt Lake City: John Walker Family Organization, 1985.

Walker, Ronald W., ed. "The Willard Richards and Brigham Young Letter to Joseph Smith from England to Nauvoo, 5 September 1840." *BYU Studies* 18 (Spring 1978): 466-75.

Walker, William Holmes. *The Life Incidents and Travels of Elder William Holmes Walker and His Association with Joseph Smith, the Prophet.* N.p.: Elizabeth Piepgrass, 1943.

Ward, Maurine Carr, ed. "John Needham's Nauvoo Letter: 1843." *Nauvoo Journal* 8 (Spring 1996): 38-42.

Wasp. www.sidneyrigdon.com/dbroadhu/LDS/wasp1.html.

Wasson, Lorenzo. Letter to Joseph Smith and Emma Smith, July 30, 1842. Printed as "Letter from L. D. Wasson." *Times and Seasons* 3 no. 20 (Aug. 15, 1842): 891-92.

_____. Statement, July 20, 1842. *Times and Seasons* 3 (Aug. 15, 1842): 892.

Waterman, Bryan, ed. *The Prophet Puzzle: Interpretive Essays on Joseph Smith.* Salt Lake City: Signature Books, 1999.

Watson, Elden J., ed. *Manuscript History of Brigham Young, 1801-1844.* Salt Lake City: Elden J. Watson, 1968.

_____, ed. *The Orson Pratt Journals.* Salt Lake City, Utah: Elden Jay Watson, 1975.

Weber, Max. *On Charisma and Institution Building.* Edited by S. N. Eisenstadt. Chicago: University of Chicago Press, 1968.

_____. *Economy and Society.* Edited by G. Roth and C. Wittich. 3 vols. New York: Bedminster Press, 1968.

_____. *The Theory of Social and Economic Organization.* Trans. A. M. Henderson and Talcott Parsons. 2d ed. New York: Oxford University Press, 1964.

Wells, Emmeline B. "A Distinguished Woman." *Woman's Exponent* 10 (Jan. 15, 1882): 123.

_____. "LDS Women of the Past: Personal Impressions." *Woman's Exponent* 36, no. 7 (Feb. 1908): 49.

_____. "Patty Sessions." *Woman's Exponent:*
13, no. 7 (Sept. 1, 1884): 51.
13, no. 8 (Sept. 15, 1884): 63.
13, no. 10 (Oct. 15, 1884): 86.
13, no. 11 (Nov. 1, 1884): 84.
13, no. 12 (Nov. 15, 1884): 94-95.
13, no. 17 (Feb. 1, 1885): 134.
13, no. 19 (Mar. 1, 1885): 150.
14, no. 11 (Nov. 1, 1885): 85.
14, no. 12 (Nov. 15, 1885): 94.

_____. "Ruth Sayers Obituary." *Woman's Exponent* 13 (Sept. 1884): 61-62.

_____. "A Venerable Woman: Presendia Lathrop Kimball." *Woman's Exponent:*
10, no. 20 (Mar. 15, 1882): 155.
11, no. 16 (Jan. 15, 1883): 123.
11, no. 17 (Feb. 1, 1883): 131.
11, no. 18 (Feb. 15, 1883): 139.
11, no. 19 (Mar. 1, 1883): 147.
11, no. 20 (Mar. 15, 1883): 155.
11, no. 21 (Apr. 1, 1883): 163.

11, no. 23 (May 1, 1883): 183.
12, no. 2 (June 15, 1883): 11.
12, no. 5 (Aug. 1, 1883): 27.
12, no. 6 (Aug. 15, 1883): 43.
12, no. 9 (Sept. 15, 1883): 67.
12, no. 10 (Oct. 1, 1883): 75.
12, no. 13 (Dec. 1, 1883): 98.
12, no. 17 (Feb. 1, 1884): 130.

Werner, Morris Robert. *Brigham Young.* New York: Harcourt Brace and Co., 1925.

White, Daniel N. "The Prairies, Nauvoo, Joe Smith, the Temple, the Mormons, &c." *Pittsburgh Weekly Gazette,* Sept. 15, 1843, 3.

Whitehead, James. "Supplement." *Lamoni Gazette* 7 (Jan. 1888), reprinted in *Autumn Leaves* 1 (May 1888): 202.

Whitney, Elizabeth Ann. "A Leaf from an Autobiography." *Woman's Exponent* 7, no. 12 (Nov. 15, 1878): 33, 41, 51, 71, 83, 90, 105, 191, 115.

Whitney, Helen Mar Kimball. Autobiography, 1881. LDS Church History Library.

_____. Letter to her children, Mar. 30, 1881. Holograph. LDS Church History Library.

_____. "Life Incidents." *Woman's Exponent* 22 (Aug. 1, 1882): 39.

_____. "Pamphlet." Salt Lake City: Salt Lake Public Library, 1882. LDS Church History Library.

_____. *Plural Marriage as Taught by the Prophet Joseph Smith: A Reply to Joseph Smith [III], Editor of the Lamoni (Iowa) Herald.* Salt Lake City: Juvenile Instructor Office, 1882.

_____. "Scenes and Incidents in Nauvoo, and Incidents from Heber C. Kimball's Journal." (Some episodes titled "Scenes and Incidents in Nauvoo after the Martyrdom of the Prophet and Patriarch.") *Woman's Exponent:*
10, no. 10 (Oct. 15, 1881): 74.
10, no. 12 (Nov. 15, 1881): 93
11, no. 1 (June 1, 1882): 1-2.
11, no. 2 (July 15, 1882): 26.
11, no. 3 (Aug. 1, 1882): 38-40.
11, no. 4 (July 15, 1882): 26.
11, no. 9 (Oct. 1, 1882): 70-71.
11, no. 10 (Oct. 15, 1882): 74.
11, no. 11 (Nov. 1, 1882): 82.
11, no. 12 (Nov. 15, 1882): 90.
11, no. 13 (Dec. 1, 1882): 98.
11, no. 14 (Dec. 15, 1882): 105-106.
11, no. 15 (Jan. 1, 1883): 114.
11, no. 17 (Feb. 1, 1883): 130.
11, no. 18 (Feb. 15, 1883): 138.
11, no. 19 (Mar. 1, 1883): 146.
11, no. 20 (Mar. 15, 1883): 153-54.
11, no. 21 (Apr. 1, 1883): 161.
11, no. 22 (Apr. 15, 1883): 169-70.
11, no. 23 (May 1, 1883): 177.
12, no. 1 (June 1, 1883): 9.
12, no. 2 (June 15, 1883): 14.

12, no. 4 (Jul. 15, 1883): 26.
12, no. 5 (Aug. 1, 1883): 34.
12, no. 6 (Aug. 15, 1883): 42.
12, no. 7 (Sept. 1, 1883): 50.
12, no. 8 (Sept. 15, 1883): 57.
12, no. 9 (Oct. 1, 1883): 71.
12, no. 10 (Oct. 15, 1883): 74.
12, no. 11 (Nov. 1, 1883): 81.
12, no. 12 (Nov. 15, 1883): 89.

_____. "Statement: Retrospection about Her Introduction to the Doctrine and Practices of Plural marriage in Nauvoo at age 15." Mar. 30, 1881. Holograph. LDS Church History Library.

_____. *Why We Practice Plural Marriage.* Salt Lake City: Juvenile Instructor Office, 1884.

Whitney, Orson F. "Heber C. Kimball." *Contributor* 8, no. 8 (June 1887): 305-13.

_____. *History of Utah.* 4 vols. Salt Lake City: George Q. Cannon and Sons, 1892, 1904.

_____. *Life of Heber C. Kimball, An Apostle: The Father and Founder of the British Mission.* 1888; rpt., Salt Lake City: Stevens and Wallis, 1945.

Whitsett, William H. "Sidney Rigdon: The Real Founder of Mormonism." 1885. Unpublished manuscript. Marriott Library.

Whittaker, David J. "East of Nauvoo: Benjamin Winchester and the Early Mormon Church." *Journal of Mormon History* 21, no. 2 (1995): 30-83.

_____. "Joseph Smith in Recent Research: A Selected Bibliography." In *Mormon Americana.* Edited by David J. Whittaker. Provo, Utah: BYU Studies, 1995, 29-44.

_____. "Joseph Smith's First Vision: A Source Essay." *Mormon History Association Newsletter,* no. 42 (Nov. 1979): 7-9.

Wicks, Robert S., and Fred R. Foister. *Junius and Joseph: Presidential Politics and the Assassination of the First Mormon Prophet.* Logan: Utah State University Press, 2005.

Widtsoe, John A. *Joseph Smith: Seeker after Truth, Prophet of God.* Salt Lake City: Bookcraft, 1951.

_____. "Temple Worship." *Utah Genealogical and Historical Magazine* 12 (Apr. 1921): 91-92.

_____. "Was Joseph Smith Honest in Business?" *Improvement Era* 49 (Sept. 1946): 577; 604-607.

_____. "What Were the Sources of Joseph Smith's Greatness?" *Improvement Era* 51 (Dec. 1948): 809, 824.

Wight, John. "Evidence from Zina D. Huntington-Young: Interview with Zina Diantha Huntington Smith Young, October 1, 1898." *Saints Herald* 52 (Jan. 11, 1905): 28-30.

Wight, Lyman. *An Address by Way of an Abridged Account and Journal of My Life from February 1844 up to April 1848.* N.p., n.d.

_____. Letter to Wilford Woodruff, Aug. 24, 1857. LDS Church History Library.

Wight, Orange L. "Recollections of Orange L. Wight." www.boap.org/LDS/Early-Saints/OWight.html (Jan. 2, 2010).

_____. "Reminiscences." Typescript, 1823-1903. Lee Library.

Williams, Samuel Otho. Letter to John Prickett. July 10, 1844. Holograph. LDS Church History Library.

Winchester, Benjamin. "Primitive Mormonism." *Salt Lake Tribune,* Sept. 22, 1889, 2.

Winn, Kenneth H. *Exiles in a Land of Liberty: Mormons in America, 1830-1846.* Chapel Hill: University of North Carolina Press, 1989.

Wood, Timothy. "The Prophet and the Presidency: Mormonism and Politics in Joseph Smith's 1844 Presidential Campaign." *Journal of the Illinois State Historical Society,* Summer 2000, 5, http://findarticles.com/p/articles/mi_qa3945/is_200007/ai n8922399/print (May 18, 2007).

Woodford, Robert J. "The Historical Development of the Doctrine and Covenants." Ph.D. diss., Brigham Young University, 1974.

Woodruff, Phoebe C. "Autobiographic Sketch of Phebe W. Woodruff." Microfilm of holograph, 1880. Bancroft Library, University of California, Berkeley. Microfilm of holograph, LDS Church History Library.

Woodruff, Wilford. "History of Wilford Woodruff." *Millennial Star* 27, no. 21 (May 27, 1865): 326-27; also www.boap.org/LDS/EarlySaints/WWoodruff.html.

_____. "The Law of Adoption." Apr. 8, 1894, General Conference Address. In Brian H. Stuy, ed., *Collected Discourses,* 4:67-81.

_____. *Wilford Woodruff's Journal, 1833-1898.* Edited by Scott G. Kenney. 9 vols. Typescript. Midvale, Utah: Signature Books, 1983-85. On *New Mormon Studies CD-Rom: A Comprehensive Resources Library.* Salt Lake City: Smith Research Associates, 1998.

Woods, Fred E. "The Cemetery Record of William D. Huntington, Nauvoo Sexton." *Mormon Historical Studies* 3 (Spring 2002): 131-63.

Woodward, Mary Brown Firmage. Interviewed by Martha Bradley, Provo, Utah, Jan. 6, 1996.

"Words of the Prophets, Sprictural [sic] Items." N.d. Holograph. LDS Church History Library.

Wright, Lucy M. "Emma Hale Smith." *Woman's Exponent* 30, no. 8 (Dec. 15, 1901): 59.

Wyl, Wilhelm. [pseud. Wilhelm Ritter von Wymetal]. *Mormon Portraits: or the Truth about the Mormon Leaders from 1830 to 1886[,] Volume First[.] Joseph Smith the Prophet His Family and His Friends.* Salt Lake City: Tribune Printing and Publishing, 1886.

Young, Ann Eliza Webb. *Wife Number 19: Or The Story of a Life in Bondage, Being a Complete Exposé of Mormonism, and Revealing the Sorrows, Sacrifices and Sufferings of Women in Polygamy.* Hartford, Connecticut: Dustin, Gillman & Co., 1876.

Young, Brigham. Address to the School of the Prophets. Historian's Office Journal, July 24, 1869. LDS Church History Library.

_____. Journal. Holograph. Brigham Young Collection, LDS Church History Library.

_____. Letter to Mary Ann Angell Young, Nov. 12, 1840. Philip Blair Collection, Marriott Library, University of Utah.

_____. Letter to Parley P. Pratt, July 17, 1842. Brigham Young Collection, LDS Church History Library.

_____. "State of Illinois, Hancock, County; City of Nauvoo." *Times and Seasons* 5, no. 10 (May 15, 1844): 537-42.

Young, Emily Dow Partridge Smith. "Account of Early Life in Kirtland and Nauvoo." Typescript. N.p. LDS Church History Library.

_____. "Autobiography." *Woman's Exponent* 13 (Dec. 1, 1884): 102-103; 14 (Aug. 1, 1885): 38.

_____. Diary and Reminiscences, 1874-99. LDS Church History Library.

_____. "Incidents of the Early Life of a Mormon Girl." [N.d.] Handwritten manuscript. LDS Church History Library.

_____. Reminiscence, 1884. www.boap.org/LDS/EarlySaints/EmPart.html (Jan. 2, 2010).

_____. "Testimony That Cannot Be Refuted." *Woman's Exponent* 12, no. 21 (Apr. 1, 1884): 164-65.

Young, James H. *The Tourists' Pocket Map of the State of Illinois, Exhibiting Its Internal Improvements, Roads, etc., 1838.* Manuscript Collection. Wisconsin State Historical Society, Madison.

Young, Zina Diantha Huntington Jacobs Smith. Address in the Tabernacle, n.d., 1. Typescript copy of holograph. Zina D.H. Young Collection, LDS Church History Library.

_____. Autobiography. n.d. [ca. 1890]. Typescript. Zina Diantha Young Collection, LDS Church History Library.

_____. Letter to Mary E. Lightner, June 8, 1887. Holograph, LDS Church History Library.

_____. Qtd. in "Joseph, the Prophet: His Life and Mission as Viewed by Intimate Acquaintances." *Salt Lake Herald, Church and Farm Supplement,* Jan. 12, 1895, 210-12.

Zimmerman, Dean R., ed. *I Knew the Prophets: An Analysis of the Letter of Benjamin F. Johnson to George F. Gibbs, Reporting Doctrinal Views of Joseph Smith and Brigham Young.* Bountiful, Utah: Horizon Publishers, 1976.

Index

Note: JS = Joseph Smith

About the Author

Martha Bradley-Evans (*née* Sonntag) is a professor in the College of Architecture and Planning and Associate Vice President of Academic Affairs and Dean of Undergraduate Studies at the University of Utah, Salt Lake City. From 2002 to 2011, she served as Dean of the Honors College. She is the recipient of the University of Utah Distinguished Teaching Award, the University Professorship, the Student Choice Excellence in Teaching Award, the Bennion Center Service Learning Professorship, the Park Fellowship, and the Borchard Fellowship. She previously taught history at Brigham Young University (Provo, Utah), where she received a Teaching Excellence Award. She has been vice chair of the Utah State Board of History, chair of the Utah Heritage Foundation, president of the Mormon History Association, and co-editor of *Dialogue: A Journal of Mormon Thought.* In 2013, she received the Leonard Arrington Award for Meritorious and Distinguished Service to Mormon History from the Mormon History Association; and in 2014 was named a Fellow of the Utah State Historical Society. Her publications include *Kidnapped from That Land: The Government Raids on the Short Creek Polygamists; Four Zinas: A Story of Mothers and Daughters on the Mormon Frontier; Pedestals and Podiums: Utah Women, Religious Authority, and Equal Rights; A History of Beaver County; A History of Kane County; A History of Summit County; Sandy City: The First 100 Years; Z.C.M.I.: America's First Department Store;* and *Plural Wife: The Story of Mabel Finlayson Allred.*

A B C D E F G H I J K L M
N O P Q R S T U V W X Y Z

a b c d e f g h i j k l m
n o p q r s t u v w x y z

a b c d e f g h i j k l m
n o p q r s t u v w x y z

This book was set in Adobe Caslon Pro, a revival of oldstyle fonts designed by William Calson in 1725. As one of the earliest British typefaces, it was popular among English and American printers, and was used in printing the United States Declaration of Independence. *Glorious in Persecution: Joseph Smith, American Prophet, 1839-1844* was printed on fifty-pound natural offset stock and case bound by Sheridan Books in Ann Arbor, Michigan.